Caribbean Security in the Age of Terror

Caribbean Basin
UNITED STATES
GULF OF MEXICO
Straits of Florida
BAHAMAS
Nassau
ANDROS ISLAND
TURKS & CAICOS ISLANDS
ATLANTIC OCEAN
Havana
WEST INDIES
GREATER ANTILLES
Yucatan Channel
MEXICO
CUBA
Windward Passage
DOMINICAN REPUBLIC
CAYMAN ISLANDS
Port-au-Prince
HAITI
Santo Domingo
JAMAICA
Canal de la Mona
VIRGIN ISLANDS
San Juan
PUERTO RICO
Leeward Islands
ANGUILLA
BARBUDA
ANTIGUA
St. Johns
ST. KITTS-NEVIS
MONTSERRAT
GUADELOUPE
Basse-Terre
DOMINICA
Roseau
MARTINIQUE
Fort-de-France
Castries
SAINT LUCIA
SAINT VINCENT
Kingstown
BARBADOS
Bridgetown
GRENADA
St. Georges
Windward Islands
LESSER ANTILLES
BELIZE
GUATEMALA
Guatemala
HONDURAS
Tegucigalpa
San Salvador
EL SALVADOR
NICARAGUA
Managua
CARIBBEAN SEA
ISLA DE SAN ANDRES
NETHERLANDS ANTILLES
ARUBA
CURACAO
BONAIRE
Willemstad
ISLA DE MARGARITA
Port-of-Spain
TRINIDAD & TOBAGO
Caracas
COSTA RICA
San José
CANAL ZONE
PANAMA
Panama
VENEZUELA
COLOMBIA
Bogota
PACIFIC OCEAN
Georgetown
GUYANA
Paramaribo
SURINAME
Cayenne
FRENCH GUIANA
BRAZIL

Caribbean Security in the Age of Terror
Challenge and Change

Edited by
Ivelaw Lloyd Griffith

Ian Randle Publishers
Kingston • Miami

First published in Jamaica, 2004 by
Ian Randle Publishers
11 Cunningham Avenue
Box 686
Kingston 6
www.ianrandlepublishers.com

National Library of Jamaica Cataloguing in Publication Data

Caribbean security in the age of terror : challenge and change / edited by Ivelaw Lloyd Griffith

p. : ill., maps ; cm.

Bibliography : p. .– Includes index
ISBN 976-637-142-3 (paperback)

I. Griffith, Ivelaw Lloyd

1. National security – Caribbean Area 2. Terrorism

355.03309729 dc 21

Published in the United States, 2004 by
Ian Randle Publishers Inc

ISBN 0-9753529-0-3 (hardback)

Cover design by Karen Resnick West
Book design by Shelly-Gail Cooper
Printed in the United States of America

This book is dedicated to
the memories of the nationals of Caribbean Basin countries who were victims of terrorism on September 11, 2001

Antigua and Barbuda (3)
Barbados (5)
Belize (1)
Bermuda (2)
Colombia (20)
Costa Rica
Dominica (1)
Dominican Republic
El Salvador
Guatemala
Guyana (26)
Haiti (14)
Honduras
Jamaica (22)
Mexico
Nicaragua
Panama
St Lucia (2)
St Vincent (1)
Trinidad and Tobago (12)
Venezuela

Editor's Note: Thanks to officials of several embassies and consulates in the United States who have supplied the names of several of the victims. However, in light of the gaps in some of the lists and the unavailability of names for some countries we are naming the countries and not the individuals. The numbers in parentheses are the numbers of victims from the various countries for which we have records.

Contents

List of Tables and Figures

List of Figures and Maps

Maps

Acronyms and Abbreviations

ACCP	Association of Caribbean Commissioners of Police
ACP	African, Caribbean and Pacific
ACS	Association of Caribbean States
ADPC	Asian Disaster Preparedness Centre
AFD	Agence Française de Développment
APG	Asia/Pacific Group on Money Laundering
AID	Agency for International Development
BNTF	Basic Needs Trust Fund
CADM	Caribbean Disaster Management Project
CALP	Caribbean Anti Money Laundering Programme
CARDIN	Caribbean Drug Information Network
CAREC	Caribbean Epidemiology Centre
CARIB	Caribbean Association of Regulators of International Business
CARIBCAN	Caribbean Canada Trade Preferences
CARIBPOL	Caribbean Police Service
CARICOM	Caribbean Community
CARIFTA	Caribbean Free Trade Association
CBI	Caribbean Basin Initiative
CCJ	Caribbean Court of Justice
CCLEC	Caribbean Customs Law Enforcement Council
CCM	Caribbean Coordination Mechanism
CDB	Caribbean Development Bank
CDERA	Caribbean Disaster Emergency Response Agency
CDI	Commonwealth Debt Initiative
CDMP	Caribbean Disaster Mitigation Project
CEHI	Caribbean Environmental Health Institute
CEPREDENAC	Centre for Natural Disaster Prevention and Coordination of Central America
CFATF	Caribbean Financial Action Task Force
CGCED	Caribbean Group for Cooperation in Economic Development
CHAMP	Caribbean Hazard Mitigation Capacity Building Programme
CICAD	Inter-American Drug Abuse Control Commission
CICTE	Inter-American Committee against Terrorism

CIMH	Caribbean Institute for Meteorology and Hydrology
CINSEC	Caribbean Island Nations Security Conference
CIS	Commonwealth of Independent States
CISN	Caribbean Information Sharing Network
CMO	Caribbean Meteorological Organisation
COE	Council of Europe
COEF	Financial Activities Supervisory Council
CPACC	Caribbean Planning for Adaptation to Global Climate Change
CSI	Container Security Initiative
CTC	Counter Terrorism Committee
CTCS	Caribbean Technological Consultancy Services
CTO	Caribbean Tourism Organisation
DEA	Drug Enforcement Agency
DMFC	Disaster Mitigation Facility for the Caribbean
EBSVERA	Enhanced Border Security and Visa Entry Reform Act
ECCB	Eastern Caribbean Central Bank
ECLAC	Economic Commission for Latin America and the Caribbean
ECS	Eastern Caribbean States
EDF	European Development Fund
EEZ	Exclusive Economic Zone
EIB	European Investment Bank
ELN	National Liberation Army of Colombia
EPA	Economic Partnership Agreements
EU	European Union
FAL	Convention on Facilitation of International Maritime Traffic
FARC	Revolutionary Armed Forces of Colombia
FATF	Financial Action Task Force
FCO	Foreign and Commonwealth Office (UK)
FIU	Financial Intelligence Unit
FTAA	Free Trade Area of the Americas
FTZs	Free Trade Zones
GAL	Guaranteed Access Level Program
GATT	General Agreement on Tariffs and Trade
GPML	UN Global Programme against Money Laundering
IBCs	International Business Corporations
IBRD	International Bank for Reconstruction and Development

ICITAP	International Criminal Investigation Training Assistance Program
ICJ	International Court of Justice
IMF	International Monetary Fund
INL	International Narcotics and Law Enforcement Affairs
INS	Immigration and Naturalization Service
IOM	International Organization for Migration
IRA	Irish Republican Army
ITIO	International Tax and Investment Organisation
JICC	Joint Information Coordination Centres
LNG	Liquefied Natural Gas
MOU	Memorandum of Understanding
NAFTA	North America Free Trade Agreement
NGO	Non-Governmental Organisation
OAS	Organization of American States
OCR	Ordinary Capital Resources
OCT	Overseas Countries and Territories
ODCCP	UN Office of Drug Control and Crime Prevention
ODPEM	Office of Disaster Preparedness and Emergency Management
OECD	Organisation for Economic Cooperation and Development
OECS	Organisation of Eastern Caribbean States
OFCs	Offshore Financial Centres
OPBAT	Operation Bahamas and Turks and Caicos
OPEC	Organization of Petroleum Exporting Countries
PAHO	Pan American Health Organization
PMO	Project Management Office
RCM	Regional Coordination Mechanism
RDIU	Regional Drug Intelligence Unit
RDLETC	Regional Drug-Law Enforcement Training Centre
ROCCISS	Regional Organized Counter-Crime Information Sharing System
RSS	Regional Security System
SALW	Small Arms and Light Weapons
SENTRI	Secure Electronic Network for Travellers' Rapid Inspection
SFR	Special Fund Resources
SICA	Central American Integration System
SIDS	Small Island Developing States
SIDS/POA	Small Island Developing States/Programme of Action

SOUTHCOM	United States Southern Command
SSU	Special Service Unit
TRIPS	Agreement on Trade Related Aspects of Intellectual Property Rights
UN	United Nations
UNCLOS	United Nations Convention on the Law of the Sea
UNDCP	United Nations Drug Control Programme
UNGASS	United Nations General Assembly Special Session
UN-LiREC	UN Regional Centre for Peace, Disarmament and Development in Latin America and the Caribbean
UNSCR	United Nations Security Council Resolution
WHO	World Health Organization
WTC	World Trade Center
WTO	World Trade Organization

Foreword

This book is partly the result of a collaborative effort involving Florida International University, the Jamaica Defence Force, and the University of the West Indies, Mona (Office of the Principal and the Sir Arthur Lewis Institute of Social and Economic Studies) in which a conference was held at the University of the West Indies, Mona in February in conjunction with the 2003 Research Day. The book fills a void in the literature on security in the Caribbean in the period after the terrorist attacks on the United States on September 11, 2001. As Professor Ivelaw Griffith, the project leader, has so cogently argued, those events ushered in 'the age of terror'.

Specifically, the volume is intended to address four related matters:

1. Survey the contemporary security arena in both the traditional and non-traditional security areas.
2. Explore the actual and potential impact and implications of the September 11, 2001 terrorist attack in regional, hemispheric and global contexts.
3. Assess the responses to those events by Caribbean states and non-state actors such as business and non-governmental organisations.
4. Examine the institutional and operational terrorism response capacity of security agencies in the region in the age of terror.

The contribution of this work to the literature on security in the Caribbean derives principally from the perspectives of the authors who address security issues in broad, comprehensive and inclusive terms. Thus, in parts I, II and III of the book the authors probe differing conceptions and contentions about security, the traditional security issues such as territorial disputes, crime, corruption and violence as well as the non-traditional security issues such as drugs, economic vulnerability, the environmental challenge and HIV/AIDS.

These issues are then placed within regional and international contexts in light of the actual and potential impact of September 11 on the Caribbean. Attention is paid to United States-Caribbean relations, Caribbean-European relations, regionalism in the greater Caribbean, the economic and trade impact of September 11, and the impact of September 11 on the migration relations between the Caribbean and the United States. In parts V and VI of the book authors coming from a variety of perspectives address issues such as the state and civil society responses to September 11, the anti-terrorism capacity of

Caribbean security forces, the priority given by the hemisphere to terrorism, and the engagement of the Caribbean on the world scene. They also examine the regional cooperation and regional law enforcement strategies. The book concludes with a perceptive assessment under the title 'Contending with Challenge, Coping with Change'.

This volume derives its unique value from the nature and the implications of the issues it examines as well as its focus on both policy and operational models. By bringing together academics, policy makers, and security operational personnel, the volume will appeal to students and scholars of Caribbean security and politics, foreign policy and international politics. It will also find a ready audience in students and scholars interested in small states security and foreign policy matters as well as in hemispheric and international security.

Yet interest in this volume will not be limited to the academic community as it also was written to inform the thinking of policy makers in the areas of security and foreign policy. Public officials in general and non-governmental organisations and international agencies, and business persons will all find the perspectives and conclusions in this book invaluable in the conduct of their work and operations.

May I use this opportunity to convey my gratitude to all the contributors for providing us with a stimulating, insightful, and timely publication.

Kenneth O. Hall
Pro Vice Chancellor and Principal
University of the West Indies, Mona

October 2003

Preface and Acknowledgements

The genesis of this book was a visit to the University of Central Florida (UCF) in Orlando, Florida, in June 2002 to deliver a series of lectures to their Fulbright Scholars Group. My wife and our two teenaged children accompanied me on that visit, as our daughter, then a high school sophomore, had UCF on her 'colleges of interest' list. While in Orlando we went to Disney World. It was while waiting in the lines to purchase tickets and then to gain entry to Universal Studios that I conceived this work.

My family had visited Disney theme parks before. The lines in June 2002 were no longer than on previous occasions. As a matter of fact there was less of a throng on that visit than on the other summer days that we had been to Disney World. But two things were different in 2002. One, it took longer to gain entry. This was directly linked to the second factor: the security measures introduced in the aftermath of the September 11, 2001 terrorist incidents, which added what I called a 'hassle factor' to a normally visitor friendly experience, in addition to significantly slowing the pace of entry.

As I stood in the lines observing the security measures at Universal Studios and thinking of the implications of a terrorist attack at that or any theme park in terms of the physical safety of patrons and the economic, psychological, and political impact on Florida and the nation, I began to extend my 'impact of terrorism' thoughts to the Caribbean. So slow was the journey into the park that I had time to sketch the architecture of this volume, jotting down points about aims, conceptual framework, contributors, timetable, and potential publishers.

A two-day conference on the subject of the volume in early 2003 was an important stage of the development of the project. It was held in Jamaica and was cosponsored by the University of the West Indies (UWI), Mona, the Jamaica Defence Force (JDF), and The Honours College of Florida International University. The conference had two main aims. One was to allow contributors to share drafts of their chapters and get comments and suggestions from other project participants. The other aim was to extend the discourse on contemporary Caribbean security to scholars and security practitioners in Jamaica.

I wish to record my enormous appreciation to my cosponsoring colleagues, Professor Kenneth Hall, UWI pro vice chancellor and principal at Mona, and Admiral Hardley Lewin, chief of staff of the JDF. Their endorsement of the idea for the conference was both immediate and unreserved. Several members of their staff rendered efficient service in organising and hosting the conference, and deserve special mention. Included here are Rose Cameron and Oliviene Burke from UWI, and Lt Col. Lenworth Marshall, Lt Sophia McDonald-James, Cpl Milton Jones, Cpl Anthony Thomas, and Lt Cpl Alton Reid from the JDF. Special thanks also to Professor Gordon Shirley, executive director of the Mona Business School for the use of the wonderful meeting facilities and for putting his staff at our disposal during the conference. Honors College research and programs coordinator Elizabeth Williams and information technology officer Juan Lopez also must be commended for the outstanding service they rendered.

Several colleagues in Jamaica played key roles in chairing conference sessions and serving as discussants, thereby contributing to the intellectual enrichment of the conference. They are Professor Denis Benn, Professor Neville Duncan, Dr Jessica Byron, Dr Anthony Harriott, Mrs Beverley Anderson-Manley, and Col. Stewart Saunders. Thanks to one and all. I also want to record my appreciation to Professor Stephen Vasciannie who responded to a last minute luncheon speaker call and provided such a provocative talk, which is characteristic of him, that I immediately invited him to write up and expand on the remarks for inclusion in the book. Ian Randle, president of Ian Randle Publishers, responded immediately and positively to the proposal for the volume. Moreover, he and his editorial and support staff were both accommodating and supportive during the gestation of the project. My thanks to Ian and his team, especially Kim Hoo Fatt, executive assistant, and Shelly-Gail Cooper, production coordinator.

Liz Williams deserves special commendation for not only expert assistance in organising and supervising the logistics of the Jamaica conference, but also for helping to manage the overall project. Thanks as well to Juan Lopez for resolving several technical issues with the manuscript, John Kneski, assistant dean in The Honors College, for preparing some of the graphics, and Dr Bill Beesting, Fellow in The Honors College, for lending his keen editorial eye to several of the chapters. Finally, I would like to acknowledge the support and patience of my wife, Francille Griffith, and our two teenagers, Ivelaw Lamar and Shakina Aisha, while I pursued this project, which took me away from the family for long periods of time on several occasions.

Ivelaw Lloyd Griffith
Miami, Florida
August 2003

Introduction: Understanding Reality, Interpreting Change

Ivelaw L. Griffith

> The greatest and the most decisive act of judgment which a statesman and commander perform is that of recognizing correctly the kind of war in which they are engaged; of not taking it for, or wishing to make of it, something which under the circumstances it cannot be. This is, therefore, the first and most comprehensive of all strategic questions.
> *Carl von Clausewitz* [1]

The words above, penned by one of the great strategists of modern history, are both timeless and timely. Timeless in that, while composed in the nineteenth century, they are still relevant in the twenty-first century, and will be for the foreseeable future. Timely in that, although written with conventional warfare in mind, they are pertinent to the unconventional conflicts in which several states currently are engaged. But it should be noted that, in the context of the globalization and interdependence characterising the contemporary world, Clausewitz speaks not only to statesmen and generals of states directly engaged in conflict. His words should also resonate with statesmen and security practitioners of states that are affected collaterally. In other words, Clausewitz's proposition is relevant to the Caribbean.

Complexity of Terrorism; Complex Terrorism

Understanding contemporary Caribbean security realities against the backdrop of the age-defining phenomenon of terrorism is, therefore, not just desirable but necessary. Pursuit of this understanding prompts two related questions: What is meant by 'age-defining phenomenon'? What do I mean by 'age of terror', which is a term that appears in the title of this volume?[2]

In dealing with these two questions, one well-known fact is worth noting here: terrorism, which involves politically-motivated acts of violence often involving innocent individuals and with drama and fear as main ingredients, is not new. As one leading terrorism scholar explained even before September 11, 2001 (hereafter called 9/11),

> even though the word *terrorism* originated during the French Revolution and the Jacobin Reign of Terror (1792-94), individual terror-violence can be traced back at least to the ancient Greek and Roman republics. By definition, the assassination of Julius Cesar in 44 BC was an act of terrorism in so far as a modern political assassination is defined as terrorism.[3]

More specific to 9/11, it has been noted that the first major terrorist attack on the financial power centre of the United States did not occur on September 11, 2001, or even in 1993 when the World Trade Center was bombed. Actually, 'it occurred on September 16, 1920, when anarchists exploded a horse cart filled with dynamite near the intersections of Wall and Broad Street, taking 40 lives and wounding about 300 others'. [4]

However, the nature, scope, and impact of 9/11 terrorism have been such that the phenomenon of terrorism now virtually defines the age in which we live. Since the terrorist act of that fateful September day, the responses to it, and the implications of those responses for foreign affairs, security, trade and economics, transportation, immigration, civil and constitutional protections, and a variety of other matters have come to define the content and context of national actions and international interactions *in every part of the world*. Moreover, the responses and implications are unlikely to be fleeting; rather, they are likely to be deep and long-lasting. Thus, it is clear to me that the global society is not experiencing only the virtues and vices of the *information age*, the anxieties and apprehensions of the *nuclear age*, the pleasures and pains of the *post-modern age*, but now also the traumas and tribulations of an *Age of Terror*. In this respect my view differs from some other scholars. For instance, British academic Andrew Hurrell feels that

> The attacks on September 11 did not usher in a new age. They reinforced powerful tendencies that were already visible in the post-Cold War order of the 1990s but also exacerbated the tensions and contradictions within that order.[5]

The evidence seems incontrovertible that terrorism has become a fulcrum around which national and international institutional behaviour now revolves. This is not merely a function of the number of terrorist incidents. Indeed, as Figure Intro. 2 shows, globally the number of terrorist incidents has declined over the last two decades. Audrey Cronin explained: 'Internationally, the number of terrorist attacks in the 1990s averaged 382 per year, whereas in the 1980s the number per year averaged 543'.[6] But the decline in numbers was not accompanied by a similar pattern in lethality. One longitudinal study found that:

> Despite a decline in transnational terrorism of nearly 50 incidents per quarter during some of the post-Cold War era, terrorism still presents a formidable threat to targets. This conclusion follows because each incident is almost 17 percentage points more likely to result in death or injury compared with the previous two decades.[7]

This has led to the plausible conclusion that terrorists appear to be getting 'more bang for their buck' by securing greater impact from fewer events.

Additional evidence of 'age definition' may also be adduced. The following statement by the UN secretary general to the October 4, 2002 meeting of the UN Security Council is both a reflection of actions and interactions spawned by terrorism and an indication of its age-defining impact:

> Terrorism is a global threat with global effects; its methods are murder and mayhem, but its consequences affect every aspect of the United Nations agenda — from development to peace to human rights and the rule of law. No part of our mission is safe from terrorism and no part of the world is immune from this scourge.[8]

Yet, more than national and international institutional adaptation is at stake; also affected are international legal regimes. For instance, international legal scholar Antonio Cassese points to changes in relation to norms and legality pertaining to the definition of crimes against immunity, the law of self defence, and general principles of international law, among other things. Cassese notes:

> The terrorist attack of 11 September has had atrocious effects not only at the human, psychological, and political levels. It is also having shattering consequences for international law. It is subverting some important legal categories, thereby imposing the need to rethink them, on the one hand, and to lay emphasis on general principles, on the other.[9]

So, although over recent decades the world has witnessed numerous, albeit declining, terrorist incidents and increasing terrorist lethality in various parts of the world as Figures Intro. 1, 2 and 3 show, the international community is no longer experiencing multiple acts of terrorism, but complex terrorism, which is both a manifestation of and contributor to complex interdependence.[10] One acknowledged terrorism authority puts it this way: 'The current wave of international terrorism, characterized by unpredictable and unprecedented threats from nonstate actors, not only is a reaction to globalization, but is facilitated by it.'[11]

Figure Intro.1
Total International Terrorist Attacks by Region, 1995-2000

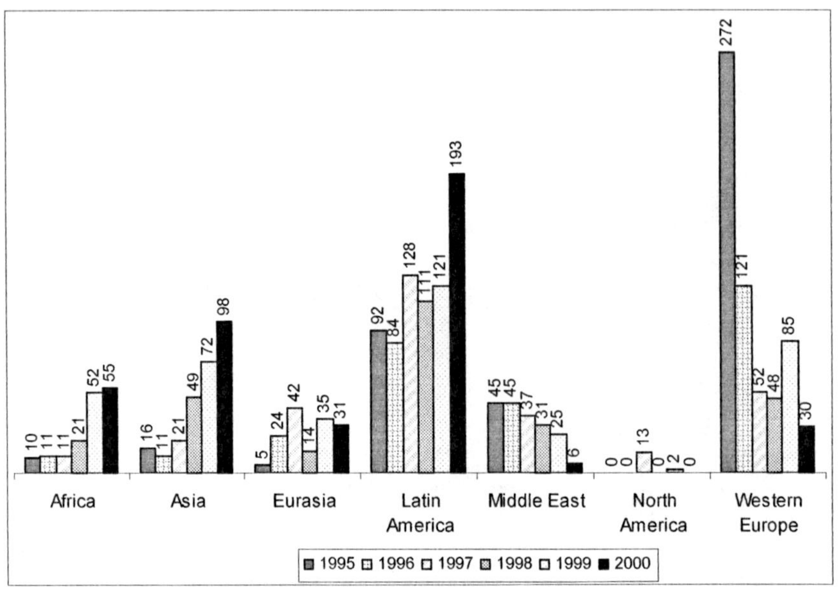

Source: US Department of State, Patterns of Global Terrorism 2000, *April 2001.*

Figure Intro.2
Total International Terrorist Attacks, 1981-2002

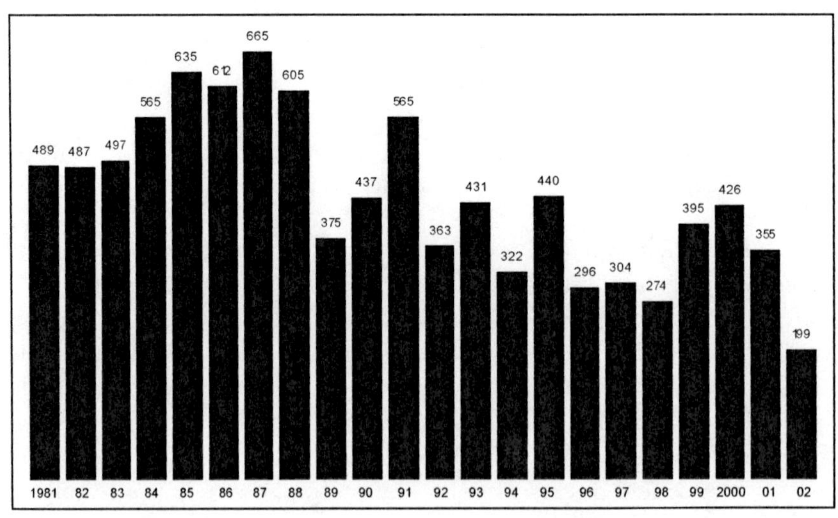

Source: US Department of State, Patterns of Global Terrorism 2002, *April 2003.*

Figure Intro.3
Total International Terrorist Attacks by Region, 1997-2002

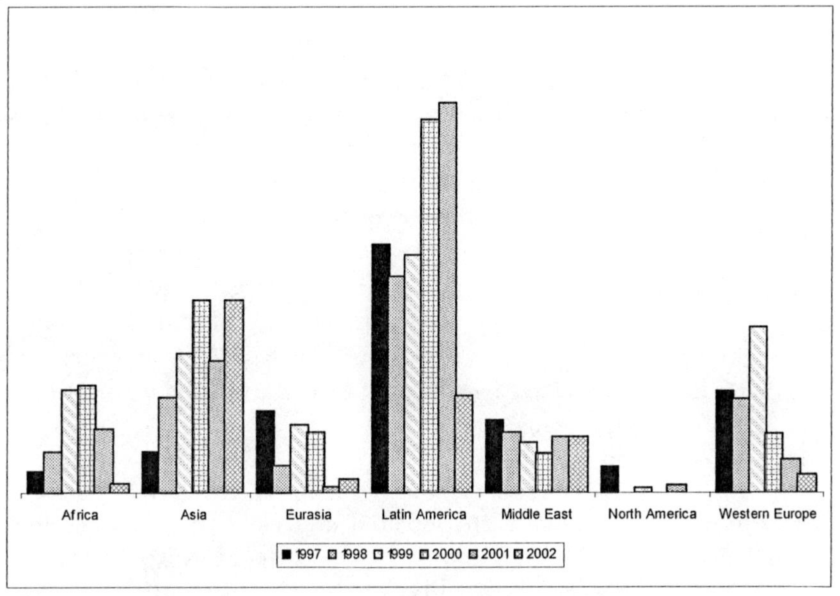

Source: US Department of State, Patterns of Global Terrorism 2002, *April 2003.*

According to Thomas Homer-Dixon, complex terrorism 'operates like jujitsu — it redirects the energies of our intricate societies against us'.[12] Whether or not one agrees with the analogy, there is credence in his proposition that complex terrorism is driven by three technological advances: more powerful weapons, dramatic progress in communications and information processing, and greater opportunities to divert non-weapon technologies to destructive ends.[13] There is more involved, though. Part of the complexity lies in the diversity of the terrorist landscape. One typology points to four basic types of terrorist operators: leftists, rightists, enthnonationalist/ separatists, and religious or 'sacred' terrorists. It is argued that all four types have enjoyed periods of relative prominence in modern times, with the first type intertwined with communist movements, the second type drawing its inspiration from fascism, and the bulk of the third type of terrorists accompanying the wave of decolonization, particularly right after the Second World War. Moreover, it is suggested that the fourth type — religious or 'sacred'— is becoming more significant.[14] Elsewhere I have pointed to terrorism as a multidimensional phenomenon with diversity among the terrorists themselves, the victims, and the religious and political fulcrums around which their actions are centred.[15]

It should be noted, however, that the complexity of terrorism is a function of much more than technological advances and diversity. Another dimension worthy of note is that identified by Robert Keohane. Although Keohane's analysis focuses on the United States, it is relevant to the broader issue of complex terrorism. For him, 'two asymmetries, which do not normally characterize relationships between states, favored wielders of informal violence in September 2001. First, there was an asymmetry of information.... Second, there is an asymmetry in beliefs.'[16]

In relation to the first asymmetry, he argues that while potential terrorists had good information about their targets the United States had poor information about the identity and location of terrorist networks within and outside the country. This is true of most terrorism target societies, one might add. Regarding the second asymmetry, after noting that some of Osama bin Laden's followers reputedly believed in rewards in the afterlife for their actions and that others seem to have been duped about the suicidal implications of their actions, Keohane states:

> Clearly, the suicidal nature of the attacks made them even more difficult to prevent and magnified their potential destructive power. Neither volunteering for suicide missions nor deliberately targeting civilians is consistent with secular beliefs widely shared in the societies attacked by Al Qaeda.[17]

Thus, the complexity of terrorism clearly contributes to its 'age-defining' character. However, this is not the only contributing factor. An additional aspect pertains to the power and role of the state that is the primary 9/11 victim. The 9/11 terrorism attacks resulted in the deaths of over 3,000 individuals from 78 nations.[18] But, as is well known, the primary victim state is the United States of America. Speaking of the United States in global power context, Joseph Nye, Jr. averred: 'Not since Rome has one nation loomed so large above the others.'[19] He also expressed the view — which I share — that, notwithstanding terrorism, American preponderance will last well into the twenty-first century. Indeed, the preponderance of American power is such that some analysts no longer describe the United States as a 'superpower' but as a 'hyperpower'.

For example, one scholar asserts:

> It is a truth universally acknowledged that the central feature of the world at the outset of the twenty-first century is the enormous power of the United States. This country possesses the most formidable military forces and the largest and most vibrant national economy on the planet.... In the

> league standings of global power, the United States occupies first place—and by a margin so large that it recalls the preponderance of the Roman Empire of antiquity. The United States is no longer a mere superpower; it has ascended to the status of 'hyperpower'.[20]

For all its preponderance of power and the history of the use of its power, though, the United States has been unique among great powers historically in not exercising direct imperium. As one writer-critic has acknowledged: 'Alone among the super-nations through history, America has generally (there are exceptions) not sought to exploit its victories to rule (directly) over other nations'.[21]

The stark contrast between the number and outcome of terrorist incidents in the United States as compared with elsewhere over recent decades, shown in Figures Intro. 1, 3, and 4, is a key indicator of the significance of the United States in the 'age definition' of contemporary terrorism. Yet, the centrality of American power is only part of the equation; another factor is American vulnerability. One writer captured this succinctly:

> September 11 and its aftermath had the paradoxical effect of demonstrating, within the space of a few months, both the unprecedented vulnerability of the United States and its unprecedented power. Its economic and military centers were more vulnerable than anyone had thought possible, and yet within several weeks Americans were displaying more power than anyone thought they possessed on one of history's toughest battlefields, Afghanistan.[22]

Figure Intro.4
Total International Terrorist Casualties by Region, 1997-2002

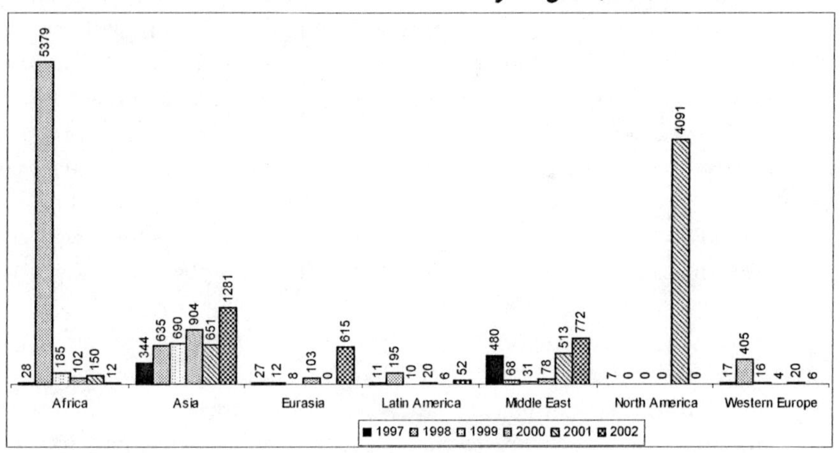

Source: US Department of State, Patterns of Global Terrorism 2002, *April 2003.*

It is in the context of the considerations above that one needs to understand the security realities facing the Caribbean. The way this volume aids an understanding of these realities therefore deserves some attention.

The Volume: Aims and Approach

This volume has four aims as part of an effort to understand reality and interpret change related to Caribbean security. First, survey the contemporary security arena. Second, explore the actual and potential impact and implications for the region of the terrorist acts of 9/11. Third, assess the responses to 9/11 by Caribbean state and by non-state actors, such as businesses and international governmental and international non-governmental organisations. Finally, examine the institutional and operational terrorism response capacity of security agencies in the region in the wake of 9/11.

The volume is organised into six main sections. The first section grapples with broad conceptual-theoretical questions and over-arching issues. It suggests that the work is guided by the view that coming to terms with security challenge and change in the Caribbean requires going beyond consideration of the traditional security arena, to examination of the non-traditional one. Thus, Parts II and III offer assessments of the main traditional and non-traditional challenges, noting the nature and scope of threats and policy responses to them. Among other things, the authors of those chapters address two common questions: What is the nature and scope of the issues — border disputes, drugs, HIV/AIDS, etc.? What are state and non-state responses to them? The assessments are region-wide, although some authors discuss national or sub-regional cases.

Following the 'reality check' in Parts II and III, attention is turned in Part IV to the dynamics of the 9/11 terrorist action, focusing on changes and implications for policy and practice by state and non-state actors. The chapters in this section are both geographically- and issue-focused. Hence, some overlapping is unavoidable. It is quite understandable that the time that has elapsed since September 2001 may be insufficient to provide assessments of the full impact of the events and aftermath of 9/11 in some areas. Thus, the chapters in Part IV offer both impact assessments based on known outcomes, and suggestions about potential impact and likely implications based on trends.

The book's fifth section provides assessments of the way Caribbean actors have coped with the aftermath of 9/11 and the requirements for adaptation to regional and international life in the Age of Terror. The aim here is to offer appraisal with both intellectual value and policy relevance; not just criticism of what has been and what is, but useful advice about what might be, as policy elites grapple with the challenges in various areas. In this respect some relevant questions are: How have state (and non-state) actors dealt with 9/11 in policy or operational terms? What are some lessons learned for adaptation in order to deal with actual attacks or collateral damage? What is the terrorism readiness capability of Caribbean security forces? What are some of the economic, political, and organisational challenges that exist or that should be considered in coping with terrorism?

Part VI of the volume goes beyond the issue of terrorism, paying attention to two central questions: What is the status of regional security and law enforcement cooperation? What are some existing challenges and opportunities in those areas? Understandably, all questions are not treatable by all the chapters. Further, it is important to note that although the volume focuses on the Caribbean, it is essential to understand the region's dynamics in hemispheric and global contexts. As 9/11 made manifest, global security interdependence is an increasing reality of contemporary life, such that developments in one country or region have effects that extend far beyond the particular target country or region. Thus, the chapters in Parts IV, V, and VI make connections between the regional landscape and the hemispheric and international arenas.

The multidimensional nature of Caribbean security and its wide-ranging policy and operational dimensions oblige us to recognise that the issues involved are important not only in relation to theory and empiricism but also to policy making and policy execution. Consequently, meaningful discussion of the various aspects of the subject is best served by having contributions from academic experts, policy makers and advisers, and people involved in 'the front lines' of policy execution. As is evident from the Notes on Contributors, the authors in this volume represent this mix. And, partly because of the nature of the group of contributors, conceptual-theoretical eclecticism is understandable — and welcome.

For reasons not appropriate to examine here, serious scholarship on Caribbean security has captured the attention of just a small number of scholars over past decades, although the subject has been garnering interest over recent years. For instance, the last decade has witnessed the publication of less than a dozen major scholarly English-language books on the subject, namely Ivelaw L. Griffith, *The Quest for Security in the Caribbean* (M.E. Sharpe, 1993); Michael Morris, *Caribbean Maritime Security* (St. Martin's Press, 1994); Jorge Rodríguez Beruff and Humberto García Muñiz, eds., *Security Problems and Policies in the Post-Cold War Caribbean* (Macmillan, 1996); Ivelaw L. Griffith, *Drugs and Security in the Caribbean: Sovereignty Under Siege* (Penn State University Press, 1997); Michael C. Desch, Jorge I. Domínguez, and Andrés Serbin, eds., *From Pirates to Drug Lords: The Post-*

Cold War Caribbean Security Environment (State University of New York Press, 1998); and Joseph S. Tulchin and Ralph H. Espach, eds., *Security in the Caribbean Basin* (Lynne Rienner, 2000).[23] These are all solid scholarly works. Nevertheless, there is a lacuna in relation to assessment of the contemporary security scene against the backdrop of 9/11 terrorism and its transformative dynamics. This work fills that void.

Conclusion

The nature and implications of the issues examined in this volume, the attention to theoretical-conceptual questions and policy and operational matters, and the broad scope of the book should make it of interest not just to statesmen and generals, the two categories referred to by Clausewitz in the epigraph. This book should be valuable to several other constituencies as well: students and scholars of Caribbean security and international politics; students and scholars interested in small state security and foreign policy matters; security policy makers and practitioners inside the Caribbean; and security and foreign policy elites outside the Caribbean who have reason to be interested in it. Mindful of Clausewitz's proposition, I commend this work to readers in all these constituencies in the hopes that it provides an understanding of the security realities confronting the Caribbean in this Age of Terror.

Notes

1 Carl von Clausewitz, *War, Politics, and Power: Selections from On War and I Believe and Profess.* Translated and edited by Edward M. Collins (Washington, DC: Regnery Gateway, 1962), p. 86.

2 This question was raised by Keith Nurse, a contributor to this volume, at the final session of the conference of project authors in Jamaica on February 1, 2003. Here I am keeping the promise made to colleagues at that session to explain what I mean.

3 Cindy C. Combs, *Terrorism in the Twenty-First Century* (Upper Saddle River, New Jersey: Prentice Hall, 2000), p. 18.

4 Office of the President of the United States of America, *National Strategy for Combating Terrorism*, February 2003, p. 5.

5 Andrew Hurrell, '"There are no Rules" (George W. Bush): International Order after September 11', *International Relations* Vol. 16 No. 2 (2002): 202.

6 Audrey Kurth Cronin, 'Behind the Curve: Globalization and International Terrorism', *International Security* Vol. 27, No. 3 (Winter 2002/03): 43.

7 Walter Enders and Todd Sandler, 'Is Transnational Terrorism Becoming More Threatening?: A Time-Series Investigation', *Journal of Conflict Resolution* Vol. 44 (June 2000): 329.

8 'Addressing Security Council, Secretary General Endorses Three-Pronged Counter-Terrorism Strategy', United Nations Press Release SG/SM/8417, SC/7523, October 4, 2002, available at www.un.org/News/Press/docs/2002/sgsm8417.doc.htm.

9 See Antonio Cassese, 'Terrorism is also Disrupting Some Crucial Legal Categories of International Law', *European Journal of International Law* Vol. 12 No. 5, (2001): 993.

10 For a discussion on complex interdependence, see Robert O. Keohane and Joseph S. Nye, Jr., *Power and Interdependence* (Glenview, IL: Scott, Foresman, 1989); James N. Rosenau, *Along the Domestic-Foreign Frontier: Exploring Governance in a Turbulent World* (Cambridge, UK: Cambridge University Press, 1997); Maryann K. Cusimano, ed., *Beyond Sovereignty: Issues for a Global Agenda* (New York: St. Martin's Press, 2000); and Stephen J. Flanagan, 'Meeting the Challenges of the Global Century', in Richard L. Kugler and Ellen L. Frost, eds, *The Global Century: Globalization and National Security* (Washington, DC: National Defense University Press, 2001), pp. 7-32.

11 Cronin, Ibid., p. 30.

12 Thomas Homer-Dixon, 'The Rise of Complex Terrorism', *Foreign Policy*, (January-February 2002) p. 58.

13 Homer-Dixon, Ibid., p. 54.

14 Cronin, Ibid., p. 39. Cronin makes the important point that there is some overlap among the four categories, as many groups have a mix of motivating ideologies.

15 See Ivelaw L. Griffith, 'Terrorism and Transnationality', *Diversity Exchange*, (Spring 2002) p. 21.

16 Robert O. Keohane, 'The Globalization of Informal Violence, Theories of World Politics, and the "Liberalization of Fear"', *Dialog-IO* (Spring 2002) p. 34.

17 Keohane, Ibid., pp. 34-35.

18 United States Department of State, Patterns of Global Terrorism 2001, April 2002, p. 1.

19 Joseph S. Nye, Jr., 'Limits of American Power', *Political Science Quarterly* Vol. 117 No 4 (Winter 2002-2003): 1.

20 Michael Mandlebaum, 'The Inadequacy of American Power', *Foreign Affairs* Vol. 81 No. 5 (September-October 2002): 61.

21 Michael Kelly, 'A Transformative Moment', *The Atlantic Monthly* Vol. 291 No.5 (June 2003): 27. The word 'directly' in parenthesis is my addition. Interestingly, Kelly, a former editor in chief of *The Atlantic Monthly* was one of the 'embedded' journalists killed in Iraq during the 2003 conflict.

22 Michael Hirsh, 'Bush and the World', *Foreign Affairs* Vol. 81 (September-October 2002): 21.

23 Of course, Caribbean security issues have also featured in works on Latin America, such as Jorge Dominguez's *The Future of Interamerican Relations* (Interamerican Dialogue, 1999), Tom Farer's *Transnational Crime in the Americas* (Routledge, 1999), Joseph Tulchin, et al's *Strategic Balance and Confidence Building in the Americas* (Stanford University Press, 1998), Jorge Dominguez's *International Security and Democracy: Latin America and the Caribbean in the Post-Cold War Era* (University of Pittsburgh Press, 1998), and Richard Millett and Michael Gold-Bliss, eds., *Beyond Praetorianism: The Latin American Military in Transition* (North South Center Press, 1996).

1

Probing Security Challenge and Change in the Caribbean

*Ivelaw L. Griffith**

We need to start afresh, to relax in our gardens, emulate [Isaac] Newton and ponder the scene around us, allowing ourselves to be puzzled by those recurring patterns that seem self-evident but that somehow have never been adequately explained.
James N. Rosenau[1]

It is almost no longer controversial to say that traditional conceptions of security were (and in many minds still are) too narrowly founded. That advance does not, however, mean that consensus exists on what a more broadly constructed conception should look like.
Barry Buzan[2]

Introduction

The wisdom of the observation by academic luminary James Rosenau extends beyond the arenas of international politics and foreign policy where the observation was first made. The remark is valuable for scholars in security studies as well and, indeed, for scholars in virtually every social science field. Rosenau's observation has added value when one is dealing with an area of inquiry with significant *real world* policy implications and where the changing dynamics of domestic and international politics have so affected the terms of intellectual engagement that rethinking of core concepts and central assumptions is not merely desirable but necessary.

The redefinition of *security* as a core concept to which Barry Buzan refers followed the end of the Cold War, which witnessed the altering of power relations between, among, and within states in significant ways. Many security scholars began to do precisely what Rosenau had suggested a decade earlier – revisit concepts and theories, reexamine threats and vulnerabilities, review puzzles and patterns, and re-estimate the utility of and necessity for extant strategies. As if the post-Cold War ferment were not enough, along came the events of September 11, 2001, referred to hereafter as 9/11, making terrorism central to the security, foreign policy, and other discourse by statesmen and scholars, and renewing the salience of Rosenau's remarks. It seems hardly disputable that 'we live in the shadow of September 11,' as Barbados Prime Minister Owen Arthur suggests.[3] Terrorism itself is not new in the international or regional arena, of course. However, the dynamics of 9/11 are so powerful and potentially far-reaching for the Caribbean that it is important to examine the contemporary security scene in the context of 9/11 dynamics.

This chapter makes a modest attempt at doing this. Mine is the view that probing the security realities of the contemporary Caribbean against the backdrop of Rosenau's advice requires raising, although perhaps not completely settling, two central questions. First, what is an appropriate conceptual framework against which to examine Caribbean security realities? Second, in the context of that framework, what are some of the main security challenges facing the region? Obviously, these are not the only questions that may be raised. Another pertinent one is: What are some relevant strategies to cope with the challenges confronting states in the region? (See Chapter 21.) As might also be expected, dealing with these questions entails responding to subsidiary ones. For instance, answering the first question necessitates addressing at least two subsidiary ones: What do we mean by security? When does a national challenge become a security matter?

Pondering an Appropriate Framework

Two preliminary observations are warranted before proceeding to the first question. First, as might be expected, this is not the first attempt to develop a framework or an approach to Caribbean security, or to apply a *universal* one to the region.[4] However, this effort differs from previous ones in some notable ways. One, it adopts the *back to basics* mode advocated in the Rosenau epigraph. Two, its ambit extends beyond United States-Caribbean security relationships, or geopolitics, although it does not discount the value of focusing on these. Three, it aims to construct a holistic schema and not a partial or segmented one, and to do so in the context of twenty-first century realities.

For instance, although Robert Pastor's *whirlpool* approach is valuable and has relevance to the security area, it is (a) an approach for interpreting United States-Caribbean dynamics, and (b) not designed purely with security in mind. Similarly, Anthony Maingot's application of interdependence theory pays considerable attention to security matters, but his approach is intended essentially to explain and interpret United States-Caribbean realities writ large. James Rosenau's application of Fragmegration to the region is presented in a book on Caribbean security and it has elements relevant to the security area, but the work is essentially an analysis of the Caribbean in the vicissitudes of international politics.

Much the same could be said about Eddie Greene's schema, although Greene provides more local-regional analysis and application than Rosenau does. Leslie Manigat focuses mainly on geopolitics and ideology, while the approach by Andrés Serbin centres largely on geopolitics. Knight and Persaud deal with a regional-international architecture for security governance, and Tyrone Ferguson's framework, although comprehensive, focuses essentially on management modalities and coping strategies. My own earlier pursuit revolves around four factors – perception, capabilities, geopolitics, and ideology – the last of which has lost its salience, thereby reducing, although not eliminating, the explanatory utility of the overall framework.

The second observation is that this schema is not being presented as *the framework* for examining security in the Caribbean. It is offered as *an appropriate* one for doing so, and as a point of departure from existing ones. Moreover, it comes in the context of post-Cold War and Age of Terror realities that previous scholars did not capture because their conceptual designs did not warrant or necessitate such, or because they could not do so, given the timing of developments. Beyond this, the framework is intended to have applicability beyond the Caribbean.

Adoption of the *back to basics* approach requires attention to several issues as we approach the first question and the subsidiary questions that flow from it. Further, as is the case with the elaboration of any credible framework, design of this framework requires attention to its central building blocks, some of which are issues of structure, concept, and paradigm.

First Set of Building Blocks: Elements of Structure

States in the Caribbean share with states everywhere the reality of being in an international system characterised by what international relations scholars call *anarchy* and by complex interdependence. One analyst offered the following commentary on this structural reality:

> In previous centuries, the course of history was determined largely by events in only a few regions, particularly Europe and North America. The world's continents existed mostly apart, not influencing each other a great deal. No longer. During the twenty-first century, the struggle for progress and prosperity, as well as questions of war and peace, will be influenced by events in many disparate places.[5]

Nevertheless, Caribbean states possess a structural feature that is not common to all states in the international system: they are small states in terms of territory, population, and economy, as well as in most – and in some cases, all – elements of national power and state capacity. This structural feature accentuates their vulnerability.

It is obvious from Table 1.1 that there are intra-regional asymmetries; that Cuba, the Dominican Republic, Haiti, and Jamaica are territorial and population 'giants' compared to St Kitts-Nevis, Grenada, Barbados, and other countries; that several countries do not fit the conventional population definition of a small state—population of 1.5 million or fewer nationals.[6] Yet, it is also evident from Table 1.1 that when the capability profiles of the various states are considered overall, the characterisation of the region as one comprising small states is more than justified.

Much has been written about the security of small states over the last several decades, and although it is outside our purview to examine this literature, it should be noted that over recent years the scholarship on small state security has changed significantly. First, the preoccupation with external security has given way to recognition that internal security issues are not only important in their own right, but also they complicate, and sometimes aggravate, external challenges. Second, the distinction between internal issues and external ones is often blurred. Third, the tendency to cast security analysis in military-political terms has been replaced by acceptance that security concerns go beyond these to the economic area and also often to the environmental one. In addition, there has been growing recognition of an emphasis on the link between security and development. What Robert Rothstein noted in the mid-1980s is even more valid a decade-and-a-half

Table 1.1
Security Capability Profile of Caribbean States

Country	Size (km²)	Population	Armed Forces*	Force Make-up	Police Force (2002)	GDP Per Capita Current Prices	Real GDP Growth Rate	Foreign Debt ($ M)
Anguilla	91	12,446	None[a]	--	73	9,502	2.0	NA
Antigua-Barbuda	440	67,448	170[+]	G, CG	679[+]	9,055	3.3	406.0
Aruba	193	70,441	None[b]	--	350	1,593**	-1.2	219.7
Bahamas	13,942	30,529	860	G, CG	2,046	16,250	3.5	393.1
Barbados	432	276,607	610[+]	G, CG	1,240[+]	9,444	-2.8	667.3
Belize	22,960	262,999	1,050	G, CG, AC	776	3,144	4.6	639.7
Br. Virgin Islands	150	21,272	None[a]	--	166	36,034	NA	49.0
Cayman Islands	264	36,273	None[a]	--	166	44,571	1.5	15.8
Cuba	110,860	11,224,321	46,000	G, N, AF	20,000	2,300 (2002 est.)	2.1	27,000 (est.)
Dominica	750	70,158	None[1]	--	500[+]	3,696	-4.3	161.5
Dom. Republic	48,442	8,721,594	24,500	G, N, AF	15,000	5,800	2.7	5,400
French Guiana	90,909	183,333	None[c]	--	406 (2003)	6,000	NA	1,200
Grenada	345	89,211	None[2]	--	719[+]	3,880	-3.4	144.4
Guadeloupe	1,780	435,739	None[c]	--	660 (2003)	9,000	NA	NA
Guyana	214,970	698,209	1,600	G, CG, AC	3,350	920	1.9	1,192.6
Haiti	27,750	7,063,722	None[3]	--	5,300	478	-1.1	NA
Jamaica	11,424	2,680,029	2,830	G, CG, AC	7,756	2,982	1.7	4,146.1
Martinique	1,100	422,277	None[c]	--	603 (2003)	11,000	NA	180
Montserrat	102	8,437	None[a]	--	93	8,063	-4.2	NA
Puerto Rico	9,104	3,957,988	None[d]	--	18,543 (2003)	11,200	2.2	NA
St Kitts-Nevis	269	38,736	120[+]	G, CG	384[+]	7,450	2.4	165.5
St Lucia	616	160, 145	None	--	542[+]	4,185	-5.4	195.1
St Vincent and the Grenadines	388	116,394	None	--	789[+]	3,112	0.2	163.3
Suriname	163,270	436,494	2,040	G, CG, AC	1,064	3,500	12.3***	512
Trinidad-Tobago	5,128	1,163,724	2,700	G, CG, AC	5,424	7,069	3.3	1,637.6
Turks & Caicos	417	18,738	None[a]	--	130	11,030	0.1	8.2
US Virgin Islands	352	23,498	None[d]	--	581	15,000	NA	NA

Notes:

All figures are for 2001, unless otherwise noted
* = Active forces only ** = GDP at Constant (1995) Prices
*** = Includes informal sector NA - Not available
+= Member of the Regional Security System
a= Defence is the responsibility of the United Kingdom
b= Defence is the responsibility of the Kingdom of the Netherlands
c= Defence is the responsibility of France
d= Defence is the responsibility of the United States of America
1= Dominica had an army from November 1975 to April 1981, when it was disbanded
2= Grenada's People's Revolutionary Army was created in March 1979 and disbanded in October 1983, following the US intervention
3= The Haitian military was demobilized between November 1994 and April 1995, following *Operation Restore Democracy* in September 1994.
AC/AF= Air Component/Air Force
CG= Coast Guard
G= Ground Forces
N= Navy

Sources: Caribbean Development Bank, Annual Report 2002, March 2003; International Institute for Strategic Studies, The Military Balance 2001/02(London, 2001); Secretariat, Caribbean Commissioners of Police, 2003; International Monetary Fund, Country Information, available at http://www.imf.org/external/country/index.htm; UN Economic Commission for Latin America and the Caribbean, Economic Survey of Latin America and the Caribbean 2000–2001 (Santiago, Chile, 2002); John Collins, Caribbean Business, 2003 (data on the Police in Puerto Rico); and Col. Roger Bencze, former French Military Liaison to the Joint Inter-Agency Task Force-East, now Director of the International Liaison Division of the Joint Inter Agency Task Force-South, 2003 (data on the Gendarmarie in the French Caribbean).

later: 'The traditional concern with territorial integrity and political independence has had to be broadened to include a concern with domestic stability – and thus also a concern with prospects for, and means of, domestic development.'[7]

Moreover, what the Commonwealth Advisory Group said about the 32 small states in the 54-member-state Commonwealth of Nations is relevant to small (and medium and large) states outside the Commonwealth: 'The major threats faced by small states are to their territorial integrity and security; political independence and security; economic security; environmental sustainability; and social cohesion. Some of them are acutely vulnerable, others moderately so.'[8] The capability limitations of small states present severe security challenges to many, if not most, of them. But it is comforting to note the assessment of one recent (Commonwealth) survey: The changing international norms and the regional and international support have been such that small states generally are able to cope with their critical security challenges.[9]

Yet the fact that international norms and international cooperation help small states to cope with their security challenges does not remove another feature of small states: their vulnerability. Vulnerability arises where geographic, political, economic, or other factors cause a nation's security to be compromised. Usually, it is not a function of one factor, but several that combine to reduce or remove a state's influence or power, thereby opening it up to internal subversion or external incursion, among other things.

Some writers feel that small states are *inherently vulnerable* because they can be perceived as potentially easy victims for external aggression.[10] However, the perception of other states is merely part of the matter. Vulnerability also relates to objective geographical, economic, political, and organisational deficiencies, such as populations too small to meet security needs, limited funds to acquire defence-related material, and fragile economies to sustain development. One statesman captured some structural dynamics as follows:

> Small states are by their nature weak and vulnerable. Sometimes it seems as if small states were like small boats pushed out into a turbulent sea, free in one sense to traverse it; but, without oars or provisions, without compass or sails, free also to perish. Or, perhaps, to be rescued and taken aboard a larger vessel.[11]

Focusing on economic vulnerability, two scholars suggest that there are differing kinds of threats related to this area: economic vulnerability threats;

systemic vulnerability threats; sensitivity dependence threats; and structural dependence threats. For example, with the first, states are exposed to the transmission of external economic disturbances originating in the international system, and the second stems from transactions among states based on asymmetric relationships.[12]

In relation to our unit of analysis, it is easy to understand the reality of economic vulnerability. For instance, the Caribbean has some valuable natural resources, including oil, bauxite, gold, and diamonds. However, these resources exist in just a few countries. For example, only Trinidad and Tobago and Venezuela have large quantities of oil. Barbados, Cuba, and Suriname, to a much lesser extent, have oil industries, although there are refining and transshipment operations in many countries. Bauxite is produced only in the Dominican Republic, Guyana, Jamaica, and Suriname, and only Cuba, the Dominican Republic, Guyana, and Suriname produce gold. This limited resource availability partly explains why Caribbean economies have narrow economic bases of (a) agriculture, mainly sugar and bananas; (b) mining and manufacturing, notably bauxite, oil, gold, and apparel; and (c) services, mostly offshore finance and tourism.

The economic vulnerability is not only functional, but also structural: economies suffer from heavy reliance on foreign trade, and there is limited production and export diversification and heavy dependence on foreign capital, among other things. Much of this vulnerability has been highlighted recently as some countries suffered setbacks in the garment and tourism industries and as others faced a threat to their banana market guarantees. Moreover, the Caribbean Development Bank reported:

> 9/11 reemphasized the structural weaknesses of economies in the region and their vulnerability to external shocks. Growth was already slowing in many Caribbean economies when the closure of U.S. airspace to flights for some days and, following the resumption of air operations, the sharp decline in air travel as a result of air safety concerns, caused a massive and unprecedented reduction in tourist arrivals in Caribbean destinations.[13]

Needless to say, the vulnerability of Caribbean countries is not limited to the economic area. One Caribbean leader once eloquently described the structural and multidimensional character of the vulnerability facing states in the region:

> Our vulnerability is manifold. Physically, we are subject to hurricanes and earthquakes; economically, to market conditions taken elsewhere; socially, to cultural penetration; and now politically, to the machinations of terrorists, mercenaries, and criminals.[14]

This description is over a decade old, but it still resonates powerfully with the structural and functional realities of the region.

Second Set of Building Blocks: Core Concepts

A discussion of some core concepts is essential in order to have some definitional baselines. In this respect the plethora of definitions and the ambiguities surrounding the use of the terms *security* and *threat* make them prime candidates for this discussion.

The term *security* has long been a highly contested one, with a multiplicity of definitions and usages.[15] Most of them revolve around a few core concepts: international anarchy, survival, territorial integrity, and military power. Moreover, the definitions mostly share a common theoretical foundation in traditional realism. Although there are different variants of realism, the common denominators are: a focus on the state as the unit of analysis; stress on the competitive character of relations among states; and emphasis on military and, to a lesser extent, the political aspects of security. This approach is oriented to the international arena, which sees states as national actors rationally pursuing their interests in that arena, and considers military power capabilities as the most critical features. Traditional realism pays attention mainly to 'great powers' and views security as 'high politics'.[16]

For most of the post-World War II period there was wide consensus among political scientists and military theorists that traditional realist theory provided the appropriate conceptual architecture to examine questions of security. As might be expected, this paradigm was challenged, but not concertedly. However, the vicissitudes of international politics since the end of the Cold War have led many scholars to pursue concerted journeys beyond the traditional Realist paradigm in conceptualizing and probing security issues. A decade ago, one scholar, himself an erstwhile proponent of realism, averred:

> Realism, rooted in the experiences of World War II and the Cold War, is undergoing a crisis of confidence largely because the lessons adduced do not convincingly apply directly to the new realities. The broadened global agenda goes beyond what Realism can realistically be expected to address.[17]

As might be expected, the 'horrific tragedy', to use Prime Minister Owen Arthur's term, has served further to undermine confidence in the utility of realism. As Robert Keohane observed in 2002:

> The globalization of informal violence has rendered problematic our conventional assumptions about security threats. It should also lead us to question the classical realist distinction between important parts of the world, in which great powers have interests, and insignificant places, which were thought to present no security threats although they may raise moral dilemmas.[18]

However, it should be said that this rethinking about traditional Realism does not represent its total debunking. Quite appropriately, Richard Falk has noted:

> To challenge the centrality of realism does not imply its total repudiation. States do remain important actors, war does remain profoundly relevant to international relations, and many international settings can be better understood as collisions of interests and antagonistic political forces.[19]

In relation to our unit of analysis there is no disputing the assertion by Michael Desch that 'realism still has much to tell us about post-Cold War international relations in the American Mediterranean'.[20]

For the Caribbean, the departure from reliance on traditional realism predated the end of the Cold War and the arrival of the Age of Terror.[21] Security in the Caribbean has never really been merely protection from military threats. It has not been just about military hardware, although it has involved this; not just about military force, although it has been concerned with it; and not simply about conventional military activity, although it certainly has encompassed it. My own definition of security views it as protection and preservation of a people's freedom from external military attack and coercion, from internal subversion, and from the erosion of cherished political, economic, and social values. These values include democratic choice and political stability in the political area, sustainable development and free enterprise in the economic domain, and social equality and respect for human rights in the social arena.[22] Thus, security is multidimensional, with military, political, economic, and other dimensions. As one statesman quite rightly asserted: 'It would be a fundamental error on our part to limit security concerns to any one area while the scourge of HIV/

AIDS, illegal arms and drug trafficking, transnational crime, ecological disasters, and poverty continue to stare us in the face'.[23]

In terms of the threat arena, then, the international system or external arena cannot be the sole arena of attention. Equally important is the domestic system, or the internal arena. This is partly because of the nexus between the domestic and international arenas, but also because in many cases the source of threats and the challenges to security are not from the external environment; often the enemy is within, so to speak. In addition, the structural realities of small size and vulnerability, along with the nature and source of the threats, suggest that the definition of the relevant actors needs to go beyond the state. The state is still the primary actor in the context of the international system, but the changing dynamics of international politics, the capability limitations of Caribbean states to adequately cope with those dynamics, and the matrix of issues and actors they face suggest the need to extend the actor matrix to include non-state actors.

In this respect the remark by the late Susan Strange is quite apposite and extends beyond the area of international political economy where it was made: 'Today it seems that the heads of governments may be the last to recognize that they and their ministers have lost the authority over national societies and economies they used to have'.[24] In other words, non-state actors are equally important. Indeed, evidently from the actions of some individuals and groups engaged in drug trafficking and other criminal enterprises in the region, many non-state actors own or can mobilise more economic and military assets than some state actors.

It is partly the diminished capacity of states to cope with threats that justifies the redefinition of the actor matrix. One analyst has made the important point: 'Only when one has a reasonable idea of both the nature of threats, and the vulnerabilities of the objects towards which they are directed, can one begin to make sense of national security as a policy problem'.[25] Of course, this raises a key question: What do we mean by threat?

The two-decades-old definition by Richard Ullman has considerable explanatory utility, and will be used for our purposes:

> A threat to national security is an action or sequence of events that (i) threatens drastically and over a relatively brief span of time to degrade the quality of life for the inhabitants of a state, or (ii) threatens significantly to narrow the range of policy choices available to the government of a state or to private nongovernmental entities (persons, groups, corporations) within the state.[26]

Given our earlier definition of security as having military, political, and other dimensions, it is understandable that we would view threats in commensurate terms. Thus, threats could be military, political, economic, or environmental. Because the use of military force has the capacity to undermine national stability and sovereignty most dramatically, military threats are generally viewed as the highest priority among threats in the various dimensions.

Barry Buzan offers a sobering caution that since security has to be defined within a competitive environment, it is unwise to take the *easy route* of defining all threats as national security threats. I also agree with his suggestion that the difference between normal challenges and threats to national security necessarily occurs on a spectrum of threats that range from trivial and routine, through serious but routine, to drastic and unprecedented. And, he argues, where on the spectrum issues begin to get legitimately classified as national security problems is a matter of political choice rather than objective fact. An additional caution is needed, though, as balancing acts are critical: 'Setting the security trigger too low on the scale risks paranoia, waste of resources, aggressive policies, and serious distortions of domestic political life. Setting it too high risks failure to prepare for major assaults until too late'.[27]

Thus, threats are a function of subjective *and* objective factors. To quote Buzan again:

> The question of when a threat becomes a national security issue depends not just on what type of threat it is, and how the recipient state perceives it, but also on the intensity with which the threat operates. The main factors affecting the intensity of a threat are the specificity of its identity, its nearness in space and time, the probability of its occurring, the weight of its consequences, and whether or not perceptions of the threat are amplified by historical circumstances. Other things being equal, the more intense a threat, the more legitimate the invoking of national security as a response to it.[28]

Third Set of Building Blocks: Elements and Framework

Examination earlier of the fundamentals of structure and the core concepts involved in this design effort was an important antecedent of the next step: outlining the elements of the framework and constructing the framework itself, which I call the *Discrete Multidimensional Security Framework*. *Discrete* reflects awareness of the need to avoid inclusion of all *significant* national challenges in the security matrix, for reasons related to parsimony and policy utility. And, *Multidimensional* points both to the multiplicity of elements in the schema and the plurality of aspects of each element.

Several elements are involved, including security categories and dimensions, threat type and arenas, threats and threat intensities, and response instruments. The number and variety of elements involved make it necessary to approach the construction of the framework in component stages. Figure 1.1 maps the security categories and dimensions, showing that the *Traditional Issues* category has military, political, and economic dimensions, while the *Non-traditional Issues* category accommodates the three dimensions of the Traditional Issues category plus an additional one: environmental.

Figure 1.1
Security Categories and Dimensions

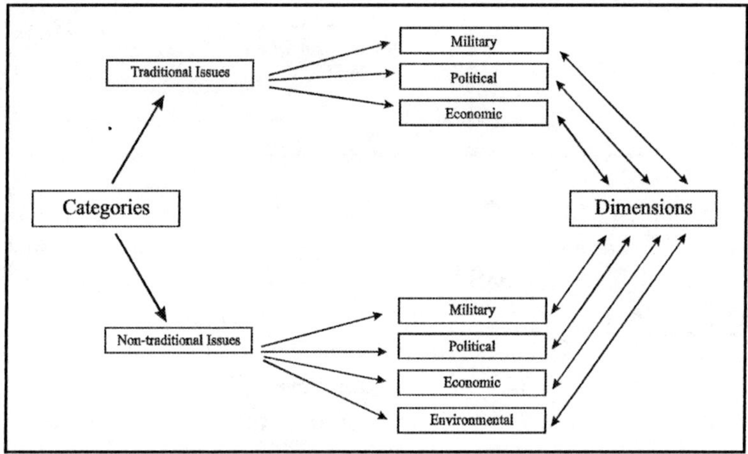

Figure 1.2 sketches threat types, threat intensities, and threat arenas. Two types of threats are identified. First are *core threats*, defined as actions or a sequence of events that affect the vital interests of nation-states, directly undermining their territorial or political integrity by jeopardising their protection against external coercion, internal subversion, or erosion of cherished political, economic, or social values. The second type of threat is the *peripheral threat*, viewed as an action or sequence of events that affects the secondary interests of nation-states by visiting collateral damage on the territorial and political integrity of the state or its cherished political, economic, or social values. Understandably this threat specification raises a key question: What do we mean by vital and secondary interests? Following

Thomas Robinson's discourse,[29] I view *vital interests* as protection of the physical, political, and cultural identity of nation-states, and *secondary interests* as matters outside the vital interests matrix but that are important to maintaining it.

Figure 1.2
Security Threat Type, Intensity, and Arena

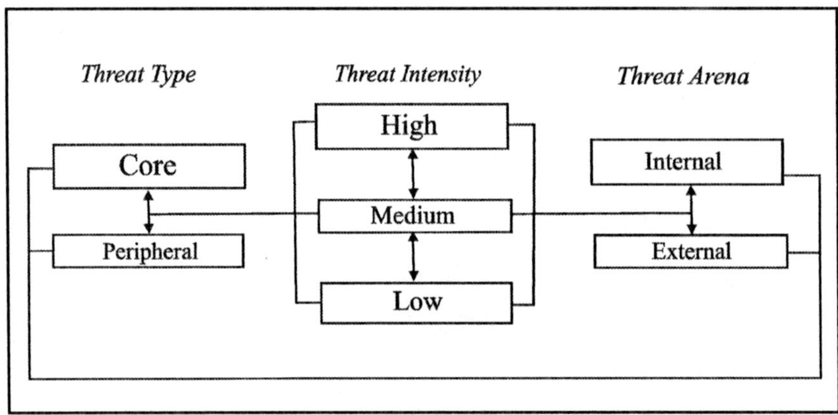

Paraphrasing George Orwell in his 1946 classic *Animal Farm*, one could observe that while all threats are important some are relatively more important than others. Hence, it is useful to distinguish among threats in terms of rank, order or intensity. Figure 1.2 therefore specifies a three-level order of threat intensity: high, medium, and low. A few observations about threat intensity and its relationship to other features in Figure 1.2 are warranted.

First, *threat intensity* is a function of both objective factors, such as the number, severity, and timing of threat actions or events and whether military force is used, and of subjective factors, largely the perception of the relevant political elites and security practitioners. On the matter of perception, Kenneth Boulding's more-than-four-decades-old remark is worth remembering:

> The people whose decisions determine the policies and actions of nations do not respond [only] to the 'objective' facts of the situation, whatever that may mean, but to their 'image' of the situation. It is what we think the world is like, not what it is really like, that determines our behavior.[30]

The second observation is that the relationship between threat type and threat intensity is variable. Thus, core threats may not always be viewed as existing at high intensity; they could be medium or low, depending on the number, severity, and timing of threat actions or events, whether military force is employed, and how the political elites define the situation. The third observation is that threat intensity is not static; the intensity of threats may change from one level to another, again, depending on objective and subjective factors.

In addition, there is no necessary correlation between threat intensity and threat arena. Put differently, not all threats from the internal arena may be high or medium; threats from either arena can be high, medium, or low, again, depending on objective and subjective factors. Finally, quite important is that there are symbiotic relationships between threat type and threat intensity, threat type and threat arena, and threat intensity and threat arena. Thus, there are dynamic relationships involving all elements of the matrix, although those relationships are not all causal-consequential in nature.

Figure 1.3
Threat Arenas, Threats, and Response Instruments

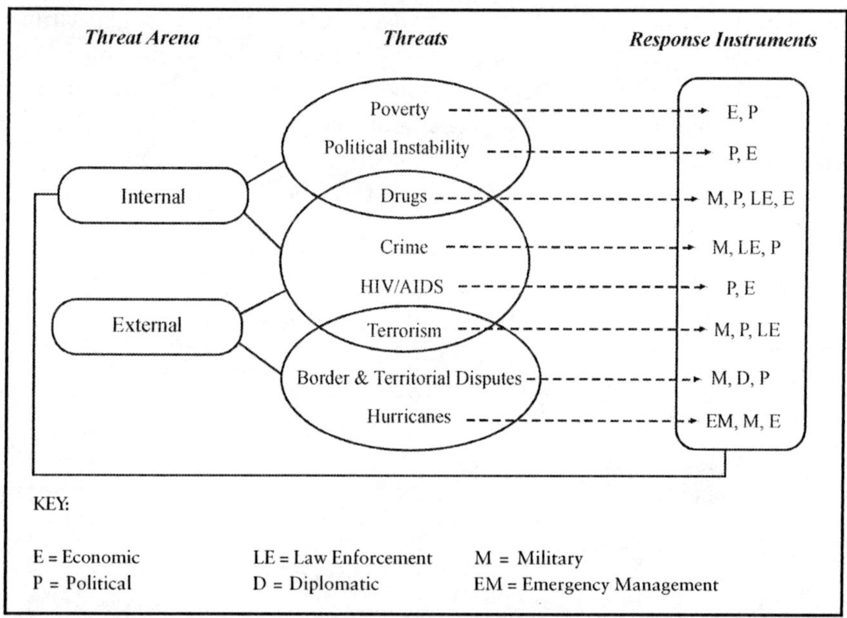

Figure 1.3 takes one component of Figure 1.2 – threat arena – and uses it to help portray the connectivity to threats and response instruments. As is evident from Figure 1.3, although some threats may be identified as being within a specific arena, most threats are a function of both internal (national)

and external (systemic) factors. They fall within the category of issues known variously as *interdependence issues*, *transsovereign problems*, and *problems without borders*.[31] It also is evident from Figure 1.3 that none of the threat issues is amenable to resolution by any single response instrument. Added to this, although the military instrument is considered to have utility in most cases, there is not universality about this. Moreover, in those cases where the military instrument is believed to be important or useful, it is but one of several instruments. Among other things, all of this supports our proposition above that some of the precepts of realism have little or no applicability to the Caribbean.

It is important to take the response instruments beyond what is portrayed in Figure 1.3 and establish linkages to the actors in the security milieu and to their engagement in that milieu. This is diagrammed in Figure 1.4.

The milieu is one where both state and non-state actors are engaged. They do so both nationally and internationally. International engagements are found at several levels: subregional, regional, and hemispheric. As is shown in the graphic, there are three kinds of actors other than governmental agencies at the national level: individuals, non-governmental organisations, and corporations. Four kinds of actors feature at the international level: states, intergovernmental organisations, international non-governmental organisations, and multinational corporations. Engagement Zones, defined as geographic spaces for policy and operational collaboration by state and non-state actors in relation to defense and security matters, exist nationally and internationally.

Figure 1.4
Instruments, Actors, and Security Engagement Zones

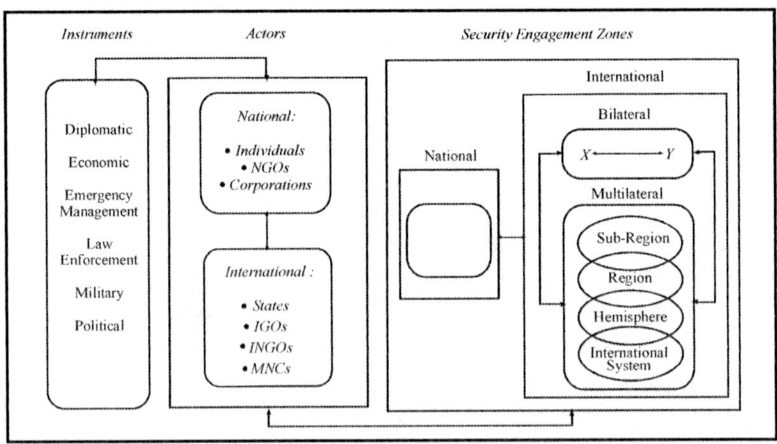

As regards the relationship between actors and engagement zones, it should be noted that the nature and capabilities of some actors make them better candidates for engagement in some zones than in others. For instance, individuals may have engagement capacity within the national zone, but they have little or none outside of it. National corporations that are part of a multinational corporate structure have a better chance of international engagement than those without it, although the interest in regional or hemispheric engagement may exist.

Also, as one might expect, there is variability in the nature and scope of engagement by the various actors and in the response instruments used. As an example, some NGOs may not be engaged in counter narcotics or counter terrorism efforts, but they may be engaged in the area of HIV/AIDS. Others may have little or no engagement capacity in relation to terrorism or territorial disputes, but rather in relation to crime or drugs. Further, depending on the nature of the actor and of the threat, the use of military or law enforcement instruments may be out of the question. Or, such capacity may very well exist but not be welcome by the managers of the state, for a variety of reasons.

In relation to the engagement zones, subregions, regions, and the hemisphere are viewed as relatively discrete spaces for analytic purposes, but they are not exclusive spaces in terms of actual engagement; they overlap. Figure 1.4 highlights both bilateral and multilateral engagements at the international level. But it does not reveal the fact that each of the multilateral zones has several non-state and state entities, with both governmental and international governmental units in the state category. Engagement instruments, such as treaties, conventions, memorandums, charters, and protocols, guide the actors at the subregional, regional, and other levels. Such instruments create the organisations that operate within the zones and define their terms of engagement.

The Discrete Multidimensional Security Framework[32] is portrayed in Figure 1.5. Developing it in stages, captured in Figures 1.1, 1.2, 1.3, and 1.4, makes mapping of the overall Framework relatively easy. As is the case with any framework, this Framework is a heuristic device. As such, it is not intended to explain each and every element or component of the social phenomenon or researchable issue being explored. The aim is to provide a conceptual architecture to facilitate explanation and interpretation of structures, patterns, and dynamics involved in the security issue area. While the Framework is being used in this assessment *of the Caribbean*, it is not designed *for the Caribbean*; it is intended for use in security assessments generally.

Figure 1.5
Discrete Multidimensional Security Framework

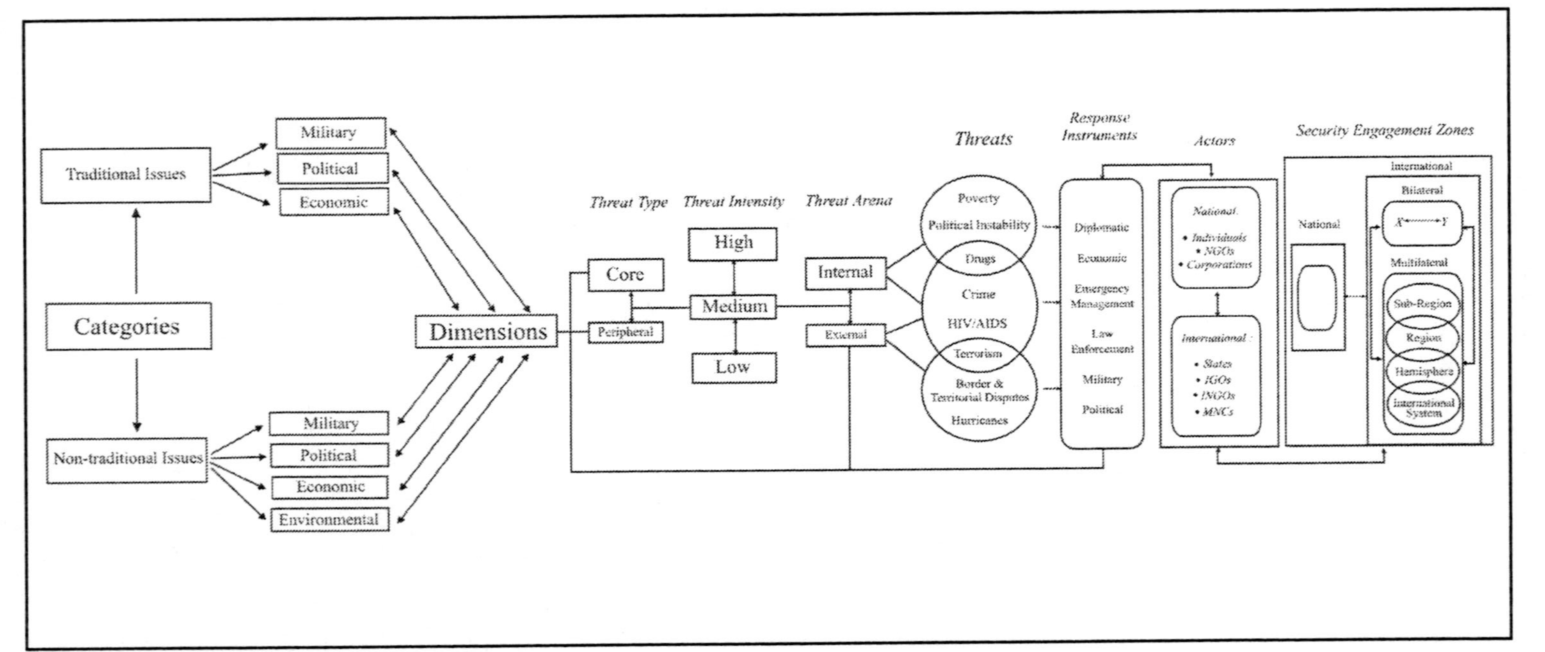

This Framework could be applied in cases where the unit of analysis is an individual state or aggregates of states, such as subregions and regions. The Caribbean region is the unit of analysis in this study. In the context of a region it is important to observe that security challenges facing one or a few states *within a region* do not automatically become *challenges of the region.* Therefore, it is important to clarify when *challenges within a region* become *challenges of the region.* This clarification is needed because of methodological considerations related to the application of the Framework. In this respect it should be stated that our assessment is an appraisal of the Caribbean in aggregate terms and not of each of the nations within it.

In terms of *challenges within a region* versus *challenges of a region*, a point made elsewhere in another context is worth stating here: regional security is relational. As such, it is difficult to appreciate the national security challenges of one state in a region without understanding the patterns of security interdependence within the region.[33] The relational aspect of regional security is central to coming to terms with the issue of *challenges within a region* and *challenges of a region.* Yet, the relational aspect alone does not resolve the issue. Needed also is a baseline or a set of parameters to facilitate judgment on the regional salience of the challenges. In the context of this Framework, *regional salience*, which is a function of the threat type and threat intensity, is influenced by three main factors: the number of states affected; the definition of the situation by the relevant elites of the states within the region; and the amount of resources being invested in the matter by state (and non-state) actors.

As regards the first factor, a reasonable approach is to use a ratio of states affected to the number of member-states in a relevant regional organisation.[34] For our purposes, the ratio will be two-thirds of membership, and the relevant regional organisation will be the Association of Caribbean States (ACS). A few observations are warranted. The first pertains to the ratio. Barry Buzan's caution against setting the security trigger too low, which was noted above, is relevant not just to the national arena, but to the regional one as well. This influences the desire here for a salience factor with a high bar for inclusion and, consequently, the adoption of a ratio of two-thirds. It is an above-minimum threshold. Partly because of this it often defines the quorum – the minimum number needed for the conduct of official business, especially for decision making – of the significant organs of international entities or the special majority decision making within them. For instance, it features in the General Assembly of the United Nations, the

General Assembly of the Organization of American States (OAS), and the Ministerial Council of the ACS.

The second observation pertains to the relevant regional organisation. The ACS is used because it is the most inclusive of the organisations of which Caribbean states are a part. It was formed in 1994 to strengthen regional cooperation and integration, preserve the environmental integrity of the Caribbean Sea, and promote sustainable development. It has a membership of 25 states (Antigua and Barbuda, Bahamas, Barbados, Belize, Colombia, Costa Rica, Cuba, Dominica, Dominican Republic, El Salvador, Grenada, Guatemala, Guyana, Haiti, Honduras, Jamaica, Mexico, Nicaragua, Panama, St Lucia, St Kitts and Nevis, St Vincent and the Grenadines, Suriname, Trinidad and Tobago, and Venezuela) and three associate members (Aruba, France on behalf of French Guiana, Guadeloupe, and Martinique, and the Netherlands Antilles).[35] Considering the ratio and the ACS membership, the numerical threshold for regional salience is 17. Incidentally, this calculation does not take account of associate membership.

The second salience factor pertains to elite perception, which, as we discussed above, is a critical variable. However, the perception factor in this case of estimating regional salience goes beyond the perception of the political elites and security practitioners of states – either those facing the challenges or those that are part of regional organisations. It extends to that of key role actors within regional organisations, such as secretaries-general and directors-general of organisations such as the ACS, the Caribbean Community (CARICOM), the Regional Security System (RSS), and the Organisation of Eastern Caribbean States (OECS). As to the third factor – amount of resources invested – the resources of relevance are not just money and manpower, but also the amount of time devoted to the matter by leaders individually and in bilateral and multilateral contexts, such as summits.

From Framework Design to Framework Application

Having dealt with the first question – What is an appropriate conceptual framework for examining Caribbean security realities? – it is now appropriate to proceed to the second one: In the context of that framework what are the key security challenges facing the region? This entails applying the Discrete Multidimensional Security Framework, which requires attention to security categories, threat type, the intensity of the threats, and the arena in which the threats manifest themselves.

Our analysis will not necessarily capture all issues deemed relevant to the security issue area by policy-makers or scholars. Moreover, application of any framework does not require that every aspect be probed whenever the framework is being applied. Consequently, dealing with our second question does not involve application of every aspect of our Framework. It does not, for instance, require probing the elements related to security engagement zones and response instruments. (These are explored in Chapter 21 in relation to the third question identified in the Introduction: What are some relevant strategies to cope with the challenges confronting states in the region?)

In terms of the security categories identified in the Framework, evidence suggests that Caribbean states face both traditional and non-traditional security challenges, although there is variable significance between the two. The extant challenges cover the spectrum of dimensions – military, political, economic, and environmental – although, again, there is variable significance among dimensions. Needless to say, we cannot examine all the possible challenges in the pertinent categories and dimensions. However, in examining the traditional category it is important to pay some attention to (a) border and territorial disputes, and (b) regional geopolitics.

Traditional Category, Various Dimensions

Border and Territorial Disputes

In relation to disputes, both land and maritime controversies are involved, as Table 1.2 shows. It is important to observe that although the term *border disputes* generally is used to refer to the controversies over land and sea, the disputes in which Caribbean states are involved are not all border disputes, which are controversies between and among states over the alignment of land or maritime boundaries. Some controversies, such as those between Venezuela and Guyana, and between Suriname and Guyana, are really territorial disputes: controversies arising from claims to land or maritime territory. As might be expected, some territorial disputes derive from controversies over border alignment. The most serious disputes involve Venezuela and Guyana, Suriname and Guyana, Venezuela and Colombia, and France (French Guiana) and Suriname.

Table 1.2
Border and Territorial Disputes Involving Caribbean Countries

PARTIES IN DISPUTE	KIND OF DISPUTE	BRIEF BACKGROUND AND SPRING 2003 STATUS
Antigua-Barbuda and France (Guadeloupe)	Maritime	Dispute reported with St Bartholemy, details unavailable. Antigua and Barbuda also object to the treaties signed by France, the Netherlands, and the United States, recognising Venezuela's claims to Islas des Aves.
Belize and Guatemala	Land	Unilateral territorial dispute: Guatemala claims half of Belize's territory south of the Sibun River based on an unfulfilled 1859 treaty. A referendum based on OAS negotiations in 2002 that created an adjustment at the Mexico tripoint, a broad Caribbean passage, and an aid package was not brought to a vote in Guatemala and postponed in Belize.
Belize and Guatemala	Maritime	At present, Guatemalan access to the Caribbean is closed off by Belize's and Honduras' territorial seas. In 2002, Guatemala did not bring the land and maritime boundary referendum forward for a popular vote over concerns of rejection. Historically, Belize objects to Guatemala's historic bay claim to the Bahia de Amatique and to linking its land boundary claims to resolution of the maritime boundary.
Belize and Honduras	Land	Honduran claims to Sapodilla Cays off Belize coast pending resolution of Belize-Guatemala dispute which proposed an international marine park.
Belize and Honduras	Maritime	No disputes identified except for Honduran claim to Sapodilla Cays. Under the OAS-negotiated Belize-Guatemala referendum, Belize and Honduras agree to create a maritime corridor for Guatemala. The Referendum has not been brought to a vote.
Colombia and Honduras	Maritime	Island disputes prevent signing. Agreement cedes Serranilla Bank to Colombia, which Jamaica, Nicaragua, and the US also claim, together with Bajo Nuevo (Petrel Bank). Nicaragua disputes the legitimacy of this agreement as it disputes Colombia's claim to waters east of 82°W (see Colombia-Nicaragua)
Colombia and Jamaica	Maritime	Two circles cut out of Joint Regime Area (JRA) for disputed Serranilla Bank and Bajo Nuevo (Low Cays). Features also claimed by US, Honduras, Nicaragua.
Colombia and Nicaragua	Land	Territorial dispute: Nicaragua claims and occupies San Andrés and Providencia islands; Albuquerque, Este-Sudeste, Roncador Cays; and the Quito Sueño and Serrana Banks on the Nicaragua Rise. During Sandinista rule, Nicaragua rejected all Colombian maritime and island claims east of 82°W, based on 1928 Treaty. Nicaragua claims, without contest, and occupies Corn Islands (Islas del Maiz). US relinquished all claims on these features in 1970s. Serranilla Bank, Bajo Nuevo (Petrel Bank) are claimed by parties along with Honduras, Jamaica, and US who reserve the right to claim these features.
Colombia and Nicaragua	Maritime	During Sandinista rule, Nicaragua rejected all Colombian maritime and island claims east of 82°W based on 1928 Barcemas-Esquerra Treaty, arguing that treaty was signed under pressure during US occupation. In 1988, Nicaraguan government maintained claim but accepts Colombian de facto occupation. (See also Colombia-Honduras)
Colombia and Panama (Caribbean Sea)	Maritime	Equidistance was not considered vis à vis the Colombian-claimed islands. Panama retains a dormant claim to the Colombian-claimed islands as they were once attached to Panama when it was a province of Colombia prior to 1903.

Colombia and United States	Land	Territorial dispute: Both states claim Serranilla Bank and Bajo Nuevo together with Honduras, Jamaica and Nicaragua.
Colombia and Venezuela	Land	Territorial dispute: Both states claim Los Monjes islands despite 1980 bilateral agreement to award them to Venezuela; numerous land boundary disputes, particularly related to Goajirá Peninsula, now largely resolved. Swiss (1922) arbitration resulted in successful demarcation in 1932. Borderland issues include illegal border crossings, Colombian migration, drug-weapons smuggling, and general lawlessness.
Colombia and Venezuela	Maritime	Venezuela occupied Los Monjes islands in 1950s. Still issue of contention despite 1980 agreement to grant them to Venezuela with limited Colombian rights in the Gulf of Venezuela (Golfo de Coquibacoa). Attempts to come to an agreement on maritime boundary around islands and to establish a bay closing line have failed with periodic resurgence of angry rhetoric. Colombia and other states protest Venezuelan closing line in gulf based on 'a historic bay, a condominium of two riparian states'.
Cuba and Haiti	Maritime	Haiti claims and Cuba rejects US claim over Navassa Island. Boundary is configured as if Navassa were Haitian, connecting to Cuba-Jamaica boundary.
Cuba and United States (Guantánamo)	Land	Cuba protests US presence on territory; $3300/year lease of 118 sq km until lease runs out in 2033 (no US checks cashed since 1962). Heavily fortified boundary.
Cuba and United States (Navassa Island)	Maritime	Cuba together with Haiti protest US administration of Navassa island off the coast of Haiti. Cuba and Jamaica ignore US claim in delimitation of joint maritime boundary.
Dominica and Venezuela (Islas des Aves)	Maritime	Dominica protests Venezuelan claim to Aves Island as a basepoint for claiming EEZ rights. It considers the features rocks and not islands.
France (French Guiana) and Suriname	Land	Territorial dispute stemming from which upstream tributary of the Morouini(Maroni)/Litani(Itany) forms boundary. Colonial rulers submitted dispute to Russian Czar (1891), and The Hague (1905). Suriname after independence (1975) adopted the Dutch line but later was willing to agree to the French line (1977) in return for joint development aid. Recent agreement awaits ratification, resolving dispute.
Guatemala and Honduras	Maritime	Belize and Honduras are willing to share a maritime corridor with Guatemala under terms of OAS-negotiated agreement. Guatemala contests Honduras' claim under the 'Maritime Areas of Honduras Act' to Sapodilla Cays, also claimed and administered by Belize.
Guyana and Suriname	Land	Boundary dispute over which upper tributary (New River or Cutari/Curuni) of Courentyne (Corantijn) constitutes primary channel, resulting in Suriname territorial claim over New River triangle in southeast Guyana. Cutari had been historical boundary until an 1841 discovery proving Cutari larger. 1939 treaty never signed and dispute became more acute after Suriname independence in 1975. A new map showing Suriname's claim on the New River triangle has frustrated negotiations, but the parties continue talking.
Guyana and Suriname	Maritime	Dispute over direction of maritime line extending from Courentyne (Corantijn) River and exact location of river's shoreline terminus. Suriname asserts a continental shelf claim directed 10° east of the meridian, and Guyana at 33°. Oil prospecting is inhibited. In 2000, Suriname's gunboats halted Guyanese-sponsored oil prospecting in the disputed wedge.
Guyana and Venezuela	Land	Territorial and boundary dispute over Essequibo river. Venezuela claims river is a natural boundary and not the 1844 Shomburgk line, which UK declared as boundary in 1886. An 1899 US arbitration resulted in bilateral concessions and demarcation in 1905. Venezuela reasserted Essequibo River claims in 1951 but in 1970 signed a 12-year moratorium with UK and independent (1966) Guyana. Venezuela refuses to renew the moratorium, surfacing and abating claims periodically.

Guyana and Venezuela	Maritime	Territorial dispute over Essequibo region prevents definition of a maritime boundary, inhibiting oil prospecting. Until the recent domestic turmoil in Venezuela, which has put the boundary dispute in hiatus, the parties had been engaged in cordial discussions. Even Guyanese seizure of Venezuelan fishing vessels for illegal fishing in 2002 did not elevate tensions.
Haiti and Jamaica	Maritime	Negotiations are planned but Haiti's claim to US-administered Navassa Island prevents creation of maritime boundary at Cuba-Haiti, Cuba-Jamaica tripoint.
Haiti and United States	Maritime	Sovereignty dispute over Navassa Island prevents establishment of maritime boundary. The US has not yet determined the limits of the fishery conservation zone around the island.
Honduras and Jamaica	Land	Territorial dispute: both states claim Bajo Nuevo and Serranilla Bank together with Colombia, Nicaragua, and US.
Honduras and Jamaica	Maritime	States have negotiations underway with resolution complicated by Serranilla Banks/Bajo Nuevo dispute also claimed by Colombia, Nicaragua and the United States.
Honduras and Nicaragua (Caribbean Sea)	Maritime	In 1986, Honduras and Colombia signed the Caribbean Sea Maritime Limits Treaty, which established a maritime boundary along the parallel as an extension of the Honduras-Nicaragua land boundary beyond the 82° meridian. Nicaragua protested treaty and subsequent Maritime Areas of Honduras Act and claimed Honduras placed troops on Cayo Sur. In 1999, Nicaragua petitioned the ICJ to resolve the boundary disputes among the three parties. As an interim measure, the OAS facilitates the disputants signing a Memorandum of Understanding (2000) and a confidence and security document (2001) to ease tensions. ICJ recently ruled in favor of Honduras' petition against Nicaragua's 35 per cent tariff on Honduran imports to retaliate against Honduras' maritime treaty with Colombia. Main ICJ boundary ruling pending.
Honduras and United States	Land	Territorial dispute: both states claim Bajo Nuevo and Serranilla Bank together with Colombia, Jamaica, and Nicaragua.
Jamaica and Navassa Island (United States)	Land	Territorial dispute: Jamaica appears to recognise Haiti's claim to Navassa Island by connecting its maritime boundary with Cuba to the Cuba-Haiti maritime boundary (that rejects the US claim).
Jamaica and Nicaragua	Land	Territorial dispute: both states claim Bajo Nuevo and Serranilla Bank together with Colombia, Honduras, US.
Jamaica and Nicaragua	Maritime	States have negotiations planned pending resolution of the Serranilla Banks/Bajo Nuevo dispute also claimed by Colombia, Nicaragua and the United States and resolution of disputed islands claimed by Nicaragua and occupied by Colombia.
Jamaica and United States	Land	Territorial dispute: both states claim Bajo Nuevo and Serranilla Bank together with Colombia, Honduras, and Nicaragua.
Nicaragua and United States	Land	Territorial dispute: Both states claim Bajo Nuevo and Serranilla Bank together with Honduras, Jamaica, and Nicaragua.
St Kitts-Nevis and Venezuela (Aves Islands)	Maritime	Saint Kitts and Nevis sent letter to the UN protesting the Venezuelan claim to Aves Island as a base point for claiming EEZ rights. It considers the features rocks and not islands.
Saint Lucia and Venezuela (Aves Islands)	Maritime	Saint Lucia sends letter to the UN protesting the Venezuelan claim to Aves Island as a basepoint for claiming EEZ rights. It considers the features to be rocks and not islands. Saint Lucia also objects to the treaties signed by France, the Netherlands and the United States, recognising Venezuela's claims to Islas des Aves.
Saint Martin[France (Guadeloupe)] – Sint Maarten [Netherlands Antilles (Leeward Islands)]	Land	Reported dispute over terminus of boundary. Only 'Schengen' European Union boundary in Western Hemisphere without customs or immigration controls. The boundary is governed by the 1648 Treaty of Concordia. Saint-Martin is part of the French Overseas Department of Guadeloupe.

St Vincent and the Grenadines and Venezuela	Maritime	Territorial dispute: Saint Vincent and the Grenadines sends letter to the UN protesting the Venezuelan claim to Aves Island as a basepoint for claiming EEZ rights. It considers the features to be rocks and not islands. Saint Vincent and the Grenadines object to the treaties signed by France, the Netherlands, and the United States, recognising Venezuela's claims to Islas des Aves.

Source: Adapted from Raymond J. Milefsky, 'Territorial Disputes and Regional Security in the Caribbean Basin,' in this volume.

As Table 1.2 also indicates, some countries are involved in multiple disputes. For example, Guyana is facing a claim by Venezuela for the western five-eighths of its 214,970 km^2 territory, and one by Suriname for 15,000 km^2 to the east. The long-standing Guatemala claim against Belize is also a massive claim. A milestone in efforts to settle that dispute was reached in August 2002. The settlement grew out of negotiations facilitated by Paul S. Reichtler for Guatemala and Sir Shridath Ramphal for Belize, under the auspices of the OAS.

The Ramphal-Reichtler proposals pertain to five key issues: land issues (including the boundary and the community of Santa Rosa); maritime issues (including territorial seas, exclusive economic zones and continental shelves, and the Belize-Honduras-Guatemala Ecological Park); a development trust fund; trade, investment, and functional cooperation; and transitional arrangements. In relation to the fifth area, the two nations took the settlement process one step further in signing an agreement about the transition process and confidence-building measures on February 7, 2003. Later the same month, OAS officials went to the two countries to establish an OAS office in the Adjacency Zone. This office will verify any transgressions of confidence-building measures as the agreement is implemented.[36]

The above discussion of border and territorial disputes suggests that at this writing (Summer 2003) although many Caribbean states face this challenge it constitutes a core threat for only a handful of states, and a peripheral one for many of them. In terms of regional salience, when one considers the issue of security interdependence and the regional salience factors – number of states affected, elite perception, and resource investment – the issue of border and territorial disputes must be viewed as a regional security challenge and not merely a challenge for a few states within the region. However, the threat intensity level is either medium or low for most of the relevant states.

As of summer 2003 the Guyana-Suriname dispute is the only one with medium-to-high intensity. After a lull of nearly three years, the dispute took a fairly dramatic turn in March 2003 when the Guyana Defence Force (GDF) high command deployed the GDF coast guard flagship, *M.V. Essequibo*, from the eastern town of New Amsterdam to patrol the waters off the Guyana-Suriname border following publication by Suriname of a map showing the disputed area as part of its territory. The GDF explained that the deployment 'to the median line in the Courentyne River to ensure there is no breach of our territory' was meant to signal the 'firm response' of Guyana to the actions by Suriname, which it deemed as 'provocative'. In response, Suriname's Defence Minister, Ronald Assen, placed the Suriname Defense Force navy on 'alert' status.[37]

Geopolitics

It is important to state at the outset that regional geopolitics – defined here as the relationship between physical and political geography and national power – as a traditional security concern does not constitute a threat as such; it provides the context in which vulnerabilities and threats may develop or be accentuated, or national power enhanced. The geopolitical context – and significance – of the Caribbean lies, generally, in its possession of strategic materials, in the location of vital Sea Lanes of Communication (SLOC) there, and in the security networks of powerful states in the area.

As regards strategic materials, Caribbean states own and produce natural resources that are important for military and civilian purposes. Some materials noted in the discussion about vulnerability above are key in this regard: petroleum and natural gas, bauxite, gold, nickel, silver, and diamonds. It might be useful to note some of the military and civilian uses of some of these strategic materials. For instance, in the military area bauxite is very important for the manufacture of a variety of military vehicles and of ammunition. In the civilian area, the use of petroleum extends beyond gasoline for automobiles; petroleum products are used also for heating, chemicals, and plastics. In relation to petroleum, although many countries do not produce this strategic material, they have considerable oil industry value, because of refining and transshipment operations conducted there. Among them are Aruba, the Bahamas, Curaçao, the Dominican Republic, Jamaica, Puerto Rico, St Lucia, and the US Virgin Islands.

In relation to SLOC, two of the world's major 'choke points' are in the Caribbean area; one is the Panama Canal and the other is the Caribbean

Sea. The Canal, which started operations in August 1914, links the Atlantic and Pacific oceans. It is 50 miles long from deep water in the Atlantic to deep water in the Pacific, and saves 8,000 miles and 20 to 30 days of steaming between the two oceans. The Canal has both military and civilian value. It has been observed, for instance, that 'From a narrow military perspective, the Panama Canal remains useful for the rapid transit of military supplies from one theater to another, particularly in a "two major regional contingency" scenario', and that 'the efficiency and routine operation of the Canal itself remains of critical commercial importance to the United States (over 10% of all US trade passes through the Canal; two thirds of all transits either originate or terminate in the United States)'.[38] It is widely accepted that while the Canal is now less important to the United States than two decades ago, other countries are still very dependent on it, among them Chile, Ecuador, and Japan.

Once ships leave the Canal from the Pacific Ocean, they must use one or more of the several Caribbean Sea passages shown in Figure 1.6, en route to destinations in the United States, Europe, Africa, and elsewhere. The Florida Strait, Mona Passage, Windward Passage, and the Yucatan Channel are the principal SLOCs for ships entering or leaving the Caribbean. Needless to say, the strategic significance of the Caribbean Sea predates the creation of the Panama Canal. European leaders recognised its importance soon after the 1492 encounter between Europe and the Americas. Thus, it is quite natural that powers great and small, and near and far, would, over the centuries, consider it strategically important.

Figure 1.6
Caribbean Sea Lanes of Communication

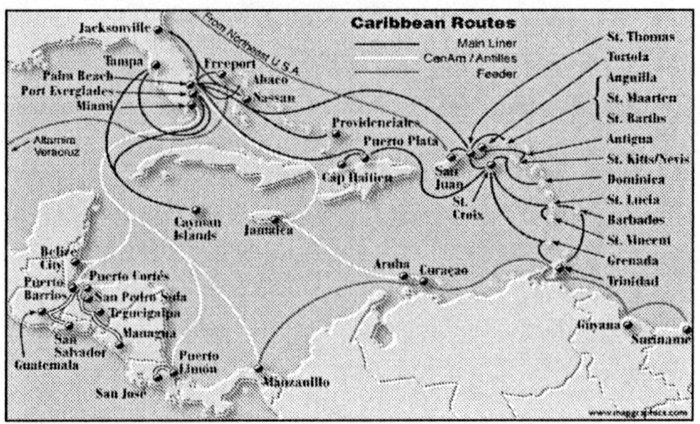

In terms of security networks, up until the early 1990s United States officialdom considered the Caribbean its 'southern flank', its 'strategic rear'. (Now the region is considered the 'Third Border' of the United States.) A considerable force presence was maintained there, mainly in Puerto Rico, at the Atlantic threshold of the Caribbean; in Panama, at the southern rim of the Caribbean Basin; and in Cuba – at Guantánamo Bay – on the northern perimeter. In 1990, for instance, the United States maintained 4,743 military and civilian personnel in Puerto Rico, 20,709 army, navy, and air force personnel in Panama, and the naval operations in Cuba had a personnel establishment of 3,401. Other bases and installations were also maintained throughout the region. Much has changed since 1990, though, including strategic redesign and force redeployment. Puerto Rico is now home to fewer forces, and the US Southern Command (SOUTHCOM) relocated from Panama to Miami in 1997. Guantánamo, long viewed as having little strategic value, began to serve essentially as a political beachhead in the hemisphere's last remaining communist outpost. However, 9/11 changed things somewhat; Guantánamo became an important detention staging post as the United States prosecuted its 9/11 and counter-terrorism battles.[39]

As might be expected, 9/11 did more than renew the strategic value of Guantánamo; it also precipitated changes in US national security posture and architecture, some of which relate to the Caribbean. For instance, it caused a major revision of the Unified Command Plan (UCP), which is the overall military schema that guides all unified commands by (a) establishing missions, responsibilities, and force structures, (b) delineating geographic areas of responsibilities (for geographic combat commanders), and (c) specifying functional responsibilities (for functional commanders).

The revision became effective October 1, 2002. It has several elements, including:

- increasing to 10 the number of geographic and functional commands, including the creation of the US Northern Command (NORTHCOM);
- merging the Space Command and the Strategic Command into an expanded Strategic Command (STRATCOM); and
- realignment of the missions of several commands, including SOUTHCOM, Joint Forces Command, and the European Command.[40]

The five geographic commands are: European, Pacific, Southern, Central, and Northern. The five functional commands are: Space, Strategic, Transportation, Special Operations, and Joint Forces (formerly Atlantic).

The geographic commands relevant to the Caribbean are NORTHCOM and SOUTHCOM, as Figure 1.7 shows. NORTHCOM, which is headquartered at the Peterson Air Force Base in Colorado, has an Area of Responsibility (AOR) that covers the continental United States, Alaska, Canada, and Mexico and the surrounding waters out to 500 miles. Its mission entails preparation for, prevention of, deterrence of, preemption of, defense against, and response to threats and aggression directed toward US territory, sovereignty, domestic population, and infrastructure. As regards the Caribbean, although Figure 1.7 shows Cuba, the Bahamas, and a few other places as being within the NORTHCOM sphere, SOUTHCOM remains responsible for contingency planning, operations, security, and force protection in relation to Cuba, the Bahamas, British Virgin Islands, and the Turks and Caicos Islands.[41]

Figure 1.7
The Caribbean in NORTHCOM and SOUTHCOM

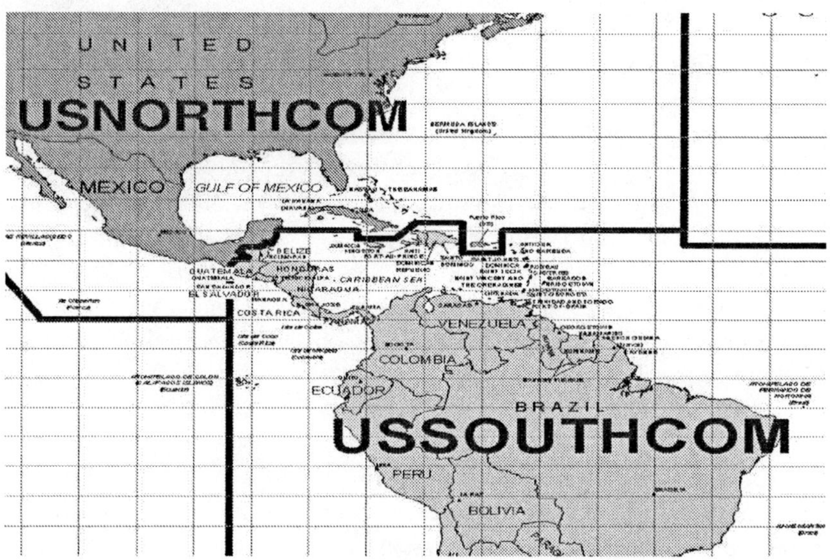

Of course, the United States has not been the only 'big power' with security networks in the area. Notable in this respect were the bases and networks maintained by the USSR, especially in Cuba. During the heyday of Cold War geopolitical games in the Americas, the Soviet-Cuban connection was said to have three main aims: fostering of political-military changes in the region to eventually facilitate Soviet-Cuban expansion there; promotion of conflict situations that could entrap or encumber US forces were they to intervene in the Central American conflict; and creation of greater dissension between the United States and the other countries in the hemisphere.[42]

During the 1980s the Soviet military presence in Cuba included modern docks and repair facilities, airport facilities for reconnaissance aircraft, and satellite and other surveillance operations. The 28-square mile facility at Lourdes had three functions: monitoring US missile tests; intercepting satellite communications, and relaying microwave communications between the USSR and its diplomatic posts in the Western Hemisphere. At the time, the Lourdes facility was reputedly the largest such operation the Soviets maintained outside the USSR. As the USSR progressively collapsed, in September 1991 President Mikhail Gorbachev announced discussions with Cuban officials about the withdrawal of 11,000 troops from the island. The Soviet military presence was progressively reduced from November 1991 onward. However, the intelligence facility at Lourdes was maintained until October 2001 when President Vladimir Putin ordered it closed.[43]

Non-traditional Category, Various Dimensions

Drugs, crime, political instability, HIV/AIDS, and poverty are the primary non-traditional security concerns. These are not the only concerns, of course; illicit arms trafficking, environmental degradation, and illegal migration also feature. There is no uniformity in the importance statesmen and scholars ascribe to these issues, but a comparison of the two categories – traditional and non-traditional – would reveal that they place a higher premium on the non-traditional area than on the traditional one. Of course, some states, such as those in the Eastern Caribbean, have few traditional security concerns. But, public security issues, related to drugs and crime, are of particular concern.

As might be appreciated, all the primary (or secondary) issues in the non-traditional category cannot be discussed here. However, some of them deserve some attention. The issue of drugs tops the list.

Drugs

The Caribbean lies at 'the Vortex of the Americas'; it is a bridge or front between North and South America. European actors recognised the strategic importance of this vortex soon after Columbus' first voyage. This strategic importance has persisted over the centuries, and it was dramatised in geopolitical terms during the Cold War. However, the region's strategic value lies not only in its geopolitical significance as viewed by state actors engaged in conflict and cooperation. Over recent decades the region has also been viewed as strategic by non-state drug actors, also with conflict and cooperation in mind, not in terms of geopolitics, but geonarcotics.

The concept of *geonarcotics* suggests the dynamics of three factors besides drugs: geography, power, and politics. As Figure 1.8 reveals, it posits, first, that the narcotics phenomenon is multidimensional, with four main problem areas (drug production, consumption abuse, trafficking, and money laundering); second, that these problem areas give rise to actual and potential threats to the security of states around the world; and third, that the drug operations and the activities they spawn precipitate both conflict and cooperation among various state and non-state actors in the international system.

Figure 1.8
Geonarcotics Framework

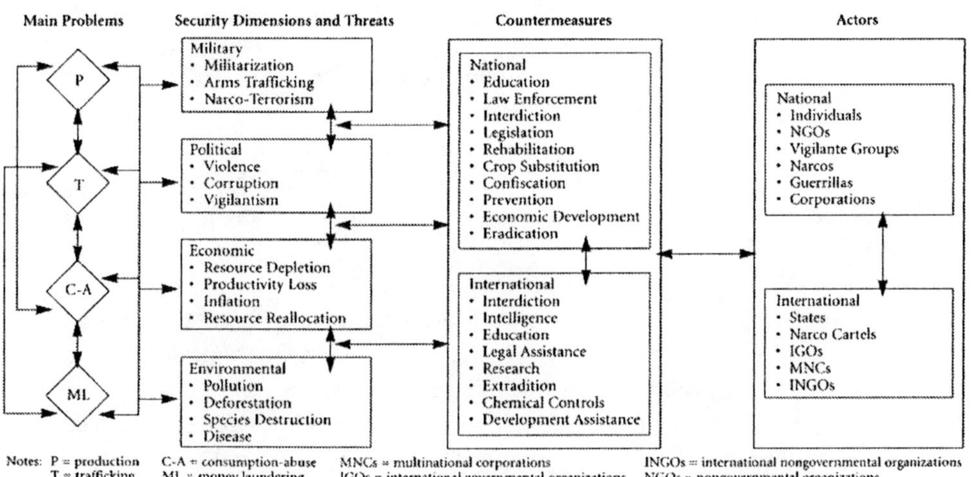

Source: Ivelaw Lloyd Griffith, Drugs and Security in the Caribbean: Sovereignty Under Siege *(University Park, Pa: Pennsylvania State University Press, 1997).*

Geography is a factor because of the global dispersion of drug operations, and because certain physical, social, and political geography features of many countries facilitate drug operations. *Power* involves the ability of individuals and groups to secure compliant action. In the drug world, this power is both state and non-state in origin, and in some cases non-state sources command relatively more power than states. *Politics* revolves around resource allocation in terms of the ability of power brokers to determine who gets what, how, and when. Since power in this milieu is not only state power, resource allocation is correspondingly not exclusively a function of state power-holders. Moreover, politics becomes perverted, and more perverted where it already was so.

The geonarcotics milieu involves a variety of state and non-state actors, which differ in how they affect and are affected by the various problems, and in their countermeasures. Drug operations generate two basic kinds of interactions: cooperation and conflict. These are bilateral and multilateral, and do not all involve force. Some involve non-military pressures, such as economic and political sanctions by the United States against countries that it considers not proactive enough in fighting drugs. Some actors engage simultaneously in both cooperation and conflict. The relationships between the United States and Colombia and Mexico over the last decade, and between the United States and Jamaica and Barbados during the late 1990s, reveal this.

The geonarcotics approach does not view the 'war on drugs' purely as a military matter. Hence, the application of military countermeasures alone is considered impractical. Moreover, international countermeasures are necessary, especially since all states – even rich and powerful ones – face resource constraints. However, collaboration among states may result in conflict over sovereignty and varying perceptions of the nature and severity of threats and, therefore, conflicts over appropriate responses.[44] The geonarcotics relationship between the Caribbean and the rest of the world, especially North America, perhaps, is best known in relation to drug trafficking. However, the relationship entails more than the movement of drugs from and through the region; involved also are: drug production, drug consumption and abuse, money laundering, organised crime, corruption, arms trafficking, and sovereignty conflicts, among other things.

Thus, what generally is called 'the drug problem' in the Caribbean really is a multidimensional phenomenon. However, the phenomenon does not constitute a security matter simply because of its multidimensional character. It presents threats to security so essentially for four reasons. First, the operations have multiple consequences and implications – such as marked increases in crime, systemic and institutionalised corruption, and arms trafficking, among other things. Second, the operations and their consequences have increased in scope and gravity over the last two decades. Third, they create dramatic impacts on agents and agencies of national security and good governance, in military, political, and economic ways. Fourth, the sovereignty of many countries is subject to infringement, by both state and non-state actors, because of drugs.

Two decades ago it was impolitic for most Caribbean leaders to accept that their countries were facing a drug threat. But over the years the scope and severity of the threat increased and became patently obvious to observers within and outside the region. Caribbean leaders no longer were able to deny the existence of the problem. Helping to catapult the issue on to the policy radar screen was the sobering assertion made by the West Indian Commission in 1992: 'Nothing poses greater threats to civil society in CARICOM countries than the drug problem; and nothing exemplifies the powerlessness of regional Governments more'.[45] Thus, it was understandable that at the special CARICOM drug summit of December 1996, leaders would acknowledge: 'Narco-trafficking and its associated evils of money laundering, gun smuggling, corruption of public officials, criminality and drug abuse constitute the major security threat to the Caribbean today'.[46]

Later, at a June 2000 multinational high level meeting on criminal justice in Trinidad and Tobago, that country's attorney general made the following declaration in speaking on behalf of the Caribbean:

> There is a direct nexus between illegal drugs and crimes of violence, sex crimes, domestic violence, maltreatment of children by parents and other evils.... Our citizens suffer from drug addiction, drug-related violence, and drug-related corruption of law enforcement and public officials. The drug lords have become a law unto themselves.... Aside from the very visible decimation of our societies caused by drug addiction and drug-related violence, there is another insidious evil: money laundering.... It changes democratic institutions, erodes the rule of law, and destroys civic order with impunity.[47]

Our discussion of drugs suggests that this challenge constitutes a core threat for most states at the time of writing (Summer 2003). Similarly, the threat intensity level is high or medium for most of them. As regards regional salience, when one considers the issue of security interdependence and the regional salience factors – number of states affected, elite perception, and resource investment – the issue of drugs could be viewed as a regional security challenge and not merely a challenge for a few states within the region. Indeed, the above-mentioned 1992 assertion by the West Indian Commission in relation to CARICOM countries – 'Nothing poses greater threats to civil society in CARICOM countries than the drug problem; and nothing exemplifies the powerlessness of regional governments more' – is true for all Caribbean countries a decade later.[48]

Crime

The above statement by Attorney General Ramesh Maharaj points clearly to the nexus between drugs and crime. Indeed, crime is a component of the drug phenomenon. Crime could be viewed in several ways typologically. One study sees two basic categories of drug crimes: *enforcement* crimes, and *business* crimes. The former involves crimes among traffickers and between traffickers and civilians and police, triggered by traffickers' efforts to avoid arrest and prosecution. The latter category encompasses crimes committed as part of business disputes, and acquisitive crimes, such as robbery and extortion. Another typology posits three types of crime: *consensual* ones, such as drug possession, use, or trafficking; *expressive* ones, such as violence or assault; and *instrumental* or property crimes, such as theft, forgery, burglary, and robbery.[49]

Regardless of the typology used, there is a wide range of drug-related criminal activity in the Caribbean. Several connections are noteworthy. First, murder, fraud, theft, and assault and bodily harm, the crimes that present the greatest challenge to most countries in the region, are precisely the crimes associated with drugs. Second, in some countries, notably Jamaica, Puerto Rico, Haiti, the Dominican Republic, and Trinidad and Tobago, there is clear evidence of a linkage. For instance, Jamaica reported 561 murders in 1991, 'a 75 per cent increase [over 1990] in the incidents of murder linked directly or indirectly to drug trafficking'.[50] A decade later murders had more than doubled: to 1,131 murders in 2001, 28 per cent more than in 2000 and a huge proportion of them drug-related.[51]

Also noteworthy is that the countries with the high or progressive crime reports in the theft, homicide, and serious assault categories are the same ones featuring prominently over the last decade as centres of drug activity. These countries include the Bahamas, the Dominican Republic, Puerto Rico, Jamaica, Trinidad and Tobago, Haiti, the US Virgin Islands, Guyana, and

St Kitts-Nevis. Thus, what the Jamaican national security minister reported to Parliament in June 2002 has a relevance that extends far beyond Jamaica:

> Madame Speaker, when you look at a breakdown of the murder figures, it becomes clear that reprisals and drug/gang related killings constitute the highest percentage of murders in the country.... Current analysis based on available intelligence suggests that the illegal drug trade has become the taproot for crime and violence in our country today. It has become the principal factor underpinning the organized criminal networks, which are at the heart of the problem.[52]

Dudley Allen, a former Jamaican commissioner of corrections, once remarked:

> It is no longer possible to think of crime as a simple or minor social problem. Mounting crime and violence have been declared leading national problems, and the issue of law and order has assumed high priority in national planning and policymaking. Fear of crime is destroying freedom of movement, freedom from harm, and freedom from fear itself.[53]

Allen first made this statement in 1976, but it is still relevant over a quarter-century later, and now even more dramatically so. He also was speaking mainly in the Jamaican context, but the observation now has region-wide validity.

For a variety of reasons that cannot be explored here, crime has skyrocketed in many parts of the region. It was the widespread regional scope and the severity of crime that prompted CARICOM leaders to create the Regional Task Force on Crime and Security at their July 2001 summit in Nassau, Bahamas. And, the first report of the Task Force which was presented to the leaders at the summit in July 2002 in Georgetown, Guyana, testifies to the widespread scope and the severity of crime. (The report also examines some of the complex reasons for crime and provides both policy and operational recommendations for coping with it.)

There is a local-global nexus in the region's drug-related crime, reflected in the fact that some of the crime is transnational and organised, extending beyond the region to North America, Europe, and elsewhere.[54] Groups called *posses* in Canada, the Caribbean, and the United States and *yardies* in Britain perpetrate the most notorious organised crime. They are organised criminal gangs composed primarily of Jamaicans or people of Jamaican descent, but increasingly involving African-Americans, Guyanese, Panamanians,

Trinidadians, Nigerians, and Dominicans. Although the posses are known most for drugs and weapons trafficking, they also have been implicated in money laundering, fraud, kidnapping, robbery, prostitution, documents forgery and murder.[55]

Another aspect of the local-global nexus pertains to deportees. Criminal activity within some Caribbean countries is complicated and aggravated by the activities of nationals who are convicted, sentenced, and later deported from elsewhere. In a July 1993 speech to the Jamaican Parliament, National Security Minister K.D. Knight, stated: 'Nearly a thousand Jamaicans were deported from other countries last year, with over 700 coming from the United States. Most of them, nearly 600, were deported for drug-related offenses.'[56] That was just the tip of the iceberg. Between 1993 and 2000, more than 8,000 Jamaican deportees were returned to the island, mainly from the United States.

Although most of the deportees come from the United States, the United States is not the only country that sends criminals back to their homelands. Of course, Jamaica is not the only Caribbean nation to be forced to accept nationals from the Diaspora who have walked on the wrong side of the law. As a matter of fact, Jamaica is not the Caribbean country to which most deportees are returned. That dubious distinction falls to the Dominican Republic. Moreover, criminal deportation is also an intra-regional reality; Caribbean countries send each other's nationals back to their countries of origin. Barbados, for example, reportedly deports an average of 20 Caribbean nationals weekly, mostly to Guyana, St Lucia, St Vincent and the Grenadines and Trinidad and Tobago.[57]

Yet, it is not merely the fact of deportation and the numbers that are troubling to many Caribbean jurisdictions. Part of the challenge is the fact that deportees generally have a troubling criminal profile, with the capabilities and disposition to perpetrate crime in the new jurisdiction. Moreover, because of economic deprivation, there are ample opportunities for the committal of crime. When these factors are combined with the manpower, equipment, and training deficiencies of Caribbean law enforcement agencies, the outcomes negatively affect state and society in the region.[58]

Calling the deportee matter a 'contested issue', the report of the Regional Task Force on Crime and Security quite rightly calls for more empirical study of the relationships between criminal deportation and domestic criminal behaviour. Overall, it offers measured commentary, noting that '... a basic descriptive study of the Barbadian deportee problem and preliminary studies in Jamaica would seem to support the idea that the deportee danger may have been overestimated'. Nevertheless, it makes the following point: 'Although imperfect, the existing information suggests that there is nothing particularly dramatic about the quantitative impact of deportee crimes. The qualitative impact of deportee crimes is, however, of great concern'.[59]

Understandably, while crime is widespread in scope it is not uniform in pattern. Over recent years, the jurisdictions that stand out in relation to violent crime have been Jamaica, Haiti, Puerto Rico, the Dominican Republic, Trinidad and Tobago, and Guyana. Yet, in some places where crime has come to define the national image if not the socio-political landscape, crime actually has declined. For instance:

- In May 2002, Trinidad's national security minister, Howard Chin Lee, reported that the murder rate for February to April 2002 had dropped by 14 per cent compared with the same period in 2001;[60] (Later developments led to a different profile, though, as the nation's murder figure for 2002 was 172 compared with 150 during 2001.)
- In August 2002, Jamaica's national security minister indicated that murders had declined by 11 per cent over the last year; rape had been reduced by 11 per cent also; carnal abuse by 17 per cent, and breaking and entering by 14 per cent;[61]
- On January 3, 2003, Jamaica's commissioner of police announced that the country's 1,045 reported homicides in 2002 represented an 8 per cent decline in the homicides for 2001; the number of people killed with guns in 2002 was 711 while it was 789 in 2001; robberies declined from 1,523 in 2001 to 1,392 in 2002; indeed, there was a decrease in almost every area of major crime in 2002, compared with 2001, except for shootings and larceny.[62]
- In March 2003, Jamaica's Ministry of National Security reported a reduction in all category of crimes, except sexual offenses, during the first two-and-a-half-months of the year: 29 per cent decline in murders; 11 per cent reduction in shootings; and 28 per cent decline in larceny, among other reductions.[63]

However, crime sprees developed elsewhere, particularly in Haiti, Guyana, and Trinidad and Tobago, with dramatic episodes of criminal temerity and new or heightened criminal forays. These include attacks on police stations (already happening in Jamaica, Haiti, and elsewhere), kidnappings and assassination of law enforcement officials. Indeed, it was said of Guyana in summer 2002:

> Even to those untrained in the detection of patterns of criminal behavior, it now appears obvious that Guyana has transcended the bounds of ordinary banditry and is engulfed in a crime wave that suggests methodological planning, sinister motives, and the lethal means to stun the nation into a state of fear-induced vulnerability.[64]

A new murder record was set there in November 2002: 14 criminal murders in the capital and neighbouring towns and villages within a 25-day period (November 4 to 29), along with three killings by the police as they tried to cope with the crime spree.[65] Political discontent in Haiti, Guyana, and the Dominican Republic, with an overlay of racial issues in Guyana and Trinidad and Tobago, has served to complicate the situation in those countries.

This examination of some of the crime dynamics suggests that the crime challenge constitutes a core threat for most states at the time of writing. Similarly, the threat intensity level is high or medium for most Caribbean nation-states, and the threat has cross-cutting impact on citizens and state and non-state actors in dramatic ways. As regards regional salience, when one considers the issue of security interdependence and the regional salience factors – number of states involved, elite perception, and resource investment – the issue of crime is indisputably a regional security challenge and not merely a challenge for states within the region. Nevertheless, as was noted earlier, crime is but one of several non-traditional security challenges facing the region. As well, attention must be paid to terrorism.

Terrorism

Brian Jenkins was correct in calling terrorism 'violence for effect'. Terrorism is, he maintains, 'not only, and sometimes not at all, for the effect on the actual victims of the terrorists. In fact, the victims may be totally unrelated to the terrorists' cause.'[66] Terrorism – and the consequences of state action to cope with it – has become an unwelcome, but undeniable, reality for citizens of the United States and elsewhere, including the Caribbean. Terrorism and its consequences have given a new meaning to the definitions of power and of powerlessness.

The assessment of one respected international politics scholar in this regard warrants full replication:

> Our failure to anticipate the impact of terrorist attacks does not derive from a fundamental conceptual failure in thinking about power. On the contrary, the power of terrorists, like that of states, derives from asymmetrical patterns of interdependence. Our fault has rather been our failure to understand that the most powerful state ever to exist on this planet could be vulnerable to small bands of terrorists because of patterns of asymmetrical interdependence. *We have overemphasized states and we have overexaggerated power.*[67]

What, then, does 9/11 mean for weak, vulnerable states in the Caribbean? The 9/11 attack has affected the Caribbean in several ways, both as a direct consequence of the economic and military fallout from the impact on the United States, and as a result of the region's security vulnerability. It is notable, for instance, that according to the US Department of State, some 160 Caribbean nationals were victims of the actions against the World Trade Center and the Pentagon. Moreover, the domino effect of 9/11 has had a deleterious effect on the region's tourism industry, which is key to the economic security of several countries. A few examples should suffice.

In Jamaica, where tourism earns some US$1.2 billion a year and employs more than 30,000 people, the impact was very dramatic, with Air Jamaica losing US$11 million within the week following the attack. In Barbados, where tourism contributes about US$1 billion to the economy, the authorities anticipated a US$30.3 million decline in receipts, a 30–35 per cent reduction in the cruise enterprise, US$857,000 less from the head tax, and a drop in tourist spending of US$9.2 million.[68] Indeed, the tourism impact is expected to be so far reaching that the Second Caribbean Tourism Summit, held in The Bahamas on December 8–9, 2001, decided on a package of special measures to salvage the industry, which in 2000 provided gross foreign exchange earnings of US$20.2 billion and employed an estimated one in four persons in the Caribbean.[69]

Undoubtedly, though, the impact goes beyond tourism. As CARICOM leaders noted at the October 2001 special summit:

> We are concerned that the attacks and subsequent developments have been especially devastating to our tourism, aviation, financial services, and agricultural sectors, which are the major contributors to our Gross Domestic Product (GDP), foreign exchange earnings and to employment in our Region. We are particularly conscious that our ongoing efforts to combat money laundering must now take specific account of the potential for

> abuse of financial services industries by terrorists, their agents, and supporters in all jurisdictions.[70]

Needless to say, some of the very realities of the region's geopolitics and geonarcotics can create opportunities for terrorist pursuits, either as ends in themselves or allied to drug (or illegal migrant smuggling) operations.[71]

A full assessment of the economic, political, military, and other impact and implications for the Caribbean is partly the task of the volume of which this chapter is a part. And, while this chapter will not comprehensively examine the subject, it is important to note that several effects in addition to those mentioned above have begun to be felt in the immigration, banking, transportation, and other areas.[72] Moreover, the CARICOM Regional Task Force on Crime and Security raised the prospects of several likely threat possibilities; that

- the region's maritime and air networks could be used for conveyance of terrorist operatives and operational assets;
- terrorists could use the region's banking and other financial systems to finance their pursuits; and
- regional port or air facilities could be used to stage terrorist operations, either targeted to places in the region or elsewhere.[73]

It certainly is crucial to discuss scenarios and possibilities of external terrorist actions and their collateral impacts. Still, it should be remembered that although the Caribbean was not the target of the dramatic 9/11 terrorist operations, the region has not been immunised against terrorism. Leslie Manigat noted quite rightly that although the transition from colonial rule to independence in the Anglophone Caribbean was largely peaceful and non-violent, there were notable 'ideologically-Zionist' bombings in Trinidad, 'independentisa bombings' in Puerto Rico, and 'nationalist bombings' in Guadeloupe. Moreover, there was the fatal car bombing of scholar-politician Walter Rodney in Guyana in June 1980, and the destruction of 11 Puerto Rican National Guard planes, worth US$45 million, in January 1981 by the Puerto Rican nationalist group called *Macheteros*.[74]

Undoubtedly, though, the most devastating terrorist incident within the Caribbean occurred on October 6, 1976, when a bomb aboard a Cubana Air flight from Guyana to Cuba was blown up shortly after departing Barbados, where it had made a transit stop. All 73 people on the flight – 57 Cubans, 11 Guyanese, and five North Koreans – were killed. Anti-Castro exiles based in

Venezuela later claimed responsibility for the action. (On August 1, 1998, while on a visit to Barbados, President Fidel Castro dedicated a monument to the victims of the incident.)[75] Moreover, Cuba suffered a dozen bombings of tourist locations during 1997, allegedly orchestrated by anti-Castro Cuban exiles in Miami and Central America.[76]

Our terrorism discussion suggests that as of summer 2003 this issue constitutes a core threat for very few states, and a peripheral one for some. As well, the threat intensity level is low and medium for most states, and largely because of exogenous factors related to hemispheric and global interdependence generally, and the economic, military, and political linkages with the United States in particular. As regards regional salience, when one considers the issue of security interdependence and the regional salience factors – number of states involved, elite perception, and resource investment – the issue of terrorism could be deemed a regional security challenge and not merely a challenge for states within the region. However, the region faces another kind of terrorism; one with similar salience but greater intensity. That 'terror' comes in the form of HIV/AIDS.

The Terror of HIV/AIDS

In many respects the HIV/AIDS pandemic has created a form of terror for the Caribbean. It has been traced to the 1980s, with the first case reported in Jamaica in 1982, just one year after the first reported case in the United States. The following year, eight cases involving gay or bisexual men were reported in Trinidad and Tobago. Yet, two years later – 1985 – female and paediatric AIDS cases made up about 28 per cent of total cases reported to the Caribbean Epidemiology Centre (CAREC) by its 21 member countries.[77] Among other things, this indicated that the disease was becoming a concern for the general population and not merely a problem restricted to gay or bisexual men.[78]

The epidemic has spread rapidly since 1982. A March 2002 report notes:

> The alarming acceleration of the epidemic is highlighted by the fact that more AIDS cases have been reported between 1995 and 1998 than since the beginning of the epidemic in the early 1980s. In 1998, among the CAREC countries, the Bahamas, Turks and Caicos, Barbados, Trinidad and Tobago, St Vincent and the Grenadines, Bermuda, Guyana, Jamaica, and Suriname reported the highest number of new AIDS cases. Together, Haiti and the Dominican Republic account for 85 per cent of the total

number of cases in the Caribbean. However, because of their size and tourism dependent economies, the small island nations remain vulnerable to the epidemic.[79]

Figure 1.9
Reported AIDS Cases in CAREC Member Countries: 1982-2000

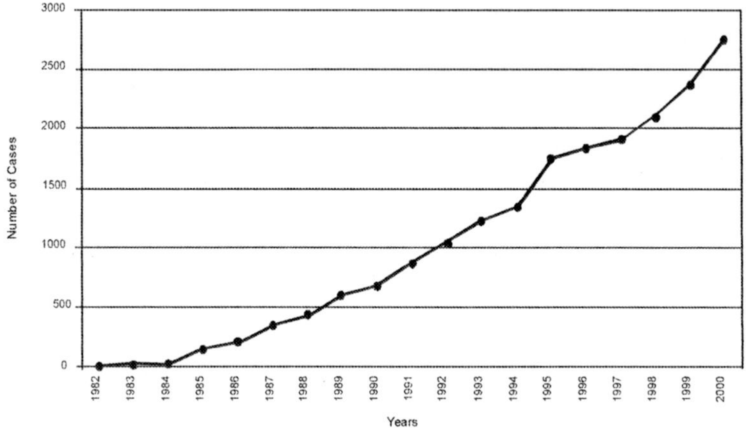

Source: Bilali Camara, '20 Years of the HIV/AIDS Epidemic in the Caribbean', Caribbean Epidemiology Centre, 2002.

Indeed, the AIDS epidemic has spread so rapidly that the Caribbean is the second hardest-hit region, the first being sub-Saharan Africa, with an overall prevalence of 2.11 per cent among adults and 501,500 people living with the virus, up to the end of 2000.[80] Figure 1.9 provides a dramatic portrait of the pandemic. Understandably, there is variability both in the prevalence among countries, as suggested above, and in the impact on differing segments of the populations of countries. For example, data for 2000 indicate the following incidence among infants: Jamaica: 5 per 1000 live births; Trinidad and Tobago: 6 per 1000 live births; Belize: 15 per 1000 live births; and Guyana: 21 per 1000 live births.[81] However, it is not only the number of people involved that makes the HIV/AIDS epidemic a security matter for the region; what makes it so serious are the demographic, economic, and social implications and the impact on the long-term socio-economic stability and governability of Caribbean nations.

For instance, 73 per cent of the cases reported between 1982 and 2000 are in the 15–44-years age range, a range critical for the region's economic and social productivity. One study put the total direct and indirect cost for the (CAREC) region in 1995 at US$20 million and predicted a rise to US$80 million in 2020. Moreover, it estimated that, as a result of the epidemic, the GNP in Jamaica and Trinidad and Tobago will be lowered by 4.2 per cent and 6.4 per cent, respectively; and that savings will decline by 10.3 per cent in Trinidad and 23.5 per cent in Jamaica.[82] One expert notes that indirect costs include the following: losses on societal investment in persons dying prematurely; costs for the care of orphans; the additional health care costs due to the increased incidence of other diseases, ensuring the safety of blood supplies, laboratory and hospital precautions, and health education and other prevention measures. Also, it is estimated that by 2010 the region's population will be 95 per cent of what it would have been without AIDS, and a mere 92 per cent by 2020.[83]

Understandably, there are other long-term effects on the demographics of Caribbean countries. One example will suffice. As the disease disproportionately affects younger age groups, one could expect life expectancy to decline over time. And, suggests the Partnership for AIDS report:

> As more people are generally expected to live for shorter periods of time, their expected contributions to national economic and social development becomes smaller and less reliable. This is of particular concern in small countries that lose large numbers of skilled individuals that are not easily replaced.[84]

All of the above amounts to compelling evidence that HIV/AIDS in the Caribbean is not simply a health crisis; it is a security challenge as well.[85] It is easy to understand this when one remembers three things. First, our definition of security: protection and preservation of a people's freedom from external military attack and coercion, from internal subversion, and from the erosion of cherished political, economic, and social values. Second, national security should not be viewed merely in relation to the immediate-term impact of issues, but also their medium- and long-term impact. Third, the disease will have a deleterious effect on the capacity of Caribbean states in the next 10–15 years to provide and sustain human capital and security capabilities. The former is key to maintaining some of the values, and the two are needed for the maintenance of formal sovereignty and the exercise of positive sovereignty, which entails having the economic, technical, military, and other capacity to declare, implement, and enforce public policy at the domestic and international levels.[86]

Thus, as of Summer 2003, HIV/AIDS constituted a core threat for many Caribbean states and a peripheral one for most of them. Further, one could assert that the threat intensity level is high or medium for most countries. Added to this, HIV/AIDS has near- and long-term impact on individual citizens and state and non-state actors in dramatic ways. As regards regional salience, when one considers the question of security interdependence and the regional salience factors – number of states involved, elite perception, and resource investment – the issue of HIV/AIDS is undoubtedly a regional security challenge and not merely a challenge for a few states within the region.

Conclusion

Sociologist Anthony Maingot once remarked: 'If it is a cliché that generals always fight the last war, it is equally true that civilian elites (including academics) tend to hold on to theories long after events have rendered them irrelevant.'[87] The statement is often true not only for theories, but also for paradigms from which they spring and frameworks to which they give rise. Our discussion suggests the validity of the statement in relation to at least one theory related to security and to approaches applied to the Caribbean. But although revisiting theories and frameworks periodically is important, also crucial is the strategy for doing this. The question must be asked: Will it be marginal modification or 'back to the basics' as advocated in the James Rosenau epigraph?

The effort in this chapter to probe security challenge and change in the Caribbean has aimed at the latter. Moreover, in doing so, this writer has been mindful of the following observation:

> The first-rate social scientist does not regard a research design [or a theory] as a blueprint for a mechanical process of data-gathering and evaluation. To the contrary, the scholar must have the flexibility of mind to overturn old ways of looking at the world, to ask new questions, to revise designs appropriately, and then to collect more data of a different type than originally intended.[88]

It is for others to judge whether or not the overall research profile of this writer warrants his entry in the 'first-rate social scientist' category. Nevertheless, this work is offered modestly with flexibility in mind and with a view to posing new questions, sketching new designs, and gathering and interpreting new data.

Notes

* I wish to acknowledge the assistance of Liz Williams of The Honors College @ FIU in gathering some of the research material and of John S. Kneski of The Honors College @ FIU in preparing some of the figures. Thanks also to Professors Emilio Pantojas García of the University of Puerto Rico, Clifford Griffin of North Carolina State University, W. Andy Knight of the University of Alberta, Canada, and Bill Beesting of Florida International University for reading and commenting on the first draft of this chapter.

1. James N. Rosenau, *The Scientific Study of Foreign Policy* (London: Frances Pinter, 1980), 237.
2. Barry Buzan, *People, States, and Fear* (Boulder: Lynne Rienner, 1991), 14.
3. Owen Arthur, prime minister of Barbados, *Address by Prime Minister Owen Arthur at the Inaugural Session of the 32nd General Assembly of the Organization of American States*, Bridgetown, Barbados, June 2, 2002, 2.
4. Some notable works in this respect are: Robert A. Pastor, *Whirlpool: United States Foreign Policy toward Latin America and the Caribbean* (Princeton: Princeton University Press, 1992); Anthony P. Maingot, *The United States and the Caribbean* (London: Macmillan Caribbean, 1994); James N. Rosenau, 'Hurricanes are not the only Intruders: The Caribbean in an era of Global Turbulence', in Michael C. Desch, Jorge I. Domínguez, and Andrés Serbin, eds., *From Pirates to Drug Lords: The Post-Cold War Caribbean Security Environment* (Albany: State University of New York Press, 1998); J. Edward Greene, 'External Influences and the Stability in the Caribbean', in Anthony T. Bryan, J. Edward Greene, and Timothy M. Shaw, eds., *Peace, Development, and Security in the Caribbean* (New York: St Martin's Press, 1990); Leslie Manigat, 'The Setting: Crisis, Ideology, and Geopolitics', in Jorge Heine and Leslie Manigat, eds., *The Caribbean and World Politics* (New York: Holmes and Meier, 1998); Andrés Serbin, *Caribbean Geopolitics: Towards Security Through Peace?* (Boulder: Lynne Rienner, 1990); W. Andy Knight and Randolph B. Persaud, 'Subsidiarity, Regional Governance, and Caribbean Security', *Latin American Politics and Society* Vol. 43, No 1 (Spring) 2001: 29–56; Tyrone Ferguson, 'A Security Management Model for the Small Island Developing State', OAS Committee on Hemispheric Security, OEA/Ser.G, CP/CSH-436/02, February 22, 2002; and Ivelaw L. Griffith, *The Quest for Security in the Caribbean: Problems and Promises in Subordinate States* (Armonk, NY: M.E. Sharpe, 1993).
5. Stephen J. Flanagan, 'Meeting the Challenges of the Global Century', in Richard L. Kuger and Ellen L. Frost, eds., *The Global Century: Globalization and National Security* (Washington, DC: National Defense University Press, 2001), 7.
6. See Commonwealth Advisory Group, *A Future for Small States: Overcoming Vulnerability* (London: Commonwealth Secretariat, 1997), 9.
7. Robert L. Rothstein, 'The Security Dilemma and the "Poverty Trap" in the Third World', *The Jerusalem Journal of International Relations* Vol. 8, No. 4 (1986): 8–9.
8. Commonwealth Advisory Group, Ibid., ix. Dame Eugenia Charles, former prime minister of Dominica, led the Advisory Group.
9. See Barry Bartmann, 'Meeting the Needs of Microstate Security', *The Round Table Issue*, 365 (2002): 361–75.
10. See, for example, Commonwealth Study Group, *Vulnerability: Small States in the Global Society* (London: Commonwealth Secretariat, 1985), 15.
11. Sir Shridath Ramphal, *Opening Address by Sir Shridath Ramphal at the first meeting of the Commonwealth experts on small state security*, July 1984.

12. See Edward Azar and Chung-in Moon, 'Third World National Security: Toward a New Conceptual Framework', *International Interactions* 11, No. 2 (1984): 103–35.
13. Caribbean Development Bank, *Annual Report 2001* (Bridgetown, Barbados, March 2002), 22–23.
14. L. Erskine Sandiford, prime minister of Barbados, Address by Prime Minister L. Erskine Sandiford, to the 1990 CARICOM Summit in 'Communiqué and Addresses – Eleventh Meeting of the Heads of Government of the Caribbean Community', *CARICOM Perspective* (Special Supplement) 49 (July–December 1990): 6.
15. For a discussion of various definitions and usages of the term, see Joseph S. Nye, Jr. and Sean Lynn-Jones, 'International Security Studies: A Report of a Conference on the State of the Field', *International Studies Quarterly* Vol. 12 (Spring 1988): 5–27; Buzan, *People, States, and Fear*, 16–24; Joseph J. Rohm, *Defining National Security: The Non-Military Aspects* (New York: Council on Foreign Relations Press, 1993); Edward Page, 'Human Security and the Environment', in Edward Page and Michael Reedclift, eds., *Human Security and the Environment: International Comparisons* (Cheltenham, UK: Edward Elgar, 2002), 27–44; and Rob McRae, 'Human Security in a Globalized World', in Rob McRae and Don Hubert, eds., *Human Security and the New Diplomacy* (Montreal: McGill-Queens University Press, 2002), 14–27.
16. For a notable recent exposition on realism and application of the theory, see John J. Mearsheimer, *The Tragedy of Great Power Politics* (New York: W.W. Norton & Co., 2001). Mearsheimer calls his variant 'offensive realism'.
17. Charles W. Kegley, Jr., 'The Neoidealist Moment in International Studies? Realist Myths and the New International Realities', *International Studies Quarterly* Vol. 37 (June 1993): 141.
18. Robert O. Keohane, 'The Globalization of Informal Violence, Theories of World Politics, and the "Liberalism of Fear"', *Dialog-IO*, (Spring 2002): 41.
19. Richard Falk, 'Theory, Realism, and World Security', in Michael T. Klare and Daniel C. Thomas, eds., *World Security: Trends and Challenges at Century's End* (New York: St Martin's Press, 1991), 10.
20. Michael C. Desch, 'Conclusion', in *From Pirates to Drug Lords*, 148.
21. For some of the evidence of this, see Alma H. Young and Dion E. Phillips, eds., *Militarization in the Non-Hispanic Caribbean* (Boulder: Lynne Rienner, 1986); Bryan, Greene and Shaw, *Peace, Development, and Security in the Caribbean*; Ivelaw L. Griffith, ed., *Strategy and Security in the Caribbean* (Westport, Conn: Praeger, 1991); and Ivelaw L. Griffith, 'Caribbean Security: Retrospect and Prospect', *Latin American Research Review*, Vol. 30, No. 2 (1995): 3–32.
22. This definition was developed initially in Griffith, *The Quest for Security in the Caribbean*, Ch. 1.
23. Arthur, 'Address', Ibid., 3.
24. Susan Strange, *The Retreat of the State: The Diffusion of Power in the World Economy* (Cambridge: Cambridge University Press, 1996), 1.
25. Buzan, Ibid., 112.
26. Richard H. Ullman, 'Redefining Security', *International Security* Vol. 8 (Summer 1983): 133.
27. Buzan, Ibid., 115.
28. Buzan, Ibid., 134.
29. See Thomas W. Robinson, 'National Interests', in James N. Rosenau, ed., *International Politics and Foreign Policy* (New York: The Free Press, 1969), 182–90.
30. Kenneth E. Boulding, 'National Images and International Systems', in Rosenau, *International Politics and Foreign Policy*, 423. Boulding's paper was written in 1958. [Only] is added by this writer.

31. See James N. Rosenau, *Turbulence in World Politics* (Princeton: Princeton University Press, 1990) on interdependence issues, 106; Maryann K. Cusimano, 'Beyond Sovereignty: The Rise of Transsovereign Problems', in Maryann K. Cusimano ed., *Beyond Sovereignty: Issues for a Global Agenda* (New York: St Martin's Press, 2000), 1–40 on transsovereign issues; and Kofi Anan, 'Foreword', in United Nations Office for Drug Control and Crime Prevention, *World Drug Report 2000 (*New York: Oxford University Press, 2001), 1 on problems without borders.
32. The concept of Multilateral Security Engagement Zones was first proposed in Ivelaw L. Griffith, 'The Caribbean Security Scenario at the Dawn of the 21st Century: Continuity, Change, Challenge', which was commissioned for the Conference on Building Regional Security Cooperation in the Western Hemisphere, sponsored by the US Army War College, the North-South Center, and the United States Southern Command, held in Miami, Florida March 2–4, 2003, and published as North-South Center Agenda Paper No. 65, September 2003.
33. For more on this see Griffith, *Quest for Security in the Caribbean*, 276–77.
34. Although not in the context of a framework design, a ratio was used in an earlier work, but in relation to the Americas. The ratio factor was one-third and the organisation of relevance was the OAS. See Ivelaw L. Griffith, 'Organized Crime in the Western Hemisphere: Content, Context, Consequences, and Countermeasures', *Low Intensity Conflict and Law Enforcement* Vol. 8, No. 1 (Spring 1999), 3.
35. For a discussion on the ACS, see Nancy Zaretsky, 'Caribbean Integration: the Association of Caribbean States and its Economic Impact on Florida'. Occasional Paper of the Latin American and Caribbean Center, Florida International University, 1996; and Norman Girvan, 'The Association of Caribbean States (ACS) as a Caribbean Cooperative Zone', in Ramesh Ramsaran, ed., *Caribbean Survival and the Global Challenge* (Kingston, Jamaica: Ian Randle Publishers, 2002), 212–19.
36. For the text of the proposals, see 'Belize-Guatemala Differendum, Proposals from the Facilitators Presented to the Secretary General of the OAS, 30 August 2002', available at http://www.belize.gov.bz/features/proposals/belize_guatemala_differendum.html. As regards the February 2003 agreement, see 'Belize and Guatemala Sign Agreement', OAS Press Release No. E-026/03 February 7, 2003, available at http://www.oas.org/library/mant_press/press_release.asp?sCodigo=E-026/03. In relation to the visit to create the Adjacency Zone, see February 26, 2003 Press Release, Press Office, Government of Belize, 'OAS Officials Visit Belize', available at http://www.belize.gov.bz/pressoffice/press_releases/26-02-2003-2466.shtml.
37. See 'Guyana Sends Gunboat into Waters Disputed with Suriname', Canadian Broadcasting Corporation, March 23, 2003, available at http://www.cbc.ca/cp/world/030314/w031464.html. For more on the Guyana-Suriname dispute, see http://www.guyana.org/guysur/guyana_suriname.html.
38. Hans Binnendijk and L. Erik Kjonnerod, 'Panama 2000', *Strategic Forum* No 17, (June 1997), 2.
39. See, for example, Martin O'Malley, 'Guantánamo Bay', available at http://www.cbc.ca/news/indepth/targetterrorism/backgrounders/guantanamo.html; 'Guantánamo One Year Later: Detention for all Terrorists or Not', *Miami Herald*, available at http://www.miami.com/mld/miamiherald/news/opinion/4837099.htm.; and Indira Lakshmanan, 'Ex-detainees: Guantanamo not Bad', *Miami Herald*, March 27, 2003, 3A.
40. See Col. Daniel Smith, USA (Ret.), 'The Impact of Sept. 11, 2001 on the Unified Command Plan', Center for Defense Information Terrorism Project, May 22, 2002; and 'Unified Command Plan', available at www.fefenselink.mil/specials/unifiedcommand/.

41. See 'U.S. Northern Command', at www.globalsecurity.org/military/agency/dod/northern.htm.
42. See Edward Gonzalez, *A Strategy for Dealing with Cuba*, Rand Corporation, R-2954-DOS/AF, September 1982; and US Congress, House, Committee on Foreign Affairs, *Soviet Posture in the Western Hemisphere*. Hearings, Subcommittee on Western Hemisphere Affairs, 99th Congress, 1st Sess., Feb. 1985.
43. See 'Lourdes (Cuba) Signals Intelligence (SIGINT) Facility', available at http://www.fas.org/irp/imint/c80_04.htm; and Susan B. Glasser, 'Russia to Dismantle Spy Facility in Cuba', *Washington Post*, October 18, 2001, A34.
44. The geonarcotics concept was developed in Ivelaw L. Griffith, 'From Cold War Geopolitics to Post-Cold War Geonarcotics', *International Journal* Vol. 48 (Winter 1993–4): 1–36. For empirical studies based on it, see Ivelaw L. Griffith, *Drugs and Security in the Caribbean: Sovereignty Under Siege* (University Park, Pa: Pennsylvania State University Press, 1997); and Padideh Tosti, 'GPEN: Framing Narcopolitics', *Security Policy Group International Working Paper*, 2002, available at www.spgi.org/articles/tosti_gpen.shtml.
45. West Indian Commission, *Time For Action* (Bridgetown, Barbados, 1992), 343. The Commission was a 15-member group of eminent persons formed by CARICOM leaders in 1989 to help chart a course for the region into the 21st century. It was led by Sir Shridath Ramphal, former foreign minister of Guyana and secretary general of the Commonwealth of Nations. At the time, he was chancellor of both the University of Guyana and the University of the West Indies.
46. *Communiqué, Fifth Special Meeting of the Conference of Heads of Government of the Caribbean Community*, Bridgetown, Barbados, December 16, 1996, 2.
47. Ramesh Lawrence Maharaj, attorney general and minister of legal affairs of the Republic of Trinidad and Tobago, *Remarks by the Hon Ramesh Lawrence Maharaj. at the Opening of the Caribbean-United-States-European-Canadian Ministerial (Criminal Justice and Law Enforcement) Conference*, Port of Spain, Trinidad, June 12–13, 2000. Available at http://usinfo.state.gov/regional/ar/islands/maharaj.htm.
48. For recent assessments and portraits of the phenomenon, see United Nations International Narcotics Control Board, *Report of the International Narcotics Control Board for 2002*, Doc. No. E/INCB/2002/2/1, February 2003, 37–43; and US Department of State, *International Narcotics Control Strategy Report for 2002*, March 2003, V1–3–54.
49. See Mark A.R. Kleiman, *Marijuana: Costs of Abuse, Costs of Control* (Westport, CT: Greenwood, 1989), 109–17; and M. Douglas Anglin and George Speckart, 'Narcotics Use and Crime: A Multisample, Multimethod Analysis', *Criminology* Vol. 26, No. 2, (1988): 197–231.
50. Planning Institute of Jamaica, *Economic and Social Survey 1991* (Kingston, Jamaica, 1992), 21.3–21.4.
51. See '1,131 Violent Deaths', *Jamaica Gleaner*, December 31, 2001, available at www.jamaica-gleaner.com/gleaner/20011231/news/news3.html.
52. Peter Phillips, Minister of National Security 'Restoring Law and Order in Society', *Presentation by Dr the Hon. Peter Phillips at the 2002–2003 Budget Sectoral Debate, June 18, 2002*, 7, 10.
53. Dudley Allen, 'Urban Crime and Violence in Jamaica', in Rosemary Brana-Shute and Gary Brana-Shute, eds., *Crime and Punishment in the Caribbean* (Gainesville, FL: University of Florida, 1980), 29.
54. For more on transnational crime in the Caribbean, see Douglas Farah, 'Russian Mob Sets Sights on Caribbean', *Miami Herald*, September 29, 1997, 8A; Anthony P. Maingot, 'The Decentralization Imperative and Caribbean Criminal Enterprise', in Tom Farer,

ed., *Transnational Crime in the Americas* (New York: Routledge, 1999), 143–170; Anthony T. Bryan, *Transnational Organized Crime: The Caribbean Context* (The Dante B. Fascell North-South Center, University of Miami, October 2000); and Charles Clifton Leacock, 'Internationalization of Crime', *New York University Journal of International Law and Politics*, Vol. 34 (Fall 2001): 263–79. Leacock is the Director of Public Prosecutions in Barbados.

55. For more on posse and yardie operations, see Laurie Gunst, *Born Fi' Dead: A Journey Through the Jamaican Posse Underworld* (New York: Henry Holt, 1995); Geoff Small, *Ruthless: The Global Rise of the Yardies* (London: Little, Brown, and Company, 1995); Serge Kovaleski and Douglas Farah, 'Organized Crime Carries Clout in Islands', *Washington Post*, February 17, 1998, A1; and Duane Blake, *Shower Posse: The Most Notorious Jamaican Criminal Organization* (New York: Diamond Publishing, 2002).
56. K.D. Knight, minister of national security and justice of Jamaica, *Presentation of the Hon K.D. Knight at the Budget Sectoral Debate, July 15, 1993*, 11.
57. See Maria Bradshaw, 'Illegal Haven', *The Nation*, June 5, 2002, 1.
58. For more on the issue of deportees, see Margaret H. Taylor and T. Alexander Aleinikoff, 'Deportation of Criminal Aliens: A Geopolitical Perspective', Inter-American Dialogue Working Paper, June 1998; Ivelaw L. Griffith, 'The Drama of Deportation', *Caribbean Perspectives* Issue 5 (January 1999), 10–14; Privat Precil, 'Criminal Deportees and Returned Teens: A Migration Phenomenon, A Social Problem', *mediaNET Bulletin*, No. 2 May 1999, available at www.panosinst.org/Haiti/h5-99e.shtml#Caribbean.; and Clifford E. Griffin, 'Criminal Deportation: the Unintended Impact of US Anti-Crime and Anti-terrorism Policy along its Third Border', *Caribbean Studies* Vol. 30 No 2 (July-December 2002): 39–76.
59. *Report of the Regional Task Force on Crime and Security to the Heads of Governments and States of the Caribbean Community and Common Market*, CARICOM Secretariat, Georgetown, Guyana, July 2002, Section 6, 4. An interesting experience for Jamaica, mostly unrelated to drugs, is the increasing deportation of children from the United Kingdom over recent years. See 'More Jamaicans Minors Being Deported', *Jamaica Gleaner*, January 5, 2003, 1.
60. See 'Trinidad Businessmen Seek Better Security after Kidnapping', *Jamaica Gleaner*, May 14, 2002, available at www.jamaica-gleaner.com/gleaner/20020514/business/business1.html.
61. See 'Project Launched to Reduce Crime Among the Youth', *Jamaica Gleaner*, August 27, 2002, available at http://www.jamaica-gleaner/gleaner/20020827/lead/lead1.html.
62. 'Police Commissioner Targets 20 per cent Reduction in Homicides', *Jamaica Information Service Press Release*, January 4, 2003.
63. See 'Gov't New Anti-crime Initiative Gets Good Results', *Jamaica Gleaner*, March 21, 2003, 1.
64. 'Crime: From Bad to Worse', *Guyana Review* Vol. 10, No. 116 (August 2002): 16.
65. See 'Death Warrant', *Guyana Review* Vol. 10, No. 120 (December 2002): 20–23. Ironically, the November 2002 crime spree began the day the nation began observance of Diwali, the Hindu festival that celebrates the conquering of darkness by light.
66. Brian Jenkins, *International Terrorism: A New Mode of Conflict* (Los Angeles: Crescent Publications, 1975), 1.
67. Keohane, 'The Globalization of Informal Violence', Ibid., 35. Emphasis in the original.
68. Anthony T. Bryan and Stephen E. Flynn, 'Terrorism, Porous Borders, and Homeland Security', *North-South Center Update*, October 22, 2001, 5.
69. See 'Meeting the Challenge of Change: Address Delivered by the Secretary General of the Caribbean Tourism Organization, Mr. Jean Holder, at the Second Caribbean

Tourism Summit, Nassau, December 8–9, 2001', 1. Holder provides a comprehensive analysis of the travails of tourism.

70. *Nassau Declaration on International Terrorism: The CARICOM Response Issued at the Conclusion of the Special (Emergency) Meeting of Heads of Government of the Caribbean Community*, October 11–12, 2001, 1. The Bahamas.
71. Narco-terrorist possibilities prompted a US Congressional visit to the region during August 2002 to hold talks with security, corporate, and other officials. Led by Rep. Mark E. Souder, Chairman of the Subcommittee on Criminal Justice, Drug Policy, and Human Resources of the Committee on Government Reform, the delegation included six members of Congress and the Chief of Operations of the U.S. Drug Enforcement Administration, Rogelio Guevara. See David Paulin, 'Congressional Team Warns of Powerful Narco-terrorist Alliance in the Caribbean', *The Jamaica Observer Internet Edition*, August 21, 2002, available at http://www.jamaicaobserver.com/news/html/20020821T210000-05.
72. See, for instance, 'Caribbean Drug Traffic up 25%: U.S. Law Enforcement Focusing on Terrorism', *The Baltimore Sun*, October 18, 2001; Greg Fields, 'Caymans to Share Information on Bank Customers with US', *Miami Herald*, November 28, 2001.
73. *Report of the Regional Task Force on Crime and Security*, Section 5, 1.
74. Manigat, 'The Setting: Crisis, Ideology, and Geopolitics', *Ibid.*, 35.
75. For more on the incident, see Dion E. Phillips, 'Terrorism and Security in the Caribbean: the 1976 Cubana Disaster off Barbados', *Terrorism* Vol. 14/4 (1991): 209–19. Regarding the 1998 dedication, see 'Castro to Dedicate Monument to Cubana Crash Victims', *Barbados Nation*, August 1, 1998, 1.
76. See Larry Rohter, 'Cuba Arrests Salvadorean in Hotel Blasts', *New York Times*, September 12, 1997; and Ann Louise Bardach and Larry Rohter, 'Bomber's Tale: A Cuban Exile Details a "Horrendous Matter"of a Bombing Campaign', *New York Times*, July 12, 1998.
77. The member countries of CAREC are Anguilla, Antigua and Barbuda, Aruba, Bahamas, Barbados, Belize, Bermuda, British Virgin Islands, Cayman Islands, Dominica, Grenada, Guyana, Jamaica, Montserrat, Netherlands Antilles, St Kitts and Nevis, St Lucia, St Vincent and the Grenadines, Suriname, Trinidad and Tobago, and Turks and Caicos.
78. Bilali Camara, 'An Overview of the AIDS/HIV/STD Situation in the Caribbean', in Glenford Howe and Alan Cobley, eds., *The Caribbean AIDS Epidemic* (Kingston, Jamaica: University of the West Indies Press, 2000), 2.
79. Pan-Caribbean Partnership on HIV/AIDS, *The Caribbean Regional Strategic Framework for HIV/AIDS 2002-2006*, March 2002, 3.
80. Pan-Caribbean Partnership on HIV/AIDS, Ibid., 1, and Bilali Camara, '20 Years of the HIV/AIDS Epidemic in the Caribbean', 2002, Slide No. 3.
81. Camara, '20 Years of the HIV/AIDS Epidemic in the Caribbean', Slide No. 20.
82. Pan-Caribbean Partnership on HIV/AIDS, Ibid., 5.
83. Camara, 'An Overview', Ibid., 16.
84. Pan-Caribbean Partnership for AIDS, Ibid., 5.
85. Interestingly, HIV/AIDS was declared by the United States to be a national security threat in 2000. See Barton Gellman, 'AIDS is Declared Threat to US National Security', *Washington Post*, April 30, 2000, AI. See also National Intelligence Council, *The Global Infectious Disease Threat and its Implications for the United States*, National Intelligence Estimate 99–17D, January 2000. More recently, see 'Tenet: AIDS Impacting National Security', *NewsMax.com*, February 13, 2003, available at www.newsmax.com/archives/articles/2003. Tenet is director of the US Central Intelligence Agency.

86. My use of the concept *positive sovereignty* follows the approach by Robert H. Jackson in *Quasi-States: Sovereignty, International Relations, and the Third World* (Cambridge: Cambridge University Press, 1990), 29.
87. Anthony P. Maingot, 'Changing Definitions of "Social Problems" in the Caribbean', in Joseph S. Tulchin and Ralph H. Espach, eds., *Security in the Caribbean Basin: The Challenge of Regional Cooperation* (Boulder: Lynne Rienner, 2000), 25.
88. Gary King, Robert O. Keohane, and Sidney Verba, *Designing Social Inquiry: Scientific Inference in Qualitative Research* (Princeton: Princeton University Press, 1994), 12.

2

Security, Terrorism and International Law: A Skeptical Comment

Stephen Vasciannie

Introduction

This chapter considers a number of questions concerning international law and national security, and seeks to cast a skeptical eye over certain propositions gaining currency in the field of national and international security. The international community has always had to address diverse issues of security, and the preservation of national security constitutes one of the core concerns of all states. But, even though these broad pronouncements are incontrovertible, they merely hint at the complexity and areas of uncertainty that prevail in security studies.

In the present international environment, for instance, one view gaining prominence among Caribbean analysts is that security should be perceived not only as a concept embracing traditional notions of military defence and defence against physical attack. Rather, it should be accepted as encompassing issues of social and economic significance to Caribbean states, so that considerations such as health, the environment, and poverty alleviation should be viewed essentially as security matters. This perspective is subjected to skeptical treatment in the discussion which follows. At the same time, it is suggested that the international community has no shortage of security concerns, as that term is properly understood: with this in mind, the chapter assesses some of the implications of the September 11 tragedy in the United States of America; briefly reviews the legal arguments proferred to justify the American-led intervention of Afghanistan following September 11 and discusses some aspects of the intervention of Iraq by the United States of America.

Security Concerns
Analysis

Genuine security challenges for the international community are, of course, in no short supply. September 11, 2001, stands as a major turning point in security analysis not just because of the brutality inherent in exposing thousands of civilians to sudden death for a cause with which they had no important connection, but also because the need to respond to this kind of security threat has opened up approaches and thought patterns that may be risky in themselves. And, there are certainly other security threats with which Caribbean people must be deeply concerned: to the extent that narco-trafficking preserves and sharpens criminality in the region,[1] and to the extent that the desire to fight fire with fire leads to an increase in police killings,[2] national security and human rights both undoubtedly remain seriously compromised in Jamaica, if not elsewhere in the region.

Partly in the wake of September 11, the event which presumably has crystallised today's view that we are living in the Age of Terror, there has been a noticeable tendency for political scientists to embrace broad conceptions of security and national security. In fairness, this tendency preceded September 11, for it is common enough to encounter references to environmental security, food security, and human security in the secondary literature from the 1980s and 1990s.[3] But, one suspects that September 11 has pushed the noticeable tendency over the edge into the more distinct category of a pronounced trend. In this pronounced trend, it is argued that a wide range of matters, not previously regarded as security issues, should now be so regarded. Thus, in addition to what I have already alluded to as genuine security issues, and in addition to environmental and food security, some analysts now refer, for instance, to health security, with HIV being described as a major threat to Caribbean security. And, in more all-encompassing language, the United Nations Development Programme has advocated recognition of a right to human security which includes, *inter alia*, protection from 'the threat of disease, hunger, unemployment, crime, social conflict, political repression, and environmental hazards'.[4] As part of the security nexus, others have also suggested items such as the need to prevent the undermining of social and cultural identity, and 'the ability to take actions and responsibility for improving economic conditions' in a given country.[5]

This impulse to broaden the definition of security in international relations is not driven by linguistic concerns; neither is it value-neutral. Rather, it is predicated on the assumption that there is magic in the term security. At its core, the argument, not usually made explicit, is built on three propositions:

a) security is generally acknowledged to be an important, if not the most important, social good within and across national boundaries;
b) because of its importance in all societies, special steps must always be taken to ensure security, even at the expense of other social goods; and
c) because special steps must be taken to preserve security, if the label *security* is attached to other social goods (such as health, employment or cultural identity), then special measures will need to be taken to secure the social goods which have been redesignated as security items.[6]

Is this approach useful? Undoubtedly, it is well-intentioned. In support of the concept of human security, the UNDP's *Human Development Report* puts the matter in the following terms:

> In the final analysis, human security is a child who did not die, a disease that did not spread, a job that was not cut, an ethnic tension that did not explode in violence, a dissident who was not silenced. Human security is not a concern with weapons – it is a concern with human life and dignity.[7]

It is difficult to raise objections when such noble objectives are set forth, and, particularly from a developing country perspective, there is every temptation to embrace the broader conception of security on the basis that, by placing basic human needs and human dignity into the category of security, international help may be forthcoming for those most in need.[8]

On the other hand, the skeptic should almost certainly have misgivings about the broad school approach. In the first place, this approach seems to place a gloss on the plain meaning of words, usually a signal for concern.[9] Security, as traditionally understood in international relations, is a relatively straightforward concept, connoting in essence the safety of a state, or organisation against criminal activity such as terrorism, theft, or espionage.[10] Thus, security of the state has been viewed primarily as ensuring protection of territory from external aggression, or protection of national interests in foreign policy from deliberate subversion or possibly from Acts of God. At the personal level, it also encompasses security from physical attack. When the meaning is stretched beyond what is normally understood in international discourse, this may be perceived as linguistic sleight of hand, built on the notion that words can mean what we want them to mean, essentially to suit our purposes. In short, the broad school approach to the definition of security could be regarded by the skeptic as a laudable, but questionable, exercise in what may possibly be constructive obfuscation.

Secondly, if everything is security, as long as thinking makes it so, will this approach really help developing countries, or the poor, the unemployed or the downtrodden? Again, there is room for skepticism. Developed countries have always attached high levels of priority to security issues in their national affairs, and in their international relations, proceeding on the basis that the preservation of law and order in the state – a matter of security – is the first order of business. But, though developed countries may be prepared to offer substantial assistance for security matters, it does not follow that they will be prepared to increase aid contributions when security is redefined to encompass a broader agenda that includes matters not traditionally regarded as security issues.[11] To be clear, I am not suggesting at all that developed countries have been satisfying their moral obligations in an international community characterised by income inequality and stark deprivation in some places; the point is just that when aid allocations are being determined, the redesignation of, say, unemployment or hunger, into the category of security, is not likely to advance the cause of poverty alleviation. It is, in short, a *non sequitor* to move from the proposition that security concerns are to be addressed to the view that classifying other social goods as security will mean that they will be addressed. If the concern is about unemployment, or about the environment, and these are legitimate issues meriting the highest attention, then clarity and transparency suggest that these concerns should be presented in their own terms. The AIDS pandemic is brutal and debilitating as a crisis of health care, which has security implications; one wonders, though, if anything is to be gained by classifying it as a security crisis as well.[12]

To elaborate: there is a sense in which most issues of broad social significance will have a security component. So, as just noted, the AIDS pandemic will clearly have security implications as it penetrates more deeply into Caribbean society, undermining the workforce, placing stress on medical services, and destroying family units. Similarly, as Griffith noted at the start of the 1990s, most Caribbean leaders are understandably concerned that economic and political considerations should not be excluded in any assessment of security matters within the region.[13] It is one thing, however, to say that particular social, economic and political problems may or will have consequences for national security; it is quite another to imply that these particular social, economic and political problems are themselves security problems.[14] Thus, economic vulnerability – characterised by import dependency, inflexible production structures, domestic capital shortage and related problems – may lead to genuine problems of security; but economic vulnerability is hardly synonymous with security, properly so-called. If the broad school approach leads to a divergent conclusion, it may be fairly criticised as misconstruing cause and effect.[15]

Implications

There are two additional concerns. One is that the overstretching of the concept of security could give rise to uncertainty in our understanding and interpretation of rules of international law constructed on the traditional meaning of the term. For example, the 1982 Convention on the Law of the Sea contemplates a regime of innocent passage for ships traversing the territorial waters of the coastal state.[16] In order to promote free navigation, the provisions allow ships of all states to exercise passage through foreign territorial waters without informing the coastal state. This approach to passage is sanctioned by antiquity, and works in practice. However, in order to safeguard the interests of coastal states, Article 19 of the Convention, in defining the circumstances in which innocent passage may occur, indicates that '(p)assage is innocent so long as it is not prejudicial to the peace, good order or security of the coastal state'. In this provision, security is intended to embrace the territorial integrity of the coastal State, and may be so understood even from the juxtaposition of the word security after peace and good order.[17] But what if we assume that, notwithstanding earlier practice, security should now also include the need to avoid, say, unemployment? Could a coastal state argue that a particular shipment through its territorial sea would somehow undermine its trade position and the level of local employment? And, if this approach is taken, could it lead the coastal state to challenge the passage at issue on the basis that it is non-innocent, thus undermining the general structure of innocent passage contemplated in the 1982 Convention? For some, these questions may be on the margins of plausibility, but the fact that they can be raised, highlights one of the risks of using the term security as if it has no core meaning.

As another example, the risks inherent in an unduly elastic conception of the term *security* are also apparent when reference is made to Chapter VII of the United Nations Charter. Chapter VII gives to the United Nations Security Council the power to determine the existence of threats to the peace, breaches of the peace or acts of aggression, and authorises the Security Council to take measures 'to maintain or restore international peace and security'.[18] The context and wording of the provisions in Chapter VII clearly indicate that the term *security* used here is meant to encompass military security, and not, for instance, health security or environmental security. Indeed, even the name Security Council has traditionally been taken to refer to issues of security in the narrow sense.

Similarly, when Chapter VII authorises the Security Council to take enforcement action, it has always been presumed that such action would be in response to situations that threaten international peace and security in the militaristic sense. But what if the broad school prevails, and security comes to encompass non-military matters in Chapter VII? Would this allow the Security Council, if it is so inclined, to order military action to address issues of environmental security, or issues of health security? Would, for instance, a refugee crisis without military implications, be reasonably regarded as a threat to international peace and security, triggering Security Council use of force? This possibility needs to be given further consideration by supporters of the broad school; for it is doubtful that the well-intentioned advocates of a wide reading of the term *security* would wish to extend powers of military intervention by the Security Council pursuant to Chapter VII of the United Nations Charter.

In addition, the skeptic may also be reluctant to accept the broad school approach because it could divert attention from some matters which fall genuinely within the definition of the term security as traditionally understood. During the Cold War period, the core meaning of security was understood clearly enough by countries with power; and indeed, the desire to redefine security may have been driven, in part, by the perception that, with the end of the Cold War, the so-called peace dividend should include greater attention to the human dimension of international relations.[19] So, it may be felt that with Cold War threats out of the way, funds used to deter or promote aggression could be used for socially uplifting projects.[20] This objective is, again, well-intentioned, and, following the end of the Cold War, there was arguably a window of opportunity for some countries to place less emphasis on security matters, and more on other areas. Given, however, the realities of September 11, and the understandable preoccupation of various countries with 'homeland' security, that opportunity may have passed. The Cold War may have moved into history, but security concerns – in the traditional sense – are as pronounced now as they were in the generation following 1950. But, this reality also generates a new set of considerations for the international community; some of these new considerations, and their implications for international peace and security merit further analysis, using, for the present purposes, traditional conceptions of security.

Some Policy Implications of September 11

General

The unparalleled events of September 11, 2001, by virtue of their suddenness, brutality, extensive publicity and implications have come to occupy a central place in the foreign policy perspectives of most Western powers. And, given the Caribbean's traditional ties with, and proximity to, the United States, there can be little doubt that the continued impact of September 11 will have direct bearing on the fortunes of the region. One challenge for us, then, is to form a proper understanding of the nature of the foreign policy mindset that has evolved, and is evolving, in Washington and elsewhere, and to formulate plans and strategies to address the repercussions of that date.

From the policy perspective, September 11 has, most obviously, caused the United States to concentrate more fully on national security issues, and on foreign policy questions arising from perceived 'trouble spots'. Already, the military action in Afghanistan, and the public deliberation as to possible action in Iraq, emphasises the fact that American foreign policy is likely to be directed with greatest emphasis on the Middle East for some time to come. And, by extension, it could be that CARICOM states, and our interests, may receive even less attention from the United States and the United Kingdom, as a result of Western perceptions of what is immediately important in the world.

No amount of conceptual redefinition is likely to change this in the short run, but, perhaps one area for contention will be for us continually to emphasise the nature of genuine security risks faced by countries of the region. And, in this regard, it should be recalled that, after some degree of turbulence, the Shiprider programme sailed home in 1997.[21] There is a distinct risk that the efforts to secure a Shiprider Agreement that respects national pride will drift into the margins as the United States diverts its attention to other pressing security concerns. The challenge, then, is for our foreign policy specialists to keep the question of maritime drug trafficking high on the public agenda, as a means of ensuring that Caribbean security concerns with respect to our maritime areas are not forgotten. Whether this is best ensured through the expansion of the Regional Security System is a point for discussion, but, at very least, CARICOM may benefit from negotiating about regional security issues as a single group.

More generally, the nature of the attacks on September 11 has prompted the United States to consider the choice between unilateralism and multilateralism in its International Relations. Prior to the attacks, there was no paucity of evidence of American unilateralism: its decision not to become a party to the Statute of the International Criminal Court (and the circumstances attending that decision),[22] and withdrawal from the Anti-ballistic missile treaty[23] are often cited as evidence of this trend. Now, however, given that its vulnerability has been exposed, there may be an even greater temptation for the United States to seek to impose its will on other countries.[24] In respect of terrorism and security matters, some of this may be understandable;[25] but, the risk for countries of this region is that American unilateralism may go beyond such matters and thereby permeate other areas of foreign policy. If this happens, then questions of policy in some CARICOM states, as, for example, the issue of marijuana decriminalisation in Jamaica,[26] or the vexed question of deportation of Caribbean nationals, could be given short shrift, independently of the merits or demerits of the case. There may, in other words, be less tolerance on the part of the hegemony.

But, to be fair, the case for multilateralism with respect to security matters has, so far, not been completely ignored by the United States. On one interpretation, the events of September 11 may be perceived not only as an attack on symbols of American strength, but also as a challenge to Western values such as liberalism, individualism and secularism.[27] And, if one takes this perspective, then the case may be made for the United States to try to strengthen its alliances against those who build bombs for the greater glory of terrorist ends. Generally, a reaction to terrorism may therefore require more, rather than less diplomacy.[28] This perspective could possibly prompt greater sensitivity on the part of the United States and its main allies towards the interests of developing countries in the hope that it may discourage anti-American subversion in the long run.[29] The American decision to work, at least initially, through the United Nations Security Council on the question of Iraq reflects, to some extent, respect for the multilateral approach suggested here.

Even in the Age of Terror, state policies should show deference to international law. This is so not because of esoteric notions concerning the grandeur of law and legal rules, but rather because respect for the law at both municipal and international levels helps to preserve order and justice, and ultimately promotes economic and social development. With this in mind, it may be appropriate to cast a brief look at whether two of the more important consequences of September 11 – the intervention in Afghanistan and the proposed attack on Iraq if certain preconditions are not met – actually satisfy the strictures of international law.

Intervention in Afghanistan

As to the intervention in Afghanistan, the question is whether the American response may properly be regarded as self-defence.[30] At the risk of oversimplification, international law, as enshrined in Article 2(4) of the United Nations Charter, establishes a blanket prohibition on the use of force. It requires states to refrain, in their international relations from the threat or use of force against the territorial integrity and political independence of other states.[31] Simultaneously, however, the UN Charter contemplates two exceptions to this prohibition, namely the use of force in self-defence (pursuant to Article 51),[32] and the use of force as part of the scheme for collective security set out in Chapter VII of the Charter.[33] If we assume *arguendo* that the provisions of the United Nations Charter in Article 51, and Chapter VII, specify the only permissible exceptions to the rule against the use of force in international law, this would have placed a marked restriction on American freedom of action in response to September 11.

More specifically, self-defence is traditionally understood to contemplate the situation in which one state is subject to an armed attack by another state; in that scenario, the victim state is allowed to respond proportionately to the prior attack. Article 51 states: 'Nothing in the present Charter shall impair the inherent right of individual or collective self-defence if an armed attack occurs against a Member of the United Nations, until the Security Council has taken measures necessary to maintain international peace and security.'

Arguably, the American response might fit the traditional reading of Article 51, in the sense that there was an armed attack, and the United States reacted some time later to that armed attack in self-defence. In truth, however, this approach is problematic: the traditional conception of self-defence works to drive back an attack which is in progress.[34] In the September 11 case, however, the attack had come and gone; it was atrocious, but not continuous. And, in this situation, the American use of force may be viewed as a reprisal, or a means of punishing the putative attackers, rather than a means of driving back the attacker. If that is so, then the American response of intervention in Afghanistan would be in breach of international law, for reprisals involving the use of force are contrary to Article 2(4) of the United Nations Charter.

Alternatively, therefore, to address the allegation that it is in breach of international law, the United States would need to argue that its response to the Al Qaeda attacks was not designed merely to punish the attackers (as a reprisal), but rather, it is a counterattack meant to deter future attacks from those which brought destruction to New York, Washington and Pennsylvania.[35] The response, it is suggested then, is best viewed as an act of anticipatory self-defence,[36] a form of self-defence which is acceptable in the existing customary international law according to some jurists.[37]

But, to maintain the argument based on anticipatory self-defence, the United States would need to overcome one further legal hurdle. In the traditional case of anticipatory self-defence, the state exercising that right needs to show that the attack which it is anticipating is 'instant, overwhelming, leaving no choice of means, and no moment for deliberation' (as argued in respect of the *Caroline* incident).[38] At the time the United States launched its military response to the Al Qaeda bombings, it was not entirely clear that a future Al Qaeda attack was immediately forthcoming, or even generally imminent. Should this have led to American restraint, pursuant to law? In the special and extreme circumstances of the Al Qaeda attacks, a wide reading of the concept of self-defence is reasonable, and this forms sufficient justification for the American military response. This wide reading is fully justifiable, given the unorthodox nature of the original attack, and bearing in mind the overarching need not only to rectify a grave moral wrong, but also to deter future, random acts of terrorism.[39] Those who launched the original attacks, apparently from a base of comfort and succour offered by the Taliban,[40] acted in breach of the rules of national and international law concerning murder, hijacking, conspiracy, malicious destruction of property, and other genuine security concepts. And the timing of future possible Al Qaeda attacks was almost beyond calculation. In the circumstances, it was open to the United States to exercise anticipatory self-defence, with a proportionate set of attacks on Afghanistan,[41] even if it could not point directly to another instant and overwhelming Al Qaeda attack on the horizon.[42]

Use of Force against Iraq

In contrast, the legal case in respect of possible military action against Iraq is not easily made. As a matter of politics, the current round of discussions and weapons-inspection[43] gives us a conflicting set of considerations to be weighed in the balance.[44] On the one hand, those inclined to support military intervention by the United States (and the United Kingdom) in Iraq raise concerns about the possibility of allowing Iraq to develop, retain, and use weapons of mass destruction in violation of various United Nations resolutions and contrary to the interests of humanity. In support of this perspective, it is noted that Iraq's record on security questions – including the war with Iran, the intervention in Kuwait, the treatment of the Kurdish people, and its reactions to the Security Council on weapons-inspection – hardly inspires confidence.[45] On the otherhand, it is suggested that the current round of arguments over weapons of mass destruction highlights, again, the hyprocrisy of an international system that allows some countries such weapons, but would deny them to other countries.[46] Some have also argued that military force in Iraq would never be able to ensure the end of a clandestine programme of weapons creation, would endanger innocent citizens, would exacerbate tensions in the Middle East, would widen the gap between Western perspectives and others, and would really be part of the new American imperium.[47]

As to the law, however, it is evident that a unilateral attack, without the authorisation of the United Nations under Chapter VII of the Charter, would be contrary to international law. To rely on self-defence in this instance would be to stretch that concept beyond its breaking point; and, at the same time, Chapter VII may only be used to justify the use of force where the Security Council gives approval. And yet, some who attach importance to the need for international peace and security may feel considerable unease at this conclusion. Given the history of the current Iraqi regime, must the law compel the conclusion that nothing can be done to prevent the development of weapons of mass destruction in that country?

In response to this question, it is clear that the United States is prepared to ignore international law if it perceives this course of action to be necessary following the Security Council deliberations. And herein lies a serious structural fault within international law: if the law does not accord with the highest national security interests of the most powerful countries, it will probably be ignored. This reality is food for skeptics, and, indeed, provides steady nourishment for cynics as well. But, at the same time, there may be a positive sign. Neither the United States nor Britain has sought openly to challenge International Law or the need for the rule of law even in respect of difficult cases of national interest. Instead, they have sometimes sought to shape the direction of the law either through deliberations at the United Nations or by other means. So, for instance, in the immediate case of Iraq, behind the rhetoric of the Axis of Evil and so on, there is also an attempt to suggest that given the nature of weapons of mass destruction and changes in the world since the United Nations Charter was formulated, there may now be the need for a doctrine of pre-emptive strike in international law.[48] In truth, this doctrine may really be a rationalisation for unlawful superpower action, but, in some instances, it may be necessary to safeguard international peace and security. That debate should continue, with active participation from smaller countries, such as CARICOM states, which are likely to have different perspectives from the major powers.

Human Rights in the Age of Terror

In the wake of September 11, human rights concerns have generally been relegated to a secondary position *vis-à-vis* the need to combat terrorism. Even those who may be inclined to regard this as understandable, however, should view with concern detentions without trial and other violations of due process. For Jamaica, one development which needs to be watched carefully, and avoided, is the tendency to assume that violations of the criminal law amount, by definition, to acts of terrorism. This is a point carefully made by Bernard Headley in his 2003 publication on criminal justice in Jamaica.[49] Headley notes that in recent months, the Minister of National Security has sought to identify the issue of drug transshipment through Jamaica, and its attendant features, as 'narco-terrorism'.[50] This approach seems incorrect because, in essence, terrorism is the use of violence for political ends.[51] The existence of drug-related crime in Jamaica is undeniable, and its connection between drug trafficking and the political process has always been a subject for conjecture (at least); however, there is as yet insufficient evidence to agree with the minister that drug trafficking has spawned systematic terrorist attacks on the state designed to achieve clearly identifiable political ends (other than the promotion of a greater flow of drugs through the country).

Another tendency apparently strengthened by events since September 11 lies in the argument that in the fight against criminality and violence in Jamaica, the state should be given greater powers to disregard human rights. This view – which in the past would be characterised by the Left as Fascist – is linked to September 11. In response to September 11, some restrictions of human rights have been allowed 'even in democratic America';[52] so, it is argued, why should the Jamaican authorities be slow to act against murderers and sundry criminals at a time when the very existence of the state is jeopardised?[53] One criticism of some who take this view is that they tend not to identify the particular human rights to be surrendered by individuals in the interests of security; and a second is that there is sometimes no clear linkage between the suppression of particular human rights and the enhancement of state security. Presumably, therefore, further refinement of that approach will be forthcoming.

For the moment, though, my point of emphasis is that restrictions on the human rights of Jamaicans – through, for instance, detention without trial – are not likely to help in reducing crime levels, and will instead promote even further alienation of the defenceless in society. In this regard, it should not escape our attention that there is already in Jamaican society a crisis of personal security.[54] Both in respect of murders by citizen upon citizen, and in respect of police killings, the trends indicate that the preservation of life is a daily matter of chance in some communities. For instance, in the five-year period from 1996 to 2000, 3,727 murders were reported in Jamaica;[55] in that same period, 742 persons were killed by the police, and 56 police were killed.[56] Having regard to the ratio of civilian to police death, roughly 13 to 1, there is at least scope for the view that something is amiss in terms of police treatment of civilians. This is hardly the kind of environment in which we should be keen to increase police powers in the name of security.

Conclusion

Caribbean security in the Age of Terror requires constant vigilance and careful analysis. As part of the global environment, Caribbean countries need to participate in the broader debates now current in the international arena about issues on the use of force, humanitarian intervention, immigration, drugs, the limits of sovereignty, and democratic rights, among other things. Simultaneously, we need to formulate further strategies to confront regional security concerns such as drug transshipment, gun importation, and crime. In pursuing these objectives, Caribbean countries need to show deference for International Law in the hope that this will help to provide us with credibility in our deliberations. It is debatable, though, whether we benefit much from conflating issues such as health, the environment and the economy with the concept of security. No doubt, health, the environment, the economy and other matters raise difficult and important questions of social policy for our societies, but redesignating them as security questions will probably not do much to promote conceptual clarity, and may undermine the credibility of Caribbean negotiators. Perhaps the skeptic should say no less.

Notes

1. From the extensive literature on drug trafficking in the region, see, e.g., Michael A. Morris, *Caribbean Maritime Security* (1994), especially 132–165; Ivelaw L. Griffith, *Caribbean Security on the Eve of the 21st Century* (McNair Paper 54) (1996), 33–59; Ivelaw L. Griffith, 'Drugs and Security in the Commonwealth Caribbean', *Journal of Commonwealth and Comparative Politics*, Vol. 31(July 1993): 70–102; Ivelaw L. Griffith and Trevor Munroe, 'Drugs and Democratic Governance in the Caribbean', in Ivelaw L. Griffith and Betty N. Sedoc-Dahlberg (eds.), *Democracy and Human Rights in the Caribbean* (1997), 74–97; Juan G. Toketlian, 'The Miami Summit and Drugs: A Placid Innocuous Conference?', *Journal of Interamerican Studies and World Affairs*, Vol. 36, No. 3 (Fall 1994): 75–91; James W. Van Wert, 'The US State Department's Narcotics Control Policy in the Americas', *Journal of Interamerican Studies*, Vol. 30, Nos. 2 and 3, (Summer/Fall 1998): 1–8.
2. For discussion of this problem in Jamaica see Anthony Harriott, *Police and Crime Control in Jamaica: Problems of Reforming Ex-Colonial Constabularies* (2000), 76–92.
3. See Jessica Tuchman Mathews, 'Redefining Security', *Foreign Affairs*, Vol. 68, No. 2 (1989): 162–177; Gareth Porter, 'Environmental Security as a National Security Issue', *Current History* (May 1995), 218–222; Barry Buzan, 'New Patterns of Security in the Twenty-First Century', *International Affairs*, Vol. 67, No. 3 (1991): 431–451; Michael T. Klare, 'Redefining Security: The New Global Schisms', *Current History*, Vol. 95, No. 604 (1996): 353–358; Hugh C. Dyer, 'Environmental Security as a Universal Value' in John Volger and Mark F. Imber (eds.), *The Environment and International Relations* (1996), 22–40; Caroline Thomas, 'Third World Security', in Roger Carey and Trevor C. Salmon (eds.), *International Security in the Modern World* (1992, 1996 reprint), 90–114. For the suggestion that there is widespread recognition of the need to redefine security in the post-Cold War era, and that academic writers agree on the need 'for a more holistic view of security which takes into account many non-military sources of threat', see Jessica Byron, 'The Eastern Caribbean in the 1990s: New Security Challenges', *Caribbean Quarterly*, Vol. 43, No. 3 (1997): 54–73. For a more recent proposal to measure human security as the number of years of future life spent outside a state of generalised poverty (accepting the premise of a broad definition of security), see Gary King and Christopher J.L. Murray, 'Rethinking Human Security', *Political Science Quarterly*, Vol. 116, No. 4 (2001/2):585
4. UNDP, *Human Development Report 1994*, 22. The UNDP Report identifies seven classes of threats to human security, viz., economic, food, health, environment, personal, community and political: ibid., 24–25. The vagueness inherent in this approach is apparent from the difficulty one would have in distinguishing, for instance, those personal, community and political matters that are security matters, and those which are not. See also George MacLean, 'The Changing Perception of Human Security: Coordinating National and Multilateral Responses: The United Nations and the New Security Agenda', United Nations Association in Canada, 1999 (www.unac.org/canada/security /maclean.html), cited by Gary King and Christopher J.L. Murray, 'Rethinking Human Security', *Political Science Quarterly*, Vol. 116, No. 4 (2001/2): 585–610. King and Murray quote the Japanese Ministry of Foreign Affairs to the effect that human security covers 'all the menaces that threaten human survival, daily life and dignity – for example, environmental degradation, violations of human rights, transnational organized crime, illicit drugs, refugees, anti personnel landmines and other infectious diseases such as AIDS' (*sic*): *loc. cit.*, previous note, at p. 590.

5. Diana Thorburn, 'Engendering Caribbean Security: National Security Reconsidered from a Feminist Perspective', in *Caribbean Quarterly*, Vol. 43, No. 3 (1997):77 (quoting a 1985 Report of the Commonwealth Consultative Group). The need to ensure the region's 'energy security' has been mentioned as an issue of 'capital importance': see William Perry and Max Primorac, 'The Inter-American Security Agenda', *Journal of Interamerican Studies and World Affairs*, Vol. 36, No. 3 (Fall 1994): 118. Trevor Salmon suggests it has become almost routine to echo Joseph Nye to the effect that 'Security problems have become more complicated as threats to state autonomy have shifted from the simply military, in which the threat is defined largely in terms of territorial integrity, to the economic': Trevor C. Salmon, 'The Nature of International Security', in Roger Carey and Trevor C. Salmon (eds.), *International Security in the Modern World* (1991, 1996 reprint), 2. For reference to Caribbean 'economic security', and to the pulling together of Caribbean security issues under the heading of 'vulnerability', see Anthony T. Bryan, 'Caribbean International Relations: A Retrospect and Outlook for a New Millennium' in Kenneth Hall and Denis Benn (eds.), *Contending with Destiny: The Caribbean in the 21st Century* (2000) 368–373. In his influential *Drugs and Security in the Caribbean* (1997), Ivelaw Griffith proceeds on the basis that 'security is multidimensional, with military, political, economic and environmental aspects', 4–13.
6. This is implicitly recognised in the review offered by King and Murray, *loc. cit.*, note 3, 589.
7. *UNDP Human Development Report 1994*, 22.
8. Tuchman Mathews, 'Redefining Security', 174–175; Gareth Porter, 'Environmental Security as National Security', 235.
9. For a critique, see also Robert Jackson, *The Global Covenant: Human Conduct in a World of States* (2000), 193–205.
10. UNDP, *Human Development Report 1994*, 22. On long-term conceptual imprecision of *security* see Arnold Wolfers, 'National Security as an Ambiguous Symbol', in Arnold Wolfers (ed.), *Discord and Collaboration* (1962), 10, as cited by Stephen J. Del Rosso Jr, in 'The Insecure State: Reflections on "the State" and "Security" in a Changing World', *Daedalus*, Vol. 124, No. 2 (1995): 182–183. Del Rosso acknowledges that security has for many years meant 'protection from organized violence caused by armed foreigners', but notes that this is not exclusively so. For traditional conceptions of security in the Caribbean context, see Duke Pollard 'International Law and the Protection of Small States', *CARICOM Perspective*, No. 66 (1996): 102–107, reprinted in Kenneth O. Hall (ed.), *The Caribbean Community: Beyond Survival* (2001), 514–526.
11. Cf., Porter, 'Environmental Security as National Security', 221–222 (US redefinition of national security to encompass environmental threats).
12. Wattie Vos, 'The New Caribbean Security Agenda', in Joseph S. Tulchin and Ralph H. Espach (eds.), *Security in the Caribbean Basin: The Challenge of Regional Cooperation* (2000), 189–191.
13. Griffith, 'The Quest for Security in the English-Speaking Caribbean', *Caribbean Affairs*, Vol. 3, No. 2 (April–June 1990): 68–76.
14. See also Robert Jackson, *The Global Covenant* (2000), 195–196.
15. George Washington is reported to have argued, in 1791, for more spending on the post office and related services because of their 'instrumentality in diffusing a knowledge of the laws and proceedings of Government which ... contributes to the security of the people': Ernest May, 'National Security in American History', in Graham Allison and Gregory Treverton (eds.), *Rethinking America's Security: Beyond Cold War to New*

World Order (1992), 104. Quoted by Del Russo to support idea that broader conceptions of security have long been incorporated into US political discourse; notice, though, that the quotation from Washington only concedes that greater expenditure on postal services could lead to greater security, a rather uncontroversial proposition if one views the matter in terms of cause and effect: Del Russo, 'The Insecure State', *Daedalus* Vol 124, No. 2 (1995): 183. Griffith's distinction between security capability and security also helps to clarify that the factors which may impinge on security are not necessarily security issues in themselves, see 'Securing the Region's Borders', *Caribbean Affairs*, Vol. 7, No. 3 (1994): 82. Subsequently, Griffith inclines to the broader view of security, see 'Drugs and the Emerging Security Agenda in the Caribbean', in Joseph F. Tulchin and Ralph H. Espach (eds.), *Security in the Caribbean Basin: The Challenge of Regional Cooperation* (2000), 137–150.

16. United Nations Law of the Sea Convention, Part II, Articles 17 to 32.
17. This reading would be in keeping with the *ejusdem generis* rule which sometimes serves as an aid to treaty interpretation: generally, see Lord McNair, *The Law of Treaties* (1961), 394–399.
18. United Nations Charter, Article 39.
19. Joseph Muravchik has given some indication of the magnitude of the peace dividend by noting that in the first five budget years following the end of the Cold War, American defence spending was $350 billion below the amount projected in the last Cold War budget: 'Affording Foreign Policy', *Foreign Affairs*, Vol. 75, No. 2 (1996):8–13.
20. For a discussion on US security concerns in Asia in light of post-Cold War changes (which relies on traditional conceptions of security), see Crowe Jr and Romberg, 'Rethinking Security in the Pacific', *Foreign Affairs*, Vol. 70, No. 2 (1991): 123–140.
21. See Vasciannie, 'Political and Policy Aspects of the Jamaica/United States Shiprider Negotiations', *Caribbean Quarterly*, Vol. 43, No. 3 (1997): 34–53; Kathy-Ann Brown, 'The Shiprider Model: An Analysis of the US Proposed Agreement Concerning Maritime Counter-Drug Operations in its Wider Legal Context', *Contemporary Caribbean Legal Issues*, Issue No. 1 (1997); Abrams, 'The Shiprider Solution: Policing the Caribbean', *National Interest*, No. 43 (Spring 1996): 86–92; Beardsworth, 'Maritime Counternarcotics Agreements: The Cop on the Beat', in Tulchin and Espach (eds.), *Security in the Caribbean Basin* (2000), 197–202. On the issue of drug certification by the US, see Mathea Falco, 'Passing Grades', *Foreign Affairs*, Vol. 74, No. 5 (1995): 15–20.
22. For the official US perspective on the International Criminal Court, see Address of Ambassador Scheffer to the American University School of Law, September 14, 2000, reprinted in Office of the Legal Adviser, Department of State, *Digest of United States Practice in International Law 2000* (2001): 273–279; Address of Ambassador Scheffer to the annual meeting of the American Society of International Law, March 26, 1999, ibid., 279–285; Letter to the secretary-general of the UN Regarding the Rome Statute of the International Criminal Court, *International Legal Materials*, Vol. XLI, No. 4 (July 2002), 1014. For criticism, see, Monroe Leigh, 'The United States and the Statute of Rome', *American Journal of International Law*, Vol. 95, No. 1 (2001), 124–131.
23. For comment, see John Steinbruner and Jeffrey Lewis, 'The Unsettled Legacy of the Cold War', *Daedalus* (Fall 2002):6–7.
24. 9/11 attacks may have provided political justification for the US to act as a hegemon. The view, however, that the US has tended to act in this way well before 9/11 has no shortage of protagonists: see, Charles William Maynes, 'The Perils of (and for) an Imperial America', *Foreign Policy*, No. 111 (Summer 1998): 36–49; Yong Deng, 'Hegemon on the Offensive: Chinese Perspectives on U.S. Global Strategy', *Political*

Science Quarterly, Vol. 116, No. 3 (2001): 343–366; Robert Kagan, 'The Benevolent Empire', *Foreign Policy*, No. 111 (Summer 1998): 24–34. On the nature of American power in general, see Stepehen G. Brooks and William C. Wohlforth, 'American Primacy in Perspective', *Foreign Affairs*, Vol. 81, No. 4 (2002): 20–33. For the view that the end of US hegemony began from the 1970s and only accelerated by the events of 9/11, see Immanuel Wallerstein, 'The Eagle Has Crash Landed', *Foreign Policy* (July/August 2002): 60–68.

25. See also Stanley Hoffman, 'On the War', *New York Review of Books*, Vol. XLVIII, No. 17 (2001), 4.
26. For the proposal made by the National Commission chaired by Professor Barry Chevannes in favour of decriminalising marijuana for personal use in Jamaica, see *A Report of the National Commission on Ganja to Rt. Hon. P.J. Patterson, Q.C., M.P., Prime Minister of Jamaica*, August 7, 2001. Generally, see also Vasciannie, 'Re Ganja: International Law and the Decriminalisation of Marijuana in Jamaica', *West Indian Law Journal*, Vol. 26, Nos. 1 and 2 (2001): 1–49; Oswald G. Harding, 'Decriminalization of Ganja: Jamaica's Treaty Obligations', ibid., Vol. 27, No. 1 (2002): 99–122.
27. For an account of how these values and others have come to be associated with Western societies, see, Buruma and Margalit, 'Occidentalism', *The New York Review of Books*, Vol. XLIX, No. 1 (2002) 4.
28. Some of the factors that could guide the US choice between unilateralism and multilateralism in particular contexts are canvassed by Nye, in 'Seven Tests: Between Concert and Unilateralism', *National Interest*, No. 66 (2001/2002): 5–13.
29. This is not to suggest that there is a direct relationship between US sensitivity to developments in the Third World and a reduction in international terrorism. It is essentially to note that some roots of terrorism have been linked, in rhetoric and in fact, to actions of the United States government. For a recent critique of the 'root causes' argument in the context of terrorism, see Dick Howard, 'The Left Agenda after September 11: An American View', *Internationale Politik und Gesellschaft*, Vol. 4/(2002).
30. Because the UN Security Council did not authorise the use of force by the American and British coalition *vis-à-vis* Afghanistan, the Chapter VII exception to Article 2(4) of the UN Charter is inapplicable here. Security Council Resolution 1373 of 2001 called on states to take certain actions against terrorism, but did not sanction the use of force. For a different reading of Resolution 1373, see Michael Byers, 'Terrorism, The Use of Force and International Law after 11 September', *International and Comparative Law Quarterly*, Vol. 51, Part 2 (2002): 401–402.
31. Sources on the prohibition of the use of force include: The 1970 Declaration on Principles of International Law Concerning Friendly Relations and Co-operation Among States in Accordance with the Charter of the UN, UN General Assembly Resolution 2625, United Nations General Assembly, *Official Records*, 26th Session, Supp. No. 28, p. 28; *Military and Paramilitary Activities in and against Nicaragua (Nicaragua v. United States of America)*, ICJ Reports 1986, 14.
32. For discussion, see Sir Robert Jennings and Sir Arthur Watts, *Oppenheim's International Law* (9th ed., 1992), Vol. 1: 416–427. John F. Murphy, 'Force and Arms', in Schachter and Joyner (eds.), *United Nations Legal Order*, Vol. 1 (1995): 247–317.
33. On Chapter VII generally, see Christine Gray, *International Law and the Use of Force* (2000): 144–199; Rosalyn Higgins, *Problems and Process: International Law and How We Use it* (1998 reprint), 254–266.

34. For *dicta* from the ICJ that attach significance to the pre-condition of an armed attack before self-defence may be invoked, see *Nicaragua v. The United States of America*, ICJ Reports 1986, 103–105; but cf., the position taken by Judge Sir Robert Jennings on this point: ibid., 542–544.
35. On concerns that the American response may be viewed as a reprisal, see also Christopher Greenwood, 'International Law and the "War against Terrorism"', *International Affairs*, Vol. 78, No. 2, (2002): 311–312. See also Derek Bowett, *Self-Defence in International Law* (1958), 188*ff*.
36. For reliance by the US and the UK on anticipatory self-defence in respect of future Al Qaeda attacks, see letter, dated October 7, 2001, from the US ambassador to the president of the UN Security Council, UN Doc. S/2001/946, and letter, dated October 7, 2001, from the UK charge d'affaires to the president of the UN Security Council, UN Doc. S/2001/947.
37. For the view that the prohibition in Article 2(4) of the UN Charter did not undermine the nature and scope of the right of self-defence under the pre-Charter customary law, see Bowett, *Self-Defence in International Law* (1958), 182*ff*. Cf., Brownlie, *International Law and the Use of Force by States* (1963), 257–261.
38. Quotation from US secretary of state, Daniel Webster, reprinted in J. Moore, *Digest of International Law* (1906), 412.
39. The degree of urgency required by the *Caroline* formulation is presumably accepted by states because it reduces the likelihood of state abuse: an imminent attack, leaving no choice of means, indicates that the state exercising self-defence has no non-violent option: Myres McDougal and Florentino Feliciano, *Law and Minimum World Public Order: The Legal Regulation of International Coercion* (1961), 231. Similarly, the surreptitious nature of terrorist attacks may be said to leave violence as the only realistic method of counterattack. The surreptitious nature of the 9/11 attacks also gave rise to obvious, and difficult, problems of evidence. Here, it is a matter of judgement as to how much latitude should be offered to the victim state in its identification of putative attackers: for comment, see Jonathan I. Charney, 'The Use of Force against Terrorism and International Law', *American Journal of International Law*, Vol. 95, No. 4, (2002) 836; Phillip Wilcox Jr, 'The Terror', in Robert B. Silvers and Barbara Epstein (eds.), *Striking Terror: America's New War* (2002): 7–8.
40. On the responsibility of the Taliban under International Law, see Greenwood, 'International Law and the War against Terrorism', *International Affairs*, 313; see also Thomas Franck, 'Terrorism and the Right of Self-Defense', *American Journal of International Law*, Vol. 95, No. 4 (2001): 840–841.
41. On proportionality as a factor in determining legality in instances of self-defence, see, Brownlie, *International Law and the Use of Force by States* (1963), 261–264.
42. UK support of the US may be justified as collective self-defence. According to the ICJ, collective self-defence is legally permissible where the state that is the victim of an armed attack requests assistance from another state: *Nicaragua v. United States of America*, ICJ Reports 1986, 14 para. 232.
43. For skeptical views on the efficacy of UN arms inspection in Iraq, see Gary Milhollin and Kelly Motz, 'Iraq: The Snare of Inspections', *Commentary*, Vol. 114, No. 3 (2002): 50–53; Daniel Byman, 'A Farewell to Arms Inspections', *Foreign Affairs*, Vol. 79, No. 1 (2000): 119–139. For a criticism of continued reliance on economic sanctions against Iraq, see Dennis J. Halliday, 'Iraq and the UN's Weapon of Mass Destruction', *Current History*, Vol. 98, No. 625 (1999): 65–68.
44. For a concise review of the issues, see Brian Urquhart, 'The Prospect of War', *New York Review of Books*, Vol. XLIX, No. 20, December 19, 2002: 16–22.

45. For the view that Saddam Hussein's record in starting two wars in the region is no worse than that of states such as Egypt or Israel, see John J. Mearsheimer and Stephen M. Walt, 'An Unnecessary War', *Foreign Policy* (January/February 2003): 51–59.
46. For this line of analysis in the context of India's nuclear weapons programme, see, Jaswant Singh, 'Against Nuclear Apartheid', *Foreign Affairs*, Vol. 77, No. 5 (1998): 41–52. On the case of Pakistan, post-9/11, see Farzana Shaikh, 'Pakistan's Nuclear Bomb: Beyond the Non-Proliferation Regime', *International Affairs*, Vol. 78, No. 1 (2002): 29–48.
47. On the danger of US over-reaching in the context of Iraq, see, Anthony Lewis, 'Bush and Iraq', *New York Review of Books*, Vol. XLIX, No. 17, November 7, 2002: 4–6; John Ikenberry, 'America's Imperial Ambition', *Foreign Affairs*, Vol. 81, No. 5 (2002): 44–60.
48. For the general comment that the doctrine of pre-emption 'puts the final nail in the coffin of Article 51 of the UN Charter', see Gary Schmitt, 'A Case of Continuity', *National Interest*, No. 69 (2002): 11. For a critique of the National Security Strategy report for 2002, and on related pronouncements by President Bush on the doctrine of pre-emption, see, John Lewis Gaddis, 'A Grand Strategy of Transformation', *Foreign Policy* (November/December 2002): 50–57.
49. Headley, *A Spade is Still a Spade: Essays on Crime and the Politics of Jamaica* (2003), 5–21.
50. Ibid., 6–7. For a view similar to that taken by the Minister of National Security and Justice, see Garth Rattray, 'Time to Tackle Domestic Terrorism', *The Gleaner* (Jamaica), November 5, 2002.
51. Walter Laqueur accepts the definition of terrorism as 'the substate application of violence or threatened violence intended to sow panic in a society, to weaken or even overthrow the incumbents, and to bring about political change': 'Postmodern Terrorism', *Foreign Affairs*, Vol. 75, No. 5 (1996): 24-25. This approach is also apparent in the definition of terrorism set out in the International Convention for the Suppression of the Financing of Terrorism (1999), UN Doc. A/RES/54/109, Annex, reprinted in United Nations, *International Instruments related to the Prevention and Suppression of International Terrorism* (2001),113–133. On difficulties in defining terrorism post-9/11, see, Byford, 'The Wrong War', Foreign Affairs, Vol. 81, No. 4 (2002): 34–43.
52. The US has sought to justify reliance on military tribunals, rather than criminal courts for persons accused of terrorist activities as part of the Al Qaeda effort: see Presidential Military Order of November 13, 2001, on Detention, Treatment and Trial of Certain Non-Citizens in the War against Terrorism, 66 Fed. Reg. 57833 (2001), reprinted in *International Legal Materials*, Vol. XLI (January 2002), 252–255; United States Department of Defense, Military Commission Order No. 1, March 21, 2002, reprinted ibid., Vol. XLI, No. 3 (2002); United States, 'Response of the United States to Request for Precautionary Measures —Detainees in Guantanamo Bay, Cuba', April 15, 2002, reprinted ibid., Vol. XLI, No. 4: 1015–1027. See also Abraham D. Sofaer and Paul R. Williams, 'Doing Justice During Wartime: Why Military Tribunals Make Sense', *Policy Review*, No. 111 (February & March 2002): 3–14. For review of military courts in general, see A.P.V. Rogers, 'The Use of Military Courts to Try Suspects', *International and Comparative Law Quarterly*, Vol. 51, Part 4 (October 2002): 967–979. For criticism of the US approach to human rights post-9/11, see Ronald Dworkin, 'The Threat to Patriotism', *New York Review of Books*, Vol. XLIX, No. 3, 2002: 44–49. There is evidence that US citizens have mixed feelings about the treatment of suspected terrorists on grounds of civil liberties, and that they are wary about surveillance policies put in place by the US Government following 9/11: Leonie Huddy, Nadia

Khatibe, Theresa Capelos, 'The Polls – Trends: Reactions to the Terrorist Attacks of September 11, 2001', *Public Opinion Quarterly*, Vol. 66, No. 3 (2002): 418–450.

53. The British legislative reaction is encapsulated in their Anti-Terrorism, Crime and Security Act (2001); for a critical assessment, see Helen Fenwick, 'The Anti-Terrorism, Crime and Security Act 2001: A Proportionate Response to 11 September?', *Modern Law Review*, Vol. 65, No. 5 (2002): 724–762.
54. Issues of personal security, though clearly linked to questions of national security, have their own, distinct place in the debates on social policy. For the view that perceived conflicts between personal and national security have been substantially reduced in the post-Cold War era, see Jack Donnelly, 'Rethinking Human Rights', *Current History*, Vol. 95, No. 604 (1996): 387–391.
55. See Stephen Vasciannie, *International Law and Selected Human Rights in Jamaica* (2002), 46–52.
56. Ibid., p. 49. Nor is the high level of police killings for the period 1996 to 2000 unique. Harriott notes that the average number of police killings per year fell from some 200 per year in the 1980s, to an annual average of 132 in the 1990s: *Police and Crime Control in Jamaica* (2000) 82.

3

Territorial Disputes and Regional Security in the Caribbean Basin

Raymond J. Milefsky[1]

> There are no intrinsically good or bad boundaries... A boundary, like the human skin, may have diseases of its own or may reflect the illnesses of the body.[2]

Introduction

Land and maritime border disputes represent a traditional threat to Caribbean security. Such disputes arise from competition over resources: mainly offshore hydrocarbons and living resources but extend to other natural and manmade cultural assets, such as coral reefs and shipwrecks. Today, border disputes affect the region less intensely than domestic instabilities and transnational criminal activities, but dormant disputes do sometimes re-erupt in violent conflict. This chapter explains borders boundaries, limits, and disputes from a Caribbean perspective, comprehensively reviews the status of all Caribbean boundaries, and provides channels for regional states to resolve border disputes. For the purposes of this discussion, the Caribbean basin includes the Gulf of Mexico states, Leeward and Windward Caribbean islands, Bermuda and the north shore states of South America.

Understanding Land and Maritime Limits and Boundaries

Land Limits and Boundaries

Ancient peoples and some nomads today in sparsely populated regions identified the *limits* of their domain by physical features. Occasionally they built walls to assert those limits. As dominion expanded with the creation of armies and navies, limits were extended by conquest and nation-states were formed. Where the balance of power clashed and limits overlapped, adjacent states sometimes allied against other states and agreed to establish common *boundaries.*

A land boundary affixes the limits of sovereignty of adjacent states with a two-dimensional perpendicular plane that extends into the air, on the surface and underground. That plane, represented notionally on maps as a line, can extend along *physical features* (peaks, ridges, drainage, streams, etc.), *geometrical configurations* (straight lines, arcs) or around and along *man-made features* (rail lines and roads, settlements, property lines). A body of law in the form of treaties evolved to codify and define the alignment and conditions related to boundaries. In medieval Western Europe, sovereigns mirrored their early boundary treaties on Roman property law. Today, a body of international law and practice defines the 322 international land boundaries that divide up the entire landmass of the planet into independent states, dependencies, and areas of special sovereignty.[3]

Land boundaries differ with respect to their legal and political status. Legally a boundary is either *de jure* (alignment agreed upon by treaty or other internationally recognised instrument) or *de facto* (based on mutually accepted reality on the ground). Some states maintain historically *de jure* boundaries, which means the lines were established during colonial times but have no formal post-colonial agreement. This situation fortunately does not exist in the Western Hemisphere. Politically, the majority of international land boundaries or segments of boundaries are described as either definite or indefinite. *Definite* boundaries are usually *de jure* and are usually clearly demarcated with pillars or other fixed points on the ground.[4] *Indefinite* boundaries or certain of its segments, by contrast, may lack current legal substance, may be delimited but exist undemarcated or poorly defined. Indefinite segments are still found in sections of remote, unpopulated Brazilian jungle. The newly-created states of the former Soviet Union and former Yugoslavia have indefinite boundaries that lack bilateral agreement regarding their delimitation and demarcation.

A boundary *dispute* exists when both states cannot agree on the alignment of the line, its segments, or special arrangements related to navigation, the transit of local populations and the like along the border. Disputes can occur among *de jure* and *de facto*, definite and indefinite boundaries and result from changing geography and political realities on the ground: streams shift courses, valuable mineral resources are discovered, populations resettle, and – most importantly – governments change.

Official maps reflect the foreign policy of states, so disputant states and third parties may or may not label or depict boundaries in the same way and employ different names for adjacent features. Cartographers may also label sections of boundaries as 'approximate' when the sources they are using to compile the map conflict or lack sufficient information to draw the line correctly. 'Approximate' is not a political or legal term. Besides definite and indefinite international boundaries, 'other lines of separation' exist. They relate to temporal sovereignty divisions, often resulting from unresolved conflicts or negotiated arrangements, frequently mandated by third parties. They include armistice lines, ceasefire lines, claim lines, demilitarised zone lines, ground security zone lines, military disengagement zone lines, military base lines, peace-keeping zone limits, occupied territory and no-man's-land limits, and the like. In the Western Hemisphere, such lines of separation are presently limited to the:

- Belize-Guatemala Line of Adjacency (an Organization of American States brokered line of convenience created in 2000 to deal with Guatemalan squatters in Belize's rain forests);
- US military base boundary in Guantánamo, Cuba.

Maritime Limits

International limits no longer exist on land,[5] but claims to the waters and seabed extending from the shoreline constitute the largest form of delimitation at sea. Because limits are *unilaterally claimed*, other states may protest these claims but they are to be respected. Several states, for example, protest Venezuela's right to claim an exclusive economic zone around Aves Island as well as Nicaragua's claimed 200 nautical mile territorial sea.

Before the Second World War, maritime powers asserted territorial limits seaward out to three nautical miles.[6] This was based on the range of standard eighteenth-century twelve-pounder cannon. After the Second World War, countries recognised the need to expand their territorial seas for defence as well as to protect and claim offshore living and mineral resources. Today most states[7] subscribe to the United Nations Convention on the Law of the Sea (UNCLOS), which sets guidelines for various types of limits:

1) *Baselines* consist of either straight-line tangents from projecting coastal features or the coastline itself at a certain tide. Waters behind coastal and straight baselines are called inland waters and have the same

sovereignty status as land, including denial of innocent passage to foreign vessels.

2) *Bay and river closing lines* are straight-line tangents closing off rivers and bays of a certain width or historically claimed by states. Several states protest Venezuela's claim to a historic bay closing line to the Gulf of Venezuela.
3) *Archipelagic closing lines* are straight-line tangents connecting the outer islands of an archipelagic state. Archipelagic waters are much the same as inland waters except for proscribed transit lanes that permit foreign vessels innocent passage. Several Caribbean states have asserted archipelagic closing lines.
4) *Territorial seas limits* are made up of buffered arcs extending territorial sovereignty seaward from the coastal baselines, usually out to 12 nautical miles as stipulated under UNCLOS. Innocent passage of foreign vessels is guaranteed. The Dominican Republic uniquely retains a six nautical mile territorial sea. Ecuador, El Salvador, Nicaragua and Peru established and still assert 200 nautical mile (nm) territorial seas before UNCLOS. Brazil, Panama, and Uruguay amended their 200 nm claims several years ago to conform to UNCLOS.
5) *Contiguous zones limits* extend an additional 12 nautical miles beyond the territorial sea limits to prevent and punish infringements of national customs, fiscal, immigration, and sanitary regulations under UNCLOS. Venezuela declares only a three nautical mile contiguous zone beyond its territorial sea.
6) *Exclusive economic zone (EEZ) limits* may extend from the baseline 200 nautical miles out to sea under UNCLOS, allowing states to explore and exploit resources in the seabed, subsoil and the water column to the exclusion of all other states. The waters are considered open seas for all navigation.
7) *Continental shelf limits* may extend 350 nautical miles out from the coast or 100 nautical miles from the 2500 metre isobath, whichever is further. States are permitted exclusive rights to explore and exploit the seabed and subsoil, but the waters are considered open seas.[8]

Beyond these limits lie the *open seas*.[9] The illustration below schematically represents the alignment of maritime limits. Geography creates certain anomalies, which make UNCLOS definitions subject to protest and dispute. These include definitions of islands, rocks, banks and sandbars; acceptable lengths of closing lines; and the extent and composition of the continental shelf. Table 3.1 below shows the maritime claims of the Caribbean Basin states and dependencies while Map 3.1 shows maritime and land disputes.

Table 3.1
Maritime Limit Claims Of The Caribbean Basin States And Dependencies

State/Dependency	Baseline Type	Territorial Sea	Contiguous Zone*	EEZ/CS**
Antigua and Barbuda	Archipelagic	12	12	0
The Bahamas	Straight	12	0	0
Barbados	Straight	12	0	0
Belize	Straight	12	0	0
Bermuda (United Kingdom)	Straight	12	0	0
Brazil	Straight	12	12	0
Cayman Islands (United Kingdom)	Straight	12	12	200
Colombia	Straight	12	0	0
Costa Rica	Straight	12	0	0
Cuba	Straight	12	0	0
Dominica	Straight	12	12	0
Dominican Republic	Straight	6	18	0
France (French Guyana)‡	Straight	12	12	200
France (Guadeloupe)‡	Straight	12	12	200
France (Martinique)‡	Straight	12	12	200
Grenada	Straight	12	0	200
Guatemala	Coastline	12	0	200
Guyana	Coastline	12	0	200†
Haiti	Straight	12	12	200
Honduras	Straight	12	12	200
Jamaica	Archipelagic	12	12	200
Mexico	Straight	12	12	200
Netherlands Antilles/Aruba (Netherlands)	Straight	12	0	200
Nicaragua	Coastline	200	0	0
Panama	Coastline	12	12	200
St Kitts & Nevis	Coastline	12	12	200
St Lucia	Coastline	12	12	200
St Vincent & the Grenadines	Archipelagic	12	12	200
Suriname	Coastline	12	0	200
Trinidad & Tobago	Archipelagic	12	12	200
Turks & Caicos (United Kingdom)	Straight	12	0	0
United States	Coastline	12	12	200
Venezuela	Straight	12	3	200

**Distance beyond territorial sea   **Exclusive economic zone or continental shelf.*
† UN Maritime Treaty website claims Guyana claims only a 200 nautical mile fishing zone.
‡ French Guyana, Guadeloupe, Martinique and associated islands are overseas departments of France and are considered administrative divisions rather than dependencies.

Source: Summary of National Maritime Claims, US Department of State/OES, June 1, 2002.

Map 3.1
Maritime Boundaries and Territorial Disputes of the Countries and Dependencies in the Caribbean Basin

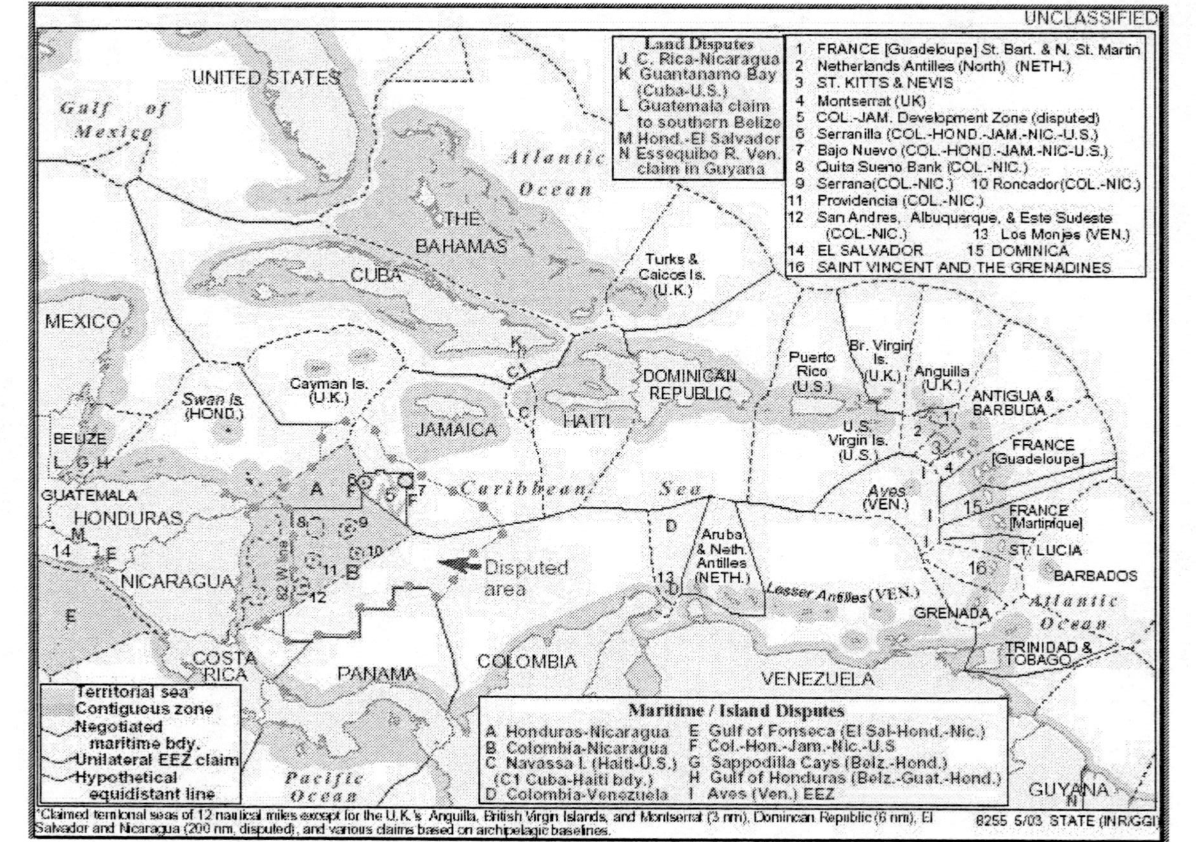

Maritime Boundaries

States unilaterally declare maritime limits. In cases where states are adjacent or opposite to one another and where maritime limits overlap, they may act bilaterally to create maritime boundaries under agreement. Land boundaries go back centuries into early recorded history and their segments are crafted often as a consequence of multiple treaties, arbitrations, diplomatic manoeuvers, demarcations and wars. Most maritime boundaries date after the Second World War when states realised they needed to protect and could exploit offshore resources in the water and the seabed.[10] Generally, only one treaty or agreement governs a maritime boundary.

Of the potential 420 areas of the world where maritime boundaries could be created, only 132 boundary treaties are presently in force.[11] Like land boundaries, maritime boundaries are permanent; they are established when competition over identifiable offshore resources or the need to protect the maritime ecology demands a precise allocation of the seabed, subsoil or water column. Where no compelling grounds for dispute exist, adjoining or opposing states largely make do with informal arrangements and accept hypothetical boundaries. The Caribbean states have the highest density of established maritime boundaries in the world.

States may opt to create temporary or renewable *joint fishing or development zones* in lieu of or in addition to establishing maritime boundaries. Such zones are popular where states do not feel ready to establish permanently binding boundaries, yet feel compelled to address amicably their claims to the water and seabed. Maritime boundaries, like limits, represent varying levels of sovereignty. A territorial sea boundary separates sovereign waters, the seabed, subsoil and airspace above, but an exclusive economic zone (EEZ) boundary only establishes the exclusive limits for the undersea economic exploitation. A continental shelf boundary relates only to the seabed and subsoil and not to the water column. Fishing zones usually pertain only to the water column, and even joint development zones often leave the seabed to further negotiation. Second and third party states are entitled to innocent passage through all maritime zones (sometimes subject to prior notification restrictions).

The definitions of legal and political land boundary status (*de facto*, *de jure*, definite, indefinite) do not pertain to maritime boundaries. Instead, one references whether a boundary treaty is 'in force,' meaning that it has been ratified by the states and registered with an international organisation. Otherwise, the status of the boundary is considered provisional. A hypothetical equidistant boundary can be constructed as a notional, but non-binding separation between states.

Maritime boundaries between opposing and adjoining states can be built of equidistant and median lines measured from coastlines, straight lines or arcs. Equidistant lines can be simplified or modified depending on the negotiating parties and geographical circumstances. Adjacent boundaries can also be formed from perpendiculars to the general direction of the coast, extensions of parallels and meridians (latitudes and longitudes), or some other agreed-upon configuration.

Maritime boundaries are seldom demarcated with light buoys except in narrow passages. Because a straight line drawn on a Mercator projection map (loxodrome line) forms an arc on the earth's ellipsoid surface and *vice versa* (geodesic line), disputes may sometimes arise over the precise location of maritime boundaries if the treaty does not specify the type of straight line. Other technical ambiguities occur when the datum of coordinate points is not specified.

Border Disputes

Categories of Border Disputes

Border is a generic term that relates to the invisible line separating sovereignties as well as to the territories, peoples, and resources adjacent to that line. Border disputes therefore fall into three categories: 1) divergent interpretations over the alignment of the boundary (*boundary disputes*), 2) issues related to the flow of people and resources (legal and illegal) across the boundary (*borderland disputes*), and 3) claims to territory (*territorial disputes*).[12] Land boundaries can obviously be more easily demarcated and monitored with walls, fences, signs and guns than maritime boundaries, but both can fall subject to the three categories of border disputes. Furthermore, the viability of both land and maritime boundaries remains dictated by the same incalculable admixture of political prowess, armed security, regional alliances, economic development, endowment of natural resources, and favourable geography.

Border disputes are not necessarily bilateral. One side may assert historical rights to lands, peoples, and resources on the opposite side of the boundary that the other side ignores or counters with similar rights. Also, one of the parties may dispute special conditions imposed by border treaties, such as river navigation or water sharing rights, or challenge the locations of features referenced in the treaties, such as the upstream sources of boundary streams, which Guyana and French Guiana contest with Suriname.

Intensities of Border Disputes

Not all border disputes are belligerent and destabilising. Some states accept the fact that they interpret (especially small or remote segments of) their boundary differently and choose not to reconcile those differences. Many states maintain managed disputes that continue on at the diplomatic level or between boundary commissions, sometimes for decades, without upsetting overall bilateral relations. Parties with managed disputes establish working administrative arrangements while pursuing claims. Unfortunately, managed or dormant disputes can turn hostile when other political frictions ignite old animosities. On the other hand, parties managing a dispute often turn to third party mediation if political will to settle is present. Disputes become bellicose when border populations fall prey to popular violence, armed incidents, criminal or illegal activities. Such destabilising bellicosity can, however, push the states to settle long-festering differences and avoid war. The figure below outlines a notional scale reflecting the escalating intensity of border disputes.

Figure 3.1 Border Dispute Intensity Levels

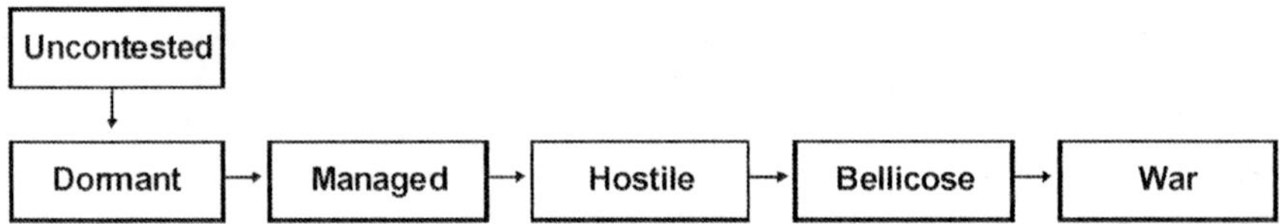

Border Disputes in the Caribbean Basin

At the start of the twenty-first century, only a few moderated, yet pernicious, land boundary and territorial conflicts remain among the many bloody disputes of the last two centuries. They have been eclipsed by more intense borderland conflicts involving smuggling, illegal migration, and drug trafficking. The Caribbean Basin contains 26 independent states (13 continental, 13 insular), eight insular dependencies plus three French overseas departments. They share a total of 19 land boundaries and 86 actual and hypothetical maritime boundaries. The comprehensive table (Table 3.2) identifies each boundary by category (land/maritime), type (physical configuration), length, current treaty status, treaty dates, current dispute status and background, and dispute intensity. Island territorial disputes are inventoried as a type of land boundary dispute.

Land Boundaries

Although maritime boundaries outnumber land boundaries by more than 4:1, land border disputes (which include boundary, territorial and borderland issues) outnumber and are more intense than maritime disputes. In several cases land disputes prevent the creation of adjacent maritime boundaries.

Boundary and Territorial Disputes:

- Belize-Guatemala: Guatemalan territorial claims in Belize (hostile)
- Cuba-United States: Cuba's protest to the US base on Guantánamo (managed)
- Guyana-Suriname: New River triangle dispute (managed to hostile)
- Guyana-Venezuela: Essequibo region dispute (managed to hostile)
- Saint-Martin (France) [Guadeloupe]-Saint Maarten (Netherlands Antilles): segment of land boundary dispute (uncontested to managed)

Borderlands Issues:

- Brazil-Suriname: illegal migration, smuggling (managed)
- Colombia-Venezuela: illegal migration, smuggling (managed to hostile)
- Costa Rica-Nicaragua: San Juan river border patrols (managed)

Furthermore, there are persistent territorial disputes over islands:

- Navassa island: Haiti-United States (managed)
- San Andres, Providencia islands; Albuquerque, Este-Sudeste, Roncador cays; Quito Sueno, Serrana banks: Colombia-Nicaragua (managed to hostile)
- Sapodilla Cays: Belize-Guatemala-Honduras (managed)
- Serranilla Banks and Bajo Nuevo: Colombia, Honduras, Jamaica, Nicaragua, United States (dormant to managed)
- West Breaker, Middle, East/Beacon cays: Colombia-Honduras (dormant to managed)

The protracted South American bickering over lands in Suriname and Guyana stem from divergent interpretations of colonial treaties and serve as a vehicle for regional states to assert regional power and compete for potential oil resources on and offshore. The convoluted island claims on the Nicaraguan Rise derive less from historical claims than projections of regional identity mixed with a latent hope for oil riches.

The most serious regional dispute, which seemed, until recently, headed toward resolution, remains between Belize and Guatemala. For the last several years, the Organization of American States (OAS) with United Kingdom and United States participation crafted a territorial differendum wherein Guatemala would renounce its territorial claims to Belize in exchange for a slight adjustment to the land boundary; Belize would accept Guatemala's Bay of Amatique closing line; a broad maritime channel would be carved from Belizean and Honduran waters; the disputed Sapodilla Cays would become a tri-national ecological park; and the US and UK would provide $200 million in development aid. Fearing popular rejection, however, the Guatemalan leadership withdrew the referendum on the differendum just before the vote was to be taken. The referendum may be either deferred until a more propitious time or the dispute referred to the International Court of Justice in The Hague for complete reconsideration.

Maritime Boundaries in the Caribbean Basin

Only 23 maritime boundaries out of a potential 86 are governed by treaties in force in the Caribbean Basin. Cuba's two boundaries with the Mexico and United States are *de facto* in force, maintained through the periodic exchange of diplomatic notes. Colombia and Costa Rica have a similar *de facto* arrangement to their unratified treaty. Colombia and Honduras dispute several small keys, keeping their signed treaty from coming into force and Nicaragua contests the treaty, claiming Colombian and Honduran islands and waters. The United Kingdom and the Dominican Republic and France (Guadeloupe) have unratified agreements that are not disputed. Brazil and French Guiana must sort our whether their ratified agreement intended a loxodrome or geodesic line, and several states persist in their claims to Serranilla Banks and Bajo Nuevo. The Dominican Republic has unilaterally asserted boundaries with the US territory of Puerto Rico and Haiti in the south.

No maritime boundaries exist for the remaining 58 potential allocations in waters in the Caribbean Basin. Several states are currently in various stages of negotiating delimitations: Jamaica with Haiti, Honduras, Nicaragua, and the UK (Cayman Islands); and Honduras with Cuba. Forty of the potential boundaries have no identified disputes and hypothetical equidistance boundaries appear to serve adequately in lieu of actual treaty boundaries.

Eighteen potential boundaries have identified disputes ranging in intensity:

Dormant: 2

- Belize-Guatemala-Honduras: Sapodilla Cays
- Jamaica-Nicaragua: Serranilla Banks, Bajo Nuevo

Managed: 10

- Antigua and Barbuda-France (St Bartholemy [Guadeloupe]): reported dispute, details unknown
- Bahamas-United States: northern continental shelf allocation
- Belize-Honduras: Guatemalan maritime corridor
- Cuba-United States: maritime access to Guantánamo base
- Dominica-Venezuela: Aves islands
- Haiti-United States: Navassa island
- Saint Martin (France [Guadeloupe])-Sint Maarten (Netherlands Antilles): land boundary dispute prevents extension at sea
- Saint Kitts and Nevis-Venezuela: Aves islands
- Saint Lucia-Venezuela: Aves islands
- Saint Vincent and the Grenadines-Venezuela: Aves islands

Managed to Hostile: 6

- Colombia-Nicaragua: multiple island disputes
- Colombia-Venezuela: boundary around Los Monjes islands
- Guyana-Suriname: Courantijn river maritime extension
- Guyana-Venezuela: Essequibo land boundary extension seaward
- Honduras-Nicaragua: extension of straight line from land boundary
- Belize-Guatemala: Caribbean access corridor for Guatemala

Littoral states harbour most of the more serious maritime conflicts in the region. The island states of the Caribbean have managed their boundary relations rather peaceably. The dependencies, in particular, have the highest ratio of settled boundaries to political entity. One might ascribe this peaceful arrangement to the islands possessing fewer hydrocarbons, smaller militaries, and a longer tradition of regional cooperation. Problems with illegal migration and the use of islands to facilitate narcotics smuggling, however, represent a borderlands management problem exacerbated by the lack of maritime boundaries.

Approaches to Resolving Caribbean Regional Border Disputes

Today the states and dependencies in the Caribbean have access to a number of internationally accepted, non-belligerent means to resolve border disputes. Regardless of the approach, resolution is possible only if the parties negotiate in good faith. External pressure seldom sustains good faith but it can facilitate it. On the other hand, states which maintain managed disputes and otherwise maintain balanced, stable relations can defer resolution for long periods.

Bilateral Diplomatic Negotiations

Unless neighbouring states become involved in a border dispute,[13] two states can attempt to negotiate their differences bilaterally. This, however, requires that the negotiating parties exercise the internal political will to seek a solution that will likely involve compromise and sacrifice. States can call upon non-binding and binding third parties to assist them with services ranging from informal mediation to international court decisions. Services vary in costs, demands, and deliberative periods.

Non-Binding Third Party Negotiations

In non-binding processes, third parties help the disputants seek solutions to a dispute. Third parties have included semi-public mediators, retired statesmen, the Pope, international organisations like the Organization of American States, CARICOM, as well as the foreign ministries of neighbouring states, larger regional powers, and former colonial states. They can be brought in to prepare, lead, manage, or arbitrate the negotiations, as well as provide technical assistance in the form of cartographic and imagery support. They suggest venues, conditions, terms, goals and expected outcomes. Joint negotiations can take place in the same room or as consecutive talks in separate rooms, depending upon the parties. In all cases, the third parties must remain neutral with the disputants actively participating in the deliberations.

OAS assistant secretary general, Ambassador Luigi Einaudi, perhaps the finest living boundary negotiator in the Western Hemisphere, established a series of proven, successful negotiating rules that apply to non-binding third party deliberations:

1) Maintain unity among all the third parties leading the negotiations by assuring that someone takes the lead to represent the negotiators.
2) Keep an eye on where the people with the guns stand to ensure that armed might is available to back up rather than undermine the decision. Assure, too, a proper balance of military-diplomatic involvement.
3) The two parties must see themselves as taking the lead out front and not simply following the negotiator's instructions. Private sector, professional facilitators and mediators are particularly good at this.
4) Follow the law. While negotiations must generally be held under conditions of the strictest confidence, they must be above board and conform to the principles of international law. Legal improprieties subvert any decision.
5) Keep sights high and do not hesitate to keep making proposals to the parties.[14]

Common forums for non-binding third party negotiations include:

- Intercessory 'good offices' of respected negotiators to keep the parties talking and arbitrate a decision,
- Mediation through offering proposals to forward discussions, and
- Commissions of inquiry to substantiate and gather facts for the disputants.

Requesting such services does not mean that they will implement decisions reached in the deliberations. In fact, the disputants can summarily rebuff and reject advice after days of deliberations, particularly when all realise that the 'good faith' the parties exhibited to negotiate was ephemeral.

The OAS Fund for Peace is an important regional resource for assistance in resolving border issues in the Western Hemisphere. The OAS has a long history of successful boundary dispute resolution and its Fund provides an added incentive to utilise the OAS in conflict resolution. The Rio Treaty security umbrella was established to deal with terrorism, natural disasters, and other non-traditional threats. It may also prove to be beneficial in redressing border disputes. The US Institute for Peace is also intended to assist states in dispute mediation and conflict resolution.

In May 2002, Mexico proposed the Caribbean Maritime Boundary Initiative, whose intent is to facilitate, but not adjudicate, the resolution of seaward disputes within a regional forum by creating a database of pending disputes and low-cost technical expertise through a joint trust fund. Participating states will be obliged to 'register' the records of their bilateral negotiations with the regional forum for the database. Few states in the Caribbean Basin have yet to sign on to the Initiative due to skepticism over motives and the belief that boundary negotiations are fundamentally unique, sensitive and bilateral in nature.

Third-Party Binding Processes

Disputing parties can also call upon international organisations to render a binding decision for them under international law. The three main binding processes include conciliation, ad hoc arbitration, and adjudication. Under *conciliation,* a court chamber settles minor controversies through agreement by the parties without recourse to litigation. The court decision is considered binding but not authoritative. This process is rather swift, generally taking months, to render a decision on generally straightforward cases.

Likewise, *ad hoc arbitration* is quasi-judicial, conducted through independent commissions whose rulings are considered authoritative. Commission arbitration is used when communications between the parties are difficult but both have agreed through an armistice or cease fire to seek a solution in good faith. It could take several months to years to find that solution. Commissions may have members representing both sides or be made up of all disinterested parties. *Adjudication* is the most time consuming (over three years on average) and costly (millions of dollars) means of receiving an authoritative ruling from the courts. The International Court of Justice (ICJ) is commonly called upon to rule on boundary disputes but signatories to the UN Convention on the Law of the Sea can also adjudicate maritime disputes through that organisation.

Rulings can be based on equanimity (*ex aequo et bono*), historical precedent, a strict interpretation of the treaties, or some combination, depending upon the conditions outlined by the parties and mediators. *Uti possidetis juris* (as you possess so shall you rule) judgements respect boundaries as they existed at independence. This principle was first applied in the nineteenth century to adjudicate numerous boundary disputes in the Western Hemisphere. The court can likewise resort to *effectivités* (evidence of the effective exercise of territorial juristiction) and *actualités* (evidence of present-day jurisdiction in the region) to allocate territory, depending upon the guidelines set by the disputants.

International court decisions are considered to be binding and irrevocable. Without an international enforcement mechanism, however, binding processes assume that the parties will honour the decision and submit to international law.[15] In most cases, states conform, but in the case of the 1992 International Court of Justice ruling for El Salvador-Honduras, the parties have yet to demarcate the adjudicated sections of boundary on account of technical ambiguities in the Court's allocation. Furthermore, in September 2002, El Salvador requested that the ICJ revisit its 1992 ruling for one of the sections based on newly acquired historical evidence.

Table 3.2
Boundary Disputes and Territorial Demarcations of the States and Dependencies in the Caribbean Basin

BOUNDARY PAIR	CAT.	TYPE	LENGTH	TREATY STATUS	DATE	DISPUTE STATUS	DISPUTE INTENSITY
ANGUILA (UNITED KINGDOM)-ANTIGUA AND BARBUDA	Maritime	Hypothetical maritime boundary		None		No disputes identified	
ANGUILLA (UNITED KINGDOM)-ST MARTIN/ST BARTHOLEMY (FRANCE [GUADELOUPE])	Maritime	7-segment equidistance maritime boundary	83 nm	Signed, not in force	1996	No disputes identified	
ANGUILLA (UNITED KINGDOM)-VIRGIN ISLANDS (UNITED KINGDOM)	Maritime	Hypothetical maritime boundary		None		No disputes identified	
ANGUILLA (UNITED KINGDOM)-VIRGIN ISLANDS (UNITED STATES)	Maritime	1-segment maritime boundary	1.34 nm	In force	1995	No disputes identified	
ANTIGUA AND BARBUDA-FRANCE (GUADELOUPE)	Maritime	Hypothetical maritime boundary		None		Dispute reported with St Bartholemy, details unavailable. Antigua and Barbuda also protests the treaties signed by France, the Netherlands and the United States, recognising Venezuela's claim to full effect to Islas des Aves and thus continental shelf/EEZ	Managed
ANTIGUA AND BARBUDA-MONTSERRAT (UNITED KINGDOM)	Maritime	Hypothetical maritime boundary		None		No boundary disputes identified but Antigua and Barbuda objects to the treaties signed by France, the Netherlands and the United States, recognising Venezuela's claim to full effect to Islas des Aves and thus continental shelf/EEZ	
ANTIGUA AND BARBUDA-ST KITTS AND NEVIS	Maritime	Hypothetical maritime boundary		None		No disputes identified	

ANTIGUA AND BARBUDA-VENEZUELA (Islas des Aves)	Maritime	Hypothetical wedge between Saint Kitts and Nevis separates these features.		None		Antigua and Barbuda also objects to the treaties signed by France, the Netherlands and the United States, recognising Venezuela's claim to full effect to Islas des Aves and thus continental shelf/EEZ	
BAHAMAS, THE-CUBA	Maritime	Hypothetical maritime boundary		None		No disputes identified. The Bahamas have had to deal with Cuban refugees in recent years.	
BAHAMAS, THE-HAITI	Maritime	Hypothetical maritime boundary		None		No disputes identified. The Bahamas have had to deal with Haitian refugees in recent years.	
BAHAMAS, THE-TURKS AND CAICOS (UNITED KINGDOM)	Maritime	Hypothetical maritime boundary		None		No disputes identified	
BAHAMAS, THE-UNITED STATES	Maritime	Hypothetical maritime boundary		None		No disputes identified related to Hypothetical equidistant line except at Bahamian northern limit where US claims the parallel and not an equidistant boundary. Dispute inhibits maritime treaty settlement. Borderland disputes over fishing, illegal smuggling across Hypothetical boundary.	Managed
BARBADOS-FRANCE (MARTINIQUE)	Maritime	Hypothetical maritime boundary		None		Maritime boundary dispute reported; no details available.	
BARBADOS-GUYANA	Maritime	Hypothetical maritime boundary		None		It is unclear whether the Trinidad and Tobago-Venezuela boundary precludes this boundary.	
BARBADOS-ST LUCIA	Maritime	Hypothetical maritime boundary		None		No disputes identified	
BARBADOS-ST VINCENT AND THE GRENADINES	Maritime	Hypothetical maritime boundary		None		No disputes identified	
BARBADOS-TRINIDAD AND TOBAGO	Maritime	Hypothetical maritime boundary		None		No disputes identified. The seaward extension of the Trinidad and Tobago-Venezuela continental shelf boundary may intersect with Barbados' southeastern limits precluding a common boundary with Guyana.	

BARBADOS-VENEZUELA	Maritime	Hypothetical maritime boundary		None		In 1989, Trinidad and Tobago and Venezuela extended their maritime boundary out to nominal Barbados water, thereby eliminating any Hypothetical boundary between Barbados and Guyana and Guyana and Trinidad and Tobago.	
BELIZE-GUATEMALA	Land	Two straight line segments, one stream. Demarcated, definite.	266 km	Ratified	1786 1856 1859 1991	Unilateral territorial dispute: Guatemala claims half of Belizan territory south of Sibun river based on an unfulfilled 1859 treaty. A referendum based on OAS negotiations in 2002 that created an adjustment at the Mexico tripoint, a broad Caribbean passage, aid package is not brought to a vote in Guatemala and postponed in Belize.	Hostile
BELIZE-GUATEMALA	Maritime	Hypothetical adjacency in Gulf of Amatique; proposed channel into Caribbean		None		At present, Guatemalan access to Caribbean is closed off by Belize, Honduras territorial seas. In 2002, Guatemala did not bring the land and maritime boundary referendum forward for a popular vote over concerns of rejection. Historically, Belize objects to Guatemala's historic bay claim to the Bahia de Amatique and linking its land boundary claims to resolution of the maritime boundary.	Hostile
BELIZE-HONDURAS	Land	Offshore islands		None		Honduran claims to Sapodilla Cays off Belize coast pend resolution of Belize-Guatemala dispute which proposed an international marine park.	Managed
BELIZE-HONDURAS	Maritime	Hypothetical maritime boundary		None		No disputes identified except for Honduran claim to Sapodilla Cays. States agree to an OAS negotiated maritime corridor for Guatemala separating Hypothetical boundary as part of Belize-Guatemala referendum.	
BELIZE-MEXICO	Land	Physical boundary mostly along streams; N-S/E-W straight lines through Chetumal Bay; one straight line segment over land. Demarcated, definite	250 km	Ratified	1859 1893	No disputes identified. Mexico once claimed down to Sibun river, but 1859 treaty moved line northward. Treaties conveyed after Belize independence in 1973	
BELIZE-MEXICO	Maritime	Hypothetical adjacency boundary		None		No disputes identified	
BRAZIL-FRANCE (FRENCH GUIANA)	Land	Physical boundary along remote streams (definite) and across uninhabited jungle watershed (indefinite). Undemarcated.	673 km	In force	1815 1817 1822	No disputes identified. Boundary has never been in dispute.	

BRAZIL-FRANCE (FRENCH GUIANA)	Maritime	Single line simplified direction of coast perpendicular, territorial sea/EEZ adjacency boundary	(200 nm)	In force	1981	No disputes have been identified, but the treaty does not specify whether the line is a loxodrome or geodesic, resulting in a significant difference in area.	Dormant
BRAZIL-GUYANA	Land	Physical boundary based on Amazon basin and Essequibo-Courantyne rivers watershed. Demarcated, definite	1119 km	Ratified	1904 1926 1936	No disputes identified. Brazil-UK boundary undefined until 1904 arbitral decision in Rome and 1926 watershed demarcation.	
BRAZIL-SURINAME	Land	Physical boundary along Tumuc-Humac Mountains watershed dividing northern Amazon tributaries from streams flowing into Atlantic	597 km	Ratified	1906 1936	Watershed line agreed to in 1906, with Brazil, Netherlands, and UK agreeing to tripoint in 1936. Brazil is not party to Suriname's disputes with Guyana and French Guiana. As many as 40,000 Brazilian gold diggers occupy Guyana as illegal aliens and Brazil is concerned about drug trafficking through Guyana.	Managed
BRAZIL-VENEZUELA	Land	Physical boundary consisting largely of remote Orinoco and Amazon watersheds. Demarcated, definite.	2200 km	Ratified	1777 1852 1928 1939 1970?	No disputes identified although remoteness of region continues to inhibit identification of some stream sources in establishing watershed.	
BRITISH VIRGIN ISLANDS (UNITED KINGDOM)-PUERTO RICO/US VIRGIN ISLANDS (UNITED STATES)	Maritime	Simplfied equidistance maritime boundary of 50 points		In force	1995	Common treaty for Puerto Rico and US Virgin Islands.	
CAYMAN ISLANDS (UNITED KINGDOM)-COLOMBIA	Maritime	Hypothetical maritime boundary		None		Colombia does not appear to assert any claims to waters extending up to the Cayman Islands in its agreement between Colombia and Honduras.	
CAYMAN ISLANDS (UNITED KINGDOM)-CUBA	Maritime	Hypothetical maritime boundary		None		No disputes identified	
CAYMAN ISLANDS (UNITED KINGDOM)-HONDURAS	Maritime	Maritme boundary treaty		None	2002	Treaty establishes maritime boundary.	
CAYMAN ISLANDS (UNITED KINGDOM)-JAMAICA	Maritime	Hypothetical maritime boundary		None		Negotiations underway	

COLOMBIA (Albuqerque Cay, Este-Sudeste Cay, San Andrés Island) -COSTA RICA (Caribbean Sea)	Maritime	2-segment non-equidistance maritime boundary	116 nm	Signed, de facto in force	1977	No disputes identified.	
COLOMBIA-DOMINICAN REPUBLIC	Maritime	1-segment, equidistance maritime boundary; includes a common scientific and fishing zone	103 nm	In force	1979	No disputes identified. Trijuctions with Colombia-Haiti Boundary	
COLOMBIA-HAITI	Maritime	1-segment, non-equidistance maritime boundary	65 nm	In force	1979	No disputes identified	
COLOMBIA-HONDURAS	Land	Offshore islands		None		Both states claim Bajo Nuevo, Serranilla Bank, West Breaker, Middle and East/Beacon Cay	Managed
COLOMBIA-HONDURAS	Maritime	6-segment maritime boundary where first line follows parallel, second follows meridian; others are around various cays.	195 nm	Signed but not in force	1986	No disputes identified. Agreement cedes SerranillaBank to Colombia, which Jamaica, Nicaragua, US also claim together with Bajo Nuevo (Petrel Bank). Nicaragua disputes the legitimacy of this agreement as it disputes Colombia's claim to waters east of 82°W (see Colombia-Nicaragua)	
COLOMBIA-JAMAICA	Maritime	4-segment modified equidistance maritime boundary; portion of boundary beyond 200 nm (continental shelf); 4500 sq nm Joint Regime Area for fishing		In force		Two circles cut out of JRA for disputed Serranilla Bank and Bajo Nuevo (Low Cays). Features also claimed by US, Honduras, Nicaragua.	Managed
COLOMBIA-NICARAGUA	Land	Offshore islands.		None		Territorial dispute: Colombia claims and occupies San Andres and Providencia islands; Albuquerque, Este-Sudeste, Roncador cayes; and the Quito Sueño and Serrana banks on the Nicaragua Rise. During Sandinista rule, Nicaragua rejected all Colombian maritime and island claims east of 82°W based on 1928 Treaty. Nicaragua uncontestedly claims and occupies Corn Islands (Islas del Maiz). US relinquished all claims on these features in 1970s. Serranilla Bank, Bajo Nuevo (Petrel Bank) are by claimed parties along with Honduras, Jamaica, and US who reserve the right to claim these features.	Managed to Hostile

COLOMBIA-NICARAGUA	Maritime	Maritime boundary		None	1928	During Sandinista rule, Nicaragua rejected all Colombian maritime and island claims east of 82°W based on 1928 Barcemas-Esquerra Treaty, arguing that treaty was signed under pressure during US occupation. In 1988, Nicaraguan government maintained claim but accepts Colombian *de facto* occupation. (See also Colombia-Honduras)	Managed to Hostile
COLOMBIA-PANAMA	Land	Physical boundary dividing water partings. Demarcated, definite	225 km	In force	1924 1938	No boundary disputes identified. Overlapping ethnic-cultural region in Darien Gap. 1924 Treaty recognises 1855 former provincial boundary as international, which was demarcated in 1938.	
COLOMBIA-PANAMA (Caribbean Sea)	Maritime	Simplified equidistance and along latitude, longitude maritime boundary		In force	1977	Equidistance was not considered vis à vis the Colombian-claimed islands. Panama retains a dormant claim to the Colombian-claimed islands as they were once attached to Panama when it was province of Colombia prior to 1903.	
COLOMBIA-UNITED STATES	Land	Islands		None		*Territorial dispute*: Both states claim Serranilla Bank, Bajo Nuevo together with Honduras, Jamaica and Nicaragua.	Dormant
COLOMBIA-VENEZUELA	Land	Physical boundary along streams, ridges	2050 km	None	1842/4, 1881 1922 1932	*Territorial dispute*: Colombia recognises the 1980 award of Los Monjes islands to Venezuela, but challenges its maritime claims extending from them; Numerous land boundary disputes, particularly related to Goajirá Peninsula, now largely resolved: Swiss (1922) arbitration resulted in successful demarcation in 1932. *Borderland issues* include illegal border crossings, Colombian migration, drug-weapons smuggling, general lawlessness.	Managed, occasionally Hostile.
COLOMBIA-VENEZUELA	Maritime	Venezuela has juridicial claim to most of Gulf of Venezuela		None		Venezuela occupied Los Monjes islands in 1950s. Colombia recognises the 1980 award of Los Monjes islands to Venezuela, but challenges its maritime claims extending from them and limited Colombian rights in the Gulf of Venezuela (Golfo de Coquibacoa). Attempts to come to an agreement on maritime boundary around islands and to establish a bay closing line have failed with periodic resurgence of angry rhetoric. Colombia and other states protest Venezuelan closing line in gulf based on 'a historic bay, a condominium of two riparian states'.	Managed, occasionally Hostile.
COSTA RICA-NICARAGUA	Land	Stream (right bank), overland in straight line segments, 32m contour above L. Nicaragua. Demarcated, definite	309 km	Ratified	1965 2002	Nicaragua protests Costa Rica using armed patrols on the San Juan river which is sovereign Nicaraguan territory. 1983 agreement called for joint patrols of borders. Unresolved dispute is currently quiet. The 2002 redemarcation disclosed large survey error, resettlement of Costa Rican village may be required to establish border clearing but parties concur with realignment.	Managed

COSTA RICA-NICARAGUA (Caribbean Sea)	Maritime	Hypothetical maritime boundary		None		No disputes identified	
COSTA RICA-PANAMA	Land	Mostly physical boundary (streams, peaks, ridges, watersheds), straight line segments (51 km). Demarcated, definite	330 km	Ratified	1838 1941 1944	No disputes identified. Largely 1838 Central American Federation and Gran Colombia boundary with disputed sections that defied French (1896) and US (1910) arbitration until states sign treaty (1941) and demarcate (1944).	
COSTA RICA-PANAMA (Caribbean)	Maritime	One straight line continental shelf boundary	96 nm	In force	1982	No disputes identified. Connects to Colombia-Costa Rica and Colombia-Panama lines	
CUBA-HAITI	Maritime	Equity and equidistance maritime boundary	170 mn	In force	1978	Haiti claims and Cuba reject US claim over Navassa Island. Boundary is configured as if Navassa were Haitian, connecting to Cuba-Jamaica boundary.	
CUBA-HONDURAS	Maritime	Hypothetical maritime boundary		None		Negotiations underway	
CUBA-JAMAICA	Maritime	105 equidistance segments, maritime boundary	175 nm	In force	1994	No disputes identified	
CUBA-MEXICO	Maritime	12 equidistance segments, maritime boundary	352 nm	Dip Notes (*de facto* in force)	1978	No disputes identified	
CUBA-UNITED STATES	Maritime	Equidistance opposite coasts boundary to 200 nm limit	313 nm	Dip Notes (*de facto* in force)	1978	Maritime boundary agreement not ratified, but renewed by biennial exchange of notes; no disputes. No agreement exists on the delimitation of the boundary westward beyond 200 nm limits allocating the continental shelf. *Borderland issue*: Cuban refugees continue to cross into US waters	Managed
CUBA-UNITED STATES (Guantanamo)	Land	Leased military base		Lease	1894	Cuba protests US presence on territory; $3300/year lease of 118 sq km until lease runs out in 2033 (no cheques cashed since 1962). Heavily fortified boundary.	Managed

CUBA-UNITED STATES (Guantanamo)	Maritime	Hypothetical territorial sea adjacency line		None		Operational maritime boundary in effect based on leasing agreement protested by Cuba but defended by US	Managed
CUBA-UNITED STATES (Navassa Island)	Maritime	Hypothetical maritime boundary		None		Cuba together with Haiti protest US administration of Navassa island off the coast of Haiti. Cuba and Jamaica ignore US claim in delimitation of joint maritime boundary.	
DOMINICA - FRANCE (GUADELOUPE)	Maritime	Equity and equidistance maritime boundary	298 nm	In force	1988	No disputes identified	
DOMINICA - FRANCE (MARTINIQUE)	Maritime	Equity and equidistance maritime boundary	294 nm	In force	1988	No disputes identified	
DOMINICA - VENEZUELA (Islas des Aves)	Maritime	Hypothetical maritime boundary		None		Dominica protests Venezuelan claim to Aves Island as a basepoint for claiming EEZ rights. It considers the features rocks and not islands. It also objects to the treaties signed by France, the Netherlands and the United States, recognising Venezuela's claim to full effect.	Managed
DOMINICAN REPUBLIC-HAITI	Land	physical boundary along streams (160 km), ridges, peaks, plains. Demarcated, definite	358 km	Ratified	1929	No disputes with boundary line but Treaty called for de-militarised strip and joint use of hydrology and border road. Borderland issue with Haitian economic refugees	
DOMINICAN REPUBLIC-HAITI (north)	Maritime	Hypothetical adjacency territorial/EEZ boundary		None	1980	No major maritime disputes identified. Reported 1980 treaty established maritime boundary (confirmation details not available). Problems with Haitian boat refugees entering Dominican Republic.	
DOMINICAN REPUBLIC-HAITI (south)	Maritime	Hypothetical adjacency territorial/EEZ boundary		None		No major maritime disputes identified. Problems with Haitian boat refugees entering Dominican Republic.	
DOMINICAN REPUBLIC-NETHERLANDS ANTILLES (Bonaire, Curaçao)/ARUBA	Maritime	Hypothetical maritime boundary		None		No disputes identified	

DOMINICAN REPUBLIC-PUERTO RICO (UNITED STATES)	Maritime	Hypothetical maritime boundary		None		No disputes identified	
DOMINICAN REPUBLIC-TURKS AND CAICOS (UNITED KINGDOM)	Maritime	Simplified 4-segment equidistant EEZ boundary from straight baselines	283 nm	Signed, not in force	1996	No disputes identified	
DOMINICAN REPUBLIC-VENEZUELA	Maritime	Continental shelf boundary in 2 lines (western in 6 segments, eastern in 1 segment) separated by U-shaped Netherlands Antilles-Venezuela boundary	335 nm	In force	1982	Venezuela coordinated this boundary together with Colombia and Dominican Republic to secure oil shipping lanes. No disputes identified	
FRANCE (FRENCH GUIANA)-SURINAME	Land	Physical boundary along streams. (Demarcated?), disputed upstream segment is indefinite.	510 km	Not ratified	1891 1905 1977	Territorial dispute stemming from which upstream tributary of the Morouini(Maroni)/Litani(Itany) forms boundary. Colonial rulers submitted dispute to Russian Czar (1891), The Hague (1905), and Suriname after independence (1975) adopted the Dutch line but later was willing to agree to the French line (1977) in return for joint development aid. Recent agreement awaits ratification, resolving dispute.	Managed
FRANCE (FRENCH GUIANA)-SURINAME	Maritime	Hypothetical territorial and EEZ/ continental shelf boundary		None		No disputes identified	
FRANCE (GUADELOUPE)-MONTSERRAT (UNITED KINGDOM)	Maritime	Hypothetical territorial and EEZ/ continental shelf boundary		None		No disputes identified	
FRANCE (GUADELOUPE)-NETHERLANDS ANTILLES (Leeward Islands)	Maritime	Hypothetical territorial and EEZ/ continental shelf boundary; Adjacent boundary on east and west coasts of St Martin-Saint Maarten land boundary		None		French Department of Guadeloupe includes Guadeloupe (Basse-Terre, Grand-Terre), Marie-Galante, Désirade, Iles des Saintes, Saint Barthélemy, Saint Martin; Netherlands Antilles (Leeward Islands) include Saint Maartin, Saint Eustatius, and Saba. Saint Martin-Saint Maarten land boundary prevents creation of maritime boundary	Managed
FRANCE (GUADELOUPE)-ST KITTS AND NEVIS	Maritime	Hypothetical territorial and EEZ/ continental shelf boundary		None		No disputes identified	

FRANCE (GUADELOUPE)-VENEZUELA	Maritime	Non-equidistant straight line maritime boundary		In force	1983	Franco-Venezuelan treaty separates French Departments from Aves Islands along common meridian 62°48'50"W	
FRANCE (MARTINIQUE)-ST LUCIA	Maritime	Equidistance territorial sea and maritime boundary in 18 points	166 nm	In force	1981	No disputes identified	
FRANCE (MARTINIQUE)-VENEZUELA	Maritime	Non-equidistant straight line maritime boundary		In force	1983	Franco-Venezuelan treaty separates French Departments from Aves Islands along common meridian 62°48'50"W	
GRENADA-ST VINCENT AND THE GRENADINES	Maritime	Hypothetical maritime boundary		None		No disputes identified	
GRENADA-TRINIDAD AND TOBAGO	Maritime	Hypothetical maritime boundary		None		No disputes identified	
GUATEMALA-HONDURAS	Land	Physical boundary along stream medians, elevations, drainage, watersheds. Fully demarcated, definite	256 km	Ratified	1930 1936	No disputes identified. Disputes rising from break-up of Central American Federation (1843) went unresolved until 1930 Special Boundary Tribunal ruled in favour of 1821 colonial line, a 1933 tribunal, and 1936 demarcation. Minor borderland issues persist over transnational banana plantations and overlapping ethnic groups.	
GUATEMALA-HONDURAS	Maritime	Hypothetical maritime boundary		None		Belize and Honduras are willing to share a maritime corridor with Guatemala under terms of OAS-negotiated referendum agreement. Guatemala contests Honduras' claim under the 'Maritime Areas of Honduras Act' to Sapodilla Cays, also claimed and administered by Belize.	Dormant
GUYANA-SURINAME	Land	Indefinite, physical boundary along streams	600 km	Colonial agreement, unratified	1794 1815 1841 1939	Boundary dispute over which upper tributary (New River or Cutari/Curuni) of Courantyne (Corantijn) constitutes primary channel, resulting in Suriname territorial claim over New River triangle in SE Guyana. Cutari had been historical boundary until an 1841 discovery proving Cutari larger. 1939 treaty never signed and dispute became more acute after Suriname independence in 1975. Recent Commission talks were hindered by a new map showing Suriname's claim on the New River triangle. The parties continue talking but cannot reconcile language for a joint statement.	Managed to hostile

GUYANA-SURINAME	Maritime	Hypothetical maritime boundary		None		Dispute over direction of maritime line extending from Courantyne (Corantijn) river and shoreline terminus. Suriname asserts a continental shelf claim directed 10° east of the meridian, and Guyana at 33°. Oil prospecting inhibited.	Managed to hostile
GUYANA-TRINIDAD AND TOBAGO	Maritime	Hypothetical maritime boundary		None		No common boundary can be created as a result of the extension of the Trinidad and Tobago-Venezuela boundary	
GUYANA-VENEZUELA	Land	Complex arbitrated boundary follows surveyed markers, several streams, watershed, straight lines, several peaks. Demarcated, definite	743 km	Ratified	1899 1905 1970	Territorial and boundary dispute over Essequibo river which Netherlands and Britain controlled since 1794 but Venezuela claims is a natural boundary and not 1844 Shomburgk line which UK declares as boundary in 1886. 1899 US arbitration results in bilateral concessions and demarcation in 1905. Venezuela reasserts claims in 1951 but in 1970 sign a 12-year moritorium with UK and independent (1966) Guyana. Venezuela refuses to renew, surfacing and abating claims periodically without offering resolution.	Managed to hostile
GUYANA-VENEZUELA	Maritime	Hypothetical maritime boundary		None		Territorial dispute over Essequibo region prevents definition of a maritime boundary, inhibiting oil prospecting. Until the recent domestic turmoil in Venezuela, which has put the boundary dispute in hiatus, the parties had been engaged in cordial discussions. Even the Guyanese seizure of Venezuelan fishing vessels in 2002 did not elevate tensions.	Managed to hostile
HAITI-JAMAICA	Maritime	Hypothetical maritime boundary		None		Negotiations are planned but Haiti's claim to US-administered Navassa Island inhibits creation of maritime boundary at Cuba-Haiti, Cuba-Jamaica tripoint.	
HAITI-TURKS AND CAICOS (UNITED KINGDOM)	Maritime	Hypothetical maritime boundary		None		No disputes identified.	
HAITI-UNITED STATES	Land	Offshore island		None		Haiti claims and protests US administration of Navassa Island as an unincorporated territory.	Managed
HAITI-UNITED STATES	Maritime	Hypothetical maritime boundary		None		Sovereignty dispute over Navassa Island prevents establishment of maritime boundary. The US has not yet determined the limits of the fishery conservation zone around the island.	Managed

HONDURAS-JAMAICA	Land	Islands		None		Territorial dispute: both states claim Bajo Nuevo and Serranilla Bank together with Colombia, Nicaragua and US	Dormant
HONDURAS-JAMAICA	Maritime	Hypothetical maritime boundary		None		States have negotiations underway with resolution complicated by Serranilla Banks/Bajo Nuevo dispute also claimed by Colombia, Nicaragua and the United States.	Managed
HONDURAS-NICARAGUA	Land	Physical boundary, primarily along stream medians (716 km), hilltops, a watershed, into the Gulf of Fonseca. Well demarcated, definite; Islands	922 km	In force	1888 1904 1961	No significant disputes identified since final demarcation in 1961, ending 140 years of disputes in eastern areas. Western area demarcated in 1904. 1906 King of Spain arbitration confirmed by 1960 ICJ decision. Territorial dispute both states claim Bajo Nuevo and Serranilla Bank together with Colombia, Jamaica, and US.	Dormant
HONDURAS-NICARAGUA (Caribbean Sea)	Maritime	Hypothetical straight line boundary based on parallel (Honduras) or equidistance (Nicaragua)		None		In 1986, Honduras and Colombia sign Caribbean Sea Maritime Limits Treaty, which established a maritime boundary along the parallel as an extension of the Honduras-Nicaragua land boundary beyond the 82° meridian. Nicaragua protests treaty and subsequent Maritime Areas of Honduras Act and claims Honduras placed troops on Cayo Sur. In 1999, Nicaragua petitioned the ICJ to resolve the boundary disputes among the three parties. As an interim measure, the OAS facilitates the disputants signing an MOU (2000) and a confidence and security document (2001) to ease tensions. ICJ recently ruled in favor of Honduras' petition against Nicaragua's 35 per cent tariff on Honduran imports to retaliate against Hondura's maritime treaty with Colombia. Main ICJ boundary ruling pending.	Managed to hostile
HONDURAS-UNITED STATES	Land	Islands		None		*Territorial dispute*: both states claim Bajo Nuevo and Serranilla Bank together with Colombia, Jamaica, and Nicaragua	Dormant
JAMAICA-NAVASSA ISLAND (UNITED STATES)	Land	Islands		None		Jamaica appears to recognise Haiti's claim to Navassa Island by connecting its maritime boundary with Cuba to the Cuba-Haiti maritime boundary (that rejects the US claim).	Uncontested
JAMAICA-NICARAGUA	Land	Islands		None		*Territorial dispute*: both states claim Bajo Nuevo and Serranilla Bank together with Colombia, Honduras, US	Dormant

JAMAICA-NICARAGUA	Maritime	Hypothetical maritime boundary		None		States have negotiations planned pending resolution of the Serranilla Banks/Bajo Nuevo dispute also claimed by Colombia, Nicaragua and the United States and resolution of disputed islands claimed by Nicaragua and occupied by Colombia.	Dormant
JAMAICA-UNITED STATES	Land	Islands		None		*Territorial dispute:* both states claim Bajo Nuevo and Serranilla Bank together with Colombia, Honduras, Nicaragua.	Dormant
MEXICO-UNITED STATES	Land	Physical boundary, 2/3 of which is Rio Grande river, as well as 2 overland segments and a section of the Colorado river. Well demarcated, defined	3140 km	In force	1848 1853	No boundary disputes at present. Mexican cession of lands to the Rio Grande (1848) and Gadsen Purchase (1853) establish boundary. Current borderland issues related to Mexico's 'water debt' to the United States under 1944 agreement, illegal migration, post-9/11 delays at border crossings, Mexican truck transport in the US. Mexico reports that it is committed to delivering the minimum water quota of 431 cubic metres based on the minimum annual average for the 2001–2003 period.	
MEXICO-UNITED STATES (Caribbean)	Maritime	Territorial sea, EEZ boundaries based on simplified equidistance in five segments; 'Western Gap' continental shelf boundary based on equidistance	347 nm (EEZ); 130 nm (gap)	In force	1972 1978 1997 2001	No disputes identified. EEZ boundary ratified and in force in 1997. The first fixed point of the maritime boundary is 2000 feet offshore to take the shifting course of Rio Grande into the Gulf of Mexico into consideration (1972, 1997). Continental shelf boundary area is established within the 'Western Gap' (2001).	
MONTSERRAT (UNITED KINGDOM)-ST KITTS AND NEVIS	Maritime	Hypothetical maritime boundary		None		No disputes identified.	
MONTSERRAT (UNITED KINGDOM)-VENEZUELA	Maritime	Hypothetical maritime boundary		None		No disputes identified.	
NETHERLANDS ANTILLES (Bonaire, Curacao)/ARUBA-VENEZUELA (mainland)	Maritime	U-shaped 12-segment maritime boundary based on simplified equidistance		In force	1978	No disputes identified	
NETHERLANDS ANTILLES (Leeward Islands) - PUERTO RICO/US VIRGIN ISLANDS (UNITED STATES)	Maritime	Hypothetical maritime boundary		None		No disputes identified.	

NETHERLANDS ANTILLES (Leeward Islands)-ST KITTS AND NEVIS	Maritime	Hypothetical maritime boundary		None		No dispute has been identified between the Netherlands' lesser Antilles islands of Saba and St Eustatius from the islands of St Kitts and Nevis.	
NETHERLANDS ANTILLES (Leeward Islands)-VENEZUELA (Islas des Aves)	Maritime	1 small equidistance segment maritime boundary		In force	1978	No disputes identified	
NICARAGUA-UNITED STATES	Land	Islands		None		*Territorial dispute*: Both states claim Bajo Nuevo and Serranilla Bank together with Honduras, Jamaica, and Nicaragua.	Dormant
PUERTO RICO/US VIRGIN ISLANDS (UNITED STATES)-VENEZUELA	Maritime	21 equidistant segments forming maritime boundary	304 nm	In force	1980	Treaty separates St Croix and Puerto Rico from Aves Islands. No disputes identified	
SAINT KITTS AND NEVIS-VENEZUELA (Aves Islands)	Maritime	Hypothetical EEC/Continental Shelf boundary		None		Saint Kitts and Nevis sends letter to the UN protesting the Venezuelan claim to Aves Island as a basepoint for claiming EEZ rights. It considers the features rocks and not islands.	Managed
SAINT LUCIA-SAINT VINCENT AND THE GRENADINES	Maritime	Hypothetical EEC/Continental shelf boundaries		None		No disputes identified	
SAINT LUCIA-VENEZUELA (Aves Islands)	Maritime	Hypothetical EEC/Continental Shelf boundary		None		Saint Lucia sends letter to the UN protesting the Venezuelan claim to Aves Island as a basepoint for claiming EEZ rights. It considers the features to be rocks and not islands. Saint Lucia also objects to the treaties signed by France, the Netherlands and the United States, recognising Venezuela's claims to Islas des Aves.	Managed
SAINT MARTIN [FRANCE (GUADELOUPE)] - SINT MAARTEN [NETHERLANDS ANTILLES (Leeward Islands)]	Land	Boundary runs across rolling hills a lagoon and an oyster pond.	9 km	Unknown	1648	Reported dispute over terminus of boundary. Only 'Schengen' European Union boundary in Western Hemisphere without customs or immigration controls. The boundary is governed by the 1648 Treaty of Concordia. Saint-Martin is part of the French Overseas Department of Guadeloupe.	Managed
SAINT VINCENT AND THE GRENADINES-TRINIDAD AND TOBAGO	Maritime	Hypothetical EEC/Continental Shelf boundary		None		No disputes identified	

SAINT VINCENT AND THE GRENADINES-VENEZUELA	Maritime	Hypothetical EEC/Continental shelf boundaries: Aves Islands, Venezuela		None		Saint Vincent and the Grenadines sends letter to the UN protesting the Venezuelan claim to Aves Island as a basepoint for claiming EEZ rights. It considers the features to be rocks and not islands. Saint Vincent and the Grenadines objects to the treaties signed by France, the Netherlands and the United States, recognising Venezuela's claims to Islas des Aves.	Managed
TRINIDAD AND TOBAGO-VENEZUELA	Maritime	21 equidistant segments forming maritime boundary	304 nm	In force	1980	Treaty separates St Croix (US Virgin Islands) and Puerto Rico from Aves Islands. No disputes identified	
TRINIDAD AND TOBAGO-VENEZUELA	Maritime	Equidistance and hydrocarbon equity arrangements in territorial sea, maritime boundary delimitation.	440 nm	In force	1942 1989 1991	1991 treaty replaced previous treaties and besides making technical rectifications, it extended claims out into continental shelf into waters that nominally would include Barbados-Guyana Hypothetical boundary. No disputes identified, however.	

Notes

1. The views and analysis expressed in this chapter are solely those of the author and do not necessarily reflect those of the US Department of State and the United States Government.
2. Stephen B. Jones, *Boundary Making: A Handbook for Statesmen, Treaty Editors and Boundary Commissioners* (Washington, DC: Carnegie Endowment for International Peace, Division of International Law, 1945), 3.
3. According to the Office of the Geographer and Global Issues, US Department of State, based on the Office's official list of Independent States, Dependencies and Areas of Special Sovereignty at www.state.gov. Note that the United States Government does not recognise sovereignty claims on Antarctica.
4. Generally speaking, a boundary treaty is initialled by a joint border commission or foreign ministries, signed by the heads of state, and ratified by both parliaments before it is considered in force. Today, treaties are also registered with international organisations, such as the United Nations, which provide recourse to arbitration in the event of a later dispute.
5. Exceptions include the limits of temporary military or peacekeeping zones and patrol areas, none of which exist at present in the Caribbean Basin.
6. 1 nautical mile = 1852 metres or approximately 1 minute of latitude (1843 metres at the equator to 1861.6 metres at the poles).
7. See US Department of State, Bureau of Oceans and International Environmental and Scientific Affairs, *Limits in the Sea*, No. 26: 'National claims to Maritime Jurisdictions', 8th Revision (2000), which lists all maritime limits declared by independent states.
8. Additional language in UNCLOS also permits states to extend the continental shelf along undersea ridges if geological evidence can prove the ridge is a true contiguous extension of the shelf. No claims have been accepted to date.
9. The UNCLOS text can be accessed through http://www.un.org/Depts/los/index.htm
10. The notable exceptions are 1) the 1867 Russia-United States treaty establishing a Convention Line in the Bering Sea, which was reconfigured in 1990 but the treaty still awaits Russian parliamentary ratification; 2) the 1942 Trinidad and Tobago-Venezuela maritime boundary treaty, replaced by an expanded new treaty in force since 1991; 3) The 1928 Colombia-Nicaragua treaty dividing claims along the 82nd meridian, which Nicaragua currently rejects.
11. US Department of State, Bureau of Oceans and International Environmental and Scientific Affairs (OES), *Limits in the Seas*, No. 108: 'Maritime Boundaries of the World' (1990). See also http://www.un.org/Depts/los/LEGISLATIONANDTREATIES.
12. Friedrich Kratochwill termed his sovereignty dispute taxonomies as 'positional, functional, and territorial' in his *Peace and Disputed Sovereignty* (Boston: University Press of America, 1985), 18.
13. Disputes over tripoints (where the boundaries of three states come together), multiple territorial claims, and cross-national refugee, illegal or criminal transactions transcend boundaries of more than two states.
14. Lecture presented by Ambassador Einaudi at a conference on Central American border issues, US Department of State, INR, October 19, 2000.
15. For a comprehensive discussion of the limits and principles of international law, particularly as they relate to the adjudication of border disputes, see the World Court Digest of the Max Planck Institute (http:/www.mpiv-hd.mpg.de).

4

A Portrait of Crime in the Caribbean: Realities and Challenges

Ramesh Deosaran

Introduction

The first part of this chapter provides a very brief overview of the political status of the relevant Caribbean states and the institutions dealing with crime and justice. It will then examine some very dramatic crime events that helped to expose the weaknesses in the region's crime-fighting institutions, and which also stimulated the region's keenness for security. It will examine some trends from official police records and discuss the implications. Finally, it will provide a brief discussion on the way forward in forging better public safety and security.

CARICOM States: Political Status

Geographically, the Caribbean region is usually viewed as that part of the world which is located in the Caribbean Sea, bound by the United States in the north, Central America in the west, South America in the south and the Atlantic Ocean in the east. In terms of political, legal and judicial systems, however, there is a significant diversity among these 21 island-states. For example, there is Puerto Rico, a dependency-state of the United States, and the United States Virgin Islands. Then there are the very small island-states of the British Virgin Islands and Bermuda. Haiti is French-speaking while the Dominican Republic has a mix of Spanish and French languages.

Added to this Caribbean diversity is the fact that three of the states which are now included in the Caribbean Community (CARICOM), largely a trading bloc, are lodged in different parts of the American mainland. Belize is in Central America, and Guyana and Suriname are at the north of South America. Guyana is a former British colony; Suriname a former Dutch colony. As further examples, Cuba has been largely Spanish-driven in both language and institutions, and have had for over 40 years a one-party state. Then there is French-speaking Martinique and Guadeloupe as parts of those islands in the Caribbean Sea. This cultural and institutional diversity was largely formed by the adventurism and colonial policies of European powers, mainly the British, French and Spanish, between the fifteenth and nineteenth centuries.

The majority of Caribbean states, however, now politically independent and English-speaking, have had a history of British colonialism, of African slave labour and, in the case of Guyana and Trinidad and Tobago, particularly, a history of both slave and East Indian indentured labour. This chapter focuses mainly on 12 member states of CARICOM: Jamaica, St Kitts and Nevis, Bahamas, Belize, Antigua and Barbuda, Dominica, St Lucia, St Vincent and the Grenadines, Barbados, Grenada, Trinidad and Tobago and Guyana. These nations have inherited their political, legal and judicial systems from the British and, unlike Suriname, Martinique or Haiti, they now possess institutions that largely reflect British antecedents, with legal and judicial systems generally derived from British common law. These former British colonies, from Jamaica in the north to Guyana in the south, form the bulk of the Commonwealth Caribbean and CARICOM. Difficult as it is to gather data across these 12 separate CARICOM countries, they will be the major focus of this discussion on crime and punishment in the Caribbean.

Before we look at some crime trends and comparisons, it is useful to make a few comments on the state of crime data and the responses to it across these CARICOM countries. There is the *culture of secrecy* within police organisations in the Caribbean, a feature that makes it difficult for researchers to gain access to police data and other related crime data for analysis. Unlike the release of the Uniform Crime Reports in the USA, or crime data by the British Home Office, there is no tradition in the Caribbean of having the crime figures published regularly. In fact, the figures are normally released when they suit the political directorate to do so: or when some kind of public pressure is brought to bear upon the police to do so. And even when released, there is some attempt to present the figures in ways that help to put the police in the best possible light. The resistance to open up the crime report database has been quite obvious over the years. In fact, a 2001 proposal by a consultant to provide transparency and improve the methods of both collecting and reporting crime data remains securely shelved by the police and the Ministry of National Security in Trinidad and Tobago.[1]

All this makes it quite difficult to provide smooth generalisations about crime across the Caribbean. There is much unevenness. Apart from the laws that define crimes, the quality of data from crime reports compiled by the police varies very much from one state to another. Recently, however, there have been proposals to standardise, as far as possible, the statutes which define the same crime (for example, robbery, assault, etc.) in the different states within CARICOM.

Institutions

Crime in this region cannot be well understood by an exclusive reliance on official police data or cross-country comparisons derived from percentages. When dealing with crime and justice in the Caribbean, it is therefore useful to consider the relationships between the key institutions of state. Such relationships tell us a lot about the processes of control, adjudication and accountability in the areas of crime management and reduction. These Caribbean states with British antecedents practise multi-party democracy and have institutionalised the separation of powers among the executive, legislative and judicial branches of government. In practice, however, the lines of policy-making and implementation are quite blurred between the executive and legislative branches in the particular sense that the executive through the Cabinet of Ministers dominates the legislative outcome in Parliament. This result is due to the fact that the Cabinet (that is, the executive) is derived from the ruling party (or coalition) in the Legislature (that is, the Parliament) where it typically enjoys a majority.

Mainly for this reason, and apart from matters that may travel on appeal to the courts, there are no institutional checks and balances on the policy-making processes of the executive such as those used by the US Congress (except for certain laws which require a special parliamentary majority). This means, in effect, that policies of crime and punishment, and their relevant implementing departments and institutions fall largely under the jurisdiction of the relevant ministries of government, that is, the executive. In the pervasive calls for constitutional reform across CARICOM states, such very centralised authority has come under intense scrutiny to the point where the parliaments of the various states have been impolitely described as 'mere rubber stamps'.

Government ministries related to crime and justice have different names across the Caribbean. For example, in Jamaica it is called the Ministry of Justice and National Security, and in Trinidad and Tobago it is the Ministry of National Security and Rehabilitation. In Barbados, such matters of crime and punishment fall under the Attorney General's Office. In St Lucia, there is shared jurisdiction between the Ministry of Legal Affairs and the Office of the Attorney General. Jurisdiction over the police in such CARICOM states is not statutorily defined. Such complexities of jurisdiction and functions largely arise from the fact that with these Caribbean governments, there are no constitutionally-entrenched patterns of nomenclature or of designated functions for ministries (except for the attorney general). Such ministerial assignments are left to the discretion of the prime minister, as head of government. Typically, however, it is the attorney general who advises Cabinet on legal and judicial matters and quite often also brings the relevant legislation to Parliament.

The agency responsible for handling crime reports from citizens, and carrying out pertinent investigations and prosecutions is the Police Service. Some Caribbean countries like St Lucia and Barbados still retain the colonial nomenclature of *Police Force*. Others like Trinidad and Tobago changed theirs to *Police Service*. The police across these states are subject to a large measure of *civilian* control mainly through the relevant minister and the director of public prosecutions who must approve or direct further investigations or prosecutions. This procedure is particularly notable, for example, when charges against the press are contemplated. The other form of control over the police comes from the line ministry which provides for the police budget and other resources, and which also determines with Cabinet who will be recommended as the commissioner of police. The final determination for such appointment is the relevant Service Commission – wherever one exists. In some Caribbean states, for example, Trinidad and Tobago, there is a Police Service Commission while in others, for example, in St Lucia, steps are now being taken to establish one.

Although there have been intermittent tensions between the judiciary and the executive, mainly in terms of functions and judgements, the judiciaries of the Commonwealth Caribbean are quite independent from direct political interference. It is important to note as well that Barbados, Grenada, St Vincent and the Grenadines, St Lucia, Antigua and Dominica have the Eastern Caribbean Supreme Court, located in St Lucia, which serves as their Appeal Court. The other five states have their own respective Appeal Courts and, with the exception of Guyana, all these countries have the Judicial Committee of the Privy Council in London as their final court of appeal. However, these countries have recently indicated through a heads of government meeting in February 2001 that they intend to establish a Caribbean Court of Justice to replace the London Privy Council as their final court of appeal. Jamaica,

Trinidad and Tobago, Barbados, Guyana and St Vincent and the Grenadines are expected to be the first clients of this new court. Other CARICOM states are expected to follow in due course.

Subversive Threats

What all this indicates is that matters of crime and justice in the Caribbean are in a state of flux in several ways. There is tremendous pressure on the relevant institutions of each CARICOM state to respond effectively to the increasing threats of crime and security. Apart from public concerns over traditional crimes (for example, robbery, rape, assault, etc.), these pressures upon CARICOM governments to escalate effective crime management and crime reduction measures have been largely stimulated by five distinctive security threats.

The first is the 1979 overthrow of the corrupt regime in Grenada by a socialist group, the New Jewel Movement, which itself in 1983 suffered murderous internal conflict and was removed by US intervention. The second is the 1990 insurrection in Trinidad and Tobago by a group of Islamic fundamentalists, the Muslimeen, when the country's Parliament was attacked and the prime minister and several cabinet ministers, among others, were held hostage for about one week. At this same time the Muslimeen drove a car loaded with explosives into the police compound where it exploded. At least ten persons were killed and US$30 million lost in looting, damaged buildings, etc. (see, for example, Deosaran, 1993; Ryan, 1991). While this unprecedented episode ended in a Muslimeen surrender to the armed forces and an elite US squad, the Privy Council did not bring a clear closure to the case against the Muslimeen nor on the particular point of whether or not the 'conferred' amnesty to them was valid. Since then, the Muslimeen figures prominently and quite controversially in every general election with the field support they provide to political parties. The prolonged controversy mainly revolves around their beneficial relationships with the ruling political parties and their alleged threats to national security.

The third threat involves the intermittent, but very violent ethnic (African-East Indian) conflicts in Guyana, conflicts which are surrounded by kidnappings, murders and police shootings. In the years 2000–2003 in particular, such violent episodes have kept the Indian-dominated People's Progressive party (PPP) Government and the entire country of Guyana under intense political turmoil and ethnic strife. There have been repeated allegations that these acts of kidnapping and political violence are instigated, or at least implicitly supported, by the opposition party, the African-dominated People's National Congress (PNC) which in turn has repeatedly accused the ruling PPP of racial discrimination against Guyanese of African descent.

In Jamaica, the role of the drug-ridden *garrisons* continues to plague the country's internal security. These garrisons are divided into two opposing camps, one blessed with political support from one of the two major political parties, the other similarly blessed by the other party. In exchange, the garrison community provides political support to the patronising political party. A central feature of this subversive scenario is the number of deaths which result from police-garrison shootings. In the last five years, the average for such police shootings is beyond the 100 mark, a trend which has earned sharp rebuke from several civic and human rights groups, including Amnesty International. In each of the years, 2001 and 2002, over 1,000 persons have been murdered in Jamaica (population 2.6 million).

All these episodes signal to us that crime in the Caribbean cannot properly be understood through the 'official crime statistics' alone. Apart from the range of other criminogenic features (for example, poverty and inequity, unemployment, community and family fragmentation, etc.), there are dysfunctional political connections that add to the subversion of civil societies in the Caribbean. Faced with strong civic opposition to such alliances, the respective political directorates in Trinidad and Tobago and Jamaica explain that they court these *community leaders* in order to control the crime rate, or at least, to help dissuade these community leaders from further crime and violence. It is widely known that such community leaders and their followers play a part in assisting political parties during election time. This underlying feature continues to be a substantial obstacle to having effective policy action against crime, or at least some forms of crime.

To make matters worse for the Caribbean, there has been an apparent intensification of deporting criminals who, as non-citizens, are found guilty of crimes in Canada and particularly the USA. There is as yet no reliable figure, but estimates indicate that in the last five years, the rate of such deportees stands at around 1,000 per year. The police complain that the deportees usually reach their native land with the relevant documentation arriving some time afterwards, thus making it difficult for monitoring the deportee and also for keeping the figures up to date. The Jamaican police have indicated that these deportees have indeed been engaged in many serious crimes, from rape, robbery to murders. In Trinidad and Tobago and Guyana, the authorities have expressed the view that deportees instigate many of the recent kidnappings. In fact, in Trinidad and Tobago and Jamaica, the deportees have formed themselves into 'an organisation' to look after the rights and comfort of their deportee members.

Legislation is now being brought to the Jamaican Parliament to provide a monitoring and rehabilitation system for such deportees. The concerns over the subversive and criminal actions of these deportees remain a very sore point in US-Caribbean relations. Several attempts have been unsuccessfully made to have the US 'ease up' on the deportee rate or at least to provide some financial support for treating with them when they do arrive in the Caribbean. This issue of deportees, alongside the *political-community leader* alliances, will very likely present serious problems for effective law enforcement across the Caribbean. More recently, from 2001 to 2003, there has been a very frightening spate of kidnappings in Trinidad and Tobago and Guyana especially. Trinidad and Tobago has experienced a rise in reported kidnappings from 56 in 1995 to 156 in 2000, to 227 in 2002 – a 300 per cent increase between 1995 and 2002. Guyana has had over 20 reported kidnappings between 2002 and June 2003 – an unprecedented number. The overall detection rate is way below 30 per cent, a feature that aggravates public fear.

Overall, these crime trends and the surrounding political contexts help expose a serious problem in the crime-fighting capacity of the Caribbean: the fragility and vulnerability of the relevant state institutions. Born of Westminster traditions, these institutions – from the police to the Parliament – easily buckle under pressure from serious security attacks. The 1979 coup in Grenada was preceded by a barrage of substantiated charges of state corruption that were not well attended to. The Grenada police itself faced serious charges of brutality and political conspiracy. All this helped to pave the way for significant support for the 1979 coup, after which the major institutions in Grenada (for example, Parliament, the police and the judiciary) were left in virtual shambles – a condition which turned murderous with the socialist prime minister, Maurice Bishop, and other officials murdered by some cabinet conspirators, a violent turn which facilitated the US intervention of 1983. The court trial in 1984 sentenced 17 politicians and army officers to death for murder and treason, but these are still languishing in Grenada's Richmond Hill Prison (one is out for medical reasons), (see Deosaran, 1989 for a summary).

The 1990 violent insurrection in Trinidad and Tobago has also exposed several weaknesses in the political, police and judicial institutions. Today, the 114 members of the Muslimeen who were charged for treason remain free. In fact, the state was ordered to pay compensation to the Muslimeen (so far over US $300,000 has been paid). The Muslimeen is yet to pay the state the sums which the court also ordered. However, the Muslimeen remain free on the technical point of whether the conferred amnesty was valid or not. The Privy Council in London ruled that while it might be invalid, it would be 'impolitic' for the state to pursue the matter. Today, protracted public controversies over the role of the Muslimeen in crime and politics persist.

The CARICOM Response

In 2001, the Caribbean states (through a CARICOM Heads of Government meeting) established a CARICOM Task Force on Crime and Security as a means of developing 'an action plan' to fight crime in the region. There were already several regional security groupings: for example, the Regional Security System (RSS) and the Association of Caribbean Commissioners of Police (ACCP). There were also anti-money laundering and anti-drug agencies as well as several UN agencies such as the UN Office on Drugs and Crime, all of which provided some form of cooperation and support to the respective CARICOM governments. The 2001 CARICOM Task Force on Crime and Security, however, was expected to draw from all these agencies and from The University of the West Indies, in order to produce its final action plan against crime and regional security.[2]

Reflecting the widespread concern over crime in the Caribbean region, the secretary-general of CARICOM in March 2003 issued a statement to the region in which he said: 'No issue has concerned us more than the rising crime wave which threatens to envelop the region.' At that time, the murder rate across the Caribbean was alarming. In Jamaica, especially (population 2.6 million), there were 1,040 murders in 2002, with 171 in Trinidad and Tobago (population 1.2 million), and 152 in Guyana (population 800,000). Almost 40 police officers were killed during 2002 and 2003 across the Caribbean.

So far, two progress reports from the CARICOM Task Force on Crime and Security have been submitted to the CARICOM Heads of Government. These reports have singled out the following for special and urgent action: illegal drugs and arms smuggling, narco-terrorism, transshipment drug locations, violence and murder, community policing, penal and police reform, alternatives to sentencing, school violence and delinquency, escalating gang warfare, kidnappings and crime by deportees from North America. Some areas not considered by this Task Force are: use of force by police, state and political corruption and misconduct in public office. As articulated in these two progress reports and by the Heads of CARICOM Governments themselves, the successful implementation of the Task Force action plan will depend a lot upon international financial and logistical assistance. In fact, the US is expected to play a significant role in lending maritime and aerial support for the fight against drugs and narco-terrorism and expert assistance in crime detection. Such reliance, though justifiable, helps reveal the 'dependency' nature of Caribbean societies when it comes to dealing with internal and external insecurity.

As facilitating mechanisms for building community support and effective policing, several Caribbean states are now considering establishing National Crime Commissions. In fact, St Lucia has already led the way in 2002 by having its National Crime Commission put into legislation, completing a national fear of crime survey in 2002, and linking both to its growing community policing programmes. This three-cornered strategic linkage, first proposed in St Lucia, is now being actively considered for implementation in other CARICOM states.[3]

With all these currents flowing into the conditions and prevalence of crime in the Caribbean, it is no wonder that in the last 10 years there has been increasing momentum within the research and policy making community for a 'Caribbean criminology'. Some writers feel that given the tourist and economic dependency profile of most Caribbean states, the modes of collecting data and crime management will have to be significantly altered in order to understand crime in the Caribbean (for example, Bennett and Lynch, 1996; Bennett et al., 1997). A few suggest that there is no longer any time to tolerate traditional theories, except the radical Marxist approaches since the Caribbean region has been too long a subject to 'capitalist forces of exploitation' (for example, Headley, 1994; Pryce, 1976).

Others argue that the explanations and perspectives on crime in the Caribbean have been unduly distorted by 'tourist criminologists' who do not know enough about the vagaries of Caribbean history and culture (for example, Jones, 1999; St Jean, 1999). Still others have argued, however, that some existing theories on crime are still able to accommodate the unfolding data on Caribbean crime until such time as the data clearly needs a different explanatory paradigm (for example, Birkbeck, 1999; Deosaran and Chadee, 1997). However, even in this compromising position, the troublesome question still remains: Since data is usually collected within a predisposing perspective, how will we know with certainty that the data needs a new perspective, or theory? Of course, this is a perennial problem for criminology and social science generally. We need to note here, however, that this question has now crept into the current debate over what exactly a 'Caribbean criminology' should look like.

To help provide a scientific basis for the analysis of crime and its implications in the Caribbean, the Centre for Criminology and Criminal Justice was established on the St Augustine Campus of the University of the West Indies. In 1996, the *Caribbean Journal of Criminology and Social Psychology* was established under the auspices of the Centre for Criminology and Criminal Justice and continues to publish papers and ideas useful to developing an understanding of crime in the Caribbean.

Crime

We now turn to some specific crime trends. In these Caribbean states, there have always been widespread official and public concerns over crime, especially over such serious crimes as murder, rape, assault, dwelling-house larceny and robbery. One of the major reasons for such panic-driven concerns is the sociological nature of these Caribbean societies. Not only are they small in population (for example, 60,000 people in St Kitts and Nevis; 116,000 in St Vincent and the Grenadines), but they are small in geographical size too (for example, 390 sq km in St Vincent and the Grenadines). Furthermore, they are regularly spotted with hundreds of little villages and well-worn streets, but especially in the smaller states such as St Kitts and Nevis, St Lucia or Antigua, the residents have a rather close familiarity with one another mainly through their religious institutions. Panic over crimes against the person or property spread rapidly. The fear of crime rate across the Caribbean is between 40 and 70 per cent.

From Jamaica to the north, through all the Eastern Caribbean countries (St Lucia, Barbados, St Vincent and the Grenadines, Grenada, St Kitts and Nevis, Antigua), Trinidad and Tobago to Guyana in the south, the respective governments and the police services are under constant pressure from opposition politicians, the media and the various interests groups (for example, labour and business) to 'deal with' crime and criminals. Crime, therefore, has become a leading issue in general elections across the Caribbean. Apart from the social impact and local fears generated by crime in these states, the additional pressures upon the various governments to 'take action' have emerged from the fact that these states depend heavily on foreign investment and the tourist trade. The economics of crime, or more precisely, the economic dependency of the Caribbean states, have added much tension to the debate over crime in the Caribbean. The issue over crime in the Caribbean therefore includes, but goes far beyond, the personal safety of citizens.

Jamaica, St Lucia, Antigua, St Kitts and Nevis, Trinidad and Tobago and the Bahamas all invest very heavily in attracting tourists from North America and Europe. The service industries that support the tourist trade contribute between 40 to 60 per cent of the total number of employed persons in these countries. The state of crime, the local media, the treatment of crime on the Internet, and the public fear of crime all have serious implications for the economy of these countries. In 2002, for example, the British government issued a warning that is a 'travel advisory' to its citizens regarding the alarming 'levels of crime' in Trinidad and Tobago.

This crime advisory sent the Trinidad and Tobago government into a tailspin, so much so that the prime minister and several cabinet ministers struggled to explain that there was no need to be alarmed about crime in the country. In fact, a special delegation, headed by the country's minister of foreign affairs, quickly visited London and New York to have the crime advisory withdrawn. Mainly prompted by gang warfare, police-bandit shoot-outs and politically-motivated violence in 2002 and early 2003, the US government issued similar travel advisories for Jamaica which brought a great downturn to the tourism sector. Foreign embassies in the Caribbean now dispatch regular intelligence to their home offices on the state of crime and security in the Caribbean. For the smaller Caribbean states such as St Kitts and Nevis or St Lucia, a travel advisory on crime will be disastrous for the economy. The threat of such crime advisories serves as a strong motivator for the respective governments to keep crime under control.

Over the past 20 years and, more so at present, drug abuse and especially drug-trafficking have become serious targets for police, customs and immigration departments. The police have estimated that at least 60 per cent of the crimes in these countries are 'drug-related'. The drug trade typically emanates from South America on to North America and Europe, with these Caribbean countries, especially Trinidad and Tobago, being the transshipment point. Given the rise in Internet usage and the increased use of information technology in business, there are mounting concerns over fraud and other related white-collar crimes.

Generally, the existing database and methods of collecting crime, justice and prisons' data in these countries are quite deficient and even archaic. There are no active, coordinated, computerised systems for data collection and analysis, nor for making reliable assessments of the crime and punishment trends across these 12 Caribbean countries. There is also a great unevenness in the manner of compiling and reporting data on crime. For example, the categories used for compiling crime reports or offenses are not consistent from one country to another. The three countries that are relatively advanced in this respect are Jamaica, Barbados and Trinidad and Tobago. Even so, these countries are still at the stage where gross national figures are commonly used for policy.

The task of configuring the crime data into crime rates applicable to particular sections of the country, for example, are not yet in effective force. The social and demographic characteristics of offenders and victims are slowly becoming part of the crime reporting profile (see, for example, Deosaran, 2001). However, several proposals for systematic improvement have been put before some CARICOM states, particularly Trinidad and Tobago and Barbados. This general situation has been well noted by several international agencies that are seeking to provide loan assistance to help remedy the problem (see, for example, IADB, 2000).

Murder, Robbery, and Rape Rates for Selected Countries

From available data (1980–1996), the incidence and rate of murder increased in all Caribbean countries from the 1980s to the 1990s. Jamaica, which possessed the highest murder rate in the 1980s with 21.4 per 100,000 population, saw its rate increase to 27.7 in the 1990s. The United States Virgin Islands closely followed with a rate of 20.1 per 100,000 population in the 1980s and 24.2 in the 1990s (see, for example, de Albuquerque and Mc Elroy, 1999).

Guyana's murder rate averaged 14.0 per 100,000 in the 1980s but rose to 16.8 in the 1990s whilst the St Kitts and Nevis rate of 5.9 in the 1980s rose to 10.2 in the 1990s. A similar pattern unfolded as Trinidad and Tobago's murder rate in the 1980s, which stood at 7.0 per 100,000, increased to 8.8 in the 1990s while Antigua and Barbuda's murder rate moved from 5.6 in the 1980s to 7.2 in the 1990s. The average murder rate for Barbados in the 1990s was 7.2 as compared to 6.5 in the 1980s. Dominica's murder rate for the 1980s stood at 5.4 per 100,000 but increased to 5.9 in the 1990s while the murder rate for Grenada was 7.1 for the 1990s. It can be clearly seen from the above data that the rate of murder increased in Caribbean countries, but by different proportions, thus requiring specialised policy treatment.

Similar to murder rates, the rates of robbery increased in countries across the Caribbean from the 1980s to the 1990s. For example, in the United States Virgin Islands the average rate of robbery in the 1980s was 411 per 100,000 population but it increased to 575 for the 1990s. For Guyana, it almost doubled from 245 in the 1980s to 450 in the 1990s. The robbery rate for

Jamaica rose from 199 per 100,000 in the 1980s to 207 in the 1990s, while for Barbados it rose drastically from 65 in the 1980s to 212 in the 1990s. The robbery rate increased from 42 per 100,000 in the 1980s to 69 in the 1990s for Antigua and Barbuda. For Dominica, the rate of robbery almost tripled from 12 per 100,000 in the 1980s to 32 in the 1990s while it also increased in St Kitts and Nevis from 13 in the 1980s to 59 in the 1990s. The rate was 42 in the 1990s for Grenada. These data suggest that robbery continues to be a major problem facing Caribbean countries as seen by lofty increases in its incidence rates.

Similar to murder and robbery, the rate of rape increased from the 1980s to the 1990s across Caribbean countries. For example, the rate almost doubled from 39 per 100,000 in the 1980s to 77 in the 1990s for Dominica. For the United States Virgin Islands, it increased from 66 in the 1980s to 74 in the 1990s. For Antigua and Barbuda, the rate increased from 58 per 100,000 in the 1980s to 72 in the 1990s and for St Kitts and Nevis from 56 in the 1980s to 72 in the 1990s. The rape rate for Jamaica increased from 40 in the 1980s to 52 in the 1990s. The rate increased from 21 per 100,000 in the 1980s to 30 in the 1990s for Barbados and from 13 in the 1980s to 17 in the 1990s for Guyana. The rate was 18 in the 1990s for Grenada.

Burglary and Larceny Rates for Selected Countries

Unlike murder, robbery and rape rates that increased consistently in Caribbean countries over the last two decades, the rates for burglary varied, that is, sometimes it increased and at others decreased. For example, in Antigua and Barbuda, burglary rates increased from 1,300 per 100,000 population in the 1980s to 1,937 in the 1990s. Similarly with St Kitts and Nevis, it increased from 779 in the 1980s to 1,365 in the 1990s and in Dominica, from 863 in the 1980s to 1,219 in the 1990s. In Barbados, the burglary rate increased from 717 per 100,000 in the 1980s to 1,143 in the 1990s and for Guyana it increased from 407 in the 1980s to 581 in the 1990s.

For some Caribbean countries, burglary rates decreased over the last two decades. For example, in the United States Virgin Islands, it dropped from 3,741 per 100,000 population in the 1980s to 3,041 in the 1990s as well as for Trinidad and Tobago it decreased from 666 in the 1980s to 607 in the 1990s. Similarly, in Jamaica, the rate dropped from 360 per 100,000 in the 1980s to 269 in the 1990s while it was 855 in the 1990s for Grenada. Similar to burglary rates, the rate of larceny across Caribbean countries either increased or decreased. For example, larceny increased from 3,284 per

100,000 in the 1980s to 3,311.4 in the 1990s in the United States Virgin Islands and from 1,318.0 in the 1980s to 1,758.1 in the 1990s for Antigua and Barbuda. For Barbados, it increased from 1,039.1 in the 1980s to 1,149.0 in the 1990s. In St Kitts and Nevis, the larceny rate increased from 183 per 100,000 population in the 1980s to 386 in the 1990s. Similarly for Trinidad and Tobago and Dominica the rate increased. For the former country it increased from 200 in the 1980s to 234 in the 1990s; in the latter from 30 in the 1980s to 55 in the 1990s. However, larceny rates decreased for Guyana from 266 per 100,000 population in the 1980s to 136 in the 1990s and from 105 in the 1980s to 62 in the 1990s for Jamaica. The rate was 924 for Grenada in the 1990s.

Drug Trafficking

Drug trafficking is a major problem in the Caribbean and a nagging menace to Caribbean society and has resulted in the development of several subregional, regional and international programmes and policies. In 1982, the Barbados-based Regional Security System (RSS) was formed as a regional alliance to combat drug trafficking. Further, the United Nations has sponsored several drug control treaties, for example, the United Nations Convention Against Illicit Traffic in Narcotic Drugs and Psychotropic Substances of 1988. The US and individual Caribbean islands have signed several bilateral treaties. For example, in 1992, Belize and the US signed the Mutual Legal Assistance Treaty (MLAT).

By 1995, several other Caribbean countries signed a similar treaty commonly known as the 'Shiprider Agreement' – Antigua and Barbuda, Dominica, Grenada, St Lucia, St Vincent and the Grenadines, Dominican Republic and Trinidad and Tobago. The participants agreed to observe the six counter-narcotic measures: shipboarding, shiprider, pursuit, entry-to-investigate, over flight and order-to-land. It should be noted that both Jamaica and Barbados have agreed in principle to most of the treaty provisions, but they retain the authority to grant or deny permission to US law enforcement personnel in counter-drug efforts. This represents a significant departure from other Caribbean countries that have given the US standing authority to unilaterally combat drug trafficking in foreign waters.

Cocaine and Marijuana

Data from the Caribbean Drug Control Coordination Mechanism (2000) revealed that for the five-year period (1995 to 1999), 143,571 kilos of cocaine were seized in the Caribbean, averaging 28,714.2 kilos per year. Puerto Rico had the highest seizure, with 59,058 kilos, followed by Cuba with 13,067 kilos and the Cayman Islands with 10,849 kilos. Other Caribbean islands and their cocaine seizures (kilos) for this period are shown in Table 4.1. The Caribbean Coordination Mechanism (CCM) also revealed that, as regards marijuana in the Caribbean for the same five-year period, 467,383 kilos were seized with an average of 93,476.6 kilos per year. The countries with the highest seizures were Jamaica with 205,704 kilos followed by Guyana with 96,365 kilos and Cuba with 25,997 kilos. Other Caribbean islands and their marijuana seizures (kilos) for the same five-year period are highlighted in Table 4.2.

Table 4.1 Cocaine Seizures in the Caribbean 1995–1999

Country	Seizure (kilos)
Dominican Republic	10,566
Bahamas	8,279
Haiti	6,065
Belize	5,264
Jamaica	4,836
Turks and Caicos Islands	4,435
British Virgin Islands	4,304
Guyana	3,468
Netherlands Antilles	2,780
Suriname	2,057
Aruba	1,558
Guadeloupe	1,400
Anguilla	900
Barbados	548
Trinidad and Tobago	522
Antigua and Barbuda	269
Grenada	266
Dominica	223
St Kitts and Nevis	166
Martinique	136
Bermuda	47
St Vincent and the Grenadines	44
Montserrat	2

Source: Caribbean Drug Control Coordination Mechanism, 2000

Table 4.2 Marijuana Seizures in the Caribbean 1995–1999

Country	Seizure (kilos)
Puerto Rico	23,862
Trinidad and Tobago	18,530
Cayman Islands	18,447
Haiti	18,286
Bahamas	16,003
St Vincent and the Grenadines	13,893
Barbados	5,872
Dominican Republic	2,913
Montserrat	2,683
Antigua and Barbuda	2,508
Guadeloupe	2,467
Belize	2,462
Grenada	2,412
Netherlands Antilles	2,113
St Lucia	1,795
Dominica	1,507
British Virgin Islands	878
Aruba	456
Suriname	399
Bermuda	361
St Kitts and Nevis	122
Anguilla	100
Turks and Caicos Islands	68

Source: Caribbean Drug Control Coordination Mechanism, 2000

Number of Police Officers in Selected Countries

Police officers, soldiers, coast guards, prison officers, probation officers, etc. are all critical components in terms of manpower to deal with crime. However, usually the police are the first called upon to serve whenever a problem arises. With regard to the manpower distribution of this important crime-fighting agency in selected countries, Table 4.3 is very instructive.

Table 4.3 Police Establishments in the Caribbean

Country	Population (1997)	No. of Police Officers
Dominican Republic	8,107,000	24,000
Jamaica	2,554,000	10,317
Haiti	7,492,000	6,500
Trinidad and Tobago	1,307,000	7,000
Guyana	848,000	3,570
Bahamas	289,000	2,391
Barbados	265,000	1,450
Suriname	412,000	1,056
Belize	230,000	826
Grenada	96,000	724
Antigua and Barbuda	66,000	687
St Vincent and the Grenadines	112,000	565
St Lucia	159,000	542
Dominica	74,000	442
St Kitts and Nevis	41,000	430

Source: Caribbean Drug Control Coordination Mechanism, 2000

Police Complaints Offices and Community Policing in Selected Countries

Sometimes the need arises for the introduction of special measures, especially when members of the public may not be satisfied with the service received from the police. As such, some countries have established a special office to deal with such complaints. In some countries, the office is part of the police service while in other countries it is an independent specialised unit. Countries in which a police complaints office exists include the Bahamas, Barbados, Guyana, Haiti, Jamaica, St Vincent and the Grenadines and Trinidad and Tobago. In Belize and St Lucia, the Ombudsman's office functions as the police complaints office. Caribbean countries in which there is no specific police complaints office include Antigua and Barbuda, Dominica, Dominican Republic, Grenada, St Kitts and Nevis and Suriname.

Community policing is increasingly being adopted as a new thrust in policing in the Caribbean. In the 1990s, several countries formally adopted this new method in policing and have accordingly initiated the required structural changes. These include the Bahamas, Barbados, Belize, Guyana, Jamaica, St Vincent and the Grenadines, Suriname and Trinidad and Tobago (see, for example, Deosaran, 2000). However, other countries are still working to have community policing as an integral part of their crime prevention and crime reduction programmes. These are Antigua and Barbuda, Dominica, Grenada, Haiti, St Kitts and Nevis and St Lucia. In 2001, the Association of Caribbean Commissioners of Police (ACCP) collectively adopted community policing as a 'modernised' policing mission and have, in fact, in collaboration with the Centre for Criminology and Criminal Justice at the University of the West Indies, established a Special Task Force to help pursue the deepening of community policing across all police jurisdictions of the Caribbean.

Forensic Laboratories and Criminal Investigation in Selected Countries

Forensic laboratories are increasingly playing a crucial role to effectively deal with criminal investigation and prosecution. To this end, there are some countries in the Caribbean that possess such facilities. These countries include Antigua and Barbuda, Bahamas, Barbados, Belize, Dominica, Dominican Republic, Guyana, Haiti, Jamaica, St Lucia and Trinidad and Tobago. However, there are countries without such facilities. They are Grenada, St Kitts and Nevis, St Vincent and the Grenadines and Suriname.

There is some variation across Caribbean countries as to who undertakes criminal investigations. For example, the police and the director of public prosecutions undertake criminal investigation in Antigua and Barbuda and Dominica. In Suriname, the police and the Office of the Attorney General perform this function. The police, magistrates and judges in Haiti also perform this function. In the Dominican Republic, the prosecutor police and the instruction judge undertake criminal investigation. The police alone perform this function in the Bahamas, Barbados, Belize, Grenada, Guyana, Jamaica, St Kitts and Nevis, St Lucia, St Vincent and the Grenadines and Trinidad and Tobago.

In some Caribbean countries, the police usually serve as prosecutors. For certain cases, state or privately-contracted lawyers lead the prosecution. These countries include Antigua and Barbuda, Bahamas, Barbados, Belize, Dominica, Grenada, Guyana, St Kitts and Nevis, St Lucia, St Vincent and the Grenadines and Trinidad and Tobago. In the Dominican Republic, the police usually perform this function. This contrasts with other Caribbean countries such as Haiti, Jamaica and Suriname where the police do not generally perform this function.

Portrait of Inmates in Selected Countries

From the available data, it can be seen that the Dominican Republic has the largest number of inmates with 15,000 followed by Jamaica with 4,200, Haiti with 3,500 and the Bahamas with 1,200. Guyana has 1,000 inmates while Barbados has 750 and Belize with 600. St Lucia has 320 inmates, St Vincent and the Grenadines has between 200–400 inmates whilst Grenada has 300. There are 192 inmates in Suriname and 175 in St Kitts and Nevis. For Trinidad and Tobago, in 1997 the daily average number of prisoners was 4,685 (see, for example, *Annual Statistical Digest 1997, No. 23*).

With regard to the number of spaces available for inmates, from the limited data available, the Dominican Republic has 7,000 spaces followed by Bahamas with 500, Guyana 400, Barbados 380, Grenada 250, Belize and St Lucia 200 spaces each, St Kitts and Nevis and St Vincent and the Grenadines 75 spaces each and Suriname 25. Prison overcrowding is now a hotly debated issue across the Caribbean. Recently, too, the problem of recidivism has been gaining a lot of public attention, especially in the context of estimated recidivism rates of between 40 and 60 per cent across the Caribbean (see, for example, a recent research and policy report by Deosaran, 2003a).

The data available reveals that the bulk of inmates reflects a relatively young population. For example, it is 18–24 years in the Bahamas, 20–23 years in Belize, 26 years in the Dominican Republic, 28 years in Grenada, 18–30 years in Guyana, 17–25 years in Jamaica, 21 years in St Kitts and Nevis, 20–29 years in St Lucia, 25 years in St Vincent and the Grenadines and 20–25 years in Suriname.

There are many countries in the Caribbean without any systematic, sustainable prison rehabilitation programmes, among them Antigua and Barbuda, Dominica, Dominican Republic, St Kitts and Nevis, St Lucia, St Vincent and the Grenadines and Suriname. However, attempts to insert firm rehabilitation programmes in these countries are now receiving serious official consideration. Some programmes of varying quality now exist in the Bahamas, Guyana, Jamaica, Belize, Grenada and in Trinidad and Tobago. But in all cases there is a lack of a sustainable supporting infrastructure and dedicated budget. These are matters which now form part of several penal reform packages now occupying the attention of several Caribbean governments, including St Lucia, St Vincent and the Grenadines, Jamaica, Grenada, Trinidad and Tobago.

Legal Representation and Criminal Responsibility in Selected Countries

The estimated number of lawyers (members of the Bar) in Caribbean countries varies considerably. For example, there are 22,240 lawyers in the Dominican Republic followed by 2,500 in Jamaica, 1,000 in Haiti, 1,000 in Trinidad and Tobago, 600 in the Bahamas, 300 in Barbados, 200 in Guyana, 120 in St Lucia, 80 each in Antigua and Barbuda, Dominica and Suriname, 80 in Belize, 68 in St Vincent and the Grenadines, 50 in Grenada and 45 in St Kitts and Nevis.

The age of criminal responsibility varies across Caribbean countries. For example, it is five years in St Vincent and the Grenadines, seven years in Belize, Grenada and Trinidad and Tobago, 10 years in Guyana and Suriname, 11 years in Barbados and 12 years in Dominica, Jamaica and St Lucia. The most common juvenile offences found across Caribbean countries include burglaries, thefts, drug offences (transport and peddling), vandalism, behaviour/language. By 1993, all CARICOM countries ratified the United Nations Convention on the Rights of the Child.

Family Courts have been established in several Caribbean countries: for example, Belize, St Lucia, St Vincent and the Grenadines and Jamaica. Some countries (for example, Trinidad and Tobago) have indicated plans to introduce such courts in the near future. In Trinidad and Tobago, mediation as an alternative to litigation for certain categories of offenders and offences are available (see, for example, *the Community Mediation Act, No. 13 of 1998*). Community Service as a sentence from the courts is available in some Caribbean countries, for example, Belize, Suriname, Trinidad and Tobago and Montserrat. In Dominica and St Lucia it is available, but not for juveniles. Parole is available only in Suriname, Belize and St Vincent and the Grenadines while a suspended sentence is available in Belize, Dominica and Suriname. A curfew can be prescribed in the Turks and Caicos Islands.

The Death Penalty

There are persistent controversies over punishment, alternatives to imprisonment, and in particular, the death penalty. In the case of the death penalty and from repeated surveys conducted, over 80 per cent of the Caribbean population support the death penalty for convicted murderers. In the last ten years, however, there have been several pressures especially from the Privy Council (Judicial Committee of the House of Lords) to abolish the death penalty in the Caribbean. The Catholic Church has expressed strong opposition to the death penalty and it is quite likely the Anglican Church will soon express its opposition to the death penalty as well.

All in all, and in the midst of public concerns and a growing research enterprise in the Caribbean, the various governments of the region are undertaking serious and deliberate steps to improve policies and strengthen the institutions to deal with crime and the administration of justice. Some countries are of course moving more quickly than others in these respects; two of the major hurdles being a lack of financial resources and appropriate databases. Given the relatively conservative nature of Caribbean societies and the general fear of crime, governments have found it more politically feasible to put more emphasis on punitive legislation and law enforcement than on programmes of crime prevention, rehabilitation and restorative justice. Nevertheless, the movement towards the latter options have begun to pick up some speed in recent times.

Conclusion: The Way Forward

There are five key areas in which urgent attention and sustained remedies are required. The first is on police reform and revisiting the objectives and operations of police work. The second pertains to the administration of justice, that is, the processing and determination of cases. The third key area is politics and public policy. The fourth is the need for a more sophisticated and responsive crime reporting, data collection and retrieval system. The fifth is penal reform and sentencing. Brief comments will be provided on these five key areas.

Policing in the Caribbean remains stuck with a conceptual and operational dilemma. Spawned by the narrow security needs of the plantation system and supported by the British tradition of imperial control, Caribbean policing has been largely confined to functions of social control of the working classes (Mahabir, 1985; Trotman, 1986). While social control is a typical function of the police across the world, because of the plantation labour and race antagonisms in the Caribbean, there has been a very hostile divide between the police and the mass of citizens. In recent times, however, the serious attempts to introduce a socially-oriented form of community policing has been met with little or no success.

The main reason for such failure is the growing and highly visible need for law enforcement measures. On the face of widespread public and government concerns over the serious crime rate, from Jamaica to Guyana, the rhetoric for community policing is shoved in the shadows with the pressures for heavy law enforcement in great public demand. While in the long run, and as a crime prevention and information-gathering device, community policing will certainly greatly help these Caribbean countries, the public mood and political expediency make it a dim prospect, at least in the near future.

In terms of decision-making theory, a person is likely to commit a crime if he knows the odds of detection and conviction are relatively low. The rate of crime detection across the Caribbean remains around 30 per cent, with the conviction rate for reported serious crimes at around 10 per cent. Added to this is the well-known, heavy case backlog in the Supreme Courts and especially in the Magistrates' Courts across the Caribbean. Such inefficiencies and blockages within the administration of justice attract further criminality. Public policy on crime has been driven largely by the fluctuating moods of the electoral and political expediency. For example, even though the death penalty is almost now impossible to carry out in the Caribbean, and though the murder rate still climbs, no CARICOM government sees any virtue in abolishing the death penalty.

Further, in Jamaica and Trinidad and Tobago, several Crime Committees and Crime Commissions were appointed between 1990 and 2002 to examine the problem of crime and violence. What the political directorates select for implementation are usually the very short-term recommendations with public appeal such as longer sentences and more legislation. Other long-term recommendations such as alternatives to incarceration or community strengthening, and so forth, are left on the shelves.[4]

The fourth key area – crime statistics – remains a very neglected aspect of policing. In order to drive effective policing on the basis of strategic intelligence, and especially for crimes such as kidnapping and terrorism, a sophisticated system of crime reporting, compilation, retrieval and dissemination is an imperative. The traditional methods of bookkeeping and storage still persist in many CARICOM states. The problem is not only the methods of compilation and retrieval. The fact is that even with available computers, crime information is usually stored in such global fashion, thereby making it impossible at any required moment to find out exactly what the crime trends are at any particular police station district (see Deosaran, 2001 for a fuller examination of this problem and its adverse effects upon community policing). The related deficiency is the lack of victimisation surveys across the Caribbean as a means of supplementing the official police records.

With a prisoner recidivism rate of around 60 per cent across the Caribbean, one would think that Caribbean governments would be in a haste to seek alternatives to such imprisonment. Indeed, some countries, for example, Barbados and Trinidad and Tobago, are looking this way, but still too slowly given the enormity of the problem. For example, while the recommended ratio is four prisoners to a cell, in almost all Caribbean countries the ratio is around eight prisoners per cell. Apart from prisons being heavily overcrowded, the need to rehabilitate prisoners remains a burning issue in order to reduce the rather high rate of recidivism across the Caribbean. These matters therefore range from institutional strengthening to process management and public confidence. Such matters as outlined above need urgent attention by the governments in order to deal effectively with the serious and escalating problems of crime in the Caribbean.

Notes

1. See, for example, research/policy report by R. Deosaran (2001), *Crime Statistics, Analysis and Policy Action: The Way Forward.*
2. The author is an advisor to this CARICOM Task Force on Crime and Security.
3. See, for example, a research and policy report by R. Deosaran on *A National Commission on Crime* (2001), submitted and accepted by the government of St Lucia; news items by R. Deosaran, 'Set Up a Crime Commission', *Sunday Express*, July 31, 1977, 4–5 and 'Let's Have Some Frank Talk on Crime', *Sunday Express*, November 20, 1977, 4–5 and *Report on Crime and Violence in the Caribbean* by R. Deosaran and A. Harriott (2002), submitted to CARICOM Task Force on Crime and Security.
4. See, for example, some research and policy reports by R. Deosaran: *Quality Benchmarking and Police Performance: Readiness for Community Policing* (2002), *A Human Resource Survey of Community Policing and Organisational Readiness in the Trinidad and Tobago Police Service* (2002), *Community Policing: Towards Quality Performance and Benchmarking* (2001) and *The Dynamics of Community Policing: Theory, Practice and Evaluation* (2000). Also refer to *Report of the National Committee on Crime and Violence in Jamaica*, June 2002 by a Bipartisan Committee appointed by Government of Jamaica, 2001.

Selected References

Bennett, R. & Lynch, J. (1996). 'Towards a Caribbean Criminology: Problems and Prospects'. *Caribbean Journal of Criminology and Social Psychology*, *1* (1), 8–37.

Bennett, R., Shields, W.P. & Daniels, B. (1997). 'Crime and Development in the Caribbean: An Investigation of Traditional Explanatory Models'. *Caribbean Journal of Criminology and Social Psychology*, *2* (2), 1–35.

Birkbeck, C. (1999). 'By Your Theories You Shall be Known: Some Reflections on Caribbean Criminology'. *Caribbean Journal of Criminology and Social Psychology, 4*(1&2), 1–31.

Caribbean Drug Control Coordination Mechanism. (2000). *Drugs in the Caribbean Region – 1999/2000 Trends*. Barbados: Caribbean Drug Control Coordination Mechanism.

Caribbean Journal of Criminology and Social Psychology, 6(1&2). (2001). Special issue on Policing and Policy in the Caribbean.

Central Statistical Office. (1999). *Annual Statistical Digest 1997*. Port of Spain, Trinidad: Central Statistical Office.

de Albuquerque, K. & Mc Elroy, J. (1999). 'A Longitudinal Study of Serious Crime in the Caribbean'. *Caribbean Journal of Criminology and Social Psychology, 4* (1&2), 32–70.

Deosaran, R. (l989). *The Grenada File*. Trinidad: The University of the West Indies, Extra Mural Studies Unit.

Deosaran, R. (1993). *A Society Under Siege: A Study of Political Confusion and Legal Mysticism*. (A Study of the Muslimeen Insurrection in Trinidad and Tobago). Trinidad and Tobago: The University of the West Indies, Psychological Research Centre.

Deosaran, R. (2000). *The Dynamics of Community Policing: Theory, Practice and Evaluation*. Trinidad: The University of the West Indies, St Augustine Campus, Centre for Criminology and Criminal Justice.

Deosaran, R. (2001). *Crime Statistics, Analysis and Policy Action: The Way Forward*. Research and Policy Report. Trinidad: The University of the West Indies, St Augustine Campus, Centre for Criminology and Criminal Justice.

Deosaran, R. (2002). 'Community Policing in the Caribbean: Context, Community and Police Capability'. *Policing: An International Journal of Police Strategies and Management*. Volume *25*(1), 125–146. (Special Journal Issue on 'Community Policing: An International Perspective).

Deosaran, R. (2003a). *Prison Recidivism: Towards Reduction, Rehabilitation and Reform*. Research and Policy Report. Trinidad: University of the West Indies, St Augustine Campus, Centre for Criminology and Criminal Justice.

Deosaran, R. (2003b). 'National Security and Community Policing: Police Leadership and the Civic Alliance'. *Caribbean Perspectives*, 22–31. A Leadership Research Publication of the Eastern Caribbean Centre, University of the Virgin Islands, Eastern Caribbean Centre.

Deosaran, R. (2003c). *From Concepts to Practice: The Caribbean Challenge in Community Policing*. Paper presented at Annual Conference of the Association of Caribbean Commissioners of Police (ACCP), Fairmont Hamilton Princess Hotel, Bermuda. May 22, 2003.

Deosaran, R. & Chadee, D. (1997). 'Juvenile Delinquency in Trinidad and Tobago: Challenges for Social Policy and Caribbean Criminology'. *Caribbean Journal of Criminology and Social Psychology*, *2* (2), 36–83.

Forst, B. & Bennett, R. (1998). 'Unemployment and Crime: Implications for the Caribbean'. *Caribbean Journal of Criminology and Social Psychology, 3*(1&2), 1–29.

Friedrichs, D.O. (1998). 'Responding to the Challenges of White Collar Crime as a Social Problem: Implications for Caribbean States'. *Caribbean Journal of Criminology and Social Psychology*, *2* (2), 84–99.

Headley, B. (1994). *The Jamaican Crime Scene*. Washington, DC: Howard University Press.

IADB. (2000). *Challenges of Capacity Development: Towards Sustainable Reforms of Caribbean Justice Sectors*. Report 2000 IADB/CGED. Washington, DC: IADB.

Jones, M. (1999). 'Towards a Caribbean Criminology: Of, or For the Caribbean?' *Caribbean Journal of Criminology and Social Psychology*, *4* (1&2), 233-253.

King, J. (1997). 'Paradise Lost? Crime in the Caribbean: A Comparison of Barbados and Jamaica'. *Caribbean Journal of Criminology and Social Psychology, 2* (1), 30–44.

King, J. (1998). 'Conflict and Cooperation in the War on Drugs: The Caribbean Experience'. *Caribbean Journal of Criminology and Social Psychology*, 4 (1&2), 83–95.

Laws of the Republic of Trinidad and Tobago. (1998). *Community Mediation Act, No. 13 of 1998.*

Mahabir, C. (1985). *Crime and Nation Building in the Caribbean: The Legacy of Legal Barriers.* Cambridge, MA: Schenkman Publishing Company, Inc.

McCormack, R.J. (1999). 'The Caribbean, Sovereignty and the War on Drugs: Historical Factors and Current Perspectives'. *Caribbean Journal of Criminology and Social Psychology*, 4 (1&2), 71–84.

Pryce, K. (Ed.). (1976). *Crime in the Caribbean. Caribbean Issues*, 2(2). (Entire Issue).

Ryan, S. (1991). *The Muslimeen Grab for Power.* Trinidad: Imprint Publications.

St. Jean, P.K.B. (1999). 'Caribbean Criminology: An Empirical Question – A Further Critique'. *Caribbean Journal of Criminology and Social Psychology, 4* (1&2), 210–232.

The World Bank. (1999). *World Bank Atlas – 1999.* Washington, DC: The World Bank

Trotman, D.V. (1986). *Crime in Trinidad: Conflict and Control in a Plantation Society 1838–1900.* Knoxville, TN: The University of Tennessee Press.

United States Information Agency. (1997). *Partnership for Prosperity and Security in the Caribbean.* Washington, DC: United States Information Agency.

5

The Challenge of the Corruption-Violence Connection

Anthony P. Maingot

Introduction

Anyone following the news emanating from the four corners of the world will quickly notice the repeated juxtaposition of two phenomena: widespread corruption and persistent conflict and violence. Note the link between corruption, violence and underdevelopment made by the highly influential Nicholas Kristof of the New York Times:[1]

> Corruption has undermined the efficiency of capitalism in South America and eroded support for markets. It's one reason too many South Americans see foreign investors and lenders only as exploiters.... Unless we pitch in to fight corruption, unless we help build the case for markets, then much of South America will spin out of control – ultimately looking like that angry street scene in Caracas.

In the mid-1990s in Jamaica, the fear that violence would undermine the nation's economy led to the secondment of Col. Trevor MacMillan from the army to the police. It was the beginning of the militarisation of the war against violence, akin to what was being called 'the war on drugs'. Col. MacMillan, however, saw it as a battle against 'criminality, corruption and power abuse', even in the police services.[2] Clearly the juxtaposition of social trends, even where a correlation is proven, is not the same as establishing a causal link. Is there a causal relationship between widespread corruption and violent conflict? Note that the dependent variable is *violent* conflict, not simply conflict. The latter can safely be presumed to exist in varying degrees in all social interactions and social change. Democratic systems can and do coexist with even relatively high levels of conflict. Violence, including acts of terrorism, on the other hand, involves a qualitatively different order of social relations. Violence involves a breakdown in the pattern of expectations and assumptions about social relations either at the point of goals and/or at the level of means towards those goals.

It is this breakdown which can properly be called a *crisis* in the social system, a crisis which often has – intended or unintended – destabilising consequences for political systems, whether democratic or not. Indeed, it is evident that this destabilisation is the intended goal of terrorist violence. Other forms of violence, such as kidnapping, even though it does not have the intended goal of political destabilisation, do contribute to doubts about the effectiveness of the system. At what point does lack of confidence in the effectiveness of the system begin to reduce legitimacy? What, then, is the causal relationship between widespread corruption, violent conflict and its contribution to a crisis in existing social, economic and political order?

Theoretical Approaches

The enormous contemporary interest in the subject is evident in the most important compilation published so far, that of Arnold J. Heidenheimer.[3]The variety of theoretical approaches evident in that volume attest to the universality of the phenomenon but also to the absence of any single body of theory with which to study it. Each student starts the theoretical debate anew. The comprehensive and incisive study by Stephen D. Morris[4]begins with a long discourse and analysis of the existing theories and why they do not apply to his case. Other studies tend to repeat such disclaimers. Not surprisingly, the applicability of Morris' model has yet to be tested by others. The conclusion one must reach is that there is no single, widely accepted body of theory for the study of corruption much less is there any theorising on the possible links between widespread corruption and violence. A review of the literature will illustrate the point. In 1967, J.S. Nye published one of the early social science analyses of corruption.[5]He telescoped his basic premise by prefacing his essay with a 1714 quote from one Bernard Madevile who maintained that 'private vices by the dexterous Management of a skilful Politician may be turned into Public Benefits'. This represented an early version of what has been labelled the *realist* or *functionalist* approach to corruption. Nye joins their ranks when he concluded that the topic was 'too important a phenomenon to be left to moralists'. Indeed, he strongly argued that in both the United States and Russia, corruption had 'probably been, on balance, a positive factor'. Corruption, far from generating conflict, did the exact opposite: it smoothed the path to modernisation, helping to avoid severe conflicts.

In other words, corruption is a mechanism of conflict-avoidance. Just how widespread this theoretical assumption has been can be seen in the 1921 statement by Spanish philosopher Jose Ortega y Gasset who pointed out that the United States, where 'public immorality flowed like a Mississippi River' went on to become one of the world's most 'stellar' nations.[6]

In 1968, two highly influential books on *modernisation* appeared. They differed on the particular role of corruption in the modernisation process, but agreed on some basic points. To Samuel P. Huntington, quoting Nye's 1967 piece, there was some benefit to 'a little corruption' in developed traditional societies: it acted as 'a welcome lubricant easing the path to modernization'.[7] That same year, 1968, Swedish economist Gunnar Myrdal provided a radically different interpretation in his monumental *Asian Drama: An Inquiry Into the Poverty of Nations.* Chapter 20 of Volume Two was a devastating critique of what he called 'the opportunistic rationalizations' which portray corruption as either unimportant or somehow useful in development. Myrdal portrayed corruption as one of the key forces preserving what he called the 'soft state' where development is arrested by inertia, inefficiency and irrationality.[8] Myrdal, like most other theorists, was interested in development so he never made a major connection between corruption and violence and their role in undermining democracy. The focus was always on modernisation as economic development.

Functionalist theory was dominant in the 1960s and part of the 1970s and it assumed that legitimacy minimised conflict. Indeed, it was assumed that political party competition was a substitute for open class conflict. The key elements were the rates of social mobility and change.

During the 1970s and 1980s, with the emphasis on Marxist and *dependency* and world systems paradigms, the term corruption was a way of characterising whole economic systems, national and international. Whole classes were *corrupt* by their very location in the capitalist development and trading arrangements between *core* and 'peripheral' societies. At the more micro-sociological level, explanations tended to be based on Marxian notions of social conflict and social strain. In this theoretical perspective, it is assumed that, due to the obstacles to legitimate social mobility and advancement, people will resort to either corruption or outright violence in order to overcome those obstacles. Needless to say, there was a propensity to consider violence legitimate if it came in a revolutionary package. Since the macro-sociological system was intrinsically corrupt, only the uprooting of the whole system could combat corruption. For example, René Dumont wrote about the dramatic reduction in corruption in the early stages of the Cuban revolution and compared it to the opposite results of change in many African states which were transiting from colony to independence. He lauded the 'spirit of service and dedication' of the Cubans, to which the Africans compared unfavourably.[9] To be sure, Dumont never mentioned the state-sponsored violence such as executions which was occurring at the time in Cuba and which, in fact, made the change possible. Since fighting corruption was a major theme of the Cuban Revolution the draconian measures of the early stages of the revolution had widespread public support.

This conflict school overlapped with another: theories of the rational actors making free choices. A pioneer was Susan Rose-Ackerman whose 1978 study laid out the key aspects of this approach: the role of opportunities, incentives, risks and costs of engaging in corrupt behaviour.[10] The emphasis in this approach tended to be on how to reduce incentives or increase risks and costs. In other words, how to *combat* corruption by increasing the costs to the corrupt agent. This rational actor economist approach to combating corruption became the standard approach, even in studies of corruption in Latin America. This was, to say the least, surprising given the cultural focus which studies of corruption had always had in that region.[11]

Quite plainly, there was nothing in the *development, modernisation or rational actor* literature which made an effort to analyse the links between levels of corruption and violent conflict. Unfortunately, the body of theoretical literature which followed did nothing to close the explanatory gap.

In the late 1980s and 1990s, advocates of a return of cultural explanations began to challenge the functionalist, the conflict and economist/rational actor theories. Without being mentioned by name, Talcott Parson's culturally-based theory of *pattern variables* re-emerged. Societies were again described in terms of normative systems which emphasised 'particularistic specificity and ascription' and those which emphasised 'universalistic' and 'achievement-based' norms. Most non-European cultures were again found to respond to the former normative system. In fact, there was a general return to the cultural studies approach pioneered by Edward Banfield. In his study of Southern Italy, Banfield spoke of 'amoral familism': a culture in which 'no one will further the interest of the group or community except as it is to his private advantage to do so. In other words, the hope of material gain in the short-run will be the only motive for concern with public affairs'.[12] In a perverse sort of way amoral familism acts as a block to outright social conflict and violence against the system because it stifles any *idealistic* (*revolutionary*?) notions that it will do any good. Banfield did assume that whatever group was in power would be self-serving and corrupt and that it would use state-sponsored violence to avoid wider, and authority-threatening, violence.

No one should be surprised to find Banfield's analysis of Southern Italy applied by analogy to much of the Catholic Third World. This partly explains why one of the hottest selling books on Amazon.com in 2001 is the one edited by Lawrence E. Harrison and Samuel P. Huntington, *Culture Matters* (2000), a book the editors dedicate to the memory of Edward Banfield. Virtually all the studies in the 'culture matters' theoretical school advance culture as the dominant independent variable. In the words of one of them, 'culture is the mother and...institutions are the children'.[13] Predictably, the index of culture matters contains only one entry on *conflict.* This reference is to an essay by the African, Daniel Etounga-Manguelle in which there is a barely concealed lament that Africa's 'excessive conviviality' (akin to Banfield's 'amoral familism') pushes the African to avoid conflict. This in turn means that neither is true justice done nor anomic violence avoided. Naturally, the book does contain a chapter on corruption. In a highly sophisticated study involving several regression analyses, Seymour Martin Lipset and Gabriel Salman Lanz provide three explanations of corruption.[14] Two are culturally based: 1) inadequate means to achieve culturally prescribed goals, and 2) the role of particularistic norms inherent in amoral familism, as described by Banfield. The third explanation is social-structural: the positive correlation between economic success (income) and democracy. The authors return to culture even in terms of the third explanation since they find that the highest correlation between income and democracy is found in Protestant countries. 'Protestantism,' they conclude, 'reduces corruption, in part because of its association with individualistic, non-familistic relations.'[15]

The key question is this: If culture is the key explanatory-predictive factor in economic and political development, does it also explain and predict the presence or absence of violent conflict? The new culture theory, like all the previous ones, provides no answer because the question is never posed. The reality is that the present state of research on corruption is such that no deductive theory is possible. We still are, says Robert Klitgaard, at the stage of hypotheses and of policy analysis used heuristically. This holds especially for any attempt to link corruption to violent conflict or the absence of violent conflict.[16]

If the various schools of theory on corrupt behaviour do not address the question of corruption and violent conflict, the time might be right to reverse the research process: operating inductively, that is, going from case studies to theory (or at least hypothesis) formulation. This is certainly the appreciation of Ibrahim Shihata who, as senior vice president of the World Bank, has had to deal directly and programmatically with the issue of corruption. Understanding the impacts of corruption, according to Shihata, requires two approaches: First, an analysis of local context and circumstances of the level and nature of corruption in any given country, and secondly, an understanding that corruption is, in his words, 'a highly complex set of interlocking economic, political, social, moral, and historical phenomena'. One should, therefore, avoid 'narrow approaches advocated by any one social discipline'.[17]

Unable, thus, to operate deductively from established theory, and lacking definitional clarity we turn to inductive analysis in the form of two country case studies and one regional one. The hope is that they will contribute to both useful theoretical insights and to definitional clarification.

The Colombia Case

Throughout the Greater Caribbean one hears repeatedly that a process of *Colombianisation* is taking place. Occasionally this is meant to indicate the actual presence of Colombian drug operatives in the region but more often than not it is meant to indicate a link between widespread corruption and increasing violence similar, it is believed, to what exists in Colombia. How accurate are these analogies and what can be learned from a Colombian case study, albeit a brief one?

In the more widely read literature on politics in Colombia since 1952, the theme of corruption hardly figured. T. Lynn Smith never even mentions the word. He has one paragraph on what Colombians call *corbata*: sinecures.[18] Robert H. Dix's very comprehensive study also limits his single, and brief, analysis of corruption to the issue of employment, and this within the following general context: 'Colombian administration is reputed not to be particularly corrupt in the more flagrant sense of large-scale bribery. But nepotism, "connections" (*palanca)*, petty bribery, and similar means of acquiring private influence and advantages are widespread'.[19]

In one of the most provocative studies of the period, James L. Payne presented the issue again as one of employment opportunities, this time, however, placed within a broader sociological framework in which three key variables interact: high social status consciousness, weak barriers to social mobility, and availability of status-providing jobs.[20] Everett E. Hagen also emphasised the status-consciousness of Colombian society and saw the highland elite's denial of status to the *antioqueños* as the basis of the latter's motivations and entrepreneurial energies. Never is the issue of corruption raised.[21]

Interestingly enough, it was the *US Army's Area Handbook for Colombia* that had the most useful conceptual formulation for an understanding of the particular political culture in which corruption prospers.[22] A key element, they noted, was the survival in Colombia of the colonial notion of the *fuero*: No one general law applies to all and at all times; each individual is regulated by whatever 'law' he can secure from his leaders and a politician was expected to demonstrate his ability to shield his supporters from the rigorous application of the laws. The constant and all-pervasive quest of any leader, thus, is to secure prerogatives for one's subordinates. The one who does that best is, in the local parlance, *un verraco* (a real man); the one who does not seek – or cannot secure – such prerogatives is *un pendejo* (a stupid weakling). This could well be describing a Jamaican *don* for instance. Again, however, the *Handbook* does not speak of corruption *per se*.

There are two probable explanations for this absence of discussion on corruption in the literature on Colombia. First, and as already noted, the topic had not yet become a subject for study anywhere. Not until Gunnar Myrdal's categorical assertion that corruption was fundamental to the development process did the problem become a serious topic for social science analysis. Up to that point, it was regarded as either innocuous or even beneficial – because it cut red tape – and best relegated to the preaching of moralists. Second, there appears to have been an excess of caution and cultural sensitivity about passing judgment about probity and honesty in other cultures. Such total relativism is evident in Glenn Caudill Dealy's assertion that the favouritism, nepotism, and graft that characterise Latin American public and private relations cannot be judged or called corrupt by 'cultural outsiders'. The 'insider', says Dealy, knows that this system is really 'the law of reciprocal favors', which 'foreshadows and reinforces culture-wide rationality in Latin America.'[23]

Mercifully, Colombians need not be concerned with this false insider-outsider dichotomy. It is true that they started really late in the game. It is a universal characteristic of studies in corruption, as it is of most historical research: they are *post facto*. In the case of corruption, it is only once the terrible consequences are evident that the need to understand both the causes and the consequences is felt. Be that as it may, there are some pioneering studies done by Colombians which are revealing.

The very important study by Fernando Cepeda Ulloa fills a long-felt need.[24] It is not Cepeda's purpose to be theoretically innovative. His purpose is to introduce Colombian decision makers and scholars to the systematic study of the phenomenon. As such, Cepeda adopts Robert Klitgaard's policy-oriented framework which stresses seven variables: institutional inefficiency, scope of individual discretion in decision making posts, degree of monopolisation over the values desired, benefits that can be derived from those monopolies, probability of being discovered, weight of punishments meted out, and level of condemnation of corrupt acts by society as a whole.[25] It is evident, however, that unless one can attach causal weights and causal sequences to these variables, the framework operates more as a taxonomy than as an explanatory-predictive theory. The question then becomes: Can there be a theory which links corruption and violence in the sense of an 'if...then' explanatory system that has general applicability? Equally important, can such an explanatory framework assist policy-makers to formulate strategies to combat both corruption and violence?

That this question is central to the issue at hand is evident in the work of Francisco Thoumi, foremost authority on drug-related violence in Colombia. The first issue, argues Thoumi, is that of causality. The common assumption is that the drug industry in that country resulted from a conjuncture of international factors, fundamentally US demands for drugs. According to Thoumi, if this thesis was true, then the causal sequence would be clear; from illegal drugs to massive corruption and from there to systemic violence. This, however, is not how he interprets the causal chain. In fact, says Thoumi, it went the other way: a social, political and economic environment dominated by corruption and patronage created the ideal conditions for the drug industry to locate in Colombia. 'In that case,' he argues, 'the illegal drug industry has acted as a catalyst and accelerator in a process that had already begun.'[26] Thoumi pursues this causal sequence in a variety of studies, all of which emphasise three key factors: 1) the long history of corruption (mostly through contraband) in Colombia, 2) the delegitimisation of the state and government system generally, and 3) the growth of the informal economy specifically. It was the *antioqueño,* says Thoumi, who was best, though not exclusively, situated to take advantage of these Colombian conditions to exploit the opening of the US drug market.[27]

What had occurred was that the higher stakes and payoffs of the drug trade pushed one form of *corruption* (call it *clientelism* or *patrimonialism*) into a qualitatively and quantitatively different form of corruption. This created a crisis in the normative and legal systems to such an extent that existing definitions, social and legal, of corruption were no longer adequate. Thoumi discusses the US pressure on Colombia to try President Ernesto Samper for corruption. Independent of whether Samper knew about or authorised or condoned the entrance of drug moneys to his campaign coffers, Thoumi argues that the legal case against Samper was very weak. First, illicit enrichment legislation had not been *typified*; that is, the crime itself had not been defined so that the legislation was unenforceable. Second, most drug funds came from legal companies that fronted for the cartels and contributed cheques from legal accounts in approved banks. In other words, there was no anti-money laundering legislation on the books. Third, the illicit enrichment legislation required Samper's personal net worth to have increased, which did not happen since all moneys were spent on his presidential campaign. The trial, says Thoumi, was an attempt to turn a political issue into a criminal one. This whole process can be labelled *Colombianisation* and the question is, can it be applied to the case of the Caribbean?

In order to answer that question, we need a conceptualisation of organised crime. This conceptualisation of what has been generalised in the term *Colombianisation* should help us answer questions such as: Are the three reputed *mafias* in Trinidad (organised, as these groups tend to be worldwide, on ethnic lines), or the Jamaican *posses*, or the Dominican *mafias*, subordinate to the Cali cartel? Or are they autonomous players that act sequentially, segmentally, and locally in a chain of individual conspiracies running from producer to consumer? Because of the secrecy involved, direct empirical evidence is difficult to come by. This means that any attempt to illuminate the structure of the Caribbean drug business will have to depend on a series of assumptions.

One assumption is that there is a natural and logical tendency among all those involved in the *business*, Colombian producers and Caribbean transshippers alike, to maximise the gains of their participation, to increase their profits by controlling more and more links in the chain – that is, centralising the operation. Call it the centralisation imperative. The other assumption is that this attempt at centralisation engenders considerable violence. It is logical to assume that since the centralisation imperative operates in all groups, there will be violence to increase and maintain profitability. The process through which all this takes place can be called *Colombianisation*. The group best organised in terms outlined in the conceptual scheme (Table 5.1) will emerge victorious in the *Colombianised* environment. A few cases will illustrate this progression from generalised corruption to a state of *Colombianisation*, of organised crime.

Table 5.1 –Defining* 'Organized Crime'*: Conceptual Approximation

1. Despite a preference for laissez-faire ideologies, it is *nonideological* in an opportunistic way.
2. Its *capacity to adapt* in order to meet a variety of demands for its services provides it with *strong continuity* over time.
3. The adaptability and continuity are facilitated and enhanced by (i) milieus of *generalised corruption* which are not of its creation, indeed, they precede the emergence of the organisation; (ii) the acquiescence or indifference over long periods of major military actors creating 'blowback situations'; (iii) the total or significant control of a given territory (urban or rural) in which it can operate freely and profitably.
4. It is most efficient when based on ethnic ties utilising ethnic loyalties among its overseas diasporas and networks.
5. It has an organisation which is hierarchical and whose top command has the *capacity* to coordinate and implement (enforce) at least the following:
    1. the use of force or the credible threat thereof
    2. recruitment: access and membership
    3. control of the bulk of the profits (value added) from any series of transactions through total or near monopoly control
    4. strategical planning to achieve a range of goals, especially the 'control' or at least neutralisation through corruption or/and violence of crucial political/civilian/military actors
    5. enforcement of secrecy and loyalty

Sources: *F. Hangan, 'The Organized Crime Continuum: A further specification of a new conceptual model'*, Criminal Justice Review, *8 (1983): 52–57; M. Maltz, 'On Defining Organized Crime'*, Crime and Delinquency, *22 (1976): 338–46; Dennis J. Kenny and James O. Fluckenauer*, Organized Crime in America *(Belmont, CA: Wadsworth, 1995), 1–28; Diego Gambetta*, The Sicilian Mafia *(Harvard University Press 1993).*

The Case Of Haiti

The news out of Haiti has not been good for decades.[28] Contrary to expectations, the reestablishment of the elected government of Jean Bertrand Aristide appears to have done little to stem the tide of the drug trade with its sequel of corruption and violence. What appears to have happened is that Haitian society is experiencing a ratcheting up of corruption and violence, a process we have already identified as *Colombianisation*. Following Francisco Thoumi's strictures on the direction of causation and the conceptual scheme on Table 5.1, one has to begin the analysis with the reign of the Duvalier dynasty (1957–1986).

To understand the nature of a kleptocratic state (that is, Myrdal's *soft state* carried to its maximal expression) is to understand how the poorest country in the Western Hemisphere – where the per capita GNP was (and is less than) $250 a year and the per capita government expenditure to health was $2 per year – provided Duvalier, his relatives, and his wife's relatives with such enormous fortunes. After Duvalier, it continued to provide new elites with magnificent lifestyles. Typical is the oft-repeated assertion of Emmanuel Edouard that to work for the state in Haiti was 'to be in politics', which meant – by definition – to be eternally distrustful, false and conniving. It was a particular subcultural norm that to steal from Haitian state revenues did not engender reprobation, but outright envy.

The fine-tuning of the kleptocratic state occurred with the marriage of Jean-Claude to Michelle Bennett. A system of power through tyranny was joined to an expanding system of private economic despoliation and plunder. As one of Jean-Claude Duvalier's former aides once remarked to this author, 'Money for his father [Papa Doc] was a way of keeping power. Power for Jean-Claude was a way of making money.'

Comprehending how this money was made requires the dismissal of several myths about corruption in Haiti. The first is that Jean-Claude Duvalier's rule and misuse of state funds fit a traditional Haitian system of corruption whereby favouritism and nepotism operate to exploit loosely regulated state finances. The new Haitian kleptocratic state was nothing of the sort. Baby Doc's system was the modern institutionalisation of corruption through the nationalisation of the economy – usually under the ideological guise of defence of the national patrimony. Dictators such as Rafael Leonidas Trujillo in the Dominican Republic and the Somoza dynasty in Nicaragua had discovered the same formula.

The second myth is the misunderstanding of the status of Haiti's armed forces during these years. Before the senior Duvalier came to power, they were – whether manipulated or autochthonous – 'kingmakers'. Duvalier destroyed this military capability by creating counter-forces: first the Tontons Macoute and then the Volontaires de Securité Nationale (VSN), three times the size of the regular army. Under Baby Doc, the regular army lost even more ground; between 1972 and 1982 there were relative declines in military expenditures and size, and the official incomes if the paramilitary forces were also squeezed. Corruption was thus deepened. Instead of payment by the state, the paramilitaries were given even wider state licence to collect their rewards from the population – not unlike the *letters of patent* given by European monarchs to their privateers. And since the military did not participate collectively in the spoils of the official corruption, individual senior officers were encouraged to take private initiatives and make their own private arrangements. Predictably, the military went into business.

A final myth is the widely held belief in the United States that Haitian fortunes – such as that of Duvalier-Bennett – came primarily from skimming off foreign aid, especially from the United States. This was done, to be sure, but furnished only a minor part of the take. Between 1976 and 1982, Haiti received $618 million in foreign aid. Only $218 million of that came from the United States; of this, half was spent directly through private organisations without the involvement of the Haitian government. The balance went into the Haitian budget, but even there much of it was under the supervisory control of the Agency for International Development (AID) and other United States agencies.

While stealing from the Haitian state could be done with total impunity, stealing from international aid carried severe penalties. The crisis the regime faced in 1985 stemmed partially from foreign responses to Duvalierist thievery. Marc Bazin, called 'Mr. Clean' when he was minister of finance for six months in 1982, later related to this author how the Duvaliers stole $20 million of the $36 million he had secured from the IMF. Similarly, oil provided under an agreement with Venezuela and Mexico was cut off when it was discovered that substantial amounts were being resold on the world market, especially, it appears, to embargoed South Africa. All this came back to haunt the regime.

Clearly, the as yet undetermined millions with which the Duvalier-Bennett clan absconded had to come from other, more 'risk free' sources. In a country as poor as Haiti, where the middle and upper classes had developed time-honoured ways of escaping form the insatiable grasp of the state, it was the Haitian masses who provided the greater part of the take, increasing their collective anger. The bulk of the monies came from two sources. The most obvious, but probably not the most lucrative, was a network of private businesses owned by seven members of the Duvalier family, seven from the Bennett family, and assorted relatives, military men, and friends. The list of firms is long, the hidden ownerships difficult to trace. It is abundantly evident, however, that above and beyond the gains derived from its links to the state, the private sector enjoyed an additional privilege: by conducting most transactions in United States dollars, these families benefitted from the sale of dollars at black market rates as well as from the ability to easily open hard currency accounts in foreign banks.

The most bountiful, continuous, and risk-free source of the Duvalier-Bennett fortune, however, was the 'take' from state enterprises, which squeezed the working class to the point of bringing on further malnutrition and general despair. The scheme operated through control over essential services and monopoly ownership of critical commodities such as flour, sugar, oils, and cement. It was 'risk-free' because it involved national, not foreign, money. The weakness of civil society allowed the regime to skim large sums off budget items invariably labelled 'social works' or 'national defence.' In Haiti, the so-called public services passed the costs on to consumers and served as a major source of income for the state. The state electric company, for instance, had the highest rates in the Caribbean, the rates of the state telephone utility were exorbitant, and the national airline, Air Haiti, charged much more to ship cargo than did most of the other carriers in the region (the country's other airline, Haiti Air, was owned by the Bennetts).

State control of manufacturing provided the greatest opportunity for plunder. Under Jean-Claude Duvalier, the Ministry of Finance and the Central Bank were intimately linked to it. Their technical skills were essential for the complex chicanery that systematically fattened various secret foreign bank accounts and permitted the skimming of funds from state-owned enterprises. Here, in a nutshell, was the kleptocratic state as it operated until 1986. The critical aspect of this generalised corruption was that since it was centralised in the state which also had a monopoly of force, the levels of violence were relatively low. Considerable violence did accompany the fall of the Duvalier dynasty that year, called *dechoukage* to indicate the uprooting of corruption. Unfortunately, it did not bring this system to an end. It merely meant a widening in the number of recipients, many of whom were now eager to enter a higher level of corruption engendered by the drug trade.

On the surface it might appear that Haiti, since the restoration of Jean Bertrand Aristide, reflects a return to the pattern of corruption existing under the Duvaliers. It is and it is not. There is no military as before but there is a new police force with equal independent abilities to engage in major acts of corruption. The police now no longer has its own source of economic power, that is, jobs in the remaining state enterprises and the democratisation of smuggling – especially drug smuggling. Today, they are dependent on individual political figures. On the other hand, these political figures operate very similarly to how the Duvaliers operated, which is the only way to explain their luxurious lifestyles and capacity to fund what can only be called political enforcers.

The evident continuity in the history of elite corruption invariably followed by the use of violence to hold on to that power has been escalating. The assassination of journalists pursuing questions about the operation of local mafias, threats to judges and heads of commissions investigating political murders, are all parts of the *Colombianisation* of the island. Again, it did not start with Aristide but it certainly has not been stopped by Aristide. As the widow of assassinated journalist Jean Dominique put it from her exile in New York: 'When he [Aristide] first lost power, then came back, he felt it was not going to happen again. If that meant corruption so be it.... Power is now the name of the game'.[29] The 'adaptability and continuity', cited as characteristic of organised crime (Table 5.1), is certainly present in Haiti as are, indeed, many of the other characteristics cited in the conceptualisation.[30]

Important as any case study is to an understanding of the links between corruption and violence, one should not lose sight of two other characteristics: control over a territory and the role of ethnic ties. All this is evident in the following analysis of what might be called the regional nature of organised crime in the Caribbean.

The 'Regional Arena'

Despite its relative insignificance in the total scheme of US geopolitical and geoeconomic concerns, the Caribbean retains a certain *droit de regard.* Its location, the shared mutual interests, and its potential for causing a good deal of trouble to the United States all make it so. The Caribbean not only provides bridges between the producer and the consumer of drugs; in addition, its modern banking system provides virtually impenetrable shelter for the profits and investments of that criminal industry. In fact, there are a few more cases of corruption and, ultimately, violence than the so called Ochoa case in Cuba in 1989. To read the transcript of the trial which led to the execution of General Arnaldo Ochoa and three other high officials of the Cuban government is to understand the region-wide operation which took tons of drugs from Colombia to Cuba and from there to Miami by speed boats originating in that city. Panamá and its banks figured prominently in that scheme.[31] The case studies of Colombia, Haiti and Cuba should be seen in terms of a regional perspective which includes San Andrés, Central America, the Dominican Republic and Puerto Rico.

A Vital Geographical Link: San Andrés and Honduras

The Archipelago of San Andrés y Providencia belongs to Colombia and is located some 110 kilometres southwest of Jamaica.[32] It is inhabited by English-speaking people of West Indian descent, who, like the people of the Bay Islands off Honduras, have long existed as fishermen, as crew on ocean and inter island vessels, and as smugglers. Because San Andrés has always been a free port serving mainland Colombians, the smuggling business was always more important than it was in the Bay Islands. Yet San Andrés never brought in the kind of money and wealth that the *sanandresianos* began to notice starting some 20 years ago. The erstwhile bucolic existence of these islands has been replaced by high-rise hotels, fancy discos, shops with expensive clothing and merchandise, and yacht havens chock-full of vessels of every description and price.

The islanders know exactly to what this wealth is attributable and colourfully dub it the 'lobster route'. This is an operation which began with the Medellín cartel, initially controlled by the Cali cartel and today by what is generally known as the '*carteles de la Costa*'. Drugs and fuel are flown in from the mainland, either delivered at the airport in San Andrés or dropped offshore and picked up by speedboats the islanders call *voladores.* These cargoes are delivered to larger vessels which ply the Caribbean. The word is that the Mosquito Coast of Nicaragua was once their principal destination; today it is the Bay Islands, Jamaica, Cuba and the Dominican Republic. According to a well-placed source, a Colombian police report called San Andrés the 'epicenter' of the nation's drug export.[33] In addition to drugs, the archipelago trades in arms, precursor chemicals, and counterfeit dollars, and it provides the services necessary for money laundering.

Another major service, according to a report of the Colombian navy, is that: 'They can take an old ship, restore it to service, pack it with a ton of cocaine, and have it off the Jamaican coast, all in 30 hours'.[34] All these activities, noted the source, take place with brazen openness. Soon after that report was made public, *Cambio 16* reported that 'the major' drug dealer on San Andrés had been arrested. The individual was said to be at the service of the Cali cartel and to have business associations with Italians and Jamaicans established on the island. On this critical launching point, there can be no doubt that the Colombian cartels, first the Medellín, then the Cali cartel and now a variety of groups are in full control. Their control spread throughout Central America and the Caribbean. Honduras is an example of this expansion.

Judging from newspaper reports, citing sources in the DEA, by the late 1980s, Honduras had become a significant transshipment centre for cocaine that the Medellín cartel was shipping north.[35] This development was facilitated by the dramatic relaxation of ethical standards generally and in the Honduran armed forces specifically that accompanied the US use of the country as a base for insurgency against the Sandinistas of Nicaragua. In other words, Honduras was another of the many 'blowback' states in the region. The military were in an excellent position to take advantage of the proceeds of this trade. The civilian powers were thoroughly corrupt and not interested in probing too deeply into military corruption. No one else, at times not even the US Embassy, it appears, was interested in probing either, since national security and geopolitical concerns had priority. Additionally, the military controlled the police and, as such, had a monopoly of force and surveillance. As if all this did not give them latitude enough, the military also administered the country's airports (three out of the 215 airstrips had surveillance) and ran the nation's merchant marine.

No evidence surfaced of a direct and ongoing link between the military itself and the Medellín cartel. Instead, officers appear to have relied in the 1980s on a Honduran national, José Ramón Ballesteros, who was also connected with Col. Antonio Noriega in Panamá. As reported by US Senator John Kerry: According to antinarcotics officials, he was the contact between the Colombian cocaine suppliers and the Mexican smugglers. He heads the so-called Padrino trafficking organisation, which supplies cocaine to the United States...operates in Perú, México, Colombia, and Honduras.[36]When US pressure was finally applied on the military, they promptly arrested Mata and secretly moved him to the United States. With that, a major link between the Colombians and the Hondurans was broken, and a big gap was left in the whole operation. It is difficult to say just what quantity of drugs is presently moving through Honduras.

Whatever drugs do move out of Honduras through the Caribbean route, rather than up through Mexico, probably leave from the Bay Islands which lie off the northern coast of Honduras. A number of conditions make this an ideal transshipment point. Aside from the obvious geographical one of being able to escape the surveillance of US radar and being within range of the Colombian islands of San Andrés and Providencia, there are ethnic and economic reasons. Settled in the early nineteenth century by English-speaking Belizeans and Jamaicans and other West Indians, the Bay Islanders share a common ethnicity with the inhabitants of other archipelagos in the Western Caribbean as well as similarities in economic life. Besides fishing, the Bay Islanders have traditionally served as crew on regional and oceanic vessels and engaged in small-scale smuggling. For the past two decades, the islands have been experiencing a boom in the tourist industry, and the once-peaceful islands are now littered with pleasure craft of all sizes and nationalities but with little surveillance and control by the Honduran armed forces. The islands are ideal stop and drop-off points for the flow coming through any group of neighbouring islands.

In Honduras there appears to be a differentiated situation: on the mainland, the tendency was towards localisation; on the offshore Bay Islands, the Colombians probably had the upper hand. In the final analysis, however, the major movement up to Mexico, Guatemala, and the United States went through the local cartel dominated by Mata Ballesteros. Colombian operations appear to be exercised through subordinates on the islands of San Andrés y Providencia.

Dominican Republic and Puerto Rico

It should come as no surprise that the drug trade and the accompanying corruption of officials are today a major problem in both Puerto Rico and the Dominican Republic. At a 'Technical Anti-Drugs Summit' held in Puerto Rico in May 1995, the head of Puerto Rico's DEA office spoke of the Colombianisation of the region.[37] He was not the first to so characterise it, but the characterisation seems especially apt for the situations in Puerto Rico and the Dominican Republic. The most tragic evidence that this is indeed so is the increase in professionally executed murders of those in the trade, of those combating the rot, and of those involved and soiled but fallen from grace. There is also a real effort to influence the nation's politics. In late March 1996, Puerto Rican authorities seized $511,592 in $20 bills hidden in food cans. The destination was the Dominican Republic and there, according to the then Dominican drug czar, Contraalmirante Julio Cesar Ventura Bayonet, it was an attempt by Dominican narcos to influence the upcoming elections.[38]

Today, the first point of contact for the Puerto Rican operators is the Dominican Republic. The rest of the Caribbean plays an essentially supporting role to this US/New York/Miami/Puerto Rico/Dominican Republic axis. The DEA claims that Colombians are directly organising groups and routes in the Dominican Republic. It is nevertheless indisputable that the Dominicans have a formidable set of their own organisations. Michael Woods claims that the role of Dominican criminals has 'dramatically evolved' as a result of their association with the Colombians. Previously, Dominicans were limited to acting as pickup crews and couriers assisting Puerto Rican criminals in drug-smuggling ventures. 'Now,' says Woods, 'Dominican traffickers are smugglers, transporters, and wholesalers.'[39] Through their infrastructure support from Colombian traffickers, they have been able to dominate a significant portion of the market in US east coast cities. Like the Jamaicans, the Dominicans have created truly binational societies between the US and the Dominican Republic. The US-based Dominicans are called Dominicanyorks and are resented in the Dominican Republic, in major part because they have been stereotyped as being drug dealers. They are, of course, not all drug dealers, but there is no doubt that there are powerful Dominican drug rings operating in New York with very tight contacts with the trade back home.

Additionally, with no Dominican legislation against money laundering, the Dominican drug lords have literally flooded the island with dollars and in that way have penetrated the island's banking, business, judiciary, police, and even Congress. According to much of the growing literature on the subject, this penetration and corruption of the Dominican system has taken place virtually unhindered and certainly with near-total impunity.[40] The establishment of a new Dominican National Directorate for Drug Control is part of the expansion of such local efforts throughout the Caribbean. This is one case, however, where the evidence does not warrant optimism about controlling the crime wave. One obstacle is the apparent absence of a mafia controlled by one or even a few *capos*. The state fights a Hydra of decentralised and localised gangs without hierarchy or enduring central control, opportunistically engaging in whatever conspiracies are necessary to carry on the lucrative business.

Finally, and crucially, the consequences of globalisation have swept up the Caribbean in dramatic changes. For the small nations of this region, this means closer commercial and other ties with the United States, including offshore services of all types such as tourism, banking, electronic betting, and medical schools. Puerto Rico has 75 daily flights to the mainland and no exit immigration controls. The seaport of San Juan is the third busiest in the United States. Competing with San Juan to be the hub of inter-Caribbean trade and transportation is Miami, a virtually open city and locus of many illicit activities ranging from gun-running and alien smuggling to money laundering. It is a sobering thought that any drug ship captured is only one of 111,000 vessels that entered US seaports yearly in the 1990s; less than five per cent of this traffic is ever inspected. A significant element in the mass migratory movement is the problem of the new binational criminal gangs, as we saw in the case of Jamaica- US posses and the so-called Dominicanyorks. This is a new phenomenon as far as the Caribbean is concerned, and the full implication for the islands of this growing phenomenon – the migration and then deportation of criminal aliens has yet to be fully analysed. It stands to reason that if they are considered threats to US national security, the violence they are capable of surely must be even larger threats to their country of origin.

The fact is that there exists such criminal-influenced states in the Caribbean which continue to operate democratically. Quite evidently, democratic politics has not prevented the ratcheting up of violence linked to the drug trade.

Conclusion

If at a time there was a tendency to study the potential damage of corrupt behaviour on the immediate economic development context, today the focus has expanded to include virtually all aspects of governance and development: human rights, property rights, professional standards, environmental standards, rights of women and children; as well as major aspects of the international system – money laundering. The debate over causes has moved a long way since 1968 but not in the direction of explaining its probable links with violent conflict. And yet, there are interesting insights which can be gleaned from the case studies presented here as they reflect on established theory.

To return to the two theorists with whom we started, we note that both Huntington and Myrdal coincided in the fundamental explanation they provided of the causes of corruption: the loss of a normative system in periods of rapid social change. Modernisation to both meant changes in the system of moral norms and values. As old norms and values are challenged by the demands of modern development, there is the danger that a period ensues when, as Huntington put it, the 'legitimacy' of all standards tends to be undermined. To Huntington, these are dangerous periods when the functions, as well as the causes of corruption, are similar to those of violence. Both corruption and violence are encouraged by modernisation, both are symptomatic of the weakness of political institutions. 'Hence,' he concludes, 'the society which has a high capacity for corruption also has a high capacity for violence.' Unfortunately, he does not pursue this link in depth. He moves rather to his general theoretical thrust, that the solution is not to combat corruption *per se* but to promote modernisation and institution-building, particularly political parties. The reason is evident in the general theoretical thrust: political patronage, a form of corruption, was often beneficial to political party formation and this in turn tended to reduce both major corruption and conflict.

Be that as it may, the operative part of Huntington's thesis is the notion that crisis in norms and values results in the undermining of 'all standards'. This notion is crucial to an understanding of the hypothesis that corruption's impact, while appearing to be compartmentalised, is in fact systemic. As two Latin American practitioners put it, 'Corruption erodes our faith in institutions, undermining the credibility of politicians and politics alike.'[41]

It was Gunnar Myrdal who first suggested that corrupt acts could not be isolated or compartmentalised, they invariably had systemic impacts and consequences. This explains his critique of the functionalist argument that since bribes were simply 'economic transfers', they involved no heavy societal or welfare losses. Despite the fact that his reasoning was economic, Myrdal pointed the way to a critical theoretical point: the 'ratcheting up' and 'widening out' of the effects of corruption create a 'ripple effect' which reaches all areas of society. Myrdal's focus was on bribes, only one part of what he termed 'soft' societies. His point was that where a bribe was tolerated, it became a reward which encouraged acts aimed at engendering further and larger rewards. The impact on development was evident: rather than encouraging higher efficiency and productivity, it did the opposite. To the extent that social tolerance allows the behaviour to be institutionalised, that institutionalisation becomes a costly burden and an obstruction to productivity and growth. Quite certainly this effect is evident in the case studies presented here.

Interestingly enough, other theorists have made similar arguments. Susan Rose-Ackerman is quite precise on the point that corruption may be impossible to limit to 'desirable' situations. A system which overlooks corruption in areas where it is 'economically justifiable' may find in time that corruption has spread to all aspects of the government structure. 'If trust, honesty and altruism are valuable traits in some areas of life,' says Ackerman-Rose, 'they may be impossible to preserve if dishonesty is openly tolerated elsewhere.'[42] A similar argument is advance by two Italian authors who have studied the impact of corruption on administrative efficiency, or rather, inefficiency.[43]

These views find support in the new approach taken by the World Bank which, lately, has operated on the basic premise that it is quite impossible to compartmentalise corruption. It might, as Leff, Huntington and other functionalists argue, bring advantages to specific parts of the system, but it is impossible to keep its negative effects from spreading. The World Bank has noted that persistent corruption has a high probability of undermining the legitimacy of the whole public service, often engendering a movement to change the government through violent means.[44] A similar position has been adopted by the International Monetary Fund.[45]

But as our case studies illustrate, it is not just the societal response to underdevelopment and income inequality which might be violent, the very holders of office engage in ever-increasing counter-violence to insure the continuance of their power, whether legitimate and especially when not. Corruption, says Robin Theobald, is less a promoter of political parties with ideological and programmatic goals than it is of political machines. The latter are loose coalitions of vested interests which have one goal; staying in power. 'Once in power,' says Theobold, 'the victors do everything they can to stay there – from ballot-rigging to censorship, from the imprisonment of political opponents to death squads and terror.'[46] The opposition, in turn, has few options other than to fight violence with violence. The cases of Haiti and Cuba and, to a certain extent, Honduras illustrate this.

Of course, there is also the case where a democratically-elected regime has to fight violence with violence. The case of Colombia illustrates this. But Colombia also illustrates how the erosion of public confidence, which widespread corruption brings about over extended periods, forces legitimate regimes to take even more strenuous measures which, if not successful, could backfire. The shift to a more draconian state response, as promised by 'right-wing' President Alvaro Uribe Vélez, is a direct result of the disenchantment with 'conventional' political action. Thus, an important question is: How long can that regime retain its high level of popularity if there is no reduction in violence?

In the absence of any specific deductive model linking of corruption to violent conflict, an inductively-constructed flow model is suggested (Figure 5.1). This model assumes that all major components of a social system are interrelated and that their effects are systemic. The numbers in the model refer to the specific theoretical literature from which each section is drawn.

Following the case studies presented and the flow of the model, we can conclude with two hypotheses making the link between corruption and violence.

Hypothesis 1: The greater the incentives to ratchet up the benefits of corruption, the wider the 'ripple effects' in three interrelated areas: a) decreased economic performance, including investments, b) distortions in wealth distribution with the concomitant increase in sense of relative deprivation, and c) increasing disaffection and alienation from traditional institutions.

Hypothesis No. 2: Declining economic performance, increasing senses of relative deprivation and the delegitimisation of state institutions increase the probability of violent conflict.

Figure 5.1
Corruption and Violent Conflict: Schematic Presentation Of Two fsHypotheses

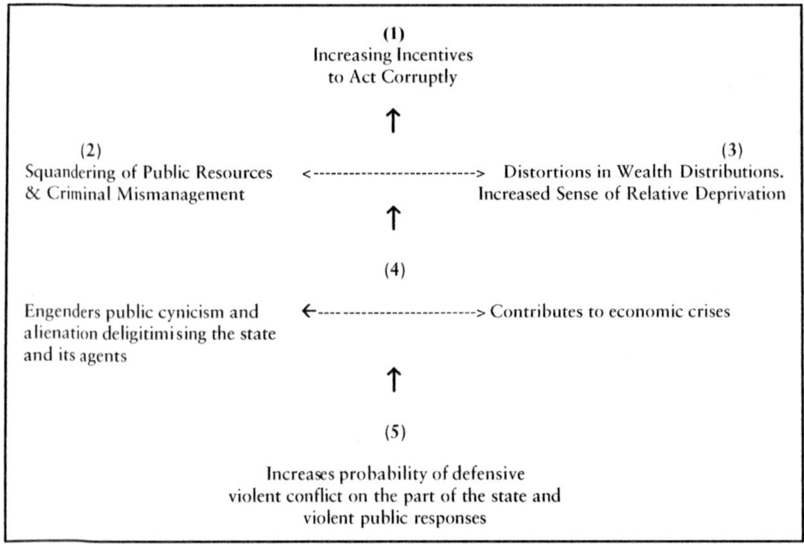

Supporting Theoretical Studies for Figure 5.1:

(1) Works by Myrdal, Rose-Ackerman and Theobold cited in study. (2) See Paulo Mauro, 1995. 'Corruption and Growth'. *Quarterly Journal of Economics* 110, 3; Paolo Mauro, 1997. 'The Effects of Corruption on Growth, Investment and Government Expenditure: A Cross-Country Analysis', in *Corruption and the Global Economy,* ed. Kimberly Ann Elliot. Washington, D.C.: Institute for International Economics). (3) World Bank, 1997. *World Development Report*. Washington, D.C.: Oxford University Press, pp. 102–104; Sanjeev Gupta, Hamid Davoodi, and Rosa Alonso-Terme, 1998. 'Does Corruption Affect Income Inequality and Poverty?' *IMF Working Papers* 98/76. Washington, D.C.: International Monetary Fund. (4) Alberto Ades and Rafael Di Tella. 1996. 'The Causes and Consequences of Corruption'. *IDS Bulletin 2* (1997), 6–10; Susan J. Pharr and Robert D. Putman, Eds., 2000. *Disaffected Democracies: What's Troubling the Trilateral Countries?* Princeton: Princeton University Press. Note the appreciation of John B. Thompson, Sociologist, Cambridge University: 'One of the

reasons scandals have become so important in our societies today is because they impinge upon the forms of trust which underpin social relations and institutions'. ('Political Scandal: Power and Visibility in the Media Age'. *New York Times,* 2/17/02, Section 4,1). (5) Hypothesised effect supported by case studies and extrapolation from existing theory.

Notes

1. *The New York Times*, 17 December, 2002, 8.
2. *Financial Gleaner*, 24 June 1994, 1.
3. Arnold J. Heidenheimer, et. al (ed.), *Political Corruption: A Handbook* (New Brunswick, N.J.: Transaction, 1989).
4. Stephen D. Morris, *Corruption and Politics in Contemporary Mexico* (Tuscaloosa, Ala.: The University of Alabama, 1991).
5. J.S. Nye, 'Corruption and Political Development: A Cost Benefit Analysis', in *The American Political Science Review*, Vol. 6 (June 1967), 417–427.
6. Jose Ortega y Gasset, *Espana invertebrada* (Madrid: Coleccion Austral [1921] 1967), 101.
7. Samuel P. Huntington, *Political Order in Changing Societies* (New Haven, Conn.: Yale University Press, 1968), 59–71,
8. Gunnar Myrdal, *Asian Drama: An Inquiry Into the Poverty of Nations* (New York: Pantheon, 1968), 951–958.
9. René Dumont, *False Start in Africa* (N.Y.: Praeger, 1966), 78–87.
10. Susan Rose-Ackerman, *Corruption: A Study in Political Economy* (New York: Academic Press, 1978).
11. See Anthony P. Maingot, 'Confronting Corruption in the Hemisphere: A Sociological Perspective', *Journal of Inter-American Studies and World Affairs,* Vol. 35 (Fall 1994), 49–62.
12. Edward C. Banfield, *The Moral Basis of a Backward Society* (New York: The Free Press, 1958), 85-86.
13. Etounga-Manguelle in *Culture Matters.*
14. Seymour Martin Lipset and Gabriel Salman Lanz, 'Corruption, Culture and Markets', in Lawrence E. Harrison and Samuel P. Huntington, (eds.), *Culture Matters*, 121–124.
15. Ibid, 120.
16. R. Klitgaard, *Controlling Corruption* (Los Angeles: University of California Press, 1988), 201.
17. Ibrahim F.I. Shihata, 'The Role of the World Bank in Combating Corruption', in Joseph S. Tulchin and Ralph H. Espach (ed.), *Combating Corruption in Latin America* (Washington, D.C.: Woodrow Wilson Centre Press, 2000), 205.
18. T. Lynn Smith, *Colombia: Social Structures and the Process of Development* (Gainesville: University of Florida Press, 1967).
19. Robert H. Dix, *Colombia, Social Structures and the Process of Development.* (Gainesville: University of Florida Press, 1967).
20. James L. Payne, *Patterns of Conflict in Colombia* (New Haven, Conn.: Yale University Press, 1967).

21. Everett E. Hagen, *On the Theory of Social Change.* (Harewood, IL: Dorsey Press, 1962).
22. *US Army's Area Handbook for Colombia* (Washington, D.C.: American University, 1961).
23. Glen Caudill Dealy, *Latin America: Spirit and Ethos* (Boulder, Colorado: Westview Press, 1992), 191.
24. Fernando Cepeda Ulloa, *La corrupción administrativa en Colombia*, 2 vols. (Bogotá: TM Editores, 1994).
25. Robert Klitgaard, *Controlling Corruption* (Berkeley, California: University of California Press, 1988).
26. Francisco Thoumi, 'Some Implications of the Growth of the Underground Economy in Colombia', *The Journal of Inter-American Studies and World Affairs* (Summer 1987), 36.
27. Francisco Thoumi, *Political Economy and Illegal Drugs in Colombia* (Boulder, Co: Lynne Reiner, 1995).
28. This section draws heavily from Anthony P. Maingot, *The United States and the Caribbean* (London: Macmillan, 1994).
29. See the excellent analysis of Marika Lynch 'Police Leadership in Haiti Worries Foreign Observers', *The Herald*, April 1, 2003, 3.
30. Quoted in *The New York Times*, March 29, 2003, 4.
31. For a full transcript of the trial and evidence see *Narcotráfico, Crimen Sin Fronteras* (Habana: Editorial José Martí, 1989). See also, Andres Oppenheimer, *Castro's Final Hour* (New York: Simon and Schuster, 1992); Jean-Francois Fogel and Bertrand Rosenthal, *Fin de Siglo en la Habana* (Bogota: TM Editores, 1994).
32. Anthony P. Maingot, 'The Decentralization Imperative and Caribbean Criminal Enterprises', in Tom Farer (ed.), *Transnational Crime in the Americas* (New York: Routledge, 1999), 143–170.
33. *Semana* (Bogotá), 21–28 Febrero, 1995, 27.
34. *Cambio 16* (Bogotá), 3–10 April, 1995, 35–46.
35. This section draws heavily from Anthony P. Maingot, 'The Decentralization Imperative and Caribbean Criminal Enterprises', in Tom Farer (ed.), *Transnational Crime in the Americas* (New York: Routledge, 1999), 143-170.
36. Testimony in the US Senate Committee on Foreign Relations, *Drugs, Law Enforcement and Policy*. Part 3. (Washington, D.C.: Government Printing Office, 1988), 154.
37. *El Nuevo Dia* (San Juan), 18 May, 1995, 26.
38. See Sandro Calvani, Foreword, UNCDCP, No One is an Island. Bridgetown, Barbados, February 1997, 1.
39. Interviews, Miami DEA Field Division, 6 Dec. 1995.
40. The literature on drug-related corruption in the Dominican Republic is growing rapidly. See the following works by M.A.Velazquez Mainardi, *El narcotrafico y el lavado de dolares en Republica Dominicana* (Santo Domingo: Editora Corripio, 1992) and; *Corrupcion e impunidad* (Santo Domingo: Editora Tele-3, 1993.)
41. Edmundo Jarquín and Fernando Carrillo-Flores, 'The Complexity of Anticorruption Policies and Latin America', in Joseph S. Tulchin and Ralph H. Espach (ed.), *Combatting Corruption in Latin America (*Washington, D.C. The Woodrow Wilson Center Press, 2000), 193.
42. Susan Rose-Ackerman, *Corruption: A Study in Political Economy* (NY: Academic Press, 1978), 8.
43. See Donatella della Porta and Alberto Vannucci, *Corrupt Exchanges* New York: Aldine De Gruyter, 1999). Chapter 9 (2), 'The Vicious Circles of Corruption' is of particular importance to the hypothesis advanced in this study.

44. While at first shying away from such wider 'political' assessment, the Bank changed its reporting policy in the early 1980s. See, *World Development Report, 1997* (New York: Oxford University Press, 1997), 102–104.
45. See Sanjeev Gupta, Hamid Davoodi, and Rosa Alonso-Terme, 'Does Corruption Affect Income Inequality and Poverty?' IMF Working Papers 98/76. Wash. D.C.: International Monetary Fund, 1998.
46. Robin Theobold, *Corruption, Development and Underdevelopment* (Durham: Duke University Press, 1990), 128–29.

6

The Menace of Drugs

Trevor Munroe

Introduction

Before and after 9/11 the Caribbean has been at the centre of the world of drugs but very much on the periphery of the world of terror. As such, for at least a decade before the September 2001 terrorist attack and its consequential highlight of the connection between international terrorism and drug trafficking, Caribbean leaders and citizens have been expressing anxiety about the magnitude of the drug problem whilst more or less ignoring the issue of terrorism. At the beginning of the 1990s the West Indian Commission set up by the CARICOM Heads of Governments and constituted by eminent leaders of the Caribbean private sector and civil society concluded that, 'CARICOM countries are threatened today by an onslaught from illegal drugs as crushing as any military excursion.'[1] This assessment was evidently shared by the man in the street. The Commission reported that:

> in .... consultations in country after country, the anxiety of citizens about these dangers... have been raised consistently. There is acute awareness that in our small societies, they spell disaster for people, for institutions, for values, for the fabric of society itself; and there is concern that the menace is steadily growing.[2]

A decade after the publication of this Report and ten Heads of CARICOM Governments Conferences later, the anxiety of the people and the concerns of the leadership remain. A MORI International survey of public opinion[3] in six

Eastern Caribbean states found in February – March 2001 that drugs and related issues of crime/law and order ranked second only to employment/jobs in the peoples' perception of the major problems facing these countries. In December 2001, continued leadership anxiety led to the convening of the 'high level meeting on Drugs and Crime' in Port of Spain attended by 24 governments, six overseas territories, nine international organisations and 12 regional institutions. This meeting heard grim words from host Prime Minister Panday, 'that there had been an increase in the addicted population with more drugs staying within the region' and that there was 'a close and undeniable connection between the illicit drug trade ... and the commission and financing of crimes and the emergence of underground communities characterised by gang culture'.[4] In the same vein, the 22nd Conference of Heads of Government held in Nassau, Bahamas in July 2001 had 'expressed concern over the new forms of crime and violence that continue to pose threats to the Region's security'.[5] The Heads set up a Regional Task Force on Crime and Security, one of whose areas of central focus would be, 'to examine the interconnected nature of the newer forms of crime, which involve illicit drugs and arms, and money laundering.'[6]

These decades-long expressions of concern among leaders and people alike have been accompanied by impressive plans of action. In May 1996, for example, representatives of 35 states and territories, the European Union, seven inter-governmental organisations, six regional bodies, a number of UN specialised agencies and non-governmental organisations met in Bridgetown, Barbados and produced a Plan of Action for Drug Control Coordination and Cooperation in the Caribbean.[7] Its 67 recommendations encompassed the development of national drug bodies and master plans in each territory, the elaboration of legislative measures, effective law enforcement, demand reduction as well as maritime and aerial cooperation. A year later, in May 1997, the first ever summit in the Caribbean between a US President and Caribbean Heads of Government endorsed the Barbados Plan and added new areas of joint US-Caribbean action in the regional anti-drug struggle.[8] A Caribbean drug control coordination mechanism was set up under the auspices of the UNDCP and periodically reviewed significant progress made in implementation of the Barbados Plan. In December 2001, a high level meeting on Drugs and Crime was held in Port of Spain, Trinidad and Tobago to further review progress in putting the Barbados Plan into effect.

Despite these efforts, however, on the eve of 9/11, the Caribbean remained at the centre of key aspects of the global illicit narcotics trade. In 2000, a little over one-third of the global supply of cocaine was intercepted and the Caribbean/Central American zone ranked number four in the world in terms of cocaine seizures. Three Caribbean territories (Bahamas, Cayman Islands and Jamaica) were among the top 20 countries in terms of cocaine interdiction. [See Figure 6.1].

'In 2001, the countries and territories that comprise the Caribbean region accounted for aggregate seizures of 24.7 MT of cocaine, 112.9 MT of marijuana, 223 kilos of heroin and over 115,000 ecstasy tablets.' With only 0.5 per cent of the world's population, the law enforcement agencies of the region contributed 7.4 per cent of the global seizures of cocaine.[9] For cocaine, heroin and marijuana this represented a significant increase over 2000 and the trend continued into 2002. 'The total amount of cocaine going through the region increased to over 400 MT'[10] and close to 50 per cent of the cocaine introduced into this US$35 billion United States cocaine market in 2001 passed through the Caribbean corridor. As Figure 6.2 shows, this was somewhat more than the percentage of the drug introduced into the United States through the Mexican corridor.

In relation to other drugs, the export market for the Caribbean's initial 'drug of choice', marijuana, has fallen victim to local production of the crop particularly in the United States and Canada. Eradication in the Caribbean territories and seizures of marijuana in the transit zone and at US ports of entry have, in effect, operated as protectionist barriers and allowed for home-grown, 'import substituted' ganja cultivation to assume dominance in the North American market. 'Caribbean marijuana has been displaced from its traditional export markets – the United States, Canada and the United Kingdom – by high quality local production, both in-doors and outdoors... the marijuana market in the Caribbean is now an internal common market rather than an export-oriented production'.[11] Concomitantly, marijuana generates only a tiny fraction of revenues now compared to that derived from cocaine trafficking. Overall, these two drugs dominate the Caribbean illicit narcotics scene, though there is evidence of the gradual introduction of heroin and ecstasy into the regional trade.

Money laundering has been a significant derivative of narcotics and other organised crime in the Caribbean. Six Caribbean territories – Antigua and Barbuda, The Bahamas, Cayman Islands, Dominica, the Dominican Republic and Haiti – are amongst the major money laundering countries 'whose financial institutions engage in currency transactions involving significant amounts of proceeds from international narcotics trafficking'.[12]

Figure 6.1 Global Cocaine Supply

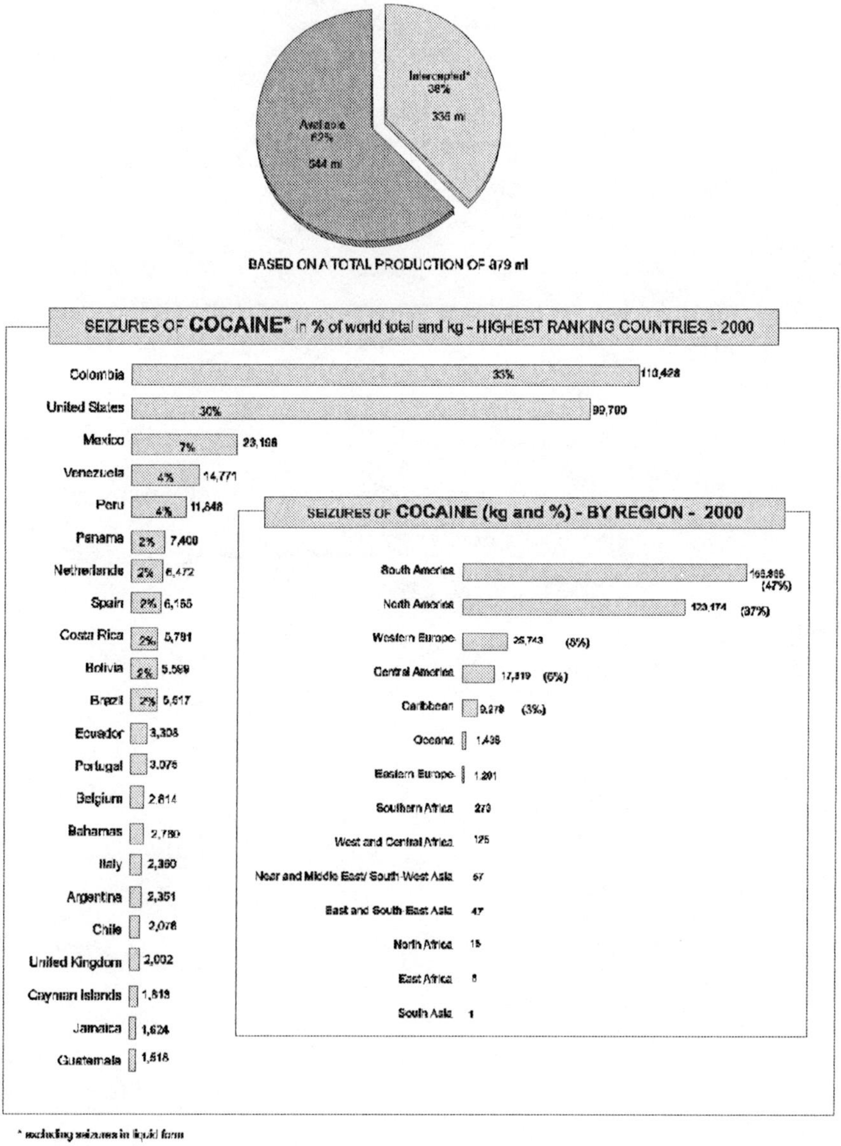

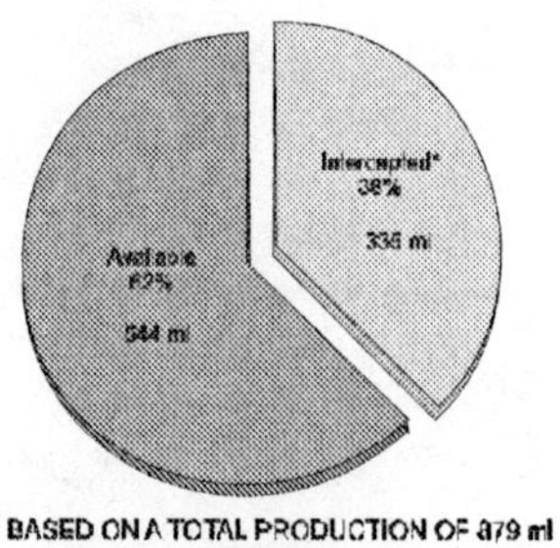

BASED ON A TOTAL PRODUCTION OF 879 mt

SEIZURES OF **COCAINE*** in % of world total and kg - HIGHEST RANKING COUNTRIES - 2000

Country	%	kg
Colombia	33%	110,428
United States	30%	99,700
Mexico	7%	23,198
Venezuela	4%	14,771
Peru	4%	11,848
Panama	2%	7,400
Netherlands	2%	6,472
Spain	2%	6,165
Costa Rica	2%	5,791
Bolivia	2%	5,599
Brazil	2%	5,617
Ecuador		3,308
Portugal		3,075
Belgium		2,814
Bahamas		2,780
Italy		2,360
Argentina		2,351
Chile		2,078
United Kingdom		2,002
Cayman Islands		1,819
Jamaica		1,624
Guatemala		1,518

SEIZURES OF **COCAINE (kg and %) - BY REGION - 2000**

Region	kg	%
South America	166,866	(47%)
North America	123,174	(37%)
Western Europe	25,743	(8%)
Central America	17,319	(6%)
Caribbean	9,278	(3%)
Oceania	1,438	
Eastern Europe	1,201	
Southern Africa	273	
West and Central Africa	125	
Near and Middle East/ South-West Asia	67	
East and South-East Asia	47	
North Africa	15	
East Africa	8	
South Asia	1	

* excluding seizures in liquid form

Source: United Nations Office for Drug Control and Crime Prevention, Global Illicit Drug Trends, *2002.*

Figure 6.2
Cocaine Introduced in the United States by Corridor, 1981-2001 (by percentage)

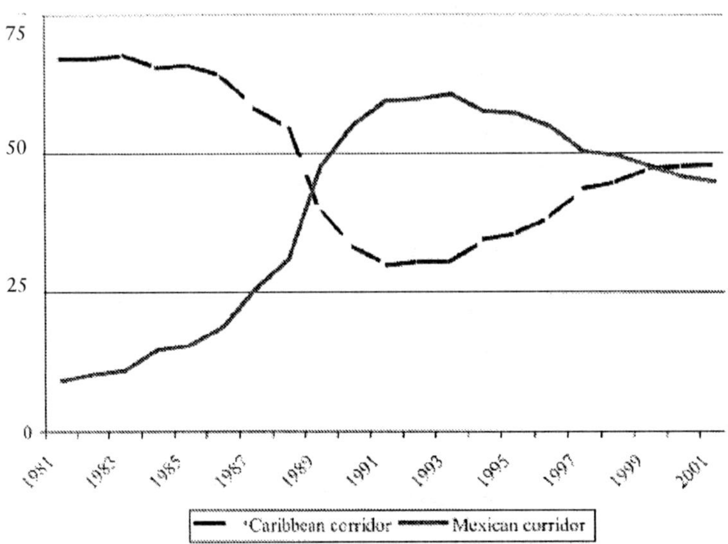

Source: Caribbean Drug Trends 2001-2002

Table 6.1 Cocaine Seizures, 1994–2002 (in Kilos)

	2002	2001	2000	1999	1998	1997	1996	1995	1994
Anguilla		926	0	0	0	0	289	611	342
Antigua and Barbuda	51	767	24	26	1	126	6	115	130
Aruba	469	266	346	465	794	408	203	153	146
Bahamas	2,450	1,468	2,774	1,857	3,347	2,565	115	392	492
Barbados	47	83	81	138	35	88	36	248	246
Belize	10	3,850	13	38	1,221	2,691	470	845	143
Bermuda		667	13	392	11	4	23	9	20
British Virgin Islands		1,334	534	0	75	838	1,765	1,194	457
Cayman Islands		1,001	1,813	1,402	1,213	1,054	2,219	143	5
Cuba		1,278	3,145	2,444	956	1,444	7,905	372	238
Dominica	4	6	10	83	29	101	3	7	1,652
Dominican Republic	1,100	1,908	1,307	1,071	2,337	1,225	1,341	4,391	2,888
French Guiana	46		25	446	3	213	9	64	0
Grenada	77	83	103	43	44	21	1,224	95	10
Guadeloupe		593	292	593	3,222	66	91	0	6,211
Guyana		31	164	37	175	167	45	51	76
Haiti	264	436	594	380	1,272	2,100	956	1,357	716
Jamaica	3,390	2,948	1,656	2,455	1,143	414	254	570	179
Martinique			15	36	46	37	17	0	0
Montserrat		0	0	0	0	1	0	1	60
Netherlands Antilles	28,939	1,043	n/a	18	639	1,302	710	11	906
Puerto Rico		2,831	5,516	9,977	10,344	15,153	11,072	12,512	15,167
Saint Kitts and Nevis	30	20	53	10	1	150	0	6	420
Saint Lucia	152	63	110	122	58	8	20	27	18
St Vincent & Grenadines	13	0	50	15	13	1	2	13	61
Suriname	340	2,510	207	180	283	117	1,413	0	219
Trinidad and Tobago	227	616	303	137	79	31	180	95	342
Turks and Caicos		4	0	0	2,075	1	393	45	20
TOTAL	37,609	24,732	19,148	22,365	29,416	30,326	30,761	23,327	31,164

Source: Caribbean Drug Trends 2001–2002; US Department of State, International Narcotics Control Strategy Report 2002.

Counter-Narcotics Measures[13] – Significant But Ineffective?

Awareness of the serious dangers of the drug menace led Caribbean states to take significant steps to implement the Barbados Plan of Action. By the end of 2001, national drug bodies were established by legislation in Barbados, Cayman Islands, Cuba, Dominican Republic, Jamaica and St Kitts & Nevis. Some assistance from the OAS/CICAD was provided to develop national drug control strategies. Mechanisms were set up to facilitate regional international coordination and cooperation – in particular the Caribbean Drug Control Coordination Mechanism (1997), the Regional Coordination Mechanism (RCM – 1998), the Caribbean Drug Information Network (CARDIN – July 2001).

In terms of legislative reform, all states ratified and implemented the UN Conventions on illicit drugs, with the exception of St Lucia in relation to the 1971 convention, and have been bringing domestic drug control laws in line with international conventions. Most jurisdictions in the region have modified traditional rules of bank secrecy, introduced anti-money-laundering legislation and have taken steps to implement recommendations of the Caribbean Financial Action Task Force. It should be noted however, that most asset seizure and forfeiture provisions have not been extended to the proceeds of all serious crimes, as recommended in the Barbados Plan, but are restricted to assets derived from drug crimes. Bilateral mutual legal assistance and extradition treaties, asset sharing and counter-narcotics agreements have been entered into. A CARICOM Regional Justice Protection Agreement providing for regional cooperation in the area of witness protection programmes has also been signed. Between 1998 and 1999, coordinated programmes of training to address money laundering issues were held for investigators, prosecutors, magistrates and judges in Belize, Guyana, Barbados, Jamaica, Trinidad, the Bahamas and St Lucia.

In terms of law enforcement, significant steps were taken to strengthen information exchange between Caribbean states. Towards this end, with assistance from France, the Netherlands, UK and USA, most states have either established or are in the process of setting up a national multi-agency law enforcement headquarters. Regional law enforcement organisations, such as the Association of Caribbean Commissioners of Police (ACCP), organise regular periodic meetings. A regional drug law enforcement training centre network was established, though reviews of national training needs have been inadequate. Equally, the development of closer Caribbean and Latin American coordination and cooperation has lagged. Where, however, such cooperation has been institutionalised, as between Jamaica and Colombia, there have been markedly positive results. For example, the largest cocaine seizures in Jamaica took place in August and September 2002 when speedboats were intercepted by joint Colombian/Jamaican counter-drug operations[14] facilitated by agreements signed between Jamaica and Colombia in April 2002.

These largely supply side measures were accompanied by efforts at demand reduction. Integrated programmes have been developed in most jurisdictions but resource constraints have meant that much of the anti-drug educational material has drawn heavily on external sources and been culturally inappropriate. There has been significant inter-regional cooperation in the review of demand reduction programmes through meetings convened at least annually by the Regional Coordination Mechanism, the CARICOM Inter-governmental Task Force, the UNDCP, and the OAS/CICAD. By and large however, the sustained collection of data on substance abuse on a national level has lagged and therefore collation and consolidation of information on a regional basis has been inadequate. Equally inadequate has been the development of Employee Assistance Programmes at the workplace.

Overall, while there has been undoubted progress in the development and implementation of Caribbean counter-narcotics plans, these have clearly fallen short. Resource shortfall from both CARICOM states and extra-regional partners has seen a deficit of social and political will to make the legislative and law enforcement changes with the urgency and thoroughness necessary to cope with the magnitude of the drug invasion on the region. Most of all, the absence of alternative development programmes in territories experiencing sluggish and inequitable economic growth, high levels of youth unemployment, rapid contraction of traditional export agriculture and an onslaught of materialistic values through intense exposure to North American media – all contributed, despite resistance, to the continuing drug menace in the Caribbean.

The Multi-Dimensional Impact Of Drugs

This menace in particular, the trafficking and consumption of cocaine, has been having a devastating effect on Caribbean civil society. This devastation has been most apparent in Jamaica but, more recently, Guyana, Trinidad and Tobago as well as smaller Eastern Caribbean states have been experiencing similar symptoms.

Rates of violent crime and, in particular, murders have risen considerably. Jamaican homicide rates place the island among the top five murder capitals of the world.[15] The illegal gun is the weapon of choice. Drug-related murders, reprisal killings and turf wars account for almost half of all murders. Transnational criminal enterprises set up by local branches and local gangs became international through the illicit cocaine trade and the associated trafficking in small arms.[16] One authoritative 1998 study identified almost 150 gangs operating in Jamaica, six of which were characterised as having high levels of activity and of organisational structure. These latter were engaged in transnational drug trafficking, extortion, money laundering and arms dealing. These gangs utilised violence to secure internal discipline, deterring external threats and for purposes of intimidating witnesses. Difficult policing environments in the context of heavily armed criminals have contributed to excessive use of lethal force and credible allegations of extra-judicial killings by the police. Conversely, fatal shootings of police officers by gunmen, particularly in Jamaica, rank among the highest in the hemisphere. These circumstances severely undermine the rule of law, an essential framework for the flourishing of civil society.

Table 6.2
Shootings in Jamaica

Fatal Shooting by Police, Security Guard, Soldier and Licenced Firearm Holder

Year	Amount
1982	236
1983	254
1984	358
1985	273
1986	179
1987	205
1988	181
1989	162
1990	148
1991	178
1992	145
1993	91
1994	125
1995	144
1996	164
1997	177
1998	156
1999	169
2000	169
2001	188
2002	170

Period	Annual Average	% Change
1980s	231	
1990s	150	-35%

Source: Ministry of National Security & Justice, Jamaica

Fatal Shooting by Police, Security Guard, Solider and Licensed Firearm Holder (1995-2002)

Years	Police	Security Guard	Soldier	Licenced Firearm Holder	Total
1995	131	4	0	9	144
1996	148	7	0	9	164
1997	149	13	5	10	177
1998	145	3	0	8	156
1999	151	8	0	10	169
2000	140	8	1	20	169
2001	148	9	4	27	188
2002	133	11	3	23	170

Year	No. Police Killed
1995	4
1996	10
1997	13
1998	14
1999	8
2000	11
2001	15
2002	16

Source: Ministry of National Security & Justice, Jamaica

The erosion of this framework paralyses entire communities, particularly in inner cities. Anarchic tendencies coexist with systems of alternative community justice. Fear of gunmen contends with fear of the police. Both contribute to personal insecurity, to low levels of job creation, sustained threats on the right to life, and frequent restrictions on freedom of movement amongst ordinary citizens. Associational life in these conditions is severely circumscribed and very often subordinated to the drug dons. Protection rackets and extortion also disrupt normal relationships.[17] In the latter regard, kidnappings, previously little known, are on the increase particularly in Guyana[18] and Trinidad and Tobago.

On the level of social values and behaviour, especially among the youth, drugs have had a seriously deleterious effect. In communities in which drug money flows, those involved in the drug business are invariably the most cash rich, drive the most luxurious vehicles, wear the most fashionable clothes and live the most lavishly – despite lack of education and despite the absence of legitimate economic activity. Given these role models, fractured family structures and limited opportunity in the legal economy, young people are socialised to elevate the drug culture and to depreciate the value of lawful behaviour, educational achievement, hard work, thrift and enterprise.

At the level of the state, the impact of drugs has been no less destabilising than in relation to civil society. Those involved at different points in the illicit narcotics trade – whether as producers, consumers, traffickers, money launderers or service providers – all have an interest in bribing political and governmental functionaries. Customs officials, members of the security forces, judges, prosecutors, correctional officers, politicians, bankers – to name but a few – are all at risk as potential facilitators of the drug trade. At the same time, the huge sums of money available to the trade make corruption of state officials not only possible but also likely. Certainly, both popular perception and elite opinion converge on the high incidence of drug-related corruption in the Caribbean.[19]

Indeed, there is much evidence of the role of drugs in corrupting state officials.[20] In 1984, following a Commission of Inquiry into drug-related corruption in the Bahamas, five government ministers resigned or were dismissed following exposure of questionable practices. In 1985, the chief minister and minister of commerce and development of the Turks and Caicos Islands were found guilty of drug related charges after a DEA investigation. In 1987 and 1988, in Trinidad and Tobago and St Lucia respectively the commissioners of police left office following drug corruption allegations. In 1990 in Antigua, in 1993 in Trinidad and Tobago, in 1994 in St Kitts and Nevis corruption allegations were found to be credible against senior ministers of government and whole sections of the police force.

In the new millennium, renewed anxieties have surfaced concerning drug-related corruption and the state. These have to do with the financing of election campaigns, political parties and election candidates. The Anglophone Caribbean is among the least regulated regions in the world on issues of political finance and, by and large, political parties are still regarded, under the law as private clubs.[21] There is no requirement of registration; no obligation to declare sources of party or election campaign funding; no prohibition relating to the sources from which donations may come or any limit on party campaign spending. Regulations relating to individual candidate election expenditure are often honoured in the breach.[22] Needless to say, there are no provisions for public funding of parties or of campaign expenditure.

At the same time, election expenditures have grown enormously across the region. Caribbean elections remain labour intensive but voluntary labour is now less available compared to the period of decolonisation and post-independence statehood. As a general rule, 'party workers' now have to be paid. At the same time elections in the region, as elsewhere, have become much more capital intensive. Expensive print media and television advertisements demand relatively considerable financial resources. In the tightening economic circumstances faced by most Caribbean businesses in the age of neo-liberal globalisation, party contributions from the legal private sector are less and less adequate. The contamination of the electoral process and party finance by drug money has therefore become a 'clear and present danger' across the Caribbean.[23]

Illicit drugs also threaten the legal economy. The UNDCP estimated that US$50 billion of drug money was being laundered across the region.[24] This is well in excess of the combined GDPs of all 17 of the borrowing member countries of the Caribbean Development Bank. In 2001, the 'total drugs GDP for the Caribbean [was] US$3.684 billion',[25] a figure surpassing the national GDP of each CARICOM state with the exception of Jamaica and Trinidad and Tobago. 'With the total drug exports transiting the region estimated at approximately US$4,800 million in 2001, this figure almost triples total CARICOM petroleum export earnings (also the number one export income earning sector) for 2000 and in fact surpasses the total of the top five CARICOM domestic exports in 2000'.[26] There can be little doubt that this magnitude of drug money is bound to enter, even, in the short run, sustain significant consumption as well as production of goods and services in the Caribbean economy. The conclusions of the 2002 Report of the International Narcotics Control Board clearly apply to the Caribbean and complicate the counter-narcotics struggle, viz 'In countries with high unemployment, illicit drug production and trafficking provide considerable employment opportunities but jeopardize the development of human capital; small farmers derive, in the short term, economic benefits from illicit drug crop cultivation...'[27]

The Post-9/11 Drug Situation

September 11, 2001 had a definite impact on the Caribbean drug situation. In the first place, the horror of the terrorist attack was felt the more directly by Caribbean people as a number of Caribbean states lost citizens in this episode. Among the victims from more than 90 countries who were killed,

26 were Guyanese, 17 victims were from Jamaica, 11 from Trinidad & Tobago, three from Grenada, two from Barbados and three from other Eastern Caribbean islands. In relatively small societies even small numbers of casualties have a comparatively large impact.

The reaction of the CARICOM states was immediate. At the meeting of OAS foreign ministers on September 21, the region was unanimous in condemnation. Three weeks later the heads of government of the community met in the Bahamas in special (emergency) session and issued the *Nassau Declaration on International Terrorism: The CARICOM Response.* The heads reiterated their 'unequivocal condemnation of terrorism in all its forms' and expressed firm commitment 'to fulfilling... individual and collective obligations under the UN Security Council Resolution 1368 (2001) and UNSC 1373 (2001) adopted by the UN in the fight against terrorism'.[28]

From the point of view of the Caribbean drug situation, two things are worthy of special note about the latter Security Council resolution, 1373, adopted just 17 days after the 9/11 terrorist attack. Firstly, the resolution noted 'with concern the close connection between international terrorism and transnational organised crime, *illicit drugs*, money laundering, illegal – arms trafficking....' Secondly, the resolution emphasised 'the need to enhance coordination of efforts on national, sub regional, regional and international levels in order to strengthen a global response to this serious challenge and threat to international security'.[29] Taken together, these two points added a new dimension to both the policy making and operational aspects of the drug situation in the Caribbean as elsewhere. The war against drugs was now to be integrally linked to the fight against international terrorism. While this connection between illicit drugs and terrorist activity had, arguably, been apparent in regions of Southeast Asia and Latin America, the linkage in the Caribbean was hardly apparent. So much so that the policy declarations, the action plans and the operational activity in relation to the fight against drugs in the Caribbean made no direct connection with the war against terrorism prior to September 11, 2001.

And for good reason. The undoubted terror of drugs on Caribbean society has not involved links with international terrorist groups or activity. None of the organisations listed in the Department of States' October 2002 Report on Foreign Terrorist Organisations as having links to drug trafficking have any Caribbean connection.[30] Indeed, terrorist organisations with or without drug trafficking links have a notable absence from the region. This is not to say that there are not criminal groups and gangs which do not engage in murder, kidnapping, reprisal killings, threats of violence and intimidation to protect and advance illicit drug activity in and through the Caribbean. Very often government officials, security force personnel and innocent civilians fall victim to this violence.

In one extreme manifestation of this tendency in July 2002, the Jamaica security forces, in an intelligence-driven search for drugs and illegal weapons, came under fire from armed elements.

> In the wake of that conflict 27 persons including one member of the Jamaica Constabulary Force... and another of the Jamaica Defence Force, were killed, and several injured. The damage to property, the loss of investment opportunities and of personal income was enormous.[31]

In the Commission of Enquiry, which followed the incident, the commissioner of police testified, 'never before in our history have we encountered so many illegal weapons turned on the security forces'. To the extent therefore that the narcotics trade utilises violence as a tool against the innocent and the 'non-combatant' in order to neutralise, defeat or overawe threats to the drug business, this activity may be termed terrorist. The absence of religious, ideological or political motivation or objective does, however, justify a distinction between drug gangs engaged in terrorism to advance the drug business and terrorist groups engaged in the drug business to advance political, ideological, or religious goals. At the risk of oversimplifying the similarities and differences between the two, the means, viz terror, are similar; the objectives different.

The Caribbean has experienced the terror of criminal gangs but not, so far, the terror of religious-political groups involved in illicit drugs. Of course, this distinction can be over-drawn. 'Narco-terrorism' for financial gain is no more nor no less terrorist than 'narco-terrorism' for political objectives. The suffering of the innocent is the same no matter the motivation nor the purpose of terrorism. Moreover narco-terrorists of one variety very often strike up alliances of convenience with narco-terrorists of the other brand. Indeed, narco-terrorism for 'business' can mutate into narco-terrorism for politics and vice versa. Even without mutation, the two types can and do inter penetrate as narco-traffickers pursue political purpose to provide protective cover and political groups utilise drug money for political causes – each engaging in terrorist activity as a means to their particular end.[32]

Nevertheless, it must be a matter of some note that the Caribbean – a major production and transit zone for illicit drugs – has been relatively free of terrorism particularly of the variety that produced 9/11. The region has even been relatively free of the incidents of terrorism that have scarred many

Latin American countries in the second half of the 1990s. In each of the five years ending in 2000, Latin America experienced the highest number of international terrorist attacks, yet the Caribbean subregion remained absent from the radar screen tracking global terrorism.

Figure 6.3 International Terrorism
International casualties by region, 1995-2000

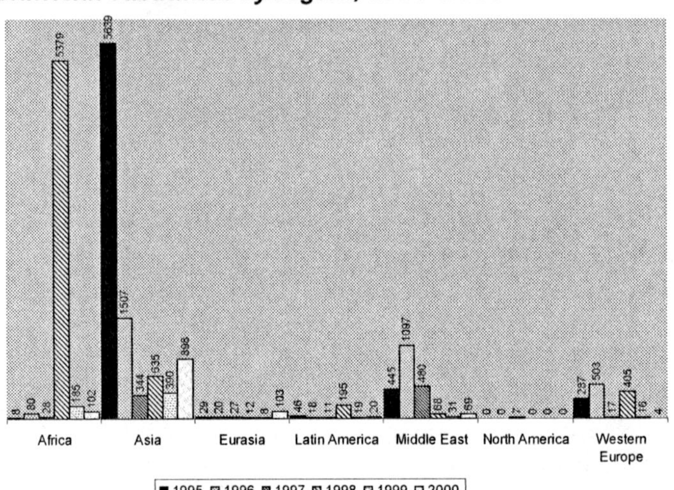

International attacks by region, 1995-2000

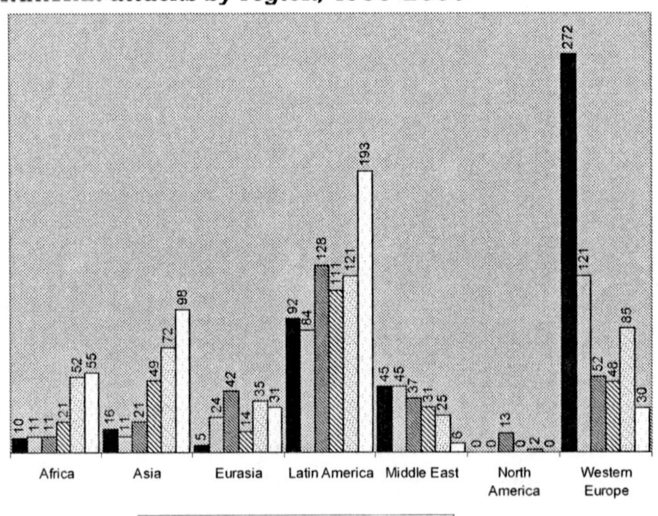

Source: US Department of State: www.state.gov.

This, of course, ought not to be a cause for complacency. And certainly inaction has hardly been evident in the aftermath of 9/11 in the region. In that regard, there has been a noticeable intensification of measures to better cope with terrorism. In June 2002 at the Annual General Assembly of the Organisation of American States, all CARICOM member states, with the exception of Trinidad and Tobago and Dominica, signed the first ever Inter-American Convention Against Terrorism. Tougher anti-terrorist legislation is being drafted or has already been passed by national parliaments. Anti-terrorist law enforcement instruments, intelligence gathering and information sharing has been strengthened across the region. Plans are underway to prepare units in the regions' security forces and infrastructure agencies to better cope with terrorist threats and attacks. In this last regard cooperation with United States and United Kingdom law enforcement bodies has been strengthened and mutual assistance has increased.

From the Caribbean perspective, however, there are two downsides worth mentioning to post-9/11 US-CARICOM collaboration in the war on drugs. One is a mismatch between the words and the deeds of the US authorities. In words, the connection between international terrorism and illicit drugs is acknowledged. In practice, however, attention to the war against drugs in the Caribbean and its potential (if not prevailing) links with international terrorism on the US 'Third Border' is being subordinated to preoccupation with *homeland security*, Afghanistan and most recently the war in Iraq. The downgrade of assets assigned to the Caribbean transit zone was evident before 9/11.[33] In the months following the attacks, however, the shift became more dramatic.

> Some three-quarters of the United States Coast Guard cutters, helicopters and other assets and a large part of the personnel that were used to search the scene – especially the Caribbean area – were reassigned to protect warships, nuclear power plants and oil tankers in American ports, to escort cruise ships and other terrorism-related tasks. About half of the Coast Guard's special agents who usually investigated drug cases were shifted to commercial jets as air marshals.[34]

Moreover, *The Financial Times* (September 12, 2002) reported that the FBI moved some 400 agents out of counter-narcotics operations to counter-terrorism task forces.[35] Acknowledging the reality, a 2002 DEA Brief confirmed the post-9/11 'reallocation of law enforcement, intelligence and military assets from counter narcotics to counter terrorism'.[36] This evident shift prompted the United National International Narcotics Control Board to urge 'Canada, the United States and countries in Europe as the main destinations for drug shipments not to reduce their drug control assistance in favour of measures against terrorism but to look for new ways to combine both'.[37]

Not surprisingly, therefore, after brief downturn, evidence suggests that the volume of drugs transiting the Caribbean increased and the rate of interdiction declined after 9/11. 'The volume of illegal drugs confiscated in the Miami seaport fell by 37 per cent after the terrorist attacks... the partial response to fewer resources dedicated to drug related enforcement activities'.[38] At the same time 'go-fast' boat activity between Colombia and the Caribbean increased in 2002 over 2001.[39] Accordingly, one authoritative report concluded:

> the amount of cocaine crossing the Caribbean may be expected to rise in the following years because the balance of American security between the two alternative routes (Mexico and the Caribbean) has changed – increased security in the Mexican border and reduced sea patrolling in the Caribbean – changing with it the cost structure offered by drug traffickers.[40]

Not surprisingly, this revival in the central Caribbean sea route has been accompanied by closer collaboration between South America and Caribbean drug operators, in particular an upgrading of relations between Jamaican and Colombian cocaine enterprises.[41]

Map 6.1
Major Cocaine Trafficking Routes in the Caribbean

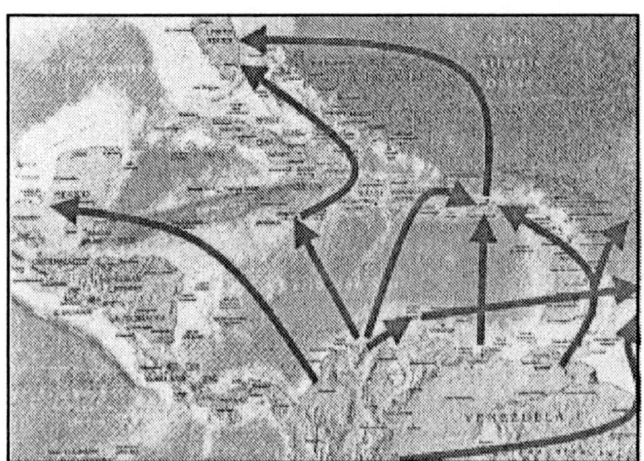

The second concern, from a Caribbean point of view, is a discernible divergence between a multi-dimensional view on security threats predominating in the region and the more narrowly focused law enforcement emphasis of the US authorities. This difference emerged at the June 2002 OAS General Assembly in Barbados. The multi-dimensional approach, in essence, places traditional security concerns, including drug-related crime and terrorism, in the context of the need to tackle factors contributing to negative security environments. In particular, security issues can be dealt with more effectively if, at the same time, conditions underlying poverty, sluggish economic development, inequality and social exclusion are also confronted. At the OAS General Assembly, Barbados Prime Minister Owen Arthur reportedly stressed that 'any meaningful definition of security can no longer be limited to the traditional military operations, but must recognise the need for an integrated approach conforming to the conditions which create instabilities in our societies and which endanger our humanity.'[42] In contrast, US secretary of state, Colin Powell, emphasised more traditionally-defined concerns and called for 'an inter-American declaration on hemispheric security, to be adopted at the special conference to be held on security'.[43]

This divergence reflects a serious and continuing historic deficit in coming to grips with not only the Caribbean but the global drug situation. The 1998 UN General Assembly's Twentieth Special Session had called for a balanced and integrated approach between demand reduction and supply interdiction in waging the war against drugs. Special emphasis was laid on the role of alternative development in drug control and development cooperation. The Action Plan adopted by the Special General Assembly on International Cooperation on the Eradication of Illicit Drug Crops and on Alternative Development stipulates the latter:

> as a process to prevent and eliminate the illicit cultivation of plants containing narcotic drugs and psychotropic substances through specifically designed rural development measures in the context of sustained national economic growth and sustainable development efforts...[44]

The 'specifically designed rural development measures' to displace illicit crops were, to some extent, evident in initiatives undertaken by Bolivia, Colombia and Peru regarding coca bush and Pakistan, Lao People's Democratic Republic, Afghanistan and Myanmar regarding poppy cultivation. In the Caribbean, one significant alternative development project was undertaken in Jamaica.[45] In general, however, there has been a huge gap between the stated resolve to undertake alternative development and the allocation of resources towards this end:

> With the exception of the main countries affected by illicit cultivation of coca bush and opium poppy, the majority of countries had not adopted alternative development programmes. In the case of Cannabis, only Brazil reported conducting some kind of alternative development.[46]

The Review of Progress after five years of implementing the recommendations of the 1998 Special General Assembly concluded that support for alternative development fell short and that:

> the international community must redouble its efforts to mainstream... the implementation of alternative development programmes into programmes and development assistance frameworks of multi-lateral and regional development agencies and financial institutions.[47]

The Caribbean has been undoubtedly among the regions that have suffered the most from the absence of alternative development strategies in dealing with the drug situation. Indeed, the decline in traditional export agriculture, accelerated by the reduction in preferential market arrangements and the processes of trade liberalisation, has savaged rural life in many CARICOM states. In the absence of viable and sustainable alternative development programmes, this decline is giving renewed impetus to the cultivation of marijuana and new opportunities for the cocaine trade. This situation is unlikely to change without 'the multi-dimensional' approach to security issues in general and the drug situation in particular.

Conclusion

Before and after 9/11, the drug situation in the Caribbean constitutes a clear and present danger to Caribbean society. Transshipment of cocaine from South to North through the region and associated illegal arms trafficking and money laundering is threatening to destabilise Caribbean civil society, economies and democratic governance. The absence of international terrorism from the region, hitherto a distinctive feature of the Caribbean drug situation, cannot be taken for granted. The vulnerabilities of the region, its strategic geographical location, the relative openness of its economies, politics and society, as well as the huge returns from drug operations in the area must make it attractive to terrorist groups seeking to strengthen funding for their operations.

As such, the policy responses and action plans of Caribbean states and civil societies, so far significant, nevertheless need strengthening. Law enforcement priorities related to intelligence gathering, information sharing, legislative reform and the upgrading of regional security capabilities need to be sustained and implemented with a greater sense of urgency. In this regard, the significant post-9/11 shift from counter-narcotics to anti-terrorism priorities by US agencies, whilst understandable, is shortsighted and must be corrected. The link between drugs and terrorism requires a dual focus and the raising of proactive US-Caribbean collaboration on these fronts to new levels. In addition, however, renewed efforts need to be made to develop consensus in the direction of a multi-dimensional approach to security, paying due attention to non-traditional socio-economic factors which incubate both the drugs and terrorism threats. 'Alternative Development' programmes and projects with appropriate multi-lateral support emphasised by the UN anti-drugs plan and so absent from the Caribbean must be introduced as a matter of urgency. Continued failure in this regard is bound to complicate and aggravate the growing menace of drugs to Caribbean society.

Notes

1. West Indian Commission, *Time For Action: The Report of the West Indian Commission*, The West Indian Commission, Black Rock, Barbados 1992, 352.
2. Ibid., 344.
3. Selwyn Ryan, *Levels of Satisfaction with Governance in the Eastern Caribbean and in Guyana and Trinidad and Tobago*, 1–2. http://salises.uwimona.edu.jm:1104//sa62a/satisgov.htm.
4. *Report of the High Level Meeting on Drugs and Crime*, 'Meeting the Challenges of the 21st Century', Trinidad & Tobago, 14–16 December 2001 (mimeo), 3.
5. *Twenty-third Meeting of the Conference of Heads of Government of the Caribbean Community*, Georgetown, Guyana, 3–5 July 2002, 3. http://caricom.org/23hgc-index.htm.
6. Ibid.
7. *Plan of Action for Drug Control Coordination and Cooperation in the Caribbean* 1996 (mimeo).
8. *Partnership for Prosperity and Security in the Caribbean* (incorporating the Bridgetown Declaration of Principles and Plan of Action), Bridgetown, Barbados, May 10, 1997.
9. United Nations Office on Drugs and Crime, *Caribbean Drug Trends 2001–2002*, Caribbean Regional Office, Bridgetown, Barbados, W.I., February 2003, 15.
10. Ibid., 4.
11. Ibid., 10.

12. US Department of State, *International Narcotics Control Strategy Report 2002* (Released by the Bureau for International Narcotics and Law Enforcement Affairs, March 2003) Introduction, 3. http://www.state.gov/g/inl/rls/nrcrpt/2002/html/17940pf.htm.
13. The overview of drug control measures draws substantially on the UNDCP Caribbean Regional Office's report – *Progress in Implementation of the Plan of Action For Drug Control Coordination and Cooperation in the Caribbean* (mimeo).
14. *The Jamaica Gleaner*, August 14, August 20, September 12, 2002.
15. United Nations Office on Drugs & Crime, *Seventh United Nations Survey of Crime Trends and Operations of Criminal Justice Systems*, covering the period 1998–2000, 11–12.
16. Donna Moncrieffe, *Gang Study: The Jamaican Crime Scene*, The Ministry of National Security & Justice, November 1998, unpublished monograph.
17. Caroline Moser and Jeremy Holland, *Urban Poverty and Violence in Jamaica*, The World Bank, Washington D.C. 1997.
18. In the months leading up to mid-April 2003, there were reportedly 18 kidnappings, cf 'Kidnapped US diplomat held in Buxton Church', *Stabrock News*, April 15, 2003 http://www.stabrocknews.com/topstory.htm.
19. See also, Trevor Munroe, 'Governance under Threat: The Impact of Corruption and the fight against Corruption', unpublished paper presented to UWI Mona Academic Conference 2002, August 30 – September 1.
20. See also Ivelaw Lloyd Griffith, *Drugs & Security in the Caribbean: Sovereignty under Siege* (University Park, PA: Pennsylvania State University Press, 1997) Chapter 5.
21. Michael Pinto-Duchinsky, 'Political Financing in the Commonwealth', Workshop on *Money and Democratic Politics* organised by the International Institute for Electoral Assistance (IIEA) and the Commonwealth Secretariat in cooperation with the Election Commission of India and the Confederation of India Industries, New Delhi, 21–24 November 2001; 'Financing Politics: A Global View', *Journal of Democracy,* Vol. 13, Number 14 (October 2002), 69–86.
22. In his capacity as a senator in the Jamaican Parliament, the author asked questions of the government relating to the extent to which general election candidates or their agents had observed the requirements of the Representation of the People Act concerning reportage of candidate election expenditure. The answers indicated that a substantial percentage of candidates had not filed electoral returns within the legally required time and that none had been prosecuted for this offence.
23. *The Jamaica Gleaner*, February 24, 2002.
24. UNDCP *Activities Report*, 1998, United Nations International Drug Control Programme, Caribbean Office, Bridgetown, Barbados, 3.
25. Caribbean Drug Trends 2001–2002 *op.cit*, 6–7.
26. Ibid.
27. *Report of the International Narcotics Control Board* for 2002, 10. http://www.incb.org/e/ar/2002/menu.htm.
28. *Nassau Declaration on International Terrorism: the CARICOM Response* (Issues at the Conclusion of the Special [Emergency] Meeting of Heads of Government of the Caribbean Community, 11–12 October 2001, The Bahamas) http://www.caricom.org/archives/nassaudeclaration.
29. United Nations *Security Council Resolution 1373* (2001). Adopted by the Security Council at its 4,385th meeting, on September 28, 2001.
30. See also endnote 3, US Drug Enforcement Administration, *Statement of John B. Brown, III,* Acting Administrator Drug Enforcement Administration, before the United States House of Representatives Committee on Appropriations, Subcommittee for the

Departments of Commerce, Justice, the judiciary and Related Agencies, March 20, 2003. http://www.usdoj.gov.dea/pubs/cngrtest.

31. *Report of the West Kingston Commission of Enquiry*, Volume 1, Main Report, June 2002 (unpublished), p. vii.
32. See also Chapters 1 & 2, Douglas J. Davids, *Narco-Terrorism: A Unified Strategy to Fight a Growing Terrorist Menace* (N.Y. USA: Transnational Publishers 2002) for a useful discussion of definitions and relationships of narco-terrorism.
33. Cf Trevor Munroe 'Cooperation and Conflict in the US-Caribbean Drug Connection' in *The Political Economy of Drugs in the Caribbean*, Ivelaw L. Griffith, ed. (Great Britain: MacMillan 2000), 187–188.
34. Caribbean Drug Trends 2001–2002 *op.cit.*, 22.
35. Ibid.
36. US Drug Enforcement Administration Drug Intelligence Brief, *The Evolution of the Drug Threat: The 1980s through 2002*, 8. http://www.usdoj.gov/dea/pubs/intel.
37. *Report of the International Narcotics Control Board* for 2002 , 37. http://www.incb.org/e/ar/2002/menu.htm.
38. Caribbean Drug Trends *op.cit,* 22.
39. US Department of State, *International Narcotics Strategy Control Report 2002* (Released by the Bureau for International Narcotics and Law Enforcement Affairs March 2003) cf. e.g. The Caribbean. The Bahamas p.3. 'Detected shipment by go-fast both through the Bahamas in 2002 increased by 32 per cent over 2001.'
40. Caribbean Drug Trends *op.cit,* 23.
41. US Department of State INSCR 2002 The Caribbean *op.cit.*, 29.
42. Ricky Singh, 'Cracks in Solidarity for OAS Security Strategy', *Guyana Chronicle*, June 4, 2002. http://www.landofsixpeoples.com/news02/nc206046.htm.
43. US Department of State Remarks at the Organisation of American States General Assembly, Secretary Colin L. Powell, Sherbourne Conference Centre, Bridgetown, Barbados, June 3, 2002, 2.
44. *Declaration of Feldafing*, Germany, January 2002, Feldafing Conference on the Role of Alternative Development in Drug Control and Development Cooperation.
45. cf Ivelaw L. Griffith and Trevor Munroe, 'Drugs & Democracy in the Caribbean' *Journal of Commonwealth & Comparative Politics*, Vol. 33, No. 3 (November 1995), 372.
46. United Nations Economic & Social Council, *Commission on Narcotic Drugs 46 Session*, Vienna, 8–17 April 2003, Report of the Executive Director, 12.
47. Ibid., p.18.

CITATION ON FINAL PAGE.

Globalisation and Economic Vulnerability: The Caribbean and the 'Post-9/11 Shift'

Emilio Pantojas-García and Thomas Klak

Introduction

The vulnerability of the Caribbean to shifts in the international political economy has been amply documented from studies of dependency to the more recent studies of the impact of globalisation (Beckford and Girvan 1989; Klak 1998; Pantojas-García 2001). The Editor's Introduction to the proceedings of the first Conference of Caribbean Economists begins by affirming this consensus view:

> The acute degree of dependency of Caribbean economies on the world economy in general, and on the economies of their main metropolitan trading partners in particular, is an historical and contemporary fact. This dependency not only stems from the structural features which are shared, to a greater or lesser extent, with all developing economies; but also from the relatively small size of most of the countries, and their current or recent political relationships with colonial powers. (Beckford and Girvan 1989: ix)

Whatever the paradigm selected to approach the study of the Caribbean, the position of the region as colonial, neo-colonial, dependent, peripheral, or price takers within the international political and economic communities is a necessary point of departure. Hence, critical economic and political events, such as oil shocks (sharp and sudden increases in oil prices), the fall of the Berlin Wall (and the subsequent collapse of the socialist bloc), or the conclusion of the Uruguay Rounds of GATT negotiations (and the creation of the World

Trade Organization), have a critical impact on and accentuate the vulnerabilities of the Caribbean economy and polity.

Against this backdrop of enduring, region-wide vulnerability, we ask how conditions have changed since the dawn of the twenty-first century. It could be argued that 9/11 is a critical event that marks the beginning of the new century in the American hemisphere if not the world.[1] This event resulted in a major shift in the foreign policy doctrine of the United States. The concept of *homeland security* represents a new understanding of the linkage between foreign and domestic policy. Terrorism is now the centre of attention of US foreign and domestic policy alike. The axis of American foreign policy shifted from securing US interests throughout the world – i.e., *national security* – to that of *securing the integrity of its national territory* through a range of new and enhanced interventions both at home and abroad.

Put another way, the logic of 'globalisation' (the process of trans-nationalisation of political, social and economic life) has brought forth the linkage between foreign and domestic policies for the United States. The old priorities have been redefined, making international terrorism the new fulcrum of foreign policy. The twin problems of drug trafficking and money laundering, which sometimes overlap but are nonetheless distinctive, have now become subsumed under the label *narco-terrorism*. The issue of undocumented or illegal immigration to the United States is now approached from the perspective of an anti-terrorist policy aimed at securing the borders of the United States continental land mass. The available evidence shows that the 9/11 perpetrators entered through various points in the northern part of the hemisphere, the US and Canada. Nevertheless, the Caribbean and Mexico are now seen and treated as potential points of entry for terrorists.

It is important to note also that the events of 9/11 took place as the American economy was initiating a downward turn after nearly eight years of sustained growth. The convergence of recession and the fear of terrorism in the US has resulted in a heightened sense of socioeconomic as well as strategic insecurity. The calls of President Bush to the American citizenry to go on with their lives, travel and spend, have translated into more domestic travel and spending, rather than into travel and spending abroad (CTO 2002: 9). This cut-back of US international travel since 9/11 follows a pattern seen after the war with Iraq in 1991. Then, US citizens became more fearful of flying abroad and Caribbean tourism, otherwise unrelated to the source of fear, suffered. Responding to their president's call, American patriotism since 9/11 has been turned into an 'inward-oriented' economic device, although it has not reversed the downward trend in the US economy.

The war on terrorism, and the war with Iraq in 2003, impacted heavily on the spending decisions of the American business owners and public in general, as well as on that of its hemispheric neighbours and European allies, as oil prices show signs of instability. The spectre of unstable oil prices is compounded by the unresolved political crisis in Venezuela; the fifth largest oil exporter in the world, a major oil exporter to the United States and the only OPEC member in the western hemisphere.[2] The policy and travel shifts induced by the 9/11 terrorist attacks and the downturn of the American economy have enormous implications for the Caribbean economies, many of which depend heavily on trade and investment from the United States. According to the Caribbean Tourism Organisation, for example, the United States is the most important tourist market for the Caribbean region, accounting for approximately half of all arrivals (CTO 2002: 9). The EU and Latin America have followed a pattern similar to the United States. Cuba relies less on US tourists than the rest of the Caribbean but tourism there has similarly softened, in part because of fewer Diaspora visits.

In the aftermath of the 9/11 events, Caribbean industries such as tourism and offshore banking have been affected negatively in the short-term. But the negative impact to these economic sectors is not attributed to a single critical event but rather to a series of developments that were already unfolding before 9/11, as we explain below. Moreover, the shift in US foreign and domestic policies entails foreseeable negative medium and long-term consequences for the Caribbean economies. Preoccupied with the war effort in Iraq and the political situation in the Middle East, the United States and Europe may further neglect the importance of the need for sustained economic exchanges with the Caribbean region. Unstable oil prices and tougher controls on immigration, visa allocations, travel, and financial transactions may affect the flow and trans-national circulation of people and resources within the Caribbean Diaspora and their families living in the Caribbean region, threatening important income sources for these families (Potter et al. 2004).

This chapter pursues the issues just introduced and explores their immediate impacts on, and future implications for, the Caribbean region. We examine the impacts by dividing the discussion of the Caribbean situation temporally into the recent past, the immediate-term, and the longer-term. First, we describe how Caribbean countries have developed various new sources of foreign exchange and employment over recent decades and note the associated vulnerabilities, most of which were already clear by 9/11. This discussion provides some essential context setting for exploring the post-9/11 situation in the remainder of the chapter. Second, the chapter examines the short-term impact of 9/11, and the policies that followed, on the Caribbean economies. Third, it assesses some possible future scenarios. We conclude by summarising some of the main aspects of Caribbean vulnerability and by stressing the importance of negotiating effectively in international arenas to represent and protect Caribbean interests.

The Caribbean in the Process of Globalisation

The Caribbean was born as part of the modern global economy. Yet, until the 1970s, it was part of colonial networks that hindered international trade and investment. In the past two decades, the Caribbean Basin economies have undergone major changes and structural adjustments to open or trans-nationalise their economic spaces. In the 1980s, most Caribbean countries and territories moved the axes of their economies away from agriculture toward promoting export manufacturing. In the 1990s, a second shift began toward international services, especially tourism, offshore financial services, and other telecommunications-based services.

In the late eighties and early nineties, under the impetus of the US trade preferences known as the Caribbean Basin Initiative and the Guaranteed Access Level Program for apparel industries (CBI/GAL), Caribbean governments adopted policies to promote export manufacturing industries or *maquiladoras*. The Caribbean Basin developed into a region with one of the largest concentrations of Free Trade Zones (FTZs) in the world. The complex of Caribbean FTZs were linked to what some analysts described as an 'apparel triangle' that configured a trans-national commodity chain linking apparel and textile producers and contractors in the United States, Asia, and the Caribbean Basin manufacturing for export to the US market (Bonacich et al. 1994: 3–4; Bonacich and Waller 1994: 21–41). By 1995, the Dominican Republic, Jamaica, St Lucia, and Haiti had become the largest beneficiaries of CBI/GAL trade preferences in the insular Caribbean, with Honduras, El Salvador and Guatemala being the major beneficiaries in Central America (USITC 1996; Pantojas-García 2001: 62). Caribbean *maquiladoras* have since declined, putting additional pressure on various service industries to provide employment and revenues.

The CBI-induced entrepreneurial climate favouring greater economic openness was reinforced by other developments: the signing of the Nassau Understanding by CARICOM leaders in 1984; the successful completion of the Lomé III Convention also in 1984, and the passage of the Canadian package of preferences known as CARIBCAN in 1986 (Dietz and Pantojas-

García 1994). The positive entrepreneurial climate created by these events benefited other economic sectors such as tourism, offshore financial services, and telecommunications-based international services. The United States Agency for International Development (USAID), the Overseas Private Investment Corporation (OPIC) and other entities promoted and financed 'business missions' for American entrepreneurs looking for investment opportunities in CBI beneficiary countries. A number of small- and medium-sized companies and investing groups participated in these missions. Special programmes were set up for financing and providing risk insurance to the new ventures that came out of these missions (Pantojas-García 1985: 123; Deere et al. 1990: 168–171).

According to the Caribbean Tourism Organisation (CTO), Caribbean tourism has grown steadily since the 1970s. The creation of the Caribbean 'all inclusive' resort concept in 1976 in Jamaica, and the concerted promotional efforts of regional tourism entrepreneurs and governments through the CTO to counter the effects of the economic uncertainties created by the oil crisis in the seventies, turned the Caribbean into the major warm weather vacation destination in the world (CTO 2002: 8; Super Clubs 2002).[3] The cruise ship industry became another form of all-inclusive Caribbean package bolstering tourism in the region. While Jamaica was the initiator and has been the main beneficiary of the all-inclusive package resorts, the main beneficiaries of the cruise ship industry have been the Bahamas, the US Virgin Islands, and Puerto Rico (McKee 1988: 68–73). Companies such as Holland America, Royal Caribbean, and Carnival Cruises have made the Bahamas, Puerto Rico, the US Virgin Islands and other Caribbean countries major cruise hubs.

The growth of Caribbean tourism has been led by North American and European hotel and cruise ship companies. Chains such as Hilton, Hyatt, Marriott, Sheraton, Holiday Inn, Club Med, Cunard, Holland America Cruise, St James Beach Hotels, Leisure Canada, and Delta Hotels have operated in the region for nearly three decades. Although there are trans-national chains owned by regional companies such as Super Clubs and Sandals, the Caribbean tourist sector is highly trans-nationalised and depends on imports for food, beverages, and equipment, much of which comes from the United States or is manufactured by US and European TNCs in the region (Momsen 1998).

International offshore financial activities began to be developed in the Caribbean in the 1960s and 70s, and earlier in a few cases. From the 1960s on, Great Britain encouraged its overseas dependencies to create legislation to become Offshore Finance Centers (OFCs). The British Foreign Office pursued this policy to help generate new sources of tax and other revenues in the dependencies and thereby reduce their reliance on subsidies from the UK (Hampton and Christensen 2002).

Since the 1960s, many British dependencies have achieved independence but, as the Bahamas illustrates, the newly independent governments have continued to pursue the offshore banking sector. Quite a few OFCs came into being in the 1980s, fostered by a variety of factors including: a tightening of the financial legal structure in the OECD; a growing global mobility of electronic capital; two rapid increases in oil prices in the 1970s that created a surge in the volume of Eurodollars (dollars traded outside the United States); and a surge in other internationally-tradable currencies in search of interest-bearing deposits (Corbridge 1993). The majority of these OFCs were established among the world's smaller jurisdictions (both independent and dependent). Of the 43 offshore banking jurisdictions in existence by the early 1990s, what might be called the first wave of OFCs, the Caribbean region had the greatest concentration, 15. The others were distributed into four additional regional groups: Europe (12), Southwest Asia (5) and two clusters in the South Asia-Pacific region (9). Only two of these OFCs are in Africa – Liberia and Mauritius.

Trade Liberalisation: Turning the Caribbean into an International Service Centre

In the 1990s, other external pressures on the competitiveness of Caribbean agriculture and manufacturing exports emerged, serving to further prioritise international services as the region's economic base. The debates that led to the signing of the North America Free Trade Agreement (NAFTA) in 1994, as well as the discussions in its immediate aftermath, made clear that the Caribbean *maquiladoras* and free trade zones would be adversely affected. Indeed, in the short run, the duty free access granted to Mexico by NAFTA, combined with its low wages, devalued peso, and proximity to the United States caused the value of Mexican textile and apparel exports to the United States to grow exponentially while the value of the four larger Caribbean exporters sagged. Between 1994 and 1996, the first two years of NAFTA (using 1994 as the base year), the value of Mexican textile and apparel exports to the United States grew by 123 per cent, while the combined exports of the Dominican Republic, Jamaica, St Lucia and Haiti grew by only 14 per cent. Exports from the Dominican Republic, the largest Caribbean exporter to the United States, grew by only 12 per cent in this period. In the three-year period, previous to NAFTA, 1992 to 1994, the growth rates for these exports were 70 per cent for Mexico, 54 per cent for Jamaica and 29 per cent for the Dominican Republic, with an overall growth of 29 per cent for the Caribbean four. The volume of exports followed a similar pattern to that of export value (USITC 1996, and unpublished 1996 figures from the US International Trade Commission; Pantojas-García 2001: 61–62).

Likewise, the current wave of trade liberalisation leading to the Free Trade Areas of the Americas (FTAA) will probably result in further negative impacts for Caribbean *maquiladoras* as well as for some of its agricultural products. This was the case of the 'second' banana war in which the United States government joined with Ecuador, Guatemala, Honduras, and Mexico to complain to the World Trade Organization (WTO) that the import preferences of the European Community to Eastern Caribbean banana exporters constituted an illegal practice under the WTO system.[4] The agreement reached under the WTO conflict resolution mechanism provided increased access to US trans-nationals such as Del Monte, Dole and Chiquita to the European market. The mechanism restricted the market preferences for Eastern Caribbean exporters who are members of the ACP and signatories of the Cotonou Convention (formerly known as the Lomé Convention) and export bananas through the European trans-national company Geest (CBEA, 2003, WTO 2001a,b).

Anticipating the negative impact of NAFTA for export manufacturing, Caribbean governments and international institutions such as the World Bank's Caribbean Group for Cooperation in Economic Development (CGCED)[5] began exploring economic alternatives and, in the mid-nineties, recommended promoting international service industries such as tourism, offshore banking, data processing, consulting services, and export services as alternative economic activities (World Bank, 1994, 1996). The actual turn of events has compelled Caribbean governments to formulate economic policies that more strongly favour international services and knowledge-intensive segments of industries. Tourism, offshore financial services, entertainment, and data processing are leading the process of economic restructuring and various other initiatives to attract investment in informatics and telecommunications-based services such as telemarketing, gambling, and entertainment.[6]

Tourism

The policies of structural adjustment and economic liberalisation begun in the 1980s have turned the Caribbean into a world-class tourism centre.

The relaxation of foreign exchange controls, liberal policies for foreign ownership of property, and even relaxed requirements for acquiring citizenship have bolstered the Caribbean's role as a tourist centre. In the year 2000, the CTOs member countries received 20.3 million visitors, which is 15.8 per cent of all visitors to the American Hemisphere. According to the CTO, the Caribbean 'has evolved into a global brand as a warm weather destination... arguably [becoming] the premier warm weather destination in the world' (WTO 2002, 3, 8). Whether or not this is a benign exaggeration, the Caribbean has become a choice destination for US, Canadian, and European tourists looking for alternatives to the more expensive and (for North Americans) further away warm weather destinations such as Hawaii, the Mediterranean coast, and the Greek islands. By 2001, the Caribbean had become the world's largest cruise destination, accounting for just under half of the cruise bed days (CTO 2002, 13).

However, the revenue gains have grown significantly less than Caribbean all-inclusive tourism itself. This is because the majority of all-inclusive tourism spending for both resorts and cruise ships is done prior to the trip and/or ends up in the metropolitan countries where the tourists live and the international tourism operators are headquartered (Pattullo 1996). As has proven to be the case with other offshore services such as e-commerce, the growth of trans-national communications has generated new interest in Caribbean locations and products. However, the advanced development of communication technologies in the metropolitan centres compared to Caribbean locations means that the associated revenues continue to be concentrated in the metropolitan centres where trans-national corporations are headquartered (Klak 2002; Pantojas-García 2001, 59–60) or in offshore corporate accounts.

As one might expect, there are other constraints on Caribbean revenue gains from cruise ships. According to one Caribbean tourism industry veteran (Pattullo 1996), the cruise lines push potential ports of call to compete against one another so as to reduce landing fees. Further, the few hours that cruise passengers are in port are hardly conducive to large amounts of tourist spending, particularly spending that reaches the islands' working people as opposed to the trans-national duty free industry that clusters near the docks. On average, around 80 per cent of expenditures on cruises go to the cruise lines with the remaining 20 per cent distributed between the various ports of call (McKee 1988, 68).

Offshore Financial Services

A second wave of OFCs appeared in various parts of the world in the 1990s although, as in the first wave, they were concentrated mainly in the Caribbean. New OFCs include Dominica, Grenada, St Lucia, St Kitts and Nevis, and Belize.[7] At least 20 Caribbean jurisdictions now offer offshore banking services, more than any other region (Klak, 2002). The Caribbean region also includes five of the world's few remaining British dependencies. The Cayman Islands, Anguilla, Montserrat, the Turks and Caicos Islands, and the British Virgin Islands have all become significant OFCs, particularly for money from the United States. The British Virgin Islands, for example, now has 400,000 registered International Business Corporations (IBCs) along with thousands of other foreign depositors, but only 20 regulators. This should convey a sense of both the scale of offshore financial activity in the Caribbean region and the limited authority many OFCs have over it. Many of these second wave OFCs have come under harsh OECD criticism for allegedly harbouring tax evaders or money launderers, as discussed below.

Offshore banks typically offer depositors a range of benefits compared to banking in most core countries. These include:

- banking secrecy laws
- asset protection against creditors or lawsuits originating outside the host country
- the ability to maximise corporate returns by setting up holding companies and subsidiaries and using transfer pricing
- lower income tax rates on the earnings from bank deposits (some jurisdictions offer tax free investment categories), and
- higher interest rates paid on tax-free bank accounts (this is possible because of lower capital reserve requirements and therefore the ability to lend out a larger share of deposits)

Lucrative and secretive bank accounts are only part of the offerings of offshore financial service centres. Others include insurance, shipping registration, trusts and even citizenship.

As a result of the trends outlined above (specifically, tightening of the OECD's legal structure, growing global electronic mobility of capital, surge in the volume of Eurodollars and in other internationally-tradable currencies, and the increased range of services and benefits OFCs provide), today there is at least $5–6 trillion deposited offshore, according to the US government.

Even more striking are a variety of estimates that place 50–60 per cent or more of the world's wealth in OFCs. The enormous scale of money involved has provoked aggressive policy actions to snare a share of it by peripheral and core governments alike.

Well before 9/11 (since 1988 to be exact), the OECD began drawing attention to the 'harmful tax practices' of peripheral OFCs and was pursuing policies to bring them under financial regulations that conform to its own (Hampton 1996). Such harmonisation would of course be to the distinct disadvantage of the OFCs themselves, who benefit from being relatively underregulated. The OFCs have therefore fought the OECD efforts through a range of tactics, including the creation of international organisations to consolidate and represent their interests.

To defend regional interests, CARICOM in 2000 created the Caribbean Association of Regulators of International Business to formulate and implement strategies. Then early in 2001, Caribbean and other OFCs created the International Tax and Investment Organisation (ITIO) to represent their interests against the OECD. The ITIO represents a disparate group of 13 offshore banking jurisdictions (Anguilla, Antigua and Barbuda, The Bahamas, Barbados, Belize, British Virgin Islands, Cayman Islands, Cook Islands, Malaysia, St Kitts and Nevis, St Lucia, Turks and Caicos Islands and Vanuatu).

The united front of OECD countries against microstate OFCs began to fray when the Bush administration came to power in January 2001. The ideological basis of the dispute is in the contrast between the social democrats who predominate in Western European countries, and therefore in the OECD, and the more conservative free marketers in the Bush camp. The Bush administration wanted international banking reform limited to information exchange between core countries and OFCs. It rejected international tax harmonisation and the idea of trying to extend and enforce OECD banking rules on foreign soil (Armey 2000). However, the Bush team's opposition to the OECD campaign to regulate OFCs ended with 9/11, as discussed below.

Other Entertainment Services

The Dominican Republic now offers a range of offshore telephone services to customers in the United States and Latin America. Television and newspaper ads for 'psychic consultants' now appear throughout the western hemisphere. Calls connect to 'psychic' wage labourers in the Dominican Republic. As has become standard practice in the Caribbean in recent decades, the Dominican Republic government offers telecommunications firms tax holidays if they will set up there. The sometimes-lengthy phone calls have been profitable for US telecommunication and telemarketing firms, and for the US-based celebrities who lend their names to the psychic services. Benefits are fewer, however, for the low-wage Caribbean workers and for government budgets (Pantojas-Garcia, 2001).

Another international service that is flourishing in the Caribbean is Internet and tele-gambling. From early on, Caribbean and Central American countries realised their locational advantages. These advantages include the region's proximity to the world's largest gambling market (the United States), legal restrictions on electronic gambling within the United States, the region's 'tropical getaway' atmosphere that is attractive to North American operators (some of these entrepreneurs have boasted of making a fortune while wearing shorts and flip-flops!), a time zone within one hour of that of the Eastern US, and (for the Caribbean) convenient telephone area codes as in the United States.[8] To exploit these locational advantages, Central American and Caribbean countries established some of the world's first offshore regulatory environments for Internet gambling (Martin, 2001).

As of May 2001, there were about 1,400 offshore gambling sites in the world operated by about 250 companies. All of these online gambling sites are located outside of the United States, and most are in Central America and the Caribbean. Costa Rica hosts about 15 per cent of the world's gambling sites. Its start-up fees of less than US$10,000 are far below some Caribbean sites that charge as much as US$250,000. Host countries also charge annual renewal fees. In Costa Rica, about 3,000 workers, mostly college students and foreigners staying on after teaching English, earn US$4–5 per hour taking bets or answering customer queries over the phone. Staff includes speakers of at least nine languages, from English, Spanish, and German to Japanese, Italian and Portuguese (Delude 2000).

'Cyber bookies' operating in places such as Antigua or bookies using '800 and 900' lines operate gambling facilities that range from virtual card and bingo games to the lottery and international sporting events. Extrapolating from recent trends, the number of offshore tele-gamblers increased to about 43 million people by 2001. Besides the United States, gamblers are concentrated in Canada and Asia. The industry made at least $1.6 billion in 2000, and was projected to take in $5 billion by 2003. The industry is so sophisticated that it has online magazines and news WebPages and deals with electronic money transactions, sometimes disguised as legal financial transactions in other entertainment activities (e.g., sweepstakes) to avoid prosecution by authorities in the United States, where gambling in sports is illegal except in Las Vegas.[9] Here again, local labour is minimal and the cash 'spent' passes through the trans-national telecommunications network but does not trickle down except in the form of wages to a few operators and minimal operational costs (fees, rent, utilities).

The big casinos in the United States have not sat idly by as gambling revenues move to the Caribbean region, however. They have gotten a foot in the door by offering online gambling in which one can win prizes, but not win or lose money. The casinos are also lobbying the US government to legalise online gambling inside the country. For now, and so long as US law restricts Internet gambling within its borders, Caribbean countries that host offshore gambling sites can earn some foreign exchange and create some jobs for English-speaking or foreign language proficient residents. But this is a highly tenuous offshore services sector because its advantages would be eliminated if the US were to legalise Internet gambling.

As we can see, by the turn of the twentieth century, the insular Caribbean appeared positioned to shift from an export platform for agricultural and industrial products, to an international service centre led by tourism and financial and entertainment services. The terrorist attacks of 9/11 appear to have put a damper on the unfolding of this already-tenuous neoliberal project for the Caribbean, as the next section explains.

The Post-9/11 Shift: Short and Medium-Term Scenarios

September 11 and its aftermath have brought forth a number of issues that are immediately converging to shape Caribbean economic prospects:

- the pre-9/11 global economic downturn is now deepened and lengthened;
- US *homeland security* replaces *national security*;
- fear of flying in the US and EU depresses Caribbean tourism;
- US shifts away from multi-lateralism and toward uni-lateralism;
- the global war on terrorism overrides various pre-9/11 concerns;
- US joins the OECD to pursue regulation and oversight of offshore financial centres;
- tighter controls on entering the US restricts the trade- and circulation-dependent Caribbean; and
- the Caribbean faces economic uncertainties from its tenuous and elastic offshore service sectors.

Short-Term Scenarios

One of the immediate effects of the 9/11 attacks was a generalised fear of flying internationally among citizens of the United States and some countries in Europe (e.g. Britain, France, Germany). The stricter security measures adopted after 9/11 may also have a discouraging effect on leisure travel. The negative effect on leisure travel was reflected in a noticeable short-term reduction in travel to the Caribbean. Caribbean tourism was impacted negatively even in locations where European tourism is stronger than American tourism such as Barbados, the Dominican Republic, and Cuba. During the first semester of 2002, European tourist arrivals to the Dominican Republic declined by 17.1 per cent and to Barbados by 13.1 per cent. For Cuba, where tourism is now the major source of foreign exchange earnings,[10] arrivals during the same period declined by 15.6 per cent from Germany, 10.4 per cent from France, 8.9 per cent from the United Kingdom and 2.7 per cent from Spain (CTO 2002: 23). The data for Spain reflect a decline in the VFR (visiting friends and relatives) market category which, for Cuba, also includes many people living in the US. The VFR decline after 9/11 is the most important factor behind Cuba's slump in GDP growth from 5.5 per cent in 2000, to 3 per cent in 2001, and only 1.5 per cent in 2002.

Table 7.1 shows the dramatic contraction of tourism following September 11, 2001 for a range of Caribbean destinations. Instead of the steady growth in the number of tourists experienced over previous years, there was a decline in virtually every case. The associated revenue loss has in turn markedly reduced Caribbean imports from the US (see chapter by Palmer in this volume). The only jurisdiction that did not decrease the number of stay-over arrivals was Puerto Rico which advertised after 9/11 focusing on the fact that, as a US possession, the agencies in charge of airport and travellers' security on the island were the same US federal agencies that were doing the job at mainland US airports.

By comparing the trends for the first semester with the yearly totals, a slight improvement can be noticed after the first three months of 2002. The full year figures show a reversal of the negative trend in stay-overs for Antigua and St Lucia and a reduction in the decline for the rest of the region. The war with Iraq, however, sent tourism into a tailspin again. The CTO announced in a March 25, 2003 'War in Iraq' bulletin that there have been 'fewer cancellations than expected'. However, Air Jamaica, after surviving an $80 million financial loss in 2002, saw reservations fall by almost 40 per cent during the first two weeks of hostilities. This decline forced Air Jamaica to reduce flights to some US cities that it regularly serviced, thereby worsening the decline in passengers (Jacobs 2003). Tourism reservations for Mexico similarly declined by 17.1 per cent overall and by more than 30 per cent from US visitors (CTO 2003 a,b).

Table 7.1 Percentage Change in Tourist Arrivals: Major Caribbean Destinations 2001-2002

	First Semester		Whole Year	
Country	*Stay-Over*	*Cruise*	*Stay-Over*	*Cruise*
Aruba	-8.8	23.5	-7.1	19.5
Antigua & Barbuda	-2.1	-23.8	2.5	-23.6
Bahamas	-6.1	7.4	-1.8	9.8
Barbados	-5.8	-2.1	-1.8	0.3
Dominican Republic	-9.1	N/A	-2.6	N/A
Jamaica	-6.7	-8.4	-0.8	3.0
Puerto Rico	0.1	-17.6	3.8	-9.7
St Lucia	-0.2	-21.0	1.3	-21.0
St Maarten	-12.0	N/A	-5.4	21.6
US Virgin Is.	-5.1	-6.3	-1.9	-8.3

Source: *Caribbean Tourism Organisation, 'Tourists stop-over and Cruise Arrivals in 2002.' http://www.onecaribbean.org/information.documentodownload.php?rowid=262 (12/20/02; 4/7/03).*

The war's obvious negative economic implications for the Caribbean were enough to push CARICOM to issue a resolution in February 2003 opposing a US invasion of Iraq. The US Assistant Secretary of State for Hemispheric Affairs, Otto Reich, responded to CARICOM's declaration with a thinly veiled threat that some Caribbean leaders found patronising:

> I would urge **CARICOM** to not only study very carefully what it says, but the consequences of what it says.... We are not going to take retaliatory action or punitive measures, but the American people do listen and our Congress listens. It is not just the executive branch. These kinds of resolutions and this kind of language doesn't help lead to a better understanding between our countries (BBC 2003).

Given CARICOM's pre-existing vulnerability to exogenous forces and its trade dependency with the United States, Reich's warning is of serious concern. Reich's reaction illustrates a regional dilemma: Should the Caribbean support US policies seen as contrary to regional interests (let alone policies seen as immoral or unlikely to promote global stability), or should it prepare to face 'the consequences'?

Although the war turned out to be short in duration, its consequences are still uncertain. Caribbean tourism entrepreneurs are trying to sell the region as a secure one, unlikely to be impacted by terrorism and marginal in terms of global security concerns and oil politics (with the exceptions of Trinidad and Tobago and Venezuela). Every government and tourism organisation in the Western Hemisphere is toeing the same line: We are marginal to the Middle East conflict and we are more secure than the rest of the world.[11] The emergence of the Asian SARs crisis may indeed prove this view to be right in the aftermath of the war.

As was argued earlier, 9/11 was a critical event that concurred with the beginning of an economic recession in the United States and triggered a series of events that led to a significant shift in US domestic and foreign policies. Hence, what could be termed 'the post-9/11 shift' refers to a combination of negative factors around the 9/11 critical event: fear of flying, tighter travel security measures, economic recession, the call to Americans to continue on with their lives and encouraging domestic spending and the war in Iraq. The post-9/11 shift has thus created a new international environment that negatively impacts Caribbean economies and particularly its international services sector.

The post-9/11 shift also brought about a reversal in American international financial policy that in the short-term is likely to have a negative impact for Caribbean OFCs. The US government's opposition to regulating global financial flows ended on September 11. Within days of the attack the Bush administration reversed its earlier position and publicly advocated the use of strong sanctions 'to pressure countries with dangerously loose banking regulations to adopt and enforce stricter rules'. This regulatory offensive, coming on the heels of Bush's declaration that 'either you are with us, or you are with the terrorists', muted much of the public opposition to US policies throughout the world. Fear of landing on the enemy list became widespread. A previously defiant CARICOM under Owen Arthur's leadership issued a supportive declaration in October 2001:

> We undertake, as part of our contribution to the international coalition against terrorism, to redouble our efforts to prevent the use and abuse of our financial services sectors by fully co-operating with the United Nations and the international community in the tracing and freezing of the assets of terrorists, their agents and supporters.

Note, however, that although CARICOM commits to the anti-terrorism effort, it strategically places authority in the hands of the United Nations rather than the United States. But the Bush administration's opposition to the UN makes this manoeuvring academic.

The Bush administration is taking aggressive actions to identify and cut off international sources of financing for terrorist actions against the United States. A major component of these efforts is directed at disclosing sources of money laundering. They include blacklisting suspected individuals and organisations, freezing of assets and investigating the internal records of US banks and their foreign affiliates. The Bush team is also pressuring OFCs with bank secrecy laws to cooperate with the FBI and other US government agencies by providing information on depositors. Nearly all offshore banking centres are cooperating. The result, according to a British international financial investigator quoted in *The Observer* of London (February 24, 2002), are treaties that 'make your eyes water when you see them. It's classic US extra-territorial lawmaking.'

We should note, however, that these US efforts appear to be curiously out of sync with the basic features of the September 11 plot, as *The Economist* (October 26, 2001) observed:

> For one thing, the main asset that the terrorists had was not money, but the willingness to commit suicide. Experts reckon that the whole operation on September 11th cost no more than $200,000, which almost any determined group could raise and distribute. A second problem is that money laundering is traditionally defined as the transfer of dirty money – the proceeds of drug trafficking, for example – through the financial system in an attempt to make it look clean.... But Mr. Bin Laden's terrorists seem mostly to be doing the reverse, taking what is often clean money – officials believe that al-Qaeda is financed by donations from Saudi businessmen, often via charities – and using it for criminal purposes. This is much more difficult to detect.

It is too soon to know the full impacts of this US-led campaign against the international financing of terrorist activities on the efforts of peripheral governments to benefit from offshore banking. Developments so far suggest that the US government is casting a very wide net with its anti-terrorism rhetoric, surveillance and interventions, military or regulatory. This US campaign is likely to serve as a check on the further advance of the Caribbean and other peripheral states' efforts to reach a favourable settlement with the OECD. With the US no longer dissenting, the OECD is stronger and more unified in its prosecution of weakly regulated OFCs. All 17 Caribbean OFCs that the OECD labelled as uncooperative tax havens prior to 9/11 have since met OECD demands for tax policy reform and have cleared its 2002 blacklist (Klak 2002). The more regulatory oversight of OFCs by core countries, the fewer advantages OFCs have that can attract mobile capital, criminal or not. It is therefore probable that one result of all of this will be a reduction of capital flows through, and therefore revenues going to, Caribbean OFCs, at least the smaller, poorer, and less regulated ones.

Medium-Term Scenarios

Recession and the US war on Iraq are likely to result in increased economic insecurity. The post-9/11 crisis of US air transportation also threatens to affect negatively not only American tourism but also the cost structure of tourist packages in the Caribbean. These factors substantially affect spending on vacations abroad. The post-Iraq war international reshuffle is likely to affect Europe as well, because of its dependence on Middle Eastern and OPEC sources of oil. At the beginning of the war, Iraq was the world's ninth oil exporter and the second in oil reserves. Crises in these countries mean crises for OPEC, and the potential for higher oil prices for Europe and the Caribbean. Even though American oil reserves are high, and prices have not been negatively affected by the war in the short-term, the post-Iraq war oil market may allow companies to increase oil prices, adding to the cost of transportation so vital to the Caribbean tourism industry. The Venezuelan crisis, which is far from settled, adds to the uncertainties over the managing of Iraq's oil industry and reinforces the negative international economic climate, as it enhances the perception of potential oil shortages or corporate manoeuvring that favour oil price increases.

So, diplomatic initiatives that affect OPEC will have a substantial impact on the Caribbean, directly increasing energy and transportation costs, and indirectly reducing the spending power of the major consumers of Caribbean vacations. The reality or perception of shrinking disposable income for Americans, Europeans, and Canadians, the main Caribbean markets for international consumer services such as tourism and entertainment, will restrict their spending and will encourage them to avoid additional personal debt. Additionally, combined European and American blacklisting of offshore banking centres in the Caribbean and Asia restricts growth in heavily American-influenced areas, particularly the Caribbean, and in turn favours growth in European centres such as Switzerland, Luxembourg, Liechtenstein,

Andorra, and the Isle of Man, where, as an extreme example, financial services account for 41 per cent of GDP (Cobb 2002). Finally, the American victory in Iraq is unlikely to abate the 'fear' of terrorist attacks and fear of flying. This is bound to reduce leisure travel even to destinations outside of immediate danger of attack, as is happening already.

Fears, economic contraction, and the tightening of immigration, visa allocations, travel, and financial transactions may affect the flow and transnational circulation of people and resources within the Caribbean Diaspora and their families living in the Caribbean region. This would, in turn, threaten important income sources for these families and the Caribbean economies.

Conclusions

The vulnerability of the Caribbean to international events and economic fluctuations is a function of its role as a 'price taker' rather than a 'price setter' of international tradable goods and services. The 'pricing out' of many Caribbean economies successively as agricultural exporters, manufacturing export platforms, and now international service centres places them in the path of what could be termed 'peripheral post-industrialisation' (Pantojas-García 2001). The post-9/11 shift lays bare the persistent vulnerability of the Caribbean to international economic and political events. Their governments and entrepreneurs cannot influence the international economic and political frameworks that condition their policy options. Even in their new role as international service and entertainment centres, Caribbean economies remain highly vulnerable (arguably even more so) to changes in the international prices of commodities and trade and financial regulations. Put simply, they remain on the periphery of the globalising economy and world-system (Gwynne et al. 2003).

The OFC policies that are now under attack by the OECD and the US unilaterally are a prime example of such vulnerability. These policies were earlier promoted by some of those same core governments in the OECD. Britain encouraged its dependencies to create OFCs, while the US role was less direct. In the 1990s, Congress loosened constraints on capital leaving the country. Enron is the most notorious of the major firms that avoid US taxation through hundreds of Caribbean subsidiaries, but it is certainly not alone. One can see parallels to other sectors that were once core promoted in the Caribbean and later undermined. From the 1950s Britain heavily promoted the planting of bananas in its overseas colonies as a substitute for sugar cane when Commonwealth Caribbean sugar became 'too expensive' in the international market (Mandle 1996). Ironically, bananas now run the same fate, being priced out of the market by global trade liberalisation and lower priced bananas from Central America and Ecuador (CBEA 2003).

The post-9/11 international campaign reveals how global priorities are set. The anti-terrorism campaign demonstrates how a critical event in advanced countries can quickly and decisively shift and focus global priorities, marginalise and effectively discredit other concerns, and dominate the global agenda. In the realm of international finance, the campaign targets jurisdictions alleged to have loose financial regulations, banking secrecy, money laundering and other associated activities. The campaign provides insight into the structure of power in the contemporary world-system. Many of the earlier priority issues for people and governments outside (and indeed inside) the core regions, whether they concerned financial flows or broader themes of equity, access or ecology, have been muted.

But the Caribbean's accentuated vulnerability in the post-9/11 world cannot be interpreted as powerlessness. Non-traditional threats, fears, and security concerns in the post-9/11 world (e.g., sabotage of various sorts, drug trafficking, computer as well as biological viruses, money laundering) require different global geopolitical responses than traditional ones. Caribbean leaders have a long history of skilful negotiation with their metropolitan centres. Eastern Caribbean leaders demonstrated such diplomatic skills during the recent 'banana war'. During the negotiation sessions at the WTO, they successfully admonished international negotiators by arguing that eliminating trade preferences for Eastern Caribbean banana farmers could turn them to marijuana growers and stimulate drug trafficking, thus getting the US to retreat from its original aim of total elimination of the banana preferences under the Lomé Convention and the Cotonou Agreement. Negotiators delayed assigning the EUs tariff rate for each banana exporting country until 2006. This delay gave Caribbean exporters a reprieve of several years and leaves open the (narrow) possibility that they could still serve the EU market.

As in World War II and the Cold War, the Caribbean remains an important line of defence for the United States' security concerns. Under the new homeland security policy, combating narco-terrorism necessitates a stable Caribbean and the solidarity of the Caribbean citizens and their Diasporas living in the continental territory of the United States. The US Drug Enforcement Administration (DEA) knows well the ways in which drug lords use the Caribbean as a launching platform for the sale of drugs in the United States (DEA 2001). Clearly, small economies such as those of the insular Caribbean have limited negotiating power. But the challenge for the Caribbean leaders is to convince the United States, the European Union, and Japan that the prosperity of small Caribbean economies is crucial to demonstrating to the world that globalisation may benefit the weak and the poor. If the new global order cannot meet the needs of small peaceful nations such as those of the Caribbean archipelago, how can international organisations involved in the implementation of the global trade liberalisation agenda (the WTO, World Bank, UN Development Program, OAS, Inter American Development Bank) claim that global economic liberalisation is beneficial to all?

While it is impossible to tell the exact shape of the Caribbean negotiating agenda for the twenty-first century, some of its components are obvious. It shall include an end of the agricultural subsidies to OECD farmers, and the elimination of the double standard in looking at the activities of European financial havens *vis-à-vis* peripheral OFCs. The Bush administration will also be encouraged to recognise that the Caribbean needs real opportunities to develop service industries and that cheaper is not always better. And until a realistic phase-in program for free trade is worked out, the disadvantages of globalisation will continue to foster popular protest from Patagonia to Chiapas.

Notes

1. Prior to 9/11 there was little doubt that the collapse of the Berlin Wall and Communist Party states throughout Central and Eastern Europe and the USSR in 1989–91 marked the beginning of a new era, most notably in wider Europe. But the extent to which the world has been caught up (willingly or not) in the US-led 'war on terrorism' suggests an alternative demarcation point, particularly, as we will argue, for the American hemisphere.
2. In 2001, 63 per cent of Venezuela's oil exports went to the United States (OPEC 2001: 97).
3. John Issa, a Jamaican entrepreneur of Lebanese descent, credits himself with introducing the 'all-inclusive' hotel concept in 1976 with the Negril Beach Village resort. Issa explains on the Super Clubs home page that he devised the all-inclusive marketing strategy to counter the economic uncertainties of the mid 1970s (<http://www.superclubs.com/sc_about.sap) (accessed December 27, 2001).
4. The 'first' round of banana wars were 1898–1934 when the US government and US owned banana plantations established their hegemony in the Caribbean Basin (Langley 2002).
5. The World Bank created CGCED in 1977. It includes Antigua and Barbuda, Bahamas, Barbados, Belize, Dominica, Dominican Republic, Grenada, Guyana, Haiti, Jamaica, St Kitts and Nevis, St Lucia, St Vincent and the Grenadines, Suriname, and Trinidad and Tobago.
6. US telecommunications TNCs (Sprint, Verizon, AT&T, TRICO – subsidiary of Motorola) are taking advantage of geographical proximity, shared time zone, relaxed regulatory standards, low wages and demand for bilingual services to establish the Dominican Republic as a hub for telecommunications services for the United States Latino market. Meanwhile, the Jamaican government promoted the creation the

Jamaica Digiport International through a consortium of the privatised Telecommunications of Jamaica, Cable and Wireless and AT&T, to stimulate the development of an international data processing industry, following an agreement with the IMF and the World Bank (World Bank 1996; Mullings 1998: 144; C/LAA 1997: fs171).

7. Operators of a web site linked to Belize (but located in California) illustrates how less regulated 'second wave' OFCs attempt to lure money from the United States and/or from more regulated OFCs by making the following claims: 'You pay no taxes whatsoever, there are NO TAXES of any kind whatsoever assessed on offshore Trusts or International Business Company's formed in Belize....Compare our price of USD$1500.00 for our Premier IBC package which includes an offshore bank account, to that of a Nevada promoter who charges USD$4,995.00 for Bahamian IBC.' http://www.eclientservices.com/cgi-bin/online/the_offshore_advantage.html (accessed January 2003)
8. While writing this paper, one of the authors received an email warning that originated at Verizon and AT&T. The warning concerned a phone number with an 809 area code that US residents have been finding on their answering machines or in their email accounts with instructions to call due to a family emergency, a sweepstakes win, or some other reason. Callers have later found charges of up to $24,000 or more on their phone bills owed to a company in the Dominican Republic. Regarding Caribbean vulnerability, the most important line in the warning is: 'DON'T EVER DIAL AREA CODE 809.' Because of this scam, US customers will be less likely to telephone legitimate Caribbean businesses. For more information see http://www.att.com/fraud/home.html#three (accessed February 2003).
9. Gambling Online Magazine, http://www.gamblingonlinemagazine.com, and Online Casino News, http://www/onlinecasinonews.com, are two of the industry's magazines.
10. Tourism contributed 12.9 per cent of Cuba's GDP by 1999, up from 0.3 per cent in 1981 and 5.6 per cent in 1993. Cuba has been capturing a growing share of the Caribbean's international tourist arrivals. Its portion grew from 2 per cent in 1990 to 9.3 per cent in 1998. Like the Caribbean in general, however, Cuban tourism suffers from a high leakage ratio, with 60 per cent of revenues exported to pay for inputs (LeoGrande and Thomas 2002).
11. A feature article in the business section of *El Nuevo Día* (San Juan), highlights this point discussing alternative destinations in the Western Hemisphere such as Machu Picchu in Peru, Costa Rica and even El Salvador (not a traditional tourist destination). Elena Irazu, *Ventaja Turística la Seguridad del Caribe*. 23 de Marzo de 2003, Negocios 16.

References

Armey, D. 2000. 'Letter from US House of Representatives Majority Leader Dick Armey to US Treasury Secretary Lawrence Summers.' http://www.taxnews.com/asp/res/st_offshorefuture_28_09_00.html.

Association of Caribbean States (ACS). 1999. Declaration for the Establishment of the Sustainable Tourism Zone of the Caribbean. Second Summit of Heads of State and/or Government of the States, Countries and Territories of the Association of Caribbean States. Santo Domingo de Guzmán, Dominican Republic, 16–17 April. <http://www.acs-aec.org/Summit/English/DecSTZ_eng.htm> (May 18, 2000).

BBC (BBC Monitoring International Reports). 2003. 'CARICOM Should Rethink Its Opposition To US-Led War On Iraq, USA's Reich Says', April 3.

Beckford, George and Norman Girvan, editors. 1989. *Development in Suspense; Selected Papers and Proceedings of the First Conference of Caribbean Economists*, Kingston, Friedrich Ebert Stiftung/Association of Caribbean Economists.

Bonacich, Edna, Lucie Cheng, Norma Chichilla, Nora Hamilton, and Paul Ong, editors. 1994. *Global Production: The Apparel Industry in the Pacific Rim*, Philadelphia, PA: Temple University Press.

Bonacich, Edna, and David V. Waller. 1994. 'Mapping a Global Industry: Apparel Production in the Pacific Rim Triangle'. In *Global Production: The Apparel Industry in the Pacific Rim,* ed. Edna Bonacich et al. Philadelphia, PA: Temple University Press. 21–41.

Caribbean Tourism Organisation (CTO). 2003a. *War In Iraq: Caribbean Tourism Response Center.* Bulletin Number 1, March 25. http://www.onecaribbean.org/information/documentdownload.php?rowid=181 (April 7, 2003).

CTO. 2003b. *Mexico's Tourism Hit Hard by War.* http://www.onecaribbean.org/information/documentdownload.php?rowid=1226 (April 7, 2003).

CTO. 2002. *Caribbean Tourism One Year After 9/11.* (Prepared by Gail Clark, November). http://www.onecaribbean.org/information/documentdownload.php?rowid=850 (December 31, 2002).

Caribbean/Latin America Action (C/LAA). 1997. *1998 Caribbean Basin Profile.* Washington, D.C.: Caribbean Publishing Co., ABCE Co., and C/LAA.

CBEA (Caribbean Banana Exporters Association). 2003. 'The Dispute Settlement'. http://www.cbea.org/home2.cfm (January 17, 2003).

Cobb, Sharon. 2002. Offshore Financial Services and the Internet: Creating confidence in the use of cyberspace? Paper presented at the annual meeting of the Association of American Geographers, Los Angeles, March.

Corbridge, Stuart. 1993. *Debt and Development.* Oxford, UK: Blackwell.

DEA. 2001. Congressional Testimony. Statement by: Donnie R. Marshall, Administrator

Drug Enforcement Administration Before the Senate Caucus on International Narcotics Control. May 15. <http://www.usdoj.gov:80/dea/pubs/cngrtest/ct051501.htm>(24 January 2003).

Dietz, James L., and Emilio Pantojas-García. 1994. 'Neoliberal Policies and Caribbean Development: From the CBI to the North American Free Trade Agreement'. *21st Century Policy Review* 2, 1–2 (Spring): 17–40.

Deere, Carmen Diana (coordinator) et al. 1990. *In the Shadows of the Sun: Caribbean Development and U.S. Policy.* Boulder, Colo.: Westview.

Delude, J. 2000. 'Las Vegas of the Internet: Americans flock to Costa Rica to set up online casinos'. *The San Francisco Chronicle,* July 20, A12.

Griffith, Ivelaw L. 1995. 'The Money Laundering Dilemma in the Caribbean'. *Cuadernos de Trabajo* 4. Institute of Caribbean Studies, University of Puerto Rico, Río Piedras.

Gwynne, R., Klak, T., and Shaw, D. 2003 *Alternative Capitalisms: Geographies of 'Emerging Regions.'* London: Edward Arnold Publishers, and New York: Oxford University Press.

Hampton, Mark. 1996. *The Offshore Interface: Tax Havens in the Global Economy.* New York: St Martin's Press.

Hampton, Mark and John Christensen. 2002. 'Offshore Pariahs? Small Island Economies, Tax Havens and the Re-configuration of Global Finance.' *World Development,* 30 (9), 1657–73.

Jacobs, Stevenson. 2003. 'Caribbean leaders seek solutions to drop in tourism'. *Associated Press,* April 8.

Klak, Thomas, ed. 1998. *Globalisation and Neoliberalism: The Caribbean Context.* Lanham: Rowman and Littlefield.

Klak, Thomas. 2002. 'How Much Does the Caribbean Gain from Offshore Services?' in *The Association of Caribbean States (ACS) Yearbook* (5th Edition). Edited by Mark Blacklock. Port of Spain and London: ACS and International Systems and Communications Limited, 88–103.

Langley, Lester. 2002. *The Banana Wars: United States Intervention in the Caribbean, 1898–1934* (revised edition). Wilmington, Delaware: Scholarly Resources.

LeoGrande, William and Julie Thomas 2002. 'Cuba's Quest for Economic Independence'. *Journal of Latin American Studies.* Vol. 34, 325–63.

Mandle, Jay. 1996. *Persistent Underdevelopment: Change and Economic Modernisation in the West Indies*. Amsterdam: Gordon and Breach.

Martin, A. 2001. 'A Sure Thing'. *Harper's Magazine*, April, 96.

McKee, David L. 1988. *Growth, Development, and the Service Economy in the Third World.* New York: Praeger.

Momsen, Janet H. 1998. 'Caribbean Tourism and Agriculture: New Linkages in the Global Era?' in Thomas Klak, ed. *Globalisation and Neoliberalism*, 115–34.

Mullings, Beverley. 1998. 'Jamaica's Information Processing Services: Neoliberal Niche or Structural Limitation?' In *Globalisation and Neoliberalism: The Caribbean Context*, Thomas Klak, ed. Lanham: Rowman and Littlefield, 135–54.

OPEC. 2001. *Annual Statistical Bulletin 2001.* <http://www.opec.org/publications/AB/pdf/AB002001.pdf> (9 January 2003).

Pantojas-García, Emilio. 1985. 'The U.S. Caribbean Basin Initiative and the Puerto Rican Experience: Some Parallels and Lessons'. *Latin American Perspectives* 12, 4 (Spring): 105–128.

Pantojas-García, Emilio. 2001. 'Trade Liberalisation and Peripheral Postindustrialisation in the Caribbean'. *Latin American Politics and* Society 43, 1 (Spring): 57–77.

Pattullo, Polly. 1996. *Last Resorts: The Cost of Tourism in the Caribbean.* NY: Monthly Review Press.

Potter, Robert, David Barker, Dennis Conway and Thomas Klak. 2004. *The Contemporary Caribbean.* Essex, UK: Addison Wesley Longman and Prentice Hall.

Super Clubs. 2002. Home Page; About Us <http://www.superclubs.com/sc_about.sap> (27 December 2001; 4 January 2003).

Tradewatch Newsletter. 2000. WTO Members Move Forward in Services Negotiations. <tradewatch@carib-export.com> (7 June 2000).

United States International Trade Commission (USITC). 1996. *Annual Statistical Report on U.S. Imports of Textiles and Apparel: 1995.* Washington, D.C.: USITC Publication no. 2987.

Wilkinson, Paul. 1997. *Tourism Policy and Planning: Case Studies from the Commonwealth Caribbean.* Elmsford, NY: Cognizant Communications Corp.

Wilkinson, Bert. 2003. 'Caribbean: Unified Front on Iraq Restored Despite U.S. Pressure' *Inter Press Service*, April 17.

World Bank, Caribbean Division. 1994. *Coping with Changes in the External Environment.* Washington, D.C., World Bank Report no. 12821 LAC.

_______. 1996. *Prospects for Service Exports from the English-Speaking Caribbean.* Washington, D.C., World Bank Report no. 15301 CRG.

WTO. 2001a. *European Communities – Regime for the Importation, Sale and Distribution of Bananas, Complaints by Ecuador, Guatemala, Honduras, Mexico and the United States (WT/DS27).* <http://www.wto.org.english/tratop_e/dsipu_e/banana_e.htm> (27 July 2001).

_________.2001b. *European Communities - the ACP-EC Partnership Agreement; Decision of 14 November 2001.* <http://www.wto.org/english/thewto_e/minist_e/mm01_e/mindecl_acdp_ec_agre_e.htm> (5 January 2002).

8

The Environmental Security Challenge

Jeremy Collymore and Elizabeth Riley

Introduction

Environmental concerns have emerged as one of the critical non-traditional security challenges facing the Caribbean region in this century. These issues existed before, and continue to exist beyond the 9/11 event and span the wide spectrum of disciplines comprising *environmental studies*. They include matters related to climate change and sea level rise, natural and technological (man-made) disasters (Table 8.1), waste management, coastal and marine resources, freshwater resources, land resources, energy resources and biodiversity resources.

This brief chapter cannot hope to address the full scope of environmental security concerns facing the region. Rather, it seeks to explore some of the key issues and challenges facing regional policy makers as they address environmental security matters, such as trends in policy approaches and the implications of the two main environmental security threats faced by the region. Finally, this chapter will discuss the role played by institutional mechanisms and human resource capacity in addressing environmental security.

Table 8.1
Natural and Technological Hazards facing Caribbean States

Natural Hazards	Technological Hazards
• Hurricanes • Tropical Storms • Storm Surge • Extreme rainfall events • Floods • Drought • Landslides • Earthquakes • Volcanic eruptions • Tsunamis	• Fire • Oil Spills • Industrial accidents • Hazardous material accidents • Aircraft accidents • Shipping accidents

Environmental Security –A Definition

To facilitate discussion on *environmental security* it is first necessary to define the term and then understand its character, particularly within our regional context. Interpreted in its widest sense, the term *environment* encompasses the physical surroundings and conditions, both natural and man-made, within which any organism, group or object exists. It is this definition which is used within this chapter. *Security* refers to the secure condition of any entity, in this case the state. The term *environmental security* will therefore be defined as those environmental problems or challenges which may create or add to instability in a geopolitical region or threaten the sovereignty of a state. This *geopolitical region* may range from an individual nation to a geopolitical grouping such as CARICOM. Bearing this general definition in mind, it is necessary to outline four of the specific features which characterise the Caribbean region.

First, it must be stated that environmental security is but one component of the larger regional security challenge. It has been clearly recognised that the character of Caribbean regional security is multi-dimensional and includes not only environmental concerns but also military, political and socio-economic dimensions (Griffith 1997) with each component offering its peculiar challenge to development. Thus any attempts to address environmental security within the region must also address these larger, already emergent challenges: threats from both external and internal forces; limited capacity; internal bureaucratic politics and sovereignty and its particular power dynamics.

However, one advantage of the multi-dimensional nature of regional security is that approaches to environmental security benefit from lessons learnt and successful practices identified in dealing with these other challenges. These include: recognition of the need for collaboration among regional partners and the need to tackle problems from a national, regional and international level; and recognition of roles of both state and non-state actors. The larger security issues therefore combine with the peculiar characteristics of environmental considerations to establish the current security climate.

Secondly, environmental security within the region is characterised by a wide diversity of concerns, which impact individual states to differing degrees. Therefore, any actions taken by individual states in response to an environmental security issue depend on the degree of importance attributed to that issue. While recognising the inherent limitations of works which seek to give regional synopses, the review of regional progress towards implementing the Small Island Developing States Programme of Action (SIDS/POA, 1994) (ECLAC, 2001) provides some illustration of this. For example, climate change and sea-level rise have received significant attention throughout the region, indicated by the participation of 12 countries in the Caribbean Planning for Adaptation to Climate Change (CPACC) Project and the achievement of regional consensus on the need for a regional climate centre to address these matters. Conversely, although freshwater resources have been identified as a regional priority, at the time of publication, only Barbados, Cuba, Jamaica and Trinidad and Tobago had completed a full assessment of water resources.

The third key point is the particular vulnerabilities of Caribbean small developing states and the critical role played by the environment in the countries within our region. Small states are characterised by special development challenges which include: remoteness and isolation; a high degree of openness of the economies to global influences; a high susceptibility to natural disasters and environmental change; limited diversity in production and exports; limited capacity to address many of the challenges of globalisation and poverty (Commonwealth Secretariat/World Bank 2000). The limited size of small developing states means that environment and development are inextricably linked and inter-dependent (SIDS/POA 1994).

The final point is that environmental security issues vary in magnitude and time frame. The dynamics of addressing climate change impacts and the associated uncertainty will certainly vary as compared to addressing the threat posed by nuclear transshipments through our region. The diversity of time frames and scale associated with environmental security issues poses yet another dimension to the challenge of addressing them.

Policy Context

Within the Caribbean context, environmental security is certainly not a new concept. Recognition of the threat which non-traditional forces such as the environment can pose to small island and low-lying states is most clearly evidenced through the Programme of Action for Small Island States (1994). Subsequent to this, the special security concerns of small states have been actively promoted in a number of fora, most notably through the Summit Process and resultant dialogue within the Organisation of American States (OAS) Committee on Hemispheric Security and also within the ambit of the Commonwealth Secretariat and World Bank.

Thus, the environmental security of the region has largely been addressed at the international level under the umbrella of vulnerabilities of small states. It is the vulnerable character of our countries and region which contributes to the larger security challenges. Central to this view has been the limited resources base of these states and the heavy dependence on natural resources for economic survival. This, compounded by narrow economic diversification, renders these states highly vulnerable to the potential impact of climate change and to the extreme weather events expected to be associated with the climate change phenomenon. The role played by environmental security in the vulnerability of small states was recognised within the Quebec Plan of Action emerging from the third Summit 2000, where the Summit nations agreed to:

> Support the efforts of Small Island Developing States (SIDS) to address their special security concerns, recognising that for the smallest and most vulnerable states in the Hemisphere, security is multi-dimensional in scope, involves state and non-state actors and includes political, economic, social and natural components, and that SIDS have concluded that among the threats to their security are illicit drug trafficking, the illegal trade in arms, increasing levels of corruption, environmental vulnerability exacerbated by susceptibility to natural disasters and the transportation of nuclear waste, economic vulnerability particularly in relation to trade, new health threats including the Human Immunodeficiency Virus (HIV)/Acquired Immune Deficiency Syndrome (AIDS) pandemic and increased levels of poverty.(Plan of Action Summit of the Americas Quebec 2000)

A more detailed summary of these concerns emerged from the discussions of the OAS Committee on Hemispheric Security during a meeting convened to discuss the Special Security Concerns of Small Island States in March 2001. At this meeting, environment (particularly climate change and natural disasters) was clearly identified as one of three priority non-traditional security concerns within the Caribbean region to be addressed within the proposed model by Ferguson (2001) along with drugs and related criminal activity and HIV/AIDS.

Within the Caribbean, subsequent to 9/11, the key environmental security concepts to be tackled relate to two main areas:

1. The potential threats posed to national (and regional) security by natural systems. This refers particularly to natural disasters and climate change.
2. The potential threats posed by man-made threats to national (and regional) security particularly in the aftermath of the 9/11 event.

Regional Environmental Security Concerns

While not a new issue for the region, environmental security has certainly been identified as an area which needs to be addressed with a new urgency. The urgency associated with this matter has been recognised by the regional political directorate, and is reflected in the '...coherent activist campaign on the diplomatic plane to gain recognition of the special circumstances of small states' (Ferguson 2001). Evidence of the actions taken in this area is provided by the numerous OAS resolutions on the Special Security Concerns of Small Island Developing States.

Environmental Security Implications of Natural Disasters, Climate Change and Climate Variability

The environmental security threat posed by natural disasters and climate variability and change must necessarily be viewed as part and parcel of each other. Disasters are caused by hazards impacting upon vulnerable aspects of our built, natural and human environment and as such climate change must be viewed as one of a suite of hazards facing our region.

The vulnerability of our region to hazards is not new and past events have already exposed the severity of the security threat posed by the impact of these phenomena on our countries and on the economic, social and environmental security of the region (Table 8.2). The impact of Hurricane Gilbert (1988) on Jamaica resulted in damages equal to 65 per cent of Gross Domestic Product (GDP) (CDERA 2001a). Hugo (1989), a category 5 hurricane, resulted in damages to the value of US$ 412 million in five countries of the region. In recent times, two extreme flood events have affected the island of Jamaica – in October 2001 and more recently in May 2002 – causing significant damage to infrastructure and loss of life. The former resulted in damages estimated at US$ 48 million (ODPEM 2001). Droughts in the Caribbean are often associated with the El Niño phenomenon (CDERA 2001c). Although in most cases impacts on the natural environment are not fully quantified within damage assessments, they have also been severe and include extensive destruction of vegetation cover.

An appreciation of the true environmental security threat posed by natural hazards to the economies of small states becomes visible on examination of the impacts on critical economic sectors such as agriculture and tourism. Following the impact of Hurricane Georges in St Kitts & Nevis in 1998, the islands experienced an approximate 10 per cent decline in the 1999 tourist arrival figures as compared to 1998 (CDB 2002). In addition, The annual change in GDP (constant prices %) moved from 7.3 per cent for 1997 to 1.0 per cent for 1998 (CDB 2000). It is likely that these indicators were influenced by the hurricane impacts.

Table 8.2
Losses from Disaster in CDERA Member Countries 1970–1999

1970–1999				
Country	No. of Occurrences	Total Fatalities	Economic Losses (1998 $m.)	Economic Losses as % of GDP (1995)
Antigua & Barbuda	7	7	105.7	18.1
Bahamas	4	5	290.4	9.5
Barbados	5	3	148.4	6.3
Belize	6	5	33.8	5.4
Dominica	7	43	133.4	55.0
Grenada	4	0	30.1	9.5
Guyana	5	0	29.8	4.6
Jamaica	19	271	1,988.1	29.3
Montserrat	5	43	323.7	899.0
St Kitts & Nevis	7	6	312.5	116.5
St Lucia	8	54	1554.6	272.3
St Vincent	9	5	47.0	16.5
Trinidad & Tobago	8	9	16.7	0.3

Source: From Table 1.10 in the IDB Research Department Report, 'Natural Disasters in Latin America and the Caribbean: An Overview of Risk', October 2000.

The climate change phenomenon threatens to exacerbate these existing climatic extremes, adding a new dimension to the environmental security threat. The potential impact of global climate change to which the Caribbean region is most vulnerable are changes in sea level, sea temperature, precipitation, wind and ocean currents (MACC Project Concept Document

2001). The IPCC Working Group 1 (2001) report concludes that globally averaged surface temperatures have increased 0.6 +/- 0.2 degrees C over the twentieth century and that for a range of modelled scenarios, the globally averaged surface air temperature is projected to warm 1.4 to 5.8 degrees C by 2100 relative to 1990 (IPCC 2001). Increased average surface temperatures have associated consequences for sea level rise. Through modelling, the IPCC Working Group 1 (2001) report projects the globally averaged sea level to rise 0.09–0.88 m by 2100.

Climate change therefore has the potential to increase the frequency and severity of these climatic extremes already experienced by the region. A major concern for the Caribbean region is the potential for increased frequency and severity of tropical storms and hurricanes (IPCC 2001). During the period 1978–1988, the Caribbean region was affected by only three hurricanes of a category 4 or higher strength (www.wunderground.com, 2002) on the Saffir-Simpson Scale (Table 8.3). In contrast, during the period 1989–2001, 11 hurricanes of either category 4 or 5 strength affected the region (Table 8.4).

Table 8.3
Saffir/Simpson Hurricane Scale

Category	Central Pressure Mean (millibars)	Winds mph (km/h)	Surge (ft)	Damage	Example of a Storm
1	980 or more	74–95mph (119–151km/h)	4–5	Minimal	Anges 1972
2	965–979	96–110mph (152–176km/h)	6–8	Moderate	Kate 1965
3	945–964	111–130mph (177–209km/h)	9–12	Extensive	Elena 1985
4	920–944	131–155mph (210–248km/h)	13–18	Extreme	Hugo 1989
5	less than 920	more than 155mph (248km/h)	more than 18	Catastrophic	Gilbert 1988

A further threat posed by the climate change phenomenon is that of sea level rise. It is anticipated that the effects of sea level rise will be highly variable both among countries and within them (IPCC 2001; Nicholls 1998), and that coastal areas will be most vulnerable. The coastal zone of many of the Caribbean nations is home to a large percentage of the population; in Guyana this figure is approximately 90 per cent (Nicholls 1998). Moreover, a large percentage of the critical infrastructure and tourism infrastructure is located in this critical zone. Over 65 per cent of the approximately 77, 500 hotel rooms in the Commonwealth Caribbean are located in coastal areas (Jackson 2002).

Table 8.4
Category 4 & 5 Hurricanes Affecting the Caribbean 1979-2001

Year	Name	Maximum Sustained wind speed (mph)	Minimum Central Pressure (millibars)	Category Saffir-Simpson Scale
1979	David	170	924	5
1980	Allen	190	899	5
1988	Gilbert	185	888	5
1989	Hugo	160	918	5
1992	Andrew	155	922	5
1995	Luis	150	935	4
1996	Hortense	140	935	4
1998	Georges	155	937	5
1998	Mitch	180	905	5
1999	Floyd	155	921	4
1999	Lenny	155	933	5
2000	Keith	135	942	4
2001	Iris	140	950	4
2001	Michelle	135	933	4

Source: www.wunderground.com (Accessed June 4, 2002).

A number of studies have been undertaken utilising various methodologies for assessment of coastal vulnerability to sea level rise. Nicholls (1998) gives an informative review of many national and regional analyses. Nicholls cites Kahn & Sturm (1995) who utilised the IPCC Common Methodology to examine the vulnerability of Guyana to accelerated sea level rise. Results estimate that, given a 1 m rise in sea level and present conditions, 400,000 people (rising to 600,000 in 2020) would require relocation. In addition, in the absence of adaptation measures, the country could sustain billions of dollars in damage and losses. National level assessments on the impacts of sea level rise have been carried out, often on selected sites within the countries of Nevis, Antigua and Barbuda. What has been identified from these studies is the need to assess potential impacts of damage through detailed inventories of coastal resources and infrastructure. In addition, as suggested in the results of the Guyana study, relocation as a broader disaster management issue may require examination.

In summary, the security concern posed by the potential impact of climate change on the region is a function of the level of risk posed by the potential hazards combined with the level of vulnerability within countries. From a climate change perspective, vulnerability is defined as 'the degree to which a system is susceptible to, or able to cope with, adverse effects of climate change, including climate variability and extremes' (IPCC 2001). Within the region as well as within countries, therefore, there will exist large variations in levels of vulnerability to climate change impacts and, by extension, variations in the level of environmental security concerns.

Policy Responses

CDERA has made numerous capacity-building interventions within the region to enhance preparedness and response capability including training in emergency telecommunications, shelter management, community disaster preparedness, relief supplies and donations management and Emergency Operations Management. The adoption of Comprehensive Disaster Management (CDM) has provided a framework within which the role of both state and non-state actors has been recognised and defined. However, the vulnerabilities exposed in past experiences combined with IPCC projections highlight the need for urgent strengthening of preparedness and response capability at the national and regional levels.

Disaster Management Implications of 9/11

September 11, 2001 highlighted a dimension to regional environmental security to which little attention had previously been paid, that of technological or man-made disasters. Whilst the potential threats of oil spills, aircraft or boating accident and nuclear transshipment have always been identified as environmental security concerns, the threat of biological and chemical weapons has introduced an environmental security concern for the region which challenges the traditional role and approach of the emergency manager.

Hazard Management and Disaster Planning

Terrorism adds new dimensions to the principles of Hazard Management and Disaster Planning. Whilst the fundamental tenets of a disaster management system — threat identification and analysis; monitoring, alert and warning; evacuation; shelter; relief and recovery — are still essential to the management of the consequences of a terrorism event, an effective response to such an event is highly dependent upon effective organisation and communication (Demuth and Platt 2002). However, evaluations of recent disaster events and disaster management in the Caribbean highlighted inherent weaknesses in these two critical areas. (Collymore 1999, 1995, 1992, 1989).

Therefore, in seeking to develop effective consequence-management systems building on current capacity it will be important to fully reflect on the lessons learnt from recent natural impacting events. It is also important to note that, despite the similarity in the consequences of a terrorism event and natural or technological hazard, the issue of causation is critical. Terrorism is the deliberate causing of harm (Platt 2002) and is often calculated, cold blooded and may even be 'criminal'. Additionally, the manifestations of terrorism events are largely unpredictable as to form, location and magnitude and the effects may spread more rapidly than those generally associated with technological and natural hazard events (Bloem, 2002). What this suggests is that the time and resource demands for managing the consequences of terrorism-related events will amplify significantly the short-comings in our emergency management systems. In seeking to improve the organisation and communications for preparedness and response planning there is a need to reassess the process for determining the threats that can compromise our development, their probability and consequences that flow there from.

Disaster Management

Disaster management is one dimension of the environmental security portfolio that clearly highlights some of the critical policy and strategy issues confronting small island developing states in this Age of Terror. It allows for an easy definition of how traditional policies and approaches must be altered to deal with the challenges of this emerging environment security agenda. More importantly, it provides a framework within which to consider the utility of the Ferguson model for security management.

The basic tenets of the Ferguson model are that:

- issues of environment and security are of trans-national or global importance;
- they involve several actors thus requiring clear definition of roles and responsibilities at national, regional and international levels; and
- the roles and functions must be managed in a comprehensive and holistic approach.

Efforts to recognise and forge the links between environment, disasters, development and security initially raised in Agenda 21 (UN 1992) and the United Nations Convention on Biological Diversity, have been constrained by the essential characteristics of smallness and fragility. The issues associated with this Age of Terror, the consequences of weapons of mass destruction (WMD) have reinforced the global dimension of the problem and its solution as well as the need for multi-level actions within a coordinated mechanism. These two driving forces, national and international security considerations and the need to protect the environment, seek to ensure that potentially hazardous biological and chemical materials are not abused (Pearson, 1997).

The tenets of the Ferguson Security Management model are underpinned by two cross-cutting themes, communication and organisation. The communication component encompasses those issues associated with threat assessment, monitoring, alerting, responding and recovery as well as collection, collation and analysis of information and its dissemination for support of decision making are primary activities here. Organisation embraces the institutional arrangements and relationships that allow for the sharing and application of the information for preventative and countermeasure programmes and policies. It elaborates the roles and functions of the multi-level actors and the mechanism and processes for their coordination and cooperation.

The major natural hazards which threaten the Caribbean include hurricanes, volcanoes and earthquakes. They are trans-bounding in nature, even through an event may be experienced in a particular jurisdiction. The effective preparedness for and management of an event requires monitoring and information sharing from several activities and from a diversity of players (Scott, Berridge, Collymore 1994). This is so for the hurricane hazard and especially so for the seismic and volcanic hazards.

Currently, preparedness and response planning systems are marginally fact based. They are seldom informed by hazard identification and analysis, including probability of occurrence and related consequence scenarios. This shortcoming has been recognised and within the last decade there have been periodic interventions to address these. Building on these initial efforts, the Caribbean Hazard Mitigation Capacity Building Project (CHAMP) and Caribbean Disaster Management Project (CADM) are seeking to provide a more systematic approach to the development of regional capacity for fact-based disaster management interventions. The CDB, through its DMFC, is also committed to and partnered with this process.

Clearly, in preparing themselves for this Age of Terror, the emergency management systems in the Caribbean will need to focus on the new threats, and on changes to our monitoring and warning systems, the roles and relationships of the actors, the nature of Damage Assessment and Needs Analysis (DANA), equipment and operational standards and the legal authority associated with them. Terrorism brings additional threats that result in widespread death and disease and the destruction of societal infrastructure (Jenkins 1997).

Threat Assessment

National and regional emergency managements, in this era of terror, will need to assess the threats to the environment, paying particular attention to the probable nature of consequences and the implication for monitoring and management. The September 2001 and anthrax experiences in the United States have signalled the need to examine the potential use of biological and chemical agents for the spread of disease, widespread death and the disability of critical societal infrastructure including transportation, food water and utility supply.

The nature of the monitoring systems to be established will be informed by the character of the threat in each jurisdiction and its cross-boundary implications, whatever the agent of transfer. Biological and chemical agents require different kinds of preparedness and response systems (McSwegan 2000) which add to the capacity demands of already weak institutions with limited budgets. Threats associated with chemical agents are likely to be acute, localised and immediate while biological agents (other than toxins) may be more subtle, their effects less immediate and less discernable, with the potential for very widespread dissemination.

An important dimension of this assessment process in the Caribbean must be an examination of the current biological and chemical agents in our society and the potential for causing significant disease and death by intent or through negligence. The second element of the threat assessment process must be the determination of the possible opportunities for the introduction of these agents into our jurisdiction with intent to create mass destruction. Indeed, this process should be urgently initiated to allow for a more informed consideration of the WMD risk in the Caribbean and targeted strategic policies and programmes to address these.

In the context of the Ferguson Model, the issues of priority, the incorporation of new actors and levels of intervention are important. Firstly, when the results of the threat assessment are analysed there will be a need to determine how terror-related WMD hazards rank when juxtaposed with our traditional hazards, especially natural hazards. Prioritisation will involve consideration of not only the consequences of threats, irrespective of source, but of the capacity to change the loss potential there from, the short and medium-term investments required in counter measure planning, the probability of occurrence and the existence of international, regional or bilateral arrangements that can support the process.

New actors and new relationships between existing actors will also be required. The results of threat assessments for natural and technological hazards, except for those that are terrorism based, are usually public knowledge, even if not utilised. Threat assessments for terror hazards are usually restricted to the security forces and elements of the diplomatic community, even though the consequences will be required to be managed by a much wider set of players (Ferguson 2001).

The nature of the new threats associated with terror calls for several layers of cooperation. At the national level, this entails more organised and structured dialogues between the security and emergency management community. It will also require more regional and international cooperation among security forces (already emerging in the fight against drugs) and stronger civil and military protocols for sharing threat information.

Monitoring, Alert and Warning

In the Caribbean, our infrastructure for monitoring the hazards that are more predictable in terms of form, location and seasonability have been subject to ongoing concern (Scott, Collymore, Berridge 1994 and 1990 RAIV Meeting Report). Even for the most frequently anticipated and experienced hazard, the tropical cyclone, the monitoring equipment has been, generally, limited. Only now are the defective radars within the region being replaced. The Seismic Research Unit is now beginning to acquire some important resources to enhance its monitoring capacity.

The monitoring of new environmental and security-related threats, such as sea level rise and WMD, will impose a substantial additional demand on already weak monitoring systems and stretched fiscal resources. Given the dependence of reliable response and preparedness systems on effective monitoring and surveillance this must be at the frontier of our capacity development. It is also an important first step in improving the communications in our response operations (Demuth and Platt 2002). If biological or chemical agents are critical hazards to our community then some investment in enhanced surveillance systems that include instrumentation for better detecting these agents will be required. The more efficient use of existing metal detection systems and basic surveillance practices are immediate low-cost options for improving current practice.

The use of the monitoring information to generate alert and warning decisions will require more integration of the threat information databases and networks, and ongoing analysis of the threat situations. Since much of this information may now fall in the realm of *national intelligence* or be classified *highly restricted*, careful and immediate consideration must be given to the timing and the modes of its access by the alert-and-warning decision makers and consequence managers, who are not now normally included in the intelligence/security group.

Beyond that, there must be concomitant investment in the training of the medical and scientific partners in rapid diagnostic approaches so that monitoring information can result in timely and appropriate alerts and or warnings. Given the security elements associated with terrorist activities, the integration of the databases of the actors in this widened monitoring network will require reflection on data validity and integrity issues, capacity constraints and privacy. The idea of a national electronic network to monitor reports of unusual medical events and medical databases from hospitals and other sources, including emergency agencies to provide real-time valid information, critical detection and early warning, has already been proposed (Waeckerle 2000).

In the Caribbean, the Caribbean Epidemiology Centre (CAREC) and Caribbean Security Chiefs (CANSEC) mechanisms provide an embryonic infrastructural foundation upon which the idea could be built to forge links between intelligence and disease monitoring. The Caribbean Information Sharing Network (CISN) provides a potential technological framework for accommodating cooperation in this area, within specific invited communities around a common goal whilst still maintaining secrecy.

Response and Relief Operations

A recent CDERA audit of disaster preparedness within its 16 participating states indicated that despite the number of hazards to which they are exposed, and which have been experienced, there is a low level of readiness for disasters other than hurricanes. Even for this event the capacity is highly variable (CDERA 2001). Many hazard preparedness plans are very detailed and generally effective up to the pre-impact phase but inadequate in managing post-impact situations. This, despite the many models and guidelines developed for such critical areas as shelter management, relief policies, emergency housing assistance, donations management and supplies management.

Response planning, which includes consideration of terrorist mass destruction events, raises many issues centred around roles, responsibilities and authority. It necessitates intense consideration of the civil-military relationships in disaster events management. Already in the Caribbean, there is an ongoing effort to build the operational parameters for civil-military relations in disaster response (CDERA Regional Coordination Plan 1998). These plans and operational guidelines do not address the issue of security. Even with this infrastructure in place, which is frequently reviewed and exercised, there is still an inclination to see the military as the primary manager of disaster events resulting from natural and technological hazards.

The inclusion of terrorism consequence management in the response planning of the Caribbean Disaster Emergency Response Agency has a high potential for straining the tenuous civil-military coordination arrangements. A terrorist originated disaster will require health emergency response and law enforcement. Authority and control in this very dynamic operating theatre needs to be proactively considered and addressed.

Saving lives of victims of the event, whilst minimising potential for loss of other lives, requires the engagement of both emergency health professionals and detection and law enforcement personnel. The safety from terror and safety from the consequences thereof mandates the establishment and understanding of a common incident management and decision making protocol. Early dialogue on the character of Incident Management Systems that accommodates the functional integration of personnel from different organisations is required. These operational integrative mechanisms are built on standard terminology, protocols for chain of command, communications and flow of information and an emphasis on logistics planning (Christen et al 2001). The Unified Management Systems approach may provide the framework for defining the actors and the nature of their engagement at the varying levels of operation – national, regional and international. It also provides a mechanism through which performance and equipment standards can be agreed upon and cooperative training and capacity development structured.

The Regional Response Plan, managed by CDERA, attempts this, with the exclusion of security issues. It establishes monitoring and alerting protocols, communications and information flow protocols, command and control principles and minimum resource commitment levels. Enhancing this system to accommodate management of terrorism consequences could be a first point of departure in addressing the issues of communication and organisation in the restructured efforts to protect the environment and improve security and safety. Whilst an enhanced Regional Response Plan Mechanism can provide the operational blueprint for addressing the issues of agency and jurisdictional coordination, these must be founded on basic national actions and decisions in relation to authority and legality.

The threat of terrorism will demand further innovations from regional response mechanisms. Psychological preparedness for catastrophic events with extensive loss of life, devastation of social and physical landscapes is a new element of preparedness and response planning for environmental security in this Age of Terror. Only recently have we in the Caribbean started to address the issue of trauma management amongst victims and emergency workers. Contingency plans for managing public hysteria and disruption of health care delivery systems will be an essential addition to response planning (Simon 1997). More attention will need to be paid to the adoption and application of Critical Incident Stress Management Systems as part of the disaster planning dispensation.

This capacity and capability can be achieved through regional and international cooperation in plan development and training. There will also be a need to determine if there is a legal authority to mandate mass vaccinations, quarantining or evacuation, if considered essential (Cole 1997). These require national-level actions and decisions that can be informed by lessons from regional and international states. Terrorism consequence management as a key element of our environment security challenge will also necessitate a revisit of current relief and recovery policies. Presently, these are very rudimentary in the CDERA Community, though guidelines exist (CDERA Disaster Relief Policy 2000). In addition, the issue of the role and nature of support to and from the private sector will loom large.

Contaminated environments will necessitate more pre-event consideration, not only in relation to the nature of the information to be collected, but the preparation for undertaking it. Dress and equipment standards and debriefing protocols for joint health and law enforcement officials will also need to be established. The provision of resources for these new dimensions of contingency planning will need to be evaluated within the context of the region's sustainability agenda. An assessment of the threat to our present and future development in this Age of Terror may call for more adequate funding for basic preparedness and the consolidation and interfacing of existing regional cooperation mechanisms and frameworks.

Regional Building Blocks for Managing the Environmental Security Challenge

The management of the environmental security challenges, whether these consist of the consequences of natural hazards or terrorist acts, requires a holistic integrated approach built on risk identification, analysis and management. More importantly, this must be linked to the region's sustainable development agenda if the low level of attention in public decision making is to be reversed (Ferguson 2001; Simon 1997). The recognition that our community of limited resources cannot afford to meet all the costs of enhanced monitoring and surveillance systems, specialised response equipment and related training, means that attention must therefore be directed toward the use of existing regional security, environmental monitoring and emergency preparedness systems to address and mitigate these additional security challenges.

Already in existence are sector stakeholder mechanisms for regional cooperation with established links to the international community. The CAREC and the Caribbean Environmental Health Institute (CEHI) are regional organisations that bring together many of the actors in health intelligence, public health policy and training. Regional security chiefs meet within the framework of the CANSEC, a facility supported by the government of the United States. Disaster preparedness is coordinated within the CDERA mechanism, with the Caribbean Meteorological Organisation (CMO), through the Caribbean Institute for Meteorology and Hydrology (CIMH), bringing specialised knowledge and practice in the monitoring of climatological hazards and the Seismic Research Unit bringing expertise in the area of volcanoes and earthquakes.

A first step in defining a Comprehensive Regional Strategy and mechanism to combat the consequences of the terrorism challenge to our environmental security would necessitate an analysis of the best arrangement for harmonising the assets of these organisations. The creation of a Ministerial Security Committee as proposed by Ferguson (2001) is one option for consideration. The operationalisation of this institutional arrangement should be informed by the principles of the Unified Management System (Christen et al 2001). Decision making within this Unified Management System can be enhanced by the development and use of an Integrated Decision Support System (IDSS). IDSS is a set of processes and tools that are intended to assist in providing actors in the disaster management system, at all levels of the operation, with a common operating picture. Such a system is under consideration for the Caribbean with the support of the US Southern Command through the Asian Disaster Preparedness Centre (ADPC 2002).

We recognise the cost implications of and constraints to planning for environmental security breaches – that is, low-probability, high-impact events with system-wide failures. However, we believe that the existing regional cooperation infrastructure, coupled with new technologies, makes it possible to create mechanisms, policies and infrastructure for managing these with some flexibility (Arens and Rosenbloom 2002).

What is outlined here has focused extensively on consequence management issues. The Regional Strategy and Results Framework for Comprehensive Disaster Management (CDM – see www.cdera.org) acknowledges the link between risk management and development, the diversity of actors and the complexity of priority setting. Its strategic objective is linked to sustainable development and thus provides the overarching link to development and environment security issues. It represents a strategic planning and communications tool for linking the actors in the risk management sector into the larger development discourse. It is offered as a medium for contextualising the identified priorities for managing environment security within the larger sustainable development dialogue, thus rescuing it from the margins of policy debate.

Conclusion

Environmental security exacerbates the challenges of development planning and finance in the Caribbean island and developing states, especially in a global environment of increasing terror. These new and growing challenges should not be allowed to generate a sense of despondency. The potential infrastructure for structuring and improving strategic and operational coordination already exists, and ever-emerging new technologies will support the decision making process therein. However, environmental security must be one of the strategic goals of the Caribbean Single Market and Economy programme. Its criticality to sustainable development goals requires its elevation in our political discourse.

References

Arens, Y. and Rosenbloom. Report of the Workshop on Responding to the Unexpected, New York, USA, February 27–March 1, 2002, USC/Information Science Institute.

Asian Disaster Preparedness Center (ADPC). Integrated Decision Support: Concept Paper presented at the Integrated Decision Support System Status Briefing and Workshop, Barbados, January 8–9, 2002.

Bloem, Ken. Natural Disasters and Terrorist Attacks: Are US Hospitals Prepared? Presentation at the Natural Disaster Roundtable Forum on Countering Terrorism: Lessons Learnt from Natural and Technological Disasters, Washington, DC, Feb 28–March 1, 2002.

Caribbean Development Bank (2002) *Social and Economic Indicators for Borrowing Member Countries 2001 Volume VII.*

Caribbean Disaster Emergency Response Agency. A Strategy & Results Framework for Comprehensive Disaster Management in the Caribbean; Prepared by Bisek et. al. with the Support of USAID and UNDP, 2001a.

Caribbean Disaster Emergency Response Agency. The Status of Disaster Reduction Initiatives in the Caribbean; Contribution prepared for the ISDR Global Report on Disaster Reduction, 2001b.

Caribbean Disaster Emergency Response Agency. Status of Disaster Preparedness of CDERA Participating States, 2001c.

Caribbean Disaster Emergency Response Agency. Guidelines for (a) National Disaster Relief Policy, 2000.

Caribbean Disaster Emergency Response Agency. Regional Coordination Plan, 1998.

Christen, H. et al., 'An overview of Incident Management System', *Perspectives on Preparedness* No 4, September 2001.

Cole, Thomas B., 'When a Bioweapon Strikes, Who Will Be in Charge?' *JAMA*. Vol 284 No.8 (1997).

Collymore, J McA., Environmental Disaster Preparedness: Review and Considerations for Caribbean Small Island Developing States. Paper prepared for the Environmental Management Conference, Port-of-Spain, Trinidad and Tobago, March 20–24, 2000.

Collymore, J McA. 'Disaster Planning Lessons for the Caribbean. The Gilbert Experience'. *Disaster Management.* Vol 2, No. 2 (1989): 87–93.

Collymore J McA. 'Planning to Reduce the Socio-economic impacts of Natural Hazards on Caribbean Society'. *The Journal of the Geological Society of Jamaica.* Special Issue 12. Natural Hazards in the Caribbean (1992): 88–97.

Commonwealth Secretariat/World Bank, Small States: Meeting Challenges in the Global Economy, Report of the Commonwealth Secretariat/World Bank Joint Task Force on Small States, 2000.

Demuth, Julie L. and Platt, Rutherford H., Summary of the Natural Disasters Roundtable on Countering Terrorism: Lessons Learnt from Natural and Technological Disasters, Washington, DC, Feb 28–March 1, 2002.

Ferguson, T. 'A Security Management Model for Small States'. Keynote presentation delivered to the Committee on Hemispheric Security Meeting on the Special Security Concerns of Small Island States, March 30, 2001 – Rapporteur's Report.

Griffith, Ivelaw. Caribbean Regional Security in National Defense University Strategic Forum Institute for National Strategic Studies Number 102, 1997.

Intergovernmental Panel on Climate Change *'Climate Change 2001: Impacts, Adaptation and Vulnerability, Summary for Policy Makers'*, A Report of Working Group II of the Intergovernmental Panel on Climate Change.

Jenkins B.M., 'Understanding the link between Motives and Methods' in Roberts B, ed. *Terrorism with Chemical and Biological Weapons; Calibration Risks and Responses*, 43-52 Alexandria, Virginia: Chemical and Biological Arms Control Institute, 1997.

Mainstreaming Adaptation to Climate Change (MACC) Project Concept Document, 2001.

McSwegan E., Review of 'Chemical and Biological Terrorism; Research and Development to Improve Civilian Medical Response'. *JAMA* 283, 1.15 (2000).

Nicholls, R., '*Coastal Vulnerability Assessment for Sea-Level Rise – Evaluation and Selection of Methodologies for Implementation*', 1998. www.cpacc.org/ifownframe.htm.

Office of Disaster Preparedness and Emergency Management (ODPEM, 2001) '*Tropical Depression 15 – Floods of October 29, Summary Update, November 20, 2001*'.

Organization of American States, 2001 Committee on Hemispheric Security Meeting on the Special Security Concerns of Small Island Developing States, March 30, 2001 Rapporteur's Report.

Pearson, Graham S., 'The Complementary Role of Environmental and Security Biological Control Regimes in the 21st Century', *JAMA*. (1997): 369–372

RAIV Hurricane Committee Meeting Report, 1990.

Scott, J., Berridge, C.E. and Collymore, J. A Study of the Early Warning Capabilities of the CMO and CDERA. A Report prepared for the United Nations Department for Policy Coordination and Sustainable Development, Barbados, April 1994.

Simon, Jeffrey D., 'Biological Terrorism'. *JAMA* 278 (1997): 428–430.

Third Summit of the Americas – Quebec Plan of Action, 2000. http://www.summit-americas.org/Documents.

United Nations Economic Commission for Latin America and the Caribbean (2001) The SIDS Programme of Action Agenda Twenty One The Road to Johannesburg, 2002.

UNDESA Barbados Programme of Action for Small Island Developing States, 1994.

Waeckerle, Joseph F., 'Domestic Preparedness for Events Involving Weapons of Mass Destruction', *JAMA* Vol 283, No 2 (2000).

9

The Caribbean, HIV/AIDS and Security

Caroline Allen, Roger McLean, and Keith Nurse

Introduction

As a global pandemic, HIV/AIDS is forecast to claim more lives than any other outbreak of disease in human history. However, the impact is not uniform across the globe. HIV/AIDS has already wreaked havoc on the social, economic and political fabric of sub-Saharan Africa, which is the most affected region. In North America and Western Europe, the relative affordability of anti-retroviral treatment has reduced HIV/AIDS-related mortality, while there has been a steady increase in the number of people living with the virus. Prevalence is on the rise in regions such as Southeast Asia, the countries of the former Soviet Union, and South and Central America. In the Caribbean, adult prevalence of the virus is second only to that of sub-Saharan Africa (see Table 9.1 below).

With its impact on life expectancies and wider socio-economic and political consequences, HIV/AIDS has begun to reverse the developmental gains for many of the world's most vulnerable groups, nations and regions as well as create an additional source of instability, including military conflict. Recognition of the grave threat that AIDS poses has only recently gained prominence in global policy debates. At the closing session of the International AIDS Conference in Durban, South Africa in 2000, Nelson Mandela declared that 'a tragedy of unprecedented proportions is unfolding in Africa. AIDS today in Africa is claiming more lives than the sum total of all wars, famines and floods...' Mandela's words highlight the gravity of the HIV epidemic in Africa by comparing its impact with that of war, a traditional security concern, and natural or man-made disasters.

The HIV/AIDS pandemic has moved from being defined purely as a health issue to be seen as a development as well as a security threat. In addition, the AIDS pandemic has emerged as a security concern for both high and low prevalence countries and regions. The problem of AIDS is increasingly viewed as a part of the 'global commons' and not just as a problem that can be easily contained within the boundaries of affected nation-states. The adequacy of the traditional state-centric, militaristic approach to security has been thrown into question with the recognition of biological threats, emanating from diseases carried across borders by travellers as the pace of globalisation quickens.

Table 9.1
Regional HIV/AIDS Statistics and Features, end of 2002

Region	Epidemic started	Adults and children living with HIV/AIDS	Adults and children newly infected with HIV	% Adult prevalence rate (*)	% HIV-positive adults who are women	Main mode(s) of transmission (#) for adults living with HIV/AIDS
Sub-Saharan Africa	Late 70s early 80s	29.4 million	3.5 million	8.8	58	Hetero
North Africa & Middle East	Late 80s	550,000	83,000	0.3	55	Hetero, IDU
South & South-East Asia	Late 80s	6.0 million	700,000	0.6	36	Hetero, IDU
East Asia & Pacific	Late 80s	1.2 million	270,000	0.1	24	IDU, hetero, MSM
Latin America	Late 70s early 80s	1.5 million	150,000	0.6	30	MSM, IDU, hetero
Caribbean	Late 70s early 80s	440,000	60,000	2.4	50	Hetero, MSM
Eastern Europe & Central Asia	Early 90s	1.2 million	250,000	0.6	27	IDU
Western Europe	Late 70s early 80s	570,000	30,000	0.3	25	MSM, IDU
North America	Late 70s early 80s	980,000	45,000	0.6	20	MSM, IDU, hetero
Australia & New Zealand	Late 70s early 80s	15,000	500	0.1	7	MSM
TOTAL		42 million	5 million	1.2	50	

* The proportion of adults (15 to 49 years of age) living with HIV/AIDS in 2002, using 2002 population numbers.
\# Hetero (heterosexual transmission), IDU (transmission through injecting drug use), MSM (sexual transmission among men who have sex with men).

Source: UNAIDS/WHO, AIDS Epidemic Update, 2002.

Outline

The chapter firstly analyses the emerging security discourse and international relations practice and looks specifically at the development of US policy towards HIV in developing countries. Attention is given to the threats to state governance and connections are made with issues such as travel and tourism, migration, the drug trade and military operations. The second section presents data on the epidemiological profile and health impact of HIV/AIDS in the Caribbean. The major characteristics of the Caribbean epidemic are presented along with factors associated with vulnerability in the region. The third section evaluates the current and prospective security risks for the Caribbean. The focus is largely on the mobility of populations and the possible socio-economic and political implications of the disease. The fourth section examines the international and regional response to the epidemic. Particular attention is given to the Caribbean response from a security perspective. The concluding section provides a critical perspective on the security concept and its applicability to the Caribbean HIV/AIDS epidemic. Traditional concepts of security concerned with the territorial integrity of nation-states are considered, along with notions of human security that extend the focus from the state to the safety and welfare of other collective groupings and to individuals.

HIV/AIDS and Security

In 2000, President Clinton declared HIV a security threat to the United States. Since then, James Wolfensohn, head of the World Bank, speaking at the UN Security Council on the issue of AIDS argued, 'we face a major development crisis, and more than that, a security crisis'. In the US, the State Department and the CIA are on record as stating that the AIDS crisis is a threat to national security. The statement by the US under-secretary of state, Paul Dobriansky, that 'HIV/AIDS is a threat to security and global stability, plain and simple', exemplifies this Singer 2003).

In July 2000, the United Nations Security Council under Resolution 1308 delineated the dangers that HIV/AIDS poses to worldwide stability and particularly to the role of international peace-keeping personnel. Resolution 1308 requests the secretary-general:

> To take further steps towards the provision of training for peacekeeping personnel on issues related to preventing the spread of HIV/AIDS and to continue the further development of pre-deployment orientation and on-going training for all peacekeeping personnel on these issues. (UN Security Council 2000, 2).

Numerous international agencies and policy makers are now linking the issues of HIV and security, asserting that the epidemic poses a threat to international stability. Generally, the security concept remains focussed on military considerations and the state in this discourse. UNAIDS has recently launched an initiative on HIV and security, with three main components:

- National security. The initiative aims to establish national programmes to address the spread of HIV among national uniformed services, including armed forces and the civil defence force.
- Community security. HIV/AIDS awareness, prevention, care and treatment strategies should be incorporated into actions that respond to emergency situations, including armed conflict, humanitarian emergencies and natural disasters.
- International security. Personnel involved in international peace-keeping operations should be provided with HIV/AIDS awareness and training, including a gender component (UNAIDS Humanitarian Unit 2002).

The discourse on AIDS as a security issue emerged firstly from the US, and US perspectives have largely defined the debate. In April 2000, the US government declared HIV/AIDS a threat to American national security, marking the first time ever that a disease had been entrusted to the National Security Council. The US Office of National AIDS Policy now has an explicit international focus, and the Bush administration, since his inauguration in January 2001, continues to regard HIV as a national security problem (Gow 2002). Former president, Bill Clinton is now co-chair (with Nelson Mandela) of the International AIDS Trust.

In the late 1990s, President Bill Clinton expanded US political interest in the African epidemic, and the flow of funding to that cause increased. Legislation enacted during the 106th US Congress increased HIV/AIDS funding worldwide (Gow, 2002). In January 2000, the US National Intelligence Council launched a document entitled *The Global Infectious Disease Threat and its Implications for the United States* (National Intelligence Council 2000). Infectious diseases, and particularly HIV, were considered as *non-traditional* threats to US national security. Immigration, international travel and returning US military forces were seen as a means of mass transmission to US citizens. The US was thought to be vulnerable 'as a major hub of global travel, immigration, and commerce with wide-ranging interests and a large civilian and military presence overseas'. Among the concerns were that:

- Infectious diseases would be imported by growing numbers of migrants.
- US military personnel, particularly those deployed in support of humanitarian and peace-keeping operations in developing countries, would be at high risk of infection.
- Drug resistance would diminish the effectiveness of medical treatment.
- The infectious disease burden would diminish the military capabilities of America's allies.

- The slowing of economic development resulting from disease would challenge democratic development in some countries.
- Infectious disease-related embargoes and restrictions on travel and immigration would cause frictions among and between developed and developing countries
- 'The severe social and economic impact of infectious diseases, particularly HIV/AIDS, and the infiltration of these diseases into the ruling political and military elites and middle classes of developing countries are likely to intensify the struggle for political power to control scarce state resources. This will hamper the development of a civil society and other underpinnings of democracy and will increase pressure on democratic transitions in regions... where the infectious disease burden will add to economic misery and political polarization.' (National Intelligence Council, 2000)

Analysis

The emerging perspectives on security and HIV/AIDS appear to be driven by two interconnected concerns. The first is with the infection through contact with mobile populations such as migrants (including asylum seekers and refugees), sex workers and military personnel. This is associated with concern about the decline of good governance or state failure arising from social, economic and political instability in high prevalence countries and regions. The view is that high prevalence could lead to a vicious cycle of disease and conflict.

These views illustrate the universality and interdependence of the HIV/AIDS pandemic. However, the policy response seems to be moving towards externalising the threat and pursuing containment strategies for the low prevalence, high-income countries and their military personnel. This route is not without historical antecedents. Analysts have observed that in previous epidemics, after the early phase of denial the next steps are to impose restrictive measures and to identify groups to blame (Whiteside and FitzSimons 1992, 33). This view is shared by Barnett and Blaikie who argue that in the contemporary context ... an undercurrent of opinion is beginning to suggest that AIDS is under control in Europe and North America, that it can now be seen as 'just' another tropical disease – like malaria – against which the people of Europe and North America can protect themselves by means of simple precautionary measures. Such attitudes are easy to adopt, they fit well with established prejudices along class, gender and ethnic lines. They insidiously penetrate research agendas (quoted in Whiteside and FitzSimons 1992, 33).

The Caribbean and HIV/AIDS

Since the first case of AIDS was diagnosed in Jamaica in 1982, the number of cases in the Caribbean region has risen consistently every year. By 2000, the annual number of new cases per 100,000 population was three times higher than in North America and six times higher than in Latin America.[1] It is now estimated that in the Caribbean, 2.4 per cent of adults in the age group 15–49 were living with HIV/AIDS (UNAIDS/ WHO 2002). This rate is the highest in the Western hemisphere and second highest in the world after sub-Saharan Africa. It is now the leading cause of death in both male and female 15–49 year olds in the region. More than half a million people in the Caribbean were reported to be living with HIV/AIDS at the end of 2000: 137,000 in member countries of the Caribbean Epidemiology Centre,[2] 112,000 in the Dominican Republic, 250,000 in Haiti and 2,500 in Cuba.

In the Caribbean, HIV is primarily sexually transmitted. Intravenous drug use is rare and accounts for only 1.5 per cent of cases reported since 1982. Almost two-thirds of cases since 1982 were reportedly transmitted heterosexually, while 11 per cent resulted from homo- or bisexual behaviour (Camara 2002).[3] While the proportion attributed to male homosexual behaviour is thought to be an underestimate (De Groulard et al 2000), the predominantly heterosexual character of the epidemic in the Caribbean is also evident from the fact that females have accounted for an increasing proportion of HIV and AIDS cases ever since 1985. This is similar to the pattern in sub-Saharan Africa, and contrasts with the pattern in North American and European countries, where homosexual transmission accounts for the majority of cases among nationals.

Figure 9.1 indicates that the highest numbers of AIDS cases in the Caribbean are in the age groups 25 to 34 and 35 to 44. This is precisely when people have the largest measure of responsibility for emotional and financial care of their families, and when workers can be expected to be at the height of their productive powers. This age distribution suggests that many people are becoming infected in the young adult age group 15 to 24.

Young women are particularly vulnerable. In women 15 to 24 years old, HIV prevalence is two to four times higher than in all other female age groups and three to six times higher than in males of that age group. This pattern is consistent with the finding from several surveys conducted in the Caribbean that females usually have their first sexual experience with an older male. Qualitative research has shown that females choose older men partly because they can gain access to goods offering status such as brand-

Figure 9.1
Age Group Distribution of Reported AIDS Cases in CAREC Member Countries, 1982-2000

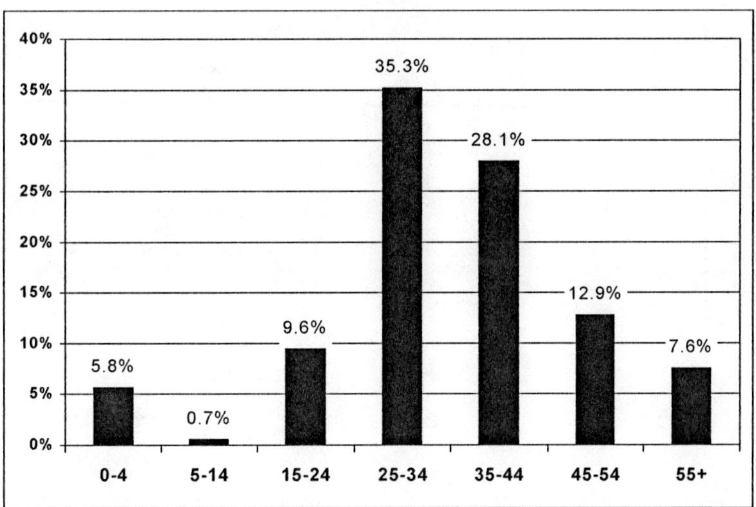

Source: Camara, 2002

name clothes, fast food and rides in cars. However, surveys show that males' first sexual experience also tends to be with an older partner; the data do not allow us to determine whether the partners are mostly female or male (Allen et al 2001). This may suggest sexual abuse of young people. The PAHO Adolescent Health Survey had a sample of 15,695 school students age 10–18 in Antigua and Barbuda, Bahamas, Barbados, British Virgin Islands, Dominica, Grenada, Guyana, Jamaica and St Lucia. In this survey, almost half of females (48 per cent) and a third of males (32 per cent) said their first intercourse was forced ('yes' or 'somewhat') (Pan American Health Organization 2000).

Figure 9.2 presents HIV prevalence data for Caribbean countries where prevalence exceeds 1 per cent. It will be seen that there is no obvious correlation between rates of HIV and social and economic indicators. For instance, the rate is highest in Haiti, where income per capita is lowest, but rates are also high in the Bahamas and the Turks and Caicos Island where income per capita is relatively high. This suggests that a complex mixture of factors is at work in determining rates of HIV in each country.

Figure 9.2
Caribbean Countries with Adult Prevalence of HIV Greater than 1%, 2001

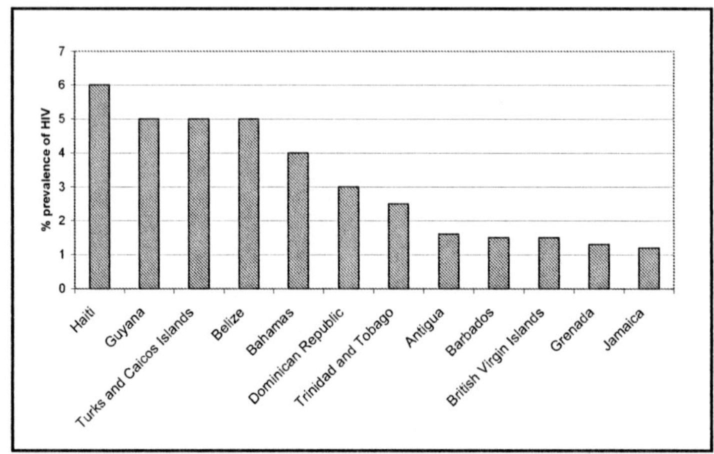

Source: Camara, 2002

Figure 9.3 shows the rates of HIV found among pregnant women in various Caribbean countries. This is an indicator of rates among the sexually active female population.

Figure 9.3
Prevalence of HIV among Pregnant Women in Selected Caribbean Countries

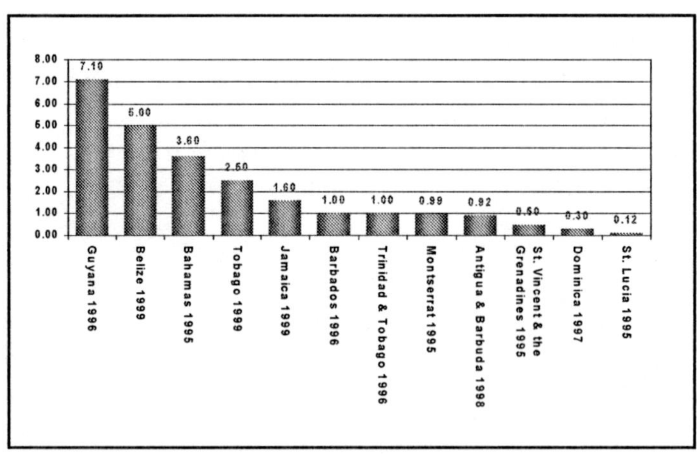

Source: Camara 2001

High rates among pregnant women translate into high rates of mother to child transmission. Indeed, the proportion of AIDS cases accounted for by mother to child transmission, at 6 per cent, is the highest outside sub-Saharan Africa. In the 21 CAREC member countries, some 3,000 children are born each year to mothers with HIV, and about 1,000 are infected (Camara 2001). Surveys have been conducted of prevalence of HIV in certain vulnerable groups, showing far higher HIV prevalence than in the general population. Comparing individual Caribbean countries, it has been found that HIV prevalence ranges from 2 to 21 per cent among patients with Sexually Transmitted Infections (STIs) to 18 to 40 per cent among men who have sex with men (MSM), to 3 to 45 per cent among female sex workers (Camara 2001).

Studies have shown that most Caribbean people know that condom use is a primary HIV prevention method for people who are sexually active, particularly if they have more than one partner. Given the risk, condom use on each occasion of sexual intercourse is advisable for sexually active people. However, a review of sexual behavioural studies conducted across CAREC member countries among youth (age 10–24) and general adult populations (age 18 and over) showed that consistent condom use for adults ranged from 7 to 29 per cent and for youth 16 to 56 per cent. Generally, a minority of Caribbean people, male or female, are reporting consistent condom use, and the true percentages may be smaller if there is a tendency to exaggerate safer behaviour. The studies showed that younger adults were more likely to use condoms than older adults, whereas the reverse was true in youth studies (Allen et al 2001).

The Caribbean HIV/AIDS Security Problem

How does the Caribbean situation relate to these security concerns? Pertinent Caribbean security issues relate to mobile populations including tourists, migrants and military troops. Other threats emerge from socio-economic and political instability arising from the impact of the epidemic on the social fabric of the region.

Travel and Tourism

Tourism is the mainstay of most Caribbean economies, having surpassed the traditional agro-based and natural resource-based export economy in terms of foreign exchange earnings and employment. Over 17 million stay-over and 8 million cruise ship visitors came to the region in 1999. Among stay-over visitors, US visitors account for approximately 46 per cent while Europeans account for 28 per cent (Caribbean Tourism Organisation 2000). Relative to other regions in the world, the Caribbean has the highest level of dependence on the industry when tourism receipts are compared with services and merchandise exports (Nurse 2002).

The first reported Caribbean AIDS cases in Haiti, Jamaica and Trinidad and Tobago were among gay men who had had sex with North American men in North America or in the Caribbean. This observation is reinforced by the fact that molecular distribution of the HIV has shown that the same Clade B is circulating in both North America and the Caribbean (Camara 2002). This is an illustration of the role of international travel in the spread of the epidemic.

With tourism, the commercial demand for sex from Caribbean people of both sexes has grown, though local men also purchase sex from sex workers. Both females and males sell sex, with male sex work in tourist zones often involving the purchase of goods such as a pair of jeans or a night's entertainment rather than monetary payment (Russell-Brown and Sealey 1998; De Moya and Garcia 1999). Homosexual behaviour has played a crucial role in the epidemic, especially in the early phase. In some senses the Caribbean shares the causes of HIV with its North American neighbours, as this was the initial transmission route.

Many Caribbean women and men sell sex outside their country of origin, including other Caribbean countries and in North America. Not all derive their full income from sex work, with many, including petty traders, selling sex as and when they perceive an economic need (Kempadoo 1999). There is very little data on the travel patterns of Caribbean people who sell sex. Rates of HIV among women selling sex in the Caribbean have been shown to range from 3–45 per cent and condom use among them is low, but studies specific to mobile female populations who sell sex have not been conducted (Allen 2002). It is notable that tourism dependent economies are among the most affected in the Caribbean, having high HIV seroprevalence and reported AIDS incidence, i.e. the Bahamas, Barbados, Bermuda, the Dominican Republic, Turks and Caicos, the Montego Bay and Kingston areas of Jamaica, St Maarten/St Martin and Tobago (Camara 2002).

Extra-Regional Migration

The Caribbean region has one of the largest diasporic communities in the world as a proportion of population. It is estimated that the Cubans and

Dominicans in the US are equivalent to 8 per cent of their respective populations of origin (UNECLAC 2002, 237). Some of the mini states in the region like St Kitts and Nevis, Grenada and Belize export as much as 1–2 per cent of their population to the US thereby transferring their population growth (Mittelman 2000, 60).

The significance of the Diaspora to the region is exemplified by the fact that the region receives more money from financial remittances than from international aid. In territories like Jamaica and the Dominican Republic, remittances account for 10.8 per cent and 8.5 per cent of GDP, respectively (UNECLAC 2002, 247). Extra-regional migration is predominantly to the US and Canada, with diminishing migration to the UK and Europe. Intra-regional migration is substantial, with people moving predominantly from poorer countries to richer ones in search of economic opportunities. Migrants are especially vulnerable to HIV because of their isolation, insecure jobs and living situations, fear of government services and lack of access to sexual and reproductive health care (UNAIDS and IOM 2001). This scenario is further compounded by undocumented migrants who are more likely to be exposed to abuse because of the lack of legal protection. In the US most of the undocumented Caribbean migrants fall under the category of 'non-immigrant overstays'.

In the high-income countries, the epidemic has shifted increasingly to marginalised populations like the urban poor, migrants and other mobile populations. For the UK and Europe it is documented that 'a large share of the heterosexually transmitted HIV infections are being diagnosed in persons who originate from, or who have lived in or visited, areas where HIV prevalence is high'. In the US the epidemic is 'the leading cause of death for African-American men aged 25–44 and the third-leading cause of death for Hispanic men in the same age group' (UNAIDS 2002, 23–24). Caribbean migrants are largely to be found among the above-mentioned demographic groups (e.g. the urban poor, migrants, the African-American and Hispanic population). The susceptibility of the region's migrants is evident in that 46 per cent of the immigrants diagnosed with AIDS in New York City are from the Caribbean, while 27 per cent are from Latin America and 17 per cent from Eastern Europe (Camara 2002).

Intra-Regional Migration

The region's HIV/AIDS scenario also has an intra-regional dimension. A US Centres for Disease Control study conducted among internal migrant workers in Guyana's mining industry found 6 per cent HIV prevalence. This is a population essentially of young males migrating from the coastal area to the hinterland to work in the mining industry. Immigrants from Haiti working in the sugar cane industry in the Dominican Republic were found to have a rate of HIV infection of 15 per cent in 1997, up from 7 per cent in 1991. At the end of 2001, 25 per cent of AIDS patients in the Bahamas were non-Bahamian, specifically Haitian immigrants. A similar situation exists in the Turks and Caicos Islands where there is a large migrant population living and working in the construction and tourism sectors (Camara 2002).

Many people living with HIV/AIDS (PLWHA) travel, and often seek to migrate, to countries where quality of care is superior (Whiteside and FitzSimons 1992). The US and most Caribbean countries conduct mandatory HIV testing on applicants for migrant status, and HIV positive applicants are rejected unless a waiver is granted by the immigration authorities. Co-operative agreements between governments on meeting the care needs of HIV positive travellers and migrants are extremely limited, with private individuals and non-governmental organisations making most of the supportive arrangements for PLWHA (Rodriguez 2002).

The Drug Trade, Military Operations and Prison Populations

The Caribbean is a minor producer but a major transshipment route for the drug trade as it enters North America. Drug-related crime, in the context of rising poverty and increasing materialism, has become the major source of domestic insecurity and has the potential to affect state and corporate governance through corruption and money laundering. The Caribbean epidemic, being predominantly heterosexual, has not been impacted by the transmission of HIV/AIDS through intravenous drug use. The drug trade has been more important in terms of promoting the trade in sex for money to obtain drugs, thus increasing HIV risk. HIV among sex workers has been found to be associated with the use of illegal drugs (particularly cocaine) and high consumption of alcohol (Allen et al 2002).

In several sub-Saharan African countries, rates of HIV have been found to be several times higher among male military personnel, and significantly higher among domestic police and security personnel than in the general adult population (National Intelligence Council 2000; Ostergard 2002). High rates of infection are explained by the indiscriminate sexual culture among security forces, their use of sex workers and, occasionally, violence against women (Healthlink Worldwide 2002). Despite such evidence from elsewhere, there has been little attention to the threat of HIV among Caribbean military, police and security personnel. There are no published studies of rates of HIV among these forces in the Caribbean.

The Caribbean is not currently a major zone of military conflict or humanitarian relief efforts. The region has seen peace-keeping operations in recent years, in the case of Haiti in the mid-1990s. Haiti is the country in the region with the highest prevalence of AIDS (6.1 per cent) as well as the country that is the most unstable politically and likely to see the deployment of humanitarian and peace-keeping forces. US concerns about the impact of HIV on (its own) military forces are of the highest relevance here. The relevance of the US concern about potential infection of its own troops applies where the US becomes involved in further major military operations in the region. Caribbean forces were involved in the Haiti peace-keeping mission but no data is available on this matter.

Prisoners are predominantly from poor and marginalised groups that are vulnerable to HIV infection. Furthermore, isolation from regular sexual partners places them at risk of homosexual transmission within the prison environment. A survey in the Dominican Republic found 19 per cent HIV seroprevalence in prison populations (Camara 2002). Caribbean governments have found it difficult to confront the issue of HIV in prisons by providing HIV education and condoms to prisoners. In August 1997, in Jamaica, six inmates were killed in three days of prison riots sparked by a government official's proposal to distribute condoms to inmates and guards. Union leaders of prison guards who went on strike said the proposal had implied the guards were homosexuals. This illustrates the high level of stigma associated with homosexuality and HIV in Jamaica. The US government has a policy of deporting foreign prisoners who have served their sentences in the United States. Policies to reintegrate the former prisoners in their countries of origin focus on prevention of crime, not HIV. Given high rates of HIV among prisoners in the US, this presents another avenue for the escalation of the epidemic in the Caribbean.

Socio-economic Instability

High prevalence of HIV has many repercussions at the microeconomic and macroeconomic levels. Figure 9.4 shows how the illness or death of an individual with HIV/ AIDS impacts negatively on the fulfilment of multiple roles within the society and economy.

Figure 9.4
Microeconomic Impact of HIV/AIDS

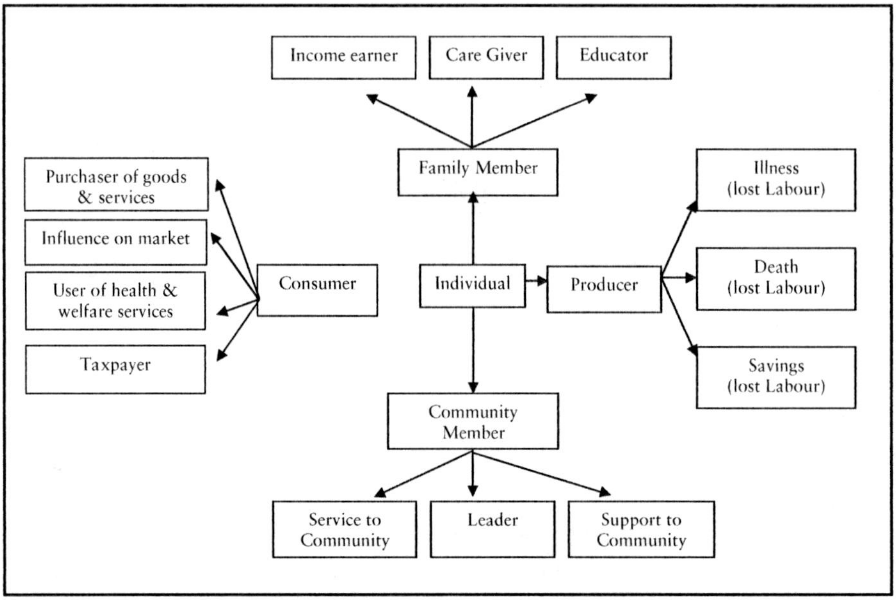

Source: Whiteside and Sunter, 2000

The erosion in the performance of social roles in turn tends to diminish overall levels of national wealth by reducing the supply of labour and capital. HIV/AIDS erodes the labour supply, thereby affecting production quotas and incurring higher medical costs and ultimately a higher unit cost of production. The most labour-intensive sectors are most adversely affected. The Caribbean epidemic is likely to have a severe impact given the labour-intensive nature of production, for example in services and agricultural commodities. Additionally, there is likely to be a greater demand on savings (away from investment) as increased resources are demanded to address health and other related concerns (Nicholls et al 2000). In the Caribbean, savings are predominantly translated into consumption, and HIV/AIDS is likely to further weaken the investment climate. Economies are highly dependent on foreign investment which is likely to decrease if productivity falls.

The aggregated impact of HIV on all sectors will therefore manifest itself in an overall reduction in the country's Gross Domestic Product (GDP) and that of specific sectors. Nicholls et al (2000) projected the impact on several macroeconomic indicators for Trinidad and Tobago and Jamaica from 1997–2005. This study projected the number of cases of HIV/AIDS to the year 2005 using a modelling technique based on a general population survey of sexual behaviours associated with risk of HIV. A macroeconomic model was then used to measure the impact of these behaviours and attributed risk of HIV on the national economy.

Table 9.2
Macroeconomic Impact on Key Variables for Jamaica and Trinidad and Tobago by 2005 (low case scenario projections)

Impact variables	Trinidad and Tobago %	Jamaica %
Gross domestic product	-4.2	-6.4
Savings	-10.3	-23.5
Investment	-15.6	-17.4
Employment in agriculture	-3.5	-5.2
Employment in manufacturing	-4.6	-4.1
Employment in services	-6.7	-8.2
Labour supply	-5.2	-7.3
HIV/AIDS expenditure	+25.3	+35.4

Source: Nicholls et al, 2000

The above table shows the low case scenario predictions, but clearly illustrates the potential of the epidemic to derail major economic indicators. The projected loss in GDP almost eclipses the proportion spent on the public health and equals the proportion spent on the national health budget for the two countries.

HIV/AIDS strikes the most economically productive people in society, with the age group 25–45 bearing the greatest burden of illness and death. With female infections rising more rapidly than male infections, we should consider this within the context of gender roles in the region. Caribbean women have a large share of economic responsibility for their families, working in the informal and formal economies, often with little or sporadic economic support from men. Infections among young women far outstrip those in young men; in young adulthood, numbers of cases of mother-to-child transmission are likely to be high and surviving children may be left to fend for themselves as women become sick and die. As in Africa, grandparents, and especially grandmothers and other older women, will see their burden of care increase. As middle-class women move into a wider range of professions and jobs, HIV/AIDS is likely to erode their gains, as well as diminish the labour force in occupations which are crucial to development, such as nursing and teaching.

The highest rates of AIDS illness and death among males are among 35–44 year olds; the disease strikes at the age group most likely to include managers and professionals, whose skills tend to be in short supply given substantial brain drain to North America and Europe. The effect of HIV on poorer and/or smaller countries, such as those of the Caribbean, is greater because the economy is vulnerable to the loss of even a few skilled people (Whiteside and FitzSimons 1992).

The likely disruption to economic activity across sectors would challenge the state's ability to address its most basic functions in an environment of increased demands on a shrinking productive base. Key among these functions is the area of social policy formulation which is geared toward fulfilling full employment, reduction of poverty and the maintenance of harmonious relationships among various social groups. This will inevitably affect the provision of key public investment programmes and other related incentives which are a critical stimulus to private investment and social policy formulation geared towards:

- increasing the productivity of the poor to better facilitate their integration into the labour force;
- promoting the integration of vulnerable groups in the mainstream of the economy; and
- the creation of a climate that can promote savings and investment, stimulate efficiency and productivity to achieve sustainable growth.

Increased poverty and marginalisation of social groups will, in their turn, feed into increased rates of HIV/AIDS. Such a vicious downward spiral is the scenario facing many sub-Saharan countries whose rates of HIV/AIDS were similar to those in the Caribbean only about ten years ago (Barnett and Whiteside 2002).

Policy Responses
International and Multilateral Responses

An important instance of international cooperation was when President Museveni of Uganda, having recognised the devastating impact AIDS was having on his country, received assistance from the World Health Organization (WHO) to develop the first ever Medium Term Plan to control AIDS. In 1990, the World Bank responded to the government's request for additional help by sending a multi-donor mission, consisting of representatives from WHO, the UNDP, the United Nations Children's Fund, the United Nations Population Fund, Britain, Denmark, Norway, Sweden and the United States. They worked with government and local NGO representatives to develop a multi-sectoral approach, coordinated by a National AIDS Commission, chaired by the president of Uganda and comprising ministers from a wide range of sectors (Armstrong 1991). This multi-sectoral approach, by involving ministries as diverse as Finance, Education and National Security as well as NGOs and the private sector, sought to address a number of dimensions of human security relating to HIV. The model has since been followed by numerous countries, and is promoted by UNAIDS, the UN body which was set up in 1996 to confront the epidemic globally (Barnett and Whiteside 2002). The case of Uganda is now widely cited as a success story, as HIV prevalence among pregnant women has fallen from a high of 29 per cent in 1992 to 11 per cent in 2000 (UNAIDS 2002a).

In January 2000, the UN Security Council convened a session devoted exclusively to the threat of AIDS to Africa. International interest in AIDS as a security issue grew, culminating in the first ever United Nations General Assembly Special Session (UNGASS) on HIV/AIDS, June 25–27, 2000 in Washington. Those in attendance included a delegation from the Caribbean, comprising representatives of several Caribbean governments, the Caribbean Regional Network of People Living with HIV/AIDS (CRN+) and the Caribbean Epidemiology Centre. The session made a *Declaration of Commitment on HIV/AIDS*, comprising measurable, time-specific targets for achievement. Countries represented at UNGASS resolved to increase annual expenditure on the AIDS epidemic to $7 to $10 billion a year, with much of the money to be raised and disbursed by a new global fund. When the fund was eventually set up, its mandate was extended, and it was named the Global Fund to Fight AIDS, Tuberculosis and Malaria (Gow 2002; Ssemakula 2002).

With increasing devotion of resources to the 'war on terrorism' since September 11, 2001, the commitment of Western governments to meet the target faltered. As of December 2002, total commitments amounted to only $2 billion. Though the Bush administration continued to pronounce that AIDS is a national security threat, by March 2002, the US government had pledged only $500 million (Gow 2002). Former president, Bill Clinton, in a speech delivered at the closing session of the International AIDS Conference in Barcelona in 2002, argued that the share that should be allocated by the US to the Global Fund according to its wealth was about $2 billion, roughly equivalent to 'less than two months of the Afghan war, less than three per cent of the requested increases for defence and homeland defence in the current budget' (Clinton 2002). The largest contribution from the private sector has been the $100 million pledged by the Bill and Melinda Gates Foundation in 2001.

In President Bush's State of the Union address on January 28, 2003, he pledged $15 billion over the next three years to fight AIDS 'in the most afflicted nations of Africa and the Caribbean'. This major boost in funding should be seen against the background of the rising tide of anxiety about security threats in general which is accompanied by increasing unilateralism by the US government. Notably, only $1 billion of the 15 is to be allocated to the Global Fund. The US government alone will make the rest of the allocation decisions for the new funds. Multilateral initiatives such as the Pan-Caribbean Partnership on HIV/AIDS (see below) are likely to be sidelined by this move. US funds for the Caribbean are to concentrate only on Guyana and Haiti.

Policy Responses in the Caribbean

The scale of financial contribution of international and bilateral development agencies to the struggle against HIV/AIDS in the Caribbean is substantial, but is difficult to compare with contributions from other sources within the countries. UNAIDS (1999) obtained information from 64 developing countries and countries in transition on their financing of HIV/AIDS activities in 1996–7. International and bilateral agencies provided more than half of the reported funds overall, and 29 of the 64 countries reported that national sources represented less than 10 per cent of HIV/AIDS monies. The proportion of funding attributable to national sources for the six Caribbean countries included in the study was reported to be 39 per cent for the Bahamas, 6 per cent for the Dominican Republic, 60 per cent for Jamaica, 41 per cent for Trinidad and Tobago, while donor funds accounted for all the expenditure in Haiti.

However, the results on national sources were based on reports on HIV/AIDS resources obligated by national AIDS programmes, and included very little information on other government spending, spending by local NGOs and institutions, funding obligated by district or municipal governments or the private sector. Furthermore, country responses centred on HIV/AIDS expenditure within the health sector, few included information on cross-sectoral spending on HIV/AIDS. Finally, though countries were asked to report on activities exclusively dedicated to HIV/AIDS care and prevention and those in which HIV/AIDS strategies were integrated into other activities, they generally reported only on the former. In countries where the state response to HIV/AIDS has been weak, such as Haiti, NGOs, churches and other private sources have supplemented foreign funds in a rather ad hoc and sporadic response to the epidemic.

In December 2002, Haiti became the first country in the Western hemisphere to receive a grant from the Global Fund to Fight AIDS, Tuberculosis and Malaria. The $25 million will assist a consortium, led by the NGO GHESKIO and including the Haitian government, to run low-cost clinics for people living with HIV/AIDS and tuberculosis. The GHESKIO clinics are recognised as a model of how countries facing political upheaval, poverty and crumbling infrastructure can combat AIDS. GHESKIO has developed methods of diagnosing sexually transmitted diseases and has found some less expensive drug combinations to treat AIDS. It and other private groups use funds provided by foundations and foreign governments to buy the medicines, which are priced far beyond the reach of most Haitians. The grant will also assist the NGO Partners in Health to provide health education and outreach to villages. Haiti's Health Ministry will receive about $1 million to help develop its planning ability and to coordinate the various projects (Gonzalez 2002).

National AIDS Programmes (NAPs) in the Caribbean were initially guided by the World Health Organization Global Programme on AIDS that later disbanded to form UNAIDS. NAPs have received technical support and guidance from agencies such as CARICOM, the Caribbean Epidemiology Centre (CAREC), Pan American Health Organization (PAHO) and UNAIDS. In 1998, the Caribbean Task Force on HIV/AIDS was formed with a mandate to co-ordinate and strengthen the regional response to the epidemic. The Task Force was chaired by the CARICOM Secretariat and included experts in key HIV/AIDS programming areas, such as the Caribbean Regional Network of People Living with AIDS (CRN+), UNAIDS, CAREC, PAHO/WHO, the University of the West Indies, the Caribbean Development Bank and the Caribbean Conference of Churches. A critical policy initiative of the Task Force was the formulation of the Regional Strategic Plan (RSP).

This plan provided the framework to inform and direct the expanded response to the problem of HIV in the region as well as at the national and sector levels. The objective of the plan was therefore to provide support and guidance to national efforts to prevent and control the spread of HIV and mitigate its consequences. The plan identified a number of key areas of intervention which include:

- advocacy, policy development and legislation;
- care and support for PLWHA;
- prevention of HIV transmission among young people;
- prevention of HIV transmission among especially vulnerable groups;
- prevention of mother to child transmission of HIV;
- strengthening the nation and regional response capability; and
- resource mobilisation.

Regional finance ministers endorsed the plan at the June 2000 Meeting of the Caribbean Group on Cooperation in Economic Development (CGCED) held at the World Bank.

It was eventually recognised that more was required to ensure sustained commitment at all levels across the region. It was agreed that the Task Force be expanded to what is now the Pan Caribbean Partnership against HIV/ AIDS (PANCAP). The Partnership, established on February 14, 2001, aims to 'scale up' the regional response. It operates under the aegis of the Caribbean Community (CARICOM) Secretariat and is charged with providing support to the priority actions specified in the Regional Strategic Framework. It comprises governments, regional institutions, non-governmental organisations, associations of people living with HIV/AIDS, bilateral donors and the United Nations organisations, and aims to be the regional coordinating committee for addressing the epidemic. PANCAP covers Caribbean countries including CARICOM and CARIFORUM member states, CARICOM associate members and other states and territories in the Caribbean. These include Puerto Rico, Aruba, Cuba, the Netherlands Antilles and the US Virgin Islands.

PANCAP aims to promote collaborative action and establish an environment through which a broad coalition of key stakeholders under the leadership of regional governments can curtail the spread of the HIV epidemic. This is to be achieved by:

- coordinating the resources of government, regional institutions and the international community with those of civil society, including PLWHA and the private sector; and
- ensuring an integrated approach to planning and monitoring where partners complement each other and work with a shared strategic agenda and common targets and principles.

PANCAP has made significant strides in the mobilisation of political support from the region's leaders for the expanded response to the epidemic. As a result, Caribbean leaders were able to put the region's agenda on the table at UNGASS. The sustained commitment was further illustrated at the meeting of CARICOM Heads of States in Nassau in 2001 where it was declared the 'The Health of the Region is the Wealth of the Region'. The decision was also supported to revise the Regional Strategic Plan of HIV/AIDS to address, among other things, the input of additional stakeholders in such areas as treatment and care. This momentum was continued into the 2002 International AIDS Conference in Barcelona, Spain, where in several special sessions and presentations the Caribbean was highlighted by the international community as a priority area in responding to the epidemic. The most recent achievement of PANCAP has been the submission of a regional proposal to the Global Fund to Fight AIDS, Tuberculosis and Malaria as a means of further scaling up the regional response to the epidemic.

Several Caribbean prime ministers have been vocal advocates on HIV/AIDS both nationally and at the regional and international levels. Prime Minister Dr Denzel Douglas of St Kitts/Nevis and Prime Minister Owen Arthur of Barbados have spearheaded efforts for the establishment of high-level commissions to manage the multi-sectoral response to HIV/AIDS in their countries. National AIDS Programmes are also under the leadership of or directly influenced by the president or the prime minister in the following countries: Bahamas, Trinidad and Tobago, Haiti, Dominican Republic and Belize. All the governments in the region are taking steps to accelerate access to care and treatment for PLWHA and are seeking support from CARICOM and its development partners in this effort. The Caribbean ministers of health, as part of the CARICOM-led Pan Caribbean Partnership, negotiated with the pharmaceutical companies and have successfully achieved significant price reductions for HIV/AIDS care and treatment in the region.

The increased commitment to HIV/AIDS has also been reflected in increased budgetary allocation to HIV/AIDS as part of national spending in many Caribbean countries. For example, the governments of Trinidad and

Tobago, Barbados, Dominican Republic, Jamaica and St Kitts and Nevis allocated significant resources within their national budgets for HIV/AIDS prevention and control. A number of Caribbean countries have also been able to access or have requested World Bank loans for their expanded HIV/AIDS response programme through the Bank's Caribbean Multi-Country HIV/AIDS Prevention and Control Adaptable Lending Programme, and have moved to the development and costing of their National Strategic Plans for HIV/AIDS to this end.

The Caribbean, HIV/AIDS and Security: A Critical Perspective

The discourse on HIV as a security issue emerged firstly in the United States and, initially, was concerned with protection of the US population from a disease seen as emanating predominantly from beyond US borders. Given the geographical proximity and strong historical links between the Caribbean and the US, the question arises, is the Caribbean epidemic a threat to US security, and more broadly, to that of richer countries in the North?

In *The Global Infectious Disease Threat and its Implications for The United States* (National Intelligence Council 2000), immigration, international travel and returning US military forces were seen as means of mass transmission to US citizens. The Caribbean region has one of the largest diasporic communities in the world as a proportion of population, with the US receiving the largest number of migrants and travellers. Given that HIV prevalence in the Caribbean is on average about four times higher than in the US, there is cause for concern in the US. For instance, 46 per cent of the immigrants diagnosed with AIDS in New York City are from the Caribbean.

The usual security response to concerns about immigration and travellers is to impose embargoes and restrictions on travel, and to impose these more heavily on countries from which threats are supposed to emanate. Can we therefore anticipate increased restrictions on movement of Caribbean people to the United States? Specifically in relation to HIV/AIDS, will the US not only maintain mandatory HIV testing of Caribbean applicants for immigrant status, but also increase the rate of rejection of applicants from the region? If the answer to either of these questions is 'yes', it is in fact doubtful whether this will be a successful strategy of containment. Firstly, such an approach assumes that immigrants are infected in their countries of origin. Reasons for the vulnerability of migrants to HIV infection in destination countries are numerous, and include:

1. Lack of access to services
   Migrants generally:
- have little legal or social protection in the host community. This places them at risk of sexual and other forms of abuse by employers and service providers;
- have limited or no access to HIV information, health services, condoms, STI treatment and voluntary counselling and testing;
- are not included in HIV strategic planning activities;
- are unfamiliar with the place and culture and thus do not know how to use services effectively; and
- avoid contact with services if they are illegal immigrants or engaged in illegal activity.

2. Discrimination
- Blaming immigrants for spreading HIV is one form of discrimination, and tends to further discourage migrants from seeking access to services which may prevent HIV, such as treatment for sexually transmitted infections.
- Xenophobia, racism, and ethnic discrimination likewise increase the isolation of migrants and contribute to risky behaviour.
- Migrants often live in poor and ghetto communities where rates of HIV are higher than the national average.

3. Psychological effects of migration
- Far away from familiar faces and surroundings, migrants often feel insecure and lonely, and seek comfort in new sexual relationships and encounters.
- Many countries do not allow the family of a migrant worker to migrate with him or her. This aggravates isolation and the risk that s/he will engage in risky behaviour.
- Distance from the social constraints of home allows migrants to engage in risky behaviour they may not engage in at home (IOM and UNAIDS 2002).

The International Organization for Migration and UNAIDS (2002) suggest that, instead of imposing restrictions on migration, destination countries should collaborate with countries of origin to develop services responsive to the HIV prevention and care needs of migrants. Migrants and NGOs representing them should be involved in the development of services which are culturally appropriate and responsive to their needs. Responses should address HIV/

AIDS prevention, care and support pre-departure, as migrants travel, in host communities and after they return home.

IOM and UNAIDS also advocate for the elimination of mandatory testing of migrants, pointing out that this simply contributes to a climate of discrimination which makes illegal immigration and associated HIV risk more likely (see also Shtarkshall and Soskolne 2000). A collaborative approach is not only more likely to be productive, but it would also remove the concern that political frictions between states would arise from embargoes and restrictions on travel.

A second reason why restrictions on the travel of Caribbean people is unlikely to succeed in containing the epidemic is that it ignores the issue of tourism and other travel to the Caribbean by people from lower prevalence countries. It seems highly unlikely that low prevalence countries would countenance placing restrictions on the leisure, business and other travel of their own people to high prevalence areas in an attempt to control the epidemic. Yet sex tourism is growing as an industry, and tourists tend to have a large number of sexual partners. The following diagram presents evidence on the numbers of sexual partners reported by a UK general population sample, showing that females reported on average two partners, and males 3.7 while travelling in the last five years.

Figure 9.5
Rates of Partner Acquisition Abroad by UK Residents
Mean number of new overseas sexual partners whilst travelling abroad in the past 5 years

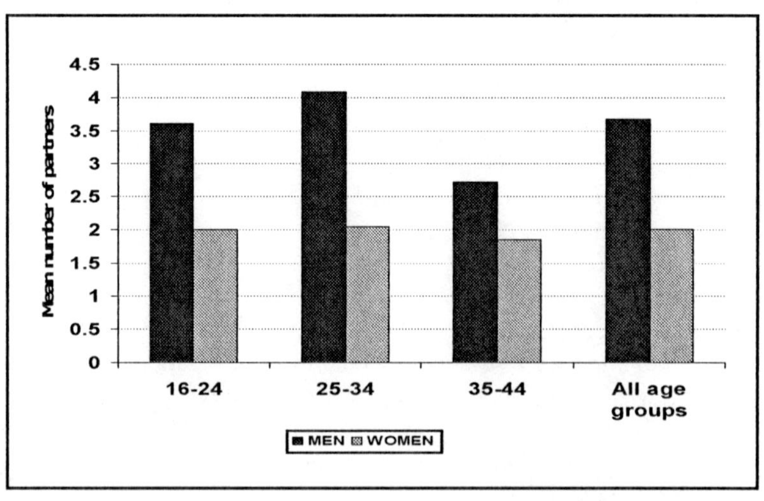

Source: UK National Survey of Sexual Attitudes and Lifestyles, 2000.

Of the aspects of security highlighted by the US National Intelligence Council, the impact of HIV on military forces has received the most attention by UNAIDS and other international organisations. However, the Caribbean is not currently a major zone of military conflict or humanitarian relief efforts. Nevertheless, the potential impact of HIV on Caribbean security services is an area deserving of further attention and policy initiatives.

The threat to state stability from HIV is real and may, in the long run, lead to the engagement of military forces in the region. This threat is, of course, of concern to Caribbean people and not only to outside countries with interests in the region. The discourse on HIV and security, as it now stands, is primarily concerned with the risk of infection to *developed* countries from *developing* countries and not vice versa. It is centred on the interests of richer, low prevalence countries. In this chapter, however, we have largely been concerned with answering a second question, is the HIV epidemic a security threat to Caribbean people?

From our analysis, it is clear that the HIV/AIDS epidemic presents a threat to state stability through the many dimensions through which the virus affects the social and economic indicators at both the micro and macro levels. The threat to the health sector is likely to be immediate as the sector is subjected to the initial impact and charged with the initial response. The state will need to make 'hard choices' in the face of competing demands, leading to frictions between social groups. The epidemic will significantly impact on the efficiency and effectiveness of policy initiatives geared towards poverty alleviation, income distribution and overall economic growth and development. Investor confidence will fall, further eroding the ability of the state to carry out its functions. The concentration of the epidemic among marginalised social groups (such as, sex workers, prisoners, migrants) poses further challenges for security forces working with these groups. Unless the health sector response to the epidemic across the region is carefully coordinated, the potential for the creation of new drug resistant strains of the virus is quite real. This speaks for the need to integrate HIV/AIDS into the wider development dialogue.

It is also necessary to broaden the concept of security from its traditional focus on military considerations and the stability of the state. The prevailing security approach is characterised by short-term action planning and an emphasis on direct forms of violence. However, the adequacy of such a conception is questionable in the case of HIV/AIDS. The disease does not pose the immediate danger presented by a prospective military attack and cannot be addressed by the use of physical force. In contrast with other diseases, HIV has no clear symptoms during its long latency, so that people cannot rely on recognisable signs and symptoms to avoid infection.

Economic, food and environmental insecurity are both causes and consequences of HIV/AIDS, with poverty being the major driving force behind sex work and an important explanatory factor behind low condom use, multiple partnerships and early initiation of sex. Gender-based norms and discrimination mean that women find it difficult to assert a wish for safer sex, while men are impelled by cultural expectations towards less safe behaviour. Discrimination and repression of sexual, cultural, religious or ethnic minorities by the state or by the society at large weakens their ability to access health care and to adopt protective behaviour (UNAIDS and IOM 2001). Personal, community and political security are components of a safer environment where the risks of HIV infection can be minimised.

The globally differentiated impact of the HIV/AIDS pandemic (that is, between high-income and poor regions) and the necessity of long-term, diverse and sustained responses are among the reasons that it is not a popular campaign issue among politicians (Ostergard 2002; Parker 2002). Individuals are infected, not states and within states it is usually the most marginalised populations who are the most vulnerable to infection: for example, disadvantaged racial and ethnic minority communities, commercial sex workers, economic migrants and men who have sex with men. From this perspective, it can be argued that the HIV/AIDS pandemic is not just a cause but also a consequence of global structural inequalities. Addressing HIV/AIDS as a security concern thus means focusing on the interests and concerns of marginalised groups and minorities and attacking the root causes of global and local inequalities.

In recent years, considerable progress has been made within the Caribbean in developing regional strategies to address the challenges of HIV/AIDS. The formation of the Pan-Caribbean Partnership is unique, worldwide, in aiming to coordinate the efforts of many national governments in a region, and is especially necessary in this region given the small size and limited capacity and influence of individual countries. Important achievements include successful negotiations with pharmaceutical companies for reduced prices for anti-retroviral drugs. Several Caribbean presidents and prime ministers have followed the example of President Museveni of Uganda in heading commissions to manage the multi-sectoral response in their countries. However, for further progress to be made, it will be necessary to deepen the response within the countries and address sources of vulnerability within the region.

Areas for strengthening the response within countries include the following:

- The human resource capacity to address the epidemic must be substantially increased. There is a need for more specialist medical and social scientists, counsellors, home care workers and nurses. HIV/AIDS awareness programmes should be incorporated into the training of a wide range of staff, notably police forces, prison officers, immigration officials, NGO leaders and civil servants. Substantial funds have been donated or loaned to the region to address the epidemic, but the disbursement record has been poor. Without substantial investment in human resources, opportunities will be lost to stem the tide of the epidemic. Education and training institutions should be strengthened to address the additional demands.
- Confidential voluntary counselling and testing for HIV should be widely available. The vital importance of maintaining the confidentiality of client information should be emphasised to staff, and sanctions imposed on staff who break the confidence of clients. Effective treatment and care interventions also require that laboratories be equipped to conduct CD4 tests and other related tests at the minimum and be equipped to provide effective diagnosis for a range of opportunistic infections.
- Given the high prevalence of HIV among women, the low-cost drugs which exist to prevent mother-to-child transmission of the virus should be made universally available as part of antenatal care. This will reduce the impact on future generations.
- Vulnerable groups such as sex workers and men who have sex with men should be actively involved in the development of programmes appropriate to their needs. Professionals who work with them should receive specialist training and supervision to ensure that they are responding sensitively and in a non-discriminatory manner.

Concerted regional approaches are needed in the following areas:

- Programmes to increase access to anti-retrovirals must be carefully coordinated to prevent the development of resistant strains of the virus.
- Mandatory testing of migrants for HIV should be stopped. National leaders must recognise that Caribbean countries are 'all in the same boat'; the extent of intra-Caribbean migration and travel threatens public health in each and every country, whether these countries are primarily of origin or destination. Cross-national alliances should be

formed to develop programmes to address the HIV prevention and care needs of travellers and migrants pre-departure, at transit points, in the destination countries and on their return to countries of origin. Migrants and organisations representing them should be involved in strategic planning and the development of programmes.

- Caribbean governments should work with the tourism sector to develop health promotion measures such as staff health education and the provision of condoms and information in hotel rooms.
- Caribbean governments should seek to increase their own contributions and thus self-sufficiency in addressing the epidemic. To date, a number of Caribbean territories have accessed World Bank loans or have expressed an interest in doing so. This increases the indebtedness of Caribbean countries and may reduce their capacity to spend in crucial areas of HIV prevention such as poverty alleviation. Note that several costings of National Strategic Plans have been conducted as part of the operationalisation of the Regional Strategic Plan of the Pan-Caribbean Partnership, as a means of indicating the financial requirements of the country's response. A look at the cost of a sample of the strategic plans developed reveals some interesting facts as seen in the table below.

Table 9.3
Breakdown of Cost of a National Response per annum by Selected Country

Country	Cost of response US$M	Share of cost to GDP %	Projected impact US$M
Trinidad & Tobago	18.07	0.2	453.0
St Kitts & Nevis	1.7	0.8	10.4
Barbados	10.0	0.4	125.0

Source: National AIDS Programmes

Based on table 9.3, the cost of the national strategic plans have, to date, amounted to less than 1 per cent of the country's Gross Domestic Product, quite small particularly when juxtaposed against the projected impact. It therefore begs the question, why would countries forego the financing of their National HIV/AIDS plans internally and seek external funding, thereby increasing debt burden and jeopardising fiscal stability, particularly in light of the poor track record in utilising aid funding for the social sector in the past?

More broadly, an adequate response to HIV requires a shift in the security perspective away from the traditional concern with power politics, national interest, territorial sovereignty and external aggression (for example, military invasion, terrorism) and towards the pursuit of democratic security via sustainable human development (Johansen 1991; Busumtwi-Sam 2002). At present, it may be said that this orientation to the epidemic has strengthened the hand of the state by creating anxieties about 'undesirable elements' in the society who are blamed for spreading the virus. Without a fundamental re-think of the concept of security as it applies to HIV, the response may be to strengthen the forces of repression against sexual and other minorities. Quite apart from ethical concerns, there is every reason to suppose that this will be counter-productive.

Instead, responses to HIV must be fundamentally respectful of difference within the state (sexual, ethnic or otherwise) and must involve a wide variety of social groups in developing strategies which are appropriate to their own needs. Human security is about removing or reducing sources of insecurity and vulnerabilities and promoting human participatory development. In broad terms, human security is defined 'as freedom from want as well as freedom from fear' (UNDP 1995). The four essential characteristics of human security as defined by the UNDP (1995) are particularly pertinent to the HIV epidemic:

- Human security is a universal concern. It is relevant to people everywhere, in rich nations and poor.
- The components of human security are interdependent. There are no longer isolated events that are confined within national borders. Their consequences travel the globe.
- We have seen that, not only does HIV/AIDS traverse national boundaries, but sources of vulnerability within a country are conditioned by the position of the country within the world economy.
- Human security is easier to ensure through early prevention than later intervention. It is less costly to meet these threats upstream than downstream.
- We have presented evidence of the profound social and economic costs of the epidemic in the absence of concerted, coordinated and cooperative multisectoral action, nationally, regionally and internationally.

- Human security is people-centred. It is concerned with people's freedom of choice, access and peace.
- The prevailing concept of security shapes people's attitudes and moral commitments, making it easier for them to accept that people seen as different from themselves can die from HIV/AIDS in their millions (Johansen 1991). A people-centred concept of security is a pre-requisite for a democratic and effective response to the epidemic.

Notes

1. The number of new AIDS cases in North America started to fall from a high of 27 per 100,000 population in 1992 following the introduction of anti-retroviral drugs. In 1994, the rate in the Caribbean began to surpass that in North America. By 1996 the rate in North America stood at 13 per 100,000 while that in the Caribbean was 37 per 100,000.
2. CAREC member countries are Anguilla, Antigua and Barbuda, Aruba, Bahamas, Barbados, Belize, Bermuda, British Virgin Islands, Cayman Islands, Dominica, Grenada, Guyana, Jamaica, Montserrat, Netherlands Antilles, St Kitts and Nevis, St Lucia, St Martin, St Vincent and the Grenadines, Suriname, Trinidad and Tobago and Turks and Caicos Islands.
3. This is an imperfect estimate as it does not take into account the different sexual behaviour patterns between the sexes and between those women who are pregnant and those who are not, nor the higher biological susceptibility to HIV among females. This indicator is often used because it is the most accessible as the blood of pregnant women is routinely screened. There is not a similar 'captive population' for screening among males.

References

Allen, Caroline F., Dusilley Cannings, Wendy Kitson-Piggott, Karen De Souza, Morris Edwards, Uli Wagner, Maxine Swain and Carol Trotman. 2002. *Employing peers and women's group members as researchers in an HIV seroprevalence and behavioural survey among female sex workers in Georgetown, Guyana.* Poster presented at the International AIDS conference, Barcelona, July 7-12. Abstract TuPeF5338, book of the XIII International AIDS Conference.

Allen, Caroline F. 2002. 'Gender and the transmission of HIV in the Caribbean', *The Society for Caribbean Studies Annual Conference Papers*, 3. Available: http://www.scsonline.freeserve.co.uk/olvol3.html.

Allen, Caroline F., Sheila Samiel, Tiphani Burrell, Cheryl O'Neil and C. James Hospedales. 2001. *HIV risk behaviour in the Caribbean among adults and young people.* Paper presented at the conference on the Social History of Medicine and Public Health Policy in the Caribbean, University of the West Indies, Cave Hill, Barbados. (Port of Spain, Trinidad and Tobago: Caribbean Epidemiology Centre/Pan American Health Organization/World Health Organization).

Armstrong, Jill. 1991. 'Socioeconomic implications of AIDS in developing countries', *Finance and Development*, 14–17.

Barnett, Tony and Alan Whiteside. 2002. *AIDS in the Twenty-First Century: Disease and Globalization*. Basingstoke and New York: Palgrave Macmillan.

Bezanson, Keith. 2002. *Will a global public goods approach at the Monterrey Conference lead to additional resources for development co-operation?* Brighton, UK: Institute of Development Studies. Accessed November 19, 2002 at: http://www.ids.ac.uk/ids/news/Archive/globalgoods.html.

Busumtwi-Sam, James. 2002. 'Development and human security: whose security, and from what?' *International Journal*, Spring: 253–72.

Camara, Bilali. *2001. Nineteen years of the HIV/ AIDS epidemic in the Caribbean: a summary*. Port of Spain, Trinidad and Tobago: Special Programme on Sexually Transmitted Infections, Caribbean Epidemiology Centre/Pan American Health Organization/World Health Organization.

Camara, Bilali. 2002. *Twenty years of the HIV/ AIDS epidemic in the Caribbean*. (Port of Spain, Trinidad and Tobago: Special Programme on Sexually Transmitted Infections, Caribbean Epidemiology Centre/Pan American Health Organisation/World Health Organisation.

Clinton, Bill. 2002. *Action against AIDS: for the global good*, speech delivered at the closing session of the International AIDS Conference, Barcelona, on Friday, July 12, 2002. Accessed 20/11/02 at: http://www.kaisernetwork.org/aids2002/transcript/transcript_webcast_12_a1.html.

De Groulard, Michel, Godfrey Sealy, Pauline Russell-Brown, Uli Wagner, Cheryl O'Neil, Caroline F. Allen and Emmanuel Joseph. 2000. *Homosexual Aspects of the HIV/AIDS Epidemic in the Caribbean: A Public Health Challenge for Prevention and Control*, abstract book of the International AIDS Conference, Durban, South Africa, 9–14 July, Volume 1.

De Moya, E. Antonio and Rafael Garcia. 1999. 'Three decades of male sex work in Santo Domingo'. In P. Aggleton, ed. *Men who sell sex: international perspectives on male prostitution and HIV/AIDS*. London: UCL Press, 127–139.

Frenk, Julio and Octavio Gomez-Dantes. 2002. 'Globalization and the challenges to health systems', *Health Affairs*, 21, 3: 160–165.

Gonzalez, David. 2002. 'A Haitian Doctor's Success in the Fight Against Disease', *New York Times*, 22 December.

Gow, Jeff. 2002. 'HIV/ AIDS in Africa: implications for US foreign policy', *Health Affairs*, 21,3: 57–69.

Healthlink Worldwide. 2002. *Combat AIDS: HIV and the World's Armed Forces*. London: Healthlink Worldwide.

Homer-Dixon, Thomas F. 1996. 'Environmental scarcity, mass violence, and the limits to ingenuity', *Current History*, 95, 604: 359–365.

Hsu, Lee-Nah. 2001. *HIV subverts national security*. Bangkok: United Nations Development Programme South East Asia HIV and Development Project.

Johansen, Robert C. 1991. 'Real security is democratic security', *Alternatives*, 16, 209–42.

Kaul, Inge, Isabelle Grunberg and Marc A. Stern, eds. 1999. *Global Public Goods: International Cooperation in the Twenty-First Century*. New York: Oxford University Press.

Kempadoo, Kamala, ed. 2000. *Sun, Sex and Gold: Tourism and Sex Work in the Caribbean* Lanham, MD: Roman and Littlefield.

Klare, Michael T. 1996. 'Redefining security: the new global schisms,' *Current History*, 95, 604: 353–358.

Luo, Robert F. 2002. 'Understanding the threat of AIDS', *Medical Student Journal of the American Medical Association*, 288: 1649.

Mills, Anne. 2002. *Technology and science as global public goods: tackling priority diseases of poor countries*, paper prepared for the Annual World Bank Conference on Development Economics, Barcelona. Accessed November 15, 2002 at: http://wbln0018.worldbank.org/eurvp/web.nsf/Pages/Mills/$File/MILLS.PDF.

Mittelman, J.H. 2000. *The Globalization Syndrome: Transformation and Resistance*. Princeton: Princeton University Press.

National Intelligence Council. 2000. *The Global Infectious Disease Threat and its Implications for The United States*. Washington: National Intelligence Council. Accessed 19 November 2002 at http://www.cia.gov/nic/pubs/other_products/inf_diseases_paper.html.

Nicholls, Shelton, Roger McLean, Karl Theodore, Ralph Henry, Bilali Camara and team. 2000. 'Modelling the macroeconomic impact of HIV/AIDS in the English-speaking Caribbean', *The South African Journal of Economics* 68, 5: 916–32.

Nurse, Keith. 2002. *Festival Tourism in the Caribbean*. Washington D.C.: Inter-American Development Bank.

Ostergard, Robert L. 2002. 'Politics in the hot zone: AIDS and national security in Africa', *Third World Quarterly*, 23, 2: 333–350.

Pan American Health Organization. 2000. *A Portrait of Adolescent Health in the Caribbean*, Minnesota: WHO Collaborating Centre on Adolescent Health, University of Minnesota/Barbados: Caribbean Program Coordination Office of the Pan American Health Organization/World Health Organization.

Parker, Richard. 2002. 'The Global HIV/AIDS Pandemic, Structural Inequalities, and the Politics of International Health', *American Journal of Public Health*, 92, 3: 343–346.

Pettiford, Lloyd. 1996. 'Changing conceptions of security in the Third World', *Third World Quarterly*, 17, 2: 289–306.

Rodriguez, L.R. 2002. *The Air Bridge Network: coordinated care across cultural and geographic boundaries*. Poster presented at the International AIDS conference, Barcelona, 7–12 July. Abstract MoPeF4126 of the XIII International AIDS Conference.

Russell-Brown, Pauline and Godfrey Sealey. 1998. *Gay Research Initiative in the Caribbean: a Technical Report*, Port of Spain, Trinidad and Tobago: Caribbean Epidemiology Centre/Pan American Health Organization/World Health Organization.

Shtarkshall, R. and V. Soskolne. 2000. *Migrant populations and HIV/ AIDS: the development and implementation of programmes*. Paris: UNESCO and Geneva: Joint United Nations Programme on HIV/AIDS.

Singer, P.W. 2003. 'AIDS and International Security', *Survival*, 44, 1: 145–58.

Ssemakula, John K. 2002. 'The impact of 9/11 on HIV/AIDS care in Africa and the global fund to fight AIDS, tuberculosis and malaria', *Journal of the Association of Nurses in AIDS Care*, 13, 5: 45–56.

UNAIDS. 2002. *Report on the global HIV/AIDS epidemic*, Geneva: Joint United Nations Programme on HIV/ AIDS.

UNAIDS. 1999. Level and flow of national and international resources for the response to HIV/ AIDS, 1996–97, Geneva: Joint UN Programme on HIV/AIDS.

UNAIDS and International Organization for Migration. 2001. *Population Mobility and AIDS*. Geneva: Joint United Nations Programme on HIV/AIDS.

UNAIDS Humanitarian Unit. 2002. *UNAIDS Initiative on HIV/ AIDS and Security*, Geneva: Joint UN Programme on HIV/AIDS. Accessed 16 November 2002 at: http://www.unaids.org/security/Issues/human%20security/docs/SecurityInitiative.ppt.

UNAIDS/WHO. 2002. AIDS Epidemic Update.

UNAIDS. 2002a 'Report on the Global HIV/AIDS Epidemic'.

UNDP. 1995. 'Redefining security: the human dimension', *Current History*, 94, 592: 229–236.

UNECLAC. 2002. *Globalization and Development*. Santiago, Chile.

UN Security Council. Resolution 1308.

Walker, Robert B.J. 1990. 'Security, sovereignty and the challenge of world politics', *Alternatives*, 15, 3–27.

Whiteside, Alan and David FitzSimons. 1992. *The AIDS epidemic: economic, political and security implications*. London: Research Institute for the Study of Conflict and Terrorism.

Whiteside, Alan and Clem Sunter. 2000. *AIDS, The Challenge for South Africa*. Cape Town: Human and Rousseau Tafelberg.

Williams, Simon. 2001. 'From Smart Bombs to Smart Bugs: Thinking the Unthinkable in Medical Sociology and Beyond', *Sociological Research Online*, 6:3, <http://www.socresonline.org.uk/6/3/williams.html>

Yeager, Rodger and Stuart Kingma. 2001. 'HIV/AIDS: destabilising national security and the multi-national response', *International Review of Armed Forces Medical Services*, Official Organ of the International Committee of Military Medicine 4,1: 3–12.

10

United States-Caribbean Relations: The Impact of 9/11

Dorith Grant-Wisdom

Introduction

The attacks on the World Trade Center and the Pentagon on September 11, 2001, were strongly condemned by practically every government in the world, as was terrorism in a general sense. There were unwavering denouncements of these acts by commentators from across the political spectrum. In his Havana speech, Castro enunciated that 'The unanimous anger caused by the human and psychological damage inflicted on the American people by the unexpected and shocking deaths of thousands of innocent people, whose images have shaken the world, is perfectly understandable.' Other Caribbean leaders expressed similar sentiments as the world bemoaned the tragedy. But beneath this basic agreement were many differences of opinion as to how best to respond to this horrendous disaster that has left an indelible mark on the thinking and practice of international relations.

This chapter focuses on the nature of the response by the United States since September 11 and the impact this is having on US-Caribbean relations. It employs a conceptual and ontological approach to the goals, principles and strategies that have been central to the hegemonic role the United States has historically played in the Western Hemisphere. In so doing, the chapter takes into consideration the history of US-Caribbean relations, the types and forms of interactions at the policy level, and the nature of the worldview that informs the context in which such interactions are generated. This enables an understanding of the extent to which the US response represents a break with earlier policies and, if so why, and the likely consequences for US-Caribbean relations.

Overview of US-Caribbean Relations

It is impossible to recount here all of the history of United States-Caribbean relations, but it is necessary to consider key threads of development over time to aid an assessment of the impact of September 11. Beginning with the 1823 Monroe Doctrine, the history of the United States has been one of territorial and economic expansionism that fits within the wider context of the growth of colonialism, and the increasing struggle among powerful states to secure a dominant position in the global political economy. So, despite periods of isolationism, the United States has been able to influence the agenda of issues that Caribbean nations face, as well as shape the context and contours for choices and decisions made by the governments of the region.

As Gilderhus asserts, 'The modern age in relations between the United States and the countries of Latin America began in 1889 at the First International American Conference'.[1] Reflective of a *paradigm shift* in the views and implementation of US foreign policy, diplomatic practice moved away 'from the reactive, improvisational style so characteristic of the immediate post-Civil War era and toward a more systematic, expansive approach'.[2] Amidst the economic downturns, 'social malaise' and intense global rivalry among the Great Powers, 'the Old Diplomacy could not respond to new realities coherently and effectively'.[3] Change in foreign policy occurred 'when anomalies and inconsistencies debilitated the traditional ways of doing things and rendered them inadequate'.[4]

The Spanish-American War of 1898 marked the beginnings of US involvement in the Caribbean. So, by 1913, the US had created protectorates, practised intervention in the Caribbean region and established its hegemony through affirmations of power expressed in policies such as the Roosevelt corollary to the Monroe Doctrine, and 'dollar diplomacy'. This rise to regional dominance 'required the subordination of Latin American sensibilities to US preferences...'[5] Consequent to the First World War, the United States became the largest capitalist economy, displacing the European powers. In light of its newly acquired economic status, the US began to consolidate its advantage within the region in order to neutralise the European influence and presence in the hemisphere and to promote the development of client states. The scores of military interventions and occupations which took place to keep 'friendly' governments in power, as well as seizures of land for United

States bases (in Cuba, Haiti and Dominican Republic) had a tremendous impact on the formation of Caribbean political economy.[6] Despite the shift from direct interventionist practices to the more subtle techniques of President Franklin Roosevelt's Good Neighbour Policy, the United States continued to maintain dominance by promoting policies of commercial expansion and regional collaboration.

With the onset of World War II and the Cold War, the Good Neighbour Policy lost its viability as a basis for US regional relations. The United States navigated its interests between those conservative nationalists who defended the tenets of the Monroe Doctrine and the universalists who favoured the creation of a post-war system of collective security. The result was a regional system of security consisting of a military alliance – the Rio Pact – and a political complement – the Organization of American States (OAS), and the United Nations whose Article 51 'sanctioned the exercise of regional prerogatives within the context of the world organization'. The Rio Pact, otherwise known as the Inter-American Treaty of Reciprocal Assistance, embraced the concept of collective security for the American states, provided for peaceful settlements before appealing to the United Nations, and proposed the use of collective action based on a two-thirds majority vote.

Enthusiasts lauded the move for hemispheric cooperation, but critics saw it as a system that 'emanated from US hegemonic aspirations and functioned essentially as an alliance between the United States and the established elites of Latin America in defense of the status quo'.[7] Interestingly, this move towards a new hemispheric solidarity coincided with the broad *Open Door* approach of the US that emerged under the Truman Doctrine in particular. The Monroe Doctrine was recast at the level of the global as Truman warned against any attempt to impose foreign domination and politics in areas deemed vital to US security. It is also critical to note that no equivalent of a Marshall Plan was envisioned for Latin America. In response to a query at a press conference, Truman stated: 'I think there has always been a Marshall Plan in effect for the Western hemisphere. The foreign policy of the United States in that direction has been set for one hundred years, known as the Monroe Doctrine'.

With the balance of power cast in its favour, the United States sought to build an international liberal economic order through key institutions such as the United Nations, World Bank, International Monetary Fund and GATT. However, its global leadership was stymied by the presence of the Soviet Union, and 'as the contest between East and West intensified, the United States grew more and more determined to protect its own backyard by maintaining the *status quo* and squashing any externally impelled movements for change'.[8] The Cold War set the tone for relations for the next 40 years as it first diverted attention away from the Americas. But as fears of communist threats increased, the countries of Latin America in general and the Caribbean in particular gained in importance, not because of anything intrinsic to them but because of their links with the wider struggle between the US and the USSR. In regard to the actual direction of foreign policy and the strategy that was applied, there were voices from the more conservative streams that advocated an all-out offensive against the USSR, introducing the *roll-back* strategy. This was tempered by a strategy of *containment* used to deter Soviet expansionist aims by applying counter pressures.

Although the character of US-Caribbean relations evolved over the duration of the Cold War, a pattern persisted that illustrates the larger historical pattern of United States dominance. Security concerns within the framework of containment became a focal point in the Caribbean after the 1959 Cuban Revolution. This was highlighted by the 1961 Bay of Pigs invasion, the Cuban missile crisis, and the resulting policy of political and economic isolation of Cuba. In an effort to prevent further radical revolutions in the hemisphere, the Alliance for Progress was launched in 1961 to support economic and social reforms. As most of the other nations had not attained independence, the main beneficiaries in the Caribbean of this ten-year aid program were Haiti and the Dominican Republic. Despite the emphasis on economic and social reforms, US-Caribbean relations continued to be dictated by the predominant concern of anti-communism.

The ensuing decades witnessed the constant opposition to radical regimes in the Caribbean and Latin American region. In 1965, the United States engaged in direct military intervention in the Dominican Republic preventing 'the return to power of a democratically elected leader who had been overthrown in 1963'.[9] Notwithstanding the efforts by the Carter administration to redefine Cold War policies, the anti-communist strategy intensified under President Reagan with a military intervention in Grenada. Military action was bolstered with the return to earlier policies of supporting and sustaining friendly authoritarian leaders and opposing the possibilities of having another Nicaraguan situation. The Reagan administration also launched the Caribbean Basin Initiative (that provided some aid and lower tariffs on exports to the United States) as a means to increase trade and investment. However, the programme served the political purpose of rewarding those countries that implemented free market economic reforms.

It was during the presidency of George Bush, from 1989 to 1993, that the Cold War came to an end. One major consequence of this was a shift in the policy agenda from the fears of Soviet encroachment and communist expansionism. Although it altered the debate over interventionist activities in the region, the Bush administration engaged in a unilateral invasion of Panama in December of 1989 in which Noriega was removed and a new government installed. Overall, United States policy toward Latin America and the Caribbean reflected the new conditions, suggesting continuity as well as change. Amidst the uncertainty of this new age, and a lot of speculation about the emerging order, a general consensus materialised in the Washington circles that stressed democratic development and economic reform as the overarching norms in hemispheric relations. These provided the subtext for focusing on key issues such as consolidating democracy and human rights, economic integration, trade and investment, trafficking of illicit narcotics, immigration and refugee problems.

Exhibiting a propensity for diplomacy and negotiation in the Caribbean Basin rather than military action, the Bush administration placed emphasis on economic issues within the framework of neo-liberalism as a means to addressing the economic woes that plagued the region. So, in 1990, President Bush made two major announcements that had significant impact on US-Caribbean relations. First, there was the intention to negotiate a free trade agreement (FTA) with Mexico, which was later expanded to include Canada in a North American Free Trade Area (NAFTA). The second announcement built on the Caribbean Basin Initiative by introducing the Enterprise for the Americas Initiative with the objective of creating a hemispheric free trade area. Using NAFTA as a precedent, bilateral trade and investment 'framework agreements' with countries of the region were proposed as a step towards a hemispheric FTA. Notwithstanding concerns of capital flight towards Mexico and fears of losing preferential treatment and increasing trade competition, most Caribbean countries have signed framework agreements with the US.

The momentum for building hemispheric free trade was picked up by President Clinton but it was heavily laden with a discourse of liberal internationalism. However, despite the Clinton administration's more multilateral stance, the United States continued to unilaterally determine the framework of US-Caribbean relations. This unilateral action sparked some controversy as Caribbean countries pointed to a number of problems related to preferential trade treatment, US deportation of criminals, and the Shiprider Agreement. Interestingly, Barbados and Jamaica refused to sign the latter agreement intended to develop international drug cooperation between the

US and the Caribbean. The two countries highlighted the need for cooperation that took into account democratic principles and respect for sovereignty. Consequently, the Bridgetown Accord in 1997 established a basis on which the US and CARICOM could cooperate on a wide range of issues of concern and interests to both sides. Despite this, relations continued to be shaped by the overarching principle of unilateralism but it afforded some space for Caribbean countries to address their concerns.

Towards a New Grand Strategy –The Emerging Bush Doctrine

The new environment of the post-Cold War era necessitated a restructuring of foreign policy, as the United States was 'required to *think* again, at a depth not required in two generations'.[10] The first President Bush's declaration of a *new world order* reflected this thinking and 'his first steps towards defining that order were his police action against the Noriega regime in Panama and his organisation of a UN action to counteract Iraq's invasion of Kuwait'.[11] A variety of ways of conceptualising this new world order and America's role in it began to surface. But regardless of the differences, the collapse of the Soviet Union was generally interpreted as an opportunity to consolidate a position of unchallengeable global leadership and hegemony. The question centred on what grand strategy would replace the grand strategy of global military containment and multilateral economic openness that characterised foreign policy in the past 40 years. The disagreement about the nature of threats to American interests was manifested in the number of tentative doctrines that were proposed during the 1990s. These ranged from maintaining a *balance of power*, to developing a *liberal community of peace.*[12]

A significant point of departure was the development of the concept of a *unipolar moment* developed by conservative columnist, Charles Krauthammer in 1991. Calling attention to the unchallenged superpower status of the United States, Krauthammer denounced the pretence of multilateralism by claiming, 'It is largely for domestic reasons ... that the American political leaders make sure to dress unilateral action in multilateral clothing'.[13] The 'best hope for safety', according to him, 'is in American strength and will to lead a unipolar world, unashamedly laying down the rules of world order and being prepared to enforce them'.[14] This proposal may have appeared far-fetched at the time as no one approach proved sufficiently comprehensive as a grand strategy for the new era.

In addition, there was not a major overarching threat or danger that could enable enough support from most Americans for the resources to sustain such a strategy. However, this changed with September 11 as the attacks on the World Trade Center and the Pentagon were cast in the same light as the attack on Pearl Harbour. Terrorism was now the fundamental threat to the United States, its way of life and its interests. This presented a moment in which the second Bush administration could reconfigure foreign policy and enunciate an emerging grand strategy that is altering the relationships and nature of international relations of which the Caribbean is a part.

The new strategy being put in place 'begins with a fundamental commitment to maintaining a unipolar world in which the United States has no peer competitor'.[15] President Bush has emphasised the intention of limiting rivalries and keeping US military and other strengths beyond challenges. In his State of the Union address in January 2003, Bush stated, 'The course of this nation does not depend on the decisions of others. Whenever action is necessary, I will defend the actions and freedom of the American people'. Recalling the words of Charles Krauthammer, it is critical to note that the view of asserting US global dominance and capturing the unipolar moment is not new. In fact, a member of the first Bush administration shared this view, but in a post-September 11 scenario, the goal is to make US advantages permanent, thereby setting new global standards.[16]

A shift in foreign policy is also reflected in the decision and determination of what constitutes threats on a global scale. The New National Security Strategy put forward in September 2002, speaks of 'shadowy networks of individuals that can bring great chaos and suffering'. In his 2002 State of the Union address, Bush portrayed an image of thousands of 'dangerous killers' who were 'ticking time bombs' roaming the globe. Terrorism is thus defined as a war of global dimensions that involves anyone and everyone. The essence of the emerging Bush Doctrine is captured in the following statement from *The National Security Strategy of the United States of America*:

> The struggle against global terrorism is different from any other war in our history. It will be fought on many fronts against a particularly elusive enemy over an extended period of time. Progress will come through the persistent accumulation of successes – some seen, some unseen.

The fact is that viewing terrorism as war reduces concern for individual culpability. Evidence need not be 'of courtroom quality; intelligence reporting will suffice' and 'focus is not on the accused individual but on the correct identification of the *enemy*'.[17] What is significant is that the National Security Strategy speaks not only of stopping the enemy's efforts, but also of acting 'against such emerging threats before they are fully formed'. Threat comes not only from actual enemies but also from potential attackers. It states that the 'immediacy of today's threats, and the magnitude of potential harm' create a sense of urgency requiring that the war must be taken to the enemy. Therefore, success does not come by relying solely on a 'reactive posture', and 'traditional concepts of deterrence' that characterised the Cold War period. Instead, the US must 'adapt the concept of imminent threat'; in fact, the 'United States will, if necessary, act preemptively'. A fundamental premise of this kind of *preemptive war* is the application of a quick first strike attack that seeks to defeat an adversary (potential or real) before it can put together a retaliatory response.

A final aspect that shapes the contours of the Bush Doctrine is, instead of defining the horrendous violence of September 11 as a crime against humanity, it was perceived as an act of war. In so doing, it couched the issues in nationalist sentiment and separated the US from other nations despite the fact that so many people from other states were killed. Among the many that perished were at least 160 persons from 15 Caribbean countries. Given the fact that this took place on US soil and the character of international relations, it would be remiss not to state that the United States does have a leadership role in response to the September 11 attacks.

However, instead of fostering a concerted international effort that would accommodate open discussion, the United States seised the unipolar moment to apply force and mete out justice as it saw fit. In waging an indefinite war, President Bush claimed it 'will not end until every terrorist group of global reach has been found, stopped and defeated'. Participation of the rest of the world was assumed and determined by the new global fault lines envisaged by the US. As Bush noted: 'Every nation in every region now has a decision to make. Either you are with us or you are with the terrorists'. Indicative of the *new realism*, the Bush Doctrine projected a global outlook but is still driven by the *zero-sum*, *us-versus them* worldview that characterised previous eras. Such a view of national security inevitably relies on unilateral solutions with consequences that are substantially determined by policy choices made within the United States.

In adapting a particular image of terrorism's character and primary causes, the Bush administration was drawn to a particular set of policy recommendations. These include making no concessions to terrorists and striking no deals; bringing terrorists to justice for their crimes; isolating and applying pressure on states that sponsor terrorism to force them to change their behaviour; and bolstering the counter terrorist capabilities of those countries that work with the US and require assistance. The war on terrorism commenced with the massive bombing of Afghanistan on October 7, 2001 and the Iraq war in March of 2003; but based on the premise of fighting war on multiple fronts, the offensive has adopted a variety of tactics and approaches in different countries. As far as the Caribbean is concerned, Washington is working on two tracks. The rest of this chapter will therefore situate the analysis of the impact of September 11 within the framework of these two tracks bearing in mind the historical context of US-Caribbean relations.

The Bush Doctrine and the Caribbean

In regard to the first track on which Washington is working, the conditions are being set for the US to intervene anywhere and anytime to preemptively destroy the terrorist threats. The war on terrorism is different not only in scope but in the principles that are used to justify how and where it is waged. The Iraq War has demonstrated the overwhelming nature of US military power and its willingness to use it as a display of unipolarity. It is also a key example of what is perceived as an imminent threat and the right of the US to eradicate such potential threats. On March 17, in his address to the American people, Bush stated: 'We are acting now because the risk of inaction would be far greater. In one year, or five years, the power of Iraq to inflict harm to free nations would be multiplied many times over.'

Such preemption not only stops Iraq from taking future action but the show of extreme strength – shock and awe – indicates to others what they should expect if they do not fall in line. The message is a global one and it certainly resonates for the Caribbean region In addition, the US 'must be prepared to stop rogue states and their terrorist clients before they are able to threaten or use weapons of mass destruction...' This statement begs the questions as to what is a *rogue state* and who defines it. Is a rogue state one that challenges, directly or indirectly, American interests? How is this challenge conceptualised relative to America's national security? Defining global terms solely from an American viewpoint privileges the US. America's enemy automatically becomes an enemy of all states.

As far as the Caribbean is concerned, the only country in this hemisphere that is on the list of *rogue* and terrorist states is Cuba. Taking into consideration Cold War policy and the political pressure from exiles in Miami to isolate Cuba, one is left to wonder what the real reasons behind the inclusion of Cuba are. Defence of American interests in an era of global terrorism is one thing, but to place emphasis on the rogue nature of its perceived foes rules out deeper analysis, limiting its options to offensive action. This is implicit in US Senator Robert Byrd's floor speech made before the invasion of Iraq. He said, 'The doctrine of preemption...is being tested at a time of world-wide terrorism, making many countries around the globe wonder if they will soon be on our – hit list.' He further claimed that the war in Iraq 'represents a turning point in US foreign policy' and that the new doctrine 'appears to be in contravention of international law and the UN Charter'. This apparent defiance is linked to how key concepts are being redefined and reinvented in order to bring justice to enemies and reaffirm US dominance and leadership regionally and globally.

The National Security Strategy makes no distinction between terrorists and those who knowingly harbour or aid them. *Terrorists* and *terrorism* are distinctive yet vague enough to be subject to political manipulation. Linking states to terrorists and terrorism can be done without providing any factual substantiation or credible evidence to support such a claim. It also establishes a basis for intervention regardless of geographical boundaries, and justifies US intrusion into the affairs of others using war as the definitive instrument. But this has serious implications for the concept of sovereignty – a cardinal principle of international relations. Of course, it must be emphasised that the violation of sovereignty is certainly not a new phenomenon, especially in relation to developing states.

As history has illustrated, the United States has done this in the Western Hemisphere since the nineteenth century and, despite the formal independence of Caribbean states, in reality there was substantial control from Washington. The critical point is, regardless of the various forms of intrusion, which did not exclude armed intervention, there was the necessity to give the appearance that states had some internal control. Whether it was a Good Neighbour Policy or containment of the Soviet encroachment, there was some degree of deterrence in terms of overt intervention. As in the case of Guatemala, the United States was not a direct participant in the civil war of 1960 to 1996, but it funded, armed, trained and provided intelligence support to the Guatemalan government forces. Unlike previous periods, the difference now lies in the Bush administration's inclination to apply sovereignty 'on a global basis, leaving to itself the authority to determine when sovereign rights have been forfeited, and doing so on an anticipatory basis'.[18] So, for states such as those in the Caribbean region, the already limited view accorded to sovereignty is no longer a given as there is less inclination to view US intervention as compromising a state's independence.

One of the clearest articulations of the conceptualisation of sovereignty from the perspective of the Bush administration is by Ambassador Richard Haas, director of the State Department's Policy Planning Staff.[19] He begins by pointing out that the components of sovereignty – internal authority, border control, policy autonomy, and non-intervention – are now challenged by new realities. The US must therefore adjust its thinking and actions as these realities pose serious threats to its national security. First, *failed states* that lack sovereign capacities can be breeding grounds for extremism and havens for criminals, drug traffickers, and terrorists. So, today's troubled countries must be prevented from becoming tomorrow's failed states. The second challenge to sovereignty, according to Haas, is globalisation that provides tangible 'goods' but facilitates the flow of many 'bads'. Thirdly, there is the challenge to sovereignty from the voluntary pooling or delegating of the rights of sovereignty to gain the benefits of multilateral cooperation. The final challenge that Haas highlights is when sovereignty is taken away – a result of an emerging global consensus that sovereignty is not a blank check.

In light of this growing consensus, Haas asserts that the principle of non-intervention does not hold for at least three circumstances.

> The first qualification of sovereignty comes when a state commits or fails to prevent genocide or crimes against humanity on its territory...the second point...countries have the right to take action to protect their citizens against those states that abet, support, or harbour international terrorists, or are incapable of controlling terrorists operating from their territory. Finally, states risk forfeiting their sovereignty when they take steps that represent a clear threat to global security. When certain regimes with a history of aggression and support for terrorism pursue weapons of mass destruction, thereby endangering the international community, they jeopardise their sovereign immunity from intervention including anticipatory action to destroy this developing capability.

What provides justification for these circumstances is the view that sovereignty is not a*bsolute* but *conditional*. The contingency of sovereignty lies in striking a 'balance between the rights and responsibilities of states'. As far as the war on terrorism is concerned, this balance is weighing heavily on the responsibilities and obligations that states must fulfil as opposed to the rights that have been traditionally bestowed on them. This worldview is reflective of the conservative ascendance to a governing and advisory role in the US administration. Taking pride in its realism, this stream of contemporary conservatives views US superiority as a special condition that confers not only rights but also duties. This view rests upon an assumption that inequality of status and achievement are inevitable, and just as individuals in society hold unequal positions, states in the international system share asymmetrical relations. It therefore proceeds from an ontological premise that takes for granted the hierarchical nature of the international system.

Such values run counter to the more all-embracing and inclusive tendencies of contemporary liberals or moderates such as Bill Clinton. In fact, it has tilted the scale to the right of the Post-World II ethos that balanced realist policies with liberal multilateral institutions. There is a basic mistrust of international institutions, coupled with a disbelief in egalitarianism at the multilateral level. Eschewing the importance of such institutions facilitates the general argument put forward by realism for the primacy of the state in international affairs. At the concrete policy level, September 11 created an ideological opportunity to project an image of the special condition of US superiority and its duty to the world as a whole, and to specifically lead the war on terrorism. From this perspective, multilateral mechanisms based on notions of egalitarianism cannot work in a world driven by natural tendencies to struggle for power and one in which the evil forces of terrorism will try to gain the upper hand. What will keep the system in check is the ability of the strong to lead, and its capability to hold others accountable for their actions. Given the unipolar moment, the US has no choice but to assume its responsibility. Thus, global security is dependent on and synonymous with the national security of the United States.

It is significant to note that the National Security Strategy points out that US national security begins with its strength. The US is portrayed as a modern society with 'inherent, ambitious, entrepreneurial energy', and its strength 'comes from what to do with that energy'. In an affirmation of the supremacy of US capitalism and military might in the war on terrorism, the National Security Strategy claims,

> In building a balance of power that favours freedom, the United States is guided by the conviction that all nations have important responsibilities...For freedom to thrive, accountability must be expected and required... The United States possesses unprecedented – and unequalled – strength and influence in the world. Sustained by faith in the principles of liberty, and the value of a free society, this position comes with unparalleled responsibilities, obligations, and opportunity. The great strength of this

> nation must be used to promote a balance of power that favours freedom...The United States welcomes our responsibility to lead in this great mission.

In the exercise of its leadership, based on a 'distinctly American internationalism that reflects the union of our values and our national interests' the US 'will respect the values, judgment, and interests of our friends and partners', but 'will be prepared to act apart when our interests and unique responsibilities require'. The momentum to make the world safe under the supremacy of US power engenders a conception of sovereignty that is *absolute* for the US but *conditional* for the rest of the world. In a sense, one could indeed argue that this kind of American exceptionalism is not necessarily new. What is new is the shift in the thinking and the attempts to create a global political and legal order that will make such exceptionalism the norm. The focal principle then would not be *whether* but *how* to pursue a policy of intervention.

It is this new conception of sovereignty that establishes the framework for the second track on which Washington is working in its war on terrorism. Operating from a premise that assumes the possibility of military intervention, this track lays out the different tactics and channels that the US is employing in the Caribbean to ensure its national security. These are in keeping with the necessity to strengthen weak and failed states, regulate globalisation's downside, and accommodate cooperation to combat terrorism. At the broadest level, there is the need to develop a 'coalition of the willing' in which states will 'voluntarily pool or delegate sovereign rights to gain the benefits of cooperation'. Bolstering solidarity in the hemisphere and building a cooperative defence strategy give credence to President Bush's declaration that 'This is the fight of all who believe in progress and pluralism, tolerance and freedom'. The OAS is the designated institution for rallying such a support and its arm, the Inter-American Committee Against Terrorism (CICTE), becomes the means to accomplishing its purpose.

As a show of support, the OAS approved two resolutions ten days after September 11. In the first resolution, the members of the Rio Pact activated its key provision on collective security thereby labelling the attacks against the US as an attack against all. The whole body of the OAS later supported this in a second resolution. Under the rubric of cooperation, both resolutions expressed concerted efforts to deny terrorist groups the ability to operate in their territories; to pursue, capture, prosecute, and extradite terrorists, to engage in the exchange of information; and to get all states to ratify the international convention for the suppression of financing terrorism. Significantly, the Inter-American Convention against Terrorism was adopted in June 2002 and has been signed by all but one of the OAS member states.

Notwithstanding the need for real and genuine cooperation, the OAS as a whole and the CICTE in particular provides a crucial backdrop for the specific requests the United States is making of individual countries. Occupying the position of chair before it was passed to El Salvador, the US was well placed to set the tone and direction of the CICTE. A Washington file staff writer recounts the statements of Roger Noriega, the US ambassador to the OAS, at a briefing in January 2003:

> As 'an instrument for applying the rule of law to criminal groups that seek to do our people harm,' CICTE 'has really transformed itself into a ground-breaking body and is a model for the rest of the world to follow'...CICTE will examine 'the practical ways each of these countries goes about applying rule of law,' helping government officials keep track of 'who's doing business in their countries, who's moving across borders, what sort of financial transactions are going on, and (whether they are) structured in a way that is apparently designed to evade detection'.[20]

The strategy entails the development of protocols to enhance coordination at the regional level. The CICTE is not only expected to carry out the functions listed in the above quote. Its members are also expected to sign, ratify and implement the 12 UN conventions against terrorism and the OAS convention and convert them into national legislation as well as make or increase financial or other tangible commitments to CICTE. To get the ball rolling at the CICTE session in January 2003, the US Customs Commissioner reiterated US commitment to the OAS/CICTE and pledged 'financial support in the amount of $1 million to further seed the Secretariat and nurture CICTE's growth...' In keeping with this US initiative, other member states were encouraged to follow suit. Such cooperation not only ensures its input and guidance but also creates a framework from which the US can apply pressure on an individual basis. As Ambassador Noriega further pointed out, in addition to using multilateral channels for combating terrorism, the United States 'continues to pursue bilateral agendas with individual countries'. But this two-pronged strategy is wrought with its own contradictions of providing the desired symbolic effects of cooperation and generating areas of tension as states are pressured to conform to external requirements.

One contradiction lies in the Bush administration's readiness to press the Caribbean and Latin American states to create cooperative efforts while it circumvents multilateral efforts in order to wage war on Iraq. The US has not joined the International Criminal Court for fear that its citizens would be at the risk of politically motivated prosecution; and it has withdrawn from the Kyoto Protocol because it would bring a disproportionate burden to the US. From this standpoint, cooperation means first pre-determining the agenda then dragooning other countries into agreement or acquiescence. Operating from this distinctly realist position of exceptionalism, a former policy director to the White House, special envoy for the Americas, lauds the resolutions of the OAS and the Rio Pact, but adds: 'In and of themselves, however, they are insufficient. Unless Latin American and Caribbean nations truly own the issue of global terrorism... the region's efforts will be overshadowed and fears of renewed US policy neglect could well come to pass ...' He also notes, 'The fight against global terrorism is the first test of the new century, and the question remains, will Latin American and Caribbean nations pass or fail? The answer will determine in part the strategic importance that the United States ascribes to the region well into the future'.[21]

There is therefore pressure for Caribbean countries to conform to certain demands geared towards the adoption and implementation of anti-terrorism policies and activities. These demands are made mainly through political and diplomatic instruments. The message is clear in Secretary of State Colin Powell's speech at the United Nations Security Council on January 20, 2003. In ridding the world of terrorism, Powell claimed, 'We must wage our campaign at every level, with every tool of statecraft, for as long as it takes.' He further stated, '...this war has many fronts, from money laundering and the illicit trade, to arms trafficking and the proliferation of weapons of mass destruction. We must fight terrorism on all of these fronts.' It follows that the identification of terrorist cells is significant but it is not the major reason why the Caribbean is critical to the war on terrorism. In an era of globalisation there is the imperative for Caribbean states to regain sovereign control over cross-border flows that may endanger security. As a 'third border', the Caribbean's strategic location relative to the movement of drugs, arms and peoples holds some degree of importance for the United States. Linking US homeland security with its foreign policy has resulted in the merge between the war on terrorism and the war on drugs.

One of the most visible impacts of this has been the expansion of the FBI, DEA, and CIA operations and presence across the region. This is also in keeping with the first major re-organisation of the executive branch since the Truman era including the creation of the new Department of Homeland Security that encompass 22 existing federal agencies. The centralisation and direction of war efforts from this new department have immediate repercussions not only for domestic affairs but also for regional and global relations as priorities become shuffled on the US policy agenda. This signals a move towards the direct coordination of security measures in the Caribbean from the Department of Homeland Security. It means that the institutional divisions between the US and the Caribbean are becoming blurred as this Department extends its tentacles into the region.

At a concrete level there are a number of policy issues that have attained high priority in relation to the Caribbean. Denying safe-havens to terrorists is a major requirement. This entails the improvement of intelligence sharing at the national level, within the region and with the United States. In addition, governments will have to increase surveillance activities and take appropriate law enforcement action. Pressure has been brought to bear on regional governments to regulate their financial and banking systems as a means to cutting off terrorists' financial support. Previously under attack by the OECD, offshore financial jurisdictions have come under closer scrutiny by the United States to ensure that they will not be used to fund terrorists or their activities. There has been a great amount of compliance on this front as Caribbean governments seek to meet international standards.

Another issue that is high on the agenda is transportation and border security, and a number of measures have been introduced from Washington. There is a move towards developing *smart borders* based on a layered management system that will incorporate air, sea, and land continental transportation systems of the United States, Canada and Mexico. So, people, goods, and vehicles bound for any of these three countries will be prescreened for greater visibility. Accordingly, one measure being implemented by the US Customs Service is the Container Security Initiative (CSI). Along with US presence, governments are expected to identify and prescreen high-risk cargo containers for terrorist weapons at the point of departure instead of the port of arrival.

The Aviation and Transportation Security Act of 2001 that requires the screening of all airline passengers, baggage and cargo is also in operation. In addition, prior public-private partnership programs such as the Business Anti-Smuggling Coalition and the carrier Initiative Programs that have been expanded to improve security practices. Overall, some of the recommended steps that states have been obliged to take include better application of risk-management principles; automated, advanced data on goods and people; and the use of some level of detection technology for inspections. In addition to mandating these regional cooperative efforts and the regulation of cross-border flows, the US takes the position that its global responsibilities envelope political and economic freedom, peaceful relations and respect for human dignity. Thus, it uses economic, technical, and military assistance to ensure that vulnerable countries can fulfill the responsibilities of sovereignty through effective governance. Does this constitute a substantial change in US-Caribbean relations or is it business as usual?

The mandate for Caribbean countries to develop *best practice* approaches to security certainly raises a number of concerns. First, there is no doubt that the war on terrorism will be expensive. Security precautions are indeed costly and will certainly take their toll on budgets as governments divert policies and resources towards fighting terrorism. This is further exaggerated by a decline in foreign direct investment, regional tourism, slow growth in the global economy, and growing difficulty in gaining access to the American economy. As a means to fostering peace and prosperity, the National Security Strategy seeks to expand the circle of development by opening societies and building the infrastructure of democracy.

In a stated attempt to correct the failures of past development assistance, the Bush administration created a Millennium Challenge Account (MCA) as a new form of foreign aid up to $5 billion by 2006. There is no denying the significance of such aid, and the HIV/AIDS initiative is a step in the right direction. However, this assistance comes with conditions for national reforms. Eligibility is dependent on governments committing themselves to ruling justly, promoting economic freedom, and investing in people. It is not that states must not be held accountable, but in dealing with countries on a bilateral basis puts the US in the unique position of sole arbiter. As history can attest, conditionalities have invariably favoured the interests and objectives of the US, given the political basis for providing such aid. The MCA also reduces the move towards greater coordination of assistance at the international level and will most likely operate on a selective basis. The question remains as to how many Caribbean countries will be able to benefit from this initiative. In addition to the MCA, the increased assistance to the controversial *Plan Colombia* is being touted as an example of how the US is helping governments to defeat violent challenges to their sovereign authority.

Weak states like Colombia certainly need support for democratic institutions – particularly in regard to the rule of law and the promotion of human rights. After all, US officials have recognised that a lack of democracy helps to feed terrorism. Despite this acknowledgement, 'the question after September 11 is whether the era of human rights has come and gone'.[22] For one, the infringement on civil liberties within the US has raised concerns about the priority status of human rights in foreign affairs. In addition, by building a coalition of the willing, Washington has joined forces with regimes that have had a history of human rights violations. This has provided an opportunity for governments to handle internal threats as they see fit, in the name of the war on terrorism. The Cold War period is a constant reminder of the ills that accompany the propping up of dictators and turning a blind eye to the atrocities of friendly regimes. Sensitive issues such as intelligence and increased surveillance activities could also amplify tensions in civilian-military relations especially in a period of economic decline.

As mentioned earlier, expanding the circle of development also entails opening societies to commerce and investment. Free trade is therefore promoted as the catalyst for economic development. In sync with the tenets of neoliberalism, it requires the Caribbean states to reduce barriers and open their economies to the free flow of goods and people. But the push for free trade is a one-way street for there is silence when it comes to opening US markets to Caribbean exports. This response in the economic sphere is no different from the past and mirrors the predisposition to impose conditional sovereignty on others while reserving for the US the status of absolute freedom. The nature of this kind of asymmetrical relationship is not only historical but opens up an interesting paradox. On the one hand, there is the imperative for Caribbean states to ensure economic liberalisation and openness. On the other hand they are being empowered to tighten border controls in order to filter out the 'bads' of globalisation. Governments are imbued with sovereignty when it comes to the regulation of security issues that fall under the rubric of the war on terrorism. But they are disempowered when it comes to curbing the 'bads' of structural adjustment policies and opening economies to the dominance of market capitalism.

The Free Trade Area of the Americas (FTAA) has been touted as one way Caribbean economies would be able to make positive adjustments in an era of globalisation. Because security has now displaced trade on the US agenda, the need to forge alliances could also lead to a reconsideration of the terms for hemispheric trade. The FTAA could be restructured to accommodate commitments to hemispheric security. Bilateral free trade agreements such as the US-MERCOSUR could receive new impetus in the drive to alleviate the threat of international terrorism. This all amounts to the conclusion that there is no real attempt to address the economic woes that plague the Caribbean states although they have been tasked with the responsibility of engaging in the war on terrorism. With an economic future that appears very bleak the US has to bear in mind the well being of all its Caribbean and Latin American neighbours for it is integrally tied to national security and has important implications for the future.

Conclusion

It can be said by way of conclusion that the expectation for the Caribbean to 'truly own the issue of global terrorism' based on US national security strategy raises concerns of sovereignty and US unilateralism and their effects on United States-Caribbean relations. Real multilateral cooperation involves setting up international structures that are democratic, transparent, and accountable to the people, institutions, and governments of the world. For Caribbean states, the stage is being set to reduce the effectiveness that multilateral action can provide for the international community and to establish a kind of order that legally reinforces stratification at the international level.

The asymmetry of power, wealth and influence has been a constant in US-Caribbean relations. The fundamental nature of US relations with the Caribbean shows a line of continuity over the years and remains the same even after September 11. In that sense, there is no change. The basic framework remains in place but is enhanced in important ways. The key factor is as the course of events change, so does the thinking that guides the policy choices of the US. New strategies that can further the cause of such policies must also be developed. The end of the Cold War required new strategies, and there were many on the drawing board. But it was September 11 that tilted the scales in favour of the neo-conservatives in the American political system. This has pushed the present administration towards an excessive reliance on its military strength. The US is now operating from a worldview that distinctly favours the exercise of military power and is setting new conditions for the acquiescence of its neighbours.

What if the Caribbean states should refuse to acquiesce to US demands? The answer lies in the nature of their subordinate status in this relationship. Vulnerability has always been a major obstacle for Caribbean nations in its relations with the giant in the north. The response to September 11 increased this vulnerability with some worrisome implications and consequences. The threat of military intervention has certainly increased. But whether or not the US resorts to the use of military intervention, the Caribbean states will be faced with a situation in which there are increasing constraints on the state to live up to its responsibilities as externally dictated by the US. The rise in tensions will not only be in response to US exceptionalism and unilateral actions but will also come from within. As citizens encounter hardships and face bleak futures, governments will be caught in the quagmire of trying to fulfil its responsibilities both from above and from below.

Notes

1. Gilderhus, p 1.
2. Ibid., p 2.
3. Ibid., p 4.
4. Ibid., p 4.
5. Ibid., p 32.
6. Thomas, p 42.
7. Gilderhus, p 114.
8. Thomas, p 43.
9. Sullivan, p 4.
10. Allison and Treverton, p 17.
11. Ernest R. May, 'National Security in American History', in Allison and Treverton, p 112.
12. Allison and Treverton, pp 24-25.
13. Charles Krauthammer, 'The Unipolar Moment', in Allison and Treverton, p 296.
14. Ibid., p 306.
15. Ikenberry, p. 49.
16. Ibid., p 50.
17. Lesser, p xii.
18. Ikenberry, p 53.
19. This and following excerpts are taken from an adaptation from his remarks on 'The Changing Nature of Sovereignty' to the School of Foreign Service and the Mortara Center for International Studies at Georgetown University in Washington on January 14, 2003, Washington File, Office of International Information Programs, US Department of State.
20. Monsen, Lauren, 'OAS Conference on Terrorism Will Focus on Coordinated Response, Say Officials', The Washington File, Office of International Information Programs, US Department of State, 2003.
21. Farnsworth.
22. Ignatieff, p. 103.

Bibliography

Allison, Graham and Gregory F. Treverton., eds., *Rethinking America's Security: Beyond the Cold War to New World Order.* New York: WW Norton & Co, 1992.

Gilderhus, Mark T. *The Second Century: U.S.-Latin American Relations Since 1889.* Wilmington, Delaware: Scholarly Resources Inc., 2000.

Farnsworth, Eric. 'Latin America's Role in the Battle against Terror', Hemisphere Focus, IX: 6 (10/30/2001).

Hoge, James F., Jr., and Gideon Rose., eds. *How Did This Happen? Terrorism and the New War.* New York: Council on Foreign Relations 2001.

Ignatieff, Michael. 'Is the Human Rights Era Ending?' in *Perspectives on Terrorism: How 9/11 Changed U.S. Politics*. Boston: Houghton Mifflin Company, 2002.

Ikenberry, G. John. 'America's Imperial Ambition'. *Foreign Affairs*, 81:5 (2002).

Lesser, Ian O. et al. *Countering the New Terrorism*. Santa Monica, CA: Rand Corporation, 1999.

Sullivan, Mark P., 'Caribbean-US Relations' in *The Caribbean Basin: Economic and Security Issues,* Study Papers submitted to the Joint Economic Committee of the United States Congress, Government Printing Office, Washington, DC, January, 1993.

Thomas, Clive Y., *The Poor and the Powerless: Economic Policy and Change in the Caribbean,* New York: Monthly Review Press, 1988.

Websites

The Washington File, Office of International Information Programs, US Department of State (http://usinfo.state.gov).

Hemisphere Focus, IX:6 (10/30/2001) (http://www.csis.org/americas/pubs/h01130.htm).

11

Caribbean-European Relations: Did 9/11 make a difference?

Peter Clegg

> Europe's presence in the Caribbean is the product of a long and eventful history. At one time or another nearly all the major European powers have identified a Caribbean interest and more than any other region of the world the Caribbean bears the impress of the era of European colonialism ... The European presence is rooted in the foundations and the fabric of the area and is reproduced in countless ways in nearly every aspect of the economic, social and political life of the modern Caribbean.[1]
> *Paul Sutton*

Introduction

The ramifications, both politically and economically, of the September 11, 2001 terrorist attacks have been profound for the Caribbean and Europe. Caribbean states have been adversely affected by the decline in international economic confidence, particularly in regard to the tourist sector. In addition, the region's offshore banking sector has been criticised for its lax regulation and lack of transparency, issues of paramount importance in an era of heightened concerns over security and terrorist financing. Indeed, across a wide range of matters related to regional and international security, and political and economic good practice Caribbean countries have been challenged to meet the obligations necessary to survive in a more uncertain international environment. Similarly, European states as well as the European Union (EU) have been forced to recognise and respond to the impact of September 11.

Within the context of this chapter, however, rather than assessing the respective issues of concern for the Caribbean and Europe, an evaluation is made as to whether the terrorist attacks of September 11 have altered the dynamics and nature of the long-standing relationship between these two regions. The first part of the chapter considers the Caribbean region's relationship with those European states, the UK, France and the Netherlands, which have particularly close ties with the Caribbean, while the second part concentrates on the Caribbean's relationship with the EU.

Caribbean relations with European states post-9/11

As the epigraph indicated, the nature of Caribbean-European relations is long-standing and complex, with a great deal of historical baggage underpinning ties between the two regions. As will be seen in the second part of the chapter, the EU is an important and growing component within the fabric of Caribbean-European relations. However, individual states within Europe retain significant links with the Caribbean region. In order to fully comprehend whether the nature of Caribbean-European relations has altered after the terrorist attacks of September 11, an assessment needs to be made of the relationship between the Caribbean and those European states with a particular interest in the region. Within the context of this chapter, the relationship that the Caribbean region has with the UK, France and the Netherlands is considered. All three countries have links with the Caribbean going back almost four centuries, first as colonising powers, and then much later with their own particular post-colonial political and economic arrangements. The first section considers the nature of these different relationships, and the state of political relations in the aftermath of 9/11.

Caribbean-European political relations: an overview

The Caribbean-UK relationship

The nature of the UK's relationship with the Caribbean has been underpinned in large measure since the 1960s by cooperation involving independent states. Since 1962 the vast majority of the UK's Caribbean colonies have gained their independence. However, the UK still oversees five very small territories: Anguilla, British Virgin Islands, Cayman Islands, Montserrat and Turks and Caicos Islands. Formerly referred to as British Dependent Territories, they were renamed British Overseas Territories in May 2002 as part of the *British Overseas Territories Act*. The Act, emanating from a policy review started in 1997, altered the form if not the substance of the relationship between the UK and its territories, with an emphasis on partnership and mutual obligations and responsibilities. The legislation provided greater autonomy for the territories to run their own affairs, albeit under the continued supervision of UK-appointed governors.

In addition, the Act granted the right of UK citizenship to all inhabitants of Britain's Overseas Territories, although without providing them with full voting rights and representation in the UK Parliament. In return, the UK expected the territories to meet 'the highest standards of probity, law and order, good government and observance of Britain's international commitments' ('Partnership for Progress and Prosperity', FCO website). This has meant tighter controls being imposed on the territories' offshore financial sector and their use of corporal and capital punishment. While homosexual acts between consenting adults in private have now been decriminalised, these changes have been imposed in many cases without the full agreement of the territories themselves and this has created tensions within the relationship. However, it is important to recognise that though the *British Overseas Territories Act* came into law after the terrorist attacks of 9/11, the first ideas for reform were apparent in 1997, a full four years before the September 11 outrage.

As with the UK's relationship with the Caribbean Overseas Territories, measures have been undertaken to reform the links with the independent Commonwealth Caribbean states, prior and without reference to the September 11 attacks on the United States (US). The relationship between the Commonwealth Caribbean and the UK since 9/11 has, to a great extent, continued on the lines set in 1997 and 1998. The present relationship was established with the accession to power of the British Labour Party in 1997. The approach developed at that time after the Commonwealth Heads of Government Meeting in Edinburgh in November 1997, when the new UK prime minister, Tony Blair, and foreign secretary, Robin Cook, failed to meet Caribbean leaders as a group away from the main conference gathering. The Caribbean leaders were not pleased with such a perceived snub, and as a consequence vented their displeasure with the British government. The roots of this more disengaged relationship on the part of the UK originated in the 1970s and 1980s when the UK divested itself of most of its dependent territories likely to be candidates for independence and concentrated on the efficient management of the remainder.

In response to the clear displeasure of Caribbean leaders, Foreign Secretary Cook took action in an attempt to mollify the region's leaders by establishing the UK-Caribbean Forum, with the first meeting being held in Nassau, The Bahamas in 1998. The UK-Caribbean Forum, made up of ministers of Foreign Affairs from the UK and the Caribbean, continues to be at the heart of the relationship and the key point of contact. The Forum was established to strengthen and institutionalise the relationship between the UK and the Caribbean. It is based on biennial meetings held alternately in the UK and the Caribbean. After Nassau, the Forum subsequently met in London (2000) and Guyana (2002). From the outset, the Forum recognised the need for more central management of a relationship that required change away from a diffused system based largely on trading relations, particularly in the core commodities of bananas and sugar. It was hoped that more regular contacts between the UK and the countries of the Caribbean would be established. Indeed, contacts at the ministerial level are now more regular and Prime Minister Blair has made a commitment to meet Caribbean leaders at the Commonwealth heads of government summits held every two years.

The work of the UK-Caribbean Forum has meanwhile been given a stronger direction after a Ministerial Task Force on UK-Caribbean Relations was held in September 2001. Heads of government who had met in Kingston on July 29, 2001, established the Task Force to assess the future of relations between the UK and the region. The Task Force, involving ministers from the UK and the Caribbean, reaffirmed the link between economic progress, democracy and governance, while also recommending that heads of government should set the overall strategy of the UK-Caribbean Forum. It was hoped that the work of the Forum would be more focused and effective if the group was accountable to the British prime minister and Caribbean leaders.

The first formal recognition of the political and economic effects of September 11 on the Caribbean within the context of the UK-Caribbean Forum came in April 2002 during the group's third biennial meeting in Georgetown, Guyana. It was at this gathering that the first collective ministerial discussions took place regarding the changed international environment. In the joint communiqué released at the end of the Forum it was stated that:

> [Ministers] acknowledged the particular impact of the terrorist attacks of 11 September 2001. They recognised that the effect of terrorism on the Caribbean is costly, in terms of improving security, the loss of income from tourism and harm to the investment climate. They agreed to explore ways to address the adverse effects on the Caribbean and to continue to work together in the global fight against terrorism. (Joint communiqué issued by the UK-Caribbean Forum, April 5, 2002, FCO website).

The meeting of the UK-Caribbean Forum in Guyana and the subsequent joint communiqué are important as they highlight how UK and Caribbean ministers perceived the post-September 11 climate, the challenges and risks that the Caribbean in particular faced, and the commitment to bilateral and multilateral cooperation that was needed in order to address issues of concern. However, despite the appearance given within the communiqué of a new approach, little in fact changed in terms of policy priorities and forms of cooperation. Indeed, any change has been mostly one of rhetoric, with few practical adjustments having taken place.

One exception to this, where the terrorist attacks did have some effect on existing UK-Caribbean relations, was within the context of international relations, and the safeguarding of Caribbean interests within international forums more particularly.

At the Commonwealth Heads of Government Meeting in March 2002, in tandem with the gathering of the UK-Caribbean Forum the following month, a change of policy emphasis was forthcoming that took account of the new geo-political environment after September 11. In particular, it was agreed that a so-called UK-Caribbean Transmission Mechanism should be enacted. The UK is a member of a number of international groups such as the G8 and the EU, whose actions affect the Caribbean but to whose deliberations the region is not party. As a consequence it was hoped that the transmission mechanism would ensure that Caribbean interests are taken into account when issues are discussed within these fora. In practice, it was agreed that the UK should inform Caribbean leaders of the timing of international meetings that are likely to deal with issues that might have an impact on the Caribbean, and also their outcomes. Further, the mechanism would give Caribbean leaders an opportunity to advise the UK about their position on particular issues.

A number of specific areas for which the transmission mechanism would be used were highlighted at the third UK-Caribbean Forum in April 2002. It was agreed that the Caribbean would need to be given special assistance for them to cope with the end of non-reciprocal trade access to EU markets. Further, it was recognised that the UK and Caribbean would work together within the context of the World Trade Organization (WTO) so that Caribbean countries could derive greater benefit from international trade (Joint communiqué issued by the UK-Caribbean Forum, April 5, 2002, FCO website). There was a clear commitment on the part of the UK, therefore, that despite the changing dynamics of international relations post 9/11, the voices of small Caribbean states should not be forgotten or ignored.

Nevertheless, there is a limit to the commitments that the UK government is prepared to give when assisting Caribbean states in international forums, particularly in relation to the World Bank and the International Monetary Fund. With the increased economic pressures caused by September 11 and the move away from preferential access for certain key commodities, the Caribbean states have asked the UK to support their request for special dispensation within international economic bodies. In particular, the Caribbean has asked for support in easing the level of interest repayments on loans and in lengthening the period allowed for loan repayments to be made. However, the UK government has declined to support such special treatment, believing that all countries, regardless of their size or special circumstances, should be required to adhere to the same fiscal and monetary discipline. The position of the UK government is that if the Caribbean was given special loan provisions, they might take advantage of them, thus reducing their commitment to institute fundamental economic reform to meet the challenges of the new international trading environment. It is clear therefore that although the UK has attempted to be more responsive to Caribbean concerns in post-9/11 there are limits to the extent of their accommodation.

The Caribbean-French Relationship

As with the UK, France has two different kinds of relationship with the Caribbean region. First of all Guadeloupe, Martinique and French Guiana are departments of France, a status these territories have had since 1946. The *départements d' Outre-Mer* (DOM), sometimes also referred to as *départements français d'Amérique*, have the same status as any other part of France. The overseas departments, for example, use the euro, while their citizens have the same passport, rights and duties as any other French person. A complex set of local, departmental and national administrative arrangements bind the DOM to the French metropolis, with a Paris-appointed prefect representing the interests of the national government in each department. A separate body, meanwhile, based in Guadeloupe connects the various local levels of government in the Caribbean.

Traditionally, the balance of the relationship between the DOM and the metropolis has been strongly in favour of the latter, although in recent years reforms have been undertaken to decentralise policy making and administrative tasks. The pressure for reform was strengthened in the late 1990s because of increasing unrest on the DOM precipitated by continued high unemployment, concerns over the direction of education policy, and the prescriptive and unaccountable nature of metropolis rule. A major reform came in December 2000 when the *Loi d'orientation pour l'Outre-Mer* (Overseas French Act) was passed, which attempted to reenergise the DOM through greater freedom of action in the political, economic and social spheres in order that local needs could be better met. The move towards greater decentralisation was extended further in early 2003 when legislation was passed to devolve power and resources away from central government to the regions across France. Though the reforms are not specifically focused on the DOM, their influence will be felt in the overseas departments, with the transfer of education, housing, health and transport issues taking place in June 2003. The impetus behind such a reform programme came from concerns over the functioning of French democracy after the 2002 French presidential election, and the serious instability on the island of Corsica caused by secessionist forces. The changes to the framework of relations between the DOM and the metropolis are important, but it will take a while before a proper assessment of these changes can be made.

The second form of relationship that France has with the Caribbean is between sovereign states. However, the French have historically lacked a coherent policy for the wider Caribbean, placing the majority of emphasis on the DOM and the independent French speaking states such as Haiti. In spite of this, French policy is beginning to change, partially as a consequence of the constitutional reforms altering the status of the DOM. The French government hopes that the greater autonomy afforded to the DOM will allow them to develop closer political and economic ties with neighbouring independent Caribbean states. Further, the French government itself is trying to develop closer ties with the wider Caribbean. In March 2000, for example, President Chirac met Caribbean leaders in Martinique; the first time such a meeting had taken place between France and the states of the Caribbean.

The reasons for increasing French interest in the Caribbean are three fold: to challenge US power in the region by sustaining and strengthening a European presence; to safeguard the internal and external security of the DOM within a wider Caribbean setting; and to make sure the DOM are not economically isolated in a region moving to free trade with the EU and the Americas. Caribbean states also see the benefits of deepening cooperation with France in terms of developing closer trade and investment ties with the DOM, receiving French diplomatic support in international forums such as the EU and the World Trade Organization (WTO), and potentially gaining from French bilateral assistance. Although the reforms instituted by France with regard to the DOM and the independent Caribbean were in the main enacted prior to 9/11, the reform agenda is relevant in the new international geo-political climate. In particular, France's interest in challenging US hegemony in the Caribbean is indicative and symbolic of the importance that France attaches to developing a European presence on the world stage to rival that of the US.

The Caribbean-Netherlands Relationship

The relationship between the Caribbean and the Netherlands is based on two separate models of association. First of all there is the relationship involving the Netherlands, the Netherlands Antilles (incorporating the island districts of Curaçao, Bonaire, St Maarten, Saba and St Eustatius) and Aruba based on the Charter for the Kingdom of the Netherlands. Within this framework, there are three different levels of cooperation: Kingdom affairs, common and collaborative affairs, and the own (autonomous) affairs of each separate country. Under Kingdom affairs, which are overseen by the Dutch metropolis, issues such as safeguarding fundamental human rights and freedoms, foreign affairs, and Dutch nationality are dealt with. Common and collaborative affairs incorporate areas that are part of each country's own competency, but for which a single policy line is desirable. Examples include the promotion of cultural and social affairs among the countries, cooperation in aviation and maritime affairs, and the development of common legal and judicial forms. Finally, with regard to the countries' autonomous powers, all those areas of competence that are not designated specifically within the Charter as Kingdom affairs are included.

Although all three countries are legally equal within the Kingdom, the reality of the constitutional settlement is that, to a great extent, the Dutch government determines the most important policy outcomes; a situation strengthened by the fact that the Netherlands is economically and demographically much stronger than the other members of the Kingdom. Nevertheless, the Charter has survived for almost 50 years, although part of the reason for this is there no viable alternative to the existing arrangements. However, at the present time, St Maarten is challenging the status quo by threatening to break away and become independent unless the Netherlands grants it autonomy as a separate self-governing territory like Aruba. A compromise is the most likely outcome of the dispute, but it is nevertheless illustrative of the tensions that do, from time to time, challenge the existing Charter arrangements.

The second form of relationship is one between independent states, and more particularly between Suriname and the Netherlands. Suriname was a member of the Kingdom of the Netherlands until 1975, when the country gained its independence. However, as has been argued 'Suriname's independence did not fundamentally change the country's ties with the rest of the world' (Hoefte 2001, 61–62). The Netherlands continues to be the primary point of contact and source of assistance for Suriname. The nature of Dutch-Surinamese relations, however, has been at times difficult since the latter's independence, with the Dutch having failed to formulate a coherent policy towards Suriname since then (Hoefte 2001, 64). Contacts, meanwhile, between the Netherlands and the non-Dutch speaking Caribbean are virtually non-existent.

The relationship among the three countries constituting the Kingdom of the Netherlands has seen changes instituted over the last few years, particularly after 1998. A memorandum was published by the Dutch government in June 1999 entitled 'A Future in Partnership' which outlined measures to reform Dutch policy with respect to the Netherlands Antilles and Aruba. The memorandum was significant as it was an attempt by the Dutch government to reenergise and restructure its relationship with its Kingdom partners after a period of political and economic stagnation and subsequent decline. This was despite the fact that large amounts of financial support had been provided by the Netherlands to the island governments in the Dutch Caribbean over a number of years. The new policy is based on the ideas of good governance, self-reliance and financial responsibility, which are hoped will precipitate structural financial and economic reforms.

A key element of the reform programme involves the rationalising and refocusing of development policies, with a greater emphasis on measurable objectives and assessment. Indeed, the changing nature of Dutch-Caribbean relations over the last few years can be compared with what has been happening within the context of the Anglo- and Franco-phone Caribbean. The emphasis on improving the effectiveness of political relations has been important for all three European countries in their relations with the Caribbean; a sign of the changing perceptions of governance and cooperation over the last few years. However, the changes had little to do with the September 11 terrorist attacks, focusing as they did on longer-term political, economic and social concerns.

Overall, therefore, the underlying nature of the relationships between European states and the Caribbean after September 11 did not drastically change. The main determining factor is the long lead in time for any changes in policy to take place. As a consequence, both European and Caribbean states have found it more convenient and effective to retain their existing structures and policy programmes, rather than to dramatically reform their modes of cooperation to take on board the challenges of the post-9/11 environment. It is therefore difficult to see any fundamental differences in the relationship at the present time. Any changes that have been made are so small within the wider policy context that they are of marginal significance. However, it can be argued that due to the nature of the policy framework that existed prior to September 11, aspects of Caribbean-European relations could be reconfigured to take on board the new demands created by the fallout from the terrorist attacks. Although, the overall nature of the relationship appears to be relatively unchanged, it is nevertheless important to assess the dynamics of Caribbean-European relations in more detail, in order to identify the nuances of policy change since September 11, 2001.

Regional Security and Law Enforcement

Two related areas that drew a great deal of attention in the aftermath of the terrorist attacks on September 11 were regional security and law enforcement. In terms of Caribbean-European relations, the issues of drug trafficking and criminal activity, more generally, have been particularly important. However, as has been suggested previously, although these issue areas were given a slightly higher priority after September 11, existing policies were maintained to a large degree. Indeed, the relationship between European states and the Caribbean has been underpinned by long-standing commitments to improve the capacity and capability of law enforcement agencies and the criminal justice system in the Caribbean.

In terms of UK-Caribbean law enforcement activity, a vitally important component is a cross Whitehall group (which includes representatives from the Metropolitan Police Service, the Foreign and Commonwealth Office (FCO), the Home Office, the Department for International Development (DfID), the National Crime Squad and National Crime Intelligence Service). Significantly, however, the group was established in early 2001, well before the tragedy of September 11. Indeed, the origins of the group came a few months earlier when Deputy Assistant Commissioner Michael Fuller, head of Operation Trident, a project organised by London's Metropolitan Police to tackle drug-related crime in the capital, visited Jamaica in December 2000. Commissioner Fuller talked to the Jamaican government and the Jamaica Constabulary Force about ways of improving cooperation between the British Police Service and police forces in Jamaica and the Caribbean more generally. In addition, Mo Mowlam, then UK minister for the cabinet office, undertook a follow-up visit in January 2001.

The outcome of these high level visits was the establishment of the Whitehall Group. Since the group's creation, it has focused attention on two particular areas of law enforcement. On the one hand, measures have been undertaken to improve police management and officer training in the region, while on the other improving crime management techniques, including forensics, has been a priority. A number of projects, related mainly to police training and improving operational activity, are now underway in Jamaica and elsewhere in the region. The projects overseen by the cross Whitehall Group are complimenting DfID's Jamaica Constabulary Force modernisation project (DfID Country Strategy Paper 2001, 12).

One particularly important element of the fight against crime in the Commonwealth Caribbean has been the Law Enforcement Enhancement Project launched at the UK-Caribbean Forum in 2000. A sum of £400,000 was provided for the setting up of training centres in Kingston, Bridgetown and Port of Spain (UK-Caribbean Forum Joint Communiqué, May 12, 2000, Government of Belize website). The training aimed at improving law enforcement and administering justice began towards the end of 2000, and was due to cease in 2002. However, as a direct response to the terrorist attacks of September 11, the project has been extended. The continuation of the Law Enforcement Enhancement Project is illustrative of the overall nature of the UK-Caribbean relationship post-9/11. Although not a new programme, there is sufficient flexibility within the cooperation arrangements between the UK and Caribbean, that the unexpected turn of events precipitated by the terrorist attacks can be accommodated without drastic changes to the overall structure of UK-Caribbean relations.

A similar change of emphasis came with the downgrading of the EU Caribbean Drugs Initiative at the end of 2001. Though the initiative was coming to an end, the importance of it was recognised by the UK and the Caribbean, particularly so after the events of September 11 and the heightened concern over international crime. It is estimated that 65 per cent of all cocaine reaching Europe transits the Caribbean region ('Tackling the Major Drugs Threats', FCO website). As a consequence, the UK has now taken the lead in providing bilateral counter-drug assistance to the region. Recent and ongoing programmes include the British Military Advisory and Training Team Eastern Caribbean based in Antigua, sniffer dog training in the Eastern Caribbean, and support for the Association of Caribbean Commissioners of Police and the Caribbean Customs Law Enforcement Council. The UK also funds the Project Management Office for Maritime Cooperation and Training based in Barbados ('Tackling the Major Drugs Threats', FCO website). This example again illustrates that existing programmes can be adapted to respond to the new security concerns post-9/11.

A more recent example of heightened concern over the drug trafficking issue can be seen in the context of UK-Jamaica relations. In April 2002, the two countries established a joint operation against drug smuggling, code named 'Operation Airbridge'. The operation involves British law enforcement officers being stationed at Jamaican airports and the extensive screening of passengers departing from there. This is part of a UK £2 million programme to create a 'customs strike force' that will help train Jamaican police officers to operate machines, at airports, that will identify anyone who has had recent contact with cocaine (*Caribbean Insight*, May 24, 2002). Jamaican national security minister, Peter Phillips, and the UK under secretary of state, Bob Ainsworth, supplemented this programme in November when a Memorandum of Understanding was signed. The agreement allows Jamaican narcotics police to be posted at UK airports to assist in restricting the flow of drugs to the UK. On signing the agreement, Mr Philips said that it will 'enhance both the UK intelligence capabilities and the Jamaican intelligence capabilities as we galvanise our efforts to focus on the violent criminal gangs operating in Jamaica and the UK' (*Caribbean Insight*, November 22, 2002).

Early evidence suggested that cooperation was effective in reducing the number of drug couriers travelling from Jamaica to the UK (*Caribbean Times*, March 14, 2003). However, it is apparent that the centre for cocaine trafficking is shifting from Jamaica to the Eastern Caribbean, and particularly to St Maarten in the Dutch Antilles. The drawback of bilateral cooperation, as against multilateral cooperation, can be seen here with the transshipment of cocaine just moving to a different part of the Caribbean. However, attempts are being made to address this lack of coordination via the UK's participation, with the US and the Netherlands in joint coast guard operations, an example being the 'Tradewinds' exercise (Ministerie van Binnenlandse Zaken en Koninkrijksrelaties 2001, 21). Although the French are not so directly involved in such drug-related operations, they participate indirectly through the sharing of intelligence.

The Dutch approach to regional security and law enforcement in the Caribbean is not greatly different to that of the UK, although there is evidence to suggest that the Dutch authorities were obliged to do more in this area after September 11 than the UK. A possible reason for this is that the Caribbean

Kingdom territories 'are not high on the list of priorities of the Dutch public or politicians, partly because the economic or geopolitical interests of the Netherlands in the region in the post-cold war era are slight' (Hoefte 2001,59). In the aftermath of 9/11, a Kingdom summit was held on terrorism and a series of agreements were subsequently signed between the Netherlands, Aruba and the Netherlands Antilles on combating international terrorism, with an emphasis on strengthened police action, judicial cooperation and investigation activities. A number of particular measures have since been taken, including the development of an Investigation Support Team for the Antillean police force and the strengthening of the police forces of the Netherlands Antilles and Aruba more generally in the fields of training, organisational, development, information exchange and staff recruitment ('Kingdom united against terrorism', Ministerie van Binnenlandse Zaken en Koninkrijksrelaties website).

In the related area of narcotics smuggling the Netherlands has provided assistance to help track down drug couriers at the airports of Curaçao, Bonaire and St Martin, to recruit more prison staff to stop drug couriers from being set free in the Netherlands Antilles, and to allow the coastguard operating in the water around Aruba and the Netherlands Antilles to maintain a permanent role in tracking down drug traffickers ('Dutch government wants to help Netherlands Antilles fight drug trafficking', Ministerie van Binnenlandse Zaken en Koninkrijksrelaties website). The latter development is important, particularly in the post-9/11 environment, as the Dutch supported coast guard has been asked by the US to undertake more operations in the Caribbean Sea. Further, from May 2002 Curaçao-based Dutch Caribbean Airline began screening passengers before allowing them to purchase tickets in an attempt to stop drug smuggling on flights to the Netherlands (*Caribbean Insight*, April 17, 2002). It seems that some progress is being made in the Netherlands Antilles against drug trafficking with 6,500 kilograms of drugs being confiscated by the authorities during 2002, more than double the amount seized in 2001 (*Caribbean Insight*, January 24, 2003). The Dutch government also extended its cooperation to Suriname with an agreement in October 2002 to provide Suriname's police force with training and equipment to help fight drug trafficking along the country's borders. The UN Drug Control Agency estimates that over 20 metric tons of cocaine is smuggled through Suriname to Europe each year (*Caribbean Insight*, October 25, 2002).

Although France has similar regional security and law enforcement interests to the other European powers in the Caribbean region, it has also a wider set of concerns. In particular, the DOM provides France with a military and strategic capacity, which is important in safeguarding French power and influence in the international system. As has been argued, 'these territories are essential in terms of communications and, particularly, for activities related to outer space' (Martin 1996, 35). Since 1968, French Guiana has been the centre of French space activity, from where observation and telecommunications satellites have been launched. At the present time, the French military is developing for itself, and possibly the EU, an integrated information and intelligence space system which would guarantee full independence of action in the future. Guadeloupe and Martinique, meanwhile, though strategically slightly less important are both essential stopping off points in the transportation of nuclear weapons to the test sites in the French Pacific. The role that the DOM plays in French and European security is a long-standing one. However, since the September 11 attacks, the importance of such an intelligence capability has become even more crucial.

When considering the impact of the September 11 terrorist attacks on European state relations with the Caribbean in regard to regional security and law enforcement cooperation, it can be argued that though the Netherlands introduced a number of new anti-crime provisions, there was not a dramatic shift in policy on the part of the UK and France. It is true that there has been a reconsideration of priorities on the part of the two European states, but in general pre-existing programmes and policies have been retained. Perhaps the most important consequence of 9/11 is that policies that might have ended in other circumstances were continued.

Visa and Deportation Issues: a Post-9/11 Response?

A related set of issues that have had a bearing on regional security and law enforcement concerns citizens of Caribbean states visiting the UK, particularly with regard to drug smuggling and the deportation of Caribbean nationals from the UK to the Caribbean. The former issue was pushed up the political agenda after the controversy surrounding the UK government's decision to introduce a visa regime for Jamaican nationals travelling to the UK from January 9, 2003. Though the UK government strongly denied that the decision had anything to do with controlling drug trafficking and yardie crime, the suspicion on the part of some in the Caribbean was that the increased security concerns after September 11 and a number of high profile cases of black gang violence in the UK had forced the government to act.

After announcing the decision, the UK government argued that the visa requirement would help prevent delays at UK immigration control for people arriving on Jamaican flights and thus make it easier for genuine Jamaican visitors to come to the UK. The government alleged that the long delays were a result of the large number of Jamaican nationals refused entry at UK ports. The government also claimed that significant numbers absconded once granted temporary admission to the UK. In order to support their position, the Home Office released statistics, subsequently challenged, showing that a relatively large number of Jamaican nationals arriving in the UK were refused entry, while others absconded after being granted temporary leave to remain (*The Times*, January 9, 2003 and *The Sunday Gleaner*, February 2, 2003).

The Home Office denied that the imposition of visa requirements had any connection with attempts to reduce drug trafficking and yardie crime. It stated, 'the decision is based on immigration control considerations' (Home Office, Press Office Briefing Note, January 8, 2003). However, elsewhere in the Home Office's rather contradictory press statement, it was argued 'there are over 2,000 Jamaicans in UK prisons, about a third of all foreign prisoners, and it is reasonable to expect that the new visa regime will make it more difficult for those who are engaged in criminal activities or who have committed crimes from reaching the UK' (Home Office, Press Office Briefing Note, January 2002). In response, the Jamaican Ministry of Foreign Affairs and Foreign Trade said it viewed the decision with regret, although it agreed that it would be beneficial to cut the numbers rejected before arrival. While Maxine Roberts, the Jamaican high commissioner in London said, 'I am very disappointed ... [however] we have to recognise the right of the British Government to make their arrangements where they consider it is necessary' (*The Times*, January 9, 2003).

The imposition of visa restrictions on Jamaican nationals wanting to visit the UK is another interesting case in which the September 11 terrorist attacks may have influenced decisions at the margins of policy making. It is certainly the case that the issues of drug trafficking and yardie crime have been high on the political agenda in both the UK and Jamaica, and with the heightened concerns after 9/11 it might seem reasonable that policy outputs would have been influenced as a consequence. However, once again it is important not to overstate the case, as both the UK and Jamaican governments stressed that the visa issue had been on the agenda for almost two years (Home Office, Press Office Briefing Note, January 8, 2002 and *Caribbean Times*, January 17, 2003). Nevertheless, the very fact that the shadow of September 11 is mentioned within the context of immigration issues is indicative of the altered mindset of governments at the present time.

Another issue of contention in the area of population movements between the UK and the Caribbean concerns the deportation of Caribbean nationals, some of whom have been convicted of crimes in the UK, served their sentences, then returned to their countries of origin. Caribbean governments are concerned that deportations of Caribbean nationals from the UK, as well as from the US and Canada, back to their country of birth has contributed to the rising crime levels in a number of Caribbean states. In 1998, for example, 1,483 Jamaicans were deported from the US, 325 from Canada and 250 from the UK (*The Jamaica Gleaner*, February 6, 2000). Caribbean governments are concerned about the destabilising effect that such large numbers of criminal deportees are having on their societies; a fear heightened by the September 11 terrorist attacks and their subsequent desire to maintain strong domestic and regional security arrangements.

Under such circumstances, the issue of deportations was considered within the context of the third UK-Caribbean Forum held in Guyana in April 2002. During the Forum, ministers discussed the problems arising from the deportation of Caribbean nationals from the UK, including the criminal dimension and the potential threat to international security, the negative effects on economic and social development in the receiving states, and the humanitarian aspects (Joint communiqué issued by the UK-Caribbean Forum, April 5, 2002, FCO website). In subsequent negotiations, the UK government agreed to reconsider its procedures for the removal of deportees, a decision that was welcomed by the Caribbean. Indeed, only one Caribbean national was deported from the UK during 2002, a significant decline in the figure from four years before. A complementary set of agreements between the UK and a number of Caribbean states have improved the cooperation in regard to the status of prisoners in their respective gaols. In July 2002, for example, it was announced that an agreement had been signed to allow British and Surinamese prisoners to return to their native country to serve out their sentences (*Caribbean Insight*, July 5, 2002). The UK has similar agreements with Barbados, Cuba and Guyana. Thus it can be argued that in the area of deportations and prisoner detention, the influence of September 11 has been tangible. Through cooperation on a number of fronts, the British and Caribbean governments have been able to bring about concrete change in the very important areas of judicial cooperation and international security.

Financial Probity: Money Laundering and Tax Evasion

Two issues that are closely linked to the previously considered subjects of drug trafficking and drug transshipment, which have also been hot political topics since September 11, are money laundering and tax evasion. However, unlike the other issues previously discussed, the changes brought about by 9/

11 have been more significant, illustrating a clear shift in emphasis and urgency. There are two key institutions that deal with financial matters, and which involve both the Caribbean and a number of European states, including the UK, France and the Netherlands. The first is the Caribbean Financial Action Task Force (CFATF), a sub-grouping of the Financial Action Task Force (FATF). The CFATF was established in 1990 and includes 26 Caribbean countries and Bermuda. The UK, French and Dutch governments are 'Cooperating and Supporting Nations' within the context of the CFATF. The body is concerned with improving the Caribbean's ability to prevent and control money laundering in its jurisdictions (CFATF, OECD website).

The second key institution is the OECD and its Harmful Tax Practices Initiative, which attempts to bring countries together to encourage them to eliminate harmful tax practices that can distort financial and, indirectly, real investment flows. In essence, it is an attempt by the 'developed' states of the OECD to end countries' tax haven status, which they believe is being abused by criminal and terrorist organisations. The parameters of the undertaking were set in 1998 when a document 'Harmful Tax Competition', which set out criteria for determining harmful tax practices and recommendations for combating them, was published. This was followed by a progress report in 2000, 'Toward Global Tax Cooperation', which updated the work and identified 35 tax havens and 47 potentially harmful preferential regimes ('About Harmful Tax Practices', OECD website).

Though both the initiatives emanating from the CFATF and the OECD pre-date the terrorist attacks of September 11, there was a palpable shift in approach after that date. In the post-9/11 environment, the pressure on states to comply with the money laundering and tax evasion provisions was greatly increased. The main actor driving the change was the US, which became much more actively engaged in the area of international financial regulation after 9/11. In the aftermath of the attacks and as part of the US's fight against terrorism, the *Patriot Act* was adopted to strengthen measures to prevent, detect and prosecute international money laundering and the financing of terrorism. Such a strengthening of domestic provisions then fed into the international arena. In a similar vein, European states also reassessed their financial rules and regulations. For example, the UK government introduced new legislation in the fight against money laundering, while also calling for tougher action at the international level. The countries of the Kingdom of the Netherlands also committed themselves to intensify cooperation in the area. As a consequence, both the OECD and the FATF increased their commitment to meet their respective objectives, and in the case of FATF to widen its remit. At an extraordinary plenary of the FATF held in Washington D.C. at the end of October 2001, the body expanded its mission beyond money laundering to also include combating terrorist financing. An indicator of the success of this post-9/11 shift is apparent with the fact that all 17 Caribbean independent states and overseas countries and territories have since been removed from the OECDs uncooperative tax havens list (Klak 2002). With regard to the FATF, out of four Caribbean states on the body's non-cooperative countries and territories list for money laundering prior to 9/11, only St Vincent and the Grenadines now remain (FATF website).

However, there are still weaknesses within the existing regimes established to stamp out money laundering and tax evasion, as could be seen with the collapse of a six-month-long trial of four defendants accused of laundering US$25 million through the Cayman Islands-based Euro Bank Corporation. It was reported that the trial was stopped in January 2003 after it emerged that British security services had ordered the territory's lead investigator to destroy evidence in an unsuccessful attempt to keep secret the security services involvement in the case (*The Guardian*, January 18, 2003). The UK Foreign and Commonwealth Office denied that such interference had taken place, but the political fallout was significant nevertheless. The lead investigator in the case resigned having admitted to shredding evidence, while the Cayman Islands' attorney general was dismissed for his role in the trial's collapse. Commenting on the situation, David Marchant, editor of the Miami-based *Offshore Alert* newsletter, said: 'This is the latest in several fiascos involving the prosecution of offshore bankers in the Cayman Islands and further undermines confidence in the jurisdiction' (*The Guardian*, January 18, 2003). Therefore, though steps have been taken to improve the transparency and accountability of the offshore sector, a commitment sharpened by September 11, it is apparent that much still needs to be done both on the part of individual countries and territories in the Caribbean, and by those European states who have an interest in the region.

Economic Development and Diversification

Another of the key questions that the Caribbean has had to address concerns economic development and the need to diversify their economies away from the traditional export products of sugar and bananas in particular. Since the terrorist attacks of September 11 the economic climate has worsened with, for example, a reduction in the number of tourists visiting the region and a decline in the profitability of the offshore financial sector. As a consequence, Caribbean states are facing a particularly difficult set of developmental challenges. The UK, French and Dutch governments are involved both multilaterally, through the EU, and bilaterally in providing development assistance for the Caribbean. The EU dimension is considered later, with this section evaluating the contribution of individual European states. In 1999/2000, for example, the UK government provided £36.4 million of bilateral development assistance in the independent Commonwealth countries, and £29.4 million in the Caribbean Overseas Territories. The Netherlands, meanwhile, set aside 124 million euro in assistance for the Netherlands Antilles and Aruba in 2001. The disparity in funds is a concern for the Dutch, as the Netherlands Antilles and Aruba who receive a greater amount of aid than the UK OCTs are in a worse economic position than their near neighbours.

One part of the Dutch strategy is to improve economic practice and to liberalise the economies of the Caribbean Kingdoms, while the other is to address the issue of aid distribution. In response to the apparent failure of Dutch aid policy, with its bureaucratic disbursement structures, overly strict procedures and problems of project prioritisation, reforms have been undertaken to the system of disbursement. Although the majority of the funding is still funnelled through the Dutch government, the aim of the reforms is to encourage 'a more effective use of development funds, designed to encourage the greatest degree of independence of the partners in the Kingdom' (Verhoeven 2001). In Aruba, decisions concerning project proposals are now delegated to a politically independent development bank, while similar arrangements are now being finalised for the Netherlands Antilles.

The process of devolving decision making to the Dutch Caribbean is part of the commitment within the memorandum, 'A Future in Partnership', to move away from a multiplicity of fragmented projects, and towards a limited number of multi-year sectoral programmes. The intention is to improve the efficiency and effectiveness of aid disbursement through clear boundary conditions and quality assurances, and to help meet the differing needs of the island districts of the Netherlands Antilles and of Aruba. In terms of aid priorities, the focus is on three areas: sustainable economic development, institutional strengthening and education. The framing of these priorities came prior to 9/11, but they are certainly relevant to the post-9/11 situation. One area, however, which has received special assistance as a consequence of September 11, is the tourist sector. In November 2001, a 'Tourism Promotion Emergency Plan' worth almost 15 million euro was introduced. The plan was put together in an attempt to limit the damage of the downturn in the sector, with the majority of the funds being given to Aruba and Curaçao. However, within the overall context of aid disbursement the emergency aid given to the tourism sector is dwarfed by the long-standing spending commitments. Yes, the September 11 terrorist attacks had an effect, but that influence should not be overstated.

A great deal of the money from the UK is funnelled through DfID's Caribbean Regional Office in Barbados, where there is an emphasis on capacity building, strengthening good governance and supporting enterprise development. Although in this context DfID makes a distinction between those countries, such as Barbados, Trinidad and Tobago and the Bahamas, who have graduated from development assistance and those, including Jamaica, Guyana and most of the Eastern Caribbean, where assistance remains vitally important. A further policy of benefit to the latter group of countries is the UK's Commonwealth Debt Initiative (CDI), launched in 1997, which offers debt relief on the repayment of past aid loans to countries committed to eliminating poverty, rooting out corruption and applying sound economic and social policies. Between 1998 and 2000, just under £100 million of debt was cancelled, with the main beneficiaries being Jamaica and Guyana. At the present time, the CDI is relieving some £4 million a year of Jamaican debt accrued on past UK aid loans to the country ('Country Strategy Paper' – Jamaica). Among other Caribbean countries whose aid debts Britain has agreed to cancel are Barbados, Dominica, Grenada, Jamaica, and St Lucia. In the Caribbean Overseas Territories, meanwhile, DfID is funding programmes to improve good governance in the region. In Anguilla, Montserrat and the Turks and Caicos, for example, DFID is helping to modernise and reform government financial and accounting policies, systems and procedures.

The funding that the DOM receive from the metropolis is channelled through the French Ministry of Finance and the *Agence Française de Développment* (AfD), while financial assistance for the independent Caribbean is disbursed by the AfD. The main priorities of DOM funding are to support public investment, encourage private sector growth, and pay for the construction and management of social housing. Further, in 2001 the AfD granted 29 million euro to improve the health sector in the DOM, specifically to modernise, expand and restructure public hospitals (AfD Annual Report 2001, 61). The aid focus for the independent Caribbean is similar, although disbursement decisions are made to underpin developing French interests in the region. In St Lucia, for example, where a French based Creole is spoken the AfD is funding two multi-million-euro road improvement schemes (*Caribbean Insight*, May 5, 2002 and October 25, 2002).

Meanwhile, in March 2002, Cuba signed a number of cooperation agreements on scientific research, public health and Cuba's Social Development Fund. It was reported that the 'scientific research accord will allow experts from the two countries to develop joint medical, agricultural, environmental, water and biotechnology projects, permit researchers from one country to work in the other and provide graduate and post-graduate training for Cuban scientists' (*Caribbean Insight*, April 5, 2002). French aid is also provided on the regional level, and an example of this came in February 2003 when around one million euro was given to the Caribbean Epidemiology Centre to help in the fight against HIV/AIDS in the Caribbean (*Caribbean Times*, February 21, 2003).

As with other aspects of European-Caribbean relations, there is little direct evidence to suggest that the aftermath of September 11 had any profound effect in terms of altering the nature of pre-existing development cooperation. The negotiations and planning surrounding the provision of development assistance normally has a long gestation period and, as a consequence, Caribbean-European cooperation in this area had for the most part been instituted prior to the September 11 terrorist attacks. However, the effects of 9/11 can be seen to have helped re-emphasise the importance of development assistance, and to have forced a medium-term reappraisal of funding priorities.

Caribbean-EU relations in the aftermath of 9/11

The Background to Caribbean-EU relations

The institutional framework linking the independent countries of the Caribbean with the EU was set in 1975 with the Lomé Convention, which also incorporated former European colonies in Africa and the Pacific. There have been four Lomé Conventions, Lomé I was signed in 1975, while Lomé IV was signed in 1990 and expired in 2000. In the negotiations for Lomé I, the Caribbean wanted a form of relationship with the then European Community (EC) that was *sui generis* (Gonzales 1997, 72). The Caribbean called for non-reciprocity, for protection of traditional arrangements, and for no difference in treatment between independent Caribbean countries and the self-governing territories of EC member states in the region. In large measure, Caribbean states achieved their negotiating goals, with trade provisions (preferences and protocols), aid commitments, and political cooperation underpinning the Convention. Meanwhile, the Caribbean overseas countries and territories[2] (OCTs), which are constitutionally dependent on either the UK or the Netherlands, have been associated with the EU since

1957 through Part Four of the Treaty of Rome. The arrangements for the OCTs were designed to achieve four objectives: 'promoting their economic and social development; developing their economic relations with the EU; taking greater account of their diversity and individual characteristics; and accessing financial help more effectively' (Cocchi 2002, 10).

However, during the 1990s, there was considerable political and economic pressure to radically restructure the nature of the Lomé Convention and, to a lesser extent, the provisions underpinning OCT-EU relations. This was due to the ascendancy of neo-liberal conceptions of economic development, and the profound geo-political transformations that were taking place after the end of the Cold War, which dramatically altered the EU's policy agenda. In addition, the Lomé Convention was coming under increasing criticism for its disappointing results in furthering Caribbean political and economic development (Clegg 1997; Payne and Sutton 2001; and Dearden 2002). As a consequence, a new partnership agreement was signed in Cotonou, Benin, in June 2000 to succeed the Lomé Convention, while in November 2001 the EU formally adopted a new agreement on relations with the OCTs. When considering the effects of September 11 on Caribbean-EU relations, they must be viewed within the context of the newly agreed association agreements. The remainder of the chapter focuses primarily on the more important relationship between the independent Caribbean and the EU, although reference to the OCTs is made when apposite.

Caribbean-EU Trade Relations Post-9/11

A vitally important component of the Lomé Conventions was the non-reciprocal trade provisions which provided privileged commercial access, including free access, for certain Caribbean exports to the EU market, as well as guaranteed quotas for some key regional commodities, such as bananas, sugar and rum. The hoped-for result was that Caribbean exports to the EU would increase and diversify, encouraging growth and development in the exporting countries. However, despite the trade preferences, Caribbean export performance to the EU has been poor. After a rise in exports in the early years of the Lomé Convention, from ECU 0.8 billion in 1976 to ECU 1.6 billion in 1980, total exports fell to ECU 1.5 billion in 1992. In terms of market share, in 1976 Caribbean exports accounted for 0.5 per cent of the total EU imports from outside the member states, but in 1992 that figure had fallen to 0.3 per cent (Davenport et al 1995, 5). Parallel to the debate concerning the effectiveness of the Lomé trade preferences, recent developments in the international trade environment have highlighted attention on various issues relating to the political acceptability of non-reciprocal preferences, particularly within the context of the WTO. The successful action by the US and others against the EU's banana protocol was indicative of this change in approach (Sutton 2001 and Clegg 2002).

Therefore, the nature of the trade provisions in the succeeding Cotonou Agreement was fundamentally altered in order that it would fully comply with WTO rules. The parties to the Agreement committed themselves to negotiate Economic Partnership Agreements (EPA) based around existing regional integration initiatives. The negotiations of the EPAs began in September 2002 and are scheduled to end by 2008. During the preparatory period, the non-reciprocal Lomé trade preferences will be preserved. Perhaps most importantly for Caribbean countries is the fact that the sugar and banana protocols will be maintained. The sugar protocol will continue until at least 2007, while the banana protocol, though altered to meet WTO requirements, will also be sustained. The rum protocol, however, is not to end, with compensating transitional support until 2008.

The background to the Caribbean-EU trading relationship is important when the implications of the September 11 terrorist attacks are considered. Though the economic effects of 9/11 have profoundly affected the Caribbean, the medium to long-term consideration of maintaining key commodity export markets in the EU is the uppermost concern for a large majority of states in the region. Without continued market access for Caribbean exports such as sugar and bananas, the economic future of a number of Caribbean economies looks bleak, irrespective of the fallout from September 11. As a consequence a key part of the Caribbean-EU relationship is to help maintain the viability of these crucial export commodities, while on the other hand attempting to reduce the Caribbean's dependency on these industries through the promotion of economic diversification. Therefore, although the international ramifications of September 11 have been serious they have to be placed within the more specific Caribbean-EU economic context.

At the present time therefore, the Caribbean has been in negotiation with the EU to secure packages of aid for its commodity export sector. In regard to bananas, the EU Council of Ministers decided in 1999 to establish the Special Framework of Assistance (SFA) to help producers adapt to the new market conditions. Through the SFA, the EU provides a number of Caribbean countries with around 30 million euro of support each year to enhance productivity, mitigate social dislocation and promote diversification (European Commission 2002, 22). For the rum industry, the EU approved a 70 million euro assistance programme at the beginning of 2002. This money will help to underpin the Joint Declaration of Rum (XXV) in the Cotonou Agreement that recognises the importance of the rum industry to employment, export earnings and government revenues for some African, Caribbean and Pacific (ACP) states and its international competitive potential.

The situation regarding the sugar industry is slightly different in that the main priority for the Caribbean is to defend a regime that has yet to be touched by liberal international trade rules. In October 2002, Brazil and Australia initiated WTO dispute settlement proceedings against the EU's sugar regime which guarantees purchases of particular volumes of sugar at fixed prices. Caribbean producers fear that if the case is upheld it could seriously undermine their entire industry. As has been argued 'through their challenges both Australia and Brazil are threatening the livelihood of a large number of poor farmers and workers in the ACP states concerned' (ACP General Secretariat 2002). The examples of the commodity protocols emphasise that despite the importance of the legacy of September 11 in shaping international political and economic considerations, trade relations between the Caribbean and EU continue to be dominated by long-standing considerations.

A further issue related to the sugar and banana disputes during the 1990s concerns the growing importance of the WTO in trade matters. For Caribbean states in particular the WTO has been seen as an insensitive and unaccountable organisation with little concern for small less developed states. In order to increase the Caribbean region's participation in the WTO, the EU is providing funds amounting to 10 million euro. Further, in January 2002, the EU gave 1.45 million euro for the establishment of a Geneva-based office to help ACP countries increase their participation in WTO matters. The EU has also been the main contributor to the WTO Trust Fund for technical assistance on WTO's Doha Development Agenda (European Commission 2002). So again in the area of trade relations, Caribbean-EU cooperation is focussed on meeting the challenges posed by concerns more profound than those caused solely by the events of 9/11.

An aspect of Caribbean-EU relations that perhaps has a greater synergy with September 11 relates to the attempts to encourage the diversification of Caribbean economies away from one or two key export commodities and towards a broader economic base. The concern over the growing role of the WTO is a factor within this diversification drive, but a further influence has been the economic consequences of 9/11. In particular, the fragile nature of the important tourist sector has come under serious pressure since September

11 and illustrates the need for EU funds to assist Caribbean states to diversify their economic base. One particularly important area is the developing Information and Communication Technologies (ICT) sector. As is argued, 'the Caribbean is strategically located to take advantage of corporations looking to outsource information processing tasks using direct electronic communication' (European Commission 2002, 16). To encourage the region's involvement in the ICT sector, the EU is providing 750,000 euro for an institutional strengthening programme, which is focussed on rationalising and improving the Caribbean's telecommunications sector. A range of other EU funded projects within the ICT sector are also planned (European Commission 2002, 16). The ICT programmes are funded for the Caribbean region as a whole, and this is an approach favoured by the EU. For example, the EU has given the CARIFORUM[3] region 57 million euro to help facilitate greater political and economic integration (European Commission 2002, 21). In addition, the EU funds the Caribbean Community (CARICOM) Fisheries Unit, which aims to improve the management of the region's coastal and marine fisheries resources.

The region-wide programmes are an important part of EU funding, but equally important are the country-specific projects. The education sector in a number of Caribbean states has received substantial EU funds in order to develop the potential of their human capital. In the Bahamas, for example, money was provided to improve the infrastructure of the Bahamas Law School. A Language Centre at the Barbados Community College was constructed using EU funds, while in St Vincent and the Grenadines an A-level college has been built. Other schemes addressing the issues of diversification more directly have been undertaken in Belize with EU funds helping to establish a micro-enterprise credit scheme implemented by a local NGO, the Belize Enterprise for Sustainable Technology. EU funds to promote economic diversification in Dominica and St Lucia include assistance for private sector and human resource development, while funds have also been made available for an eco-tourism development programme in Dominica. In Jamaica, EU money has financed economic adjustment efforts, trade and private sector development, and infrastructure projects. In Trinidad and Tobago, the Export Development Corporation and the Caribbean Business Services project have received EU funds.

Although the various EU-funded programmes focussed on the Caribbean seem to have addressed some of the pertinent issues emanating from September 11 fallout, such as the need to support commodity exports, economic development and diversification, human resource and infrastructure capacity building, the reality is quite different. The slow disbursement of EU funds and the limited institutional capacity of Caribbean countries to handle these funds have meant that the decisions over the money now coming on stream were made years earlier. Thus, the next section assesses aid disbursement and why the attribution of funds is such a long drawn-out process.

Aid Disbursement: Institutional Inertia and the Challenge of 9/11

The provisions of EU financial and technical assistance are important for both Caribbean ACP states and OCTs. EU aid is financed through a number of different mechanisms. Money is disbursed through the five-year European Development Funds (EDF), the European Investment Bank (EIB) and the Union's own annual budget. In the period 1976–80 the amount was ECU 239.6 million; 1981–85: ECU 415 million; 1986–90: ECU 461.9 million; and 1991–95: ECU 668.7 million (European Commission 1995, 10). The majority of money is given in the form of grant aid rather than loans, and a range of programmes and projects are supported at both the national and regional levels.

Despite the importance of EU aid allocations for the Caribbean, criticism grew throughout the 1990s of problems regarding getting funding projects approved and the slow disbursement of resources. The European Commission that oversees EU aid funds admitted that the coherence of Community assistance was lost, country programming was inflexible, and there was no single point of dialogue between the Commission and the partner country. St Lucia's Minister of Foreign Affairs and International Trade, Julian Hunte, has also expressed concern about the slow pace of aid disbursement. Hunte called for a dispassionate assessment of the reasons for the inordinate delays. We need to act speedily to remove whatever shortcomings that might exist in these arrangements (*Caribbean Insight*, October 26, 2001). In practical terms, Reisen (1999) estimates that the discrepancy between commitments and payments over the period 1993 to 1999 under the EDF was ECU 25 billion. Further, the fact that there is almost 10 billion euro of unused resources from previous funds now available for the period 2001–05 also indicates the inefficient manner of aid disbursement.

In an attempt to improve the speed and efficiency of aid disbursement a number of revisions were made to the facilities at the same time that the Cotonou Agreement was being negotiated. The financial instruments were restructured and rationalised, with the EDF made more coherent. In addition, greater flexibility has been introduced for assessing the needs of individual countries relating to aid provision. However, early evidence suggests that the procedures for disbursing aid remain slow. Under such circumstances, therefore, the EU has been unable to effectively revise its aid policies with regard to the Caribbean in the light of the September 11 terrorist attacks. An extreme illustration of the lack of dynamism within EU aid practices is that funds from the fourth EDF, linked to the first Lomé Convention are still being disbursed at a time when the ninth EDF is being finalised. Other less striking examples of slow aid disbursement can also be cited. In December 2002, for example, Jamaica received 30 million euro to support its economic reform programme from the seventh and eighth EDFs (1991–2000) while 12 months earlier, Dominica was given 5.9 million euro for an eco-tourism development programme using resources from the same two EDFs (*European Development Fund Monthly Bulletin*).

A further problem with regard to organising and distributing EU aid is that many Caribbean countries do not necessarily have the institutional capacity or sufficient technical know-how to facilitate the speedy receipt of funds. For example, the small islands states in the Eastern Caribbean, such as Grenada and Dominica, have limited capacity to help smooth the progress of aid disbursement from Brussels. Even the larger states of Trinidad and Tobago and Dominican Republic are sometimes unable to fully utilise the resources available to them. Thus, the nature of EU aid mechanisms together with the capacity constraints in Caribbean countries means that sudden and unexpected events such as those of September 11 cannot be addressed in the short or even medium-term. However, even though EU aid disbursement has not been able to address the effect of 9/11 directly, many existing aid programmes and projects do coalesce with post-9/11 priorities. Previously, economic development and diversification projects were considered. Following is an assessment of programmes within the important area of regional security and law enforcement.

Financial Probity, Regional Security and Law Enforcement Post-9/11

The significance of September 11 with regard to the oversight of money laundering and tax evasion has already been considered within the context of European states' relations with the Caribbean, and more widely within the OECD and FATF. Taking their lead from the US, the UK and other European countries introduced harsher policies in the fight against money laundering and tax evasion, while also strengthening international regulations. There was evidence to suggest that a post-9/11 shift had taken place in terms of policy regarding these matters. Similarly, within the context of the EU, existing policies were revised and built upon in the aftermath of 9/11, showing that at the supranational level in Europe there has also been a post-9/11 shift in policy emphasis. Hence, the nature of Caribbean-EU relations in the areas of money laundering and tax evasion has been altered since September 11.

Before assessing the post-9/11 shift that has taken place, it is important to recognise that the EU had a crucial role to play in improving Caribbean security and law enforcement capabilities prior to September 11. Perhaps the most important scheme established prior to 9/11 was the Caribbean Anti-Money Laundering Programme (CALP). The programme began in 1999 and will last five years. Since the launch of CALP, all the countries that are members of the CFATF benefit from legal aid and help in introducing laws against money laundering. Members of the police force, customs officials, civil servants, magistrates and judges have all received various kinds of legal training. The work of CALP complements the activities of the CFATF that have been considered earlier. However, within the context of the CFATF the role of the EU is subordinate to that of member states. With the exception of CALP, the EU is more comfortable delegating funds than being centrally involved in the detailed application of anti-money laundering provisions. For example, within the CFATF, the UK, France, the Netherlands and Spain are recognised as cooperating and supporting nations, while the European Commission is just an observer. Similarly, within the context of the OECD, EU member states have a more central role than that of the European Commission.

Although playing a less central role than member states in the OECD and FATF, the EU responded quickly to the terrorist attacks of September 11, and made its contribution felt. Within a few days of the attacks, the European Commission put forward measures to address the new situation, which led to a 'Plan of Action' being adopted by a special European Council meeting on September 21, 2001. The Plan was underpinned by five principles: continued solidarity with the US; determination in the fight against terrorism; commitment to the security of all citizens in the EU; efforts to tackle root causes of terrorism; and contributions to better understanding between civilisations ('EU response to 11th September', European Commission website). Within the context of the Plan of Action a wide-range of measures have been introduced since 9/11, including agreeing to introduce a European arrest warrant, formulating a common definition of terrorism, strengthening existing anti-money laundering provisions, freezing the assets of suspected terrorists, and signing the UN Convention for the Suppression of the Financing of Terrorism. Although many of the measures have not impinged on the Caribbean directly, they have certainly altered the overall climate in which Caribbean states are operating. However, one area where the EU has had a crucial influence over the region's OCTs is in regard to its newly agreed 'Directive on the Taxation of Savings'.

The directive framed by the European Commission in July 2001, and finally agreed by the EU economics and finance minister in January 2003, attempts to reduce the amount of tax evasion by individuals in one member state who hold bank accounts in other member states. Information exchange is a central part of the agreement so that 'Member States have the necessary information to apply the level of taxation that they see fit to their own residents' (European Commission Memo 01/266). At the same time, the UK and the Netherlands agreed that the directive would also be applicable to their Caribbean OCTs (Economic and Financial Affairs Council 2003). The coverage of the directive was established in order that a key provision of the OECD's Harmful Tax Competition Initiative, that of the automatic exchange of information, could be met. There was an expectation, therefore, that the EU's Savings Tax Directive would help build a single set of international rules on the taxation of savings.

However, as part of the agreement, it was decided that Austria, Belgium and Luxembourg would not be required to exchange information on tax matters until other non-EU nations including Switzerland and the US agree to introduce similar measures (Economic and Financial Affairs Council 2003). This seems unlikely in the short to medium-term as the US government, for example, is reluctant to introduce equivalent measures that would undermine the country's modest tax burden and banking privacy laws. Without a broader agreement, the three EU states are to be allowed to apply a withholding tax on savings held by residents of other member states. This clear case of double standards with EU member states gaining exemptions, while Caribbean OCTs are obliged to impose the Savings Tax Directive in full, has provoked a great deal of ill-feeling in the OCTs. There is also deep unease within the countries of the independent Caribbean who have come under severe pressure to accede to OECD demands on information exchange by January 1, 2004. They consider the final EU agreement as being unfair and discriminatory.

Prior to the EU compromise, for example, the Cayman Net News Service warned that if the Cayman Islands government agreed to exchange tax information with EU member states, the country's economy and reputation could be seriously damaged. The news editorial stated that 'Cayman residents will pay taxes to Great Britain for savings earned in the Cayman Islands. At a minimum, the EU tax initiative would drive millions of dollars out of the country. That translates into fewer jobs and lower incomes for residents of the Cayman Islands' (*Cayman NetNews*, July 9, 2002). Further the Cayman Islands' leader of government business, McKeeva Bush, has threatened to take the matter to the European Court of Justice if the directive is imposed. While in a statement released directly after the EU agreement, Antigua and Barbuda's chief negotiator on international financial services said, 'It is now patently and blatantly obvious that no level playing field exists and jurisdictions, such as Antigua and Barbuda, that have committed to participate in the OECD Global Tax Forum are being placed at a severe disadvantage'. The statement went on to question whether any new measures need be taken with regard to the OECDs Harmful Tax Competition Initiative in the light of the EU's action (*Caribbean Insight*, January 31, 2003).

Although the origin of the EU's 'Directive on the Taxation of Savings' goes back to 1990, and therefore clearly pre-dates the terrorist attacks of September 11, 2001, the controversy over the policy is illustrative of the tensions within the international community over the issue of tax haven regulation. There is a clear breach in the fight against tax evasion and tax havens between the independent countries and OCTs of the Caribbean on the one hand, and the developed European and North American states on the other. The perception that Europe and the US are ignoring OECD provisions, while the Caribbean is being forced to implement all measures is causing a potentially dangerous rift in the international community. These apparent strains were exacerbated by the Caribbean OCTs particular reaction to the EU's 'Directive on the Taxation of Savings', believing that the measures are a step too far in attempts to improve the transparency of the international banking system. Territories such as the Cayman Islands are already struggling to meet the new demands set by the FATF and the OECD, and consider the EU's Saving Tax Directive to be an unnecessary and overly intrusive piece of policy making. The OCTs believe that, as the measure is restricted only to them and 12 EU member states, their competitors in the offshore sector, will gain an advantage if the directive is implemented. The need, therefore, to maintain competitive advantage in international offshore centres remains a dominant concern even in the post-September 11 environment; a consideration illustrating the limits of Caribbean-European cooperation.

An overarching aspect of Caribbean-EU relations that touches upon issues such as regional security, law enforcement and money laundering, and which is particularly pertinent in the post-9/11 era is the concern for good governance. The importance attached to encouraging countries in the Caribbean to improve their democratic credentials is seen as paramount in the fight against terrorism, corruption and other criminal activities. However, as with other aspects of Caribbean-European relations, the issue of good governance has been enshrined within cooperation policies for a number of years. Therefore the effect of September 11 on improving governance practices has been marginal at best. Within the context of Caribbean-EU relations, for example, no new ideas on good governance have been put forward since 9/11. In fact the greatest change in the area of good governance came in 1995 with the Mid-Term review of the Lomé Convention.

Review of the LoméConvention

The wide-ranging review of the Fourth Lomé Convention not only made the defence of human rights an objective, but Article 5 of the revised Convention recognised the application of democratic principles and the consolidation of the rule of law as 'essential elements' (European Commission 1996, 6). Significant funds were given to support institutional and reform measures, while provisions were also included to allow a country to be suspended from the Convention if the good governance criteria were violated. The provisions inserted within the Fourth Lomé Convention in 1995 were maintained in the successor Cotonou Agreement, and extended in certain areas. In the new Agreement, for example, signatories agreed to a procedure whereby, in cases of serious active and passive corruption, aid could be suspended. Therefore, the importance of good governance within Caribbean-EU relations has been clear for some time and the influence of 9/11 has been negligible. A particular Caribbean-EU relationship which has shown some flexibility in the area of good governance has been the relationship between the EU and Cuba. The following section considers the relatively good relations between Cuba and the EU since September 11, a state of affairs quite at variance with Cuban-US relations over the same period.

Cuban-EU relations: Cooperation not Isolation

Although economic relations between Cuba and the US are beginning to thaw via the emergency food programme, political relations are still extremely limited. The events of September 11 heightened the political divisions between the two states particularly with the US government retaining Cuba's name on a list of states that allegedly sponsor terrorism, along with Iran, Iraq, Libya, North Korea, Sudan and Syria. In comparison, the relationship between Cuba and the EU has been developing over recent years, particularly in the fields of trade cooperation and aid disbursement. Indeed, the countries of the

EU account for almost 40 per cent of Cuba's trade and 56 per cent of its foreign investment. In addition, the EU provides Cuba with 15 million euro a year in development aid. A clear illustration of the difference in policy approach between the EU and the US came in a European Commission report published in October 2001. The report stated the EU's strong opposition to the continuing US trade embargo placed on Cuba and the 'extra-territorial' provisions contained in some US laws, such as the 1996 *Helms-Burton Act* that allows US citizens and companies to sue foreign firms using Cuban property confiscated after the 1959 revolution.

In terms of practical cooperation, a series of projects have been funded to promote contacts between European and Cuban firms and also to improve the business administration skills of Cuban executives in charge of running companies. Under the EU's 2002 budget, line funds have been given to improve international accountancy standards in Cuban enterprises and to strengthen the country's financial sector. The EU and European investors have also been attempting to persuade Cuba to improve its investment climate. In a report submitted to the Cuban government in early 2002, a number of complaints were listed including a lack of information on business laws and regulations and their discriminatory application against foreign companies, excessive utility costs, and the requirement to pay state labour agencies high dollar wages for employees, who are then paid by the agency in pesos. The Cuban government subsequently promised to improve the country's foreign investment, keen to expand ties with the EU. More than 190 companies from across the EU now operate in the island and, as a consequence, the governments of Spain, the UK, Germany, the Netherlands, France and Belgium have all been actively engaged in trade promotion. In addition, the European Commission established an office in Havana in March 2003, intended to improve trade and investment ties.

However, although Cuba is a member of the ACP group it is not party to the Cotonou Agreement and therefore cooperation has remained on a rather ad hoc basis. The main reason for this is that although the EU stresses the importance of constructive engagement with Cuba, a joint position adopted by the EU Council of Ministers in 1996 made it clear that the conclusion of a cooperation agreement was dependent on Havana moving towards a democratic system and improving its human rights record. Despite the position taken by the EU, Cuba submitted its application to join the EU-ACP partnership in 1999. However, this was subsequently withdrawn in April 2000 after the EU supported a UN Commission resolution condemning human rights violations in Cuba. Nevertheless, from the middle of 2001, contacts were renewed with both the European Commission and the ACP countries, subsequently making clear their support for Cuba's possible incorporation into the Cotonou Agreement. However, EU member states are divided on the issue, with some countries such as Spain and France in favour of Cuba's inclusion, while others, including the UK and Sweden, feel that Cuba's membership is impossible at the present time. The latter view seems to be shared by the European Parliament after it awarded the Sakharov Prize for Freedom and Thought to leading Cuban dissident Oswaldo Payá in December 2002. Nevertheless, despite the political differences between Europe and Cuba, the nature of the relationship is far removed from the exising US-Cuban relations. In addition, within the context of the September 11 terrorist attacks, Europe has maintained and further deepened the links with Cuba, while in the eyes of the US, Cuba is seen as part of the terrorist threat.

Conclusion

The overarching theme of the chapter has been that although the terrorist attacks of September 11 have had profound effects on individual states within the international system and on the global security environment more generally, the nature of the relationship between the Caribbean and Europe has been virtually unaltered. This is primarily due to the long-standing and institutional aspects of political and economic cooperation between the two regions. Individual European states have played a role in the Caribbean since the seventeenth century, and the legacy of that involvement remains a strong influence today. Similarly, albeit within a much more recent time frame, the EU has developed extensive links with the region. In both cases there are procedures, conventions and rules that define the relationships and which, within the context of 9/11, have overridden short-term considerations.

The issue of EU aid disbursement is an excellent case in point, where the time between agreeing a policy agenda and distributing related funds can take ten years or more. A further issue that has mitigated the effects of September 11 within the context of Caribbean-European relations is the clear synergy between pre-9/11 policies and post-9/11 concerns. At both the level of individual European states and the EU, the nature of policy cooperation with the Caribbean prior to September 11 was easily applicable to post-September 11 circumstances. Key concerns after the terrorist attacks such as drug trafficking, good governance and economic decline were all being addressed within the context of Caribbean-European relations many years before September 11, 2001. Similarly, the priorities underpinning the relationship between the Caribbean and Europe were virtually unchanged after the events of 9/11. The main concerns of the Caribbean remained the safeguarding of trade advantages for its core commodity exports, the continuation of EU aid programmes and the maintenance of cooperation in the area of law enforcement.

The 9/11 terrorist attacks may have altered the rhetoric used to describe the motivations underpinning these forms of cooperation, but the substance of the programmes have remained more or less unaffected. An aspect of Caribbean-European relations that witnessed an apparent policy change after September 11 was the area of financial good practice. Although the OECD and FATF had been in existence for some time prior to 9/11, it was the terrorist attacks that altered the international financial climate. The pressure for change from individual European states and the EU via the OECD and the FATF placed added pressure on the countries and territories of the Caribbean to extensively tighten their offshore banking sectors and tax regimes. However, even with such an apparently important issue as this, there were limits to the amount of cooperation possible – the deep divisions over the EU's savings tax directive being an excellent example. Therefore, one can argue that although the terrorist attacks of 9/11 did alter certain aspects of the relationship between the Caribbean and Europe, its underlying nature was fundamentally unchanged, retaining a direction set many years before.

Notes

1 P. Sutton, 'Europe and the Caribbean', in A. Payne and P. Sutton, *Charting Caribbean Development* (London: Macmillan Caribbean, 2001), p. 204.
2 Anguilla, Aruba, Cayman Islands, Dutch Antilles (Curaçao, Bonaire, St Maarten, St Eustache and Saba), Montserrat, Turks and Caicos Islands, British Virgin Islands.
3 Forum of the Caribbean ACP States: CARICOM Member States + Cuba and Dominican Republic.

References

ACP General Secretariat, 'Brazil and Australia's claims against the EU sugar policy threaten the ACP', Press Release, October 22, 2002, available at http://www.acpsec.org/gb/press/brasause, accessed October 29, 2002.

Agence Française de Développment, *Annual Report 2001* Paris: AfD, 2002.

CARICOM, 'Prime Minister Paterson outlines Caribbean vision for new French relations', Press Release 17/2000, March 10, 2000, available at http://www.caricom.org/pressreleases/pres17_00.htm, accessed February 15, 2003.

Caribbean Financial Action Task Force, available at http://www1.oecd.org/fatf/Ctry-orgpages/org/cfatf_en.htm, accessed January 8, 2003.

Caribbean Insight, an editorially independent publication of the Caribbean Council of Europe, published in London.

Caribbean Times, 'Visa controls are not fair', January 17, 2003.

Caribbean Times, '$9m for AIDS', February 21, 2003.

Caribbean Times, 'UK's anti-drug scan machines working well', March 14, 2003.

Cayman NetNews, 'Bracing for an EU Blow, Cayman refuses to Bow', July 9, 2002, available at http://www.caymannetnews.com, accessed January 24, 2003.

Cayman NetNews, 'Cayman Standing Up To EU', January 24, 2003, available at http://www.caymannetnews.com, accessed January 24, 2003.

Centre for Tax Policy and Administration, *The OECD's Project on Harmful Tax Practices: The 2001 Progress Report*, 2001.

Clegg, P., 'Renegotiating Lomé: The Future of the EU-ACP Caribbean Relationship', DSA European Development Policy Study Group, Discussion Paper No. 7, October 1997.

Clegg, P., *The Caribbean Banana Trade: From Colonialism to Globalization* Basingstoke: Palgrave Macmillan, 2002.

Cocchi, G., 'The OCT/EU Forum 2002: trade, aid and more', *The Courier*, November–December 2002.

Davenport, M., A. Hewitt, and A. Koning, *Europe's Preferred Partners? The Lomé Countries in World Trade* London: Overseas Development Institute, 1995.

Dearden, S. (ed.), *The European Union and the Commonwealth Caribbean,* Aldershot: Ashgate, 2002.

Department for International Development, *Jamaica Country Strategy Paper*, August 2001.

Department for International Development, *Anguilla – Development Assistance*, July 2002, available at http://www.dfid.gov.uk, accessed January 8, 2003.

Economic and Financial Affairs Council, '2480th Council Meeting', 5506/03 (Presse 15), Brussels, January 21, 2003.

The Economist, 'Empire in the Americas: And forget George Washington', October 2, 1997.

European Centre for Development Policy Management (ECDPM), *Lomé Infokit*, Number 5, March 1997.

European Commission, *The Caribbean and the European Union*, DE 80, June, (Luxembourg: Office for Official Publications of the European Communities, 1995).

European Commission, Lomé IV Revised: Changes and Challenges, DE 89, December, (Luxembourg: Office for Official Publications of the European Communities, 1996).

European Commission, *Annual report on the implementation of the European Commission's External Assistance (2000),* available at http://www.europa.eu.int/comm/europeaid/reports/aidco_2000_annual_report_acp_en.pdf, accessed January 10, 2003.

European Commission, Annual *Report on the Implementation of the European Commission's External Assistance,* (Brussels, 2001).

European Commission, 'Savings tax proposal: frequently asked questions', Memo 01/266, July 18, (Brussels, 2001).

European Commission, *The Caribbean and the European Union*, DE 113, May, Luxembourg: Office for Official Publications of the European Communities, 2002.

European Commission, 'EU action in response to 11th September 2001: one year after', available at http://europa.eu.int/comm/110901/index.htm, accessed March 2, 2003.

European Development Fund Monthly Bulletin, available at http://www.europa.eu.int/comm/europeaid/projects/edf_en.htm, accessed January 10, 2003.

Financial Action Task Force, 'Non-Cooperative Countries and Territories', available at http://www1.oecd.org/fatf/NCCT_en.htm, accessed April 6, 2003.

Foreign and Commonwealth Office, 'Britain and the Caribbean: A Special Relationship', available at http://www.fco.gov.uk/servlet/Front?pagename=OpenMarket/Xcelerate/ShowPage&c=Page&cid=1007 029394527, accessed January 8, 2003.

Foreign and Commonwealth Office, 'Tackling the Major Drugs Threat', available at http://www.fco.gov.uk/servlet/Front?pagename=OpenMarket/Xcelerate/ShowPage&c=Page&cid=1007 029393609, accessed January 8, 2003.

Foreign and Commonwealth Office, 'Partnership for Progress and Prosperity: Britain and the Overseas Territories', available at http://www.fco.gov.uk/servlet/Front?pagename=OpenMarket/Xcelerate/ShowPage&c=Page&cid=1018028164839, accessed March 2, 2003.

Gonzales, A., 'The future of EU-Caribbean links', *The Courier*, no 161 (January–February 1997): 72–73.

The Guardian, 'Bungled MI6 plot led to Cayman trial collapse', January 18, 2003.

Hoefte, R., 'The Difficulty of Getting it Right: Dutch Policy in the Caribbean', *Itinerario*, February 25, 2001, 59–73.

Home Office, 'Jamaica – visa regime aims to cut delays', January 8, 2003.

Home Office, 'New visa regime for Jamaican nationals', Press Office Briefing Note, January 8, 2003.

The Jamaica Gleaner, 'Record deportations', February 6, 2000.

The Jamaica Observer, 'France maps strategy for deeper links with Caribbean', December 8, 2002.

Klak, T., 'How Much Does the Caribbean Gain from Offshore Services?' in M. Blacklock (ed.) *The Association of Caribbean States (ACS) Yearbook*, London: ACS and International Systems and Communications Ltd., 2002.

Martin, M. L. 'French Presence and Strategic Interests in the Caribbean', in J.R. Beruff and H.G. Muñiz, *Security Problems and Policies in the Post-Cold War Caribbean*, London: Macmillan, 1996.

Ministerie van Binnenlandse Zaken en Koninkrijksrelaties, Conference Report – The economic development of Caribbean overseas countries and territories: the role of their European partners (The Hague, 2001).

Ministerie van Binnenlandse Zaken en Koninkrijksrelaties, 'Kingdom united against terrorism', available at http://www.minbzk.nl/asp/get.asp?xdl=../views/bzk/xdl/Page&VarIdt=00000002&SitIdt=00000039&It mIdt=00007421&Aka=true, accessed February 5, 2003.

Ministerie van Binnenlandse Zaken en Koninkrijksrelaties, 'Dutch government wants to help Netherlands Antilles fight drug trafficking', available at http://www.minbzk.nl/asp/get.asp?xdl=../views/bzk/xdl/Page&VarIdt=00000002&SitIdt=00000039&It mIdt=00007421&Aka=true, accessed February 5, 2003.

Nurse, K. and W. Sandiford, 'Windward Island Bananas'. *Challenges and Option under the Single European Market,* Jamaica: Friedrich Ebert Stiftung, 1995.

Organisation for Economic Cooperation and Development (OECD), 'About Harmful Tax Practices', available at http://www.oecd.org/EN/about/0,,EN-about-103-nodirectorate-no-no-no-22,00.html, accessed January 8, 2003.

Payne, A. and P. Sutton, *Charting Caribbean Development*, London: MacMillan Caribbean, 2001.

Reisen, M. van, *EU Global Player: The North South Policy of the EU,* Utrecht: International Books, 1999.

The Sunday Gleaner, 'UK newspaper accuses Home Office of lying about J'cans', February 2, 2003.

Sutton. P., 'Europe and the Caribbean', in A. Payne and P. Sutton, *Charting Caribbean Development,* London: Macmillan Caribbean, 2001.

The Times, 'Blunkett imposes visa restrictions on all Jamaicans visiting Britain', January 9, 2003.

UK-Caribbean Forum, 'Joint Communiqué Issued by the UK/Caribbean Forum, London, May 12, 2000', available at http://www.belize-guatemala.gov.bz/support/uk_carib_forum.html, accessed December 12, 2002.

UK-Caribbean Forum, 'Joint Communiqué Issued by the UK/Caribbean Forum, Guyana, April 5, 2002', at http://www.fco.gov.uk/servlet/Front?pagename=OpenMarket/Xcelerate/ShowPage&c=Page&cid=1007 029394545, accessed December 12, 2002.

Verhoeven, J. 'Country report: The Netherlands, the Netherlands Antilles and Aruba', 2001.

12

Agenda Setting and Regionalism in the Greater Caribbean: Responses to 9/11

Norman Girvan[1]

Introduction

The Greater Caribbean[2] has a total population of 240 million spread over 25 independent states and 13 non-independent territories. It is the region of the developing world of closest proximity to the United States and it has close economic, social, cultural and political ties to that country. This was reflected in the significant human and economic costs incurred by countries in the region from the terrorist attacks in the United States of September 11, 2001. In the aftermath of, the attacks, political relations were shaped by the character and content of the US response, with security issues taking centre stage.

While the security agendas of the US and those of regional countries overlapped in many respects, significant differences in emphasis and perspective became evident. Human security, in its many dimensions, was counter-posed to a uni-dimensional perspective that focuses on countering terrorism. Political negotiation of these issues was conditioned by the reality of asymmetries in power in US-Caribbean and intra-Caribbean relations associated with the wide differences in size and economic strength among countries and with the political fragmentation of the region. In examining these issues, this chapter looks first at the nature of the social and economic linkages between the Greater Caribbean and the United States. We then review political responses to the crisis to show the context in which differing perspectives on security emerged. In the third part, the problems for tourism created by 9/11 are examined as a case study of regional responses to the crisis. Finally, we offer some concluding observations.

Ties That Bind: The US-Caribbean Nexus

September 11, 2001 resulted in significant loss of human life and a virtual meltdown in the US travel industry. It tipped the sputtering US economy more deeply into recession. Key elements in the resulting 'war on terror' were immigration monitoring and control; border controls and transport security; and the link between narco-trafficking, money laundering and terrorism. These events impacted significantly on the countries of the Greater Caribbean as a consequence of their close linkages with the US in migration, tourism, trade and investment.

Table 12.1
United States Population Born in Latin American and Caribbean Countries, 1990 Census

Region / Country of birth	No.	% LAC	% of the country's national population
Total Latin America and the Caribbean	9,681,024	100.00	2.28
Greater Caribbean	7,820,462	80.78	N.A.
Mexico	4,298,014	44.40	5.16
Other Mesoamerica	1,093,929	11.28	3.91
Costa Rica	39,438	0.41	1.29
El Salvador	465,433	4.81	9.11
Guatemala	225,739	2.33	2.58
Honduras	108,923	1.13	2.32
Nicaragua	168,659	1.74	4.41
Panama	85,737	0.86	3.58
Insular Caribbean	1,803,087	18.64	N.A.
Cuba	736,971	7.63	N.A.
Barbados	43,015	0.44	16.74
Haiti	225,393	2.33	3.26
Jamaica	334,140	3.45	14.1
Dominican Republic	347,858	3.59	4.89
Trinidad & Tobago	115,710	1.20	9.52
Caribbean / South America	442,036	4.57	0.8
Colombia	286,124	2.96	0.08
Guyana	120,698	1.25	15.18
Venezuela	35,214	0.36	0.18

Source: Miguel Villa & Jorge P. Martinez, 'International Migration in LAC: Social, Demographic and Economic Traits', Table 1, p. 38, in SELA Capítulos, *n° 65, May–August 2002.*

US census data for 1990 record nearly 10 million Latin American- and Caribbean-born persons living in the United States, the vast majority of whom originate in the Greater Caribbean region (Table 12.1). Mexico accounts for the largest number, but migrants from Central America and the insular Caribbean are highly significant in relation to the populations of these countries. Recent Inter-American Development Bank (IADB) studies have shown that migrants remittances to their home economies 'have a significant economic and social impact in Latin America and the Caribbean... for the most part, remittances are used for basic subsistence needs and make up a significant portion of the income of those households that receive them'.[3] Countries in the Greater Caribbean received an estimated US$18.9 billion in 2001 and US$23.8 billion in 2002 (Table 12.2). Remittances are especially important for the economies of the insular Caribbean and Central America as a supplement to foreign currency earnings and to the GDP.

Table 12.2
Remittances to Selected Greater Caribbean Countries (US$ Millions)

	2001	2002	2001	
Country			% Exports	% GDP
Mexico	9,273	10,502	6.5	1.7
El Salvador	1,920	2,206	60.0	17.0
Dominican Republic	1,807	2,111	27.0	10.0
Colombia	1,600	2,431	2.4	2.1
Jamaica	967	1,288	30.0	15.0
Cuba	930	1,138	40.0	5.0
Haiti	810	931	150.0	24.5
Nicaragua	610	759	80.0	22.0
Guatemala	584	1,689	16.0	3.1
Honduras	460	770	17.0	7.5
Total Selected countries	**18,961**	**23,825**		

Sources: 2001: Current landscape of remittances in the Caribbean, *Power point presentation by Manuel Ozorco, Director, Central America Program, Inter-American Dialogue, at the round table, 'Remittances as a development tool in the Caribbean', Multilateral Investment Fund, Inter-American Development Bank, Kingston, Jamaica, September 17, 2002;* Sending money home: an international comparison of remittance markets, *February 2003 – Inter-American Development Bank (IDB) website*: www.iadb.org/mif/website/static/en/28docb.doc.

The presence of a significant Caribbean Diaspora in the US had several implications for the regional impact of 9/11. Some 391 Caribbean persons died in the tragedy, representing 12.9 per cent of the total deaths compared to their 3.8 per cent presence in the total US population (Table 12.3)[4]. The fact that the region appears to be disproportionately represented in 9/11 deaths may be due to the concentration of its migrants in certain urban centres including New York and Washington and in certain service occupations including catering and cleaning. El Salvador, the Dominican Republic, Colombia and CARICOM as a whole suffered significant casualties. This would have deepened the psycho-social impact of the tragedy on these societies and heightened the sense of psychological and political identification with the United States. September 11, 2001 could also have reduced remittances to the region, to the extent that resulting unemployment in the US service economy affected Caribbean migrants. However, the data show that remittances increased significantly in 2002. Hence, the tragedy either had no impact on the 'natural growth' of remittances, or it might even have induced migrants to send more money home because of the negative economic impact within the region.

The attacks led to a change in the US security regime, emphasising *homeland security* as distinct from external military threats. There were heightened controls over legal and illegal migration and increased surveillance over aliens in the United States. The effects of these measures on Caribbean migrants and migration may have been attenuated by the focus on persons from other regions with presumed ties to the perpetrators of the terrorist acts. However, the Caribbean region came under heightened scrutiny for possible links to international terrorist networks through narco-trafficking and money laundering. One notable political casualty was the proposal of the Mexican administration of President Vicente Fox to regularise the status of several million Mexicans working in the United States. The US effectively shelved negotiations on this matter after 9/11.The hopes of several governments in the region for US cooperation on the practice of deporting Caribbean nationals with criminal records back to the region also received a setback in the changed security environment.

Of the 18 million tourists who visit Caribbean destinations each year, some 57 per cent are from the United States and most of the remainder are from Canada and Europe (Table 12.4)[5]. For most of the island economies of the Caribbean and in the Mexican Yucatan peninsula, tourism has become the dominant earner of foreign income and is a major employment source. Hence, the steep contraction in US and world air travel following the attacks

Table 12.3
Casualties from 9/11: Greater Caribbean Countries

Members	Missing / Unaccounted for	Source
Group1: OECS		
Antigua & Barbuda	3	Reuters
Dominica	1	Nation News (18/09/01)
Grenada		
St Kitts and Nevis		
Saint Lucia	1	Reuters
St Vincent & The Grenadines	2	Nation News (18/09/01)
Subtotal	7	
Group 2		
The Bahamas	1	Reuters
Barbados	3	Reuters
Belize	4	Reuters
Guyana	22	Stabroeknews, Guyana (14/09/01)
Haiti	2	Nation News (18/09/01)
Suriname		
Subtotal	32	
Group 3		
Jamaica	7	Reuters
Trinidad And Tobago	4	Reuters
Subtotal	11	
Subtotal CARICOM	50	
Central American Common Market		
Costa Rica	1	Reuters
El Salvador	71	Reuters
Guatemala	6	Reuters
Honduras	7	Reuters
Nicaragua		
Subtotal	85	
Non-Grouped Countries		
Cuba		
Dominican Republic	25	Reuters
Panama	3	Reuters
Subtotal	28	
Group Of Three		
Colombia	208	Reuters
Mexico	17	Reuters
Venezuela	3	Reuters
Subtotal	228	
TOTAL INDEPENDENT STATES	391	
Other Territories		
Bermuda	1	Nation News (18/09/01)
Montserrat	1	Nation News (18/09/01)
Puerto Rico	60	Miami Herald (17/09/01)
Subtotal: Other Territories	62	
GRAND TOTAL	453	
TOTAL CASUALTIES 9/11	3023	Reuters

Note: *The Reuters figures are as of Sept. 20 and were obtained from the CNN.com Victim Story Archive Special Website. http://europe.cnn.com/SPECIALS/2001/trade.center/stories.victims.html.*

involving four plane hijackings had a severe economic impact on Caribbean destinations. As shown later, the resulting tourism crisis became a test case of the response capabilities of the Caribbean at the national, subregional and regional levels. Some 51.7 per cent of the merchandise trade of the region is with the United States. The US market absorbs 68 per cent of the region's exports as a whole; 44 per cent in the case of Central America and 42 per cent for CARICOM (Table 12.5). The US economic slow-down that heightened after the attacks impacted the region's markets and economic growth. This became evident in 2002, when the majority of regional countries experienced economic stagnation, with 13 registering negative growth and two others having growth of less than 1 per cent.[6]

Investment in offshore banking centres in the Caribbean constitutes a fourth major linkage between the region and the US. Regional countries that have specialised in the provision of international financial services include Aruba, Antigua and Barbuda, Barbados, the Bahamas and the Cayman Islands. In the insular Caribbean, the financial sector showed significant growth in the 1990s.[7] Prior to September 11, Caribbean countries had been under pressure to tighten regulations over offshore financial centres to control so-called 'harmful tax competition' and the alleged use of these centres for money laundering by transnational crime syndicates. Pressure was intensified after 9/11 due to concern over the use of offshore banking by international terrorist networks for the financing of terrorist acts and to facilitate links with narco-traffickers.

The majority of states in the region have close political and security cooperation ties with the United States. The notable exception is Cuba, with which the US does not maintain direct diplomatic relations and which has been the subject of a US trade and economic embargo since 1962. US-Caribbean relations are handled mainly in bilateral mode. In the case of CARICOM, dialogue with the US also takes place through the Community's mechanism for foreign policy coordination. The US commands significant leverage in these relations because of the marked asymmetry in economic and military power that exists. This conditioned the ongoing discourse and negotiations on security matters in the post-9/11 environment.

Table 12.4
CTO Caribbean[1] Stopover Visitor Arrivals by Main Market, 2000-2001

	US	Canada	Europe	Caribbean	Total Main Markets
Thousands					
2000	10177	1234	5254	1408	18073
2001	10077	1317	4871	1385	17650
Per cent main market					
2000	56.3	6.8	29.1	7.8	100.0
2001	57.1	7.5	27.6	7.8	100.0

Source: *Caribbean Tourism one year after 9/11, prepared by Gail Clarke, Caribbean Tourism Organization (CTO), November 2002, Cancun, CARICOM countries, Cuba, Dominican Republic, UK, US and Dutch affiliated islands.*

Table 12.5
Greater Caribbean Region: Trade with the United States, 2001 (US$ Millions and percentages)

	Group of 3[1]	CACM[2]	CARICOM	Others[3]
Exports to US	160 694	5 675	3 447	11 107
Imports from US	137 389	9 077	5 214	11 743
Exports to US % total exports	81.4	44.5	42.4	13.4
Imports from US % total imports	69.2	43.3	38.9	39.3

1. Colombia, Mexico and Venezuela
2. Central American Common Market
3. Cuba, Panama, Dominican Republic, Aruba, Netherlands Antilles

Source: Main trade trends, trade policy and integration agreements in the countries of the Association of Caribbean States (ACS), UNECLAC, 2003, ACS website: http://www.acs-aec.org/tendencias_eng.doc.

Perspectives On Security

The unprecedented attacks on the financial and political centres of the United States catapulted security issues to the top of the agenda of international relations. Cooperation in security was addressed at several levels: multilateral, hemispheric, regional/subregional and bilateral. In Latin America and the Caribbean, the first round of responses mainly reflected the priorities of the US-driven security agenda. They focused on migration and border controls, the apprehension and transfer of suspected terrorists, security of transport and elimination of terrorist financing. The majority of regional countries supported and cooperated in these initiatives.[8] However, differences were to become evident regarding the scope and emphasis of definitions of *security* and in the strategy to achieve it. Stress points also became evident where security initiatives directly impacted the economic interests of countries.

The Counter-Terrorist Agenda

Hemispheric

Meeting on the very day of the attacks in Lima, Peru, the General Assembly of the Organisation of American States (OAS) condemned the atrocities and expressed full solidarity with the United States.[9] The OAS Permanent Council invoked the Inter-American Treaty on Reciprocal Assistance (Rio Treaty)[10] and assigned special tasks to the Inter-American Committee against Terrorism[11] and to the Committee on Hemispheric Security,[12] including the convening of a Special Conference on Security of the OAS. In short order the Inter-American Convention on Terrorism was prepared; this was signed by the majority of member states at the Thirty-second General Assembly of the OAS in Barbados in June 2002. The Convention calls for cooperation in the eradication of the financing of terrorism, the seizure of funds and assets, action against money laundering, border controls, law enforcement and mutual legal assistance, transfer of persons in custody, denial of refugee status and of asylum and other similar measures.[13] The OAS Convention also called for signature, ratification and implementation of all international Conventions and Protocols related to terrorism including the newly formulated International Convention for the Financing of Terrorism.

Sub-Regional

The main elements of this agenda were reflected in statements and initiatives by the Central American Integration System (SICA) and by CARICOM. On September 19, 2001, Central American leaders adopted the Declaration 'Centroamérica unida contra el terrorismo' listing measures for increased regional security and cooperation with the US, particularly with regard to migration and border controls.[14] On September 27, 2001, the Central American Commission of Defense and Security recommended measures of cooperation in the areas of migration and border controls, money laundering and coordination of police forces.[15] A Central American plan of cooperation against terrorism was approved by the governments on October 25, 2001, highlighting modification in national legislations and reinforcement of border controls.[16]

The CARICOM statement of September 20, 2001 drew attention to the loss of life and economic dislocation suffered by the region as a consequence of the attacks.[17] An emergency CARICOM summit, convened in October 2001, issued the Nassau Declaration on International Terrorism.[18] The declaration reaffirms a commitment to international cooperation in the fight against terrorism through resolutions 1368 and 1373 of the UN Security Council; and commits to enhancing and enacting national legislation relating to security, especially in relation to international transport and money laundering. Notably, the CARICOM statement also addressed the economic fallout on the subregion. It announced agreement to launch a major tourism promotion campaign;[19] called for international financial institutions and donor agencies to provide assistance to mitigate the economic consequences of the attacks;[20] and included proposals to reduce the escalating costs of insurance for international transport.[21]

Bilateral

One feature of the US 'war on terror' is the designation of certain states and organisations as being sponsors of terrorism and terrorist organisations respectively.[22] Within the Greater Caribbean, Cuba has been included in the first list, a classification that this country energetically rejects with counter-charges of its own regarding the harbouring of known terrorists within the territory of the United States.[23] US designation of the three Colombian groups – United Self-Defence Units of Colombia (AUC), National Liberation Army (ELN) and Revolutionary Armed Forces of Colombia (FARC) – as terrorist organisations brought the Colombian conflict within the ambit of the 'war on terror', adding this dimension to the anti narco-trafficking campaign. An expanded programme of US military assistance in support of the 'Plan Colombia' was approved in 2002 at a cost of US$537 million, including US$98 million for military assistance to the units protecting the oil pipeline of Caño Limón;[24] making Colombia the third largest recipient of US aid.[25]

Expanded US assistance would aim to improve Colombia's capacity to execute laws and legislation, for example regarding kidnappings; to gather intelligence and investigate terrorism; to protect key infrastructure, and to monitor persons with suspected links to other terrorist organisations and or groups. The changed political climate was signalled in May of 2002, when Álvaro Uribe was elected as president of Colombia on a platform of vigorously prosecuting the war against the FARC and the ELN, in contrast to the previous policy of allowing the FARC safe areas. The possible repercussions of these developments in neighbouring countries and zones have also been the subject of political discussion in the region.[26]

Counter-Terrorism and Offshore Banking

A major weapon in counter-terrorism is the elimination of the financing of terrorist activities through the use of domestic and transnational banking. The International Convention for the Financing of Terrorism and the OAS Convention Against Terrorism commit parties to heightened monitoring over financial transactions carried out under their jurisdiction. The US *Patriot Act* (Uniting and Strengthening America by Providing Appropriate Tools Required to Intercept and Obstruct Terrorism) of 2001 was also a significant development. It extended the US money laundering regulations offshore by 'applying record-keeping and monitoring requirements to foreign branches of US banks and foreign institutions operating in the US'.[27] As a result, Caribbean offshore banking centres came under considerable pressure to conform to the US requirements.

Hence Panama's financial analysis unit, the UAF, launched investigation into terrorist money allegations, regarding the possible connection between Osama Bin Laden, and the financial services company Al Taqwa Management organisation, established in Panama in January 2001.[28] In another example in Antigua, the Office of National Drug Control and Money Laundering Policy circulated to banks a list of terrorists and terrorist agencies compiled by US authorities. The banks were instructed to search their accounts for any of these names and report the findings to the relevant authorities, which would freeze the accounts and provide information to the US authorities.[29] Members of the Caribbean Association of Regulators of International Business (CARIB) established a regional action plan and timetable which adopts strategies for the banking, securities and insurance industries and the offshore sector. This action was taken to comply with the UN Security Council Resolution 1373 of September 28, 2001.

While governments have, for the most part cooperated, there are concerns that, by diluting the degree of client confidentiality that lies at the base of the advantage of Caribbean locations in offshore banking, the new regulatory regime may result in some loss of business from these centres and of government revenue in the host countries.

Counter-Terrorism and Trade Liberalisation

The security crisis produced by 9/11 did not materially affect US priorities in trade liberalisation through the FTAA and WTO. The official US view has been that free trade promotes economic growth and political stability and helps to undermine the social basis of terrorism. The Bush administration was quick to reaffirm its commitment to the FTAA; with some spokesmen attempting to portray trade liberalisation as another element of counter-terrorist strategy.

In a declaration issued by the members of the Trade Negotiations Committee of the FTAA, at the IX Meeting of the Trade Committee of the FTAA held in Managua, Nicaragua, 'The Vice Ministers responsible for trade in the 34 FTAA countries... reaffirm their commitment to the FTAA process... They reiterate that these events will not disrupt the economic agenda and trade integration within the Hemisphere'.[30] In January 2002, President Bush announced the US decision to negotiate a free trade agreement with the countries of Central America, reversing a previous policy stance.[31] The administration pushed successfully for the Fourth WTO Ministerial Meeting which was held at Doha, Qatar, in November 2001; and in securing Trade Promotion Authority from Congress in early 2002. The US has since concluded a free trade agreement with Chile and the negotiations with Central America are well advanced.

The Multidimensional Model

Organization of American States (OAS)

Notwithstanding their cooperation with the US in advancing the counter-terrorist agenda, countries in the region were pressing for the incorporation of wider concerns and issues relating to security at the different levels of response. These wider concerns were couched in terms of a *multidimensional* approach to security or *human security*. In the instance of Barbados as host country, the multidimensional approach was placed on the agenda of the Thirty-second General Assembly of the OAS in June 2002. In his opening address at the meeting, Prime Minister Arthur insisted that '...any meaningful definition of security can no longer be limited to the traditional military operations, but must recognise the need for an integrated approach to confronting the conditions which create instabilities in our society and which degrade our humanity'. He called for security concerns to take on board 'the scourge of HIV/AIDS, illegal arms and drug-trafficking, trans-national crime, ecological disasters and poverty....'[32] Based on a submission from Barbados, the Assembly adopted a declaration on a Multidimensional Approach to Security which, *inter alia*, declared 'that the security of the Hemisphere encompasses political, economic, social, health, and environmental factors...' and decided 'to include the multidimensional approach to hemispheric security ...as a topic on the agenda of the Special Conference on Security.'[33]

Association of Caribbean States (ACS)

The multidimensional approach was not new; it had been present in previous declarations on the subject by states in the Greater Caribbean. In December 2001, the heads of state and governments of the Association of Caribbean States (ACS), meeting at their Third Summit, adopted a declaration that condemned terrorism 'in all its forms'[34] and went on to refer to the growing threat of transnational organised crime, the traffic in persons and migrants; the illicit trade and manufacture of firearms, components and ammunition; and the worldwide drug problem. Notably the declaration emphasised 'the principle of shared responsibility'[35] in the fight against the illegal trade in drugs and arms and money laundering. It called for ratification of the Inter American Convention against the Manufacture and Illicit Traffic in Firearms, Ammunition, Explosives and other related materials. It supported the implementation of the Plan of Action of the UN Conference on the Illicit Traffic in Small and Light Firearms held in New York in July 2001 under the chairmanship of Colombia.[36]

In November 2002, the Eighth Meeting of the ACS Ministerial Council addressed 'Human Security in the Caribbean' as the theme of its political dialogue. Host country Belize presented a paper that reiterated the concerns of the Margarita Declaration but extended the consideration of security to environmental, social and economic factors.[37] Security threats and problems included vulnerability to natural disasters and climate change, territorial disputes, the challenges to small economies in the context of growing trade liberalisation, the HIV/AIDS pandemic, corruption, poverty and the diminution of the role of the state. Security would be enhanced by democracy, good governance and human rights and by the adoption of a people-centred approach and the involvement of civil society.

By 2003, the growing incidence of homicides and other violent crimes had become a source of public concern in several countries in the region and the issue of security was placed on the agenda of the ACS Executive Board at its twenty-first meeting in Santo Domingo in March. A paper from the ACS Secretariat pointed to the deleterious social consequences of violent crime as well as its negative economic impact on investment and the sustainability of tourism. It pointed to recognition that the problems are global in scope, being linked to the emergence of transnational organised crime and related phenomena together with inter-related contributory factors, including:

> The persistence of poverty and the growth of inequality within and between nations; the erosion of social safety nets and political fragmentation over large parts of eastern Europe; the end of civil conflict in some parts of the world and the growth of civil conflict in others; and the transnationalisation of finance.[38]

The meeting decided to establish an Advisory Group on Security to make recommendations to the ACS Ministerial Council and to the Fourth ACS in Summit scheduled for November 2003.[39]

CARICOM

This issue had already been taken up by CARICOM leaders at their summit in July 2001 when they set up a Regional Task Force on Crime and Security focusing on the inter-related problems of rising crime and violence and the illicit trade in drugs and firearms.[40] After 9/11, this mandate was widened to address terrorism. At their July 2002 summit, the CARICOM heads endorsed over 100 recommendations from the Task Force report, with agreed priority actions in the areas of research, intelligence sharing, border controls, drug demand reduction strategy and a regional rapid response mechanism. One notable recommendation of the CARICOM Task Force was for consideration 'as a long-term goal of a Pan-Caribbean Partnership for

Crime and Drugs [including] all the states and jurisdictions falling within the Caribbean Sea'.[41]

CARICOM recognition that effective security cooperation requires pan-Caribbean scope and coverage is a significant development and may be pursued within the framework of the ACS. Caribbean nations are concerned with the need for reciprocity in the containment of security threats, by means of stronger US efforts to stem the inflow of illegal arms as well as termination of the practice of deportations of Caribbean nationals with criminal records from the United States to the region. The activities of deportees, together with the inflow of arms associated with narco-trafficking, are held to be significant contributors to the recent increase in violent crime in many regional countries.

CARICOM countries have also highlighted the security concerns associated with the vulnerability of small states. From before 9/11, they had succeeded in having this issue inserted into the agenda of the Inter-American Committee on Security. In one response to the terrorist attacks, the Permanent Council, on October 31, 2001, passed a resolution calling for measures to alleviate the impact of 9/11 on the 'more vulnerable and smaller economies' of the region.[42] In January 2003 the second high-level meeting on the special security concerns of small island states was held in St Vincent as part of the preparatory process for the OAS Special Conference on Security.

The meeting issued the Declaration of Kingstown on the Security of Small Island States, which began by stating that

> the small island states have peculiar characteristics which render these states specially vulnerable and susceptible to security risks, threats, concerns and other challenges of a multidimensional and transnational nature, involving political, economic, social, health, environmental and geographic factors.[43]

The declaration also adopted a 'security management mode' for small island states, for consideration by the OAS Committee on Hemispheric Security and the Special Conference on Security, scheduled to be held in October 2003. The small island states will consider implementation of a Virtual Private Network for the regional sharing of criminal intelligence, information sharing among border-control authorities, joint training programmes and joint strategic planning.

Nuclear Shipments

One specific concern of these states is with the security risks posed by the passage of shipments of radioactive nuclear waste through the Caribbean Sea. After 9/11, there were heightened fears of a terrorist attack on one of these shipments. In October 2001, the Washington-based Nuclear Control Institute (NCI) reported that 'given the changed security situation since September 11...The threat of the theft or diversion [of plutonium for use in nuclear devices], as well as the threat of attack for purposes of creating a radiological event, must be thoroughly analysed...'[44]

CARICOM fears were highlighted by the head of the Antigua and Barbuda delegation in his speech to the Thirty-Second OAS General Assembly:

> We believe that the terrorists are also likely to target their venom and suicidal drive at spectacular targets. One such target may be ships carrying nuclear wastes from Asia to Europe, using the Caribbean Sea and the Panama Canal as a shipping route... Our small states are fearful that a deliberate act of terror aimed at these ships may bring an end to our very existence...[45]

A paper analysing safety and security measures for these shipments prepared by the OAS Secretariat for the St Vincent meeting failed to assuage the fears of CARICOM delegations, and the issue figured prominently in the Kingstown Declaration.[46]

Tourism as a Test Case of Regional Response/Cooperation

As already noted, tourism is a major foreign currency earner in the region: for 17 member states of the ACS it is the largest single source of foreign earnings and for 12 of these it accounts for more than 50 per cent.[47] For the ACS region as a whole, tourism generates 3.01 per cent of the GDP; but in the smaller countries, the proportion is significantly higher (Table 12.6). Tourist expenditure is one-third of the GDP in the countries of the Organisation of Eastern Caribbean States (OECS) and in the Dutch islands; 16.5 per cent in CARICOM as a whole; 10.8 per cent in the French Caribbean islands and 8.5 per cent in the non-grouped countries.

Hence the steep contraction in air travel after 9/11 severely impacted the region. Immediately after the attacks cancellations affected some 65 per cent of Caribbean bookings. The fall-off in tourist arrivals for the four-month period September-December 2001, relative to 2000, was 16.4 per cent for the Caribbean islands and 10.4 per cent for Central America (Table 12.7). This was somewhat less than the fall-off in North America (27 per cent) and South America (18.2 per cent), but its impact was magnified by the greater weight of the industry in the smaller countries, especially the island economies. The decline is reflected in the figures for tourist expenditure in 2001 compared to 2000 for most of the island economies (Table 12.8). The contraction continued through the rest of the 2001/2002 winter season, as arrivals in CTO member countries in January-February 2002 were down 13 per cent from the previous year.[48]

The crisis proved to be a test of the rapid response capabilities of tourism industry stakeholders to a problem of unprecedented nature and scale. In the months following 9/11, most regional governments implemented, on a national basis, measures aimed at minimising the fall and accelerating the recovery of visitor arrivals. These included special advertising programmes in the US and European markets to promote destinations in the region as a 'safe haven', promotion of domestic and intra-regional tourism and financial assistance to the hotel in the form of concessionary loans and tax relief. Examples of emergency advertising programmes are those of the Dominican Republic for $25 million, Jamaica $4.7 million, Saint Lucia $3.7 million and Costa Rica $1.5 million; while Barbados set up a $16 million fund to assist the hotel industry.[49] Combining solidarity, promotion and public relations, Jamaica and the Bahamas provided free vacation packages for 9/11 victims and rescue workers and their families. Governments also provided financial assistance to airlines sustaining substantial losses as a result of the attacks, including Air Jamaica and British West Indian Airways (BWIA).

While national responses were mobilised at short notice, regional initiatives took a longer time to organise and proved more difficult to implement. They involved issues of sharing of financial costs and distribution of the probable benefits of promotional campaigns and level of commitment to the idea of a common tourist product for the region or subregion. Resolving such issues requires careful planning and negotiation, for which there is little time when countries are in emergency mode. The major example of a regional tourism initiative in response to 9/11 is that of CARICOM jointly with the CTO. In the four months after the attacks, CARICOM convened two tourism summits (meetings of Heads of Government to deal specifically with tourism).[50]

The governments agreed to a CTO proposal to launch a special $18 million advertising campaign to promote the region as a single destination in North American and European markets. The cost would be borne by a

Table 12.6
Tourist Expenditure Per cent GDP, 1998

Countries	US$ M	% GDP	% Exports
CARICOM [1]	4,640	16.52	91.6
OECS	798	32.41	
Non-grouped countries[2]	4,337	8.47	39.4
French[3]	881	10.83	n.a.
Dutch[4]	1,465	35.71	n.a.
Central America	1,564	3.25	14.9
Group of 3 [5]	9,761	1.60	6.7
Total ACS	**22,648**	**3.01**	**13.2**

1. CARICOM include OECS
2. Cuba, Dominican Republic & Panama
3. Martinique, Guadeloupe,
4. Aruba and the Netherlands Antilles
5. Colombia, Mexico & Venezuela

n.a. = not available

Source: ACS database

Table 12.7
Tourist Arrivals in the Americas, 2000-2001
(% Change in Tourist Arrivals)

	2000/1999	2001/2000		
		Year	*January-August*	*September-December*
AMERICA	5.8	-7.0	0.3	-24.0
North	4.9	-8.2	-0.1	-27.0
Caribbean	6.9	-3.5	2.0	-16.4
Central	9.0	3.0	8.8	-10.5
South	2.6	-7.1	-2.2	-18.2

Source: World Tourism Organization (WTO), as cited in ACS, Effects of the Economic Situation and the Events of September 11 on international Tourist Arrivals in 2001. *Published on ACS website: http://www.acs-aec.org Sept_11_Impact_Tourist_arrivals_eng.doc.*

Table 12.8
Tourist Expenditure in Selected Caribbean Destinations, 2000-2001 (US $ Millions)

Destination	2000	2001	% Change 2001/2000
Cancun & Cozumel (Mexico)	2327.3	2367.4	1.7
Caricom	4970.8	4579.3	-7.9
- *Bahamas*	1814.0	1582.9	-12.8
- *Barbados*	711.3	686.8	-3.4
- *Jamaica*	1333.0	1233.0	-7.5
- *O.E.C.S**	836.1	804.3	-3.8
Cuba	1756.0	1721.0	-2.0
Dominican Republic	2860.2	2689.8	-6.0
Netherlands Antilles/Aruba	737.0	741.5	0.6
Puerto Rico/USVI	3564.6	3924.2	10.0
UK Overseas Territories[1]	881.5	969.8	10.0
Total Selected Destinations	21791.8	21300.0	-2.3

1. Anguilla, Cayman Islands, Montserrat, Turks & Caicos Islands

*No figures are available for the British Virgin Islands and Dominica

* No figures are available for Dominica, Guyana, Haiti and Suriname

fund contributed in equal parts by the public and private sectors; and the public sector component was to have included inputs from non-CARICOM members of the CTO. In spite of the strong level of political commitment, difficulties and delays and raising the required funds prevented the launch of the campaign in time for the winter 2001/2002 season. The programme was eventually launched in August 2002 with the theme 'Life Needs the Caribbean'. However, the funding fell short of the original target: as of October 2002, $8.9 million of the $18 million target had been identified; $5.1 million from the public sector and $3.8 million from the private sector 'in barter'.[51]

The difficulties encountered by the CARICOM-CTO initiative originated with differing perceptions among stakeholders of their respective abilities to contribute and of the ratio of benefits to costs of their participation. 'Non-traditional' destinations such as Guyana and Belize and non-CARICOM member countries of the CTO such as Cuba, the Dominican Republic and Puerto Rico failed to contribute because of perceptions of the limited benefits likely for them as individual countries. In some instances, governments preferred to put their limited resources into national programmes where the benefits were more assured. The hotel industry also preferred to make its contribution in kind, that is, to a programme of its own making and under its own control.

In Central America, the Ministerial level Tourist Council announced a joint promotion programme of the 'Mundo Maya' (Maya World) in the Central American Isthmus in the European market.[52] For the Greater Caribbean region as a whole, a notable development was the convening of an Extraordinary Meeting of the ACS Special Committee on Sustainable Tourism in October 2001 to discuss responses to the crisis within the Greater Caribbean as a whole. A paper prepared by the ACS Secretariat on the 'New Paradigm of Tourism'[53] proposed three kinds of remedial action. The first of these was the strengthening of *intra-regional tourism*. Intra-regional tourism already accounts for 7.8 per cent of tourist arrivals in the CTO area and several countries had launched special programmes to attract domestic and regional visitors in response to the decline of extra-regional visitors.

A second measure proposed was developing *multi-destination tourism* within the region that would increase the regional impact of a tourist visit. To this end, the ACS commissioned a study in 2002 and in 2003 convened meetings between airlines, tour operators and tourism agencies with the objective of facilitating the launching of one or more multi-destination packages. A third measure is *technical cooperation with respect to Safety of the Tourist and Destination*. A symposium was convened for late 2003 in Trinidad and this activity could be linked to wider pan-Caribbean cooperation on security. More broadly, ACS-wide cooperation on tourism is being developed within the framework of the Establishment of the Sustainable Tourism Zone of the Caribbean as a long-term, strategic objective.[54]

Conclusion

The terrorist attacks in the United States of September 11, 2001 dramatised in tragic fashion the close social and economic linkages between the US and the Greater Caribbean region. The region incurred significant direct human and economic costs as a result of its ties to the US in migration and tourism. The fallout from the crisis also impacted the region's trade, investment and economic growth. Its political relations with the US were to become dominated by issues related to security and migration. The global counter-terrorism offensive launched by the US government in response to the attacks emphasised military action, the apprehension of terrorists and potential terrorists, tighter migration and border controls, and elimination of facilities for the financing of terrorism. US initiatives to secure the cooperation of regional countries in these measures were pursued multilaterally through the United Nations system and the Organization of American States and bilaterally with subregional organisations and with individual countries.

Regional countries shared and supported the US counter-terrorism agenda in large measure. However, in light of the range of social, economic and political problems in the regions many countries were impelled to place the issue of security in a wider perspective. This approach proposed from within the region emphasised the multi-dimensional nature of security problems especially those facing small island states; such as environmental vulnerability and HIV/AIDS. A human security perspective centred on poverty alleviation and economic security was also proposed. Regional countries registered some success in placing these items on the agenda of multilateral and subregional fora. The crisis in regional tourism also showed the potential and the limitations of the rapid response capabilities at the regional level in this industry.

It is probably too early to assess how far the region's attempts to influence the post-9/11 security agenda have found concrete reflection in the content of development polities, partnerships and programmes in the region. The wide asymmetries in the power relations between the United States and regional countries leads to a tendency for the US counter-terrorism agenda to predominate in regional policies; as reflected in legal obligations and legislative and administrative policies. This is exacerbated by the region's political fragmentation, the wide differences among countries in size and economic interest and the relatively recent appearance of pan-Caribbean regional organisations. But the region's potential bargaining power is considerable, given an aggregate population that is comparable to that of the United States and its location as a zone of significant economic and strategic interest to that country. To realise this potential more fully, regional cooperation will need to be strengthened in the critical areas of agenda-setting and the coordination of diplomatic effort in bilateral relations and in multilateral fora.

Notes

1. I wish to acknowledge the research assistance of Raphaële Dambo and Natasha Khan in the preparation of this chapter. The views expressed are those of the author and do not necessarily represent the official views of the Association of Caribbean States or of its members and associate members.

2. The states and territories lying in and bordering the Caribbean Sea and adjacent regions; including all the islands from Bahamas in the northwest to Barbados and Trinidad and Tobago in the southeast; and the mainland countries from Mexico to French Guiana.
3. IADB, *Remittances as a Development Tool*, http://www.iadb.org/mif/v2/remitconf.html
4. This number refers to independent states in the Greater Caribbean only. It is based on newspaper and news agency reports; and may include US citizens born in the region or persons with dual nationality; 60 Puerto Ricans, one person from Bermuda and one from Montserrat.
5. The figure of 18 million includes Mexico's 'Caribbean destinations' in Cozumel and Cancun only. Including all of Mexico's 20 million annual visitors increases the Greater Caribbean total to 36 million.
6. This is not attributable solely to the effect of 9/11, as ECLAC noted that 2002 marked the fifth straight year of economic decline in the Latin American and Caribbean region. See 'Main Trade Trends, Trade Policy And Integration Agreements in the Countries of the Association of Caribbean States (ACS)', published by the United Nations Economic Commission for Latin America and the Caribbean (ECLAC): http://www.acs-aec.org/tendencias_eng.doc.
7. *The Development of Services in the Caribbean*; Doc. LC/CAR.G.717. 17. ECLAC, Subregional Headquarters for the Caribbean. January 2003; also *Selected Statistics indicators of Caribbean Countries*, vol. 14 (LC/CAR/G.666), ECLAC Subregional Headquarters for the Caribbean, Port of Spain, November 2001.
8. Cuba, one of the first states that condemned the terrorist attacks, called for action to be taken within the framework of the United Nations system. See speech of President Castro at Ciego de Ávila, September 11, 2001. Cuba is the only hemispheric state not participating in the OAS process.
9. On September 11, 2001, a Special General Assembly of the OAS was in session in Lima, Peru, to approve the Inter-American Democratic Charter. The statement by the General Assembly on that day was followed by similar statements by the OAS Permanent Council on September 19, 2001 and by the OAS Ministers of Foreign Affairs on September 21, 2001.
10. Invoking Article 12 of the Rio Treaty, the Permanent Council converted itself into an Organ of Consultation.
11. Established in 1999 by the OAS General Assembly Resolution AG/RES. 1650 (XXIX-O/99). Its basic objectives are exchange of information, to promote counter-terrorism legislation, to promote adherence to international counter-terrorism conventions, border cooperation, training and crisis management.
12. A Committee of the Permanent Council established in 1995 by General Assembly Resolution AG/RES. 1353 (XX-O/95), this body undertook the drafting of the Inter-American Committee Against Terrorism.
13. *InterAmerican Convention Against Terrorism*, Organisation of American States, Secretariat for Legal Affairs, Technical Secretariat for Legal Cooperation Mechanisms, June 4, 2002; published on www.oas.org
14. *Centroamérica unida contra el terrorismo*, Republic of Honduras, September 19, 2002.
15. 'Inicia reunión contra terrorismo', *La Prensa*, Honduras, September 27, 2001.
16. 'Plan centroamericano de cooperación integral para prevenir y contrarrestar el terrorismo y actividades conexas', Republic of Honduras, October 25, 2001.

17. *Statement from the Chairman of the Conference of Heads of Government of the Caribbean Community in the aftermath of the tragic events in the USA on 11 September, 2001*, Georgetown, Guyana, September 20, 2001.
18. *Nassau Declaration on international terrorism: the CARICOM Response*, Nassau, The Bahamas, October 12, 2001.
19. Discussed below.
20. The IDB and the EU were specifically mentioned. See 'The impact of the 11 September attacks on the region, paragraph 2: Finance and insurance', in *Communiqué issued at the conclusion of the Special (emergency) meeting of Heads of Government of the Caribbean Community*, October 11–12, 2001, Nassau, The Bahamas.
21. There was 'support for the creation of pooling mechanisms, mainly for the aviation and hotel industries in the Region, in order to mitigate the burden of high insurance and re-insurance costs, and so to provide protection above the limits that commercial insurers are willing to offer'. A working party was also set up to develop proposals on incentives to insurance companies to facilitate the strengthening of their capital reserves. See 'The impact of the 11 September attacks on the region, paragraph 1: Tourism and Transportation; and paragraph 2: Finance and insurance', in *Communiqué issued at the conclusion of the Special (emergency) meeting of Heads of Government of the Caribbean Community*, October 11–12, 2001, Nassau, The Bahamas.
22. State-sponsored terrorism: http://www.state.gov/documents/organization/20117.pdf and designated foreign terrorist organisations: http://www.state.gov/documents/organization/20119.pdf, US Department of State website.
23. *Cuba has nothing to hide, and nothing to be ashamed of*, Declaration by the Ministry of Foreign Affairs of the Republic of Cuba, May 2, 2003.
24. Press release of the US embassy in Bogotá, April 12, 2002: http://usembassy.state.gov/bogota/wwwsmg09.shtml.
25. C. Tarnoff and L Nowels, *Foreign Aid: an introductory overview of US programs and policy*, report for Congress, January 2001, US Department of State website: http://usembassy.state.gov/bogota/wwwffa01.pdf.
26. See for example *Plan Colombia and its repercussions in Ecuador*, Report by the Ecumenical Human Rights Commission of Ecuador (CEDHU), March 2001: http://www.colombiareport.org/plancolombia_ecuador.htm.
27. The Act calls for enhanced due-diligence procedures in US banks for private banking accounts opened for foreign individuals and correspondent accounts opened for foreign banks, requiring that these procedures be designed to detect and report money laundering and other illegal activities. See full text of the USA Patriot Act (HR 3162), available at http://www.epic.org/privacy/terrorism/hr3162.html.
28. www.tax-news.com, London, September 20, 2001.
29. *The Caribbean Investor*, October 2, 2001.
30. Declaration of the Members of the Trade Negotiations Committee of FTAA. Sourced from the Website: http://www.ftaa-alca.org/911_dec/dec1_e.doc.
31. Since 1992, Central America had been asking for a free trade agreement with the United States, but Washington had previously insisted that FTAA negotiations take precedence. The new policy pursued parallel negotiations in the FTAA and CAFTA (the Central America Free Trade Agreement).
32. Address by the Honourable Owen Arthur, prime minister of Barbados on the Occasion of Inaugural Session of the 32nd General Assembly of the OAS, Bridgetown, Barbados. June 2nd 2002. Sourced from the Website: http://www.oas.org/library/mant_speech/speech.asp?sCodigo=02-0343.

33. *Declaration Of Bridgetown: The Multidimensional Approach To Hemispheric Security*, AG/DEC. 27 (XXXII-O/02), June 4, 2002.
34. 'Declaration of Margarita: The consolidation of the Greater Caribbean', Third Summit of the Heads of State and/or Government of the States, countries and territories of the Association of Caribbean States, Margarita Island, Venezuela, December 11–12, 2001.
35. *Ibid.*
36. *Ibid.*
37. 'Human Security and Development in the Greater Caribbean', a concept paper for discussion in the political dialogue, 8th Ordinary Meeting of the Ministerial Council of the Association of Caribbean States, Belize City, Belize, November 28, 2002.
38. 'Security in the Greater Caribbean', Background Note by the ACS Secretariat to the 21st Meeting of the Executive Board of the Ministerial Council, Santo Domingo, Dominican Republic, March 13–14, 2003.
39. *Rapporteur's Report*, 21st Meeting of the Executive Board of the Ministerial Council, March 13–14, 2003, Santo Domingo, Dominican Republic.
40. Information in this paragraph is taken from *Statement of Mr. Lancelot Selman, Chairman Regional Task Force on Crime and Security.* Second High Level Meeting on Special Security Concerns of Small Island States; Kingstown, St Vincent, Thursday January 10, 2003.
41. *Statement of Mr. Lancelot Selman, Chairman Regional Task Force on Crime and Security*, Second High Level Meeting on Special Security Concerns of Small Island States; Kingstown, St Vincent, Thursday January 10, 2003.
42. '*The social and economic impact of the terrorist acts of September 11, 2001 on Member States and the damage done especially to the more vulnerable and smaller economies*', The Permanent council of the Organization of American States, CP/RES 799 (1298/01), October 31, 2001.
43. Declaration on the Security of Small Island States, Second High Level Meeting of Special Security Concerns of Small Island States, OAS, Kingstown, St Vincent and the Grenadines, January 12–15, 2003.
44. The Nuclear Control Institute website: http://www.nci.org/new/nci-abo.htm.
45. Statement by the Head of Delegation of Antigua and Barbuda at the Thirty-Second OAS General Assembly, Bridgetown, Barbados, June 2, 2002. Sourced from the Website: http://www.oas.org/XXXIIGA/English/speeches/speech_ Antigua.htm.
46. Declaration of Kingstown, ibid.
47. Data from the ACS database.
48. *37th Report of the Caribbean Tourist Organisation to the Board of Directors, May 30–31, 2002*, p.13. The figures refer to island Caribbean destinations only. As such, they are not directly comparable to the ACS regional data, since the latter includes all the mainland Caribbean countries (Mexico/Cancun, Central America, Colombia and Venezuela) but excludes the US and UK affiliated territories, most of which are CTO members.
49. From newspaper and other reports in the ACS files.
50. The first of these, which was held in October, had been scheduled prior to 9/11. This meeting agreed to convene a second, special summit to deal with the crisis in regional tourism resulting from the terrorist attacks for December 8–9, 2001.
51. *38th Report of the Caribbean Tourist Organization to the Board of Directors*, October 27, 2002, p. 24.

52. Information on 'Mundo Maya' was sourced by M. Weizsman PAT, Administrative Officer and Belize Public Sector Representative for the *Organización del Mundo Maya* (OMM).
53. 'The new paradigm of tourism', Note by the Secretariat to the Extraordinary meeting of the Special Committee on Sustainable Tourism of the Association of Caribbean States, Caracas, Venezuela, November 5–6, 2001.
54 'Convention establishing the Sustainable Tourism Zone of the Caribbean', 3rd ACS Summit, Margarita, Venezuela, December 11–12, 2001. See ACS website: http://www.acs-aec.org/STZC_LEGAL_DOC_AND_INDICATO.DOC.

13

Economic and Trade Impact of 9/11

Ransford W. Palmer

Introduction

Caribbean economies are vulnerable to external shocks of all kinds because they are extremely open. That is to say, their foreign trade in goods and services accounts for a large share of their gross domestic product and their exports are concentrated in one or two commodities. Over the last few decades the region has had to face a series of external shocks of varying severity. Among them were the oil shocks of the 1970s, which benefited the oil producers and penalised the non-oil producers, the shock of falling commodity prices in the 1980s, and the Asian financial shock of the 1990s. On September 11, 2001, the terrorist attacks on America precipitated a whole new era of security arrangements that gave a serious jolt to these small, trade-dependent economies.

To set the stage, it is important to underscore the character of Caribbean foreign trade, particularly its foreign trade with the United States. A significant share of the region's merchandise exports is primary products. For example, Jamaica's leading exports are bauxite and alumina while those for the small Eastern Caribbean countries are bananas and other agricultural products. Primary products are susceptible to sharp swings in market prices and they often depend on preferential arrangements with major trading partners. Furthermore, their vulnerability tends to be aggravated by the concentration of their exports to one or two large markets such as the United States and the European Union. The same is true for Caribbean tourism which is also concentrated in these markets. The consequence is that shocks emanating from them directly affect the welfare of Caribbean populations.

Policies implemented by the major trading partners of the Caribbean to protect their national interest often directly impinge on the national interest of the Caribbean. As a result, Caribbean countries must react to these policies in order to protect their own national interest. More often than not, the Caribbean, usually after some initial resistance, winds up acceding to the policies of their major trading partners in order to preserve access to their markets. The Caribbean had no choice but to comply with the security measures put in place by the United States in the aftermath of September 11. Not to do so would have had far more negative consequences for its international trade.

At this writing, it has been a little over a year since September 11, which means that not enough time has elapsed for assessment of its long-term impact. Despite this limitation, this chapter presents an analysis based on available evidence with the caution that any economic assessment of the impact of 9/11 is complicated by the fact that changes in the larger economic environment that preceded 9/11 continue to affect economic conditions in the Caribbean. An important part of the larger economic environment is the performance of the United States economy which entered a recession in the first quarter of 2001. United States economic growth fell from an annual average of five per cent to a little over two per cent while its unemployment rose to well over five per cent from a low of four per cent in the boom years of the 1990s. It is characteristic, in recessions, that the demand for luxury goods and services declines simply because their consumption is easily postponed. Vacations are in this category, especially those that require foreign travel. Consequently, Caribbean tourist destinations are the first to feel the effect of a US recession. There is also a spillover from ongoing social problems in some Caribbean countries that continue to have a negative effect on the demand for tourism. The rising crime rate in Jamaica is often cited as an example. September 11 aggravated these situations. The closing of US air space and the subsequent imposition of new security measures severely reduced the demand for air travel. Because air transportation is the life blood of Caribbean tourism and because tourism accounts for a significant share of the region's economic activity, the decline in air travel had a directly negative effect on the economic performance of the region.

Methodology

The approach chosen here focuses on the impact of September 11 as it is transmitted through the two modes of transportation that are vital to Caribbean international trade: maritime and air transportation. The schema in Figure 13.1 depicts the impact as it is transmitted through these modes of transportation to the tourist industry and merchandise trade and ultimately to the economy as a whole. New security requirements for maritime transportation are expected to increase freight and insurance charges which will add to the cost of imports. These higher costs will ultimately be shifted to local consumers.

Figure 13.1
Schema of the Economic Impact of 9/11

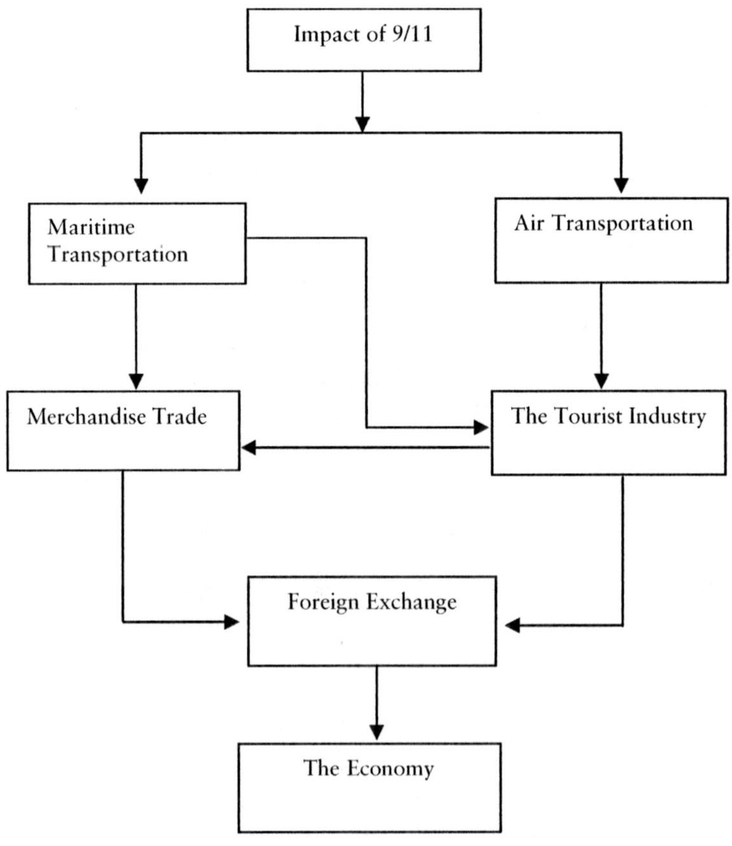

Air Transportation and Tourism

During the boom years of the 1990s in North America and Europe, the Caribbean tourist industry prospered. According to the World Tourism Organization (WTO), Caribbean tourism revenues grew from US$8.7 billion in 1990 to US$16.9 billion in 2001, an average annual growth rate in excess of 6 per cent.[1] The importance of tourism to the region is indicated in Table 13.1: tourist receipts as a percentage of Gross National Product range from 83.3 per cent for Antigua and Barbuda to 13.9 per cent for the Dominican Republic.

Table 13.1
Tourist Receipts as per cent of GNP and Exports

Countries	% of GNP	% of Exports
Antigua & Barbuda	83.3	83.3
Saint Lucia	45.9	63.4
Jamaica	26.7	37.0
Barbados	27.4	56.3
Belize	24.4	38.0
Grenada	18.1	38.0
St Vincent & the Grenadines	24.9	41.5
Dominican Republic	13.9	48.6

Source: The World Bank, 2002

For most Caribbean countries, tourism revenues have been the major source of finance for their chronic trade deficit as the experience of Jamaica and Barbados illustrates. Tables 13.2 and 13.3 show that while tourism revenues exceeded the trade deficit in Barbados, they financed 80 per cent of it in Jamaica, with worker remittances covering the rest. In both countries, the combination of tourism revenues and worker remittances exceeded the trade deficit. A disturbance in the flow of foreign exchange from these sources is a constant threat to the sustainability of the deficit. This threat is inherent in the vulnerability of tourism to any reported social and political disturbance at home and abroad.

Table 13.2
Jamaica Tourism Receipts, Worker Remittances and the Trade Gap (US$ millions).

Years	Tourism Receipts	Worker Remittances	Trade Deficit*	Tourism Receipts as % of Trade Deficit
1992	863.6	157.7	688.5	125.4
1993	945.0	187.2	1151.9	82.0
1994	970.4	457.9	946.6	102.5
1995	1068.8	582.3	1323.1	80.7
1996	1092.3	635.5	1487.6	73.4
1997	1130.8	642.3	1648.1	68.6
1998	1196.9	659.2	1639.9	72.9
1999	1279.6	679.4	1597.2	80.1

**Exports (f.o.b.) minus Imports (c.i.f.)*
Source: International Monetary Fund, Balance of Payments Yearbook, *2000.*

Table 13.3
Barbados Tourism Revenues, Worker Remittances and the Trade Gap

Years	Tourism revenues	Worker remittances	Trade deficit[1]	Tourism Revenues as % of trade deficit
1992	470.4	32.0	377.2	124.7
1993	534.4	31.5	451.6	118.3
1994	603.0	37.4	514.9	117.1
1995	669.0	42.4	617.4	108.3
1996	692.6	48.3	633.9	109.2
1997	663.5	55.0	789.1	84.0
1998	711.9	61.2	840.8	84.6

1. Exports (f.o.b) minus Imports (c.i.f.)
Source: International Monetary Fund, Balance of Payments Yearbook, *2000.*

September 11 was a disturbance of major proportions. It sharply interrupted the flow of tourists from North America and Europe – the major sources of Caribbean tourists. It triggered wholesale cancellations of tourist bookings which led to a sharp reduction in available seat miles flown to Latin America and the Caribbean by three major American airlines: American Airlines, Delta Airlines, and Continental Airlines. A seat mile is one seat flown one mile. Table 13.4 shows that in August of 2001, American Airlines flew 2.13 million seat miles; in September, this number fell sharply to 1.58 million; and in January 2002 it climbed back up to 2.02 million. Delta and Continental showed a similar pattern. By February 2002, none of the three airlines had returned to its August 2001 level. The extent to which this decline in airline capacity reduced tourism may be observed in the monthly data for Jamaica for 2000, 2001, and 2002 in Tables 13.5 and 13.6.

Table 13.4
Seat Miles Flown to Latin America by three United States Air Carriers (2001-2002)

Month/Year	American Airlines	Delta Airlines	Continental Airlines
January 2001	2,121.4	616.3	875.7
February 2001	1,925.4	545.3	797.5
August 2001	2,139.7	607.4	890.9
September 2001	1,588.7	464.3	673.5
October 2001	1,798.9	571.4	690.9
November 2001	1,735.6	550.8	651.6
December 2001	1,945.0	609.0	753.9
January 2002	2,024.2	609.0	795.6
February 2002	1,848.1	544.9	737.9

Source: Federal Aviation Administration

The month of September has historically been the month with the lowest number of tourist arrivals while December to March have been the peak arrival months. The extent to which September 11 affected arrivals in 2001 and after must be compared with the arrival pattern for 2000. Table 13.5 and 13.6 present the indices of tourist arrivals and tourist receipts calculated as a percentage of the mean for 2000.

Table 13.5
Monthly Index of Tourist Arrivals for Jamaica, 2000, 2001 and 2002

Months	2000	2001	2002
January	97.2	106.7	97.5
February	108.4	111.5	95.0
March	133.0	132.8	112.8
April	106.3	110.8	94.7
May	87.9	88.6	82.6
June	94.6	92.4	90.2
July	101.2	98.6	108.7
August	105.4	97.1	94.9
September	72.5	56.6	68.8
October	79.1	64.6	74.6
November	99.9	82.0	95.8
December	113.9	96.5	130.0

Source: Calculated from Bank of Jamaica Data.

Table 13.6
Monthly Indices of Travel Receipts for 2000, 2001 and 2002 for Jamaica

Months	2000	2001	2002
January	100.3	96.9	101.5
February	91.6	104.7	90.3
March	118.4	130.4	107.2
April	111.1	119.9	86.4
May	81.1	72.5	59.9
June	111.2	96.2	85.8
July	136.8	118.0	111.0
August	111.5	88.8	82.9
September	72.7	49.2	47.6
October	71.9	50.7	NA
November	95.2	64.4	NA
December	97.7	153.7	NA

Source: Calculated from Bank of Jamaica Data.

Figure 13.2
Jamaica Tourist Arrivals, 2000 (Year1), 2001(Year2), 2002 (Year3).

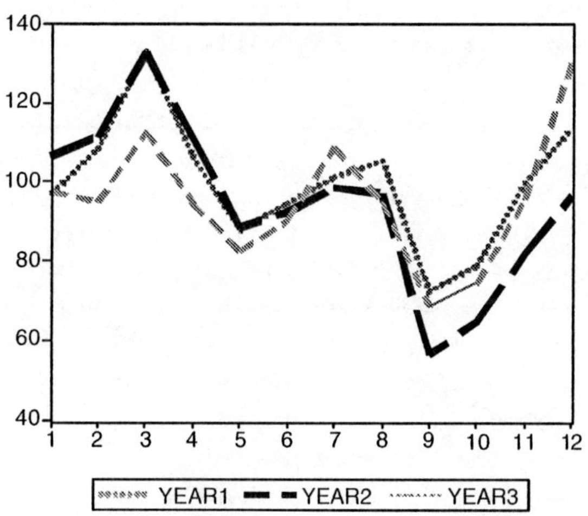

Figures 13.2 and 13.3 are graphs of Tables 13.5 and 13.6. They clearly show the similarity in the pattern of tourist arrivals and tourist receipts in each year and the impact of September 11 on that pattern in 2001 and after.

Figure 13.3
Jamaica Tourist Receipts, 2000 (TR1), 2001(TR2), 2002(TR3)

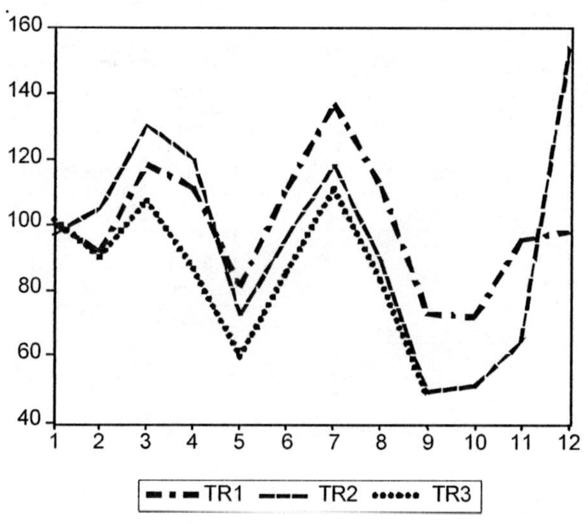

In 2000, the average monthly travel receipts for Jamaica was US$94 million a month; in 2001 it fell to US$89 million. A comparison of the data for the month of September in all three years is particularly instructive. The decline in total tourist receipts between 2000 and 2001 was US$60 million and the decline in total tourist arrivals was 114,000.

The decline in tourist receipts reduced the ability of the country to finance its trade deficit. The trade deficit is sustained by tourism. Because imports represent a large share of consumption in the Caribbean, a fall in tourism revenues is a threat to the level of consumption imports and the standard of living. A fall in tourism revenues may either reduce imports or foreign reserves if foreign reserves are used to make up the short fall in tourism revenues. A depletion of the stock of foreign reserves for this purpose could trigger the depreciation of the currency which would ultimately force a reduction in imports. It is clear, then, that the nexus between tourism and the trade deficit is crucial for Caribbean economies. Table 13.7 shows a dip in imports from the United States between the last quarter of 2001 and the second quarter of 2002. This dip is particularly observable in the monthly indices for 2001 for Jamaica's imports from the US in Table 13.8 and Figure 13.4. This dip also corresponds with the decline in tourist receipts Table 13.6.

Table 13.7
Caribbean Imports (f.o.b.) from the United States, 1st Quarter of 2001 to 3rd Quarter of 2002 (US$ million)

Countries	1st quarter	2nd quarter	3rd quarter	4th quarter	1st quarter	2nd quarter	3rd quarter
Bahamas	249.2	245.5	279.2	247.7	208.3	252.1	246.2
Barbados	74.5	67.2	73.8	70.8	68.1	58.4	66.9
Dominican Republic	1140.8	1201.3	1030.8	1062.6	1022.7	1107.8	1093.2
Guyana	32.4	35.5	40.0	33.0	27.3	35.4	29.8
Haiti	139.8	159.0	134.7	116.6	123.2	153.1	136.6
Jamaica	350.5	334.6	357.6	364.6	308.6	320.9	394.4
Trinidad & Tobago	209.5	262.4	342.1	275.5	246.1	213.7	284.8

Source: US International Trade Commission

Table 13.8
Indices of Jamaica's Imports From the United States, 2000, 2001, 2002

Month	2000	2001	2002
January	80.9	98.4	78.3
February	85.3	95.7	82.7
March	109.7	111.4	107.9
April	93.2	93.1	88.8
May	94.0	98.4	98.4
June	101.8	100.1	92.3
July	101.0	123.6	108.8
August	96.6	107.9	120.1
September	107.1	80.1	114.9
October	104.5	118.4	106.2
November	107.9	103.6	116.6
December	117.5	95.7	121.9

Source: Calculated from US International Trade Commission Data.

Figure 13.4
Jamaica's Imports from the United States, 2000 (Year1), 2001 (Year2), 2002 (Year3)

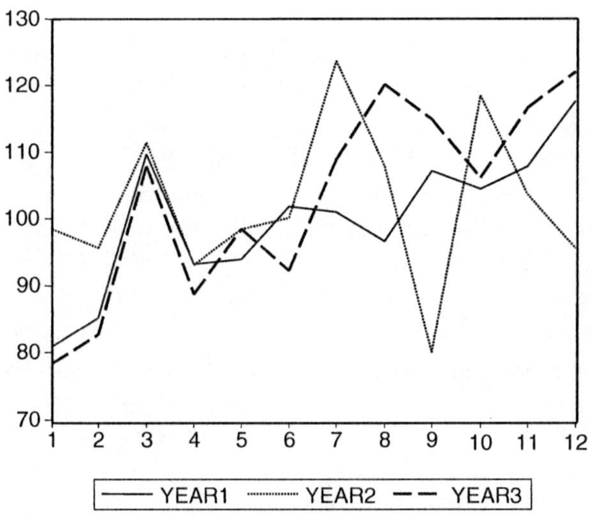

Maritime Transportation and Merchandise Trade

Since most of Caribbean merchandise trade with the United States moves by sea and since most of it is shipped in containers, the expectation is that new security measures required by the United States of vessels entering its ports will increase freight and insurance charges. These new security requirements are contained in the US Customs Container Security Initiative (CSI) which has four core elements: (1) using automated information to identify and target high risk containers;(2) pre-screening those containers identified as high-risk before they arrive at US ports; (3) using detection technology to quickly pre-screen high-risk container; and (4) using smarter, tamper-proof containers. Although the initial objective is to implement CSI at ports that send large volumes of cargo containers to the United States, the Customs Service says that 'the principles of CSI can be applied beyond CSI ports to all ports regardless of size or volume of cargo container shipped to the US'[2] The Customs Service reports that, on June 28, 2002,

> the World Customs Organization unanimously passed a resolution that will enable ports in all 161 of the member nations to begin to develop programs using CSI principles including collection of data concerning both outbound shipments in electronic form, use of risk management to identify and target high risk shipments, use of radiation detection and large-scale technology to identify containers that pose a security threat.[3]

As one of the conditions for the certification of ports involved with maritime trade with the United States, the Jamaica government has taken steps to improve its port security 'with the planned acquisition of six Vehicle and Cargo Inspection System (VACIS) X-ray machines' for its container ports at a cost of US$10.8 million. It has also established a Port Security Corps with 1,762 officers deployed at 17 locations throughout the country, including the Kingston Container Terminal and the Kingston and Montego Bay Free Trade Zones.[4] 'Trinidad and Tobago is also investing heavily in airport security, including equipment and training, while regional ports servicing the cruise tourism industry have begun to network on security systems.'[5] The result of all this investment in port security will be an increase in freight and insurance costs which will raise the price of imports. The extent to which this will affect the demand for particular imports will depend on the sensitivity of demand to price changes. Given the high share of basic consumption items in Caribbean imports, an increase in price is not likely to reduce imports by much. A more likely scenario is that foreign exchange will be diverted from capital goods imports to finance consumption imports. This will have a negative impact on economic growth.

In order to understand the significance of freight and insurance charges, it is important to understand the convention in international trade for recording the flow of goods from one country to another. Exports are normally recorded as free on board (f.o.b) or free alongside ship (f.a.s) and imports as cost, insurance, and freight (c.i.f). This means that when the exported product reaches its destination its value is increased by the amount of insurance and freight charges. Data for Jamaica and Barbados illustrate the behaviour of freight and insurance charges during the 1990s. Tables 13.8 and 13.9 show that freight and insurance charges as a per cent of imports (f.o.b.) averaged 23.8 per cent and 18.0 per cent for Barbados and Jamaica, respectively. When freight is disaggregated from insurance, its percentage is virtually fixed at 11.2 per cent and 15.1 per cent, respectively for Barbados and Jamaica. The numbers clearly indicate that for both countries, fluctuations in the percentage of freight and insurance charges together are the result of fluctuations in the percentage of insurance charges. Given the average share of insurance charges during the booming pre-9/11 period when security issues were not as dominant, it is reasonable to expect that share to rise in the security conscious post-9/11 period.

Table 13.9
Barbados Imports, Freight and Insurance Charges

Years	Imports (f.o.b.)	Sea freight	Insurance	Insurance & freight as % of imports	Insurance as % of imports	Freight as % of imports
1992	467.7	52.4	47.0	21.2	10.0	11.2
1993	514.3	57.7	67.3	24.3	13.1	11.2
1994	547.7	61.5	98.7	29.4	18.2	11.2
1995	691.2	77.1	95.3	24.9	13.7	11.2
1996	743.0	83.4	94.2	23.9	12.7	11.2
1997	807.7	99.6	90.8	21.4	10.2	11.2
1998	901.1	101.0	95.7	21.8	10.6	11.2
			Average	23.8	12.6	11.2

Source: International Monetary Fund, Balance of Payments Yearbook, *2000*

Table 13.10
Jamaica Imports, Freight and Insurance Charges

Years	Imports (f.o.b.)	Sea freight	Insurance	Insurance & freight as % of imports	Insurance as % of imports	Freight as % of imports
1992	1541.1	220.1	43.8	17.1	2.8	14.3
1993	1920.5	278.1	58.6	17.5	3.0	14.5
1994	2099.2	315.3	80.1	18.8	3.8	15.0
1995	2625.3	397.4	96.4	18.8	3.7	15.1
1996	2715.2	408.4	85.0	18.1	3.1	15.0
1997	2832.6	439.3	76.5	18.2	2.7	15.5
1998	2743.9	437.7	71.7	18.5	2.6	15.9
1999	2627.6	404.0	55.5	17.5	2.1	15.4
			Average	18.0	2.9	15.1

Source: International Monetary Fund, Balance of Payments Yearbook, *2000.*

Freight charges have fixed and variable components. The fixed component includes port charges that do not vary with the value, volume, or distance shipped. They may also include the cost of new security requirements. If higher insurance and freight charges increase the price of US imports from the Caribbean, it could put Caribbean exporters at a competitive disadvantage. Table 13.11 shows insurance and freight charges (IFC) as a percentage of US imports from the Caribbean between the first quarter of 2001 and the third quarter of 2002. A comparison of the quarterly data in Table 13.11 with the annual data in Tables 13.9 and 13.10 indicates an important difference: insurance and freight charges account for a smaller percentage of US imports from the Caribbean than of Caribbean imports from the world. Since the largest share of Caribbean imports come from the United States, the difference in the percentage of insurance and freight charges may be attributed to the difference in the character of US and Caribbean imports. The largest share of US imports from the Caribbean consists of primary goods, despite the growth of manufactured exports in recent years, while the largest share of Caribbean imports from the United States consists of manufactured goods. Manufactured goods are more valuable per ton and therefore cost more to ship than bulk goods such as petroleum and other minerals. Aside from the difference in the character of US and Caribbean imports, there is the problem of trade imbalance. According to ECLAC, 72 per cent of the containers returning from the Caribbean to the United States are empty. Shipping lines take this into account and charge higher rates.

Other factors contributing to higher transport cost include: the use of smaller vessels; high overhead costs of planning and scheduling for shipping services; multiple port calls for a limited amount of cargo; and less competition in shipping services.[6] What all this suggests is that any increase in freight and insurance charges in the post-September 11 period is likely to have a relatively larger impact on Caribbean imports from the United States than on United States imports from the Caribbean.

Table 13.11
Insurance and Freight Charges as per cent of US Imports from the Caribbean, First Quarter 2001 to Third Quarter 2002

Countries	1st quarter	2nd quarter	3rd quarter	4th quarter	1st quarter	2nd quarter	3rd quarter
Bahamas	4.19	3.54	5.89	5.78	5.45	7.79	4.10
Barbados	2.64	3.62	3.60	2.52	3.63	3.79	4.26
Dominican Republic	2.53	2.61	2.46	2.24	2.69	2.59	2.39
Guyana	11.29	9.90	13.89	10.55	9.89	13.48	10.69
Jamaica	5.22	9.32	5.72	6.18	5.95	7.02	6.28
Trinidad & Tobago	8.41	9.31	7.73	9.44	8.68	8.97	9.68
Average	5.71	6.38	6.54	6.11	6.04	7.27	6.23

Source: Tables A13.1 and A13.2.

Conclusion

The impact of 9/11 on the Caribbean was most pronounced in the tourist industry. This impact was sharp and temporary. Tourist arrivals and tourist receipts have resumed their upward growth. The industry, however, still faces the constraints of reduced air transportation capacity due to the extended recession in the United States. The impact of 9/11 on maritime transport cost will persist into the future. As a leading earner of foreign exchange the tourist industry is the main source of finance for the region's trade deficit. Any external shock that reduces tourism revenues reduces the ability of the Caribbean to sustain its trade deficit. Despite economic diversification into non-traditional industries, the foundation of many Caribbean economies still rests precariously on tourism. For some, like Jamaica, the impact of 9/11 would have been worse had it not been for the stability of remittances from nationals abroad.

If there is a pivotal lesson from 9/11 for the Caribbean, it is that a key feature of the management of Caribbean tourism must be a strategy to reduce its vulnerability to external shocks and to improve its capability to recover when shocks do occur. Part of this strategy should be a conscious effort to diversify the sources of tourists. While the magnitude of an event such as 9/11 would affect the flow of tourists no matter their source, a wider dispersion of sources would provide some measure of insulation from the effects of events occurring in any one country. This requires the close monitoring of the geopolitical situation and the events occurring in source countries that might threaten the flow of tourists. This calls for investment in serious research to develop a capability for predicting future tourist flows.

Since September 11, there has been a war in Iraq and the outbreak of SARS (Severe Acute Respiratory Syndrome) in China and its spread through air transportation to other parts of the world. These events have taken a serious toll on world tourism, especially in North America, Europe, and East Asia, and have caused a further reduction in airline capacity.[7] The Caribbean could benefit from these developments with a strategy for diversifying its sources of tourists.

Appendix

Table A13.1
United States Imports from the Caribbean, First Quarter 2001 to Third Quarter 2002 (US$ millions)

Countries	1st quarter	2nd quarter	3rd quarter	4th quarter	1st quarter	2nd quarter	3rd quarter
Bahamas	64.9	70.3	71.8	104.8	88.5	90.2	147.7
Barbados	10.8	9.4	7.3	11.9	7.1	9.1	7.3
Dominican Republic	967.0	1058.3	1107.7	1053.9	840.7	1077.2	1142.1
Guyana	30.1	31.3	29.5	34.1	27.3	26.7	21.5
Jamaica	95.7	118.0	111.7	116.4	94.0	88.2	93.8
Trinidad & Tobago	726.2	587.2	630.9	406.5	417.1	554.0	639.9

Source: United States International Trade Commission, 2002.

Table A13.2
Insurance and Freight Charges on United States Imports from the Caribbean, First Quarter 2001 to Third Quarter 2002 (US$ millions)

Countries	1st Quarter	2nd Quarter	3rd Quarter	4th Quarter	1st Quarter	2nd Quarter	3rd Quarter
Bahamas	2.7	2.5	4.2	6.0	4.8	7.0	6.0
Barbados	0.28	0.34	0.26	0.30	0.26	0.34	0.31
Dominican Republic	24.5	27.7	27.3	23.7	22.7	28.0	27.3
Guyana	3.4	3.1	4.1	3.6	2.7	3.6	2.2
Jamaica	5.0	11.0	6.3	7.2	5.6	6.2	5.9
Trinidad & Tobago	61.1	54.7	48.8	38.4	36.2	49.7	62.0

Source: United States International Trade Commission, 2002.

Notes

1. Caribbean Tourism Organisation, www.onecaribbean.org.
2. United States Customs Service Press Release, November 2002.
3. Ibid.
4. *The Jamaica Gleaner*, 'Government to Acquire X-ray Machines for Ports,' July 23, 2002. www.jamaica-gleaner.com/gleaner/20020723/shipping/shipping2.html.
5. Anthony T. Bryan and Stephen E. Flynn, *Free Trade, Smart Borders, and Homeland Security: U.S.-Caribbean Cooperation in a New Era of Vulnerability*. The Dante B. Fascell North-South Centre Working Paper Series, Paper No. 8, September 2002.
6. Joachim Fuchsluger, *Determinants of Maritime Transport Costs for the Caribbean*. UN ECLAC Experts' Meeting, Port of Spain, September 2000.
7. Scott Newman, Mitchell Ford, and Erika Lederman, 'Already Battered By Terror, Tourism Gets Double Blow,' *The Wall Street Journal*, April 8, 2003, p. 1.

14

The Impact of 9/11 on Migration Relations Between the Caribbean and the United States

Christopher Mitchell

Introduction

During the past 50 years, northward migration has become a major social, economic, and political link between the Caribbean and the United States.[1] Millions of persons from all corners of the Caribbean region reside in the US, and many maintain diverse ties with their societies of origin. A rich process of cultural exchange and interaction often connects migrants with island societies, and remittances from emigrants are a major component in Caribbean nations' international payments. Caribbean people in US cities such as New York and Miami often play significant roles in politics 'at home', and they may also exert influence over United States policy towards Cuba, Haiti, and other nations.

The terrorist attacks of September 11, 2001 (hereafter 9/11) affected US-Caribbean migration relations in diverse ways. In effect, one multi-faceted and crucial event exerted a complex impact upon a social, economic and political process that has become deeply interwoven into a score of nations surrounding the Caribbean basin. The patterns produced by that impact are far from simple, varying significantly in complexity depending on the specific societies concerned. This chapter will seek to analyze these patterns, reviewing available evidence on policy changes, legal immigration, unauthorised population movement, remittances, migrants' changing status in the United States, and other subjects. The diplomacy of Caribbean migration will also occupy our attention as we note that some existing points of stress between governments have been re-emphasised, while some new ones have been added.

In a larger sense, beyond the ongoing migration processes that have been inflected (perhaps with long-range consequences), we also will suggest that 9/11 may result in a limited recasting of migration relations between the

Caribbean and the United States. Security priorities – defined as anti-terrorism – now tend to dominate Washington's assessment of Caribbean migration issues. Previous trends in regional migration policy, tending to bring concerns about development, democracy, and transnational social linkages to the foreground, have lost momentum. A long-standing tendency towards defining migration as a subject of bilateral relations, rather than a theme for multilateral bargaining, has simultaneously been strengthened.

This chapter will begin by describing briefly the Caribbean migrant communities in the United States, and the complexity of the links they have forged with island societies. We will then review the policy changes and legislative revisions affecting migration that were put into place by the United States in the aftermath of 9/11. Most of these were rooted in global concerns or goals, but (in a sequence of events familiar to any student of past events) they have appreciably influenced Caribbean interests. The work will then review changes in legal population movement, sea-borne migration, financial flows, and the granting of visas and long-term residency to Caribbean emigrants.

In this sometimes-intricate data, we will note some signs of a stronger commitment among migrants to maintain linkages to home societies, even as – perhaps because – access to and secure status within the United States have become somewhat less certain. We will then assess several current points of political stress over migration between Washington and Caribbean nations, focusing on Cuba, the Dominican Republic, and Jamaica. The paper will conclude by examining the longer-term effects of anti-terrorist security priorities on the diplomacy of migration in the Western Hemisphere, including the Caribbean.

Changes in Migration Patterns and Policy Following 9/11

Table 14.1 provides insight into the size and diversity of the Caribbean migrant population in the US in the year preceding the 2001 terrorist attacks. Even the numbers estimated by the US Bureau of the Census – equivalent to nearly eight per cent of the total population then living in the Caribbean itself – understates the political and social weight of the migrant population since it does not include their offspring born in the US. Viewing the matter more broadly, simply counting Caribbean-born residents and their families, as though most had made a once-and-for-all northward move, provides only a minimal first suggestion of Caribbean migration's nature and impact. Complex interactions very often link migrants from the region with the societies from which they came. Travel in both directions is very active, except in the case of Cuba; 'social remittances' in the form of 'ideas, behaviours, and social capital'[2] often accompany extensive financial payments from migrant groups; Caribbean political leaders commonly seek support among compatriots in the US, while those groups frequently sponsor efforts at development in island communities. These cross-border ties are so influential and ramified that scholars have developed notions of 'transnational communities' and 'transnational consciousness' to describe them adequately.[3]

Table 14.1
Estimated Caribbean-Born Population in the United States, 2000

Country of birth	Estimated population
Bahamas	13,000
Barbados	54,000
Belize	59,000
Cuba	952,000
Dominica	9,000
Dominican Republic	692,000
Grenada	42,000
Guyana	202,000
Haiti	385,000
Jamaica	411,000
Trinidad and Tobago	173,000
Other Caribbean	82,000
Total	**3,074,000**

Source: *US Bureau of the Census, Current Population Survey, March 2000.*

Extensive population flows into and out of the United States from Caribbean nations began in the 1950s and 1960s, and have become routinised within the complex matrix of US immigration law. Following 9/11, a number of administrative and legislative changes by the United States affected migration from the Caribbean. An immediate but temporary ban on flights to and from the US contributed to a 50 per cent drop in hotel occupancy in the Caribbean in the month following the terrorist attacks, and arrivals of migrants and visitors to the US dropped by nearly 30 per cent in the same short period. In October 2001, Congress passed the USA *Patriot Act*, enhancing police authority to intercept electronic communications, and empowering the US attorney general to detain non-citizens considered to be threats to national security, while limiting judicial review of the alleged grounds for imprisonment.[4] In May 2002 a new law, the *Enhanced Border Security and Visa Entry Reform Act* (EBSVERA) was approved and signed, obliging US universities to track foreign students more carefully, and requiring more detailed scrutiny of visa applications from nations listed as encouraging terrorism.[5]

Shortly after 9/11, George W. Bush stated that the US government would become 'very diligent with our visas and observant with the behavior of people who come to this country'.[6] This approach has been implemented both within the US and abroad. Domestically, the Justice Department in the fall of 2001 promulgated rules permitting the attorney general to set aside rulings of immigration judges that would release detained immigrants on bond;[7] this power has been used in several cases involving Haitians. Internationally, partly to implement EBSVERA, programmes were set up under which the Central Intelligence Agency and FBI check visa applications from all over the world against databases of criminals and potential terrorists. The new reviews, involving lists of more than 80,000 suspects, in some cases add months to the time required for visa-processing.[8]

What was the impact of these measures, and of other events following 9/11, on migration from the Caribbean? We will begin by considering admissions of authorised immigrants and visitors to the US, with some limited information on new visas granted as well. We will also gain some insight into recent flows of unauthorised migrants, by considering the numbers intercepted at sea over the past few years. This data provides both an overview of pan-Caribbean trends, and information on migratory movements from specific societies.

Tables 14.2 and 14.3 display the admission of Caribbean people into the US in recent years, including both immigrants and non-immigrants. Flows during US fiscal years between the late 1990s and 2002 are provided; comparing data for Fiscal Years 2001 and 2002 provides a rapid snapshot of 9/11's immediate effects.[9] These tables indicate that legal population flows into the US from the Caribbean were reduced, but only moderately, in the year after the World Trade Center and Pentagon attacks. Immigrant admissions dropped by 4.7 per cent in Fiscal Year 2002; most of that change was attributable to the figures involving Haiti. On the other hand, increases in immigrant admissions were recorded in 2002 from Cuba, the Dominican Republic and Guyana.

Table 14.2
Immigrants from the Caribbean Region Admitted to the United States, Fiscal Years 1996 through 2002

	1996	1997	1998	1999	2000	2001	2002
Bahamas	768	641	602	401	768	931	811
Barbados	1,043	829	726	720	783	910	817
Cuba	26,466	33,587	17,375	14,132	20,831	27,703	28,272
Dominican Republic	39,604	27,053	20,387	17,864	17,536	21,313	22,604
Guyana	9,489	7,257	3,963	3,300	5,746	8,303	9,962
Haiti	18,386	15,057	13,449	16,532	22,364	27,120	20,268
Jamaica	19,089	17,840	15,146	14,733	16,000	15,393	14,898
Trinidad & Tobago	7,344	6,409	4,852	4,283	6,660	6,665	5,771
Other Caribbean	5,098	4,738	3,623	3,731	4,273	4,695	4,270
Total	127,287	113,411	80,123	75,696	94,961	113,033	107,673

Source: *US Department of Homeland Security, Office of Immigration Statistics*, Fiscal Year 2002 Yearbook of Immigration Statistics, *Internet advance text: <http://www.immigration.gov/graphics/shared/aboutus/statistics/IMM02yrbk/IMMExcel/table3.xls>.*

Table 14.3
Non-immigrants from the Caribbean Region Admitted to the United States Fiscal Years 1998 through 2002

	FY 1998	FY 1999	FY 2000	FY 2001	FY 2002
Bahamas	310,164	325,362	363,134	351,417	318,714
Barbados	58,521	58,116	56,003	51,914	45,284
Cuba	9,881	8,864	40,959	30,860	24,546
Dominican Republic	203,713	221,387	206,967	207,985	186,800
Guyana	24,016	25,456	24,853	25,519	28,088
Haiti	70,290	85,224	86,494	83,158	81,558
Jamaica	241,205	260,641	275,210	277,978	248,081
Trinidad & Tobago	111,475	124,676	145,070	148,170	135,170
Other Caribbean	189,908	209,588	217,023	204,214	186,066
Total	1,219,173	1,319,314	1,415,713	1,381,215	1,254,307

Source: *US Department of Homeland Security, Office of Immigration Statistics*, Yearbooks of Immigration Statistics *for years included; Internet access: <http://www.immigration.gov/graphics/shared/aboutus/statistics/ybpage.htm>.*

Non-immigrant admissions dropped more markedly (and more uniformly across the region) in 2002. Admissions of these visitors declined by nearly 9.2 per cent in 2002, with Cuba suffering a drop (20.5 per cent) that was more than double the regional average; among major migrant-source nations, only Guyana managed to eke out a 10 per cent increase. These patterns may, of course, respond to regional economic forces only loosely related to 9/11; the US economy entered a recession in March of 2001, perhaps deterring some economically-motivated population movement. In addition, applications for US non-immigrant visas dropped considerably world-wide in FY 2002, and it would not be surprising for the Caribbean to have participated in that tendency.

One reason that the arrival of immigrants and non-immigrants only declined modestly in the year following 9/11 was probably that many US visas, utilised in FY 2002, had already been issued or committed well before Al Qaeda struck US landmarks. Perhaps sharper alterations in US visa policy would be evident if one examined new grants of visas, following the terrorist attacks; Table 14.4 provides the limited available information on that score. The picture is a mixed one: fewer visitors' visas were issued in the Dominican Republic, Haiti, and (especially) Jamaica in the year after the terrorist attacks. On the other hand, slightly more immigrant visas were distributed in the Dominican Republic and Jamaica in the same year, while Haitians received 16 per cent fewer visas of that type.

Table 14.4
US Immigrant and Non-immigrant Visas Issued in Selected Caribbean Nations, Fiscal Years 1999 through 2002

	FY 1999	FY 2000	FY 2001	FY 2002
Immigrant visas				
Dominican Republic	13,505	11,685	14,606	15,392
Haiti	14,247	18,495	13,487	11,331
Jamaica	11,654	9,923	8,404	8,789
Non-immigrant visas				
Dominican Republic	69,371	50,171	52,738	49,038
Haiti	26,565	27,609	25,623	22,297
Jamaica	71,331	82,190	71,271	44,991

Source: United States Department of State.

Table 14.5
Maritime Migrant Flows Towards the United States,

	FY 1999	FY 2000	FY 2001	FY 2002	FY 2003 (first five months)
From Cuba					
Intercepted	4,076	2,793	3,201	2,047	1,036
Estimated landings*	114	18	76	0	0
From the Dominican Republic					
Intercepted	1,781	2,222	2,678	1,311	1,970
Estimated landings	1,184	1,285	1,208	1,038	1,044
From Haiti					
Intercepted	2,419	2,406	3,666	5,372	2,116
Estimated landings	19	156	38	177	75
Total	9,593	8,880	10,867	9,945	6,241

Source: United States Coast Guard, at <http://www.uscg.mil>
* *These figures apparently do not include apprehensions by the US Border Patrol in the Miami Sector, which seem to be significant. The* Miami Herald *has stated that in 1999 through 2001, 'an average of 2,150 Cubans...have reached U.S. shores [yearly]'; see Jay Weaver, 'Smuggling More Prevalent, and Deadly',* The Miami Herald, *November 21, 2001, p. 2A.*

Another important angle from which to view migration from the Caribbean to the United States, of course, involves unauthorised population flows. Some migrants from nations other than Cuba utilise non-immigrant visas for that purpose, and it is very difficult to establish the extent or rhythm of such migration. Data is available, however, on migrants who are intercepted attempting to enter the US by sea, together with estimates from the US Coast Guard and other agencies of the number of intending migrants who land successfully and elude 'interdiction' by patrol vessels; this information, since the Fiscal Year 1999 is summarised in Table 14.5.

Overall, sea-borne migration declined slightly in FY 2002, but has resumed at a brisk pace in FY 2003. Unauthorised flows from Cuba declined notably after 9/11, but have now resumed their earlier rate; those from the Dominican Republic decreased in the short-run but have now gained significant momentum; maritime migration from Haiti has risen moderately since the terrorist attacks. These trends are summarised, as average monthly flows, in Figure 14.1.

To summarise, both immigration and authorised visits to the US have declined since 9/11. This trend is somewhat stronger in the cases of immigrants from Haiti and visitors from Jamaica, where reductions in visa issuance suggest the decrease will continue. At the same time, efforts to enter the US by sea, without visas, dropped in the short-run but more recently have accelerated. While these statistical tendencies were modest in the first year after the New York and Washington attacks, if they continue in the future, late 2001 will appear as something of a turning-point.

Our analysis should consider, as well, the situation and actions of Caribbean migrants already residing in the United States, in the aftermath of 9/11. Have their prospects for stable long-term residency changed? How have they responded to the security concerns and economic downturn that have affected both the US and Caribbean nations? US processing of two important immigration credentials has slowed notably since late 2001, as administrative resources were reassigned to meet security challenges. The review of adjustment applications, often known as 'green card' requests, now requires an average of almost two years, while naturalisation papers call for one year of processing (twice President Bush's target for that function). Two of the cities where bureaucratic processing is slowest are New York and Miami, where many Caribbean migrants cluster. Figures 14.2 and 14.3 portray delays that have increased in both cities since June of 2001.[10]

Figure 14.1
Average Monthly Maritime Migrant Flows towards the US, Fiscal Years 1999-2003

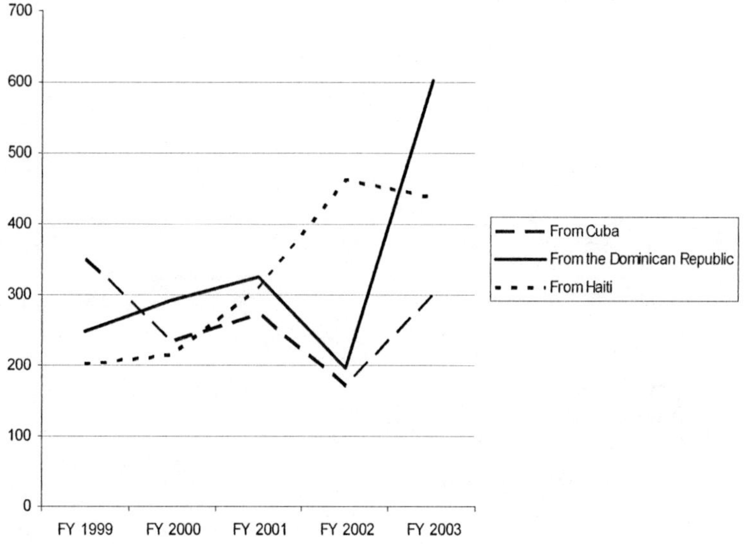

Figure 14.2
Naturalisation and Adjustment Backlogs: New York, December 2000–March 2003

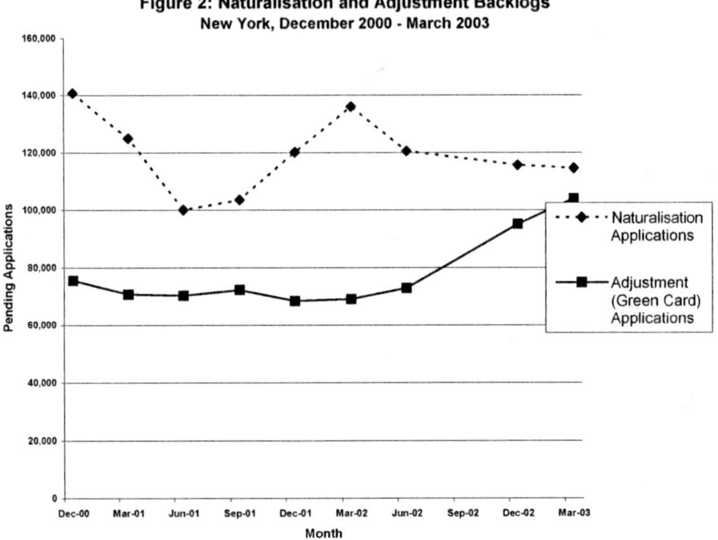

Figure 14.3
Naturalisation and Adjustment Backlogs: Miami, December 2000–March 2003

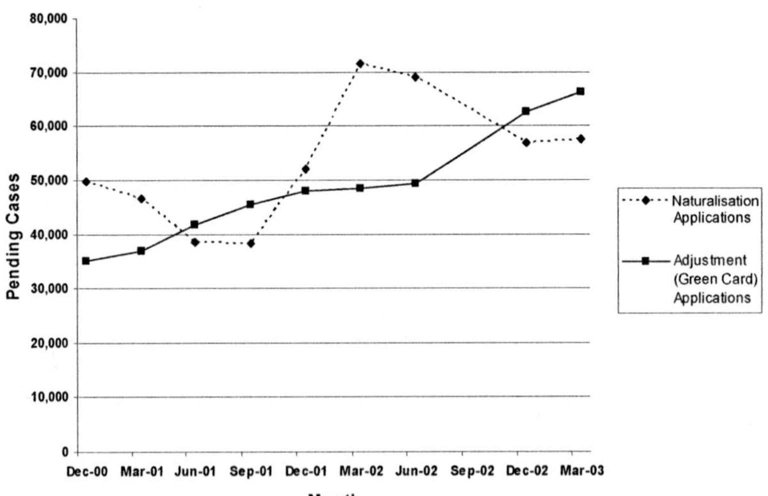

Simultaneously, with increasing uncertainty on legal immigration status, and growing unemployment in the US economy, it appears that migrants have notably increased the flow of funds they send (primarily to their families) in the Caribbean. In the third quarter of 2001, for example, Jamaica received $247 million in remittances, while in the fourth quarter of 2002 the amount had risen to $362 million; for the Dominican Republic, the corresponding figures were $384 million and $631 million.[11] These larger sums may be triggered by concerns related to immigrant status, as well as by an awareness of new economic need in Caribbean societies. Observers speculated that even legal migrants from the Caribbean, hesitant to travel to the islands at a time when immigration regulations might ensnare them, were transmitting funds from a distance rather than in person.[12]

Points of political stress in US-Caribbean migration relations

The aftermath of 9/11 has added some new tensions to US political relations with major Caribbean states, while somewhat exacerbating existing strains. The longstanding overall pattern of Washington's preponderant political influence in the region (with the exception of Cuba) has not been altered. Instead, the limited frictions that form part of that asymmetry in power have been somewhat augmented.

Perhaps paradoxically, though Cuba is the United States' major Caribbean adversary, Havana has developed the region's most institutionalised migration relations with Washington. A series of formal agreements, initiated in 1984 and modified most recently in 1995, have committed the US to issue at least 20,000 immigrant visas per year to Cuban citizens, and to return unauthorised migrants from Cuba who have been intercepted at sea. The goal of these agreements is to forestall any new mass emigration by sea from Cuba that might bring tens of thousands in small vessels to South Florida, as occurred in 1965, 1980 and 1994.

The Cuban government is critical of some aspects of US immigration policy, and US measures since 9/11 have led Havana to fear that migration incidents might present notable dangers to the revolutionary régime. Cuban President Fidel Castro has long maintained that the Cuban Adjustment Act of 1966 encourages unauthorised migration by, in effect, offering permanent residency in the United States to Cubans who reach US territory.[13] Much of that illegal movement now takes place in speed boats charging $8,000 - 10,000 per person, and from 1999 through 2001 an estimated 2,150 Cubans reached the US annually on such craft.[14] However, a series of boats and planes were hijacked from Cuba to the United States in early 2003. On April 11, 2003, Cuba executed three men convicted of hijacking a Havana harbour ferry carrying 50 passengers which ran out of fuel and was recaptured by the Cuban Coast Guard.[15]

Fidel Castro defended this measure on broad grounds of national security, in a May 1, 2003 speech in Havana:

> The Cuban Revolution was placed in the dilemma of either protecting the lives of millions of Cubans ... or sitting back and doing nothing. The US government, which incites common criminals to assault boats or airplanes with passengers on board, encourages these people, gravely endangering the lives of innocents and creating the ideal conditions for an attack on Cuba.[16]

Clearly, a possible parallel with US policy towards Iraq influenced Castro's reasoning; he claimed the Bush administration had warned Havana on April 25, 2003 that hijackings seriously threatened US security, and cautioned that 'if [Washington] were to attack Cuba like Iraq...the struggle would last a very long time.'[17]

Under the migration accords, Cuban and US officials meet twice each year to consult on implementing and maintaining the agreements. The two nations disagree, however, on proper specific themes for these encounters. The US contends they should tackle limited points of implementation, such as the specific harbours to which intercepted migrants may be returned, and the quality of medical examinations for Cuban visa applicants. The Cuban government asserts that the conclaves provide a forum to consider broader themes, and in 2000 and 2001 presented the draft of a new agreement covering migration, drug trafficking and anti-terrorist measures. The US rejected this initiative as outside the scope of the consultations, and considered it an effort to undercut the US trade embargo.[18] As might be expected, Cuba and the US have different future security concerns about migration. In addition to its worries about being invaded, with hijacking or migration as a pretext (an apprehension that US officials dismiss as illusory), Cuba focuses (albeit with less vehemence) on the pace of visa issuance since 9/11.

Especially after EBSVERA came into effect in 2002, new layers of security checks delayed the granting of visas to Cubans; by one Cuban estimate, in the first half of FY 2003, only 700 visas had been issued, against an ideal theoretical total of 10,000 in that period. US officials, it must be noted, were eager to reassure the Cuban government that there was no intention to reduce migration deliberately, and they expect to process the intended 20,000 visas in the current fiscal year. The United States, for its part, views a renewed mass boatlift from Cuba as a major security threat, in part because it would require that anti-terrorist Coast Guard patrols of the US eastern seaboard be sharply reduced. (Many patrol vessels were in fact withdrawn from the Caribbean to US home waters for three or four months following 9/11.)[19] An interagency US government working group meets weekly in Washington to assess the likelihood of a new migration crisis involving Cuba. While downplaying the prospects for such an event at present, US diplomats note that in past instances only a few days' prior warning was available.[20]

Since 9/11, migration relations between Jamaica and the US have been placed under stress by some reductions in visa issuance, and by Jamaican concerns that their nation's chosen course in other realms of foreign policy may prove costly in the field of migration. Despite assurances from the US ambassador shortly after 9/11 that 'we do not anticipate less visas being offered [in Jamaica]',[21] over the following 12 months, 37 per cent fewer visitors' visas were distributed, though processing of immigrant visas increased slightly. Jamaican diplomats described a widespread psychological impression in Jamaica that the US was not anxious to facilitate Jamaicans' access to the US in any capacity.[22]

Concerns were also expressed that nations such as Jamaica that criticised US policy towards Iraq might be penalised in other areas of bilateral relations, including migration as well as trade and aid. The heads of government in the 15-nation Caribbean Community (CARICOM) issued a 'Statement on Iraq' in mid-February, 2003. They recalled Iraq's obligation to facilitate the work of UN weapons inspectors, and affirmed their commitment to 'international efforts to combat terrorism'. In addition, however, CARICOM's statement opposed the use of armed force against Iraq 'at a time when diplomatic efforts had not yet been exhausted', and stated that regional leaders were 'deeply troubled over the humanitarian tragedy that an outbreak of war could bring about and the disastrous effects it could have on global economic stability'.[23] On March 18, some Caribbean governments received a US diplomatic note, urging them to oppose the convening of a special United Nations General Assembly session on Iraq:

> We urge you to oppose such a session and either vote against or abstain if the matter is brought to a vote...Given the currently highly charged atmosphere, the United States would regard [such a session] as unhelpful

> and as directed against the United States. Please know that this question as well as your position on it is important to the United States.[24]

In early April, the US presidential envoy to the Western Hemisphere, Otto Reich, stated in Bridgetown, Barbados, that the US did not regard the February CARICOM statement as 'particularly helpful nor based on fact'. Though he disavowed any intention to retaliate against Caribbean critics, Mr Reich added 'I would urge CARICOM to study very carefully not only what it says, but the consequences of what it says.'[25] In response, Barbadian foreign affairs minister, Billie Miller stated that Barbados was 'most offended' that Reich 'would deprecate in the most public of forums the position of the government of Barbados and other regional governments while simultaneously stressing that if there were differences of opinion the United States would wish to be told in private'.[26]

The Dominican Republic has followed a different course in dealing with the broad diplomatic consequences of 9/11. In response to the March 18 US diplomatic note, the government of President Hipólito Mejía joined the 'coalition of the willing' in endorsing the US-led invasion of Iraq, in order to maintain neighbourly relations and bilateral trade ties. (This led Foreign Minister Hugo Tolentino Dipp to resign a few days later; Tolentino had stated that 'the obligations assumed in international organizations, relative to safeguarding the peace, should not be violated by the unilateral viewpoint of any state'.)[27] Several hundred Dominican troops are slated to help patrol southern Iraq beginning in mid-2003.

Partly hoping for recompense for this diplomatic backing, the Dominican administration has sought concessions from the US on issues of migration and trade. When President Mejía visited Washington in May 2003, his delegation requested positive steps to legalise undocumented Dominican migrants in the United States, and trade benefits for the Dominican Republic as part of the negotiations for a Central American Free Trade Area. It is difficult to reduce unauthorised Dominican migration by sea to Puerto Rico (shown in Table 14.5), they contended, when the nation's economy is stagnant without new trade preferences. The Bush administration responded favourably to the trade request, including the Dominican Republic in the Central American process.[28]

However, despite a visit from President Mejía, the Department of Homeland Security did not undertake to revise US policy on deporting alien criminals to the Caribbean, a point of notable sensitivity for the Dominican and Jamaican governments.[29] As Table 14.6 shows, the Dominican Republic and Jamaica receive more than 70 per cent of the criminals 'removed' by the United States after completion of their sentences; Caribbean states contend that many such deportees became lawbreakers in the US from an early age, and that their imposition encourages criminality within the region.

Table 14.6
Aliens Deported by the United States to Caribbean Nations due to Criminal Conviction, Fiscal Years 1998–2002

Nation receiving deportees	FY 1998	FY 1999	FY 2000	FY 2001	FY 2002
Bahamas	68	64	107	92	100
Barbados	45	65	49	34	47
Cuba	26	75	71	77	56
Dominican Republic	1,705	2,343	2,257	2,149	1,990
Guyana	147	132	88	41	242
Haiti	313	302	374	354	290
Jamaica	1,224	1,379	1,347	1,298	1,517
Trinidad and Tobago	190	214	207	181	190
Other Caribbean	250	295	261	241	294
Total	3,968	4,869	4,761	4,467	4,726

Source: United States Department of Homeland Security, 2002 Yearbook of Immigration Statistics, *Internet edition: <http://www.bcis.gov/graphics/shared/aboutus/statistics/Enforce.htm>.*

Haiti has not treated migration as a major state-to-state subject for discussion since 9/11, and the two governments reportedly cooperate well in the routine administration of population movement. Most policy initiatives on migration flows from Haiti have thus fallen to the United States in recent years, and the terrorist attacks have served as one factor, stiffening Washington's long-standing restrictionist policy on this issue. Since the early Reagan administration, the US has sought to deter unauthorised seaborne migration from Haiti by energetic patrolling of sea-lanes between Haiti and Florida; if that fails, the US intercepts undocumented Haitian 'boat people' and returns the great majority to Haiti, whether or not they reachs US soil.[30]

Washington responded to a 'spike' in seaborne migration from Haiti in November and December 2001 with widespread radio advertisements in Haiti. These messages warned of dangers at sea, and of rapid repatriation. More public and political attention in the United States was drawn by the arrival in October 2002 of more than 200 Haitian migrants aboard a boat that reached Miami's Biscayne Bay unimpeded. The vessel grounded and some of the migrants waded ashore at the Rickenbacker Causeway; 207 Haitians were detained, along with nine Dominicans. The State Department recommended 'strongly' that those arrested should be detained until they could be returned to Haiti, unless they could qualify for political asylum based on a 'well-founded fear of persecution'.

Attorney-General John Ashcroft may well have needed little encouragement to detain the Haitians from Biscayne Bay, although it had been common US practice to release members of other nationalities from custody, while their asylum claims are processed. A statement included in the State Department's interagency advice on the Miami incident, however, was particularly cited by Justice Department officials: 'We have also noticed an increase in third country nationals (Pakistanis, Palestinians, etc.) using Haiti as a staging point for attempted migration to the United States. This increases the national security interest in curbing use of this migration route.'[31]

Mr Ashcroft overruled the Department of Justice's own Board of Immigration Appeals, which had granted bond to the detained Haitians; he directed that national security interests should be considered in weighing bond applications.[32] As immigration officer, Mario Ortiz, had told an immigration judge in November, 2002:

> We're concerned that very important resources of the Coast Guard and the Department of Defense would be diverted from their primary mission of protecting the homeland and fighting the war on terrorism...It sends the wrong signal of mass migration. The primary focus of this country should be in fighting terrorism.[33]

By July, 2003, 93 of those arrested at Biscayne Bay had been deported, 33 (mostly pregnant women and young children) had been released on humanitarian grounds while their asylum cases were under review, and an undetermined number had obtained both asylum and release. Thirty-two remained in custody, including two whose grants of asylum were being appealed by skeptical US authorities.[34]

Signs of a limited recasting of US-Caribbean migration relations

The 2001 terrorist attacks produced several marked alterations in the global foreign policy of the world's remaining superpower. The US narrowed its definition of national security to focus predominantly on anti-terrorism, assessing most other policy priorities in terms of their perceived contribution to that overriding goal. It has also shown a new willingness to take the initiative in world affairs, sometimes leading to a unilateralism that irks some other nations. The application of these worldwide policies in sub-regions relatively divorced from major terrorist incidents can appear unbending and severe.

These concerns and traits in US policy, while no doubt influential, do not determine in any simple way the impact of 9/11 on one transnational process – migration – in one region, the Caribbean. Both regional governments and Caribbean people, whether presently engaged in migration or not, exhibit enterprise and exert some leverage in this issue-area. In the diverse data points we have observed, one can discern the interaction of these forces. The numbers of migrants arriving in the US from the Caribbean have been modestly reduced, perhaps initiating trends that will be amplified in coming years. The legal status of some Caribbean migrants has become more uncertain in the US, but their remittances have increased. Long-standing US policies of repatriating 'boat people' have been reinforced, and newly justified in the name of counter-terrorism. Though Caribbean governments have sometimes chaffed at visa slowdowns, these limited new tensions have reminded them of the economic and social importance of migration access to the United States. Efforts (subtle and unsubtle) have been made by both migrant-sending and migrant-receiving nations to use migration as a lever to advance other policy goals, from trade to military measures in distant regions.

An important indicator of future trends in US migration policy, that may well affect the Caribbean, stems from Washington's dialogue with a much larger Western Hemisphere nation: Mexico. Just prior to the destruction of the World Trade Center and the assault on the Pentagon, the Mexican and US presidents had announced plans to conclude a sweeping new bilateral migration agreement. While the details remained to be negotiated, the diplomatic accord would probably have called for increased immigrant visas for Mexico, some degree of legalisation for undocumented Mexicans living in the US, a new guest-worker programme, and development aid targeted at major migrant-source regions in Mexico such as Puebla. The most dramatic immediate impact of 9/11 on US-Latin American relations was the unmistakable abandonment of that project by George W. Bush's administration, though Mexico remained keenly interested. American authorities devoted little time and less enthusiasm to the negotiations after September 11, and within 15 months the proposal's prime Mexican architect, Foreign Minister Jorge G. Castañeda, had resigned.

Three primary US motives help explain this radical change of direction. Increasing access for immigrants – and 'regularising' unauthorised migrants – in the wake of foreign attacks appeared unwise to US leaders, on grounds both of national security and domestic politics. In addition, the Bush administration perceived the Mexican government, led by President Vicente Fox, to be insufficiently supportive following 9/11, and Mexico's failure to back US efforts to obtain explicit endorsement from the United Nations Security Council for the 2003 invasion of Iraq only deepened that view. Finally, the impressive increases in President Bush's public-approval ratings following 9/11 placed US domestic politics on a new footing. No longer did it appear necessary, as it had since 1996, for the Republican Party to pay close attention to the partisan alignments of newly-mobilised ethnic groups, especially among Hispanic voters. A president benefiting from the strong 'rally-round-the-flag' effect in public opinion that traditionally accrues to wartime leaders, might not need the margin of support that he had sought prior to 9/11 from Hispanic people in a half-dozen states that may be electorally crucial in 2004.

The changes in US priorities that led Washington to abandon the Mexican migration initiative are likely to exert significant influence on migration affairs in the Caribbean for three reasons. First, Caribbean nations lost the opportunity to benefit from the 'new immigration deal' that was being drafted. Though both Mexico and the US described their bargaining as purely bilateral, with no involvement of other migrant-sending nations, diverse forces in US politics and international diplomacy would probably have extended some advantages to nations in Central America and the Caribbean. Since, for example, 'regularisation' for some undocumented migrants, new guest-worker programs or higher visa allocations would have had to be approved in the US Congress, legislators sympathetic to Salvadorans, Haitians, Guatemalans, Dominicans and other groups would have sought to condition their support on the inclusion of additional groups in new immigration benefits.[35]

Second, a tendency towards multilateral migration negotiations in the Caribbean has lost momentum, largely due to US coolness towards it. Beginning in the late 1990s, when Caribbean (as well as Central American) states sought to offset or reverse restrictionist US measures adopted in 1996, states in the region sometimes acted together to lobby the United States more often than in prior years. The prospect of participating in the Mexican initiative might have spurred this trend, though it might also have encouraged a spirit of 'each nation for itself'. What seems clear is that the US now has little enthusiasm for multilateral diplomacy with the Caribbean. In addition to

Otto Reich's remarks on CARICOM, Commonwealth Caribbean diplomats reported that State Department officials had complained to them, in mid-2003, that the tendency for nations from that region to consult broadly among themselves was undermining Washington's preference for dealing through bilateral channels.[36]

Third, a far lower political priority in Republican circles for reaching out to new ethnic voters has increased the influence of two groups within that party: convinced immigration restrictionists, and advocates for the most conservative Cuban-Americans in South Florida. Neither group favours the broad migration interests of Caribbean nations. In particular, as we have seen, rigid policies against Haitian seaborne migration have been reinforced, strongly encouraged by members of Congress including Florida Republicans Lincoln Diaz-Balart, Mario Diaz-Balart, and Ileana Ros-Lehtinen.

Conclusion

Avenues for individual and common action in the field of migration remain open to Caribbean nations, even in an era when, at best, few positive policy changes are to be expected from the United States. One important message of the data we have reviewed is that migration has endured as a strong link between the Caribbean and the United States, a bond that constrains both sending and receiving governments. Multilateral policy discussions on migration are only incipient in the region, and may well not be favoured by the United States at present.

However, Caribbean societies might foster such channels on their own, looking towards a day when a Caribbean consultative mechanism similar to the Regional Conference on Migration, which links Central America, Mexico, the US and Canada, could be instituted.[37] It is understandable that, barely two years after 9/11, stifling terrorism remains Washington's pre-eminent concern in international relations. That priority, however, is situated within a developing international and transnational social matrix in the Caribbean, in which both migration and the interests of migrant-source nations may well return to play a more central role.

Notes

1. As is well-known, migration within the Caribbean region has been a major social phenomenon since before colonial times. The consequences of 9/11 for population movement between Saint Lucia and Trinidad, or between Haiti and the Dominican

Republic, clearly merit examination. This chapter focuses, however, on migration flows and interactions between the Caribbean area and the United States.

2. Peggy Levitt, *The Transnational Villagers* (Berkeley and Los Angeles: University of California Press, 2001), p. 54.
3. Recent works in this scholarly enterprise include Levitt 2001, Cordero-Guzmán *et al.* 2001, and Glick Schiller and Fouron 2001.
4. See the statement of the Lawyers' Committee for Human Rights on the *Patriot Act*, October 26, 2001: <http://www.cdt.org/security/011026lchr.shtml>.
5. 'INS: EBSVERA, Visas, Border,' *Migration News* (University of California at Davis, California), Vol. 9, No. 6, June 2002, p. 1; Helen Dewar, 'Border Security Bill Clears Senate,' *Washington Post*, April 19, 2002, p. A10.
6. Somini Sengupta and Christopher Drew, 'Effort to Discover Terrorists Among Illegal Aliens Makes Glacial Progress, Critics Say,' *New York Times*, November 21, 2001, p. B8.
7. David Firestone, 'US Makes it Easier to Detain Foreigners,' *New York Times*, November 28, 2001, p. B7.
8. Christopher Marquis, 'Threats and Responses: Disruptions; Slowdown on US Visas Stalls Business, Science and Personal Travel Plans,' *New York Times*, October 13, 2002.
9. United States fiscal years run from October 1 of the preceding calendar year through September 30; thus FY 2002 began on October 1, 2001. This quirk in handling statistics happens to provide a relatively clear picture of 9/11's immediate effect, since the terror attacks occurred less than three weeks before the start of a new fiscal year. No US admissions data are yet available for the period after October 1, 2002.
10. National Immigration Forum, Washington, DC, 'Memorandum to Advocates and Service Providers,' June 27, 2003.
11. Manuel Orozco, 'Changes in the Atmosphere?: Increase of Remittances, Price Decline and New Challenges,' Inter-American Dialogue Remittances Project, Washington, DC, *Research Series*, March 2003.
12. Daisy Hernández, 'With Fewer Dollars to Go Around, More are Going Around World,' *New York Times*, July 14, 2003, pp. B1, B4.
13. Castro 1999.
14. Jay Weaver, 'Smuggling More Prevalent, and Deadly,' *Miami Herald*, November 21, 2001, p. 2A.
15. Peter Eisner, 'Cuba Executes 3 in Failed Hijacking of Ferry,' *Washington Post*, April 12, 2003, p. A13.
16. Castro 2003, p. 11.
17. Castro 2003, p. 12.
18. Interviews, US Department of State, June 27, 2003; Cuban Interests Section, Washington, DC, July 8, 2003. See also the statement by Ricardo Alarcón, President of the Cuban National Assembly, in Cuban Television, 'Informative Round Table,' 2002, pp. 21-25.
19. Interview, US Department of State, July 8, 2003.
20. Interviews, US Department of State, June 27, 2003; Cuban Interests Section, Washington, DC, July 8, 2003. Telephone interview, US Department of State, July 23, 2003.
21. Donna Ortega, 'No Intention Now to Change Visa Policy, Says US Ambassador,' *The Gleaner*, October 25, 2001.
22. Interview, Jamaican Embassy, Washington DC, July 18, 2003.
23. CARICOM's statement may be found at <http://www.caricom.org/expframes2.htm>.

24. Charles Arthur, 'Opposition too Costly,' *Latinamerica Press* (Lima, Peru), May 7, 2003, pp. 2-3; Charles Arthur, 'Fallout of War,' *Latinamerica Press* (Lima, Peru), March 26, 2003, pp. 1-2.
25. Eric Nurse, 'Leaders' Comments Upset Reich,' *Miami Herald*, April 4, 2003; Charles Arthur, 'Opposition too Costly'.
26. Saint Lucia One Stop, 'US Unhappy with Statements from the Caribbean on the War,' *sluonestop.com*, April 4, 2003.
27. Fior Gil, 'Hugo Tolentino Dipp renuncia por diferencia sobre Irak,' *Hoy* (Santo Domingo), March 26, 2003.
28. Manuel Jiménez, 'Hipólito Mejía pide regularización estatus migratorio para criollos,' *Hoy* (Santo Domingo), May 21, 2003; *Press Release*, Office of he United States Trade Representative, August 4, 2003.
29. Interview, Dominican Embassy, Washington, DC, July 9, 2003.
30. See Christopher Mitchell, 'U.S. Policy toward Haitian Boat People, 1972-93', *The Annals of the American Academy of Political and Social Science*, Vol. 534 (July, 1994).
31. US Department of State memorandum, 'State Department Position on the Disposition of Recent Boat Migrants,' Washington, DC, undated but issued in late 2002.
32. Prepared Statement of Kevin D. Rooney, Director, Executive Office for Immigration Review, US Department of Justice, before the Subcommittee on Immigration, Border Security and Claims, US House of Representatives Committee on the Judiciary, May 8, 2003, Washington, DC.
33. Andrea Elliott and Larry Lebowitz, 'Haitians a Threat, INS Says,' *Washington Post*, November 7, 2002, p. A6.
34. Rachel L. Swarns, 'Haitians are Held in U.S. Despite Grant of Asylum,' *New York Times*, July 25, 2003, p. A16.
35. Dominican diplomats make clear that their government had hoped to benefit from the impending liberalisation of migration access for Mexicans; interview, Dominican Embassy, Washington DC, July 9, 2003.
36. Interview, Jamaican Embassy, Washington DC, July 18, 2003.
37. For information on the RCM's history and projects, see <http://www.rcmvs.org/>. Among Caribbean nations, Belize and the Dominican Republic are the only members of the RCM.

Bibliography

Arthur, Charles, 'Fallout of War,' *Latinamerica Press* (Lima, Peru), March 26, 2003, pp. 1-2.

Arthur, Charles, 'Opposition too Costly,' *Latinamerica Press* (Lima, Peru), May 7, 2003, pp. 2-3.

Castro Ruz, Fidel, 'Key Statement on Illegal Migration from Cuba Promoted Throughout Forty Years by the United States of America,' Matanzas, August 3, 1999.

Castro Ruz, Fidel, 'Cuba and the Nazi-Fascism,' *Granma Internacional Digital, 2003* (<http://www.granma.cu/documento/ingles03/015.html.).

Cordero-Guzmán, Héctor R., Robert C. Smith, and Ramón Grosfoguel, eds., *Migration, Transnationalization, and Race in a Changing New York*. Philadelphia: Temple University Press 2001.

Cuban Television, 'Informative Round Table Meeting on the Statement of the Ministry of Foreign Affairs on the Important Drug Trafficker Arrested in Cuba,' March 18, 2002.

Dewar, Helen, 'Border Security Bill Clears Senate,' *Washington Post*, April 19, 2002.

Eisner, Peter, 'Cuba Executes 3 in Failed Hijacking of Ferry,' *Washington Post*, April 12, 2003, p. A13.

Elliott, Andrea and Larry Lebowitz, 'Haitians a Threat, INS Says,' *Washington Post*, November 7, 2002, p. A6.

Firestone, David, 'US Makes it Easier to Detain Foreigners,' *New York Times*, November 28, 2001.

Gil, Fior, 'Hugo Tolentino Dipp renuncia por diferencia sobre Irak,' *Hoy* (Santo Domingo), March 26, 2003.

Glick Schiller, Nina and Georges Eugene Fouron, *Georges Woke Up Laughing: Long-Distance Nationalism and the Search for Home.* Durham and London: Duke University Press 2001.

Hernández, Daisy, 'With Fewer Dollars to Go Around, More are Going Around World,' *New York Times*, July 14, 2003.

'INS: EBSVERA, Visas, Border,' *Migration News*. University of California at Davis, California, Vol. 9, No. 6 (June 2002).

Levitt, Peggy, *The Transnational Villagers.* Berkeley and Los Angeles: University of California Press, 2001.

Marquis, Christopher, 'Threats and Responses: Disruptions; Slowdown on US Visas Stalls Business, Science and Personal Travel Plans,' *New York Times*, October 13, 2002.

Mitchell, Christopher, 'U.S. Policy toward Haitian Boat People, 1972-93,' *The Annals of the American Academy of Political and Social Science*, Vol. 534 (July, 1994).

Nurse, Eric, 'Leaders' Comments Upset Reich,' *Miami Herald*, April 4, 2003.

Ortega, Donna, 'No Intention Now to Change Visa Policy, Says US Ambassador,' *The Gleaner*, October 25, 2001.

Rooney, Kevin D., Director, Executive Office for Immigration Review, US Department of Justice, Prepared Statement of, before the Subcommittee on Immigration, Border Security and Claims, US House of Representatives Committee on the Judiciary, May 8, 2003, Washington, DC.

Sengupta, Somini and Christopher Drew, 'Effort to Discover Terrorists Among Illegal Aliens Makes Glacial Progress, Critics Say,' *New York Times*, November 21, 2001

St Lucia One Stop, 'US Unhappy with Statements from the Caribbean on the War,' *Sluonestop.Com*, April 4, 2003.

Swarns, Rachel L., 'Haitians are Held in U.S. Despite Grant of Asylum,' *New York*, July 25, 2003, p. A16.

US Department of State, 'State Department Position on the Disposition of Recent Boat Migrants,' Memorandum, undated but issued in late 2002, Washington, DC.

Weaver, Jay, 'Smuggling More Prevalent, and Deadly,' *The Miami Herald*, November 21, 2001, p. 2A.

15

Coping with 9/11: State and Civil Society Responses

Isabel Jaramillo Edwards

Black Holes cannot be seen, and so they have to be detected by observing the environment around them.[1]

Introduction

The reorganisation of the global landscape in terms of geoeconomics and globalisation is a fact. The problem is the character of the changes taking place and the influence of hegemony, geopolitics and unilateralism, which must be considered in the context of these changes. The new global environment would require a new economic and financial framework in a world where contradictions mainly occur on the North/South axis. September 11, 2001 signalled transformations in the international environment and in US policy. In a context of undisputed American hegemony, multilateralism, international organisations and a legal framework are especially important for small countries.

This chapter will focus on the Caribbean's involvement in the international arena and the impact of 9/11 and its consequences for the area; issues of the security agenda – in general and in some specific cases – and the need for degrees of cooperation in the interest of the Caribbean Basin. Conclusions look at considerations on the main issues analysed, pointing out those considered relevant to the medium- and long-term prospects for the region.

The Global and Hemispheric Landscape

The international landscape is undergoing a period of widespread transition, with the convergence, among others, of a trend to multipolarity, military unipolarity, globalisation with a resulting growing interdependence[2] (*globalism* in the economic, military, environmental, social and cultural areas), a third technological revolution in an interdependent and transnationalised environment, the immediacy of communications and the re-emergence of conflicts that, although latent, did not surface in the bipolar context. Moreover, there is a struggle for the inclusion in geoeconomic and geopolitical spaces in a world marked by multidimensionality and a pervasive insecurity resulting in increased complexity and uncertainty.[3] The deceleration of global economy and the financial crises were part of the global landscape in which the United States redefined its security interests[4] and its foreign priorities.[5]

The uncertainty arising from an international context in transition is reflected in inter-American relations, traditionally characterised by the limited interest of the United States in the continent and by a policy that is still driven by crises.[6] On the basis of geopolitics, the Caribbean Basin[7] – because of its geographic proximity and levels of interdependence – will receive priority, while the Southern Cone will temporarily be relatively less significant.

The effects of social problems in Latin American and Caribbean societies – poverty, marginalisation, dissatisfied minorities, ethnic discord, lack of social justice – are central elements to consider within the hemispheric framework. They tend to create insecurity and have the potential to give rise to instability. As long as the tensions caused by these problems are present, there is the potential for the emergence of new conflicts. Recent economic troubles have fuelled unemployment, crime, and poverty, undermining the already vulnerable social fabric of Caribbean societies. At the same time, financial crises[8] and the gradual deceleration of the global economy contribute to economic insecurity. Conflicts that did not surface in the bipolar setting now take the forefront: ethnic[9] and migration issues, drugs and drug trafficking, terrorism, and traditional conflicts, such as those related to border disputes.

Convergence and contradictions between the United States, as a hegemonic power, and Latin America and the Caribbean bias the security agenda. The concepts of security in an international environment in transition will be closely linked among themselves and also to social and economic factors. Under the guise of the transnationalisation of security systems, there is the attempt at developing some policies that go against the legitimate sovereign interests of the various countries, thus contributing to insecurity.

The issues of drugs and drug trafficking, corruption, terrorism, migration, environmental problems, non-proliferation of sophisticated weapons, nuclear security, confidence-building measures, governability and stability are concerns for the entire Caribbean. In the military sphere, the main topics have to do with: the role and modernisation of the armed forces; the relationship between the civil society and the armed forces; participation in the UN peacekeeping operations and the involvement of armed forces in the control of drug trafficking. From the US point of view, natural disasters rank as 'soft threats'.[10] However, the subject of natural disasters is universal enough to unite the continent as a whole, over and above concerns of potential interference in internal affairs. Long-standing problems and those derived from integration (borders, customs, and so forth) also have substantial bearing.[11] The restructuring and homologation of judicial systems, cooperation between police and military establishments, and the exchange of intelligence to confront transnational problems – organised crime, drug trafficking and related offences – have been an important part of cooperation in the hemisphere. Moreover, the terrorist WTC/Pentagon attack of September 11, 2001 was a critical turning point in world affairs and resulted in the rearrangement of alliances at the global level.

The Caribbean

The security of the small states[12] is one of the basic topics on the Caribbean agenda. Drug trafficking and money laundering, illegal trade in arms, corruption, the transport of nuclear waste through the Caribbean Sea, organised and transnational criminal activities, illegal immigration,[13] HIV/AIDS, natural disasters, and global warming are all on the security agenda of the region and require a coordinated effort.

The Caribbean has been facing the challenges of social tensions brought about by economic depression, political alienation, unemployment, violence and social problems. A consequence of this situation is migration, which has been on the increase, although at unequal rates in the various countries. In 2000, it was estimated that 250,000 Jamaicans had migrated to the south of Florida. In the case of Haiti, with the obstacles raised by the so-called 'nation building', it is evident that development is a central element. However, to date, the policies implemented are inadequate.

The illegal drug market in the Caribbean generates an estimated income of about US$3.3 billion. This represents a 3.1 percent of the registered GDP in the region. Cocaine is the most profitable illicit drug in the Caribbean and accounts for 85 per cent of the drug market in the region. In terms of anti-drug trafficking initiatives, the Shiprider Agreement was the result of US focus on prevention and had to do with the eventual consolidation and redistribution of security tasks in the Caribbean Basin.[14] In this sense, it is significant to point out that the US rationale in the field of security in general is oriented not only at cooperation, but at the delegation of tasks and the strengthening of local forces. As to the Caribbean, the agreement was timely and implemented in accordance with the specific perspective and interests and requirements of each of the member countries.

The catastrophic effects of Hurricane Mitch in 1998 placed natural disasters at the forefront of problems in the region. Thus, the Special Committee on Natural Disasters was created in the Association of Caribbean States (ACS) and held its first meeting in Port of Spain, Trinidad, with the participation of representatives of the Caribbean Disaster Emergency Response Agency (CDERA), the Center for Natural Disaster Prevention Coordination in Central America (CEPREDENAC) and delegations from Colombia, Cuba, France and Mexico. A technical group was created with responsibility for analysing the strengths and weaknesses of each Caribbean country, identifying the projects they were implementing and, with the help of the ACS Special Fund, identifying funding sources to develop the projects included within the established priorities.[15] Other meetings intended to create a harmonised cooperation on natural disasters also were held.[16] This type of effort should be characterised by an extended cooperation for development, with the purpose of implementing security measures to prevent and confront a range of problems created by national disasters and their impact on the already precarious economic, social and environmental conditions.

As to trade, through the extension of the Caribbean Basin Initiative (CBI), the Caribbean obtained the final agreement of preferential treatment, similar to the North America Free Trade Agreement (NAFTA).[17] This initiative offered the area additional preferences to those already in place and required the eligible countries to institute 'strict and effective' customs safeguards to prevent their use as a springboard for transshipment to third countries.[18] It should be highlighted that customs laws were already amended with NAFTA, but they require constant adaptation. However, countries wishing to opt for the benefits of this law need to fulfil a series of conditions, among them a respect for the environment, the protection of labour, children and human rights, drug trafficking and corruption control, and the compliance with intellectual property rights and with several security-related measures, such as borders, customs, and anti-drug controls, among others.[19]

Development assistance to the Caribbean has been greatly reduced. In the English-speaking region, official development assistance amounted to close to $200 million in 2000. Of that amount $108 million went to a single country, Guyana, while Jamaica received a mere $10 million.[20] The argument from US government officials is 'that overseas development assistance to the Caribbean has dropped because of their high levels of human development as measured by the UN',[21] without considering the basic and increasing asymmetries between developed and underdeveloped countries and the specific characteristics of the area. On the other hand, considering the economic effect of globalisation and the present uncertain evolution of the international economy and its impact in the subregion, 'a commitment to economic growth should be assumed and at the same time prepare – in the perspective of commercial agreements – the social clauses that will help to lessen the adverse effects'.[22]

Demographics on the interrelationship between the Caribbean Basin and the United States are relevant to the impact of migration. The bulk of immigrants into the US are from Mexico, the Dominican Republic, Haiti and Cuba. Immigrants from the Caribbean and Central America are a significant source of foreign exchange income for their countries of origin through remittances, but they also contribute elements to the 'negative agenda', including criminality.[23] At the same time, the politics and culture of the countries of origin of the immigrants and those of the United States are increasingly intertwined[24] and the importance of Hispanic immigrants is becoming more decisive in the US electoral scene.[25]

Issues and Priorities for the Area

Topics gaining momentum for the United States in the hemisphere, which are part of the global agenda due to the potential increase of trade (eventually, the FTAA) and that are already present in the Caribbean Basin are: smuggling, drug trafficking,[26] traffic of arms,[27] maritime safety, airport security, money laundering, customs, security, forgery of papers,[28] immigrant trafficking,[29] nuclear waste transshipment, natural disasters and problems related to the environment. These are especially relevant in the Caribbean because of the economic importance of tourism and convergence of shipping routes. The biggest earner for most Caribbean countries is tourism and tourism needs stability. But drug trafficking through the Caribbean has been booming, and with it has come a corresponding increase in violent crime. A recent estimate by the United Nations Drug Control Programme puts the net regional earnings of the Caribbean drug industry at nearly half the GDP of Jamaica or Trinidad.[30]

The lack of resources, staff and technology in the Caribbean make it difficult to face some of the challenges and threats in this area, thus the urgency of a multilateral approach. Required are strategies such as the exchange of intelligence, police control in ports, and cooperation among regional customs, coast guards, armies and police. It should be highlighted that CARICOM has strengthened intelligence exchange with Latin America.

The Caribbean is a transshipment area for drugs to the United States, which hopes to develop and strengthen a dynamics of cooperation. But, in terms of participation, the bulk of the effort was basically Caribbean. Cooperation has to be built, and the implementation of an effort to 'share the burden' in such unequal terms does not contribute to an effective and balanced cooperation in areas that are sensitive for all the parties involved.

9/11 and its aftermath

After the impact of the WTC/Pentagon terrorist attacks, US military and logistic displacements increased the vulnerability of the Caribbean Basin in light of the sea lines of communication, air corridors, US bases and facilities in the area (Puerto Rico, US Virgin Islands, Antigua, Central America and others), the various military and nuclear facilities in the eastern and southern coasts of the US, and the danger this entails. The war situation further complicates the scenario by affecting tourism, which is integral to Caribbean economies.[31] There is also the threat of harsh economic sanctions against any foreign bank that does not cooperate with US investigators, which will affect the entire area given its large number of offshore banks. Tourism and offshore banking are the core of the economies of many Caribbean countries, and these economies are extremely sensitive to external shocks.[32]

In the immediate aftermath of 9/11 and in the area of security, one proposed alternative was:

> to combine additional security measures with careful investigation. This demands the adherence to the principles of international law and work to achieve a genuine international consensus based on the strengthening of the United Nations (UN) system. It also requires paying more attention to guaranteeing a political solution to long-standing world conflicts. The

region should carefully consider what approach suits its interests in order to achieve an international atmosphere where peace and security prevail.[33]

Cuba, for its part, spoke about the need for peace and international cooperation and the reinstatement of UN functions on both. Further, it stressed that it did not support terrorism or war.[34] The Cuban government condemned the terrorist attacks, expressed its solidarity with the people of the US and expressed its disposition to cooperate according to its modest abilities and offered its air corridors for US flights.[35] At the same time, Cuba has signed the 12 international conventions on terrorism;[36] approved a national law against terrorism and has cooperated with the United Nations Security Council on these issues. It also ratified the Treaty for Non-Proliferation of Nuclear Weapons – Tratado de Tlatelolco – that it had signed in 1995.[37] In the bilateral sphere, Cuba's proposition to the US for the adoption of a programme to combat terrorism was rejected by the American government.[38]

Cuba actively participated in the Regional Conference on Fiscalization and Drug Control in the Caribbean in 2001 and in the Second Regional Conference on Fiscalization of Drugs.[39] The island has programmes conducted by the Comisión Nacional de Drogas and it has developed a wide set of preventive programmes. Cuba has signed the main UN conventions related to drugs and has cooperation agreements in this field with 29 countries.[40] Juan Escalona Regueiro, attorney general of the Republic of Cuba, admitted at a press conference in Havana in December 2002 that Cuba 'faces grave problems' because of an increase in criminal activities in the island. Cuba applies the death penalty in exceptional crimes and those specially related to 'state security'. General (Ret) Escalona Regueiro said that in the case of Cuba it is mainly a 'deterrent'.[41]

The Cuban government's strong preventive stand on the incipient drug market in the island is translated into stronger legal sanctions for drug crimes, increased law enforcement and strict application of the law.[42] Cuba has expressed its willingness to negotiate a considerable security agenda with the US (drugs, terrorism, illegal migration) and it maintains what might be called a case-by-case coordination on migration and drugs issues.[43]

From a Caribbean perspective, security can no longer be limited to traditional military operations; there is the need for an integrated approach to 'the conditions which create instabilities in societies and which endanger our humanity', hence the need for the adoption of a 'multidimensional approach to hemispheric security'.[44] At the regional level, at its Summit in Nassau in 2001, CARICOM:

> expressed concern over the new forms of crime and violence that continue to pose threats to the region's security. These new forms of crime have implications for individual safety and the social and economic well-being of the region as a whole. The heads agreed to establish a Regional Task Force on Crime and Security to examine the major causes of crime, and to recommend approaches to deal with the inter-related problems of crime, illicit drugs and firearms, as well as terrorism.[45]

The areas on which the Regional Task Force will focus are related to the underlying causes and sources of crime; initiatives against activities that pose a direct security threat to the region and, multilateral initiatives for international security in which the region is committed to participating as co-victims of transnational crime and to build capacity through institutional strengthening, shared surveillance and other forms of cooperation among member states, and between CARICOM, the wider Caribbean and the international community.[46] In examining the wide range and complex issues surrounding the causes of crime, the Task Force considered, among others, the following factors: poverty, unemployment, social marginalisation and inequality, the illegal drug trade, corruption, the trafficking of firearms, deportation of criminals and the ineffectiveness of the existing criminal justice systems.[47]

Furthermore, CARICOM security ministers agreed on the need for a greater sharing of intelligence and coordination of counter-narcotics strategies to help fight crime in the region. The ministers highlighted the principal threats to security in the region as: illegal drugs, illegal firearms, corruption, rising crime against persons and property, criminal deportees, mainly from the US and Canada, growing lawlessness, poverty and inequity, and terrorism. They asked for more time to carry out the necessary research, analysis of crime trends and the crafting of an anti-crime and security strategies for the region.[48]

The government of Jamaica worked actively to prepare legislation to implement UN Security Council Resolution 1373 on Terrorism, which the Security Council unanimously adopted following the September 2001 terrorist attack on the United States. Instructions were also issued for the drafting of legislation to facilitate the ratification of/accession to several other international conventions on terrorism to which Jamaica is not yet a party.[49]

According to UN statistics, Jamaica has the world's third highest murder rate per capita, after South Africa and Brazil.[50] There is a widespread recognition of the social instability and fear which the high murder rate and criminal activity, among other things, has generated.[51] Strategies unveiled by Jamaica's security minister at the end of 2001 and early 2002 were not perceived as ones that would definitively tackle the country's crime problem, with 39 per cent of the people saying that the plan could not solve the crime problem, 34 per cent supporting the initiative and 27 per cent having no position either way.[52] Basically, the proposal included: anti-terrorist collaboration between the police and military; improved equipment for the police force; an increase in the number of police officers; better and more equipment for the constabulary and tougher laws to fight crime.[53]

Sentences imposed through the Gun Court in Jamaica[54] have increased in severity and some observers anticipated negative outcomes of the fight against the drug trade and other criminal activities. It was argued that 'great sacrifices will have to be made to find the material resources to equip the police force to a level where it can match the sophistication and influence of the drug criminals ... difficult choices that will involve postponement of other demands for public expenditure so [as] to provide increased resources to the security forces'.[55] At the same time, there is no national consensus on how to define the threat or, for that matter, how to confront it. In this context, civil-military contradictions are increasing; issues such as the distinction between the role of the defence forces and police forces, pervasive corruption,[56] and human rights, acquire special relevance.[57]

Guyana has been undergoing a severe crisis where racial and ethnic factors, and the stirring of racial animosities, play their role.[58] The government is moving to deal more effectively with its spate of killings and criminal violence with the introduction of a package of anti-crime legislation, including one specifically targeting acts of terrorism. The serious crime situation that affects the whole society has made it a matter of urgency to take anti-crime measures. The problem of criminal deportees is also present. The proposed amendment of the *Prevention of Crimes Act* seeks to introduce legislation to keep them under the vigilance of the security forces. The *Criminal Law (Offences) Bill* is the one that aims at toughening the penalties, including death by hanging, for those convicted of terrorist acts that resulted in the killing of anyone.[59]

Increased violence and criminal activity in Trinidad and Tobago included kidnappings,[60] and an escalation in arms and drug trafficking.[61] At the same time, 'a controversial/political organization', Jamaat-al-Muslimeen of Trinidad and Tobago was, allegedly, 'linked with terrorists' and the FBI was investigating its overseas links.[62] Vigilance is especially important in Trinidad and Tobago because 'national assets are predominantly energy based' and the country depends on the gas and oil industry, which can be easily targeted by acts of terrorism.[63] In terms of cooperation, Trinidad and Tobago reported 'Operation Ventri', a joint operation between Trinidad and Tobago and Venezuela which, together with bilateral and other maritime activities, are successful mechanisms being utilised 'to minimise the escalation of illegal manoeuvres within the hemisphere'.[64] On the other hand, Trinidad and Tobago is also 'investing heavily in airport security, including equipment and training, while regional ports servicing the cruise tourism industry have begun to network on security systems'.[65]

The mixture of race and politics, violence and criminal activity create a context of insecurity in the Caribbean.[66] These countries have been ardently discussing the death penalty issue and some have taken steps to amend present legislation to apply capital punishment. In some Caribbean countries, the population supports capital punishment as a deterrent to violent crime.[67] The effects of the new National Security Strategy of the US was perceived as a doctrine that, 'stripped of its veneer, is unilateralist in posture and unrestrained projection of American power...Partnerships have to be built and not imposed and global objectives cannot be defined only in terms of America's wishes....'[68]

Homeland security will eventually affect the Caribbean. Consequently, some believe that the area will eventually become part of the North American security perimeter, as put forward by the 'third border' concept. It is relevant to consider then that '...some Caribbean governments have recognized that it is more advantageous to be on the inside looking out of a US security perimeter'[69] At the same time 'Caribbean countries should be encouraged to participate in a genuine multilateral partnership to guarantee, as far as possible, the mutual security of North America, including the entire Caribbean region.... In this context, the United States will have to consider even closer collaboration with Cuba in global security matters, despite current policy that brands Cuba as a terrorist state'.[70] Because of sustained terrorist activity against Cuba, the island has long experience in security matters and has also developed a defensive know-how in this field.

As a result of the US logic of pushing the US 'zone of security outward', various initiatives have been designed. Among them is the Container Security Initiative (CSI), applied from February 2002, 'and designed to protect and secure the global trading system'.[71] The *Maritime Transportation Anti-Terrorist Act* 2002 verifies the vulnerability of US ports and, if extended to foreign ports, may pose a security risk for US bound ships and cargo.[72] Already strained economies will have to cope, in general terms, with the new rules applied to port security, shipping and loading containers, customs and other rules that imply 'added costs for industry, exporters and importers and an increase in port improvements'.[73]

On the side of civil society, after an overwhelming condemnation of terrorism, there is a mixed perception of the magnitude of the threat posed to Caribbean society. Widespread social instability, a significant increase in drug trafficking, crime and violence[74] and economic hardship were present before 9/11 and as a result of its impact, these conditions have tended to become more evident. Justice is a priority in Caribbean societies. Consequently, some individuals argue that, on the specific issue of race, for example, 'the Church must interpret the signs of the times and challenge the popular presuppositions that discriminate against minorities'.[75] At the same time, there is an ongoing debate in the midst of civil society about what initiatives at the family, community and national levels are adequate for the development of a balanced application of law enforcement and justice. The private sector is developing some initiatives in the context of the global fight against drugs and weapons. One such effort is the Business Anti-Smuggling Coalition (BSAC) International.[76] Finally, and also in the context of civil society, it is necessary for governments to ensure increased dialogue with the people before and after specific pronouncements that directly affect the well-being and stability of society as a whole.

A new set of challenges related to integration, including some associated with security issues, will continue to exist. Among them: international migration and immigration laws; open borders; free movement of skills; transnational criminal activities; continued tensions and risks associated with stability and governance,[77] and so on. Relevant, too, are trade negotiations with the European Union (EU) on Economic Partnership Agreements (EPA) under the Cotonou Agreement which governs aid, trade and economic arrangements between the EU and the African Caribbean and Pacific (ACP) countries. So too are FTAA negotiations and the agreement of the CARICOM countries to implement the Caribbean Court of Justice (CCJ), described as a 'demonstration of...seriousness in advancing the Caribbean Single Market Economy (CSME)'.[78] Warnings were given in relation to the changing conditions and the economic impact that 'can be decisive'.[79] At the same time, CARICOM's mandate to strengthen governance should be closely linked to political will so as to develop the adequate level of regional cooperation. This also brings to the fore the importance of consultation and deliberation with the Caribbean people on issues that are vital to the achievement of the necessary levels of confidence required to pursue a strengthened and timely[80] process of integration.[81]

Lastly, but not least, is the Iraq war, perceived in the area as one with 'ripple effects' that could have 'profound consequences for [Caribbean] economy and quality of life for some time to come'.[82] This will have a considerable impact on Caribbean economies[83] because of their dependence on petroleum imports and the significance of the travel industry. The war raised the question of the real threat to international system: pointing to the fact that the 'Bush Administration...does not conceal its contempt for the United Nations (UN)'. It has been argued that the breach of the international system is carried on through 'the stated objective of regime change in Iraq' that 'would seem to violate the UN's 1974 protocol that calls on states to settle disputes by peaceful means so as not to endanger world peace and security'.[84] Civil society, on the other hand, made its views known calling for justice, common sense and peace.[85]

Conclusions

Towards the middle of the 1990s, the United States suggested that cooperation would be at the centre of its hemispheric policy. The acknowledgement of the need for cooperation came hand in hand with some hindrances. In the case of the United States and Latin America and the Caribbean, a main element to face with realism is a legacy of mistrust and fragmentation coming from the nineteenth and twentieth centuries. It is in this context that we have to consider the agreements and disagreements between the United States and Latin America and the Caribbean in the framework of the debate on the definition of security in an asymmetrical context such as the inter-American setting.

Cooperation in the protection of the seas, of space, and of resources gives an ample perspective to the concept of neighbourliness in the hemisphere. Common interests on environmental protection and the requirement of political will transform the concept of neighbourliness into a more complex interrelationship.[86] In the area of differences on security topics, there are disagreements about the roles and functions of the armed forces and their direct commitment to the combat against drug trafficking, terrorism and organised crime.[87] The main role of the armed forces is still the defence of national territory and sovereignty. On the other hand, the differentiation between legitimate defence requirements – and thus the modernisation of the security and armed forces – and an arms race is fundamental for peace and security in the hemisphere.

The Caribbean Basin is still a priority area for the United States. In the case of the Caribbean subregion, some observers feel that cooperation within the CARICOM framework should change, basically because of a potential inclusion in the FTAA,[88] and concerns on the security of small island states are reiterated, mainly in what has to do with economic feasibility, a matter that increases violence as a result of economic and social tensions and insecurity.[89] At the same time, development continues to be a relevant issue in the Caribbean, directly related to the internal stability of each country in the area. In focusing on the issue of coping with the present situation in the Caribbean, we need to separate problems that were already present before 9/11. Such is the case of the economic slowdown which, according to some specialists, 'began in earnest' in 2000.[90] It is also the case of increased attention to security, for reasons other than terrorism.

The impact in the area of recently enacted US laws such as *Homeland Security* (PL 107–296); the *Container Security Initiative* (CSI) of November 25, 2002; *Maritime Transportation Anti-Terrorist Act* (PL 107–295); and those related to security and health, the response to biological terrorism (PL 107–188).[91] Also relevant are the concept of the third border and the issues of trade and the security agenda for the hemisphere, with special emphasis on the case of the Caribbean on migration, drugs and illegal arms. These suggest that strained Caribbean economies will have to cope with the new rules applied to port security, shipping and loading containers, customs, etc. and an increase in security expenditures. Hopefully, the technology and resources gap and increased spending on security will not hinder development.

Harnessing globalisation to national and regional ends is basic. In the present circumstances, the prevalence of and individual interest of each party must not obscure the fact that the Caribbean should think of itself politically as a region, having achieved thinking of itself as a regional economy.[92] Dealing with terrorism and other threats on a multilateral basis includes the UN international conventions, regional and subregional organisations, bilateral agreements and non-state actors perceptions, among others. One of the basic objectives should be to avoid the creation of cultures of violence.[93]

The Caribbean has condemned terrorism in all its forms, but it insists that part of the strategy must be to attempt to understand the underlying and root causes of terrorism.[94] At the same time, Caribbean countries support the need for strengthening the global role of the UN. Because security in the Caribbean is multidimensional, it is necessary to promote cooperation and exchanges between government agencies and military institutions in the region – and in the whole hemisphere. Bilateral agreements and joint maritime operations focused on organised crime and other illegal activities in the hemisphere tend to create a secure environment. Consequently, CARICOM ministers have urged regional cooperation in counter-narcotics and anti-crime measures; intelligence gathering and sharing; the coordination of mechanisms to sustain regional cooperation with regard to anti-crime and security measures; capacity building for regional law enforcement agencies; maritime cooperation and a collective approach to the problem of deportees.[95]

Increasingly, there is a need for an integrated approach to security, poverty, HIV/AIDS, illegal arms and drug trafficking; ecological disasters as well as crimes plaguing nations of the hemisphere. At the same time 'collaboration with the United States in the war on drugs is important, but it must not turn into domination'.[96] Initiatives should be directed towards cooperation for mutual benefit, with a new security system characterised by consensus, convergences and the ability to develop collective action and diplomatic maturity. The challenge is to design a coalition that strengthens the position and interests of the region and does not end in a 'fortress Caribbean' that would be inimical for sustainable tourism. The challenge for all United Nations members remains the preservation of fundamental human rights in the midst of the 'war against terrorism'. While US attention focuses on the Middle East and Asia, Latin America and the Caribbean are wary. Concern has been growing over the far-reaching new policy of pre-emption. Finally, the war in Iraq increases the uncertainty that pervades the area and has the effect of destabilising the United Nations and the international system as a whole.

Notes

1. *The New York Times*. On black holes see: www.cosmiverse.com and www.nasa.gov.
2. Interdependence has to do with situations characterised by reciprocal effects among countries and among actors in various countries. *Globalism* is a state of the world implying interdependence networks at not only regional, but also multicontinental distances. Interdependence and globalism are both multidimensional phenomena. See Robert O. Keohane and Joseph Nye, Jr. 'Globalization, What's New? What's Not (And So What?)', *Foreign Policy* (Spring 2000), 104–119.
3. Moises Naim, 'Las ansiedades de la globalización', *El País*, March 12, 2000, 16.
4. In the area of national security, a high level commission examining the topic concluded that US military superiority did not guarantee protection. See Moises Naim, op. cit. Also, M. Klare, 'The New Geography of Conflict', *Foreign Affairs* (May–June, 2001), 49; Winn Schwartau, 'Asymetrical Adversaries: Looming Security Threats', *Orbis* (Spring 2000), 197–205; and Samuel Berger, 'A Foreign Policy for the Global Age', *Foreign Affairs*, Vol. 79 No. 6 (November/December 2000), 22–39. For a perspective from the G.W. Bush administration, see Condoleezza Rice, 'Promoting National Interest', *Foreign Affairs* Vol. 79, No. 1 (January–February 2000), 5–62 and 'The US

Strategic Posture Review: Issues for the New Administration', *Strategic Forum,* No. 177, INSS, NDU (February 2001).

5. See Samuel Berger, *op. cit.*; Condoleezza Rice, *op. cit.* and 'The US Strategic Posture Review: Issues for the New Administration', *op. cit.*
6. US attention is basically focused on Russia, Chechnya because of a pipeline taking the resources of the Caspian Sea to the West, that will go through Georgia and Azerbaijan on its way to Turkey, the Middle East, the Balkans, China, East Asia, India and Pakistan, Indonesia, Africa, since it is cut off from the rest of the world in development issues. In: 'Prepared Testimony by George J. Tenet, CIA Director, Before the Armed Services Committee'. Subject: *The Worldwide Threat in 2000,* February 3, 2000.
7. The Caribbean Basin has traditionally been an area of interest for the United States. See R.A. Pastor, *Whirlpool* (Princeton University Press, 1992).
8. For a view on this issue, see Martin Feldstein, 'A Self-Help Guide for Emerging Markets', *Foreign Affairs*, vol. 78, No. 2 (March/April 1999), 93–109.
9. In some cases (such as in Ecuador, Mexico, Guatemala) national-ethnic issues.
10. With this notion in mind, the establishment of a training centre in Panama that would become operational in 2001, geared at palliating the impact of hurricanes and other disasters in the region, was being discussed. The meeting was held at Florida International University sponsored by the Center for Disaster Management and Humanitarian Assistance in this university. Guests included representatives from 16 Caribbean nations, 6 Central American countries, the White House and the Federal Emergency Management Agency and experts from the Southern Command. See: Martin Merzer, 'Talks Open to Create Center for Disaster Preparedness', *The Miami Herald*, July 25, 2000, B3.
11. For this last aspect, see S. Flynn, 'Beyond Border Control', *Foreign Affairs* (November/ December 2000), 57–68.
12. For another viewpoint, see: Summit of the Americas, Quebec, 2001, item 4. It is also an issue for discussion at the OAS.
13. Mainly from Haiti and the Dominican Republic.
14. 'Lack of economic resources' was the cause of dramatic cuts in the US Coast Guard Service, reaching 10 per cent of the federal ships, planes and patrol boats. These were mainly ships and planes to detect drug trafficking and illegal migrant smuggling. Hernando Ramirez, 'Menos barcos', *El Nuevo Herald*, March 26, 2000, A1.
15. See *Boletín de Información de la AEC*, Vol. 4, No. 2, March 2000. Homepage: www.acs-aec.org
16. Eric Green, Regional Officials Meet on Coordinating Disaster Preparedness, US, Central American, Caribbean officials discuss proposals (620), August 3, 2000, http:/ /usinfo.state.gov
17. See Text: Senate Committee Summary of Africa-Caribbean Trade Bill (Senate Passed Bill 77-19) (2800). Following is the text of the Senate Finance Committee press release summarising the Africa-Caribbean trade bill which the Senate passed 77-19, May 11, 2000, Clinton Signs Africa-Caribbean Trade Bill (Measure aims to expand two-way trade, encourage reform) (730) http://usinfo.state.gov.
18. On transshipment, see Title II of NAFTA.
19. See S. Flynn, *op cit.*
20. On the other hand, several countries attracted considerable foreign direct investment, such as Guyana and Trinidad and Tobago which amounted to almost 10 per cent of their economies and 7 per cent in Jamaica in 2000. See Tony Best, 'Caribbean Nations Forge Ahead To Improve Living Standards', *The New York CaribNews*, Week Ending August 27, 2002, 3.

21. Tony Best, *op. cit.*
22. Attending to obvious differences in terms of area and other specific issues, it is important to note the following analysis: Manuel Orozco, Latin America Advisor, Inter American Dialogue, 'Central America facing free trade: What's new?' in: *Manchester Trade's CAFTA Update*, February 2003.
23. For a critical position on the 'controversial' issue of repatriation of criminals see A. Bryan quoted in 'University of Miami Scholar advocates increased vigilance, security because of potential use of region by terrorists', *Caribbean Business*, November 15, 2001.
24. See Abraham F. Lowenthal, 'Latin America at the Century's Turn: Putting Cuba 2000 in Regional Perspective', *DRCLAS NEWS*, Harvard University (Winter 2000), 17–19.
25. States like California, Illinois, Florida and New Jersey are outstanding as to ballots.
26. Cuba has bilateral agreements on drug trafficking with 29 countries and US agencies are interested in establishing an agreement with this country, with which there already is a punctual cooperation on this issue. Another aspect to take into account in the case of Cuba is money laundering. If we consider the possibility of the establishment of a relationship between US banks and Cuban banks, the possibility of links with the Caribbean Financial Action Task Force would be present.
27. From various origins and mainly from the United States.
28. M. Lynch, 'Probe: Sniper Suspect forged US travel papers in Antigua', *The Miami Herald*, January 7, 2003, A10 and C. James, 'Antigua Wants to Question Suspect in the US', *The Miami Herald*, January 7, 2003.
29. Border with Canada, border with Mexico; also, Haiti, the Dominican Republic, and Asians, among others, who try to enter the United States through various routes and border points. With specific characteristics, it is a relevant issue also in the case of Cuba.
30. The amount is US$3.3 billion. See 'Trouble in Paradise', *The Economist* (November 23, 2002), 36–37.
31. Norman Girvan, Secretary General of the Association of Caribbean States, 'Terrorismo, turismo y comercio', *Esta Semana en el Gran Caribe*, September 20, 2001 in www.acs-aec.org.
32. John Collins, 'Devastating Impact of US terror on Caribbean', *Caribbean Business*, September 20, 2001; John Collins, 'Expert says Caribbean is in for a rough time', *Caribbean Business*, December 27, 2001.
33. Norman Givan, *op cit.*
34. Fidel Castro, 'Speech at the Open Forum held in Ciego de Avila', September 29, 2001, in *Tribuna*, Havana, September 20, 2001, 5 and 'Nuestra Discrepancia no es la lucha contra el terrorismo, sino en los metodos de luchar contra el Terrorismo', Interview with General Raul Castro, *Granma,* January 22, 2002, 4.
35. 'Declaración del Gobierno de la República de Cuba', 11 de Septiembre del 2001, *Granma,* September 12, 2001. Cuba also underlined that it has been the object of terrorist actions – from the territory of the US – for more than 40 years, including the sabotage of a Cubana de Aviacion flight in 1976 near Barbados. See Fidel Castro, Speech, October 6, 2001, in *Granma,* October 14, 2001.
36. 'Concluyó Cuba Proceso de adhesión a los doce convenios internacionales sobre terrorismo', *Granma Internacional,* December 9, 2001.
37. 'Cuba defiende Principios, no Conveniencias', Speech, Felipe Pérez Roque, Minister of Foreign Affairs of Cuba, at the 57th General Assembly of the UN, New York, September 14, 2002, in *Juventud Rebelde*, September 15, 2002, 6.

38. 'Cuba defiende Principios, no Conveniencias', *op. cit.*
39. Roger Ricardo Luis, 'Importante Contribución al Combate a la Droga en al Región', *Granma*, January 18, 2003, 8.
40. 'Comparte Cuba sus Experiencias en Foro Regional Antidrogas', *Opciones*, November 11, 2001.
41. 'El Fiscal General de la República Admitió hoy que Cuba enfrenta Graves Problemas Por Incremento de Actividades Delictivas', Conferencia de Prensa, December 3, 2002, E. Lopez Oliva, Corresponsal, monitorhavana.
42. 'Impostergable Combate para defender el presente y el futuro', Editorial, *Granma*, 10 de Enero de 2003; Decreto-Ley No. 232, 'Sobre Confiscación por Hechos relacionados con las Drogas, actos de Corrupción o con otros comportamientos Ilícitos', in *Gaceta Oficial de la República de Cuba*, Extraordinaria, Año CI, Ministerio de Justicia, La Habana 21 de Enero 2003.
43. See Peter Kornbluh, '*Cuba, Counternarcotics, and Collaboration: A Security Issue in the US-Cuban Relations*', Cuba Briefing Paper Series No. 24, Georgetown University, December 2000. Also, Roger Ricardo Luis, *op. cit.*
44. Owen Arthur, Prime Minister of Barbados, made an appeal that beyond official calls to combat international terrorism, this year's meeting of the hemispheric body makes a difference by adopting 'a multidimensional approach to hemispheric security', at 32nd Annual General Assembly of the OAS, in Rickey Singh, 'Barbados, US differ on security', *JAMAICAOBSERVER.COM*, June 4, 2002.
45. The Task Force, chaired by Lancelot Selman of Trinidad and Tobago, comprised representatives from each of the member states, the Regional Security System (RSS), the Association of Caribbean Commissioners of Police, the University of the West Indies (UWI), and the Regional Secretariats (CARICOM and the OECS). In CARICOM Secretariat, Georgetown, Guyana, Prepared for Media Clinic, June 25, 2002, in www.caricom.org.
46. CARICOM Secretariat, *op. cit.*
47. CARICOM Secretariat, *op. cit.*
48. CARICOM leaders in the Bahamas in November 2001 established a task force of their security and legal ministers to draft a Caribbean-wide response for security threats, especially in the face of 9/11 and the increasing flow of narcotics through the region. C. Clarke, 'CARICOM security ministers call for cooperation on crime', *JAMAICAOBSERVER.COM*, June 20, 2002.
49. 'Cabinet Sanctions drafting of terrorism bill', *JAMAICAOBSERVER.COM*, June 18, 2002.
50. Canute James, 'Close Contest Predicted in Jamaica Poll', *Financial Times*, September 23, 2002, www. FT.com.
51. Some argue that 'control of armed crime requires a transformation of structures and strategies and not the easy sell of incremental adjustments and an almost tedious attention to techniques and process'. Harold Crooks, 'Wrong Move, Minister Phillips' *JAMAICAOBSERVER.COM*, July 8, 2002; also, 'High Level Crime Meetings, Minister Discusses new strategies with police, army', *JAMAICAOBSERVER.COM*, July 4, 2002.
52. This picture of a divided position emerged from the poll conducted in early March by the Stone Organisation for the *Jamaica Observer*. Stone used a sample of 1,203 persons in 44 communities and the poll has a margin of error of plus or minus three percent. See *The New York CaribNews*, Week ending March 5, 2002, 7.
53. '39% Don't Believe Phillips' Crime Plan Can Solve Problems', *The New York CaribNews*, Week ending March 5, 2002, 7.
54. 'Strike hard at gun runners', *JAMAICAOBSERVER.COM*, July 21, 2002.

55. Dennis Morrison, 'As if they are your average criminal...', *JAMAICAOBSERVER*.COM, July 14, 2002.
56. 'Anti-narcotics cops urged to resist temptations', *JAMAICAOBSERVER.COM*, June 18, 2002.
57. Harold Crooks, op. cit. Also, Byron Buckley, 'Senator chides cops for improper conduct but wants police to be given necessary tools for the jobs', *JAMAICAOBSERVER.COM*, July 13, 2002; Rickey Singh, 'Reflections on sad, outrageous acts', *JAMAICAOBSERVER.COM*, August 18, 2002.
58. Rickey Singh, 'Guyana stiffening anti-race crime laws', *JAMAICAOBSERVER*.COM, August 6, 2002.
59. Rickey Singh, 'Guyana becoming "lawless republic"', *JAMAICAOBSERVER*.COM, July 28, 2002; and Rickey Singh, 'Guyana Moves for Tough Anti-Crime Laws', *JAMAICAOBSERVER*.COM, September 21, 2002.
60. Rickey Singh, 'Kidnap suspect held in T & T', *JAMAICAOBSERVER.COM*, September 4, 2002.
61. Rickey Singh, 'TT police, Panday in row over drug, missiles find at MP's home', *JAMAICAOBSERVER.COM*, July 19, 2002.
62. The Jamaat-al-Muslimeen shot to international prominence in July 1990 when it launched a coup against the government of Prime Minister ANR Robinson, and has been under close scrutiny nationally and in the USA ever since, in relation to the travels and activities of its leading members. Rickey Singh, 'Trinidad's Muslimeen linked to al-Qaeda', *JAMAICAOBSERVER.COM*, September 4, 2002
63. In the next five years, Trinidad and Tobago is poised to become the largest producer of methanol and liquefied gas in the region. *Brief Remarks of Senator the Honourable Howard Chin Lee, Minister of National Security, Opening Session of the Fifth Defence Ministerial of the Americas*, Santiago de Chile, November 18-22, 2002.
64. *Brief Remarks of Senator the Honourable Howard Chin Lee, Minister of National Security, op. cit.*
65. The Jamaican government already ordered Vehicle and Cargo Inspection System (VACIS) X-Ray machines for its container ports and has established a Port Security Corps. In Anthony T. Bryan and Stephen E. Flynn, '*Free Trade, Smart Borders, and Homeland Security: US-Caribbean Cooperation in a New Era of Vulnerability*', The Dante Fascell North-South Centre, Working Paper Series, Paper No. 8, September 2002, 6.
66. See 'The Lessons of Race, Class and Politics in the Caribbean', Carib Editorial, in *The New York CaribNews*, Week ending August 13, 2002, 15.
67. The discussion was activated by a ruling of the Privy Council in March that mandatory death sentences were unconstitutional in seven Caribbean states, including Barbados. The ruling increased resolve by Caribbean countries to form a regional supreme court and scrap their 170-year relationship with the Privy Council, which they accuse of hindering efforts to enforce the death penalty. See 'Lawmakers Make it Easier to Execute Convicts in Barbados', *The New York CaribNews*, Week Ending August 27, 2002, 10.
68. 'No to His Master's Voice', *JAMAICAOBSERVER*.COM, September 4, 2002; 'To our Friend, the United States', *JAMAICAOBSERVER*.COM, September 11, 2002.
69. Anthony T. Bryan and Stephen E. Flynn, *op. cit.*
70. Anthony T. Bryan and Stephen E. Flynn, *op. cit.*, 5. Also, see, footnote 7.
71. *Remarks of U.S. Customs Commissioner Robert C. Bonner, Center for Strategic and International Studies*, CSIS, August 26, 2002.

72. 'These foreign ports will be evaluated against standards almost identical to those in the United States. An important element of the initiative is stationing US Customs inspectors overseas in landing and transhipment ports to inspect suspicious cargo bound for the United States before it is even loaded on a ship. Nations that agree to participate are given reciprocal privileges in US ports.' In Anthony T. Bryan and Stephen E. Flynn, *op. cit.*, 5.
73. Jane Bussey, 'Building Rings of Security', *The Miami Herald*, February 24, 2003, BM16.
74. For a perspective, see Rickey Singh, *op. cit.* (note 57).
75. Devon Dick, 'Why "Rebellion to Riot"?', *Jamaica Gleaner*, February 25, 2003, jamaica-gleaner.com.
76. 'Anti-smuggling initiative Jamaica. to become first English-speaking member of int'l coalition', *Jamaica Gleaner*, February 25, 2003, jamaica-gleaner.com.
77. 'In our case, we anticipate that if we get it wrong with the EPA negotiations and the WTO, not to mention the FTAA, our GDP could decline by at least 15 per cent'. Hon. Julian R. Hunte, quoted in 'Hunte Warns on Negotiations "We Must Get It Right"', CARICOM, Press Release 38/2003, February 28, 2003, in www.caricom.org.
78. See 'Caribbean Court of Justice a Reality in 2003', CARICOM, Press Secretary of the prime minister, Basseterre, St Kitts and Nevis, February 17, 2003 in www.caricom.org; 'Hunte Warns on Negotiations "We Must Get It Right"', *op. cit.*
79. Hon. Julian R. Hunte, quoted in CARICOM, Press Release 38/2003, February 28, 2003, in www.caricom.org.
80. One of the arguments regarding the CSME is the pace of implementation that is much too slow. 'Caribbean Economic and Political Unity Back on the Discussion Table', Editorial, *NYCaribNews Online*, Week of February 12–18, 2003.
81. 'The difficult process of Caribbean integration', *JAMAICAOBSERVER.COM*, February 23, 2003; Denis Kellman, 'Caribbean unity vital to region's success', *Barbados Advocate*, February 21, 2003; Patrick Knight, 'CARICOM – Still a long way to go', *Barbados Advocate*, February 20, 2003.
82. 'The War Few Countries Really Want', *Nation Newspaper*, Barbados, February 13, 2003.
83. 'The considerable instability of the oil business, is strongly felt in the Caribbean where most of the countries of the region benefit from the preferential prices from Venezuela through the state-owned Petroleos de Venezuela (PDVSA)'. See John Collins, 'Clear Implications for Puerto Rico and the Caribbean because of dependence on massive imports of petroleum products from there', *Caribbean Business*, April 18, 2002. It is important to note that Venezuela is producing oil at its normal level at present, but the war in Iraq only adds tension to an already sensitive issue.
84. 'The War Few Countries Really Want', *Nation Newspaper*, Barbados, February 13, 2003. Eric Lewis, 'Bush wants to fight, but he'll be at home', *Barbados Advocate*, February 21, 2003.
85. 'Humanity Answers Back', *JAMAICAOBSERVER.COM*, February 25, 2003.
86. Francisco Rojas Aravena, Director, Flasco, Chile, has developed the topic of neighbourliness.
87. As is the case in Brazil.
88. Trinidad and Tobago and Jamaica have shown an interest in this topic.
89. There are also other factors, such as the influence of the media. See Mayra Buvinic and Andrew R. Morrison, 'Living in a More Violent World', *Foreign Policy* (Spring 2000), 58–73.
90. David E. Lewis, Manchester Trade Ltd., '*The CBTPA as a Mechanism to Advance Trade and Investment Opportunities for the Caribbean*', Presentation for the 27th

Annual Conference of the Caribbean Studies Association, May 28–June 1, 2002, Nassau Beach Hotel, Nassau, Bahamas.

91. Not only Caribbean countries will be affected. In the case of Chile, see 'Guerra al terrorismo podría dañar libertad de comercio', *La Hora*, Santiago de Chile, November 15, 2003,1 and 8.
92. Manuel Orozco's suggestions are relevant in this case, *op. cit.*
93. Cultures of violence 'refers to societies that have experienced high levels of communal violence over a number of years so that violence, not peace, becomes the norm'. Paul R. Viotti, Mark V. Kauppi, *International Relations and World Politics: Security, Economy, Identity*, (2nd Edition) (Pentice Hall, 2001), 255.
94. On international terrorism, Stafford Neil, Jamaica's ambassador to the United Nations, reiterated Jamaica's support for the global fight, but pointed out that ' It is imperative that the root causes of terrorism be addressed in their political, economic, social and psychological dimensions'. At the same time, he said that Jamaica was committed to the principles of the organisation and 'reaffirms its faith' in the world body. See 'Jamaica reaffirms faith in the UN', *JAMAICAOBSERVER*.COM, September 23, 2002.
95. C. Clarke, 'CARICOM security ministers call for cooperation on crime', *JAMAICAOBSERVER.COM*, June 20, 2002.
96. Jamaican Independent Senator Trevor Munroe, quoted in 'Anti-narcotics cops urged to resist temptations', *JAMAICAOBSERVER.COM*, June 18, 2002.

16

The Anti-terrorism Capacity of Caribbean Security Forces

Colvin Bishop and Oral Khan

The events of September 11th provide perhaps the most dramatic illustration to date of the extraordinary degree of global economic, political and security interdependence. ... The overnight reordering of foreign policy imperative in defence of domestic and international security, and the enormous pressure being exerted on all countries to have their anti-terrorism credentials 'certified,' has large implications for relations between states. [1]
Hon. Billie Antoinette Miller

Perhaps the clearest lesson of the past decade is that transnational security threats can only be met with multinational security cooperation. Regional conflicts ... environmental disasters, even organized crime and trafficking, these can only be solved through the broadest possible cooperation. The same is true of terrorism. [2]
Lord George Robertson

Introduction

Before the events of September 11, 2001 in the United States of America, terrorism was not an issue that generated household discussion in the Caribbean. After that date, though, there have been many human interest stories that involved Caribbean people, some about those whose lives were lost in the World Trade Center and some about those who survived by God's amazing grace. Since then, terrorism has been planted into the region's consciousness in a way that has before been unknown. The reality that there are men and women who will employ extreme violence, in ways yet to be imagined, to change a way of life when the accepted political processes do not meet their ends, is now a phenomenon no one can dismiss. The means to execute violent acts are no longer only in the hands of state actors. Modern communication systems ensure that the results of terrorist actions are transmitted in real time, and visit us directly in our living rooms. Today, no country or region could believe itself to be unaffected by what has been described by many as 'the primary security threat of the twenty-first century' – terrorism.[3]

This chapter sets out to review the anti-terrorism capabilities of security forces in the Caribbean, paying particular attention to the English-speaking Caribbean. In doing this, it will discuss the prerequisite elements of an effective security initiative. Effectiveness, though, has to be viewed in relation to credible threats. We then proffer a response framework for an anti-terror programme and then set out to outline existing regional and national security arrangements that could be brought to bear in the fight against terrorism. Specifically, the chapter will consider whether there might be a more prominent role for the militaries in the region, particularly in planning for and coordinating the response to any terror incident.

It is important to explain our use of the terms *anti-terrorism* and *counter-terrorism*. The menu of options that may be employed to protect against terrorism is traditionally described as either anti-terrorist or counter-terrorist. Although these terms are at times used interchangeably, *anti-terrorism* is the term generally applied to mean all measures intended to prevent terrorist acts. These involve measures to deny would-be terrorists the resources, the means, and the opportunity to mobilise, organise, plan and execute activities to further their objectives. Anti-terrorism could include limited offensive action. On the other hand, *counter-terrorism* is the term generally applied to measures designed to combat, defeat, disrupt or destroy terrorists and their organisations.[4]

Effectiveness and Terrorism in Perspective

Effectiveness from a security standpoint has conceptual, moral and physical components.[5] In the context of an anti-terrorist initiative, the conceptual framework required has to encompass both international and national dimensions. It involves an understanding of the world-view on terrorism, an appreciation for the social and cultural complexities that characterise relations between states and also relations between the power elite and other social groups within a state. A comprehensive doctrine and body of principles, backed by appropriate legislative arrangements, will inform and regulate operational strategy for the pursuit of terrorists, their organisations and their sponsors. The moral component addresses such issues as leadership, motivation and management. Of significance is the mobilisation of popular public support for the strategy being pursued by the state, and the maintenance of public morale.

The cohesiveness and degree of synergy achieved among the various elements participating in the effort, the quality of leadership, the level of professionalism, and the *esprit de corps* of the military and law enforcement officers are all force multipliers that affect capabilities and effectiveness. As to the physical component, it involves manpower, appropriate technology, logistics, equipment, training and readiness. The existence of this hardware, independent of sound doctrine and firm moral underpinnings, is insufficient to prevent or to combat terrorism. While force alone may not achieve an anti-terrorist victory, neither can doctrine be relied upon to succeed alone. Diplomacy may present a bold face only when bolstered by credible force. Moreover, Western democracy is in no better position to stand on its own. Both a shield and a sword are required for its protection.

Terrorism remains a vexing and complex phenomenon that continues to defy attempts at fashioning international consensus. Boaz Ganor, director of the International Policy Institute for Counter-Terrorism, noted that, based on a survey of leading academics in the field, Schmidt and Youngman cited 109 definitions of terrorism in their book *Political Terrorism*.[6] Also that these definitions all reflected the particular political bias of the authors and were designed to either include or exclude certain groups in furtherance of specific political ends. Some terrorism commentators feel there will never be a definition that is objective and internationally accepted. Further, they question whether such is necessary. For them, the ends are served by insinuating, 'what looks like a terrorist, sounds like a terrorist, and behaves like a terrorist is a terrorist.'[7]

Nonetheless, Ganor suggests that the absence of an agreed upon definition would make it impossible to either formulate or enforce any international action against terrorism. He cites, as an example, the frequently encountered difficulty in obtaining extradition for suspected terrorists, due to the explicit exclusion of political offences from some extradition treaties.[8] The terrorism literature also highlights that even within some countries, there is no definitional unanimity. As an example, the United States Subcommittee on Terrorism and Homeland Security discovered that many United States government agencies that had a responsibility for counter-terrorism had their own definition of terrorism.[9] The committee remarked on the insecurity that this created when all participants were not clear about 'what activity constituted a terrorist act and who should be designated a terrorist'.[10]

Regardless of the definitional quagmire, security planners at the strategic level have to be guided by some theoretical conceptualisation and characterisation of terrorism and who is a terrorist, what constitutes a terrorist organisation, and what actions or associations would constitute support for terrorism. Many scholars have proposed working definitions that condemned all acts, except those committed in the fight for the right to self-determination against foreign and racist regimes, and labelled these as criminal. The United Nations Security Council (UNSC), by way of Resolution 1269, went further, however, and condemned

> all acts, methods and practices of terrorism as criminal and unjustifiable, regardless of their motivation, in all their forms and manifestations, where and by whomever committed, in particular those which could threaten international peace and security.[11]

However, the issue of definition remains a pressing matter, since the international community has been summoned to support the *global war against terrorism*. With the United States of America having declared that countries would be regarded as friend or foe based on their willingness to support this war, neutrality or ambivalence could place a country in the enemy's camp.

We have, however, been left with the problem of distinguishing between those unconventional acts of violence that may stand to gain legitimacy through revolutionary movements or struggles for freedom and those that are abhorrent in public perception. The terrorist could still be mistaken for a freedom fighter. Ganor, perhaps, goes the farthest in setting the distinction. In his view, where the military, other security forces and the political leadership are the targets of a violent struggle in order to achieve political aims then what we have is guerrilla warfare. His proposed definition, which we accept, posits 'terrorism is the intentional use of, or threat to use violence against civilians or against civilian targets, in order to attain political aims'.[12] The acts are designed to be psychological attacks on public morale in order to engender a climate characterised by fear, anxiety and insecurity. Three important elements feature in his definition. The first is the use of, or threat to use, violence. Second, the aim of the activity is always political: changing the regime, changing the people in power, changing social or economic policies, and so forth. The third is that the targets are civilian. Thus, terrorism is distinguished from other types of political violence, such as guerrilla warfare and insurrection.[13]

There has been no structured discourse on the definitional issue in the Caribbean. Perhaps this is so having regard to the perceived lower threat scenario in the region, and thus the attitude has been to be a follower as far as this matter is concerned. However, some governments in the region have attempted to stretch the definition of terrorism to include heinous violent crimes, in order to secure harsh punishment for offenders. For instance, in Jamaica, the 1992 amendment to the *Offences Against the Person Law* (1864) sought to retain the offence of capital murder and the death penalty for certain classes of murder. Among the murders designated as capital murder were those 'committed by a person in the course or furtherance of an act of terrorism, that is to say, an act involving the use of violence by that person which, by reason of its nature and extent, is calculated to create a state of fear in the public or any section of the public'.[14]

Even so, the state in Jamaica may not loosely label acts of violence as terrorism, as the courts have shown intolerance for this. In a test case brought before the Judicial Committee of the Privy Council (Appeal 56 of 1995), Leroy Lamey, who had been convicted of capital murder on the basis that the circumstances of the murder constituted a terrorist act designed to drive fear in the public, had his appeal upheld. The judges rejected the argument that any murder committed in a manner that created a state of fear in any section of the public would satisfy the terrorism test. They held that there needed to be a double intent both to murder and to create fear. In their view the viciousness of a murder and the fact that it causes those who become aware of it to be fearful were therefore not sufficient conditions to label an act as terrorist.[15]

Threat

Radical Islamic fundamentalism is widely regarded as the pre-eminent transnational terrorist threat. While signs of the presence of this movement have been observed in Latin America (Israeli Embassy bombing Buenos Aries 1992 and the Panama aircraft bombing 1994), the Caribbean region has been spared of any major attention from Islamic fundamentalists for over eight years. Al Qaeda is known to have extended its network far and wide. Reports of the discovery of maps of Mexico and Brazil in a safe house in

Afghanistan have heightened concerns that Al Qaeda may be seeking partners in the Latin American region and could well find them in the cash rich drug syndicates. Historically, however, the unconventional use of force in Latin America and the Caribbean have been linked more with Marxist-Leninist ideology, and the targets of the violence were not usually civilian. Thus, according to our definition adopted from Ganor, the incidents of violence that were once observed tended to achieve legitimacy as revolutionary movements as opposed to terrorist activity. In any event, since Grenada in the period 1979–83, no government in the English-speaking Caribbean has been changed by revolutionary violence.[16]

Although the Caribbean region has continued to be relatively peaceful, the region has witnessed isolated acts of terrorism or events in which terrorist tactics have been used. The entire region shared in the tragedy when the Cubana Airline was blown up in 1976 soon after the flight departed the Grantley Adams International Airport in Barbados.[17] In Trinidad and Tobago, unexpectedly, a disaffected group stormed the national Parliament chamber and bombed the police headquarters in Port of Spain on July 27, 1990.[18] Those events in 1990 had such a significant psychological effect that any rumour that suggested the possibility of a recurrence encouraged panic buying and sent citizens home hurriedly. While the security forces were able to bring an end to the attempted coup within one week, the public openly expressed concern about the failure of the intelligence community to detect the event beforehand. In the prevailing global security environment, though, the region must be ever vigilant. The Caribbean is an integral part of a world that is driven by the dynamics of globalisation with its continuous flows of information, capital and people. The one dominant superpower is reported to be hated by some and envied by others, and is inextricably tied to the Caribbean.

The Caribbean has long been linked to the rest of the world through its economic structures. Perhaps more than anything else, these economic ties have driven the generation of concerns about the possibility of terrorist attacks, and have not allowed the region to be a bystander in the battle against terrorism. The fact that Caribbean countries depend significantly on trade and investment from the United States has heightened concerns about the possibility of attacks. It is widely accepted that, as targets within the continental United States are hardened, United States business interests and personnel abroad could become terrorist targets. Warnings of attacks on oil, gas and electricity infrastructure in the United States have thus been extended to countries, such as Trinidad and Tobago, that have large United States investment in its oil and gas sector, and where the oil companies themselves have stepped-up their security. In highlighting United States investor concerns, the ambassador to Trinidad and Tobago, in an address to an international conference held in Trinidad in May 2003, stated: 'American investors are examining very carefully how the Caribbean is responding to international organised crime and terrorism.' He also observed that the region might be in danger of losing investments to 'competitors who are better prepared to provide a safer and more secure environment', and called for the passage of legislation to support the fight against terrorism.[19]

Thus, it is clear that although by itself the Caribbean may not provide high payoff targets for a terrorist organisation seeking an international audience, the region's economic well-being requires that its security processes and critical physical infrastructure protection be given prompt attention. Security at regional airports and seaports have to be tightened in the light of the fact that the United States and Britain, as part of their own security measures, seek to ensure that people and cargo, particularly containerised cargo, are inspected using rigid standards before they reach their destinations. Given the impracticality of examining all containers on arrival, Caribbean countries are being strongly encouraged to either step up security or risk an interruption of trade. Another suggestion has been that United States customs and immigration officials be posted in the region to inspect outward-bound goods and people.[20] Caribbean countries, particularly Organisation of Eastern Caribbean States (OECS) members, have also expressed strong concern for the shipment of nuclear waste through the region in the event that transportation ships are targeted by terrorist organisations. The concerns are born out of the fact that beaches are critically important to the economic survival of these small states.

In Trinidad and Tobago, the economy is based primarily on the production and export of petroleum, petroleum-based products and liquefied natural gas (LNG). Any direct attack on these production facilities, or on the electricity and water supplies that support both the industrial and other national requirements, will have devastating effects. This effect may well be felt throughout the region given the dire economic circumstances of some islands that have already had to request regional and international financial support.[21] In addition, and connected to the concerns about physical security, there is also the matter of 'energy supply security'.[22] After a high-level meeting in March 2003 held in Washington, the minister of energy of Trinidad and Tobago reported that there was a concern about 'ensuring long term energy security' regarding natural gas.[23] United States reserves are being depleted and Canada, a major supplier itself, is predicting a shortage. According to the energy minister, this situation underlines the opportunity for Trinidad and Tobago to continue to be 'the largest supplier as a country, as a location – the largest supplier of LNG to the United States'.[24] Hence any attack against this centre of gravity has enormous destructive potential and underscores the perception that economic vulnerability is at the core of the region's insecurity.[25]

Another consideration for the region is its attractiveness as a potential staging area for terror attacks. The region's geography and topography, fairly modern communications, and political linkages could all facilitate terrorist operations. The Caribbean is easily a strategic gateway to all the Americas and Europe, and is accessible by modern air and sea carriers so that it could become a link to any part of the world. The region's largely island character permits entry from any number of approaches. The British, Dutch and French still have dependent territories in the Caribbean. These political connections provide customs, immigration, and transportation arrangements that allow easy movement of people, money, and arms. Further, as part of its own economic development, the region is moving towards the freer movement of persons within the area. Offshore banking facilities in particular could facilitate the easy movement of money. Therefore, the region provides a facilitative environment for transnational operations that could give access to both regional and international targets without potential terrorists having to face off with militarily stronger adversaries.[26]

Transnational crime and its architecture could easily facilitate terrorist operations. In this regard, a number of incidents in the region have provided indicators as to the region's vulnerability. It has been well documented that the narcotics trade presents the most pressing danger to the Caribbean region. Specific to the matter at hand is the financing of terrorist activity through the proceeds of drug trafficking and the use of established routes and arrangements to move people, money and *matériel* to target areas. In addition to the narcotic infrastructure, newspaper reports on other matters during January 2003 underline the hemisphere's interconnectivity. It was reported that Allen Muhammad, the sniper suspect in the Washington killings, made his living in Antigua and Barbuda by selling falsified documents to immigrants trying to reach the United States. It was revealed that 'Muhammad sold at least 20 falsified documents – from US birth certificates to drivers licences ....'[27] The deputy commissioner of police in Guyana reported that Guyana police were investigating whether 'foreign mercenaries' were being hired to assist in an ongoing gang war in that country. This concern was expressed after police killed 'several foreigners in gunfights during crime sweeps and have found weapons suggesting Guyanese criminals have outside help'.[28] Prior to the shooting incident, there had been no alarm about the movement of these persons into Guyana. Individual countries have also felt the impact of rising crime and the possibility of its links to terrorism. In January 2003 in Trinidad and Tobago, two British cruise ship companies stopped all visits to the country until further notice. The shipping lines'actions were driven by a notice from the British Foreign and Commonwealth Office that warned British nationals about the possibility of terrorist attacks.[29] While other cruise lines have continued to visit without incident, the advisory, nonetheless, has had its impact and the Trinidad and Tobago government had to institute a damage control plan. High-level officials were dispatched to London, Washington and New York to assure officials that Trinidad and Tobago remained a safe destination. Officials in London indicated that the advisory would remain in effect until a security reassessment reflected differently. In response, the prime minister of Trinidad and Tobago told the House of Representatives that the claims were unfounded, but following the incidents in Mombassa, Dar es Salam and Bali, governments have become extremely cautious and have adopted a doctrine of 'just in case'.[30] Another commentator noted that the advisory was 'out of an abundance of caution rather than in response to any information that *[was]* credible and worth taking seriously'.[31] Nonetheless, these events, coupled with the requests of the region's major trading partners to tighten security, have raised the security posture of the countries in the region.

Notwithstanding the region's freedom from attack from international terrorists, there are countries in the Caribbean that have witnessed waves of serious violence, notably in Haiti, Guyana, Trinidad and Tobago, Jamaica, and the Dominican Republic. This violence has severely undermined confidence in the state security machinery in those countries and, consequently, has left many citizens living in fear. Analyses of the root causes of the violence have been undertaken and it is instructive that the causes generally cited bear a striking resemblance to some of the root causes of terrorism: relative deprivation, injustice that marginalises, inequality and other social ills. While governments in the region have resisted using the terrorist label, antagonists have clearly employed terror tactics. There has been more than a hint of political motivation behind many incidents, although the political objective in some cases tended to be more local than national, that is, to seize and maintain informal control over communities and not so much over states.[32]

It might be useful to observe that civilians (non-combatants) who are the victims of violence are not so much concerned whether their attackers meet the international criteria to be called terrorists or not. They regard themselves and their communities as being terrorised. For victims, the nature of the attack and its effect upon them is of more importance than whether or not there is international support for their attackers, or whether bombs or guns or poison gas is employed, or if there is a grand political design behind it. They are concerned about their safety and the safety of their communities and will demand action from the state to protect them.

Regional Responses

The similarity between the root cause of terrorism and some of the causes of violent crimes has been earlier noted. Strategic initiatives that have sought to deal with the complex crime situation in Caribbean countries could also contribute to the prevention of terrorist acts in the region. In this regard, the work of the Regional Task Force on Crime and Security (Task Force) and its recommendations to Caribbean Heads of Government need to be considered. The Task Force was established at the Twenty-second Meeting of the Conference of Heads of Government of the Caribbean Community (CARICOM) in Nassau, Bahamas in July 2001. It was mandated by the heads to examine the major causes and contributing factors to crime and was required to present recommendations for a regional response. The Task Force focused on interrelated problems, illicit drugs and firearms and terrorism.[33]

The Task Force comprised representatives from each member state of CARICOM and from other regional organisations. These include the Association of Caribbean Commissioners of Police (ACCP), the Regional Security System (RSS), the secretariats of CARICOM and the OECS, and the University of the West Indies (UWI). The Caribbean Customs Law Enforcement Council (CCLEC) and the Caribbean Financial Action Task Force (CFATF) also were invited to participate. The Task Force has recommended to the Heads of Government a broad range of policy initiatives and specific action ideas that, in some instances, build on existing regional initiatives. Notably for the fight against terrorism, the recommendations include the establishment of collaborative arrangements with other hemispheric nations and proposals for information exchange and the development of databases with pertinent information.[34]

At the special session in the Bahamas in October 2001, heads of government recognised the wide-ranging impact of the September 11 attacks on Caribbean economic security and reaffirmed the need for the region to adopt new security standards. More specifically, the heads underlined the need for 'extraordinary vigilance and co-ordination in the future, to ensure that our territories, our institutions and our citizens, are not used in any manner to facilitate the activities of terrorists to undermine our national or regional security'.[35] In pursuit of this broad strategic objective, the meeting mandated a set of operational level goals that closely reflected the recommendations of the Task Force. These goals encompassed ensuring adherence to relevant hemispheric and international conventions; upgrading or enacting security laws; implementing best practices to secure ports of entry and to protect borders, coastlines and airspace; taking action to deny terrorist financing; and developing arrangements for intelligence gathering and sharing. The meeting further directed security agencies to conduct an urgent review of national and regional capabilities that would be needed to give effect to the operational tasks outlined and, as required, to propose any appropriate strategies.[36]

Further, in June 2002 at the Thirty-second Regular Session of the Organisation of American States (OAS) General Assembly Meeting in Barbados, Caribbean countries, except Cuba that has been suspended from the OAS, signed the Inter-American Convention Against Terrorism that was negotiated as a direct response to the September 11 attacks. The Convention built upon United Nations Security Council Resolution (UNSCR) 1373 and its stated purposes are to 'prevent, punish, and eliminate terrorism'.[37] It is intended to improve regional cooperation and to demonstrate regional solidarity in the fight against terrorism as well as facilitate the implementation of a number of the mandates directly connected to UNSCR 1373. Briefly, the Convention has sought to commit state parties to sign and ratify the relevant United Nations anti-terror instruments, to act upon the recommendations intended to prohibit terrorist financing, to create an architecture for information exchange and to deny safe haven to suspected terrorists. The Convention provides an opportunity for Caribbean states to benefit from the sharing of training and experience.[38]

Since these hemispheric and subregional decisions were taken, Caribbean countries have reached varied levels of compliance with the obligations agreed to in the Bahamas Declaration and the Inter-American Convention, and with the recommendations of the Task Force. Specific terrorism legislation has been enacted in Antigua and Barbuda, Barbados, Grenada, Guyana and St Kitts and Nevis, while legislation is being drafted in Trinidad and Tobago. Other security-related laws and practices on immigration and passports have been enacted and upgraded. One example is the new *Immigration and Passport*

Act of St Kitts and Nevis. In Jamaica, and Trinidad and Tobago, machine-readable passports are to be introduced as a response to the problem of passport fraud. However, while there has been urgent action to pass legislation, there are no indicators that point to regional collaboration in the drafting process. This legal side, therefore, would require further study to minimise or eliminate any difficulties that could potentially arise for regional security forces in the execution of their tasks.[39] Across the region, information gathering and sharing regimes are being streamlined or developed and, generally, law enforcement capacity is being upgraded. Action has also been taken at regional airports and seaports to more efficiently monitor the movement of persons and goods. In Barbados, for instance, after a thorough review at its air and seaports, new guidelines have been issued to ensure compliance with new international standards for civil aviation. The country has amended its *Money Laundering (Prevention and Control) Act*, and the M*utual Assistance in Criminal Matters Act,* and has agreed to increased cooperation in intelligence gathering analysis and dissemination with CARICOM partners.[40] In the case of Jamaica, several important pieces of legislation are in the process of being drafted. These will have the effect of tightening security at the borders, and extending the powers of the state to collect biometric data on suspects. Administrative changes are being implemented to improve the organisation for intelligence productions by the consolidation of police intelligence agencies. New technologies are being applied at the ports of entry to improve surveillance capabilities and plans are underway to also conduct electronic surveillance over other selected public spaces. These are all areas in which even incremental improvements will count.[41]

The real security policy challenge for the region, though, is not the enactment of legislation, but its implementation. The affordability issue has been the constant at the centre of the implementation challenge. Caribbean countries, constrained as they are by their limited resources, have always had leaders who viewed alleviating the social condition of their peoples as a foremost priority area for action. In these circumstances, the experience has been that security initiatives have largely been birthed and funded by extra-regional countries and, understandably, developed as part of their own defence strategy. In this regard, the regional funding of the Regional Task Force on Crime and Security, although in its early stages, has been a positive exception, and provides a possible positive signal for the future. Nonetheless, different perceptions of the nature and imminence of threats to the region have existed among countries and it is unlikely to be different in this instance. Although

Caribbean governments have made calls for action in the aftermath of events such as September 11, 2001, Grenada in 1979, and Trinidad and Tobago in 1990, the experience has been that those calls have not been translated into the allocation of significant resources. In large measure, outside of the pronouncements, CARICOM remains a part of the regional security issue. One writer has asserted: 'If it is indeed a regional priority, it was not an urgent one, except when immediate and largely unforeseeable events dictated otherwise.'[42]

A Framework for an Anti-terror Response

Since the events of September 11, 2001, numerous approaches have been proffered as to how to shape national, or in the case of the Caribbean, regional preparedness and responses to terrorism. Following the working definition of anti-terrorism noted earlier in the chapter, we have adopted the approach of Campbell and Flournoy. This has been based on three broad objectives: preventing attacks in the region; enhancing the region's ability to protect itself against attack; and if an attack does occur, developing or improving, as is appropriate, national and regional capacity to initially respond to it and manage its consequences.[43] The first objective of preventing attacks in the region must be the main effort. The Caribbean could ill-afford the costs involved in recovery if the core of any of the region's economies is attacked. Further, a secure environment is critical in order to maintain the free and relaxed lifestyle that has attracted billions of dollars in investment and a vibrant tourist trade. Plain truth be told, if tourists become uncertain about whether they will make it back home they are much less likely to visit. For the Eastern Caribbean, a subregion already prone to natural disasters and still reeling from the effects of adjusted trade practices, prevention could be life or death.

Prevention requires arrangements that would detect and neutralise threats long before they occur. The aim here should be to stop threats as far away as possible from the region. This means having countries work effectively with each other in the region, but also with hemispheric partners. This entails structuring arrangements with countries with which the region has not had traditional security relationships. Within national borders, this means partnering with private sector organisations and making full use of the resources of multinational corporations to offset resource and capability limitations. Specific to the United States, understandably, that country has shown that it intends to deal with threats before they get to its homeland.

With the Caribbean having been labelled the 'Third Border' of the United States, the region may well have to be prepared to allow some incursion on its sovereignty.[44] Consistent with this view, other writers have suggested that Caribbean countries, as part of international arrangements, should collaborate 'to guarantee as far as possible the security of the United States ...' as this is in the region's best interest.[45] They express the view that this collaboration would allow the region to take advantage of access to information and arrangements that would benefit its own security.[46]

The second objective will be to enhance the ability of the individual Caribbean countries, and then the region, to protect against attacks. This has to start with governments identifying an agency to lead the anti-terror effort and the subsequent development of a coordinated strategy and operational plan to address the threat. Who is to lead needs to be made clear to ensure that what is a complex mission is not made any more difficult than necessary. Creating the synergy that derives from unity of effort has to be the key principle that guides these operations. The lead agency must work through clearly established protocols and legal mechanisms that mandate contributing agencies to work together for the common good. This agency must be the point of contact for the terrorist response mission and must take the responsibility to educate the public and test all plans and systems. The lead agency must be responsible for the development of contingency plans in concert with other key contributors. Advance planning and war-gaming exercises are central to being able to identify problems and test solutions.

The anti-terror mission is not a law-enforcement, or intelligence, or a military one. Rather, there must be valued input from all of these and several other agencies, such as customs, immigration, the private sector, local government bodies, ministries of health, national emergency organisations and the public at large. Investigative and intelligence agencies that now work apart, have to establish mechanisms to collaborate and share information in ways that would not compromise their own operations and sources. Clearly defined roles and responsibilities must be established for each contributor as well as expectations and performance levels. Role definition must also include a frank assessment of operational units that identifies capability limitations on one hand, and any inability to deliver on required missions. These will drive training needs.

The third objective will be to develop and improve, where applicable, the ability of the region to respond to and manage the consequences of an attack. As far as a response is concerned, there must be some counter-terrorist capability that could be used to eliminate an opposing force. The experiences of others have shown that the effective management of the results or effects of an attack is the key element in maintaining public confidence and reducing the feelings of insecurity that are brought on after a terrorist attack. Fire fighters, police, the military in support of the civil authority, emergency health service/medical teams and national emergency management agencies in the region will be the most important elements of an effective consequence management. These organisations must be given the resources, equipment and training they need to do their jobs. At another level, those responsible for public works, water management, telephone services and electricity supply would be integral to ensuring that the first persons to respond could function and thus must be a part of the development and execution of contingency plans. Non-governmental agencies and local government/community organisations must be made well aware of their roles in the recovery effort.

Security Forces in the English-speaking Caribbean

As was indicated earlier, the anti-terrorism effort has to be a multi-organisation task and, as such, will involve organisations that would not be included as part of a country's security forces in the traditional sense. When the term *security forces* is used in the English-speaking Caribbean, it generally refers to both the constabulary and the military forces in the region. The more developed English-speaking Caribbean countries – Barbados, Belize, Guyana, Jamaica and Trinidad and Tobago – have standing armies and thus relatively more capability and are able to execute some tasks on their own. The Bahamas has only a coast guard whose members perform limited land operations. Of the OECS countries, only Antigua and Barbuda and St Kitts and Nevis have standing military units. The other islands have Special Service Units (SSUs) as part of their police forces. These units are generally of platoon size. The troops have been mostly trained as light infantry. The inventories include assault rifles, light machine guns, small calibre mortars and handheld antitank weapons. Guyana has an artillery battery and air defence capability, although now there is difficulty to maintain and support the unit. Some of the countries have aircraft that are used for search and rescue, surveillance and limited general transport. Generally, regional armed forces are small, not well funded, and have been dependent on foreign assistance for their training and development.[47]

Regional defence forces have twice operated under a unified command: in Operation Urgent Fury in Grenada, and Operation Restore Democracy/ UNMIH in Haiti. These experiences prove that there is sufficient commonality in doctrine and standard operational procedures to allow for effective military cooperation within the region. The fact that the majority of the officers of the defence forces in the region are trained in the same foreign military schools will serve to help maintain this commonality in doctrine. The annual regional training exercise, Exercise Trade Winds, and the annual Caribbean Nations Security Conference (CANSEC), both of which are significantly supported by the United States Southern Command (SOUTHCOM), provide additional opportunities for regional militaries to build cooperation and understanding at the tactical, operational and strategic levels. CANSEC is particularly important as it provides a forum for the heads of military forces to exchange ideas, explore issues of mutual concern and initiate mechanisms for cooperation on security-related matters.[48]

One such mechanism established by regional military heads with the support of SOUTHCOM is the Caribbean Information Sharing Network (CISN). The recommendation to establish the network was made at the May 1998 military chiefs conference, then known as the Caribbean Island Nations Security Conference (CINSEC). CISN is a subsidiary body of CANSEC. Its primary purpose is to form a collective information-sharing mechanism that meets the needs of the law enforcement and military organisations in the region during times of peace and crisis. Membership includes the countries of English-speaking Caribbean, the Dominican Republic, Haiti, Suriname, SOUTHCOM and other regional agencies.[49]

The network supports imagery, exploitation, targeting, brainstorming, working groups, audio/video conferencing, among other applications. It is intended that this will provide a platform for collaborating on transnational threats and other areas of common interest in the region. The network was designed to allow each country to progress at its own speed and requires that each member meet its own operating expenses. Since its introduction, participation in the network has been inconsistent. One can say that for most of the Caribbean countries, the capabilities of the network are untested and so it has not been given a chance to prove its credibility and reliability. The CISN Board, at its March 2003 meeting in the Bahamas, directed that there be a critical examination to determine and address the issues that create this state of affairs, as the platform could be a key piece of the regional architecture in the fight against terrorism and other transnational threats.[50]

Linked to information sharing is the production of intelligence, the key success factor in the anti-terrorism effort. Anglophone Caribbean states, perhaps with the exception of Jamaica and Trinidad and Tobago, maintain the Police Special Branch as their sole security intelligence agency. Intelligence training is not readily available in the region and foreign partners, until recently, have been reluctant to offer intelligence training above the basic level. The region is at a critical juncture. Governments must consider the establishment of intelligence agencies that may be focused on specific national and transnational threats. The information age has opened up fresh new avenues for information collection, processing and sharing of intelligence. There are hurdles to be overcome, though, before the benefits of the technology can be appropriated. These include the attitude of suspicion, concerns over propriety, and the tendency to insularity.

The Role of the Military

It has been well documented and acknowledged that the fight against terrorism requires much more than military inputs. Non-military assets have been deemed to be critical. Nonetheless, it has also been recognised that the military as an entity could bring a range of competencies to bear on the terror threat that may not all together reside in any one organisation elsewhere. The Caribbean is, relatively speaking, no different in this regard. The region is also unique in the sense that its limited resources and capacity constrain the security policy options. This uniqueness is linked as well to the fact that an attack on the Caribbean's economic and other supporting infrastructure could threaten the very existence of some countries. Foreigners may stay away and foreign firms may invest elsewhere if they feel unsafe. The anti-terrorism effort therefore has to be a priority national and regional security concern, and as such suggests the need for 'an expanded and obligatory role' for the militaries in the region.

In the current Caribbean security environment, police forces and other law enforcement agencies have primacy for law enforcement. Moreover, except in Cuba, this obtains in the context of the principle that all aspects of security policy and operations should be under the control of the civil authority. Here, the military is used to augment civilian law enforcement agencies and is always in a supporting role. However, Caribbean police forces are fully committed with their primary law enforcement mission and it is now commonplace to have armies deployed on the streets and on the seas alongside the police in support of anti-crime efforts. A legal framework guides these deployments and prescribes the processes through which assistance is sought and approved. A key point, though, is that the scope of any additional measures that would be required both to prevent and manage the consequences in the aftermath of an attack would very likely be well beyond the existing capacity of the region's police forces, and therefore will require the active involvement of the armed forces. Further examination and remodelling of the legal parameters within which the military would execute its role in any anti-terror programme is therefore a key task for the civilian authority.

Leadership of the strategic planning, operational coordination and the execution of some tactical level tasks in a multi-agency effort is a key and complex undertaking in the management of an anti-terror programme. Caribbean countries simply cannot afford to create the complex organisations as have been done in other countries, such as the Department of Homeland Security in the United States. As well, the perception of the threat differs from country to country in the region and, as such, the creation of structures that focus on the anti-terror issue would essentially be based on national and not regional interest. Under these circumstances, we would contend that the region's militaries are the best poised to provide the leadership required to mount any credible anti-terror response. Of all the security organisations in the region, the military, particularly through the training officers receive, have trained planners who could be refocused to the anti-terror mission. As was suggested earlier, military missions are now complex. This plus the region's complex environment provide good ground for military officer training, both in the region and at international military institutions. The common doctrinal base and the practice that have evolved provide a significant starting point for a regional program.

However, the delivery of security requires that the region's military forces become intimately familiar with their potential battle space. This battle space is not only the physical arrangements but also the systems and processes intended to ensure that the inter-agency challenges are identified and worked through to a point where mutual trust and confidence exists. It must be clear that the role of the military is to be the core planners and providers of the coordinating function. This will include the responsibility for testing the response systems, checking the plans for the security of critical infrastructure and supporting law enforcement as required in operational, logistical and technical aspects of anti-terror operations.

Analysis of this specific environment will reveal gaps in capabilities that require attention. Just as important, this analysis will identify which agency is best suited to deliver the capability, the actions business firms can take to harden their own potential target areas, and how actions are to be coordinated. At the political level, the ministry of government that has responsibility for the defence should be given the lead in order to facilitate the assignment of the anti-terror mission to the military. This approach also gives a focus to policy, planning, resource allocation, developing operational solutions and improving interagency cooperation. Anti-terrorism efforts can be viewed as a unique form of warfare that requires special training, tactics and equipment for success. An anti-terrorist force must be appropriately trained and equipped to defeat the potential enemy. This means dedicating troops to the anti-terror mission.

Conclusion

Protecting the Caribbean region against terror attacks is an extremely complex and challenging task, which is rendered more difficult by the openness of the region; due partly to the importance of tourism, foreign investment and other international commerce. Security has to be balanced against the freedom the Caribbean people so dearly cherish and which in itself is an attraction to visitors. Nonetheless, there is a clear need for individual countries to develop the security architecture required to coordinate the plethora of agencies that have responsibility for different aspects of an anti-terror programme. These national arrangements then have to be extended so that the region will have available a range of competencies that are appropriate for the mission.

Once plans are developed they must be implemented. Given the centrality of intelligence to the fight against terrorism and the enormity of the challenge, Caribbean governments should maximise the use of the existing CISN network for information sharing, take swift action to identify other shortfalls in current intelligence capabilities and processes and develop clear priorities and a comprehensive plan of action for addressing them. The militaries in the region are well positioned to be the main contributors to the planning and coordinating function in this effort in addition to the other tactical level tasks that would be assigned to them. In the context of the region having to make best use of its available resources, the region's defence forces cannot be overlooked for this role. The anti-terror battle is not an easy task but it is a necessary one. Governments must play their part and lead in this effort and provide the political will that is required to move ongoing initiatives beyond the planning stages.

Notes

1. Billie A. Miller, *Managing Foreign Policy in an Interdependent World,* Florida International University Honors College Occasional Paper, Vol. 1 No. 1, 2001, p. 5.

Miller was then deputy prime minister and minister of foreign affairs and foreign trade of Barbados.

2. Lord George Robertson, 'The Role of the Military in Combating Terrorism.' Speech delivered at the Second NATO-Russia Conference on the Role of the Military in Combating Terrorism, Moscow, December 9, 2002, p. 4, available from http://www.foreignpolicy.org.tr/ eng/nato/robertson_091202.htm. Robertson was secretary general of NATO from 1999 to 2003.
3. Lord Robertson, 'The Role of the Military in Combating Terrorism', 1.
4. See United States Department of Defence, *1997 Annual Defence Report,* published by the Terrorism Research Centre, 4.
5. See discussion on military effectiveness in *Design for Military Operations – The British Military Doctrine,* Army Code No. 71451, 1989, 31–36.
6. Boaz Ganor, 'Defining Terrorism: Is One Man's Terrorist Another Man's Freedom Fighter', available from http://www.ict.org.il/articles/articledet.cfm?articleid=49, p. 1.
7. Boaz Ganor, 'Terrorism: No Prohibition without Definition,' available at http://www.ict.org.il/articles/articledet.cfm?articleid=393, 1.
8. Ganor, 'Defining Terrorism,' 15.
9. This subcommittee was given the responsibility to examine and make recommendations to improve the counter-terrorism and homeland security capabilities of the USA. It assessed the Central Intelligence Agency, the National Security Agency and the Federal Bureau of Investigation after the events of September11, 2001. US Congress, House Permanent Select Committee on Intelligence, Report of the Subcommittee on Terrorism and Homeland Security, July 2002, available from http://www.house.gov/harman/terrorism/ 071702_Report.html. See pp. 2–4 of its report dated July 17, 2002.
10. Ibid.
11. United Nations Security Council Resolution 1269, October 18, 1999.
12. Boaz Ganor, 'Defining Terrorism', 7.
13. Ibid, 7–8.
14. *Offences Against the Person (Amendment) Act 1992* (14 of 1992).
15. *Lamey (Leroy) v R* 48, West Indian Reports, pp. 282–286.
16. In 1979, Maurice Bishop led the New Jewel Movement and overthrew the Sir Eric Gairy government in Grenada by force of arms. In 1983, Bishop and other key members of his government were murdered during an internal revolt that was led by Bernard Coard, the second in command of the Bishop regime. The 4-year revolution was quelled when the island was invaded in October 1983 by United States forces during Operation Urgent Fury. English-speaking Caribbean military and police forces contributed to a peacekeeping force that assisted in restoring order.
17. See Dion E. Phillips, 'Terrorism and Security in the Caribbean: the 1976 Cubana Disaster off Barbados,' *Terrorism*, Vol. 14/4 (1991):209–19.
18. On July 27, 1990, members of the Jamaat al Muslimeen, a militant group that operates outside of the mainstream Muslim community in Trinidad and Tobago, firebombed the national police headquarters in Port of Spain, the capital of Trinidad and Tobago, occupied the parliament building and the main television station. The group held the country's prime minister and other members of the government hostage in the parliament building.
19 The ambassador's remarks were made at a conference on International Crime and Terrorism: Implications for Business and Caribbean Economies that was held in Trinidad in May 2003. See 'US envoy warns T&T: Address Terrorism or lose Investors,' *Trinidad Guardian*, May 22, 2003, 7.
20. See Anthony T. Bryan and Stephen E. Flynn, 'Terrorism, Porous Borders, and Homeland Security: The Case for US-Caribbean Cooperation,' North-South Centre Update,

October 22, 2001, 4. See also 'Conference to focus on TT border security,' *Newsday*, October 14, 2002, 9.

21. See 'Dominican Prime Minister heads to IMF Headquarters,' *The Daily Observer*, May 12, 2003, 13. See also 'IDB: Caribbean survival depends on T&T economy,' *Trinidad Guardian*, May 26, 2003, 8.
22. See 'US to partly fund study of regional pipeline,' *Trinidad Guardian*, March 31, 2003, 16.
23. Ibid.
24. Ibid.
25. Anthony T. Bryan, 'The State of the Region: Trends Affecting the Future of Caribbean Security,' in Michael C. Desch, Jorge I. Dominguez and Andres Serbin, eds., *From Pirates to Drug Lords: The Post-Cold War Caribbean Security Environment* (Albany, New York: State University of New York Press, 1998), 35.
26. Lieutenant Colonel Colvin Bishop, 'Caribbean Regional Security: The Challenges to Creating Formal Military Relationships in the English-speaking Caribbean.' (Thesis, US Army Command and General Staff College, Fort Leavenworth, Kansas, 2002), 40.
27. 'Antigua wants to quiz US suspect,' *Newsday*, January 9, 2003, 25.
28. See 'Foreign Hitmen in Guyana gangs,' *Sunday Guardian*, January 19, 2003, 19.
29. See 'Cruise ships pull out ... fearful of T& T terror threat,' *Trinidad Express*, January 16, 2003. See also 'Trinidad scrambles to keep its image as a tourist destination,' *Trinidad Guardian*, January 22, 2003, 23.
30. Ibid.
31. Ibid.
32. See the Report of the National Committee on Crime and Violence of Jamaica, June 11, 2002. Among other things, the report identified the root causes of some of the major crimes of violence witnessed in Jamaica, and offered recommendations to treat with the problem. The phenomenon of the informal 'community don' as an alternate centre of influence was also addressed.
33. The Task Force Report was presented to the Conference of Heads of Government at its Twenty-Third Meeting in Georgetown, Guyana, July 3–5, 2002. A synopsis is available at http://www.caricom.org/exframes2.htm.
34. This information was presented in 2002 to a meeting of the Women's Institute for Alternative Development and the Caribbean Association for Feminist Research and Action that met to consider the impact of illegal firearms from a wider sociological perspective.
35. *Nassau Declaration on International Terrorism: the CARICOM Response*. Issued at the conclusion of the Special (Emergency) Meeting of Heads of Government of the Caribbean Community, October 11–12, 2001. 1. Available from http://www.caricom.org/archives/nassauadeclaration%20on%20 territorism.htm.
36. Ibid., 2.
37. See Inter-American Convention Against Terrorism, p. 1. Available from http://www.oas.org/juridico/english/treaties/a-66.htm. Antigua and Barbuda has since ratified the Convention. See *Newsday*, March 29, 2003, 53.
38. Ibid., 1–6.
39. See 'Hi-tech passports to fight fraud problem,' *Trinidad Guardian*, May 22, 2003, 9. The countries in the region have not all used the same sources to inform their terrorism laws. As examples, Guyana has used the Indian experience while Trinidad and Tobago has being guided by a model put out by the Commonwealth Secretariat.

40. See speech made by the Hon. Billie Miller, deputy prime minister of Barbados, to the General Debate of the Fifty-sixth Session of the United Nations General Assembly, New York, November 15, 2001.
41. See the Budget Presentation of the Rt. Hon. P. J. Patterson, QC, MP, prime minister of Jamaica on Tuesday, April 30, 2002, where he highlighted initiatives being pursued by his government to implement the recommendations of the National Committee on Crime and Violence.
42. Paul Sutton, 'The Politics of Small State Security in the Caribbean,' in Paul Sutton and Anthony Payne, eds., *Size and Survival: the Politics of Security in the Caribbean and the Pacific* (New York: Frank Cass, 1993), 17.
43. Kurt M. Campbell and Michele A. Flournoy, *To Prevail: An American Strategy for the Campaign against Terrorism* (Washington, DC: Center for Strategic and International Studies Press, 2001), 105–121.
44. See Fact Sheet: Caribbean 'Third Border Initiative,' Washington File, April 21, 2001. Available from http://usinfo.state.gov. See also *The National Security Strategy of the United States of America,* September 2002, 7.
45. Bryan and Flynn, 'Terrorism, Porous Borders, and Homeland Security,' 3.
46. Ibid.
47. Regional law enforcement agencies have their own professional groupings. Police forces have the Association of Caribbean Commissioners of Police (ACCP) and customs have the Caribbean Customs Law Enforcement Council (CCLEC). The meetings of these groups provide the opportunity to exchange best practices and experiences. Both these organisations are part of the Regional Task Force on crime and security.
48. There are many opportunities that are taken to share training experiences in the region. Exercise Red Stripe/Calypso Hop is an exchange between the British Army and the Jamaica Defence Force (JDF). There is also the Caribbean Junior Command and Staff Course, a joint project between the Canadian Army and the JDF. Caribbean defence forces contribute both instructors and students to this course. The Guyana Defence Force (GDF) and The Trinidad and Tobago Defence Force (TTDF) both conduct basic officer training courses that have regional students. It is also common to have military officers from the larger defence forces attached to OECS armies to provide expertise and training.
49. Other agencies such as CCLEC, CDERA, JIATF-S, the RSS and the United States Coast Guard District 7 also share the CISN resources.
50. The Sixth Annual CISN Conference was held in the Bahamas in March 2003. The Technical Working Group was mandated to respond to the challenges that caused the lack of participation. Consideration was also given to expansion of the network to other regional groupings such as the ACCP and the CCLEC.

Additional References

Karmon, Ely, 'The Role of Intelligence in Counter-Terrorism, 2001,' available from http://www.ict.org.il/articles/articledet.cfm?articleid=152.

Parker, Henry S., *Agricultural Bioterrorism: A Federal Strategy to Meet the Threat* (McNair Paper No. 65, Institute for National Strategic Studies, National Defense University, Washington, DC, March 2002).

The White House, *The National Security Strategy of the United States of America* (September 2002), available from http://usinfo.state.gov/ topical/pol/terror/secstrat2.htm.

Tulchin, Joseph S. and Ralph H. Espach, eds. *Security in the Caribbean Basin: The Challenge of Regional Cooperation.* Boulder, Colorado: Lynne Rienner Publishers, 1999.

17

Hemispheric Response to Terrorism: A Call for Action

John Cope and Janie Hulse

Introduction

There is an undeniable threat of terrorism in the Western Hemisphere and a determined effort to combat it. The events of September 11, 2001 launched a global war against terrorists, testing foreign and security policies across the region. Several neighbouring Latin American countries also counteract global terrorism's national equivalent. With symbiotic ties to the region's transnational criminal organisations, international and domestic terrorists have gained in sophistication and capability. Taking advantage of weak governments, they exploit porous borders and ungoverned zones at will. In this environment, homeland security has become unachievable acting alone: states must work together if the combined challenge of terrorists and associated criminal networks is to be eliminated.

The attacks on Washington and New York have prompted preliminary collaborative efforts to prevent future acts of terror. 'Smart Border' initiatives can be seen in North America; a long-standing subregional security apparatus is flexing in the Caribbean; international outreach in support of its crisis is being pursued by Colombia; and intelligence cooperation is being explored in the Tri-Border Area of Argentina, Brazil and Paraguay. Actions taken by the Organization of the American States (OAS) to react against terrorism, energising the Inter-American Committee Against Terrorism and approving an unprecedented Convention focused on prevention, are particularly hopeful.

With the United States somewhat distracted by the global war against terrorism elsewhere, there is space for the Latin American and Caribbean nations to work collectively and proactively to prevent terrorism in the Western Hemisphere. This chapter assesses the complex nature of terrorism in the Western Hemisphere and explores how states are responding individually and collectively, particularly at the hemispheric level through the OAS. The examination leads to a call for action in the region immediately and in the near term. Several suggestions are offered to meet the call. The path the chapter follows leads through a series of questions: What terrorist threats does the region face? Where are the 'hot beds'? Do national responses to terrorism follow a pattern? What role has the OAS played in fostering multinational cooperation? Can the organisation of the struggle against international terrorism be improved? We will argue for greater regional cooperation and the need to expand the OAS' authority and scope to provide a more holistic approach to counter-terrorism that could save the Americas from a repeat of September 11 or worse.

Definitions and Clarifications

Terrorism is a global phenomenon that encompasses many forms of political violence, ranging from the international jihad of Islamic extremists against Israel, the United States and Western influences in general to national or domestic resistance campaigns waged by illegal armed groups from within and outside state boundaries. It is easy to recognise but difficult to define, particularly when actors are lumped together without differentiation as occurs with the US list of foreign terrorist organisations. A review of literature suggests that practitioners and academics adapt the way the word is used to suit different interests and audiences. Washington policy makers are no exception; perceptions of terrorism differ in US security strategy documents. The global-in-scope *National Strategy for Combating Terrorism,* released in February 2003, for example, states that terrorism is 'premeditated, politically motivated violence perpetrated against noncombatant targets by subnational groups or clandestine agents'.[1] The narrowly focused *National Strategy for Homeland Security* is far more specific. It claims that terrorism is:

> any premeditated, unlawful act dangerous to human life or public welfare that is intended to intimidate or coerce civilian populations or governments...(covering) kidnappings; hijackings; shootings; conventional bombings; attacks involving chemical, biological, radiological, or nuclear weapons; cyber attacks; and any number of other forms of malicious

> violence. Terrorists can be U.S. citizens or foreigners, acting in concert with others, on their own, or on behalf of a hostile state.[2]

In the context of this chapter, terrorism is considered a political phenomenon as well as a violent means to a political end. It occurs on both international and national levels. Terrorism is premeditated and involves trained individuals. There are symbiotic international support and financial links to international organised crime – including the illegal narcotics industry, a wide range of smuggling activities as well as kidnapping and extortions. Given its many dimensions, no nation can counter terrorism effectively and successfully alone. The hemisphere's *Inter-American Convention Against Terrorism* is correct in calling for action at the national, bilateral, subregional and regional levels.

What is the nature of the terrorist threat in the Western Hemisphere? While other American governments have been unable to agree on a working definition of the threat, the model for transnational terrorist networks presented in the United States' *National Strategy for Combating Terrorism* suggests a low-grade terrorist threat in the region, one that is active primarily at the state level. Terrorists in the US model operate on three levels of transnational networks. Terrorism that occurs within a single country constitutes the lowest level of severity. This measure can be misleading because, while their external reach is limited, the activities of national terrorists can have international consequences in today's global environment. State-level groups may expand geographically if their ambitions and capabilities are allowed to grow unchecked. The second level includes terrorist organisations that operate regionally by transcending at least one international boundary. Terrorist organisations with global reach are in the third category; their operations span several regions and their ambitions can be global. The three levels are often linked together in two ways. Some organisations cooperate directly by sharing intelligence, personnel, expertise, resources and safe havens. Secondly, some groups support each other in less direct ways, such as by promoting the same ideological agenda and reinforcing each other's efforts to cultivate a favourable international image for their 'cause'.[3]

In the Western Hemisphere, the terrorist threat is at the first level of transnational networks with some regional activity by third-level groups. The Revolutionary Armed Forces of Colombia (FARC) and National Republican Army of Colombia (ELN) in Colombia and the resurgent *Sindero Luminoso* in Peru are examples of first-level networks that are developing links to counterparts in other countries and to a few second-level groups outside the hemisphere. These connections are based mainly on business transactions (arms exchanges for drugs or the purchase of technical training). The associations are not political. The Irish Republican Army (IRA), which has been in Colombia training members of the FARC on urban terrorist tactics and techniques, is an example of narco-terrorists purchasing deadly expertise. It is not clear to what extent the region's state-level groups actually cooperate with each other – sharing intelligence, personnel, expertise, resources and safe havens. The hemisphere also has 'facilitating cells' and infrastructure that are part of third-level groups, namely Hamas and Hizbollah, which are located primarily in the Tri-Border Area of Argentina, Brazil and Paraguay. Violent operations involving these cells took place in Argentina in the early 1990s. It is still uncertain if any aspect of the September 11 attacks was planned in the region, but with large Arab Diasporas in many countries and a tradition of weak national and local governance, the environment is ripe for sleeper cells and the recruitment and training of new terrorists.

While the magnitude and pervasiveness of terrorism is relatively limited in the hemisphere, Pan-American governments must not forget that international and domestic terrorists are strategic actors. They choose their targets deliberately and adapt their means based on the weaknesses they observe in defences and preparedness. Governments must be able to anticipate attacks and defend their societies against a wide range of means and methods of attack. The nations of the Western Hemisphere are vulnerable to attacks directed against symbols of the West in general or the United States or Israeli citizens in particular. The bombings in Bali and Kenya in 2002 and Morocco in 2003 could have happened in Barbados or any number of other locations in the Americas, as citizens of Argentina know. The Israeli Embassy in Buenos Aires was blown up in 1992, killing 28 people, and, two years later, the city's main Jewish community centre also was destroyed, killing 85 people in what is still the world's worst anti-Semitic attack since the end of World War II. [4]

Three important aspects of the terrorist threat in the hemisphere deserve greater attention. These elements include the connection between terrorist organisations, organised crime and drug networks and the challenges this linkage poses for policy makers; the influence of ungoverned spaces in facilitating terrorist (and drug trafficking) activities; and the role played by the lawless tri-border region of South America (also known as the triple frontier).

Terrorists and Organised Crime and Drug Networks

Terrorists are inextricably linked, often for convenience, to other illegal groups – mostly drug networks – for funding that makes their violent activities possible. While they are distinct and separate organisations, terrorists and drug traffickers have the technology to network and, in most cases, still avoid capture. However, drug traffickers are not bound by ideology like terrorists; they tend to be profit seekers unwilling to go out of their way in defence of others. The lack of loyalty between these groups creates an important vulnerability that the law enforcement and intelligence communities have been able to exploit. Such was the case when police arrested a cousin of the extremist Assad Ahmad Barakat, head of Hizbollah in the Tri-Border Area. He was in possession of more than two kilos of cocaine that he intended to sell in Syria to support Hizbollah, confirming that this South American cell has a 'wing of narco traffickers' to generate funds for their Middle Eastern cause.[5]

From a security, intelligence or law enforcement perspective, it is increasingly important to recognise and exploit the nexus between terrorist organisations and drug trafficking activity. It is equally important to understand that the line that separates terrorists from drug traffickers is blurry. Some terrorists, out of necessity or convenience, do business with drug traffickers to fund their cause while others will circumvent the intermediary and deal directly in the drug business. To complicate matters, there are also drug traffickers who use terrorism against civilians to advance their business agenda – this was more common in the days of large drug cartels that had some political aspirations (i.e. Pablo Escobar's Medellín cartel). Of most concern today are the terrorists that directly and indirectly exploit the drug trade to fund their activities. The FARC, Colombia's largest terrorist organisation, has been indicted in various countries for its direct involvement in drug production and trafficking. In May 2003, for example, police seised 33 pounds (15 kg) of cocaine in a Rio de Janeiro shantytown, five pounds of which were labelled with a symbol representing the FARC.[6] Other terrorist groups like the *Sindero Luminoso* in Peru do not appear to participate directly in the drug trade but rather 'tax' local drug traffickers who wish to transport cocaine through 'their' territory.[7]

It has long been known that terrorist organisations work with other criminal groups to advance their cause, but the September 11 attacks have heightened policy makers' awareness of the complexity of the relationship in which the latter acts as a force multiplier for the former. Success in combating terrorism requires a simultaneous crack down on national and international crime. For this reason, the United States Drug Enforcement Administration (DEA) has expanded its traditional counter-drug mandate to include some counter-terrorism operations, and established the Ad Hoc Counter-terrorism Task Force to review evidence of drug activities linked to terrorism.[8] While this approach makes sense given the inextricable tie between the two threats, it raises the issue of trade-offs between counter-terrorism priorities and counter-drug agendas. When counter-narcotics activities are pursued largely for anti-terrorism reasons, it is important to look at the degree to which they obstruct terrorist operations and whether or not they detract from the effectiveness of counter-drug efforts. Policy makers need to grapple with this issue and find the right balance between counter-drug and counter-terrorism initiatives.[9]

Ungoverned Spaces

Hemispheric security revolves in great part around the notion of sovereignty – a state's ability to exercise its authority and control throughout national territory. The truth is that few countries possess perfect domestic sovereignty. Governments' control over internal developments and trans-border movements is always problematic. Exacerbating the issue in some societies is a purposefully weak and decentralised governmental structure, which is a product of historical political arrangements often stemming from a colonial legacy. Legal, regulatory, law enforcement and defence capabilities often are inadequate to control the expanse of the nation's territory, the size of its population, or the nature and scope of its interstate commerce. And even where government authorities are present, they are sometimes corrupted to the point of being ineffective; in essence, they hand over control to illicit groups. The contemporary explosion of transnational activities, legal and illegal, increases the difficulty for public authorities to exercise control. Governments face a continuous, expensive struggle to maintain effective sovereignty, but not all states are politically willing or financially able to make the effort. The lack of government presence and control produces 'ungoverned spaces'. These can occur in urban, rural and offshore territory, free-trade zones, remote border areas, and even cyberspace.

Terrorist groups, drug traffickers and other armed criminal groups thrive in areas where local, provincial and national government either is non-existent or has been so compromised by corruption as to be defunct. Ungoverned spaces provide safe havens, logistical bases, training areas, and revenue-generating opportunities. In the view of General James T. Hill, Commander of the US Southern Command:

> the threat to the countries of the region is not the military force of the adjacent neighbor, or some invading foreign power. Today's foe is the terrorist, the narco-trafficker, and the arms trafficker. This threat is the weed that is planted, grown and nurtured in the fertile ground of ungoverned spaces....[10]

In South America, for example, the Tabatinga-Leticia corridor on the Brazil-Colombia border, the Lago Agrio area on the Ecuador-Colombia border, and the Darien jungle in Panama are a few of the places where Colombia's drug traffickers and narco-terrorists roam freely, and often control large territories. Many urban slums are in the same category. But as Luigi Einaudi, assistant secretary general of the OAS, reminds, 'It's not so much that they are 'ungoverned' urban spaces, it's that they are areas governed by illegal groups'.[11] The consequence of government inattention is evident in Rio de Janeiro's hillside slums, or *favelas*, where drug gangs often run the show. Today, the city's three main drug trafficking gangs control most of Rio's 800 *favelas*, which have a total population of around one million people. Just 5,000–6,000 'armed and active' youngsters, according to Luke Dowdney of Viva Rio, a local NGO, enforce their rule of law. They are well armed and violent. Brazilian authorities now classify some *favelas* as 'off limits' and employ military or quasi-military operations to reenter them.[12] Rio de Janeiro is one of many cities in the hemisphere plagued with ungoverned urban areas and the armed gangs that control, administer, and profit from them.

Latin American and Caribbean governments face the challenge of regaining control of ungoverned territories in a period of economic downturn. This has exacerbated existing strains on lawful business and society in general, increasing the likelihood of corruption and strengthening criminal groups' stronghold on urban and rural areas. Two notorious 'garrison communities' in Kingston, Jamaica – Tivoli and Rema – exemplify the complex issues relating to corruption in urban slums. In these places, lowly paid police officials are bribed and co-opted by the drug 'dons' or lords and there is longstanding political tribalism perpetuated by Jamaica's two main political parties that, in turn, bribe the 'dons' – the de-facto leaders of these areas – with guns and money to ensure community support for the party. The authorities are essentially providing ungoverned functional spaces for the illegal gangs to operate and the politicians are making them richer. The well-established symbiotic relationship between legitimate and illegitimate groups makes combating corruption a daunting task and creates environment ripe for exploitation by terrorist organisations. The only practical solution is to initiate the difficult process of institutional reform, modernisation and professionalisation across the broad area of law enforcement, encompassing domestic intelligence, the police, the judiciary, and the penal system.

The Tri-Border Area

The Tri-Border Area where Argentina, Brazil and Paraguay meet has long been South America's busiest contraband and smuggling centre – a corrupt, chaotic place where just about anything from drugs and arms to pirated software and bootleg whisky are available to anyone who can pay the price. With its large Arab immigrant population (more than 20,000 Middle Eastern immigrants, most from Lebanon and Syria), the area is a rich source of Islamic sympathisers who, in recent years, have legally raised or illegally laundered more than $50 million that ultimately went to support terrorist groups. Hizbollah, the Iranian-backed terrorist group, appears to be the dominant organisation. There also are 'support activities' on behalf of Hamas, Amal and the Party for Islamic Unification. Egypt's Islamic Brotherhood is believed to use the area as a haven.[13] Of the three neighbours, Brazil and Paraguay are more ambivalent to this activity, saying they need more evidence that terrorist groups have used the area as a financing, logistical and recreational centre. Despite government denials, there has been evidence of terrorist support activity along the Triple Frontier for many years.

As scrutiny of the Triple Frontier increases, activists are dispersing to smaller towns in Argentina, Brazil and Paraguay. Moreover, there are indications that Islamic extremists are gravitating toward Sao Paulo, a city of 18 million that is home to the largest concentration of Brazils' estimated 1.5 Muslims – an ideal hiding place for anyone intent on being overlooked.[14] In 2002, a map of the Tri-Border Area was recovered from an Al Qaeda safe house in Kabul,[15] raising questions about Osama bin Laden's dealings in Latin America and conjecture that Al Qaeda cells in the region may have played a supporting role in the September 11 attacks. The presence of international terrorist networks is no longer limited to the Triple Frontier. There also are signs that Islamic extremists are fanning out to nearby countries with long established Arab or Muslim communities. Mentioned most often are Iquique, Chile; Guayaquil, Ecuador; and Maracaibo, Venezuela.

Response Within the Hemisphere to Terrorism

In the aftermath of the September 11 attacks, all heads of state in the Americas have had to contemplate organising their administrations and mobilising their societies to secure their homelands from terrorist attacks. The challenge is more immediate and complex for some than it is for others, but the requirement for homeland security exists nonetheless. The United States and Canada reacted quickly to what the Bush administration describes as attacks against the very idea of civil society. To date, they have developed the most comprehensive responses to international terrorism. Latin American and Caribbean countries and the OAS are progressing at a slower pace, often having to address international as well as entrenched domestic terrorism.

National responses to this security problem follow a general pattern. It begins with a period of threat denial, followed by unilateral attempts to prevent attacks by terrorists with global reach or to combat domestic narco-terrorist groups. The complexity and sophistication of the terrorist challenge that has been allowed to develop often leads governments to pursue a bilateral approach with the United States. This usually involves US help with intelligence and, in some cases, material assistance. Common concerns about narcotics trafficking frequently provide the basis for collaboration. The final element in the pattern comes with the realisation that success ultimately requires the cooperation and support of close neighbours. At a minimum, this relationship involves sharing information about terrorist groups, eliminating legal and illegal logistical networks supporting terrorist cells and illegal armed groups that cross the border, and coordinating customs, immigration, law enforcement, and military operations along the common frontier. This part of the pattern is difficult for Latin American nations. They cherish self-reliance, nationalist traditions, sovereignty, and control. They also harbour a distrust of the United States and neighbouring countries. English-speaking Caribbean states are the exception in that they have proven more willing to collaborate.

The pattern of response to domestic terrorist activity is most developed in Colombia. In nearly 40 years of conflict with armed guerrillas, paramilitary groups and drug traffickers, Colombia has passed through all the security response phases in the model at least once and, accordingly, the United States has offered varying amounts of military and police assistance. Until recently, US aid was entirely tied to the war on drugs. This changed when the Bush administration expanded its policy focus beyond narcotics to confront the three illegal armed groups and respond to narco-terrorism. The United States continues to support Plan Colombia, which aims not only to thwart drug production and trade but also to increase the rule of law, protect human rights, expand economic development, institute judicial reform, and foster peace.

Plan Colombia, begun under the Andres Pastrana government, has been energised and broadened by the Alvaro Uribe administration. Under Uribe, the Colombian government has gone to war against the terrorists and is armed with a plan to reacquire national territory, establish permanent government presence to provide law and order, improve the economy and increase social services to the poor.[16] President Uribe recognises that Colombia cannot win this war alone and has enlisted the support of its five neighbours. He began by reaching out individually, to Brazilian President Luiz Inacio Lula da Silva and received his promise to help in detecting leftist rebels and drug traffickers along their Amazonian border. President Uribe also organised a Regional Security Ministerial in 2003 with Ecuador, Peru, Brazil, Venezuela and Panama. The group reaffirmed its commitment to fight against terrorist and drug trafficking by supporting relevant UN and OAS resolutions that call on states to implement enhanced law enforcement measures and promote a more law-abiding environment.[17] There was no agreement, however, on how to operationalise any specific cooperation.

The regionalisation of support has had some difficulties (namely accusations that President Hugo Chávez sympathises with Colombian rebels), but on the whole there has been a step-up in defensive border activity and information sharing, an increase in international awareness, and general support for Colombia's war against domestic terrorism. Furthermore, there has been some progress in the region against international terrorism, most notably in diplomatic cooperation between Argentina, Brazil and Paraguay to confront the challenges of the Tri-Border Area. The three neighbours founded the Tripartite Commission of the Triple Frontier in 1998 as a security mechanism to deal with concerns in the Tri-Border Area. The organisation met during 2003 in Buenos Aires and included the United States to discuss counter-terrorism cooperation. As a result of what is being referred to as the 'Three Plus One' meeting, the countries agreed to establish a permanent working group to examine specific counter-terrorism concerns. This four-part mechanism is proving to be an effective way to encourage action and international collaboration. In June 2003, for example, the Brazilian Army started training its troops to help the federal police supervise the traffic of vehicles, merchandise and persons at the tri-border. A civil-military task force was created to disband armed guerillas and drug traffickers in the area. The UN Office on Drugs and Crime in the Southern Cone may support this effort.[18] Greater attention to border control and black market activities, however, will be needed to secure the triple frontier.

The Tri-Border, however, is not without its issues. In a November 2002 interview, Andrienne Senna, then head of Coef, the main Brazilian body engaged in the anti-terror fight, insisted that financial support for international terrorism did not occur in the Tri-Border Area despite Argentine reports to the contrary. When asked about Argentina's allegations, she responded, 'Brazil, Paraguay and Argentina only have the border in common'.[19] Her reaction underscores the absence of unity between these neighbours exacerbated by cultural and institutional differences. The countries differ markedly in the sophistication of institutional development to counter terrorism. In Brazil, Coef has been around for years and is well established while its counterpart organisation in Argentina, the Financial Intelligence Unit, is now (June 2003) less than a year old. Paraguay has a counter-terrorism secretariat, SEPRINTE, but its Congress has rejected anti-terrorism legislation that would define criminal penalties related to terrorism; the legislature fears that a corrupt government could use the new law to target political opposition. There is a great need for neighbours to move beyond their differences and assist each other to build appropriate intelligence mechanisms and take essential preventative actions.

A notable example of a more advanced subregional security mechanism, well-suited for collaboration to prevent terrorism, is the Regional Security System (RSS) established by Memorandum of Understanding in 1982, with seven member states in the Eastern Caribbean: Antigua and Barbuda, Barbados, Dominica, Grenada, St Kitts and Nevis, Saint Lucia and St Vincent and the Grenadines. The RSS, which brings together the military and police forces of its member states, focuses on combating drug trafficking and smuggling; responding to natural disasters; and providing other forms of security-related assistance. The RSS has operational links with other national forces in the Caribbean Basin. Under the RSS, a member whose security is threatened or who needs other kinds of emergency assistance can call on other members. According to the Memorandum of Understanding, governments are obliged 'to prepare contingency plans and assist one another on request in national emergencies . . . and threats to national security'. This multi-country police/military organisation is prepared to support efforts to prevent international terrorism as well as assist, if need be, in incident recovery efforts.

The most sophisticated response to the threat of international terrorism, and a model for other neighbouring countries in the hemisphere, is the Smart Border initiatives that Washington has negotiated with Ottawa and Mexico City. After September 11, the United States and Canada recognised that they had to enhance the security of their common border while at the same time facilitating the legitimate flow of people and goods upon which both economies depend. The result was the development of a tailored bilateral programme. The US-Canada Smart Border initiative, adopted by a joint declaration in December 2001, is a 30-point action plan that identifies and expedites low risk people and goods, and concentrates on higher risk traffic. It also focuses on securing common infrastructure through information sharing and law enforcement coordination. The plan is both proactive and innovative. To increase a secure flow of people, additional immigration control officers are deployed overseas to ensure that fraudulent documents are identified before people board transportation. Also, a border-wide 'fast lane' programme called NEXUS speeds the flow of prescreened low-risk travellers. A similar programme called The Free and Secure Trade or 'FAST' programme establishes a similar 'fast lane' procedure for low-risk shipments. A bi-national steering group was created to manage protection of shared critical infrastructure in the energy, telecommunications, and transportation sectors. Agreements to secure air travel recognise each country's national standards for aviation security and create new federal transportation agencies to ensure these standards are met. Coordination of maritime surveillance and intelligence sharing also takes place systematically.

In late November 2002, the United States and Mexico signed an agreement to create a similar Smart Border programme, and each country agreed to pledge $25 million to support it. Since then, border security has improved. A Secure Electronic Network for Travelers' Rapid Inspection, SENTRI, allows northbound motorists to avoid the long waits at the San Ysidro and Otay Mesa ports of entry that link southern San Diego to Tijuana, Mexico. SENTRI participants have their vehicles equipped with a transmitter, which allows them to use an express lane. SENTRI is similar to the NEXUS programme with Canada in that it allows inspectors to focus on high-risk travellers. The first high-tech fast lane for US-bound cargo opened later in 2003. There are lingering concerns about the speed of progress with this cooperative border programme compared to joint efforts with Canada. The slower pace of the US-Mexico cooperation can be attributed in part to the political wrangling between President Bush and President Fox over issues of immigration and the Iraqi war.

The countries of the Western Hemisphere are at different stages in the pattern of response to domestic and international terrorism. (See Figure 17.1 for an illustration of the authors' view of where countries fall in this pattern). The most advanced are in North America, among Caribbean states, Colombia, and the tri-border neighbours in South America. These governments recognise the imperative for close, flexible cooperation among neighbours to prevent acts of terror or to combat narco-terrorists. In the battle of competing domestic priorities, these countries have chosen to emphasise security. (Note: While they are not the focus of this chapter, Central American nations have also proven willing to collaborate on security issues as they work to bring the US-Central American Free Trade Agreement (CAFTA) to fruition.) The remaining nations are either at an early stage in the pattern, unsure that terrorism is a threat to them, or committed to an independent response. For many of these governments a preoccupation with sovereignty and control, distrust of neighbours, and zero-sum strategies dominate policy choices. Some are unwilling to divert funds from national development. An ingredient that is common to the progressive responses to preventing terrorism is US influence and participation. This is an issue for many Latin American and Caribbean countries that fear a return to the dependency problems of old and want to protect their autonomy. A parallel track forward in hemispheric security is to work closely with programmes to combat terrorism under the auspices of the OAS.

Figure 17.1
Perceived Threat vs Level of Cooperation

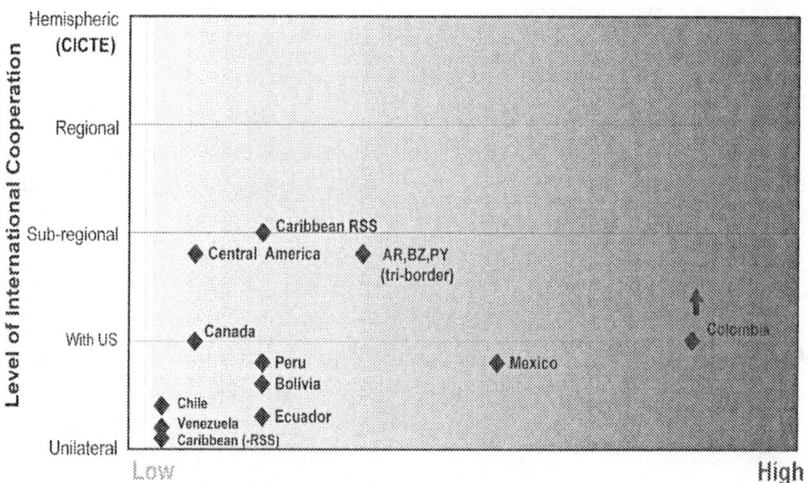

Hemispheric Response to Terrorism

Through the OAS, the Latin American and Caribbean nations responded quickly and collectively to the September 11 attacks and in the aftermath devised a legal framework to cooperate in implementing counter-terrorism action plans. The OAS, more respected today than during the Cold War when the United States tended to manipulate the body, has become an effective mechanism for governments to engage each other in the management of hemisphere affairs. It is the only forum where all governments regularly come together on an equal footing to address regional policies and issues. The challenge nations face confronting transnational terrorism has created new possibilities for regional collaboration, and a need for a coordinating clearing house to assist member governments to carry out decisions reached in this forum. In the hemispheric response to terrorism is an implicit test of Latin American and Caribbean volition to take advantage of this opportunity to act as sovereign states in furthering regional security.[20]

Within ten days of the September 11 attacks, two steps were taken by the OAS to support the United States. Member states invoked the Inter-American Treaty of Reciprocal Assistance (Rio Treaty), reaffirming that an attack on one signatory is an attack on all. Moreover, they passed the *OAS Resolution Strengthening Cooperation to Prevent, Combat and Eliminate Terrorism.* This declaration condemned the attacks and called upon all member states to take effective measures to deny terrorist groups the ability to operate within their territories. Together, these actions emphasised the need to deal with the new threats anywhere in the hemisphere.

Terrorism in the Western Hemisphere was not born on September 11, 2001. Latin American countries have struggled with domestic forms of terrorism for decades. The 2001 attacks in the United States and subsequent 2002 bombings in Bali and Kenya and Morocco in 2003 changed the perception of the threat by demonstrating to countries that no target is beyond the strategic reach and asymmetrical power of international terrorist organisations. In an important call for action with the intention of working towards preventing, punishing and eliminating terrorism, OAS member states signed a landmark Inter-American Convention Against Terrorism on June 3, 2002. The Convention, a legal instrument that is consistent with and builds upon UN conventions and protocols on terrorism and UN Security Council Resolution 1373, binds member states to regional cooperation in the fight against terrorism through exchanges of financial information, collaboration on border and customs controls, technical training, and legal assistance.

In addition to signing the Convention, member states reinvigorated the Inter-American Committee Against Terrorism (CICTE), which had languished since its creation in 1998. CICTE became the key mechanism for discussing terrorism in the hemisphere, urging compliance with the Convention, and providing limited counter-terrorism assistance. During CICTE's Third Regular Session in January 2003, the member states arrived at consensus on a detailed work plan outlining a number of concrete counter-terrorism action steps. The work plan promotes systems for early warning and intelligence sharing, the linking of migration databases, and joint training for border and migration control officers. It also outlines steps to improve the quality of identification and travel documents, customs control measures, and financial control measures.

In 2002, CICTE established a full-time secretariat that is funded by voluntary donations from OAS member states. (It is currently sustained by the United States, which contributed $1 million in late 2002.) The secretariat has three primary tasks. It manages a directory of hemispheric experts on counter-terrorism in categories such as financial controls, border controls, domestic legislation and law enforcement; maintains relevant databases and shares the information; and designs, organises and implements training and technical assistance programmes. The secretariat was working hard to bring the member countries together to discuss counter-terrorism training and prevention programmes. Its first step was a July 2003 meeting of National Points of Contacts (professionals from member states who work with counter-terrorism issues) to discuss training initiatives, communication mechanisms, and the work plan.

At present, the committee has no authority to do more than coordinate and share information among members. Nonetheless, its efforts to provide Latin American and Caribbean countries with a framework within which to shape their counter-terrorism actions appear to be on track. The existence of CICTE does not preclude countries from working together on a subregional or regional level, such as the RSS in the Caribbean and the 'Three plus One' coalition in South America's Tri-Border Area.

Domestic and international terrorism pose serious threats to national security across the hemisphere. No one country can deal successfully with the challenge. The OAS provides the forum for governments to engage each other on equal footing in coming to grips with this transnational problem, and CICTE, with its secretariat, has become the mechanism for concrete forward movement. Here is an opportunity for Latin American and Caribbean countries to show that they can work together rather than wait for the United

States to initiate action. At a May 2003 OAS-sponsored conference on hemispheric security, Joseph Tulchin, the distinguished director of the Woodrow Wilson International Centre's Latin America programme, argued that the hemisphere should not allow itself to revert to United States-led security arrangements in which Latin American and Caribbean nations merely reacted in total acceptance or complete rejection of US policy. Both responses show an absence of autonomy.[21] Today, with the United States somewhat distracted by the global war against terrorism elsewhere, there is space for the Latin American and Caribbean nations to work collectively and proactively to prevent terrorism in the Western Hemisphere. The OAS is the forum in which states can demonstrate the ability to cooperate in response to a common threat.

Call for Immediate Action

The United States and its neighbours north and south are justifiably proud of approving an Inter-American Convention Against Terrorism nine months after the September 11 attacks at last year's OAS General Assembly meeting in Barbados. The accomplishment is seen as underscoring the region's determination to protect the Americas against an enemy that knows no national or moral limits. Yet, not until June 2003 did the Convention become operable. Six states had to ratify the document for it to go into effect. As of June 2003, only Canada, Antigua-Barbuda, El Salvador, Mexico, Peru and Nicaragua have done so. President George Bush submitted the Convention to the US Congress in November 2002, but up to summer 2003 the Senate had not acted on it. (See Table 17.1 for a review of the key counter-terrorism related OAS treaties and conventions.)

The region's sense of urgency is in question. If the United States and neighbouring Latin American and Caribbean nations were really serious about terrorism and willing to work together to combat it, they would have more quickly blessed this important, proactive Convention. Ratification of the document is a test of a country's commitment on several levels:

- Commitment to help prevent another act of terrorism in the hemisphere, particularly in the United States, which is one of the principal targets for international terrorist organisations.
- Commitment to support the OAS on this initiative and strengthen its Committee Against Terrorism (CICTE), which is leading a regional effort to organise multilateral counter-terrorism cooperation.

- Commitment by Latin American and Caribbean states to play an active role in shaping contemporary hemisphere security on a strategic issue that directly affects them.

Table 17.1
OAS Counter-Terrorism Related Treaties and Conventions

OAS Member Countries	Treaty of Reciprocal Assistance – 1947* (Rio Treaty)		Convention to Prevent and Punish the Acts of Terrorism – 2001		Convention Against Terrorism – 2002		Countries w/ CICTE POC**
	Signature	Ratification	Signature	Ratification	Signature	Ratification	
Antigua & Barbuda	-	-	-	-	✓	✓	✓
Argentina	✓	✓	-	-	✓	-	✓
Bahamas	✓	✓	-	-	✓	-	✓
Barbados	-	-	-	-	✓	-	-
Belize	-	-	-	-	✓	-	✓
Bolivia	✓	✓	✓	✓	✓	-	✓
Brazil	✓	✓	-	✓	✓	-	✓
Canada	-	-	-	-	✓	✓	✓
Chile	✓	✓	✓	-	✓	-	✓
Colombia	✓	✓	✓	✓	✓	-	✓
Costa Rica	✓	✓	✓	✓	✓	-	✓
Dominica	-	-	-	-	-	-	-
Dominican Republic	-	-	✓	✓	✓	-	✓
Ecuador	✓	✓	✓	-	✓	-	-
El Salvador	✓	✓	✓	✓	✓	✓	✓
Grenada	-	-	-	✓	✓	-	✓
Guatemala	✓	✓	✓	✓	✓	-	✓
Guyana	-	-	-	-	✓	-	-
Haiti	✓	✓	-	-	✓	-	-
Honduras	✓	✓	✓	-	✓	-	-
Jamaica	-	-	✓	-	✓	-	✓
Mexico	✓	✓	✓	✓	✓	✓	✓
Nicaragua	✓	✓	✓	✓	✓	✓	✓
Panama	✓	✓	✓	✓	✓	-	✓
Paraguay	✓	✓	✓	-	✓	-	✓
Peru	✓	✓	✓	✓	✓	✓	✓
Saint Lucia	-	-	-	-	✓	-	-
Saint Vincent & Grenadines	-	-	-	-	✓	-	-
Saint Kitts & Nevis	-	-	-	-	✓	-	-
Suriname	-	-	-	-	✓	-	-
Trinidad & Tobago	✓	✓	✓	-	✓	-	✓
United States	✓	✓	✓	✓	✓	-	✓
Uruguay	✓	✓	✓	✓	✓	-	✓
Venezuela	✓	✓	✓	✓	✓	-	✓

* *Please note that most of the countries that did not approve the Rio Treaty were either not in existence at the time of signing or not part of the Inter-American system.*
** *POC (Point of Contact): Member state liaison to CICTE.*

Call for Action in the Near Term

Neighbouring states in the Western Hemisphere must make a greater effort to organise individually and collectively in the struggle against international terrorism. In responding to the September 11 attacks on the United States, American leaders immediately pledged to deal with the new threats anywhere in the hemisphere, recognising at that moment that terrorists choose targets after balancing their significance and symbolic value with their vulnerability and ease of attack. There are a large number of high-value targets in the region outside the United States. OAS member states agreed to take important legal and structural steps under its auspices, working through CICTE, that focus cooperation on early warning and the prevention of terrorist attacks. The region's energetic commitment and its strategic approach to securing itself against international terrorism, however, ended there.

The challenge of protecting an interdependent geographic network of 34 democratic homelands from international terrorism is formidable, but it can be met over time. As the United States has found, success depends on the willingness and ability to pursue three strategic objectives. Preventing terrorist attacks within the hemisphere is the first priority, and OAS member states already have a (developing) framework for action. If countries cooperate, there is great potential to make a positive contribution to inter-American security. The second and third objectives have not been addressed conjointly on a regional level; the second is to reduce the vulnerability to terrorist attack of shared critical infrastructure and key assets, and the third involves minimising the damage and recovering from attacks that may happen somewhere in the hemisphere and that affect one or more neighbouring states.

In an era of economic integration shaped by the accelerating pace of transport, telecommunication, information technology (Internet) and energy transmission, ties among American nations are closer than ever. Underpinning this interdependence are networks of shared infrastructure that may be critical to one or more countries on several different levels, regional, subregional or bilateral. Among the many sectors in the Caribbean Basin that could be affected are the Panama Canal, communication nodes, oil refineries, the chemical industry, cruise ships and tourism. Much of this infrastructure is in the private sector. If terrorists successfully attack parts of the region's critical infrastructure, they disrupt entire systems and cause serious damage to several countries simultaneously. OAS member states must pay attention to improving protection of individual assets and interconnecting systems and cooperatively securing shared structures and installations to reduce vulnerability and deter terrorists. Use of a bi-national steering group to manage the protection of shared concerns has proven successful for Canada and the United States. As an added incentive, this step also heightens the region's preparedness for natural disasters.

The scope and impact of a major terrorist attack, like a natural or health disaster, will not respect state borders. Neighbouring countries must prepare to minimise the damage and recover, the third strategic priority, despite best efforts at prevention. As all American governments have learned from recurring climatological and geological calamities, an effective response depends on being prepared with comprehensive incident management systems that bring together and coordinate the quick employment of the key response assets. Many pieces of national emergency response systems are already in place across the hemisphere, but this minimum level of preparedness must become common to all countries. Currently, there is neither incentive to take this step, nor is there interest in linking systems country to country and standardising planning, equipment and procedures.

The CICTE can play a constructive role in the hemisphere's pursuit of protection and recovery priorities as well as its current mandate for prevention. CICTE can help member states unify the hemisphere's shared infrastructure protection effort by:

- identifying the region's critical shared infrastructure and key assets;
- maintaining a database on this infrastructure with security assessments;
- managing an independent programme for evaluating the protection of shared structures and installations;
- encouraging partnerships in protection planning and execution between neighbouring governments and between national governments and the private sector; and
- providing a vehicle for sharing experiences.

In a like manner, CICTE can provide member states with assistance by becoming the hub for a hemispheric incident management system through

- establishing common norms and minimum standards for emergency preparedness and response;
- providing a mechanism for integrating national incident management plans;
- enabling the sharing of information on terrorist incidents;

- managing a regional training and evaluation system; and
- providing a vehicle for sharing experiences.

Latin American and Caribbean governments should take a longer view of the problem of combating international terrorism and encourage the OAS to expand CICTE's mandate. A focus on preventing a terrorist attack is important but inadequate to prepare properly for the magnitude of this threat and its consequences, if realised. A more comprehensive mechanism for linking, coordinating and generally managing related initiatives in a network of 34 democracies, all trying with varying degrees of effort to organise their own homeland security, is needed. The challenge is to develop interconnected and complementary systems in the hemisphere that are reinforcing and ensuring that essential requirements are met. The OAS can perform this task.

Conclusion

In facing the threat of terrorism, it is important to distinguish between its international and domestic forms – especially in the Latin American region where several countries have been plagued by domestic terror for decades and others have only recently become aware of an international terrorist threat. It is also important to view terrorists as politically motivated and inextricably linked with international criminal groups – namely drug organisations – that exploit geographic and functional spaces in countries where government authorities are weak.

The response to terrorism in the hemisphere has followed a general pattern that begins with denial and ends with full international cooperation to deal with the problem. So far, the northern states with Smart Border initiatives, the Caribbean nations with the RSS and, to a lesser extent, Colombia and the Tri-Border Area neighbours have taken concrete steps to confront the threat of terrorism. Other countries, for various reasons, ranging from a minimal threat to no perception of the danger to fear of dependency on the United States, have minimised their attention to the problem and have failed to heed the call to step up and take the initiative against terrorism. There is political space to be filled by the Latin American and Caribbean nations in the area of counter-terrorism. By working through the OAS, governments can take action proactively without compromising sovereignty. The first step is to ratify the Inter-American Convention Against Terrorism and demonstrate a willingness to implement the terrorism prevention plans laid out in 2002.

Due to the complexities and transnational nature of terrorism, countries have to work together to mitigate the threat. Counter-terrorism is a team sport that requires team players. Like all sports, there is an offence and a defence. Counter-terrorism offence includes taking preventative measures by seeking out possible threats and doing away with them. The OAS already has an offensive strategy based on prevention plans outlined in the Convention and CICTE's current work plan. Counter-terrorism defence, which includes infrastructure protection and preparation for incident recovery, is currently missing from the OAS framework. A good defence is essential to ensure a more holistic approach to combating terrorism.

The United States clearly sees the importance in playing the entire field. There may come a time in the near future (hopefully not prompted by another attack) when Washington expects its neighbours to play a solid defence as well as offence. As is the case with the war on drugs, the United States is dependent on other nations to help combat terrorism. Latin American and Caribbean states can cooperate with the United States on counter-drug and counter-terrorism efforts on equal footing working through the OAS. Should neighbours decide not to take the threat seriously, Washington may have no alternative but to pressure countries to do their part – as was the intent with the counter-drug certification process. Proving sincerity on the counter-terrorism front requires that the nations move beyond what Professor Ivelaw Griffith characterises as the Platitudes Syndrome and actually implement their rhetorical proclamations.[22] Only time will tell how hemispheric counter-terrorism policy and initiatives will take shape. But it is clear today that the domestic and international threat of terrorism in the hemisphere is real and must be dealt with cooperatively and urgently, lest the Americas experience another September 11, or worse.

Notes

1. United States Government, *National Strategy for Combating Terrorism*, February 2003, 1.
2. United States Government, *National Strategy for Homeland Security*, July 2002, 2.
3. *National Strategy for Combating Terrorism*, 8–9.
4. Larry Rohter, 'Argentine Judge Indicts 4 Iranian Officials in 1994 Bombing of Jewish Center', *The New York Times*, March 10, 2003.
5. BBC Worldwide Monitoring Service, 'Paraguayan Police Say Cocaine Arrest "Proof" Hizbollah Raising Funds from Drugs', May 12, 2003.
6. Reuters World News, 'Rio Police Seize Cocaine Linked to Colombia's FARC', May 21, 2003. *Washington File*, 'International Law Enforcement Cooperation Fights Narcoterror', May 20, 2003.

7. *Washington File*, 'International Law Enforcement Cooperation Fights Narcoterror', May 20, 2003.
8. Raphael Pearl, 'Narco-Terrorism: International Drug Trafficking and Terrorism – A Dangerous Mix', Testimony to the United States Senate Committee on the Judiciary, May 20, 2003.
9. Ibid.
10. James T. Hill in speech prepared for *Building Regional Security Cooperation in the Western Hemisphere*, A conference sponsored by The US Army War College and The Dante B. Fascell North-South Centre, March 2–4, 2003, Miami, Florida.
11. A comment made at a 2003 meeting with the authors.
12. 'What Ails Rio de Janeiro?', *The Economist*, May 10, 2003.
13. Larry Rohter, 'The Triple Frontier: terrorist safe haven in Latin America?', *The New York Times*, December 16, 2002.
14. Ibid.
15. George Gedda, Associated Press, 'Hizbollah Receives Support from South American Groups Official Says', December 20, 2002.
16. John A. Cope, 'Colombia's War: Toward a New Strategy', *Strategic Forum,* Institute for National Strategic Studies, October 2002.
17. Richard Boucher, 'Regional Security Ministerial Held In Bogota, Colombia', *State Department Press Statement,* March 18, 2003.
18. Carlos Wagner, 'Army Joins Police to Help Control Trafficking, Crime on Paraguay Border', *Porto Alegre Zero Hora* (Internet Version, FBIS LAP20030618000060), June 18, 2003.
19. BBC Monitoring Service, 'Anti-money laundering head discusses her work, tri-border allegations,' November 20, 2002.
20. Inter-American Dialogue, 'The Inter-American Agenda and Multilateral Governance: The Organisation of American States,' Washington, D.C., April 1997, pp.iv–vii.
21. Joseph S. Tulchin's speech given at the conference titled *Security in the Americas Our Hemispheric Neighborhood*, OAS Hall of the Americas, Washington D.C., May 21, 2003.
22. Ivelaw L. Griffith, 'The Caribbean Security Scenario at the Dawn of the 21st Century; Continuity, Change and Challenge,' paper presented at the conference *Building Regional Security Cooperation in the Western Hemisphere*, sponsored by The US Army War College and The Dante B. Fascell North-South Centre, March 2–4, 2003, Miami, Florida.

18

The Caribbean on the World Scene: Security Regimes, Instruments, and Actions

W. Andy Knight

Introduction

It is evident from previous chapters that the Caribbean is still trying to come to terms with the changes and evolution in security challenges to the region since the end of the Cold War. Its leaders are desperately trying to find ways to deal with a host of both traditional and non-traditional threats to both their states and their peoples. Since the nature and scope of security threats have broadened and deepened, it is imperative that Caribbean states develop comprehensive and cooperative methods of addressing them.

This chapter calls for such a policy strategy to combat security threats to the region, particularly since the 9/11 terrorist attacks on the hemispheric hegemonic power, the United States. That strategy necessarily includes: creating and building on specific regional and international regimes; utilising a combination of existing and new domestic, regional, and global mechanisms, instruments or tools; and, pursuing appropriate actions in collaboration with both state and non-state actors in the region and beyond. The essential argument here is that given the vulnerabilities of Caribbean states (viz. small, relatively weak states) to the negative fallout of globalisation and globalism processes and to the increasing pressures from the region's and global hegemonic power, Caribbean leaders have no choice but to seek out and work within broad regional and global multilateral institutions in pursuit of their policies and goals. Such institutions provide at least some insulation from the onslaught of real and serious threats to the Caribbean states' sovereignty and to the human security of its peoples.

The chapter begins by putting the Caribbean within the global context of changing security conceptions and dynamics and the constraints brought on by the imposition of US security policy in the region, particularly since the end of the Cold War. It then identifies specific traditional and non-traditional security problems and challenges to the region, including transnational security threats coming from transnational corruption and crime, money laundering, drug trafficking, migrant and immigration issues, AIDS, environmental degradation, natural disasters and, more recently, global terrorism. With respect to the latter issue, the chapter analyses some of the impacts on the Caribbean as a region of the 9/11 terrorist attack on the US and describes the official reaction of Caribbean states to this tragic event. Finally, it examines specific regimes and instruments that together form a framework for actions and potential actions of Caribbean states in response to the security challenges in this age of complex interdependence and terror.

The Caribbean in the Global and Regional Contexts

Any discussion of the security plight of the Caribbean must be placed in proper historical context. It is not possible here, given the constraints of time and space, to provide a survey of the historical developments in the Caribbean region of British, French, Spanish, Portuguese and Dutch colonialism, post-colonialism and independence, and US neo-imperialism and hegemonic dominance during the Cold War era. In any event, such surveys are readily available in other sources.[1] Basically the focus here is on placing the Caribbean within the context of post-Cold War global and regional history.

Franklin Knight and Colin Palmer made the case around the beginning of the post-Cold War period that 'since 1492, the Caribbean region has oscillated between the centre and the periphery of international affairs:

> Sometimes the victim of 'benign neglect,' other times the venue for the flexing of the American military muscle to subdue legitimate local aspirations or score points in an extra-regional geopolitical rivalry between the superpowers, the international interest in the Caribbean intensifies and wanes with predictable regularity. The local people cope with the changes as best they can.[2]

Certainly the authors were astute in their observation. In the immediate post-Cold War period, it appeared that the Caribbean would again become the victim of neglect. After all, the focus of US foreign aid policy was on assisting states in transition, especially those states of the former Soviet Union. The concern, of course, was that the new Commonwealth of Independent States (CIS) needed to be brought squarely into the capitalist fold and that a mechanism of control needed to be put in place to ensure that nuclear weapons and weapons systems located in some of these states would not pose a danger to the West. Thus, Caribbean countries could no longer use the threat of cozying up to communism/Marxism in order to attract attention and financial aid from the US. In many respects, the Caribbean Basin lost its value to the US until the so-called 'new' security threats finally came to replace the older threat that had stemmed from the old Soviet Union.

Post-Cold War Security Threats

The reconfiguration of the global security order, that occurred since the disintegration of the Soviet empire, left the US as the sole remaining hegemon. This had important implications not only for the world at large but also for Caribbean states and societies. Additionally, the end of the Cold War coincided with a shift in the conception of security that saw the concept both broadened and deepened.

The end of the Cold War removed the structural and ideological underpinnings of the superpower conflict that had reigned over the previous 40 or so years. Apart from relaxing global tensions, this changed structural condition reduced the major security threat that the world faced during the Cold War, viz. the threat of nuclear war between two military camps. But the face off between the superpowers had frozen many conflicts that were seething underneath the Cold War blanket. Lifting that blanket, in some cases, resulted not only in a thaw but also in a percolation of incipient conflicts, many of them civil conflicts. But what was even more significant about this global structural shift was the opportunity it provided for US triumphalism, best exemplified by Krauthammer's claim in 1990–91 of a unipolar moment.[3] The results of the 1990–91 Gulf War, which pitted Iraq against a US-led coalition, lent credence to this notion that the US was now the only superpower and that it was in a position to shape global order in its own likeness.

Even President George Herbert W. Bush was caught up in the headiness of the moment and prematurely declared the emergence of a 'new world order'. For him this was a new order in which US power could be wielded, in concert with 'coalitions of the willing', to bring order and stability across the globe. Clearly, only the US was in a position to do this; or so it was assumed by those in that Bush administration. As it turned out, Bush lost the next US election, and it did not take long before a 'new world disorder' was in evidence in the successor states of the former Soviet Union, across Africa, in some parts of Asia and in Latin America. One analyst had anticipated this scenario and predicted that we will soon miss the Cold War.[4] Hyper-nationalism and long-suppressed ethnic conflicts reared their ugly heads and signalled the need for either a global policeman or a more assertive United Nations. The immediate post-Cold War world got both.[5]

To a large degree, the Caribbean was spared the tumult of this new global instability. But the issue of the changing dynamics in global security began to preoccupy scholars of international relations who focused on the Caribbean. One angle taken was with the concern of some analysts that these changes would result in the decline of the strategic relevance of the Caribbean region to the United States. Peter Smith argued correctly that the countries of this hemisphere confronted 'perplexing questions' as a result of the end of the Cold War.[6]

One of those perplexing questions was: will the Caribbean find itself in a geopolitical and geostrategic vacuum now that the US was no longer concerned with the penetration of Communism into the region? The short answer to this question was yes. To a large degree the Caribbean is less important to the US since the end of the Cold War. US budgetary support and aid for several projects in the Caribbean ceased or were pared back as attention was focused on the transition states in Eastern Europe. For instance, US aid to Eastern Caribbean States (ECS) dropped from US$226 million to US$25 million between 1986 and 1995.[7] However, the answer to the question may not be as simple as that. Some of the elements of the shifting global security dynamics, such as, the interlinked 'new security threats', have forced the US to pay some attention to the Caribbean.

Negative Impacts of Globalisation

As the end of the Cold War lessened the broad military security threat that had been posed by superpower confrontation, a wide range of new problems got labelled as 'new' security issues. One of these was the economic vulnerability of small states, like those in the Caribbean, stemming from the negative fallout of an intensifying globalisation. Globalisation is linked tangentially to the unipolar thesis as well as directly to the central question of the role of the US in the post-Cold War world. This is so because the US 'is the most globalising of all world powers in the extent of its economic, cultural, political and military reach'.[8] And, as a global and regional hegemon, the US has been able to ride the crest of the wave of globalisation and use that wave to spread its influence globally and regionally. This has had important implications for the Caribbean.

The interaction between processes of globalisation and efforts to integrate regional economies has become evident. There are at least two ways of understanding this interaction. The first is the view that regional integration is simply a microcosm of the broader process of globalisation. To put it another way, regional integration could be a process of strategic adaptations to further the reach of globalisation. The NAFTA process is a case in point. In this case, there are parallels between the broader globalisation and the regional integration processes. Thus, positive and negative aspects of globalisation, according to this position, would be replicated at the regional level within the integration process. Another way to look at this interaction is to view the 'new regionalism' as a response to the broader globalisation process. Thus, regional integration in Europe can be seen as a reaction to the main tendencies of globalisation. That reaction can be acquiescent — embracing the ideology and qualities of the broader global integration processes at the regional level — or resistant, such as, creating a buffer to those broader processes in order to maintain a particular regional uniqueness (culturally, socially, politically, militarily, and so on).

Caribbean states and other small states are especially vulnerable to the negative aspects of globalisation. They are also vulnerable to regional integration processes that embrace uncritically the broader globalisation tendencies without paying attention to the impacts such tendencies will have on the entire region. When the US, Canada and Mexico decided to form a single market as part of the North American Free Trade Agreement (NAFTA), their exports to each other increased exponentially and they were able to benefit from many of the positive elements of the regional integration process. However, in the Caribbean, the economies of the region's much smaller neighbours reeled from the impact of that success and found it next to impossible to compete.[9] Despite the initiatives of the Caribbean Free Trade Association (CARIFTA) and the Caribbean Community (CARICOM), the countries of the Caribbean still find themselves operating on an un-level playing field.

The large regional trading blocs are a cause of insecurity in the Caribbean. This subregion faces the danger of being swallowed up. The recent trade dispute over bananas does not bode well for the Caribbean. In that case, the

European Union had allowed the Caribbean an 8 per cent share of the European banana market. However, under pressure from the US, the World Trade Organization (WTO) struck down this 'preferential practice'. This move by the US has been called a 'diabolical campaign to abolish European preferences that have kept the Caribbean banana – and the islands that depend on it – from going bust'.[10] Thus one can see how the US may be creating a sense of insecurity among its smaller neighbours in the region by its actions. Apart from this, there is an ongoing fear among Caribbean leaders that these large regional trading blocs may eventually lead to the reduction or loss of economic assistance, foreign investments, and preferential trading arrangements.[11]

A recent report on *Globalization and Development* being analysed at the Twenty-ninth Session of the Economic Commission for Latin America and the Caribbean (ECLAC) in Brasilia, showed that the latest phase of globalisation has worsened income inequality within Caribbean countries.[12] The primary reason for this is that capital is basically free to move anywhere in the world but the movement of labour is highly restricted as industrial states like the US tighten their immigration requirements. Private international capital markets are very unstable and contribute to the vulnerability of developing countries. In addition, the transfer of technology to poorer countries is restricted by stringent intellectual property regimes being imposed through the Agreement on Trade Related Aspects of Intellectual Property Rights (TRIPs) at the World Trade Organization (WTO).

Debt, Brain Drain, and Illegal Immigration

Added to these economic woes, is the considerable debt burden that many Caribbean countries currently face. In 1992, the 5.5 million people in the English-speaking Caribbean carried a debt totalling US$9.5 billion. This was made worse by the austerity measures taken against Caribbean countries by the International Bank for Reconstruction and Development (IBRD) and the International Monetary Fund (IMF). 'Guyana, Trinidad and Tobago, Nicaragua, Panama, Barbados, Venezuela, and Jamaica all experienced strikes, riots, demonstrations, vandalism and arson when austerity measures were introduced in the late 1980s and early 1990s.'[13] This underscores the link between economic and security concerns. Attempts to improve security of the region should be considered alongside measures to improve economic development.

Economic problems in some Caribbean states have led to the exit of large segments of their population (a veritable 'brain drain'), many of whom try to enter the US and other industrialised countries either legally or illegally. A blue-ribbon National Research Council (NRC) panel on the new US immigration concluded that an average of 200,000 to 400,000 new illegal immigrants enter the USA every year. The panel estimated that the total population of illegal immigrants in the USA at the end of the last century was between two and four million people.[14] In recent years, it has been estimated that about half of all illegal aliens in the United States enter through the US-Mexico Southern sector. Among those who 'enter without inspection', the great majority are Mexicans and Central Americans. [See Table 18.1]

The influx of illegal 'undocumented' aliens into the US poses a major problem for US policy makers and is considered by US policy makers as a 'security' concern, especially in the wake of the 9/11 terrorist attack. Thus, US patrol agents from the Immigration and Naturalization Service (INS) can be found performing their duties as far away as 8,000 miles from US shores. Whether Caribbean countries like it or not, this means that interdiction and surveillance of potential illegal aliens by these US Patrol Agents could actually take place in the Caribbean Sea – encroaching on the sovereign jurisdiction of some Caribbean nations.

Table 18.1
Deportable Aliens of Caribbean Nationality, 1997

Caribbean Country	Number of Aliens Deported from the US '000
Belize	290
Cuba	1,498
Dominican Republic	4,639
Haiti	962
Jamaica	1,926
Trinidad & Tobago	402
Guyana	256

Source: *US, Bureau of Citisenship and Immigration – a Bureau of the US Department of Homeland Security, Table 57 at http://www.immigration.gov/graphics/aboutus/statistics/enf97table.pdf.*

Drugs, Crime, and Arms

Another 'new' security concern for the region has been the drug threat.[15] The Caribbean area has become a major haven for drug trafficking, especially as a transshipment point for South American drug runners to get their products into the US. According to the US Drug Enforcement Administration, the:

> Caribbean remains a major transit route for South American cocaine destined for the United States and other world markets. The Caribbean is also a transit point for marijuana and heroin destined for the United States, and a major money-laundering centre for illicit drug proceeds. Furthermore, the shipment of synthetic drugs from Europe to the United States through the Caribbean is a growing threat. It is estimated that each year about US$60 billion in drug trafficking and organised crime proceeds are laundered in Caribbean countries.[16]

Clearly the drug issue is considered not only a human security problem for the Caribbean but also for the US where drug consumption is high.[17] Some US experts are now trying to make the link between the narco-trafficking and terrorism in light of known Al Qaeda operations.[18] Caribbean states have also recognised the links between drug trafficking and transnational organised crime.[19] Such crime has been on the rise in terms of its scope, intensity and sophistication. It is a security threat for citisens in the region and around the world in that it hampers countries' social, economic and cultural development.

The intensification of globalisation has provided abundant opportunities for the internationalisation of criminal activities. The Caribbean is not immune to this problem. Multinational criminal syndicates have significantly broadened the range of their operations from drug and arms trafficking to money laundering. Traffickers are able to move as many as four million illegal migrants globally each year, thereby generating gross earnings of up to US$7 billion.[20] The only way for Caribbean states to counter, successfully, this security threat is to cooperate among themselves and with other countries, since individual country resources are inadequate to address this problem.

Linked to the threat of transnational organised crime is the challenge posed by the proliferation of small arms and light weapons.[21] Small arms are cheap and plentiful and easily smuggled across borders. They are readily available for those who want to acquire them illegally and are difficult to track. In most cases, illegally acquired small arms are diverted for use in criminal activity.[22] The high level of crime and violence affecting some Caribbean states seems to be facilitated by the linkage between small arms, drug trafficking and illegal immigration/deportation issues, among other things. It is for this reason that Caribbean states are working with the US to ratify and implement the Inter-American Convention against the Illicit Manufacturing of and Trafficking in Firearms, Ammunition, Explosives, and other Related Materials. For small states like those in the Caribbean, the influx of small arms and drugs, and the related criminal activity pose a grave danger to law enforcement, many members of whom are usually unarmed and ill-prepared to deal with these problems. The resources needed to track these instruments of death and limit their use are just not available to most governments in the region.

Criminal activity in Caribbean states can lead to further economic and political instability and substantial losses in the tourist traffic on which much of the governments of the Caribbean depend. The links between drug trafficking, money laundering and political corruption are well known. The problem is compounded by the fact that many Caribbean governments provide tax havens that attract criminal elements. These governments stand to gain from the illicit money that is laundered and then, in some cases, used as capital for legitimate businesses. But money laundering and corruption in the financial and political sectors can also serve to scare away foreign investors and may indirectly lead to further underdevelopment and vulnerabilities in these countries.

Michael Collier has made the convincing argument that one of the major factors responsible for lack of development in some Caribbean states has been political corruption. It:

> decreases overall economic output (GDP per capita) and reduces capital formation. It also has a major effect on a state's rule of law – the more the corruption the weaker the rule of law. High levels of political corruption are also shown to have an effect on a state's educational output, societal inequalities, and on the levels of economic investment sources available, particularly foreign direct investment and domestic savings.[23]

Indeed, although more empirical studies need to be conducted on this issue, it is quite possible that political corruption could rival dependency as the primary cause of underdevelopment in some Third World countries. This threat to Caribbean economies from the above elements is very real and is being addressed, as shall be shown later.

Environmental Concerns

Another security problem for the Caribbean is environmental degradation or the potential for such catastrophes. Some Caribbean government and environmental groups have been protesting the fact that highly radioactive nuclear waste and plutonium shipments have been slipping clandestinely through the Caribbean Sea *en route* to Japan. The Caribbean Community (CARICOM), Organisation of Eastern Caribbean States (OECS), and Latin American and Central American Parliaments have in fact also issued statements of opposition to this primarily because the governments of France and Britain, from whence this nuclear waste came, refused to conduct environmental impact assessments of the waste shipments and appeared to have done little or no emergency planning in the event of a spill.[24]

Tom Clements, campaign director at Greenpeace International's Washington office warned that '[T] he plutonium industry is risking the lives and livelihoods of the people of the Caribbean and is courting an environmental catastrophe'. He went on to predict that 'an accident involving the shipment could devastate the region's travel and tourism industry and commercial fishing and shipping industries'.[25] If a ship carrying such material were to sink or experience a terrorist attack, this could pose a long-term threat to the health of marine life and to people living in the region. Ironically, this region is recognised as being the first Nuclear Weapons Free Zone (NWFZ) in the world.[26]

The high cost of natural disasters have taken their toll on Caribbean countries. They are forcing the Caribbean region, as a whole, to examine how the region plans for, and responds to, these events – especially hurricanes and volcanic eruptions. Natural disasters can decimate the tourist and agricultural industries. Since these are the two major foreign exchange earners for most Caribbean states, this can result in the devastation of local economies. Hurricanes have had devastating results on a number of Caribbean states. For instance, over the past 12 years, the Caribbean has witnessed Hurricane Gilbert in 1988, Hugo in 1989, Luis and Marilyn in 1995, Mitch and Georges in 1998 and Lenny in 1999, all resulting in major losses to local economies in the region. It is estimated that Hurricane Gilbert cost Jamaica $4–6 billion. The Eastern Caribbean Central Bank (ECCB) has reported that, because of Hurricane Luis in 1995, Antigua and Barbuda registered losses of 4,000 to 7,000 jobs – an estimated 15–25 per cent of the workforce. In Dominica, banana production fell by 22.8 per cent in 1995 because of tropical storm Iris and Hurricanes Luis and Marilyn. Economic growth slowed that year to 1.6 per cent, down from 2.2 per cent the previous year.[27]

Several issues have been identified as being contributing factors to the region's heavy losses from natural disasters. These include poor planning, inadequate building practices, and few legally enforceable infrastructure and building design standards. Therefore, natural disasters in the Caribbean can be, and has been, compounded by human failing and errors, such as man-made disasters. The absence, in some cases, of proper insurance plans, savings reserves, and catastrophe reserve funds has also made things worse, forcing tourist organisations and some in the agricultural industry to go into debt or declare bankruptcy. According to some analysts, much of the effects of these natural disasters in the Caribbean can be mitigated through designing and constructing resistant facilities and contingency planning.[28]

Terrorism and other Threats

While terrorism in the Caribbean itself has not been a major security issue for the governments there in the past, the recent terrorist attacks on American soil have affected the entire region as they have the rest of the world. 9/11 has come to symbolise a traumatic, perception-altering event that jarred the consciousness of all who witnessed it – either directly, in New York, Washington, and Pennsylvania, or indirectly via television in the Caribbean. No longer is this threat viewed as something 'out there' in Europe, the Middle East, Africa, Russia, Central Asia, the Indian sub-continent and China, but 'right here', in the region and on the North American continent.

This new reality has meant that the US would protect its homeland and shore up permeable borders (with Canada, up north, and Mexico, down south) – which inevitably involved a clamp down on civil liberties – and a complete re-evaluation of strategic alliances with countries. It has also meant that the Caribbean states, because of their proximity to the US, would be under pressure to spend more for improved customs and border practices and surveillance in the Caribbean Basin.

The events of 9/11 had some effect on the offshore financial services of several Caribbean countries, and the situation was compounded by the fact that the terrorist attacks occurred amidst a global recession that began in the third quarter of 2000. We know that small states like those in the Caribbean are especially vulnerable to such external economic shocks. But it was surprising that, although the impact on the airline industry worldwide was significant, the effects of this terrorist incident on tourism in the Caribbean were negligible. In fact, according to some reports, before 9/11, cruise and stay-over visitors were experiencing a slight decline because of the global economic recession. Yet, these figures improved after November 2001. Part of the reason for this may have been the aggressive $18 million tourism promotion and marketing campaign that the Heads of Governments in the Caribbean agreed to do in October 2001, involving mostly television advertisements in the US, the UK and Canada. These ads seemed to be successful in convincing individuals in those industrialised countries that the Caribbean islands were safe for visitors.[29]

The end of the Cold War may have meant the demise in the global nuclear threat, but for the Caribbean it has also meant a preoccupation with a number of 'new' security challenges. It is clear from that discussion that the entire concept of what constitutes security has been reformulated – broadened and deepened. The security of the Caribbean Basin has always been bound up with that of the US. However, in some cases, as has been shown above, the US itself – the global and regional hegemon – can pose a severe security threat to Caribbean nations. Just living under the shadow of this powerful hegemon can be a problem in and of itself, as even larger states like Canada and Mexico have discovered. In addition, being ignored by the hegemon may also constitute a security problem for small states like those in the Caribbean.

As the US becomes increasingly preoccupied with its global war on terrorism, its fight to transform the so-called axis of evil countries (Iraq, Iran and North Korea), its attempt to democratise the world in its own image, its desire to push a particular globalisation agenda, and its recent quest to address the AIDS crisis in Africa, the Caribbean will be affected one way or another. That preoccupation can result in redirection of US financial aid from the Caribbean to many of the above-named projects. But it may also embroil the Caribbean region in issues that it would dearly love to avoid.

The above discussion examined the main security challenges stemming from the negative aspects of globalisation and 'new regionalism', economic recession and the debt burden, the brain drain and illegal immigration, drug trafficking, transnational organised crime, the influx of small arms, societal violence, corruption and local criminal activity, environmental degradation and terrorism. The multifaceted, interlinked and trans-border nature of these problems mean that their solutions will most likely require comprehensive and multilateral measures. The following section examines some of the regimes, instruments and actions that can be used or taken to address some of these problems.

Regimes, Instruments and Actions

Both liberal institutionalists and realists have been engaged in a debate about the importance of regimes, i.e. delineated areas of rule-governed activity, in addressing specific problems and issues facing the international community. Regardless of which school of thought one agrees with, the concept of regime formation is now very much entrenched in the minds of academics and policy makers. Indeed, as Richard Little has pointed out, one of the important dimensions of living in a globalising world 'has been the establishment of worldwide regimes to foster rule-governed activity within the international system'.[30] The same can be said about the formation of regimes in specific regions like the Caribbean.

By regimes, I am referring to what Krasner identified as 'sets of implicit or explicit principles, norms, rules, and decision-making procedures around which actors' expectations converge in a given area of international relations'.[31] The construct of regimes provides a good framework for the utilisation of instruments and actions to resolve problems being confronted by a collection of actors. Thus, it is a useful conceptual tool when applied to the Caribbean's efforts to address the security challenges of the region since the end of the Cold War.

In this section, I will not try to deal with all of the regimes and instruments used by Caribbean nations in trying to address the problems these small states face. Instead, the purpose of this section is illustrative – demonstrating how a select number of the issues discussed above are being addressed, or how they ought to be addressed in the future.

Dealing with the Economic Problems and the Debt Burden

Individual Caribbean governments cannot tackle the economic problems and debt burden they face on their own. It would be a daunting task. Therefore, the attempt to create regimes within the region to deal with such issues should not come as a surprise. Since the days of the failed experimentation with a West Indian Federation back in the 1950s, Caribbean leaders have learned that certain problems do require collective action. Indeed, the demise of the West Indies Federation became a catalyst for future movements that possessed the potential to reconcile diverse elements in the region.

Caribbean states have tried to address their economic woes internationally by supporting and being part of the Group of 77, whereas, regionally, these states engaged in efforts to form a number of political and economic regimes and instruments to tackle the problem. In October 1967, a conference of the Caribbean heads of governments in Barbados led to the establishment of a Regional Secretariat, the Caribbean Development Bank (CDB), and in 1968 the Caribbean Free Trade Association (CARIFTA) was formed. CARIFTA was an attempt to address the issue of how changing global demands were affecting Caribbean exports. CARIFTA proved to be a success in the sense that, after its implementation, the value of interregional exports increased from EC$86 million in 1967 to EC$451 million by 1974.[32]

The underlying principles under which the CDB was expected to function were: to facilitate the economic integration of the region, to contribute to the harmonious economic growth and development of the member countries, and to promote economic cooperation and integration among them – having special and urgent regard to the needs of the less developed members. There are 20 regional and five non-regional members of the CDB. Its financial resources are made up of Ordinary Capital Resources (OCR) comprised primarily of subscribed capital and borrowings, and Special Fund Resources (SFR), used to make or guarantee loans of a high developmental priority. SFR loans have longer grace and amortisation periods, as well as lower interest rates than those applicable to OCR. In addition to its loan facilities, CDB also has technical assistance and grant facilities to support economic development in member countries. These include the Caribbean Technological Consultancy Services (CTCS), and the Basic Needs Trust Fund (BNTF). Since 1992, five loans totalling approximately US$33 million have been approved under SFR 3 (1992-1996), the main priority of which is the provision of concessional resources aimed at improving infrastructure, strengthening local financial institutions, and increasing productivity.

Eventually, CARIFTA was transformed into another integrative regime, the Caribbean Community (CARICOM) through the Treaty of Chaguaramus in July 1973. It was designed to preserve the traditional areas of cooperation while opening up channels for regional development. One of the unique features of CARICOM is the mandate to coordinate the foreign policies of all member states. A free trade area was created with the establishment of CARICOM and functional cooperation in non-economic areas such as education and health was established along with a Caribbean Common Market with a common external tariff.[33] These economic regimes ought to be reformed or transformed and utilised more creatively to solve some of the economic problems being faced by Caribbean states in this new era.

One possible transformation project would be the creation of more comprehensive integration arrangements, building on the existing regimes.

This would require individual Caribbean leaders to consider relinquishing some of their country's sovereignty in order to have greater harmonisation of policy among the entire Caribbean area. This, in essence, was one of the primary recommendations of the West Indian Commission (WIC). Established under the Grand Anse Declaration in 1989, the WIC was mandated to examine how the Caribbean region could prepare for the post-Cold War era, while maintaining the goals of the Treaty of Chaguaramas. Among its final recommendations were: the elimination of barriers to individual travel from one Caribbean territory to another; the free movement of skills from one country to another; increased foreign and domestic investment; enhanced mobilisation for international negotiations; and plans for a common Caribbean currency.

One concrete result of the WIC was the creation, in 1994, of the Association of Caribbean States (ACS). The ACS has gone beyond CARICOM in terms of membership to include non-English speaking Caribbean states (as members and associate members) – Aruba, Colombia, Cuba, Costa Rica, the Dominican Republic, El Salvador, Guadeloupe, Guatemala, Haiti, Honduras, Martinique, Mexico, the Netherlands Antilles, Nicaragua, Panama, Suriname, and Venezuela – thus becoming truly a regime for the 'Greater Caribbean'. The objectives of the ACS are: the strengthening of the regional cooperation and integration process, with a view to creating an enhanced economic space in the region; preserving the environmental integrity of the Caribbean Sea which is regarded as the common patrimony of the peoples of the region; and promoting the sustainable development of the Greater Caribbean. Its focal areas are trade, transport, sustainable tourism and natural disasters.[34] The desire of the ACS membership is to improve the position of the Caribbean in the international system of trading blocs. But like all integration processes, the ACS initiative has faced some obstacles; the main one being the parochialism of some Caribbean leaders.[35]

It is important, as William Demas once argued, that the Caribbean countries should unite and send out the very best people to represent the region's interests internationally.[36] The first task is to cement the regional integration process. This will require the transfer of allegiance from individual nation states to the Caribbean community as a whole and the pooling of sovereignty. So far, such regional integration efforts have not been as successful as they could have been because of the short-sightedness of some Caribbean leaders who seem more interested in preserving outmoded cultural and linguistic divisions that are rooted in the colonial history of the region.

Coping with Crime, Drugs and Small Arms

Cross-border crime is difficult to curb, even for powerful, well-endowed states. It is even more so for small, relatively impoverished states. Those involved in such crime, in drug trafficking and the illicit small arms trade are sometimes in possession of more sophisticated methods and technology than the states that are trying to track and stop them. Money laundering can threaten the entire banking system of small states and the triangulation involved in drug and arms smuggling is so complex that it takes specialised knowledge and advanced methods and technologies to counter.

It goes without saying that individual Caribbean countries cannot accomplish a dent in this illicit activity on their own. Again, the need for cooperation at the national and regional level is essential. At the global level, Caribbean states, through their membership in the UN, have contributed to the UN Convention against Transnational Crime. This Convention provides an international legal framework within which the Caribbean nations can address these problems. The whole purpose of this Convention is to promote cooperation to prevent such crimes.[37]

Alongside this global Convention emerged a regional regime – The Caribbean-US Summit Joint Committee on Justice and Security Issues – with the goal of curbing or tackling the problem of transnational criminal activity in the hemisphere. At its second meeting, held in Washington, DC, on September 8, 1999, the Committee expressed concern at the high level of crime and violence affecting partner countries and recognised the linkage between arms and drug trafficking and violent crime. It urged all partners to sign, ratify and implement the Inter-American Convention against the Illicit Manufacturing of and Trafficking in Firearms, Ammunition, Explosives, and other Related Materials. Also discussed at the meeting was the issue of deportation and its contribution to the increased levels of crime and violence in some member states. The partners acknowledged that more ought to be done to reach the objectives outlined in the Bridgetown Declaration and Plan of Action.

As a result a call was made for urgent action by partners to complete Action Plan objectives in the following areas:

- At the national political level, to continue the focus on the drug threat. All partners made a renewed commitment to formalise national drug councils and national drug strategies that include both demand and supply reduction. The US committed technical assistance for this effort.

- Reiterating their acknowledgement of the need to modernise criminal justice systems in the face of the narcotics threat, the Partners re-affirmed an earlier commitment to implement domestic legislation against conspiracy and organised crime, legislation to provide for (subject to appropriate safeguards and controlled delivery) undercover operations and telecommunications interception and electronic surveillance, and stronger asset forfeiture legislation.
- In order to complete successfully the requirement of the Action Plan to negotiate and ratify Mutual Legal Assistance and Extradition Treaties, those states that did not yet exchange instruments of ratification agreed to do so as a matter of great urgency. The US committed itself to provide partners with technical assistance for implementing relevant legislation.
- The partners agreed to revisit the issue of concluding a Memorandum of Understanding concerning criminal deportation as a matter of urgency.
- To renew efforts to combat corruption, the partners who had not yet pledged to ratify and implement the Inter-American Convention against Corruption agreed to do so.

In the case of small arms and light weapons, Caribbean states are addressing this problem through multilateral channels at the UN, realising that SALW can destabilise regions, fuel and prolong conflicts, obstruct relief programmes, undermine peace initiatives, exacerbate human rights abuses, hamper development, and foster a 'culture of violence'. The issue of SALW was first raised at the UN in 1995. But it was in July 2001 that multilateral cooperation on this issue took a substantial step forward when the UN convened a major international conference in New York on 'The Illicit Trade in Small Arms and Light Weapons in All its Aspects'.[38] From that meeting, a 'Programme of Action' was adopted to spur action and cooperation on eradicating SALW at national, regional and global levels.[39]

One way the Caribbean can further support this multilateral effort is to make consistent submissions to the UN Register of Conventional Arms that came into effect with the adoption of UN General Assembly resolution 46/36L on 6 December 1991. This Register includes data on international arms transfers as well as information provided by Member States on military holdings, procurement through national production and relevant policies. All UN member states are expected to provide this information to the Register annually.

However, some action is also being taken at the regional level as well as in the form of Conventions and Declarations. The OAS Inter-American Convention against the Illicit Manufacturing of and Trafficking in Firearms, Ammunition, Explosives, and other Related Materials was adopted in November 1997. From November 22 to 24, 2000, representatives from 22 Latin American and Caribbean States met in Brasilia to seek a common regional approach to the issue of illicit trafficking in SALW. The meeting was organised by Brazil and supported by the UN Regional Centre for Peace, Disarmament and Development in Latin America and the Caribbean (UN-LiREC). Its purpose was to prepare for the International Conference on the Illicit Trade in Small Arms and Light Weapons in All Its Aspects.

The Brasilia Declaration emphasised the importance of taking into account the specific character and experience of regions, subregions and individual countries, and recommended the adoption of concrete measures that would allow them to formulate plans that most adequately suit their specific needs. In addition, it called for the strengthening of international cooperation in the judicial, technical, financial and law enforcement fields. The participants also recognised the pivotal role that civil society can play in achieving the goals of the Conference.

With respect to tackling the issue of money laundering, Caribbean states will be taking action through the UN Global Programme against Money Laundering (GPML). This mechanism is the key instrument of the UN Office of Drug Control and Crime Prevention. Through the GPML, the UN helps member states to introduce domestic legislation against money laundering and to develop and maintain other internal mechanisms that combat this crime. The programme encourages anti-money laundering policy development, monitors and analyses the problems and responses, raises public awareness about money laundering, and acts as a coordinator of joint anti-money laundering initiatives by the UN with regional and other international organisations.

However, there is also a regional initiative – in the form of the Caribbean Financial Action Task Force – to address this problem. At a meeting in Kingston, Jamaica, from November 5–6, 1992, representatives from Caribbean and Latin American states examined the problem of money laundering as it affected each participating jurisdiction and the international community, the progress achieved in preceding years and further action required. All participants agreed to sign and ratify the 1988 UN Convention against Illicit Traffic in Narcotic Drugs and Psychotropic Substances. They also called for the creation of a mechanism to monitor and encourage progress over the next three years to ensure full implementation of this declaration. All governments were urged to take all appropriate steps necessary to ensure the integrity of their domestic and international financial systems.

Addressing the problem of crime, drugs and small arms will require Caribbean leaders to make some hard choices. First, there is a need to take a closer look at the tax shelter policy to ensure that illicit organisations and criminal elements are not taking advantage of these opportunities. But this will mean rooting out corrupt elements within governments and their bureaucracies, as well as in policing and custom agencies. Second, all Caribbean countries need to strengthen their law enforcement and judicial institutions to combat these growing problems with transnational crime, drugs and small arms proliferation. This may mean accepting financial and technical assistance from the hemispheric power or pooling regional resources to develop the requisite means for strengthening those legal and judicial bodies. The latter option makes more sense if the Caribbean states are to retain some measure of control over their pooled sovereignty.

Dealing with the threat of Terrorism

All leaders in the Caribbean expressed shock and disbelief at the despicable acts of terrorism perpetrated against the US on American soil in 2001. The immediate response was through the United Nations. At the Plenary of the Fifty-sixth Session of the General Assembly (October 5, 2001), permanent ambassadors to the UN and some Caribbean heads of state condemned all acts of terrorism, including this one, as criminal acts that are contrary to the norms of a civil society. The Dominican ambassador to the UN expressed shock at the 'macabre nature' of this act and asserted that this was not just an attack on the US but also an attack on all civil society and humankind. Indeed, several Caribbean nationals lost their lives in the series of 9/11 terrorist attacks, as many of the Caribbean representatives pointed out.

The Belize ambassador to the UN categorically rejected the claims of the 9/11 terrorist masterminds that they were championing the plight of the poor and oppressed of the Middle East. The ambassador went on to say that 'those who attack innocent civilians, support, finance, engage and encourage these criminal acts upon humanity should find no place in which to exist and operate'. The ambassador also supported 'holistic strategies at the multilateral regional and national level to combat terrorism'. As the Barbadian ambassador to the UN reminded the General Assembly, 'small countries are particularly vulnerable because they frequently do not have the logistical and intelligence assets to effectively track the activities of terrorists and other agents of transnational crime'. This is why Barbados is willing to join with other member states to elaborate appropriate measures capable of harmonising the approach of the international community to deal with the terrorist threat.

The Guyanese representative also deplored the 'criminal and monstrously destructive terrorist act' but warned as well of the imperative to guard against the bigotry that drove some to blame all Muslims and Arabs for this event.[40] The ambassador emphasised that terrorism has 'no religion, no nationality and no ethnicity.' The ambassador to the UN from Trinidad and Tobago noted that 'the manifestations of terrorism lead to the destabilisation of the world economy, and also heighten the negative impact on the economies of developing states like ours'. In his opinion, what is required is 'a consolidated and comprehensive approach to this multifaceted problem.'

The initial response of the Caribbean states to this cowardly act was to help develop a set of norms and principles around the issue of tackling terrorism. They also pushed for particular sets of actions to address the problem. There was a general feeling amongst Caribbean representatives at the UN, for instance, that international terrorism can only be properly defeated through multilateral and collective efforts aimed at not only eliminating the sources of support for terrorists but also the underlying reasons why terrorists exist in the first place. This latter point expresses an important strategic preference that the US has yet to embrace. The Grenada representative at the UN expanded on this in suggesting that 'we must consider taking steps to reduce the economic and social imbalances that exist in our world community' as a means of dealing with the terrorist threat. Echoing this sentiment, the ambassador to the UN from Antigua and Barbuda stated: 'We must address in a more meaningful manner, the underlying social, economic and political problems that cause misery, for, beyond being humanitarian, it will help to remove the atmosphere in which terrorism prospers.'

As Ed Luck has pointed out, the UN has made seminal contributions to expanding the norms against terrorism over the past 40 years.[41] This organisation has been instrumental in developing ten conventions and two protocols that essentially outlaw terrorist acts. [see Table 18.2] Clearly, the 9/11 attack provided further impetus to the UNs efforts at combating this criminal act. Those Caribbean states that did not yet ratify these Conventions and Protocols pledged to do so.

Table 18.2
Other International Conventions Established to Address Terrorism

Title	Date of signature/adoption	Date entered into Force	Caribbean state parties
Convention on Offences and Certain other Acts Committed on Board Aircraft	14 September 1963		Antigua & Barbuda, Bahamas, Barbados, Belize, Cuba, Dominican Republic, Grenada, Guyana, Haiti, Jamaica, St Lucia, St Vincent & the Grenadines, Trinidad & Tobago
Convention for the Suppression of Unlawful Seizure of Aircraft	16 December 1970	14 October 1971	Antigua & Barbuda, Barbados, Belize, Cuba, Dominican Republic, Grenada, Guyana, Haiti, Jamaica, St Lucia, St Vincent & the Grenadines, Trinidad & Tobago
Convention for the Suppression of Unlawful Acts against the Safety of Civil Aviation	23 September 1971	26 January 1973	Antigua & Barbuda, Bahamas, Barbados, Cuba, Dominican Republic, Grenada, Guyana, Haiti, Jamaica, St Lucia, St Vincent & Grenadines, Trinidad & Tobago
Convention on the Prevention and Punishment of Crimes against Internationally Protected Persons, including Diplomatic Agents	14 December 1973	20 February 1977	Antigua & Barbuda, Bahamas, Barbados, Belize, Cuba, Dominican Republic, Grenada, Haiti, Jamaica, St Vincent & the Grenadines, Trinidad & Tobago
International Convention against the Taking of Hostages	17 December, 1979	3 June 1983	Antigua & Barbuda, Bahamas, Barbados, Belize, Cuba, Dominica, Grenada, Haiti, St Kitts & Nevis, St Vincent & the Grenadines, Trinidad & Tobago
Convention on the Physical Protection of Nuclear Material	3 March 1980	8 February 1987	Antigua & Barbuda, Cuba, Grenada, Trinidad & Tobago
Protocol on the Suppression of Unlawful Acts of Violence at Airports Serving International Civil Aviation, supplementary to the Convention for the Suppression of Unlawful Acts against the Safety of Civil Aviation	24 February 1988	6 August 1989	Barbados, Belize, Grenada, Guyana, St Lucia, St Vincent & the Grenadines, Trinidad & Tobago
Convention for the Suppression of Unlawful Acts against the Safety of Maritime Navigation, done at Rome	10 March 1988	1 March 1992	Trinidad & Tobago
Protocol for the Suppression of Unlawful Acts against the Safety of Fixed Platforms Located on the Continental Shelf	10 March 1988	1 March 1992	Trinidad & Tobago
International Convention for the Suppression of Terrorist Bombings	15 December 1997	23 May 2001	Antigua & Barbuda, Barbados, Cuba, Grenada, St Kitts & Nevis, St Vincent & the Grenadines
International Convention for the Suppression of Financing of Terrorism	9 December 1999	10 April 2002	Antigua & Barbuda, Barbados, Cuba, Grenada, St Kitts & Nevis, St Vincent & the Grenadines

Source: United Nations Office on Drugs and Crime, 2003

The day after the attack on American soil the UN Security Council unanimously passed resolution 1368 which condemned the act. UN Security Council resolution 1373, which was also approved unanimously roughly two and a half weeks later, went further by calling on all UN member states to 'refrain from providing any form of support, active or passive, to entities or persons involved in terrorists acts'. It also called for the freezing of terrorists' assets, the prohibition of fundraising for terrorist activities, the denial of safe haven, passage, arms or other material assistance to terrorists, and the sharing of information between states about terrorists operations. UN member states were also obligated under this resolution to report to the Counter Terrorism Committee (CTC) about the legislative and administrative step they were taking to fulfill the above requirements. Caribbean states voted for these resolutions, so they would be expected to fulfill their end of the bargain by acting on these measures.

As members of the Organization of American States, most Caribbean nations are signatories of the Inter-American Convention against Terrorism that was adopted in Bridgetown, Barbados on June 3, 2002. In direct response to 9/11, the Twenty-third Meeting of Consultation of the Ministers of Foreign Affairs had, on September 21, 2001, entrusted the Permanent Council of the OAS with the task of preparing a Draft Inter-American Convention against Terrorism. The resulting Convention recognised that 'the fight against terrorism must be undertaken with full respect for national and international law, human rights, and democratic institutions, in order to preserve the rule of law, liberties and democratic values in the Hemisphere'. Again, this is an indication of the desire of Caribbean leaders (and others in the OAS) to address this problem within the law-based framework. It should be noted that the US has provided US$1 million to support the work of the Inter-American Committee Against Terrorism (CICTE).[42] But Brazil, Chile, and Trinidad and Tobago have also provided financial support to the secretariat of this Committee.[43]

The main purpose of this Convention is to prevent, punish, and eliminate terrorism. To accomplish this, state parties in the region have agreed to adopt certain measures and to strengthen cooperation among them. The measures include: signing on to all international Conventions designed to counteract terrorism; establishing domestic legislation and penalties to deal with terrorists and those who support them; instituting a legal and regulatory regime to prevent, combat, and eradicate the financing of terrorism; taking measures as may be necessary to provide for the identification, freesing or seizure for the purposes of possible forfeiture, and confiscation or forfeiture, of any funds or other assets constituting the proceeds of, used to facilitate, or used or intended to finance, the commission of terrorist acts; ensuring that states' domestic penal money laundering legislation also includes penalties for terrorist offences; cooperating with other states in the region with respect to the exchange of information in order to improve border and customs control measures aimed at detecting and preventing the international movement of terrorists as well as the trafficking in arms or other materials that might support terrorist activities; and enhancing the effectiveness of law enforcement bodies in the region to combat terrorism.

As shown above, Caribbean states have been part of regimes at the global and regional levels created to address these trans-border security issues. They have helped to create appropriate instruments and mechanisms through which they can carry out their actions in response to the threats to the security of states and people in the region. Further examination of these regimes, instruments and actions is needed to determine success or failure in grappling with these problems. While this goes beyond the scope of this chapter, this study should be able to help the reader understand how the Caribbean region fits into a world that is becoming increasingly globalised and interdependent and how it, as a region, is trying to deal with the security problems that confront Caribbean leaders and their civil societies. As small states, their position is at times precarious. However, through ingenuity, strategic and tactical manoeuvering, and norm entrepreneurship, this region can create the needed buffers to ensure their survival.

Conclusion

The twenty-first century will likely continue to be dominated by strategic and power calculations. While it is likely that the US may become 'overstretched' in terms of the use of its imperial power, there are few signs to indicate that its hegemonic strength will be significantly weakened anytime soon. Thus, the leaders of the Caribbean states must bear this in mind as they attempt to build a regional security regime to develop regional multilateral instruments, and to devise policy actions in response to the hegemonic policies of the sole remaining superpower.

The structure of the international system will continue to be an inhibiting factor when it comes to the development of regional regimes, instruments and policy actions in security issues areas affecting the Caribbean. The notion of cooperative security and common security is having an impact on the very structure of the international system.[44] Caribbean states, like states in other regions, must take into account the security interests of neighbours as they continue to develop a security regime for the region. There should be a shift from a preoccupation with narrow national security to an embrace of the possibility of regional and global security considerations in the development of policy throughout the Caribbean region. There is already a realisation among most Caribbean leaders that national security objectives can only be attained through broader cooperative, that is, multilateral, action – whether at the regional or international/global level. It is this realisation that continues to fuel the push towards Caribbean regional integration, despite several setbacks.

I have argued elsewhere that the development of a regional security regime in the Caribbean will have to be linked to the continued evolution of Caribbean integration and the implication that this integration movement will have for understanding the changed role of the state as a guarantor of security.[45] Traditional international relations scholarship assumes that the state can guarantee the protection of its citisens. However, we know from the experience of small and weak states that this is sometimes far from the reality. The Caribbean states, for instance, can hardly guarantee the security of their own citisens from the kinds of broadened security threats that currently exist. Even if we focused solely on the traditional security threats, a small state like Guyana, which has ongoing disputes with neighbouring countries, Venezuela and Suriname, is unable to defend itself adequately without some form of outside assistance. Indeed, as we have witnessed in the past few decades, most of the regional security arrangements in the Caribbean Basin were constructed and supported by the regional hegemon, the United States.

The scramble for foreign aid, particularly among states that are in transition from conflict, has put pressure on Caribbean governments to make greater compromises in their foreign policies and development strategies. It has led, for example, to several Caribbean countries, especially OECS states to support Japan's position in the International Whaling Commission in exchange for the promise of foreign aid. Dave Benjamin has pointed out that Grenada supported Taiwan's bid for membership in the UN in exchange for development assistance. However, the promise of foreign aid is usually greater than the actual allocation of such financial and technical assistance. In addition, the compromises made by Caribbean governments may eventually work against them in this era of globalisation. It is doubtful whether any of the foreign aid received so far has made the Caribbean any more competitive in the global economic system. And, as has been shown above, the events of 9/11 have exacerbated the vulnerability of these small states.

While mass terrorism has introduced another dynamic to the vulnerability of the small island states of the Caribbean, it is really the continuation of hegemonic pressures and hyper-liberal ideological penetration stemming from the US that may be a bigger concern in the long-run. Certainly, the new so-called Bush doctrine of pre-emptive war against regimes suspected of links to terrorism, indirectly increases the threat to Caribbean states that comes from the hemispheric 'malign' hegemon. In light of these pressures, it makes sense for Caribbean leaders to come together and develop a coherent, rational regional response. This would help them develop a single voice, in the international institutions of which they are members, on specific issues and harmonise, to the extent possible, their foreign policies.[46] Rather than constantly being reactive, the Caribbean region would be in a better position to be proactive. Rather than succumbing to US pressure on issues of concern to them, Caribbean leaders should steadfastly maintain a multilateral approach to these issues that is rooted in international law, in order to provide the region with some insulation from the onslaught.

There is an abiding hope that the Caribbean could develop a regional security regime if it is able to consolidate the regional integration movement and come to some consensus on how to respond to US security policies that are geared toward the region. This will require the summoning of diplomatic and political skill by the leaders of the entire Caribbean region and the forsaking of the parochialism that, in the past, has tended to act as a barrier to regional integration.

Notes

1. For a sampling see Donald E. Schulz and Douglas H. Graham (eds.), *Revolution and Counter-Revolution in Central America and the Caribbean* (Boulder: Westview Press, 1984); Chester Lloyd Jones, *The Caribbean since 1900* (New York: Prentice Hall, Inc., 1936).
2. Franklin W. Knight & Colin A. Palmer (eds.), *The Modern Caribbean* (Chapel Hill, NC: The University of North Carolina Press, 1989).
3. Charles Krauthammer, 'The Unipolar Moment,' *Foreign Affairs*, 70 (1990–91), 23–33.
4. See John Mearsheimer, 'Back to the Future: Instability after the Cold War,' *International Security*, 15, 1 (1990): 5–56 and John Mearsheimer, 'Why We Will Soon Miss The Cold War,' *The Atlantic Monthly*, Volume 266, No. 2 (August 1990): 35–50.
5. W. Andy Knight (ed.), *Adapting the United Nations to a Postmodern era: Lessons Learned* (Palgrave/Macmillan, 2001).
6. Peter Smith, *Talons of the Eagle: Dynamics of US-Latin American Relations*, 2nd edition (New York: Oxford University Press, 2000),1.
7. See UNDCP, 1997.
8. Richard Crockatt, 'The End of the Cold War,' in John Baylis & Steve Smith (eds.), *The Globalisation of World Politics: An Introduction to International Relations*, 2nd edition (Oxford: Oxford University Press, 2001), 108.
9. See Larry Rohter, 'Backlash From NAFTA Batters Economies of Caribbean,' *New York Times*, January 30, 1997.
10. On this issue see Brook Larmer & Michael Isikoff, 'Brawl over Bananas,' *Newsweek*, 29, 17, April 28, 1997, 43–44.
11. On this point see Ivelaw L. Griffith, 'Caribbean Security: Retrospect and Prospect,' *Latin American Research* Review, 30, 2 (1995): 18.

12. For full details on the 29th Session see http://www.eclac.cl/noticias/noticias/8/9618/infobrasil.pdf.
13. Ivelaw Griffith, 'Caribbean Security: Retrospect and Prospect,' *Latin American Research* Review, 30, 2 (1995): 24.
14. Summary of The National Research Council Report on Immigration, May 27, 1997. It can be found at http://www.usembassy-israel.org.il/publish/press/ins/in10528.htm.
15. Ivelaw L. Griffith, 'Caribbean Manifestations of the Narcotics Phenomenon,' in Jorge Rodriguez Beruff & Humberto Garcia Muniz (eds.), *Security Problems and Policies in the Post-Cold War Caribbean* (London: Macmillan, 1996), 181–200.
16. Drug Enforcement Administration, *The Drug Trade in the Caribbean: A Threat Assessment*, August 2001. See http://www.whitehousedrugpolicy.gov/international/caribbean.html. Also see the US Department of State International Narcotics Control Strategy Report, 2002 released by the Bureau for International Narcotics and Law Enforcement Affairs (March 2003) for a country-by-country summary of the drug trafficking situation as it affects the US. It can also be found at http://www.state.gov/g/inl/rls/nrcrpt/2002/html/17945.htm.
17. See a recent, comprehensive 'National Drug Threat Assessment' done by the US National Drug Intelligence Centre at http://www.usdoj.gov/ndic/pubs/716/.
18. http://www.usembassy.it/file2001_12/alia/a1120508.htm.
19. On the rise of crime in the Caribbean see, Anthony Harriott, *Crime Trends in the Caribbean and Responses*, Report to the United Nations Office on Drugs and Crime, November 12, 2002. It can be found at http://www.undcp.org/pdf/barbados/caribbean_report_crime-trends.pdf.
20. See http://www.uncjin.org/CICP/cicp.html.
21. See Keith Krause, 'Facing the Challenge of Small Arms: The UN, Multilateral Governance and Global Public Policy,' in Richard Price & Mark Zacher (eds.), *The United Nations and Global Security* (London: Palgrave/Macmillan 2004).
22. European Commission, *Small Arms and Light Weapons: The Response of the European Union* (Luxembourg: European Communities, 2001), 5.
23. A copy of this paper can be found at http://lacc.fiu.edu/publications_resources/working_papers/working_paper_05.htm.
24. See http://archive.greenpeace.org/pressreleases/nuctrans/1998feb32.html and http://www.cnic.or.jp/english/news/misc/17jan2001mox.html.
25. http://www.oneworld.net/ips2/jan98/nuclear.html.
26. See the 1967 Treaty of Tlatelolco.
27. As Dionne Jackson Miller puts it 'The Caribbean is the most tourism-dependent region in the world, with the sector raking in gross earnings of $17.9 billion in 1998, providing about 900,000 direct and indirect jobs, and contributing about a quarter of the region's foreign exchange earnings. The impact or even the threat of hurricanes can therefore have serious consequences for the region's tourism industry.' See Dionne Jackson Miller, 'Caribbean: Plan needed to mitigate impact of natural disasters,' *Third World Network* (January 15, 2003) at http://www.twnside.org.sg/title/mitigate.htm.
28. Ibid.
29. Particularly successful in this effort were Barbados and The Bahamas.
30. Richard Little, 'International Regimes,' in John Baylis & Steve Smith (eds.), *The Globalisation of World Politics: An Introduction to International* Relations, 2nd edition (Oxford: Oxford University Press, 2001), 299.
31. Stephen D. Krasner (ed.), *International Regimes* (Ithaca, NY: Cornell University Press, 1983), 2.

32. Sidney Chernick, *The Commonwealth Caribbean: The Integration Experience*, Report of a mission sent to the Commonwealth Caribbean by the World Bank, Washington, DC, World Bank, 1978, 29.
33. See Randolph Persaud, 'Social Forces and World Order Pressures in the Making of Jamaican Multilateral Policy,' in Keith Krause & W. Andy Knight (eds.), *State, Society and the UN System: Changing Perspectives on Multilateralism* (New York: United Nations University Press, 1995), 187–218.
34. See http://www.acs-aec.org/about.htm.
35. See Andres Serbin, 'Towards an Association of Caribbean States: Raising Some Awkward Questions,' *Journal of Interamerican Studies and World Affairs*, 36, 4 (Winter 1994):.72-73.
36. William Demas, *Seize the Time: Towards PECS Political Union* (Bridgetown, Barbados: West Indian Commission, 1987).
37. For the full document see http://www.uncjin.org/Documents/Conventions/dcatoc/final_documents_2/convention_eng.pdf.
38. It is estimated that there are over 600 million small arms and light weapons (SALW) in circulation worldwide. See http://disarmament.un.org/cab/salw.html.
39. UN Document A/CONF/192/15.
40. It should be noted that Guyana is a member of the Organization of Islamic Conference (OIC).
41. Edward C. Luck, 'Another Reluctant Belligerent: The United Nations and the War on Terrorism,' in Richard Price & Mark Zacher (eds.), *The United Nations and Global Security* (London: Palgrave/Macmillan, forthcoming 2004).
42. http://www.state.gov/r/pa/prs/ps/2003/16800.htm.
43. See address by the assistant secretary general of the Organization of American States, Luigi R. Einaudi, at the closing ceremonies of the Third Regular session of the Inter-American Committee Against Terrorism, San Salvador, El Salvador, January 24, 2003. See full text at http://www.oas.org/library/mant_speechspeech.asp?sCodigo=03-0008.
44. On this point see John Baylis, International and Global Security in the Post-Cold War Era,' John Baylis & Steve Smith (eds.), *The Globalization of World Politics: An Introduction to International* Relations, 2nd edition (Oxford: Oxford University Press, 2001), 253–276.
45. See W. Andy Knight & Randolph B. Persaud, 'Subsidiarity, Regional Governance, and Caribbean Security,' *Latin American Politics and Society*, vol.43, no.1 (Spring 2001), 32.
46. See Demas, 1987.

19

Regional Security Cooperation: Traditional and Non-traditional Areas

Edmund Dillon

Cooperation has become the predominant theme in discussions of security in the Caribbean Basin. Whether the specific subject is drug trafficking, migration, money laundering, natural disaster, or trade, the premise is that it is better to work together than to go it alone.
Joseph S. Tulchin & Ralph H Espach[1]

Regionalism is on the rise around the world and in the Americas, and with it comes new ways of interacting economically, politically, socially and militarily. States devote considerable thought and planning to economic issues, particularly trade, but precious little has been devoted to the security cooperation imperative that arises from these other integration areas.
Joseph R. Nunez[2]

Introduction

The quest for regional security cooperation is not new; it has been a preferred, but far-reaching, arrangement in most regions of the world. Existing collective defence arrangements, such as the Rio Treaty of the Organisation of American States, have been around since 1947. In 1960, there was the West Indian Regiment, which was formed within the English speaking Caribbean. Moreover, since 1960 the Conference of the American Armies, which includes countries from the American continent and the Caribbean, was established to collaborate and cooperate on common grounds. However, the environment in which most of these arrangements were created has changed considerably, as the contemporary security arena presents new challenges and a new focus that require solutions flowing from relevant security architectures. The two epigraphs above capture well the tone of the security environment in this Age of Terror.

Historically in the Caribbean, there have been several initiatives in respect to finding cooperative solutions for peace and security. In analysing the contemporary security situation in the Caribbean, several authors suggested that national and international issues are intertwined. In fact, many of the contemporary Caribbean security issues are not confined to the region; rather, they are transnational or have transnational consequences. The very nature of these security issues, which transcend countries, regions, and hemispheres, lends itself to some type of cooperative endeavours in the pursuit of finding solutions. The question of working together to solve security issues in the Caribbean, therefore, will always be a fundamental aspect of how we do business, as long as these security issues continue to exist in this form and the people of the Caribbean continue to seek ways of providing a safe and secure environment that is conducive to the development of the region.

It is against this background that this chapter examines continuities and challenges to regional security cooperation in the Caribbean. It is envisaged that, from a re-examination of security cooperation that occurred both in the traditional and non-traditional realm, appropriate responses can be shaped to treat with security issues in this Age of Terror. The chapter seeks to answer the question 'Can the Caribbean develop and establish regional security cooperation mechanisms to deal with traditional and non-traditional concerns in this era?' The chapter proposes a brief insight into the traditional and non-traditional areas of security cooperation by looking first at continuities and changes. Second, the relationship between security cooperation and the integration movement is examined. Finally, attention is paid to a menu of choices available to the Caribbean as it treats contemporary security cooperation issues and efforts. Within this framework, it is proposed to link the quest for integration in the Caribbean with regional security cooperation. It is hoped that regional security cooperation would be a positive outcome from the deepening and widening of integration movement.

This chapter argues that for regional security cooperation to be successful it must be intertwined with the integration movement in the Caribbean. Regional integration should, therefore, be used as the platform upon which security cooperation can be achieved. A word of caution here, however, is that, for regional cooperation to be viable, it must aim at more than the traditional model of economic integration to embrace specific projects, increased functional cooperation and a commitment to the principles of regionalism as a mechanism for achieving peace, security and development.[3]

Theoretical Framework

It can be stated from the outset that the character of security cooperation in the Caribbean has been largely a combination of reliance on external protection, on the one hand, and an attempt to guard the sovereignty of states from within the region, on the other. Moreover, issues of security have often been looked at more from national perspectives rather than a regional perspective, while the impetus and initiatives for security cooperation have mainly been externally oriented and externally driven. One way to assess this external orientation and reliance is in terms of a core-periphery security relationship between the countries of the Caribbean and the metropolitan countries. This approach derives from the work of Immanuel Wallerstein and Andre Gunder Frank who posited the idea of a core-periphery economic relationship between countries of the Third World and developed metropole.

Drawing on Wallerstein's work on World System theory,[4] in which he described the economic relationship between the countries in the developed world (core) and the underdeveloped world (periphery), the security dealings between the Caribbean and the metropolitan countries can be described as a core-periphery security relationship. Thus, this writer suggests that the security linkages between countries in North America (USA and Canada) and Europe (notably the United Kingdom, France, and the Netherlands) and the Caribbean have largely reflected a core-periphery relationship. The concept helps to demonstrate how geopolitical, cultural and national security factors provide critical influences that include the historical legacies of colonialism. In fact, colonialism introduced and maintained specific forms of linkages between small states and the metropolitan countries. These linkages are related to specific threats such as territorial integrity, sovereignty issues, challenges to democracy, the illegal drugs issue and recently terrorism, all of which affect the nature of cooperation in and with the Caribbean.

Continuities, Challenges and Changes

Security Landscape and Early Attempts at Cooperation

According to Ivelaw Griffith, the nature of the Caribbean security landscape could be seen as including both traditional and non-traditional concerns, existing side by side. Territorial disputes and hemispheric geopolitics are the core traditional concerns while drugs, political instability, HIV/AIDS, migration, illegal arms trafficking and environmental degradation are the chief non-traditional security ones.[5] Given the present international security environment and perhaps the Caribbean geopolitical concerns, terrorism must be included on the list of non-traditional threats. Additionally, with the United States-led war with Iraq in March 2003, oil producing or refining Caribbean countries such as Trinidad and Tobago and Curaçao were faced with a new threat to these resources: energy security.

As might be expected, the region's security landscape has undergone significant change over the centuries.Since the seventeenth century, Spanish, French, British, and Dutch projections of power were tied to colonial and mercantile interests in the Caribbean. This colonial relationship also shaped United States responses in the Caribbean, as the Untied States took active steps to compete directly with European activities in the region.[6] During this era, security in the Caribbean was viewed in traditional terms, through military lenses. In fact, any discussion of the Caribbean military within the international security environment cannot be complete without the mention of the key actors, such as the United Kingdom, the United States, and France and the core-periphery military relationship that was subsequently created. Except in the case of Cuba, Caribbean nations have had no international military posture, and any role played by Caribbean military forces in the international arena, in most cases, has been the role assigned by the various metropolitan powers or international agencies. Over the years, extra-regional forces did most of the regional military posturing, such that Thomas H. Moorer and George A. Fauriol have been able to conclude that regional force structure and dispositions have also been affected by the historical relationships with extra-hemispheric powers.[7]

Within the Anglophone Caribbean, the core-periphery security relationship can be seen in the tradition and culture of the military, which has its antecedence in the insertion of the British military in what was then referred to as the West Indies in the seventeenth century. By the middle of the seventeenth century, England had established permanent settlements in St Kitts (1624), Barbados (1627), Nevis (1628), Montserrat and Antigua (1632), and Jamaica (1655). It was therefore no surprise that, according to Roger Norman Buckley, the first experience of regular British soldiers in the West Indies came in 1652, when a fleet under the command of Sir George Ayscue put into Carlisle Bay, Barbados.[8]

Regional security cooperation during this period was demonstrated through the positioning of military units in several islands. In 1798, the British established a volunteer defence force known as the West India Regiment. Although primarily responsible for defending and maintaining order in Britain's West Indian colonies, the British-trained and British-commanded regiment also fought for Britain in the American Revolution, the War of 1812, and various campaigns in West Africa. The principal administrative units of the

British West Indian Army comprised the Jamaica command and the Windward and Leeward Islands command. The former, which reported separately to London on the state of the command, included bases at Jamaica, the Bahamas, Bermuda, and Belize. The latter command, with its headquarters at Barbados, comprised camps at Antigua, Barbados, Guyana, Dominica, Grenada, St Kitts, St Lucia, St Vincent, Tobago, and Trinidad.[9] Up to World War II, all troops in the British West Indies that formed the Second West Indian Regiment were under either the North Caribbean Command, headquartered in Jamaica, or the South Caribbean Command, headquartered in Trinidad. The presence of the British military in several islands of the Caribbean at this time, therefore, presented an early, rudimentary framework of regional security cooperation.

By the middle of the twentieth century, the Caribbean landscape began to change in two significant ways. First, there was the establishment of American military bases in the Caribbean, through the lend–lease arrangement whereby Britain granted the United States a 99-year lease in exchange for 40 old naval destroyers. Second, there was the formation of the third West India Regiment, which was followed by what can be described as the movements toward independence in the 1960s. During this period, also, an attempt at regional integration that incorporated a security aspect was manifested through the formulation of the Federation of the West Indies in 1958.

The security cooperation aspect of the Federation was the establishment of the West India Regiment. The Regiment, which formed the security element of the Federation, had its headquarters in Jamaica and comprised soldiers from several Caribbean islands. There were also plans to establish the second battalion in Trinidad and Tobago at a later date. Sadly, however, the Federation broke up in 1962 and the West India Regiment was disbanded as the countries moved towards gaining independence from Britain. Andy Knight and Randolph Persaud, in their article 'Subsidiarity, Regional Governance and Caribbean Security', suggested that the dissolution of the Federation did not dampen the quest for Caribbean integration, but in fact provided a catalyst for future movements that possessed the potential to reconcile diverse elements in the region.[10] The post-independence scenario in the Caribbean in the late 1960s was in fact characterised by renewed efforts to pursue integration in the region.

This pursuit of an integrated Caribbean has been described as partly a response to the real and perceived security threats that face the Caribbean; threats both to the sovereignty of individual countries and the security of individuals and groups in the region as a whole.[11] A brief discourse of the integration movement and its relationship to security cooperation is therefore pertinent here.

Integration and Cooperation

In the late 1960s and early 1970s in the English-speaking Caribbean, several regional integrated mechanisms were developed. Following the collapse of the Federation in 1962, in 1968 the Caribbean Free Trade Association (CARIFTA) was established. This was followed by the Caribbean Development Bank in 1970 and in 1973 the Treaty of Chaguaramas established the Caribbean Community (CARICOM). CARICOM maintained the traditional areas of cooperation established under CARIFTA, which facilitated and promoted economic integration while expanding on further development of the region. These further developments covered such areas as foreign policy, a common external tariff, and functional cooperation in non-economic areas, in particular, education and health. It is worth noting here that between the desolution of the Federation and the establishment of CARICOM, security cooperation was not included in the Caribbean integration agenda.

The strengthening and widening of integration efforts in the Caribbean produced the West Indian Commission which came out of the Grand Anse Declaration in 1989. This was founded to examine how the Caribbean region could prepare for the 1990s and the twenty-first century. Some of the recommendations made by the Commission included free movement of skills, increased foreign and domestic investment, elimination of barriers to individual travel, plans for a common Caribbean currency, and enhanced mobilisation for international negotiation, but still no mention of security cooperation.

The most recent product of the 1992 West Indian Commission recommendations was the establishment of the Association of Caribbean States (ACS). Formed in 1994, the ACS changed the composition and paradigm of the integration movement when it incorporated countries beyond the CARICOM area, including those in Central America and South America that fall within the Caribbean littoral. While the ACS emphasised regional trade and negotiation mechanisms, it also focused on an area that is fundamental to this study; it highlighted greater cooperation toward the establishment of regional identity that could perhaps pave the way for an expansion in areas such as regional security. Security as an issue is therefore still not treated as a pertinent topic during the quest for integration in the Caribbean.

One of the first opportunities presented to the Caribbean to cooperate with regards to a security issue in the mid-1960s was the situation between the union of St Kitts-Nevis and Anguilla.[12] In 1967, Anguilla voted to leave the union. As such, the territorial integrity of St Kitts-Nevis and Anguilla was challenged. This move resulted in confrontation between St Kitts-Nevis and Anguilla. Regional cooperation occurred on this occasion when newly independent Barbados, Guyana, Jamaica, Trinidad and Tobago, and St Kitts-Nevis and its colonial power, Great Britain, held a conference to deal with the situation. The five independent countries agreed to provide a peace-keeping force to treat with the situation. This action was evidence of cooperation. Paradoxically, it also reflected a failure of regional cooperation and the reliance on external powers when Jamaica withdrew from the agreement and the Anguillans rejected the legitimacy of the peace-keeping force. The four independent countries then called on Great Britain 'to guarantee the territorial integrity of St Kitts-Nevis-Anguilla'.[13] Britain readily accepted this challenge and intervened without the assistance from the Caribbean.

In 1981, another attempt at regional security cooperation involving the Bahamas, Barbados, Guyana, Trinidad and Tobago, Britain, and Canada occurred in relation to the territorial dispute between Belize and Guatemala. These countries, each with commonwealth ties, agreed to consult on any action deemed necessary to protect the independence of Belize. Several authors have concluded that while diplomatically this agreement worked, in terms of the positioning of force, the defence arrangement was left up to Great Britain with little or no commitment from the Caribbean countries involved in the discussion. This further demonstrated the external reliance posture of the Caribbean states. Thus, up to then, regional security cooperation was never operationalised in so far as involvement of the security forces of the Caribbean are concerned. This was to change, however, in 1983 when the United States intervened in Grenada, and in 1994 with the intervention in Haiti. This period is also significant as it marked the first time that the United States had intervened militarily in the affairs of the English speaking Caribbean.

The 1983 United States intervention in Grenada, code-named 'Urgent Fury', provided a significant milestone in the discourse on regional security cooperation in the Caribbean. It provided the catalyst for both security cooperation and a booster for regional integration while also highlighting the reliance on external powers for the security of the Caribbean. The emergence of the Maurice Bishop revolution of March 1979 in Grenada and his attempt at non-capitalist governance sent shock waves throughout the region, particularly in the Eastern Caribbean. The Eastern Caribbean States, concerned about the spread of the events in Grenada to their small states, established the Regional Security System (RSS) in 1982. The formation of the RSS was basically in response to the traditional security concerns of these East Caribbean countries, but non-traditional issues were also within its purview. The Memorandum of Understanding (MOU) that established the RSS was designed as a framework for security cooperation in the Eastern Caribbean. While the RSS did not include the wider Caribbean, it provided a significant initiative for regional security cooperation.

According to Brigadier General Rudyard Lewis, in theory the MOU stated that in the event that a member state deemed its security threatened, it has the right to request assistance from any or all of the member states.[14] Professor Vaughn Lewis, commenting on the MOU stated, 'The Memorandum of Understanding, though not a full treaty, represented the first arrangement of its kind within the Caribbean Community zone. In immediately providing the Memorandum with operational and institutional instruments for its functioning, the participating states indicated their commitment to a collective security approach'.[15] The MOU was upgraded to treaty status in 1996. Article 4, paragraph 1 of the treaty describes the purpose and functions of the System as promoting cooperation among the member states in the prevention and interdiction of traffic in illegal narcotic drugs, in national emergencies, search and rescue, immigration control, fisheries protection, customs and excise control, maritime policing duties, natural and other disasters, pollution control, combating threats to national security, the prevention of smuggling and the protection of offshore installation and exclusive economic zones.[16]

The crisis in Grenada was also the first time that regional security cooperation was effected at the operational level. This was a significant step for the English-speaking Caribbean since previous attempts at regional security cooperation never involved any commitment of personnel. On this occasion, however, troops from the Caribbean islands were actually deployed to participate in actions geared to ensure a safe and secure environment in their region.

While the involvement of personnel from the Caribbean islands provided a fillip to the regional security cooperation mechanism, it is important to note the part played by the United States in spearheading the operation, called Operation Urgent Fury. During the Grenada crisis, the Caribbean military, particularly those from the Eastern Caribbean States, Barbados and Jamaica, were integrated into the United States regional military network. The execution of the operation once again demonstrated the type of core-periphery security relationship that existed when consideration is given to the role given to the Caribbean troops in Operation Urgent Fury.

According to Humberto García Muñiz and Jorge Rodríguez Beruff, this involvement of the US with the Caribbean military started a process of regionalisation of the security forces of the Caribbean under the direction of the United States to face the threat of instability in the region.[17] Several studies have pointed out that the RSS relies heavily on external support for its continued operation, which led Paul Sutton to state that the philosophy behind the system explicitly acknowledges the role of foreign forces in an acute situation.[18] The establishment, maintenance and support for the RSS, therefore, follow a pattern within the core-periphery security relationship.

The 1990s ushered in the post-Cold War reductions of United States attention in the region and simultaneously a new thrust in the Caribbean to strengthen regional capabilities to deal with issues concerning peace and security. Two events that are worthy of mention that impacted positively on regional security cooperation are the coup attempt in Trinidad in 1990 and the US-led intervention in Haiti in 1994. The 1990 attempted *coup d'etat* in Trinidad and Tobago created another shockwave throughout the region. The situation in Trinidad provided another opportunity for cooperation among the Caribbean islands as troops from other countries were invited to assist the Trinidad and Tobago Defence Force (TTDF). It is important to note here that, unlike the Grenada situation, the crisis in Trinidad was handled in the main by the TTDF with later assistance from Caribbean troops; there were no troops from outside the Caribbean involved in the operation. The coup attempt once again acted as a catalyst, prompting participants at the Conference of Heads of the Caribbean Community held in Jamaica around the same time, to seriously consider threats to the parliamentary democracy that is a cherished heritage of the Caribbean landscape. At this conference the Heads agreed, *inter alia,* to the establishment of a regional security mechanism that would assist member states in clearly defined situations.[19]

The Trinidad and Tobago experience influenced the leaders in the Caribbean to adopt a new attitude toward regional security cooperation, as the following statements show. In 1990, then prime minister of Trinidad and Tobago, ANR Robinson, who had been held hostage in the attempted coup, stated:

> it is becoming increasingly apparent that no single state, large or small can in isolation ensure its own security from subversion or external threat. In this era of interdependence of states and the globalisation of activities relating to almost every sphere of life — economic, politic, cultural and criminal to name a few — the preservation of national security can no

> longer be seen purely in national terms. (Griffith, *The Quest for Security in the Caribbean*, 1993)

Another Caribbean statesman, Erskine Sandiford, then prime minister of Barbados, echoed similar sentiments:

> The preservation of law and order and national security contribute uniquely to growth and development through the promotion of stability. We must therefore expand our integration effort to include the area of regional security: and we must seek further cooperation with friendly governments in our region and beyond. One thing is certain; no single territory can do it alone. We have to work together if we are to ensure that [the] Caribbean remains a zone of peace, prosperity and democracy. (Griffith, *Drugs and Security in the Caribbean: Sovereignity Under Seige*, 1997)

This positive attitude towards regional security cooperation among several Caribbean leaders played a very important part in the decision to send CARICOM troops as part of the United States-led Multinational Force that intervened in Haiti in 1994 under Operation Restore Democracy. The Haitian experience is another milestone in the quest to further regional security cooperation at the operational level. This operation was the first time in the history of the Caribbean that troops from seven countries were deployed under a single command structure referred to as the CARICOM Battalion. This battalion comprised personnel from Belize, Bahamas, Jamaica, Antigua and Barbuda, Barbados, Trinidad and Tobago and Guyana, under the command of a contingent commander from Jamaica, a battalion commander and a second-in-command from Trinidad and Tobago. It is instructive to note, however, that while the battalion was Caribbean in composition, it relied heavily on the United States for logistic support with respect to clothing, vehicles, rations, accommodation, arms and ammunitions. The response from the Caribbean, however, established a working model, the CARICOM Battalion. This battalion represented an actual manifestation of regional security cooperation at both the operational and tactical levels. It is a model worthy of further analysis.

Several authors have described the Caribbean security landscape as inclusive of both traditional and non-traditional threats that have occurred side by side. The traditional concerns mentioned in the preceding paragraphs focussed on the deep-seated traditional issues related to territorial disputes and geopolitical interactions in the hemisphere. Within recent times, the territorial dispute between Ecuador and Peru is the only dispute within the hemisphere that saw military mobilisation and confrontation. While the threat and challenges are no longer states versus states, in the Caribbean there still exist some disputes involving territorial claims, such as those between Suriname and Guyana, and Venezuela and Guyana. The issue between Belize and Guatemala continues to progress towards amicable settlement. The end of the Cold War and the subsequent break up of the Soviet Union also signalled the end of the quest to pursue the non-capitalist path of governance in the Caribbean. With the exception of the historical territorial disputes that continue to exist on the South American mainland and Central America, most militaries and defence forces in the Caribbean are no longer poised to defend their country against external aggression. The focus is now on non-traditional issues that are both domestic and transnational in nature.

The above discourse on the traditional concerns and subsequent responses has demonstrated that regional security cooperation in this area has occurred over time with some degree of success and some failure. For the most part the successes were due to military security cooperation and the failures were due to lack of political will to endorse or support a particular course of action. It must also be remarked that, in some countries, non-traditional security issues are ranked higher than the traditional ones mentioned above. In fact, most of the Eastern Caribbean countries have no traditional security concerns and therefore concentrate on non-traditional issues. There are, however, some lessons and models that are fundamental to the structure and pursuit of future activities.

Non-traditional threats

There is evidently increasing attention throughout the world to non-traditional security concerns and a simultaneously increasing inclination to view security in broader, more comprehensive terms. This holds true for Europe, Asia, Africa and the Americas. Several authors have explained that the complexities of the non-traditional security issues suggest that they are best handled from a collaborative and cooperative standpoint.

Regional security cooperation in the non-traditional areas, which have been identified as illegal drugs, political instability, HIV/AIDS, migration, illegal arms and ammunition trafficking, money laundering, environmental degradation, terrorism and natural disaster, has occupied and continue to occupy the agenda of all discussions on Latin American and Caribbean security matters over the last several years. Within recent times, a review of common security concerns has revealed additional issues such as corruption, criminal deportees from North America, kidnapping and the ineffectiveness of the justice system. Kidnapping, for example, has been linked with transnational crime in the sense that it creates the accumulation of capital to carry out illegal activities associated with some of the non-traditional threats mentioned above. The United Nations Economic and Social Council's Commission on the Crime Prevention and Criminal Justice, in its resolution 2002/16 of July 2002 entitled 'International cooperation in the prevention, combating and elimination of kidnapping' condemned and rejected the practice of kidnapping.

The complexities of the various issues in the non-traditional areas suggest that they require different policies, institutional responses and courses of action from those that occurred in the traditional realm. Attempts at regional cooperation in these areas have been confined to talk shops, committee formulation and bilateral agreements that, in many cases, lack implementation. The current trend involves threat-specific bilateral or multilateral initiatives in a sort of building block approach designed to set the framework for broader regional security cooperation. A trend to note here that continues the core periphery relationship is that most of the bilateral and some of the multilateral agreements are as a result of the larger metropolitan initiatives.

The foremost non-traditional threat in the hemisphere, prior to the terrorist attack in the United States in 2001, was the multifaceted problem involving drugs. Within the realm of non-traditional threats, the narcotics phenomenon is undoubtedly the most all-inclusive issue in the Caribbean. It involves not only the Caribbean countries but it also seems to move across borders without much difficulty. Roberto Marrero-Corletto identified the Italian Mafia connection in the region; the Dutch connection through St Maarten, Aruba, Bonaire, and Curaçao; the French connection through Martinique and Guadeloupe; and the Colombian connection as external partners in the drug trade in the Caribbean.[20] Ivelaw Griffith stated that the Caribbean lies at what Jose Marti called 'the Vortex of the Americas', making it a bridge between North and South America.[21] The very geography of the Caribbean therefore lends itself not only to legal usages but also illegal endeavours. Thus, the Caribbean finds that it is strategically positioned between supply and demand in reference to the illegal drug trade and related activities such as money laundering, arms trafficking and organised crimes.

The narcotics issue infringes on the political, economic, military, paramilitary, and sociocultural dimensions of the Caribbean societies. Ivelaw Griffith has demonstrated that the narcotics issue is not a one-dimensional matter but a phenomenon that is multidimensional, both in its main problems and in its consequences. He pointed out that the nexus between drugs and security lies in the consequences and implications of drug operations for the protection and development of individuals and state and non-state entities in the hemisphere.[22]

The transnational nature of the drug trade provides a difficult scenario for the Caribbean countries to fight against with their relatively limited resources. As such, cooperation and collaboration present positive approaches to combating the problem. The efforts at cooperation to deal with this phenomenon, however, are demonstrated more in terms of bilateral arrangements, mostly with the United States, instead of a regional approach originating from within the Caribbean. In dealing with the drug phenomenon, for example, Ivelaw Griffith observed that 'The nature and gravity of the drug dilemma highlight another reality in the Caribbean: Caribbean countries cannot by themselves cope with the threats presented by drugs .... Collaboration is therefore a practical necessity if not always a political desire'.[23] In terms of bilateral arrangements, the agreement popularly known as the Shiprider Agreement is worth mentioning here, as it reflects an example of the core-periphery security relationship and a cooperative approach to dealing with a regional security issue.

This agreement, officially The Maritime and Over-flight Agreement, permits land and sea patrols by United States coast guard and navy vessels, maritime searches, and seizures and arrest by United States law enforcement authorities within the national boundaries of the Caribbean countries that are party to it. All that is required, for example, in the case of Trinidad and Tobago, is that a member of the Trinidad and Tobago Coast Guard rides on the United States navy or coast guard ship during its excursion in territorial waters and more specifically that that member is present during the arrest of the offenders. Similarly, the overflight clause allows a United States aircraft to overfly Caribbean countries and order suspect aircraft to land there. While most of the Caribbean countries have signed amended versions of the Shiprider Agreement, and while most Caribbean countries cooperate with the United States, the agreement generated both government and public hostility. It has been seen in some quarters to interfere with the national security and, in particular, the sovereignty of the islands.

Although CARICOM heads of government have described the illegal drug trafficking and its associated arms and ammunition trafficking as threats to the region, Kathy Ann Brown suggested 'there is a sense that not enough is being done to systemically uproot the drug scourge which has been both expanding and deepening.'[24] In the area of security cooperation and drug trafficking, researchers agree that the Caribbean governments have not reached a uniform, or even coordinated, policy on the drug problem in the region. However, some governments have initiated policies to deal with the drug situation while others have no policies. A point to note, though, is that the influence of the United States, and to some extent Great Britain, is present with those that have policies. In fact the funding is most times sourced from these countries to enforce the policies.

Ron Sanders captures the US interest with respect to the drug problem in the following statement:

> Caribbean governments have been subjected to more than little coercion by US agencies to allow them to select local personnel for drug enforcement units and to participate in planning, if not directing their operations. The regional governments have faced similar demands from US agencies for the establishment of National Drug Councils to review the situation in relation to drugs and take some appropriate action.[25]

Within recent times, however, there have been efforts to strengthen the region's security system. These efforts have been prompted by the desire to eradicate the drug problem and the associated issues of money laundering, arms and ammunition trafficking in the Caribbean. The RSS countries, for instance, conduct joint maritime operations within the territorial waters of individual states to stem the flow of illegal drugs and its associated activities in the region. The US Coast Guard and the Royal Navy are at times involved in these operations.

Terrorism as a non-traditional threat in the Caribbean has gained prominence over the drug issue since the attack in the United States in September 2001, once again highlighting the core-periphery security relationship. Although the Caribbean was not the direct target of the September 11 attack, the region has suffered severe economic fallout as a result. In Trinidad and Tobago, the economic growth in the first quarter of 2002 was flat as the negative fallout from the terrorist attack in the United States affected the economy, particularly the non-energy sector, according to the *Economic Bulletin* from the central bank.[26]

Terrorist acts can take place anywhere, and historically the Caribbean is not immune to this kind of activity. For example, in 1976 there was the bombing of the Cubana Air flight as it took off from Barbados. Major industrial complexes in some Caribbean countries and the large amount off foreign investments present targets of opportunity to terrorist acts. Trinidad and Tobago, as one of the more industrialised nations in the Caribbean, provides a case in terms of terrorist threat to security. It has a petroleum-based economy with heavy manufacturing activities, especially at its Point Lisas Industrial Estate. There are oil refineries, ammonia, methanol, urea and cement plants, and a steel industry that produce direct reduced iron and steel. Additionally, there are several offshore and on-land oil and industrial installations which are owned and operated by United States, British and Canadian companies. It is well noted that the international terrorists have issued warnings that they intend to target American and British interests all over the world. As such, the Caribbean cannot assume any degree of immunity, particularly given the bombings in Bali and Kenya in 2002.

The approach to dealing with the terrorist threat in the Caribbean has not been met with a regional response thus far. But there has been some encouragement from the United States, and several countries have reaffirmed their commitment to implementing the United Nations Security Council Resolution 1373. In this regard, the Legal and Constitution Affairs Division of Commonwealth Secretariat has issued a document entitled 'Model Legislative Provisions on Measures to Combat Terrorism' to assist countries with implementation of UN Security Resolution 1373. Trinidad and Tobago and some other Caribbean countries have begun drafting legislative documents to deal with the threat of terrorism in accordance with Resolution 1373. Speaking at a ceremony to celebrate United Nations Day, the Minister of Foreign Affairs of Trinidad and Tobago, Senator Knowlson Gift stated:

> We will certainly be working to strengthen the partnership with the United Nations...the near universality of membership of the UN strengthens even the cause of multilateralism, not only when the international community must address matters relating to peace and security, but also when it must deal effectively with such equally pressing global concerns as poverty reduction and the fight to halt and reverse the spread of HIV/AIDS ... multilateralism rests on the commitment of all states to join forces in pursuit of common aims.[27]

Another non-traditional regional security concern that is worthy of mention here is that of natural disasters. There is a school of thought that natural disasters do not constitute a threat as defined in the realm of security. This, however, must be put in perspective; for the people of the Caribbean, natural disasters are seen as enemies that destroy lives, homes and properties, the effect of which are similar to involvement in combat situations. There are occurrences, such as the volcanic eruption in Montserrat, as a result of which almost the entire island has become uninhabitable. Then there are hurricanes which left trails of destruction, death and mayhem throughout the Caribbean and Central America – George, Mitch, and Hugo are but a few examples of the 'enemies'. The regional response to natural disaster has been quite efficient thus far through the operation of the Caribbean Disaster Emergency Relief Agency and the Caribbean Disaster Response Unit. The former looks after the administrative and strategic issues, while the latter, consisting of military and protective services personnel from the various islands, constitutes the operational elements.

The above discourse, which re-examined the historical and contemporary issues relating to continuities and changes in traditional and non-traditional areas of regional security cooperation, has attempted to give an insight into some of the cooperation successes, failures and challenges in the Caribbean. Regional security in the Caribbean, however, cannot be treated in isolation; it must be considered together with the integration movement in the region. The integration movement is seen as the most appropriate vehicle to muster support for the political will that is required to legitimise regional security cooperation in the Caribbean. To this end, there have been several initiatives aimed at developing institutional responses to deal with security issues from a regional cooperative approach.

Institutional Measures

In examining the institutional measures adopted to pursue regional security matters, the Organisation of American States (OAS), as the overarching organisation in the Hemisphere, established a conceptual base to foster development in the area of regional security cooperation. At the Summit of the Americas in April 2001, the OAS, in its attempt to strengthen mutual confidence in regard to hemispheric security, adopted a resolution to improve the transparency and accountability of defence and security institutions and promote greater understanding and cooperation among government agencies involved in security and defence issues, through such means as increased sharing of defence policy and doctrine papers, information and personnel exchanges, including, where feasible, cooperation and training in order to improve confidence and security in the hemisphere. Within the broader hemispheric umbrella, associations such as the Conference of Commanders of American Armies (CCAA) and the Defence Ministers of the Americas Conference (DMAC) have been established in an attempt to bring the region closer in a cooperative environment to deal with regional security issues. The aim of CCAA, for instance, is the analysis, debate and exchange of ideas and experiences related to matters of common interest in the field of defence so as to heighten cooperation and integration between the armies and to contribute, from a military thinker's point of view, to security and democratic development of member countries.[28]

According to W. Andrew Axline:

> the Caribbean reflects a general trend for economic integration among developing countries to evolve beyond traditional free trade areas and customs unions, toward the establishment of regional cooperation that eschews traditional economic integration in favour of specific steps that are more relevant to problems of peace and security and development.[29]

Several authors have pointed out that security has not been a major concern of the integration movement in the Caribbean. In fact, until recently, CARICOM did not consider security as an issue. Neither did the Association of Caribbean States (ACS) make provision for cooperation in matters of regional security in its Convention. This view is beginning to change, however, as several regional institutions have placed security and specifically security cooperation on the top of their agenda.

In this Age of Terror, brought about by the effect of the events of 9/11 in the USA, security issues, spearheaded by terrorism as defined within the core-periphery security relationship, have taken prominence in formulating institutional responses. For instance, at a meeting in April 2003, the ACS committed to look at security cooperation within its membership. This move reflects a change in the focus of the ACS, which was established in July 1994 with 25 states as full members and 12 as associated members, to encourage the creation of a free trade arena among the countries of the region, coordinate their policies with respect to third parties and facilitate cooperation in other areas.[30]

At the level of CARICOM, it is only within recent times that institutional measures are being put in place to consider regional security issues in the Caribbean. The recognition of this is evidenced in the 1997 Bridgetown Declaration of Principles, which was presented at the Caribbean/United States Summit titled 'Partnership For Prosperity and Security in the Caribbean' which was held in Barbados in May 1997. In 1997, also, the CARICOM Secretariat Regional Coordinating Mechanism for Drug Control was established to coordinate Caribbean drug policy efforts. Institutions, such as the Caribbean Financial Action Task Force (CFATF), were established to develop a common anti-money laundering policy within the Caribbean, and the Caribbean Task Force on Crime and Security was established by the heads of government of CARICOM in July 2001 in response to the increase of crime in the region. The Task Force was mandated to examine the causes of rising crime and violence and propose actions for a regional response.

At the meeting of heads of government in Trinidad and Tobago in February 2003, CARICOM, agreed to recognise and institutionalise the Association of Caribbean Commissioners of Police (ACCP) as an agency of the Community. It was also agreed that this agency would report to a joint Committee of attorneys-general and ministers responsible for National Security. The Caribbean Customs Law Enforcement Council (CCLEC) is another association that is presently spearheading the thrust towards the improvement of border security in the Caribbean in this Age of Terror.

The Widening and deepening of regional cooperation

In this Age of Terror, the time is ripe for the broadening and deepening of regional cooperation. In Europe, the European Union (EU) has come into being and, thus far, is proving to be successful. In the Americas, the OAS is re-examining its position. The widening of CARICOM to include the non-English speaking countries of Haiti and Suriname speaks volumes to the cooperation effort. The establishment of the ACS, which represents a combination of both the English-speaking and the Hispanic countries within the Caribbean littoral, which now has an interest in security issues, adds value to the integration and collaboration measures being adopted. Within the Caribbean, however, geopolitics continues to play an important part in what some commentators describe as negative diplomacy between the USA and Cuba. Thus, an important question is: Can Cuba become a part of this broadening process?

The history of US-Cuban relationship and the history of US-CARICOM relationship have a great deal of bearing on this question. The events of 1990 that ushered in the end of the Cold War neither invalidated nor made this history meaningless. In fact, it only eliminated one of the essential components of the US-Cuban deadlock, the Soviet Union. The impact of shifting strategic priorities on the Caribbean, within the triangular framework of US-Cuba, US-CARICOM and CARICOM-Cuba relations, necessitates bold initiatives and independence of thinking and action. Within this framework and perspective, CARICOM must bring Cuba into its fold, while simultaneously providing a platform for the easing, and resolution of tension between Cuba and the US. In both aims, CARICOM must reiterate its uniqueness and ensure that rapprochement with Cuba occurs with CARICOM's interest in the forefront, which means not at the expense of CARICOM/US entente and cooperation.

Recommendations

Regionalism and, more specifically, regional security cooperation are on the rise around the world. However, security cooperation requires a deeper sense of partnership in dealing with the multifaceted nature of contemporary security issues. Regional security cooperation requires an understanding of political, economic and security issues that overlap and intersect within the international environment. What is required is a general framework for regional security collaboration. This collaborative effort must be looked at as a process that depends on the various sub-sets of the region coming together using a sequential approach that begins with an examination of history and establishing conceptual clarity of internal and external dynamics. Recommendations must therefore be based on the reality that regional security cooperation would embrace regional politics and economics, within the geopolitical context dominated by the United States.

Although the RSS has provided a valuable framework in dealing with the traditional and non-traditional threats to Caribbean security, it must be remembered that the RSS was created for a specific set of purposes and for countries with certain features, including very small size, the absence of a standing army (except in Barbados at creation; St Kitts and Nevis now also has a defence force), and very small economies. Brigadier General Rudyard Lewis suggested that the RSS should be expanded to include the non-RSS countries.[31] In terms of regional security cooperation, therefore, it is recommended that the RSS be used as a regional coordinator, given its established structure and experience.

Another recommendation is to coordinate the activities of the ACCP with the RSS, for the simple reason that most of the security operations in the small island states of the Caribbean involve police personnel, either operating separately or as joint police/army patrol elements. While the RSS already supports CDERA by coordinating the response and mobilisation of the Caribbean Disaster Response Unit, it is recommended that the CDRU be part of a wider structure. The argument here is that if, in the Caribbean, it is recognised that natural disasters pose a threat to security then the institutional framework to deal with this issue requires no less effort than the task performed by the CARICOM Battalion in Haiti in 1994.

Another recommendation that is closely related to the above is the development of the CARICOM Battalion itself as a model for proper command and control of any cooperative response to security issues in the Caribbean. As mentioned before, this battalion demonstrated that it could perform its tasks effectively and efficiently in a threat environment. This model can use the lessons from history and reintroduce the northern and southern command as a sub grouping within the larger cooperative efforts in the region. The concept visualises the CARICOM Battalion being made up of elements in certain zones. These elements would come together when the need arises to form the unit referred to as the CARICOM Battalion. These zones may be the Northern zone comprising Jamaica, Belize, Bahamas and Haiti; the OECS countries and the RSS in the Centre zone, and the Southern command comprising Trinidad and Tobago, Guyana and Suriname. It is suggested here that functional cooperation could become part of this zonal approach. There is also scope to expand this model, which was primarily land-based, to include a maritime and air component. What about a 'Shiprider agreement' within the Caribbean, whereby coast guard personnel from countries are posted to other island units to work with and strengthen confidence-building measures in the region?

The CARICOM Battalion model demonstrated some positive points such as the degree of equity provided to all countries in terms of command and control arrangements due to rotation of positions and appointments; the ability to understand, determine and agree on common standard operating procedures and the fact that it proved to be feasible, acceptable and suitable. The negative aspects about the model had to do primarily with the inability of the politicians in the Caribbean to agree to a memorandum of understanding to legitimise the proper functioning of the battalion. The political will to establish this organisation is crucial to the creation of the entity proposed here.

Regional security cooperation in this Age of Terror must make the best possible use of institutions, mechanisms, techniques and procedures already at the disposal of the region. According to Lloyd Best, it is not enough to prescribe desirable new agencies. Each and every intervention must be required to generate a cumulative flow of new resources for effectively taking operations to higher levels in successive stages.[32] The vision and mission of any institutional arrangement must be nested in an overarching association to ensure continuities, commonalities and consistencies. It is therefore recommended that CARICOM's security approach be nested in the ACS, which could be nested in the OAS that is linked to the United Nations.

Conclusion

Traditional issues, such as border disputes between Guyana and Venezuela, fishing issues between Trinidad and Tobago and Venezuela, the geopolitics of the region, and globalisation, continue to persist alongside non-traditional ones such as drug trafficking, money laundering, illegal sales of arms and ammunitions, natural disasters, HIV/AIDS and terrorism. These are the issues that characterise the contemporary security landscape in the Caribbean. In order to deal with these issues, a cooperative and collaborative approach must be adopted.

Today's world is interdependent. Thus, efforts to cope with traditional and non-traditional threats must consider the influence of the actors in the environment in which it has to exist and function. Regional security cooperation must not be left to chance but must be as a result of a systemic process that seeks to identify commonalities of interests and threats in a building block approach to treat with the issues. As the twenty-first century unfolds, the Caribbean countries must become responsible for their own security. As the world continues to change dramatically, countries in the Caribbean need to redefine and reconceptualise threats to regional security from a Caribbean perspective and, as such, be prepared to implement appropriate measures to deal with traditional and non-traditional security issues from within a coordinated and cooperative approach.

The vehicle to move this process forward must be the integration movement through CARICOM and the ACS in collaboration with wider hemispheric institutions under the umbrella of the OAS. CARICOM is an institution that could develop a collective consciousness among the region's politicians to instil the political will required to give legitimacy to the institutions required to pursue regional security cooperation in the Caribbean. The ACS can broaden this endeavour to include all the other countries within the littoral. Together, these institutions and associations can support the architecture that is needed for regional security cooperation in this Age of Terror.

Notes

1. Joseph S. Tulchin and Ralph H. Espach, 'US–Caribbean Security Relations in the Post-Cold War Era,' in Joseph S. Tulchin and Ralph H. Espach , eds. *Security in the Caribbean Basin: The Challenge of Regional Cooperation* (Boulder, Colorado: Lynne Rienner Publishers, 2000), 1.

2. Joseph R. Nunez, 'A 21st Century Security Architecture for the Americas: Multilateral Cooperation, Liberal Peace and Soft Power' (Carlisle, PA: US Army War College, Strategic Studies Institute, August 2002), 1.
3. Anthony T. Bryan, J. Edward Greene, and Timothy M. Shaw, eds., *Peace, Development and Security in the Caribbean: Perspectives to the Year 2000* (Basingstoke, UK: Macmillan Press, 1990), xviii.
4. Immanuel Wallerstein. *The Modern World System: Capitalist Agriculture and the Origins of the European World Economy in the Sixteenth Century* (New York: New York Academic Press, 1974), 63.
5. Ivelaw L. Griffith, 'Security, Sovereignty and Public Order in the Caribbean,' *Security and Defence Studies Review* Vol. 2 No. 1 (Summer 2000), available at http://www3.ndu.edu/chds/Journal/.
6. Thomas H. Moorer and Georges A. Fauriol, *Caribbean Basin Security* (Washington, DC: Praeger Publishers, 1984), 21.
7. Ibid., 21.
8. Roger Norman Buckley, *The British Army in the West Indies: Society and the Military in the Revolutionary Age* (Gainesville, FL: University Press of Florida, 1998), xiii.
9. Ibid.
10. W. Andy Knight and Randolph B. Persaud, 'Subsidiarity, Regional Governance and Caribbean Security,' *Latin American Politics and Society*, Vol. 43 (Spring 2001): 29.
11. Ibid., 29.
12. Lieutenant Colonel Colvin Bishop, 'Caribbean Regional Security: The Challenges to Creating Formal Military Relationships in the English Speaking Caribbean.' Unpublished thesis for Masters in Military Arts and Science, US Army Command and General Staff College, Fort Leavenworth, Kansas 2002, 11.
13. David Granger, 'Security and Stability in Small Island States: The Caribbean Community's Achilles Heel,' *Guyana Review,* (1999): 3.
14. Rudyard Lewis, 'Initiatives for Cooperative Regional Security: The Eastern Caribbean Regional Security System' in Tulchin and Espach, *Security in the Caribbean Basin*, 178.
15. Vaughn A. Lewis, 'International, National and Regional Security Arrangements in the Caribbean' in Bryan, Greene, and Shaw, *Peace Development and Security in the Caribbean*, 291.
16. *Treaty Establishing The Regional Security System*, provided to the Trinidad and Tobago Defence Force from the Central Liaison Office of the Regional Security System.
17. Humberto García Muñiz and Jorge Rodríguez Beruff, 'U.S. Military Policy Toward the Caribbean in the 1990s,' in Jorge Rodríguez Beruff and Humberto García Muñiz, eds, *Security Problems and Policies in the Post Cold War Caribbean* (London: Macmillan, 1996), 17.
18. Paul Sutton, 'Britain and the Commonwealth Caribbean,' in Rodríguez Beruff and García Muñiz, eds., *Security Problems and Policies in the Post-Cold War Caribbean*, 62.
19. See Rudyard Lewis for the conclusions reached by the Heads of CARICOM on matters of regional security in 'Initiatives for Cooperative Regional Security: The Eastern Caribbean Regional Security System' in Tulchin and Espach, *Security in the Caribbean Basin*, 178.
20. Roberto Marrero-Corletto, 'The New Caribbean Security Environment in the Caribbean,' in *Low Intensity Conflict and Law Enforcement.* No. 3 (Winter 1993), 460–491.

21. Ivelaw L. Griffith, 'The Geography of Drug Trafficking in the Caribbean', in Michael C. Desch, Jorge I. Domínguez, and Andres Serbin, eds., *From Pirates to Drug Lords: The Post Cold War Caribbean Security Environment.* (Albany, NY: State University of New York Press, 1998), 97.
22. Ivelaw L. Griffith, 'Security Collaboration and Confidence Building in the Americas,' in Jorge I. Domínguez, ed., *International Security and Democracy: Latin America and the Caribbean in the Post-Cold War Era*(Pittsburgh, PA: University of Pittsburgh Press, 1998), 174.
23. Ivelaw L. Griffith, 'Drugs and the Emerging Security Agenda in the Caribbean' in Tulchin and Espach, *Security in the Caribbean Basin*, 146.
24. George K Danns, 'Drug Trafficking and Security Cooperation in the Caribbean'. Paper presented at workshop on Strategic Capability of CARICOM Member States in National Security Policy Issues, conducted at the Institute of International Relations, University of the West Indies, Trinidad November 22–December 3, 1999, 15.
25. Ibid., 17.
26. See 'Trinidad and Tobago Affected by the Fall Out from United States Terrorist Attack,' *Newsday*, October 14, 2003, 9.
27. 'Gift Reaffirms TT's Role to Assist the UN', *Newsday*, October 26, 2002, 20.
28. CCAA website at www.redcea.org.
29. W. Andrew Axline, 'Lessons for the Caribbean from Small States of Other Regions' in Bryan, Greene, and Shaw, *Peace Development and Security in the Caribbean*, 291.
30. Association of Caribbean States, *Convention Establishing the Association of Caribbean States* (Catagena de Indias, July 24, 1994).
31. Rudyard Lewis, 'Initiatives for Cooperative Regional Security: The Eastern Caribbean Regional Security System' in Tulchin and Espach, *Security in the Caribbean Basin*, 177–83.
32. Lloyd Best, 'Reducing the CARICOM Task to Human Proportions' in Lloyd Best, ed., *Trinidad and Tobago Review*, May 2003, 3.

20

Regional Law Enforcement Strategies in the Caribbean

Clifford E. Griffin

Introduction

From the trafficking in illegal narcotics and the laundering of the proceeds to attendant activities such as gunrunning and the trafficking in human cargo, and continuing upwards to international terrorism, the Caribbean is fast becoming part of the central nervous system of transnational and international criminal activity. This activity is being facilitated at the global level by the historical political, economic, and market linkages with North America and Europe, and at the regional and local levels by the presence of an enabling environment reflecting geography, relatively sophisticated communication and transportation networks, proximity to sources of market demand, and the presence of economies challenged by the changing dynamics of the global market system. This environment enables criminals and criminal enterprises to exploit the variety of avenues made available by these linkages, including the thriving banking and offshore financial sectors, to acquire and market their illegal goods and services as well as launder the proceeds of such activities.

The region's links to drug trafficking and the susceptibility of its offshore financial sector to demands for money laundering led one US policy official to contend that

> drug trafficking, links between drug traffickers and terrorists, smuggling of illegal aliens, massive financial and bank fraud, arms smuggling, potential involvement in the theft and sale of nuclear material, political intimidation,

> and corruption all constitute a poisonous brew – a mixture potentially as deadly as what we faced during the cold war.[1]

One outcome of this contention is that small and big and poor and rich countries in the region – and around the world – have been forced to pay more attention and spend more money to improve security, especially at airports and seaports. For example, the government of Jamaica's projected investment costs for increased port security across the country, including x-ray machines for inspection of cargo at the island's two international ports, will exceed $1 billion.[2] From a law enforcement standpoint, investing in port security makes sense in light of the transnational nature of crime in Jamaica and throughout the region, and in light of the CARICOM Single Market and Economy (CSME) and the Caribbean Court of Justice (CCJ), two recent initiatives aimed at deepening the level of economic integration in the region.

But while US expectations of Caribbean countries, both express and implied, in this message are understandable in an international environment of complex interdependence,[3] law enforcement and security capabilities of Caribbean countries may be hard pressed to provide the requisite responses in terms of policy cooperation and policy coordination due to a combination of factors, including resource limitation, criminal sophistication, and unintended effects of policies undertaken by the US and other countries. For example, US anti-crime and anti-terrorism policies, as well as policies of many other countries, have resulted in the ongoing deportation of increasingly large numbers of Caribbean nationals to a number of Caribbean destinations after having been charged with a variety of criminal offences.[4] And, complicating matters for Caribbean governments, is the fact that these criminals are arriving at destinations currently experiencing escalating levels of domestic and trans-border crime. Given the apparent outcomes and implications of anti-crime and anti-terror policies of the US, Canada, the UK and other countries, the capacity for Caribbean countries to deal effectively with domestic and trans-sovereign crime, especially in light of their own development and security challenges, and in light of complex interdependence, is a matter worth probing.

Does the law enforcement architecture within the Caribbean Community and Common Market reflect the necessary preparation and requisite capability to effectively address the increasing incidence of domestic and trans-border crimes that threaten to undermine the economic, social and political fabric of these countries? This is the central question that is being probed in this chapter. And to provide a meaningful answer, I situate the analysis within the context of CARICOM's current political architecture, which, by design, if not by consequence, reflects challenges of collective problem definition, policy articulation and policy coordination within and among a confederation of mainly sovereign states. It is these challenges that merit an interrogation of the organisation's ability to meaningfully address law enforcement matters at a regional level. And it is in this regard that I make the following four arguments.

Argument one holds that, at the level of CARICOM, the most salient law enforcement issue relates to drug trafficking and money laundering and attendant crimes of larceny, burglary, bribery, fraud and murder. However, because of CARICOM's political structure, atomised by geography and autonomy, the tendency has been for individual countries to pursue their own national law enforcement strategies. Where necessary, these countries have cultivated bilateral relationships, such as the ad hoc relationships between the US and the UK, as well as the Mutual Legal Assistance Treaties (MLAT)[5] currently in force between Caribbean countries and the US and the UK, respectively.[6]

A major law enforcement shortcoming within CARICOM, therefore, reflects the fact that while the region has instituted a number of initiatives to address law enforcement issues, including the International Criminal Investigation Training Assistance Programme (ICITAP), the Association of Caribbean Commissioners of Police (ACCP), the Caribbean Financial Action Task Force (CFATF), the Caribbean Customs Law Enforcement Council (CCLEC), the Regional Drug-Law Enforcement Training Centre (RDLETC), the Bureau for International Narcotics and Law Enforcement Affairs (INL), and the Caribbean Anti Money Laundering Programme (CALP), these initiatives have all been created on an ad hoc basis, usually with extra-regional funding, and insufficient legal and institutional infrastructure. CARICOM, itself, has no independent secretariat specialised in and devoted entirely to justice and home affairs. When CARICOM proposes an initiative on home and justice affairs, such as an anti-drugs initiative, it is usually proposed and often funded by sources outside the region. Once the external funding ends, the region often experiences difficulty in sustaining the initiative. In fact, it becomes even more difficult to undertake the initiative within the broad framework of home and justice affairs. These arrangements, therefore, speak to some of the law enforcement challenges that confront the region.

Argument two holds that regarding the issue of trans-sovereign crime, CARICOM does not have an agency or an institutional structure specifically designed to address crime and criminal matters, such as a justice and home affairs agency. For example, despite its suggestive nomenclature, the CCJ, which was slated to come on stream in 2003, is functionally oriented toward interpreting the revised Treaty of Chaguaramas upon which the CSME is to be implemented. Ordinarily, a CCJ would suggest an institution designed to address, among other things, the issue of trans-border and trans-sovereign crime and criminal activity, including common classifications of crime and a common arrest warrant. But such focus is not expressly within the purview of the CCJ. CARICOM, therefore, suffers from a lack of efficacy and efficiency in the area of regional law enforcement and crime prevention.

The third argument is that where region-wide, law enforcement initiatives have been attempted, such as the Association of Caribbean Commissioners of Police (ACCP), they do not reflect direct policy interventions undertaken by CARICOM but rather the vision and goals of the organisations. The ACCP, for example, emerged out of the collective concern of the various commissioners of police, who had begun to recognise the similarity of policing and law enforcement concerns they faced, especially in the area of trans-sovereign crime. And while the ACCP has managed to achieve regional and international recognition, and while it has been able to sensitise CARICOM about regional policing matters, it has not been successful in getting the organisation to develop and implement a more integrated approach to law enforcement in the region.

Argument four holds that the only region-wide initiative with important law enforcement implications was CARICOM's decision to empanel a Task Force on Crime. This initiative was undertaken at the Heads of Government Meeting in Nassau, the Bahamas, in 2001 to address what leaders considered to be a clear and present danger to the economic and socio-political future of the region. The Task Force has presented CARICOM with a number of recommendations to manage the problem of crime and criminal activity – recommendations that have significant implications for a regional approach to law enforcement, and many of which are yet to be implemented.

This leads to argument five, which contends that given that the current scope of the CCJ is limited to economic matters; given that most regional law enforcement initiatives are ad hoc, bilateral, and externally originated and funded; and given that the ACCP is neither structurally nor functionally part of CARICOM, the reality is that the region lacks an intergovernmental police service capable of being a repository and clearinghouse for intelligence and strategy for addressing the spiralling rate of both domestic and international crime. This chapter, therefore, critically examines the shortcomings of a number of these regional law enforcement initiatives and concludes that CARICOM's obvious and urgent need is the development of an integrated law enforcement architecture to provide timely and effective, intelligence-led responses to crime and criminal matters affecting the region. The proposed cooperative and coordinated system for managing the scarce and costly law enforcement resources will provide an important contribution to the overall security architecture in the region.

Law Enforcement Initiatives in the Caribbean

The Caribbean Court of Justice (CCJ) and the Caribbean Single Market and Economy (CSME)

The issue of the role of the CCJ in the area of economic development has been given due consideration, particularly its role as interpreting the Treaty of Chaguaramas and disputes emerging therefrom.[7] However, conspicuously absent from the list of key elements for the establishment of the CSME, as well as the debate on the role and function of the CCJ, has been the element of law enforcement, national security and crime prevention. Where the issue of law enforcement and/or security has been addressed, it has been done largely in the realm of drug trafficking and money laundering. While these are fundamental issues affecting the development of the CSME, attendant issues, including the prosecution of trans-border crimes, which may or may not be related to drug trafficking and money laundering, must necessarily be considered as well because they form important components of the stock of security concerns and challenges that the many small and vulnerable countries in the region face.

To understand this issue more fully, a brief return to Chapter I of this volume is in order; there Ivelaw Griffith makes the compelling case that CARICOM countries face two types of security threats: traditional and non-traditional. Further analysis of these two classifications of security threats reveals that not only is it the case that few of these countries have genuine and indisputable traditional security issues, including latent/unresolved border disputes as well as the threat that small size presents for the protection of strategic natural resources, it is also the case that it is only this subset of countries that have security apparatuses to address non-traditional security matters. At the same time, however, all of these countries face non-traditional security issues, including domestic and trans-sovereign crime, drug trafficking, money laundering, gunrunning, and even illegal migration (alien smuggling). However, factors including size, resources and degree of vulnerability as well as the nature, threat scope and threat intensity necessitate that most of these countries employ law enforcement mechanisms to address many of these non-traditional security issues. And herein lies the dilemma. Not only does CARICOM not have any region-wide systems for addressing traditional and non-traditional security issues, many non-traditional issues are dealt with from a law enforcement standpoint. And complicating matters is the lack of uniformity in categorising crime and criminal offences across the region, and the absence of any formal CARICOM-wide extradition treaty, notwithstanding the establishment of the CCJ, as the region prepares for the creation of the CSME.

Moreover, while the CSME is aimed at facilitating the flow of goods, services, and skills throughout the region, it, paradoxically, creates increased opportunities for trans-border criminal activities as well within an environment of rising levels of crime and violence. And while the establishment of the CCJ suggests a development suited to addressing transnational crime in the region, its primary function is to interpret the Treaty of Chaguaramas and address any disputes that might arise from the implementation of the Treaty.[8] Accordingly, it does not provide much guidance in the area of law enforcement, crime prevention or even national security except in the area of drug trafficking and money laundering.

But what is more critical to assessing the law enforcement capability within CARICOM to respond promptly and effectively to the challenges of crime and criminal activity in the region, is an understanding of the constraints to policy implementation inherent in the legal expression of the organisation. For example, notwithstanding its appellation – the Caribbean Community – CARICOM remains, based upon original intent, an association of sovereign states among which the principle of sovereign equality guides decison making on substantive issues at the highest levels of the organisation. In that regard, the following must be true: that the agreement to establish the CSME necessarily reflects an agreement (expressed or implied) to create a single economic space comprising multiple, independent and/or autonomous jurisdictions. The establishment of this architecture, therefore, necessarily implies the superimposition of collective economic decisions on discrete national administrations, all of which retain, by design, autonomous decison making powers in areas of national economic development.

By extension, the institution of the CCJ implies the superimposition of collective legal/judicial decisions upon discrete national systems as well. And in order for the CSME and CCJ to be effective, the instruments of integration that define the rights and obligations of member states must be enacted into law by the various national assemblies.[9] Since the creation of a single economic space via the CSME implies increasing interdependence, it necessarily warrants the creation of a single, (common) law enforcement architecture, including uniformity in the categorisation of crimes and criminal offences as well as common arrest warrants and extradition procedures, especially for small and highly vulnerable states.

To date, however, the most far-reaching areas of cooperation within CARICOM lie in the area of drug trafficking and money laundering. Such cooperation, however, does not originate from the policy making organs of CARICOM; instead, it reflects national and bilateral initiatives secured between member countries and other international actors, whose interest in these areas coincide with those of countries within the region. For example, as a result of the 'to-ing and fro-ing' of Jamaican criminals between London and Jamaica, the country's commissioner of police, Francis Forbes and the commissioner of the London Metropolitan Police Service, Scotland Yard, have formalised a number of proposals, including increased use of ION Scan equipment and surveillance equipment at all ports, as well as training and legal support for the seizure of assets of convicts. The British are also expected to finance a special anti-narcotics squad, the first such local squad, to intensify pressure on civilians involved with drugs. An exchange of policemen is also expected.[10] The Jamaican police high command also announced the formation of a specially screened and trained anti-narcotics team of about 50 police officers that will work closely with US DEA agents and share classified information. This partnership provides Jamaica with the resources with which to upgrade or build new buildings for the narcotics team, as well as provide training and equipment.[11]

While much of this effort is formalised, it is not institutionalised within the Community. The level of cooperation and coordination between and among the various national police services is not sufficiently institutionalised to reflect a concerted regional response to crime. More important is the fact that a number of externally originating and externally funded, ad hoc regional anti-crime arrangements are in place. But what is striking is that most of them are related to illegal narcotics control, which speaks to the saliency of drug trafficking among the law enforcement/security challenges confronting countries in the region. One such programme is the International Criminal Investigation Training Assistance Program (ICITAP).

The International Criminal Investigation Training Assistance Program (ICITAP)

The US Department of Justice's 1986 International Criminal Investigation Training Assistance Program (ICITAP) was established to assist in the training of police forces in Latin America, including enhancing their professional capabilities to perform investigative and forensic functions and creating and/or strengthening their ability to respond to new criminal justice issues.[12] It provides police and criminal investigation development assistance to countries in the areas of technical advice, training, mentoring, equipment donation and internships with pre-eminent criminal justice organisations. About 1,200 Caribbean law enforcement officials have been trained between its initiation in 1986 and December 1993.[13]

But while ICITAP's mandate is not drug specific, it could be argued that all of its activities impact upon counter-narcotics because they enhance general police and investigative capabilities. It is within this context that the Government of Jamaica, drawing upon support from ICITAP, signed on to a project to establish a Regional Drug-Law Enforcement Training Centre (RDLETC) in 1995 to serve the drug control needs of the different drug control agencies in the 18 English-speaking Caribbean countries. The plans call for the subsequent inclusion of Aruba, Cuba, Dominican Republic, Haiti, Netherlands Antilles, Suriname, the three French departments and the two US Commonwealth states and ultimately, other Caribbean countries as well. The centre has the support of the CARICOM heads of state based upon their July 15, 1994 meeting in Barbados. The complaint from Jamaica, however, is that, like similar programmes with regional scope, it suffers from inadequate funding due to limited participation and low levels of cooperation, coordination and collaboration on common law enforcement matters among the countries in the region. As a result, the Government of Jamaica ends up providing most of RDLETC's funding.

In addition to ICITAP, the US Department of State, through its International Narcotics Law Enforcement Affairs (INL) programme, funds a number of anti-crime, mainly counter-narcotics programmes in the Caribbean. These include Operation Bahamas and Turks and Caicos (OPBAT) and another programme with Jamaica. Some of the objectives include: preventing the use of these territories as transit points for illicit drugs into the US; enabling these jurisdictions to conduct increasingly sophisticated investigations, effective maritime interdiction operations, drug interdiction, marijuana eradication, detection of the illegal diversion of precursor and essential chemicals; financial analyses in order to stem the flow of illegal drugs, aliens and weapons through these countries; strengthening judicial institutions so that drug traffickers, money launderers and perpetrators of other crimes will be prosecuted expeditiously, and the proceeds of their crimes seized and forfeited; developing laws and regulations to control international organised crime, especially drug trafficking, and to identify and prevent narcotics-related corruption of public officials; and assisting with drug-use prevention programmes.[14]

The US will continue to provide assistance to upgrade the capabilities of these countries in the areas of interdiction, law enforcement and administration of justice. The INL will fund increased efforts to detect and prosecute growing financial crime and governmental corruption in certain Caribbean states and will provide assistance in asset forfeiture and the development of Financial Intelligence Units (FIUs). Where appropriate, Joint Information Communications Centres (JICCs) will be established, or upgraded with new equipment, software and training, to promote more real-time interchange of cueing information from maritime and air detection platforms to law enforcement entities.[15]

As part of its anti-money-laundering programme, the INL enforcement programme recognises the need for regional-based, long-term training programmes. Accordingly, along with the European Union and the United Kingdom, the INL funds the Caribbean Anti-Money Laundering Programme (CALP), provides technical assistance and training to member countries aimed at reducing the incidence of the laundering of the proceeds of all serious crime by facilitating the prevention, investigation, and prosecution of money laundering. The CALP, which began its operations in 1999, also seeks to develop a sustainable institutional capacity in the Caribbean to address the issues related to anti-money laundering efforts at the local, regional, and international levels and, toward this end, works in conjunction with the CFATF.[16]

The Caribbean Financial Action Task Force (CFATF)

In 1989, growing concern about money laundering's threat to the international banking system and financial institutions prompted the leaders of the Group of Seven (comprising the heads of state of Canada, France, Germany, Italy, Japan, the United Kingdom, and the United States) to convene the Financial Action Task Force (FATF). This new intergovernmental policy making task force was assigned responsibility for examining money laundering techniques and trends, reviewing prior national and international action, and determining additional anti-money laundering measures. A total of 40 recommendations, adopted in 1990 and revised in 1996, apply to the three main areas of action against money laundering – legal, police and financial – and form the basis of states' strategies in their attempt to combat it. The FATF is, therefore, well known throughout the world to agents involved in combating money laundering, whether they belong to the treasury, finance ministries, justice, the police, customs or financial or non-financial institutions

The Caribbean Financial Action Task Force (CFATF), on the other hand, is much less well known because it is located in a part of the world reputed to be a paradise and renowned for the number of offshore investment possibilities. Coincidentally, the region is situated at a crossroads between the south-north drugs route, and the north-south return route taken by some of the profits from the sale of the drugs for investment purposes. This means that Caribbean countries are faced with a law enforcement challenge of global proportions given the range and scope of the illicit narcotics and transnational organised crime network. With the fight against drug trafficking being a priority in the region, the Caribbean decided in 1990 to develop effective strategies to combat crime by focusing on the enormous profits it could generate. Accordingly, in conjunction with developed countries, which have interests in the region, the Caribbean decided to set up the CFATF.

Based in Trinidad and Tobago, the CFATF comprises 27 member states and six cooperating and supporting nations (or COSUNs). Like all international organisations, the CFATF also has a number of observers, in this case organisations and banks, which are also involved in combating money laundering. Shortly after its establishment, the CFATF prepared 19 recommendations intended for application by its member states. These recommendations were adopted by all of the states present in Aruba in May 1990. They take into consideration the region's specific characteristics and expectations, and are the regional equivalent of, and complement to, those adopted by the FATF.

In November 1992, the region's ministers met in Kingston, Jamaica, and reasserted their commitment to combating money laundering. They decided that the member states should adopt the principle of ratifying the 1988 United Nations Vienna Convention on combating drugs and money laundering, and that they should also subscribe to the 40 FATF recommendations and the 19 CFATF recommendations. They also agreed that, where it was thought possible, the member states should implement the action plan of the Organisation of American States' Summit of the Americas.

The CFATF's main aim is to give practical application to the recommendations so as to prevent or control money laundering operations in the region or, at least, restrict them to a minimum. This is no easy task because the launderers are knowledgeable 'businessmen' who use every means available worldwide to conceal the criminal origin of the funds being invested. The CFATF, therefore, operates essentially at a political level and the role of the Secretariat, in cooperation with the Chairman of the organisation, is mainly to:

- develop and consolidate the member states' involvement in the organisation's affairs ('CFATF spirit');
- check that the laws and regulations adopted by the member states are in keeping with their international commitments, while remaining consistent with the FATF and CFATF recommendations;
- anticipate new 'routes' that might be used by money launderers, and take steps to reduce or minimise the effects,
- respond to the various international problems which might in the long term affect the member states; and
- gather sufficient finances to allow the organisation to function in an effective, coherent manner.[17]

At the heart of CFATF's duties and activities are the identification of potential money laundering risks in the region through typology exercises and mutual evaluation by the member states.

Like all international organisations, the CFATF depends on its members for funding, which is supplemented by voluntary contributions in the form of financial and technical assistance by the COSUNs. One of the CFATF's recurring problems is the failure of its members to pay their dues to the organisation on time. Despite the efforts of the chairman, and the secretariat, the arrears are still too great and hamper the smooth running of the operations planned by the organisation. They also directly prejudice its viability.

In that regard, Trinidad and Tobago's police commissioner Hilton Guy, past president of the Association of Caribbean Commissioners of Police (ACCP), remarked to delegates to the CALP that:

> policing [*law enforcement*] in the region...is in a reactive mode...the time has come when we must not only adopt that position where we react to the activities of those who indulge in criminal activities but the time has come, perhaps, where we should be in a predictive position...[18]

Guy, apparently, was alluding to and echoing some of the ongoing frustrations in the area of law enforcement experienced by the ACCP.

The Association of Caribbean Commissioners of Police (ACCP)

The ACCP, which turned 16 in 2003, was officially established in Castries, St Lucia on August 20, 1987. This development finally occurred after a decision to meet annually to discuss matters of interest to policing in the region was taken at a conference that regional police commissioners held in Port of Spain, Trinidad in 1972. That initial meeting emerged out of a general and growing awareness among law enforcement leaders in the region that (1) international crime and criminal activity was becoming increasingly complex and sophisticated; (2) criminals pose an ever-present threat to the safety, security and stability of the countries in the region; and (3) individual law enforcement organisations in the region face difficulties that they must confront in their efforts to discharge their responsibilities effectively.

Attempts to convene a meeting failed until 1986 when nine commissioners from the English-speaking Caribbean met in Kingston, Jamaica with representatives of the International Criminal Investigation Training Assistance Program (ICITAP) to discuss the formation of the ACCP. All agreed that the international nature of crime and the sophistication and mobility of criminals were developments that warranted coordinated and cooperative strategies. They passed a resolution calling for the establishment of an ACCP to present this united front against crime. The Commissioners also agreed at that meeting that they would seek the support and approval of their respective governments for this initiative. However, it was at the second annual conference held in St Lucia in 1987 that a resolution was passed establishing the ACCP.

The stated objectives are to promote, foster, and encourage regional cooperation in the suppression of criminal activities in such areas as narcotics, terrorism and organised crime; the exchange of information in criminal investigations; the sharing of common services which may include training, forensic analysis and research; and the effective management of law enforcement agencies. And, its mission is to be the principal Caribbean regional organisation for facilitating collaboration and cooperation in the development and implementation of policing strategies, systems and procedures in the region; professional and technical skills development of police officers throughout the region; proactive measures to prevent crime and improve police-community relations.

Any Caribbean country may be admitted to ordinary membership and may be represented by full-time executive police officers engaged in the management of a police force or service. The ordinary membership of the Association of Caribbean Commissioners of Police (ACCP) represents the following 24 police jurisdictions: Anguilla, Antigua and Barbuda, Aruba, the Bahamas, Barbados, Belize, Bermuda, the British Virgin Islands, the Cayman Islands, Curaçao, Dominica, the French Antilles, Grenada, Guyana, Jamaica, Montserrat, St Kitts and Nevis, St Lucia, St Martin, St Vincent and the Grenadines, Suriname, Trinidad and Tobago, the Turks and Caicos Islands, and the US Virgin Islands.

Policy Decisions and Activities

Most of the ACCP's policy decisions and action plans are developed during their annual meetings, which, over the past 15 years have included discussions on penal reform, given the large numbers of prisoners being held in police stations; reform programmes in Belize; customs and the criminal justice system reform in Grenada; customs reform in St Lucia; improving the image of the police force in Guyana as well as improving the management of Guyana's Crime Prevention Unit.

During its inaugural meeting in 1987, the organisation passed a resolution adopting the United Nations Code of Conduct for Law Enforcement Officers; explored the possibility of establishing a regional automated fingerprint identification system; passed a resolution to apply to the CARICOM Council of Ministers to establish a permanent CARICOM law enforcement desk to address law enforcement issues in the region; called for the establishment of a Regional Drug Intelligence Unit in the Bahamas; urged members to promote the introduction of asset forfeiture legislation in their countries; increased participation in INTERPOL; called on governments to re-examine their perception of the role, function and management of police forces in the region with a view to providing the standard and quality of policing demanded by communities; advocated installation of technology for fingerprint identification and forensic services.

Subsequently, the ACCP recommended the establishment of a National Crime Task Force in each country that would: focus on organised crime; develop approaches to deal with violent crime, particularly those involving the use of firearms; coordinate efforts in the fight against drugs and crimes against tourists; and promote the introduction of legislation allowing the use of electronic technology when collecting criminal intelligence. Members agreed during their 1994 meeting in Guyana to advise CARICOM's Council of Ministers of ACCP's intention to find the most effective means of implementing a Regional Organised Counter-Crime Information Sharing System (ROCCISS). In 1995, commissioners agreed to exchange information on illicit drugs and firearms with each other; discussed the policing implications of the issue of criminal deportees, especially from North America.

In 1996, ACCP agreed to host Haitian police officers in member countries for on-the-job training; agreed to establish a training programme to deal with the problem of domestic violence. In 1997, commissioners agreed to support the introduction of a Witness Protection Programme in the region, and in 1998 agreed to consider the establishment of an INTERPOL sub-regional office in the Caribbean. In 2000, ACCP agreed that the ROCCISS Intelligence-Led Policing should be installed and operated by all member forces/services, and that members should: take ownership and take the lead in securing support for ROCCISS; identify and appoint a middle manager with responsibility for management and promotion of ROCCISS throughout the force/service; and develop internal communication systems to process information flowing in and out of ROCCISS.

In addition, the ACCP has signed a memorandum of understanding with the Caribbean Customs Law Enforcement Council (CCLEC) because of the need for intelligence gathering and cooperation through national joint intelligence units; the development of interagency task forces or anti-smuggling units; intelligence sharing; the need for the computerisation of units involved in financial investigations, commercial and international crime; the need for harmonisation of laws to facilitate the extradition of criminals; the need to develop a regional extradition treaty to replace existing bilateral treaties; the need to have crime committed in one jurisdiction tried in the jurisdiction where the offender is to be found; the need to study the trade in illegal firearms; the need for a regional inspectorate to serve the forces in the region to include a uniform method of policing.

Challenges and Concerns for the ACCP

Like other law enforcement initiatives in the region, funding is a major concern for the ACCP. The organisation has been attempting to have a police representative in CARICOM's Project Management Office (PMO) which focuses on 29 Caribbean countries, including all members of the ACCP. One objective of the PMO is to develop a common core curriculum for officers from the various agencies engaged in drug interdiction. The curriculum would focus on three levels of training, one outcome of which would be the development of a computerised database.

Presently, the ACCP works with the Regional Police Training Centre in Barbados to develop training courses for police in the region with a goal of developing a Certificate Course in Police Studies. The ACCP has signed a memorandum of understanding with the Caribbean Customs Law Enforcement Council (CCLEC) because of, among other things, the need for:

- intelligence gathering and cooperation through national joint intelligence units;
- the computerisation of units involved in financial investigations, commercial and international crime; and
- a regional inspectorate to serve the forces in the region to include a uniform method of policing.

The real challenge for the ACCP, however, is sustainability, if the organisation is to fulfill its mission. Sustainability is critical, given the increasing levels of crime in the region and the region's potential for serving as a staging ground for anti-US/Western attacks. Sustainability is also important in light of the following:

- most experts agree that drug-related crime is rampant throughout the region;
- the creation of the Caribbean Single Market and Economy (CSME) increases the prospect for transnational crime in the region;
- transnational crimes warrant transnational rather than national responses;
- drugs are considered by Caribbean governments to be a security issue; and
- the fact that while police and defence forces often engage (security) in anti-drug activities, such activities are essentially policing functions.

Notwithstanding the existence of organisations, such as the CFATF, CCLEC, RDETC, ICITAP, and the INL, there is an obvious, if not urgent need for coordinated, concerted, and collective regional response to crime in the region.

CARICOM Responds to Crime in the Region

The prevailing view among leaders and policy makers throughout CARICOM is that drug trafficking, money laundering, gunrunning, and the criminal deportees from North America and Europe, have combined to worsen the region's murder rate and criminal violence. There are also strong suggestions that a transnational criminal underworld supplies the illegal guns and ammunition being used in an increasing number of these violent crimes alongside the enduring problem of illegal narcotics trafficking and attendant money laundering. In addition, corruption is on the rise, with a number of police and security officers being arrested and tried for breaking the social trust. As of mid-November 2002, some 27 separate allegations of police corruption were reported by both members of the police and the public, representing a more than 300 per cent increase in the number of cases reported in 2001.[19] In Trinidad and Tobago, several police officers have been arrested and charged with complicity in kidnapping for ransom. In 2002, kidnappings in Jamaica resulted in a number of deaths linked to drug trafficking and gun running crimes, while in Trinidad and Tobago, the reported 19 cases of armed abductions were primarily to meet monetary demands ranging from $200,000 to $5 million. Until 2002, kidnapping for ransom money was not a feature of serious crime in Guyana; however, three of the 60 homicides that occurred in 2002 were abductees.

These developments are reflective of an upsurge in crime and violence over recent decades and leaders and policy makers in the Caribbean have finally begun to acknowledge that this represents a worrisome economic and social problem. And while a number of factors, including rapid urbanisation, persistent poverty and inequality, political violence, all contribute to the deteriorating social situation, the more organised nature of crime (local and transnational), and the emergence of illegal drug use and drug trafficking are often cited as root causes of increases in crime and violence. Yet, the region has experienced a puzzling lack of unity among the political directorates and a lack of coordination by the disciplined forces with regard to reducing crime and combating the criminals.

In 2001, Prime Minister Lester Bird of Antigua and Barbuda proposed that the region urgently consider three initiatives:

1. creating a single, well-manned and well-resourced unit that would deal with drug-related matters on behalf of the region as a whole;
2. creating a single, well-trained, well-equipped, single rapid response unit dealing with drug-related and serious crimes; and
3. establishing one or two high security prisons for all of the countries of CARICOM.

Prime Minister Bird signalled the need to broaden the region's approach to this problem, noting that 'the international community would be responsive to any practical proposals we offer for the necessary financial and technical assistance we need'.[20]

It was not until its twenty-second meeting, held in Nassau in July 2001, that the CARICOM Conference of Heads of Government, as a unit, expressed concern over the new forms of crime and violence that continue to pose threats to the region's security. Recognising that 'these new forms of crime have implications for individual safety and the social and economic well-being of the region as a whole', the heads agreed to establish a Regional Task Force on Crime and Security to examine the major causes of crime, and to recommend approaches to deal with the interrelated problems of crime, illicit drugs and firearms, as well as terrorism. Reflecting a regional perspective, Bahamas' prime minister, Perry Christie, noted that the:

> illicit traffic in narcotic drugs and firearms and other organised crime activities underpin much of the crime our countries are experiencing. In this regard, it cannot be emphasised enough that we, the member states of CARICOM, are, by an accident of geography, the victims of the ever-burgeoning trade in illicit drugs.[21]

Chaired by Lancelot Selman of Trinidad and Tobago, the Task Force comprised representatives from each of the member states, the RSS, the ACCP, the University of the West Indies (UWI), and the regional secretariats (CARICOM and the OECS). However, the events of September 11, 2001, prevented it from beginning its work until November 2001. Five meetings were held between November 2001 and May 2002. In establishing its framework, the group acknowledged two factors:

- the multidimensionality of hemispheric security threats, concerns and other challenges; and
- the traditional ways of meeting the challenges needed to be expanded to be able to respond to new non-traditional threats, which include political, economic, social, health and environmental aspects.

Given the mandate of the heads of government, however, the task force confined itself to a definition of security which, in essence, encompassed governance. Specifically, the concept referred to a state or condition in which, within the context of a constitutional framework, freedom is enjoyed without fear of victimisation from crime and in which the functioning of governance by a constitutionally elected government is not inhibited or disrupted through criminal activity. The task force therefore established the following areas of focus:

- Issues relative to the underlying causes and sources of crime: to comprehend the causes of crime, especially in its newer manifestations, that have resulted in escalating fear and panic, with implications for law and order as well as economic prospects, social stability and the general morale of member states.
- Initiatives against activities that pose a direct security threat to the region: to examine the interconnected nature of the newer forms of crime, which involve illicit drugs and arms, money laundering, and tourism, with a view to proposing policies that would meet the challenges facing member states and the region as a whole.
- Multilateral initiatives for international security in respect of which the region is committed to participating as co-victims of transnational crime; to build capacity through institutional strengthening, shared surveillance and other forms of cooperation among member states, and between CARICOM, the wider Caribbean and the international community.

Among other factors contributing to crime, the task force considered poverty, unemployment, social marginalisation and inequality, the illegal drug trade, corruption, the trafficking of firearms, deportation of criminals and the ineffectiveness of the existing criminal justice systems. In formulating its report, the following questions, among others were considered:

- why would young women risk their lives daily by swallowing packets of cocaine and undertaking the role of drug mules from the Caribbean to North America and Europe?
- why would a young man risk losing his life by being shot for stealing tyres to feed his drug habit?
- why should the car owner feel justified in equating that young man's life to four tyres?
- should drug abuse be seen as a criminal act or is it a health problem?
- are the values we embrace in society in contradiction to our laws? and
- are traditional methods of policing effective in crime prevention?

The report contains over 100 recommendations, which have been reviewed by a joint committee of attorneys-general and ministers with responsibility for national security, and which were presented to the Conference of Heads of Government at their twenty-third meeting in Georgetown, Guyana, July 3–5, 2002.

The task force recognised that security threats, concerns and challenges in the hemispheric context are multidimensional and, consequently, sought to find a formula to ensure more effective, pre-emptive and responsive measures to deal with the upsurge in crime and threats to security at the national and regional levels. It determined that some of the fundamental causes of crime in the region revolve around poverty, inequality and social marginalisation, and are fuelled by illegal firearms and ammunition, deportees, drug trafficking and corruption. It recommended that heads of government develop a multi-sector approach through public policy planning and execution of crime prevention initiatives over a long term.

In addressing the immediate needs to arrest the escalating levels of crime and violence the heads agreed to:

- establish broad-based National Commissions on Law and Order;
- prepare and implement national anti-crime master plans;
- strengthen border control measures especially at seaports and airports;
- strengthen the information and intelligence exchange regime as an essential element in the fight against illegal drugs, firearms and terrorism;
- implement an aggressive programme aimed at removing guns from the streets;
- establish a regional mutual legal assistance regime and a regional exchange of prisoners agreement; and
- engage the international community in discussions regarding mutual support for crime control efforts and a critical review of the existing policy against illegal drugs.

The heads also recognised the need for further scientific investigations with a view to arriving at a clearer understanding of the values that underlie the social choices that lead to criminal behaviour and endorsed the recommendation of the Joint Meeting of attorneys general and ministers responsible for National Security which, in reviewing the report prior to its submission, called for more work to be done to ascertain the types of societal values and attitudes which result in behaviour breaching the Rule of Law.

And, being aware of a number of contradictions, the joint meeting of ministers recommended that drug abuse be treated primarily as a public health issue with emphasis on the reinforcement of values.

Since the deepening of the integration process through the establishment of the CSME renders the region more vulnerable because of the freer movement of capital, people, goods and services, the Conference reiterated its commitment to the international fight against drug trafficking, terrorism and transnational organised crime. Also among the recommendations is the establishment of crime commissions throughout the region and the setting up of parliamentary oversight committees on crime. The task force also proposed alternative sentencing for persons who have been convicted of minor offences.

These recommendations notwithstanding, the task force has failed to recommend and the heads of government have made no effort to centralise the process so that the efficiency and efficacy gains of greater coordination are realised. Such gains require the institutionalisation of a Caribbean Police Service or (CARIBPOL).

Conclusion
Toward a Caribbean Police Service (CARIBPOL)

One of the principal obstacles to effective and efficient law enforcement in the Caribbean is judicial limitation. Within the context of the CSME, at the very least, it is important to recognise that borderless crime cannot be fought effectively by law enforcement agencies whose reach stays within national borders. Trans-sovereign organised criminal actors regularly demonstrate readiness and ability to exploit this weakness, for instance, by residing in one member state and committing crime in another, or by moving regularly between member states in their criminal pursuit. Indeed, many criminals are also known to take refuge in other member states. These trends are expected to continue. Law enforcement in the Caribbean, therefore, must confront new realities, including the fact that the emerging pattern of crime being evidenced throughout the region involves both the physical and jurisdictional distancing between the perpetrators of crime and the countries where the victimisation takes place. Among these crimes are illegal drug trafficking and use, fraud, illegal arms possession and trafficking, illegal immigration and alien smuggling, and tax evasion – the principal revenue-generators that require money laundering – as well as car theft and major robberies.

Thus far, CARICOM has remained reluctant to establish a regional security institution, despite the findings of the task force, and the role of the CCJ in law enforcement and regional security is yet to be made clear. What CARICOM needs in the area of law enforcement is an organisation that fosters cooperation and coordination between national police services and customs departments, if necessary, for the purposes of preventing and combating crime in fields such as terrorism, drug trafficking and other serious forms of transnational crime, chiefly through the central exchange and analysis of information and intelligence. This organisation will complement existing national and transnational prevention, training and research and development programmes, and would provide leadership and support in the areas of crime, asylum, immigration, police and judicial cooperation.

Effective and efficient responses to new crime trends require well-developed police intelligence capacity. In that regard, the specific crime reports must be forwarded to a single location, analysed for common elements, and sent to the police agency in the best position to act. This is what governments of the countries of the European Union are attempting to accomplish through the European Police Office (EUROPOL); this is also what CARICOM should seek to accomplish. The development of an integrated response to crime in the form of a Caribbean Police Service or CARIBPOL would serve as a central coordinating institution for intelligence and resources in criminal matters is a law enforcement strategy whose time has come. A CARIBPOL will enable police services throughout the region to acquire new techniques in policing and measures to counter the communications intelligence and sophisticated weapons of the criminal underworld.

For this policy to work, CARICOM needs, among other things, to bring the laws of the various countries into greater harmony. With the establishment of the CCJ, CARICOM should task the attorneys general, in consultation with key stakeholders within the criminal justice system in the region, including representatives from the various directors of public prosecutions, the commissioners of police, the magistracies and the bar associations, to develop new criminal codes to reflect the harmonisation of laws in the following areas:

- agreement on a list of crimes that would be covered by a CARICOM-wide warrant;
- adoption of a common definition of terrorism;
- the setting of minimum penal sanctions for crimes ranging from extortion, to theft, to robbery;

- agreement on minimum/maximum sentences for crimes;
- empowerment of enforcement authorities to enable them to coordinate and cooperate more closely;
- agreement upon mutual recognition orders freezing assets; and
- the development of a common extradition treaty to replace the current bilateral regimes.

In sum, the current shortcomings experienced by law enforcement authorities in the region can be meaningfully addressed through greater policy cooperation and coordination. A CARIBPOL appears, prospectively, to be the region's best strategy to achieve the necessary preparation and acquire the requisite capability to effectively respond to the threats posed by a resource-abundant and highly motivated criminal fraternity.

Notes

1. See 'The Threat Posed by the Convergence of Organised Crime, Drug Trafficking and Terrorism', Testimony by Frank J. Cilluffo, Deputy Director Global Organized Crime Project, Director Counterterrorism Task Force, Centre for Strategic Studies, Washington, DC, before the US House Committee on the Judiciary, Subcommittee on Crime, December 13, 2000, at http://www.csis.org/hill/ts001213cilluffo.html.
2. See Balford Henry, 'Ja, Uk "Link-up" In Crime Fight', *Jamaica Gleaner* on-line, July 17, 2002, at http://www.gleaner.com.
3. See R.O. Keohane and J. Nye Jr. *Power and Interdependence* (Boston: Little Brown), 1977.
4. See Clifford E. Griffin, 'Criminal Deportation: The Unintended Impact of US Anti-Crime and Anti-Terrorism Policy Along Its Third Border', *Journal of Caribbean Studies*, Vol. 30, No. 2 (July–December 2002): 39–76.
5. The US currently has bilateral agreements in force with Anguilla, Antigua and Barbuda, The Bahamas, Barbados, the British Virgin Islands, the Cayman Islands, Dominica, Grenada, Jamaica, Montserrat, St Kitts and Nevis, St Lucia, St Vincent, Trinidad and Tobago, and the Turks and Caicos Islands. The UK's Mutual Legal Assistance in Criminal Matters treaty with the Cayman Islands was extended to Anguilla, the British Virgin Islands, and the Turks and Caicos Islands on November 9, 1990, and to Montserrat on April 26, 1991.
6. See 'Mutual Legal Assistance In Criminal Matters Treaties (MLATs) And Other Agreements' at http://travel.state.gov/mlat.html.
7. See, for example, Duke Pollard. *The Caribbean Court of Justice in Regional Economic Development,* Caribbean Community Secretariat, 2000; and Hugh Rawlins. *The Caribbean Court of Justice: The History and Analysis of the Debate*, Caribbean Community Secretariat, 2000.
8. Ibid.
9. See *Challenges of Capacity Development: Towards Sustainable Reforms of Caribbean Justice Sectors*, Volume 1: Policy Document, IDB/CGCED, May 2000, 2.
10. See Balford Henry, 'Ja, Uk "Link-up" In Crime Fight', *Jamaica Gleaner* on-line, July 17, 2002, at http://www.gleaner.com.

11. See Charmaine Clarke, 'Elite Squad To Fight Drugs', *Jamaica Observer*, July 6, 2002 at http://www.observer.com.
12. See International Criminal Investigative Training Assistance Program (ICITAP) at http://www.usdoj.gov/criminal/icitap/.
13. See International Criminal Investigative Training Assistance Program (ICITAP) at http://www.usdoj.gov/criminal/icitap/.
14. See Bureau of International Narcotics and Law Enforcement Affairs at http://www.state.gov/g/inl/.
15. Ibid.
16. See Ex-St Kitts and Nevis Police Commissioner Views Crime in the Caribbean, BBC Monitoring International Reports, November 5, 2002 at http://web.lexis-nexis.com/universe.
17. See Pierre Lapaque, 'The Caribbean Financial Action Task Force', *International Criminal Police Review*, No. 480 (2000) at http://www.interpol.int/Public/Publications/ICPR/ICPR480_1.asp.
18. See Ex-St Kitts and Nevis Police Commissioner Views Crime in the Caribbean, BBC Monitoring International Reports, November 5, 2002 at http://web.lexis-nexis.com/universe.
19. See Omar Anderson, 'More Good Cops Go Bad', *Jamaica Gleaner* on-line, November 17, 2002 at http://www.gleaner.com.
20. See Opening Remarks by Hon. Lester Bird, MP, Prime Minister of Antigua and Barbuda to the Fourth Joint Meeting of the Inter-Governmental Task Force on Drugs and Ministers Responsible For National Security held in Antigua and Barbuda, June 13 and 14, 2001.
21. See The *Nassau Guardian*, July 6, 2002.

21

Conclusion: Contending with Challenge, Coping with Change

Ivelaw L. Griffith

> It is essential to know the character of the enemy and of their principal officers—whether they be rash or cautious, enterprising or timid, whether they fight on principle or from chance.
> *Vegetius*[1]

> The world has certainly become a different, more dangerous place and we are required to adapt almost daily to changing circumstances and emerging threats. We have also come to accept the reality of our interconnectedness.
> *Kenny Anthony*[2]

Introduction

Vegetius and Anthony capture many of the dynamics of challenge and change that define the security scenario of the contemporary Caribbean. Of course, challenge and change are not new for the region. Indeed, they have been constants of the Caribbean experience ever since the fifteenth century, when Christopher Columbus encountered the region with his history-making geographical blunder. As one would expect, challenge and change matrixes have had differing elements since the arrival of Columbus, with new and often dangerous dimensions in the twentieth century and in this new century, precipitated or accentuated by dynamics of the security, political, and economic environments.

It is reasonable to assume from the chapters in this volume that the context of the security landscape of the contemporary Caribbean is markedly different from that about which Vegetius would have written. Nevertheless, the challenge to which he refers – to know well the enemy's leadership and modus operandi – still exists. The suggestion by Vegetius is a logical extension of that offered in the Introduction to this volume by Carl von Clausewitz: that statesmen and generals must exercise sound judgment about the kind of conflict in which they are engaged. Yet, the need for familiarity about which Vegetius wrote is predicated on much more than simply the desire to know the opponents. It is driven by necessity – for a strategy for engagement and victory that is built on more than anecdote, intuition, and luck. This need for familiarity becomes even more crucial in circumstances of complexity and interdependence, and with new and emerging threats. Such is the situation with the Caribbean, which Prime Minister Kenny Anthony captures, and which this volume has outlined.

Different chapters in this volume have addressed modes, methods, policies, and practices attempted and underway for coping with the region's challenges. As several authors have shown, some of these have been more successful than others. Some have been undermined by the absence of the two key elements that Clausewitz, Vegetius, and Kenny Anthony postulate. First, there should be more than cursory appreciation of the nature of the conflicts being waged and the character of the opposing actors. Second, there needs to be a willingness and ability by security policy makers and practitioners to be sufficiently adaptable.

Adaptation – of modes, methods, policies, and practices – becomes not just a desire; it is a necessity, amounting to a challenge of change. Thus, in pondering ways in which Caribbean states cope with the security challenges facing them and with adaptation as a challenge of change, it is essential to go beyond the largely issue-focused considerations of earlier chapters and pursue the over-arching question raised but not examined in Chapter One: What are some relevant strategies to cope with the challenges confronting states in the region? Dealing with this question requires revisiting the framework developed in Chapter 1 in order to address relevant components – pertaining to actors, response instruments, and engagement zones – that were not elaborated there. Needless to say, this analysis is by no means exhaustive or definitive.

The Framework Revisited

It is important to recall the key features of the *Discrete Multidimensional Security Framework* outlined in Chapter 1 before proceeding to discuss the issue of strategy. Use of the term *Discrete* reflects awareness of the need to avoid inclusion of all *significant* national challenges in the security matrix, and *Multidimensional* highlights the multiplicity of elements in the schema and the plurality of aspects of each element. As Figure 1.5 in Chapter 1 shows, several elements are involved, including security categories and dimensions, threat type and arenas, threats and threat intensities, and response instruments. The security categories and dimensions entail a *Traditional Issues* category with military, political, and economic dimensions, and a *Non-traditional Issues* category involving the three dimensions of the other category plus an environmental one.

As regards threat types, threat intensities, and threat arenas, two types of threats are identified. *Core threats* are actions or a sequence of events that affect the vital interests of nation-states, directly undermining their territorial or political integrity by jeopardising their protection against external coercion, internal subversion, or erosion of cherished political, economic, or social values. *Peripheral threats* derive from actions or a sequence of events that affect the secondary interests of states by visiting collateral damage on their territorial and political integrity or their cherished political, economic, or social values. Threat specification makes it necessary to define the two sets of interests at stake: *vital interests*, which entail protection of the physical, political, and cultural identity of Caribbean nation-states, and *secondary interests* – matters that are important to maintaining vital interests.

Conscious that while all threats are important and that some are relatively more important than others, I specify a three-level order of threat intensity: high, medium, and low. *Threat intensity* itself is a function of both objective factors, such as the number, severity, and timing of the threat and whether military force is used, and of subjective factors, largely the perception of the relevant political elites and security practitioners. Important too is the fact that the relationship between threat type and threat intensity is variable. Thus, core threats may not always exist at high intensity; they could be medium or low, depending on the number, severity, and timing of the threat, whether military force is employed, and how the political elites define the situation. Further, threat intensity is not static; the intensity of threats may change from one level to another, again, depending on objective and subjective factors.

In addition, there is no necessary correlation between threat intensity and threat arena. In other words, not all threats from the internal arena may be high or medium; threats from either arena can be high, medium, or low, again, depending on objective and subjective factors. Moreover, quite important is that there are symbiotic relationships between threat type and threat intensity, threat type and threat arena, and threat intensity and threat arena. Thus, there are dynamic relationships involving all elements of the matrix, although those relationships are not all causal-consequential in nature. Although some threats may be identified as being within a specific arena, most threats derive from both internal and external factors. They are 'interdependence issues'.

Understandably, there are links between the actors in the security milieu and their engagement in that milieu. The milieu has state and non-state actors, and these actors engage both nationally and internationally. *Engagement Zones*, defined as geographic spaces for policy and operational collaboration by state and non-state actors in relation to defence and security matters, exist nationally and internationally. As regards the relationship between actors and Engagement Zones, the nature and capabilities of some actors make them better candidates for engagement in some zones than in others. For example, individuals may have engagement capacity only within the national zone, and national corporations that are part of a multinational corporate structure have a better chance of international engagement than those without it. Moreover, there is variability in the nature and scope of engagement by actors and in the instruments they use. For instance, some non-governmental organisations (NGOs) may not engage in counter-narcotics or counter-terrorism efforts, but in fighting HIV/AIDS.

Subregions, regions, and the hemisphere are viewed as relatively discrete spaces for analytic purposes, but they are not exclusive spaces in terms of actual engagement; they overlap. There are both bilateral and multilateral engagements, and each of the multilateral zones has several non-state and state entities. Multilateral engagement instruments, such as treaties, conventions, memoranda, and protocols, guide the actors at the subregional, regional, and other levels. These instruments create the entities that operate within the zones and define their terms of engagement. It is essential to bear in mind that, as is the case with any framework, the Discrete Multidimensional Security Framework is a heuristic device. As such, it is not intended to explain each and every element or component of the phenomenon being explored, but to offer a conceptual architecture to facilitate explanation and interpretation of structures, patterns, and dynamics involved in the security issue area. Some of these structures, patterns, and dynamics relate to the matter of strategy, to which we turn our attention next.

Connecting Framework to Strategy

Caribbean security elites and practitioners should embrace two broad strategies: a *Strategy of Engagement*, and a *Strategy of Adaptation*. These are offered as complementary, not competing, strategic pursuits. The term *strategy* itself needs to be put into definitional context. Edward Luttwak explains that it derives from the Greek *strategos* ('general'), but it has come to be known more over time in terms of *strategike episteme* (generals' knowledge) or *strategon sophia* (general's wisdom). In this vein it has been defined both narrowly and expansively.

For instance, for Carl von Clausewitz it was 'the use of engagements for the object of war', while it is used in the *Dictionary of United States Military Terms for Joint Usage* of the US Joint Chiefs of Staff to mean 'the art and science of developing and using political, economic, psychological, and military forces as necessary during peace and war to afford the maximum support to policies, in order to increase the probabilities and favorable consequences of victory and to lessen the chances of defeat'.[3] (Understandably, the military context is not the only one in which the term is used; it is used in the economic and corporate contexts quite significantly as well).[4]

Both of the definitions above are anchored on the traditional military aspect of security. However, the approach of this chapter – and the volume overall – is that the context and content of the Caribbean's security challenges are not merely traditional military ones and should not be interpreted as such. Hence, our approach to security strategy must go beyond the military domain. Thus, for me, strategy involves *an overall schema about the use of political, economic, military, and law enforcement capabilities to preserve a nation's territorial integrity, maintain its political stability, and secure the general well being of its citizens*. In this sense, it is perspective and plan. Moreover, I share Fred Nickols' view that it is the bridge between policy and tactics, and a general framework that guides actions and at the same time is shaped by the actions undertaken.[5]

Strategy of Engagement

The underlying precept of the Strategy of Engagement proposed here is simple: *Caribbean security elites and practitioners should embrace proactive national and regional engagement in order to better cope with extant security challenges, lest the 'science of "muddling through,"'*[6] *which is practised in some places, becomes the regional norm and undermines the security and sovereignty of nations in the region.* The region's security environment requires multidimensional, multi-agency, and multi-level security engagement. This is because the threats and challenges are transnational and multifaceted, as chapters in this volume have revealed. Engagement also needs to be multiactored because (a) states are not the only actors with threatened interests, and (b) many states have such capability limitations that their individual actions are inconsequential. Thus, as is suggested in the Discrete Multidimensional Security Framework and captured in Figure 1.5, international governmental organisations (IGOs), non-governmental organisations (NGOs), and other non-state actors become important.

The multidimensionality of the security arena makes it necessary for the actors to use a range of response instruments to deal with threats and challenges, as Figures 1.4 and 1.5 in Chapter One reveal. These include modes, methods, policies, and programmes that essentially are diplomatic, economic, emergency management, law enforcement, military, and political in nature. This list is not offered in any order of importance. Noteworthy, too, is that threats require differing response instruments. Moreover, coping with specific threats may require the use of multiple response instruments. For instance, fighting drugs – which itself is a multidimensional threat – requires the use of military, law enforcement, economic, political, and diplomatic instruments. Dealing with HIV/AIDS does not require the military instruments but it does demand the use of economic, political, and some law enforcement instruments.

The dynamics of actor-instrument relationships are manifest within the security engagement zones, described above. Basically, there are two zone arenas: national and international. The latter arena has several zones, called *Multilateral Security Engagement (MSE) Zones*. Such zones exist at the sub-regional, regional, hemispheric, and international systemic levels. As Figure 21.1 suggests, although the zones are relatively discrete spaces, they are not exclusive spaces; they overlap. Also, as those illustrations reveal, each MSE zone has several state and non-state entities. Further, as with the listing of response instruments above, the agencies and networks are not presented in any order of importance.

Figure 21.1
Multilateral Security Engagement Zones

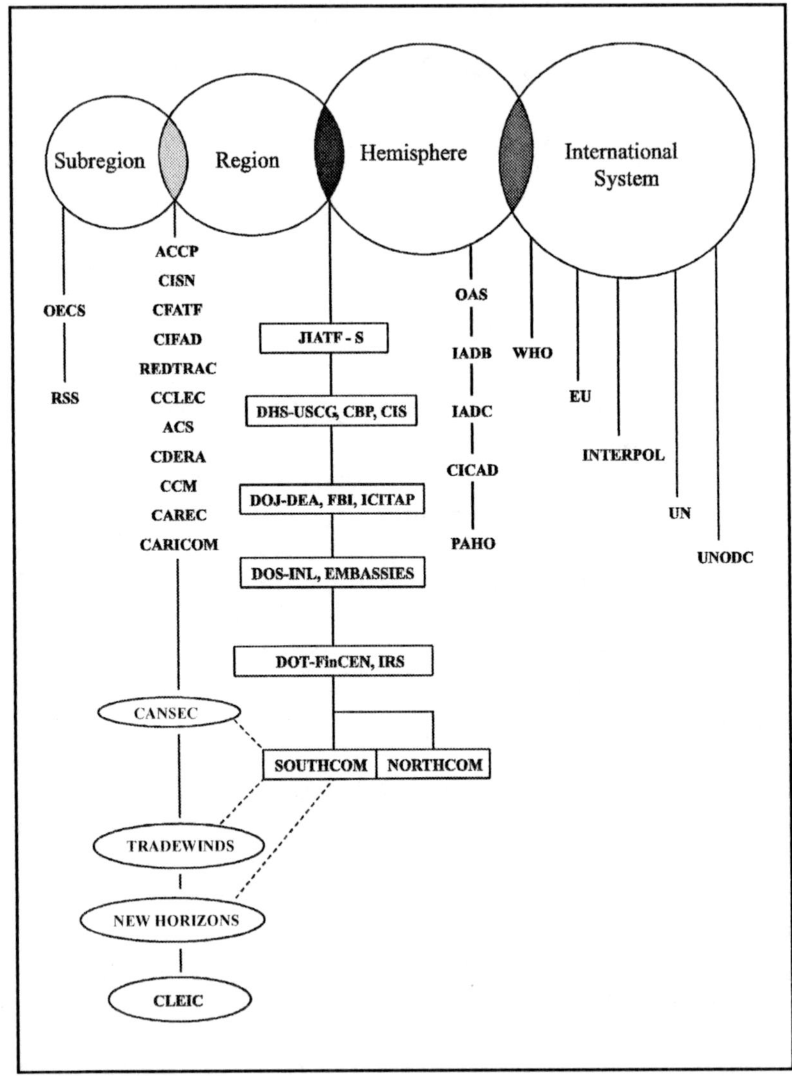

Table 21.1
Agencies and Networks in the Multilateral Security Engagement Zones

Subregional Engagement Zone
Organization of Eastern Caribbean States (OECS)
Regional Security System (RSS)

Regional Engagement Zone
Association of Caribbean Commissioners of Police (ACCP)
Association of Caribbean States (ACS)
Caribbean Community (CARICOM)
Caribbean Coordination Mechanism (CCM)
Caribbean Customs Law Enforcement Council (CCLEC)
Caribbean Disaster Emergency Response Agency (CDERA)
Caribbean Epimediology Centre (CAREC)
Caribbean Financial Action Task Force (CFATF)
Caribbean Information Sharing Network (CISN)
Caribbean Inter-Ministerial Drug Control Training Centre (CIFAD)
Caribbean Law Enforcement and Intelligence Committee (CLEIC)
Caribbean Nations Security Conference (CANSEC)
Regional Drug Training Centre (REDTRAC)

Hemispheric Engagement Zone
Bureau of Alcohol, Tobacco, Firearms, and Explosives (ATF) [Department of Justice]
Bureau of Customs and Border Patrol (CBP) [Department of Homeland Security]
Drug Enforcement Administration (DEA) [Department of Justice]
Federal Bureau of Investigation (FBI) [Department of Treasury]
Financial Crimes Enforcement Network (FinCEN) [Department of Treasury]
Inland Revenue Service (IRS) [Department of Treasury]
Inter-American Defence Board (IADB)
Inter-American Defence College (IADC)
Inter-American Drug Abuse Control Commission [Comisión Interamericana para el Control del Abuso de Drogas] (CICAD)
International Criminal Investigative Training Assistance Program (ICITAP) [Justice]
International Narcotics and Law Enforcement Affairs (INL) [Department of State]
Joint Interagency Task Force–South (JIATF-S) [Department of Defence]
Organization of American States (OAS)
Pan-American Health Organization (PAHO)
US Coast Guard (USCG) [Department of Homeland Security]
US Northern Command (NORTHCOM)
US Southern Command (SOUTHCOM)

International Systemic Engagement Zone
European Union (EU)
International Criminal Police Organization (INTERPOL)
United Nations (UN)
United Nations Office on Drugs and Crime (UNODC)
World Health Organization (WHO)

Notes:
- Agencies and networks do not fall exclusively within the Zones with which they are identified
- This is not a list of all agencies and networks in the Zones, just a representative group

United States governmental agencies and United States-led networks play key roles in some regional and hemispheric engagements, as Figure 21.1 suggests.[7] Although not shown in the illustrations, so too do a few British, Canadian, Dutch, and French agencies, notably Scotland Yard and the Royal Canadian Mounted Police (RCMP). This is because these nations have security and other interests that are affected by what happens in the Caribbean and to it, and because of the resources they possess. In other words, essentially their involvement is not driven by altruism, but by national interests. Understandably, there is a mixed record of implementation and success of the various engagements. One could appreciate, as well, that operating within the MSE zones also would carry many challenges. These deserve some attention.

Multilateral Engagement Challenges

Working within the MSE zones entails dealing with many challenges, among them challenges related to priorities, institutionalising agreements, cooperating with other actors, and sharing intelligence.[8] These challenges are not the only possible ones related to engagement in the zones. Further, they exist not only in relation to multilateral collaboration; most of them also exist in bilateral relationships. It is important also to observe that the order in which the challenges are discussed does not suggest a rank order of the challenges themselves; challenge dynamics vary in relation to several factors, including the actors involved, the zone(s) in question, and threat(s) in question.

The Prioritisation and Institutionalisation Challenges

Prioritisation is necessary for several reasons. First, as was noted earlier, the multidimensionality of the security challenges means that the response must also be multidimensional. Yet, and this is the second reason, the states involved are all small states with various budgetary, manpower, technical, intelligence, and other capability limitations.

Beyond this, as security issues are not the only issues on national policy agendas, resources have to be allocated to other areas, such as health, education, and housing. National and regional (and other) decision makers therefore have to undertake the unenviable task of setting priorities. This should be done in some rational way, guided by some policy framework or strategy, rather than in an ad hoc manner. The consequences of the latter –

and there is evidence of this consequence within the Caribbean and elsewhere – is sub-optimal use of resources, sometimes a waste of resources, and little appreciable mitigation impact on the challenge at hand.

A key test of the commitment of many states to meaningfully confront the security challenges facing them is their willingness to institutionalise the multilateral arrangements by incorporating them adequately into national policy. In practical terms this can be judged, among other things, by the following criteria:

1. Whether they sign, and later ratify, the multilateral engagement instrument, whether treaty, convention, or memorandum of understanding.
2. Whether they procrastinate on such action or act with deliberate speed.
3. Whether they adopt enabling, supporting, or collateral legislation or other domestic policy instruments.

Some countries have poor records when it comes to sustaining, and sometimes, merely launching initiatives. This is often because of financial, technical, manpower or other constraints, but often it is due to simple neglect driven by a lack of political will or administrative lethargy, or both. Sometimes it is a manifestation of what I call the *Solution By Platitudes Syndrome* found in many parts of the hemisphere. This behaviour occurs when political elites seem or prefer to believe that the delivery of a grand speech or proclamation or the signing of a convention or treaty *ipso facto* solves the problem at hand, and that they can afford to pay scant attention to the implementation, institutionalisation, and evaluation aspects involved. Political and bureaucratic elites therefore need to recognise that meaningful regional or other multilateral engagement requires rising above platitudes and going beyond signings. As leaders, they themselves are obliged to follow-through, institutionalise, and implement or delegate the appropriate tasks to other officials whom they hold accountable.

The Cooperation and Intelligence Sharing Challenges

The security challenges discussed earlier clearly are transnational in nature; they are 'interdependence issues' to use James Rosenau's conceptual construct: 'issues that [are] distinguished from conventional issues by the fact that they span national boundaries and thus cannot be addressed much less resolved through actions undertaken at the national or local level'.[9] Hence, actions to cope with security challenges must be commensurately transnational. This necessitates cooperation, which needs to be both bilateral and multilateral. These two approaches are not mutually exclusive; it is not a case of either bilateral cooperation or multilateral cooperation, but how much of each is desirable or necessary. Indeed, many times bilateral measures are preferred, as generally they can be designed and implemented more quickly.

The cooperation challenge lies partly in the fact that, whether viewed in bilateral or multilateral terms, the need for cooperation raises the prospect that conflicts may ensue in relation to capabilities and sovereignty, among other things. Capability disputes between or among cooperating states do not arise merely because of the actual money, equipment, and other constraints on the part of partners. They often occur because inherent in the capability disparities of cooperating partners is the expectation that those with fewer limitations will give relatively more to the collective effort. This is likely to be especially so in a multilateral context with many actors, and where just a few of them have meaningful resource capacity.

Effective cooperation is not always achievable, and for a variety of reasons, including political leadership changes within countries, public opinion within the more resource-endowed states, and the fact that policy makers in the relatively better-off states are sometimes unsure that there will be commensurate national interest returns on their nation's investments in the collective project. It is not that they are often against collaboration; sometimes there is uncertainty or rethinking about the amount of investment to be made in the various response mixes – unilateral, bilateral, or multilateral – and the form that investment should take.

The cooperation challenge has an additional dimension, which pertains to cooperation between and among agencies *within* countries. Problems spawned by bureaucratic politics give rise to jurisdictional and turf battles and coordination difficulties between army and coast guard, army intelligence and police intelligence, health ministries and trade ministries, foreign affairs ministries and national security ministries, and such. Thus, the cooperation within countries deserves the same emphasis as cooperation between and among countries, as 'cooperation among' and 'cooperation within' are but two dimensions of the same challenge.

Essential to 'knowing the enemy' and determining 'how to adapt', to which Vegetius and Kenny Anthony referred, is information about the adversary and the threat environment, obtained through observation, investigation, and analysis. This involves the business of intelligence. Although important, matters such as the strategic and tactical levels of intelligence, the kind of intelligence – military, drug, counter-terrorism, and so on – and the intelligence cycle are beyond the purview of this discussion.[10] But it must be noted that all these aspects are important to the security of the Caribbean, and they all are undertaken in the Caribbean and in relation to it. However, Caribbean states themselves do not have meaningful ownership of the intelligence processes or products.

The intelligence area provides dramatic evidence of capability limitations and security subordination. True, there are security mechanisms within countries, such as Joint Information Coordination Centres (JICCs) and Joint Operations Command Centres (JOCCs). But in almost all cases their establishment and operation are the result of interest and investment by non-Caribbean state actors, notably the United States and Britain. Similarly, regional intelligence networks and systems, such as the Caribbean Law Enforcement and Intelligence Committee (CLEIC), which meets monthly in Puerto Rico, the Caribbean Information Sharing Network (CISN), and the Cooperating Nations Information Exchange System (CNIES) are expressions of the twin dynamics of US and European national interests and cooperative engagement.[11]

One of the multilateral engagement challenges related to the issue of intelligence has pertained to the sharing of intelligence. Despite several significant instances of cooperation in fighting drugs and other transnational threats in the region, displeasure has often been expressed in some Caribbean security circles about the one-sidedness of the intelligence sharing relationship with the United States. In essence, this is a problem of intelligence cooperation.

Some of the criticism is justifiable. Legislative restrictions within the United States explain why some of this obtains. But perhaps more importantly, the reluctance of US and other authorities to share intelligence is based on often justifiable concerns about the integrity of Caribbean security agencies and personnel, because of corruption, operational constraints, and inefficiency. Indeed, there are cases *within Caribbean countries* where some agencies do not share information with other agencies precisely because of the concerns about integrity of personnel or systems.

The structures and orientation of intelligence networks and agencies in the region relate significantly to combating drugs and crime, with terrorism assuming a higher profile since 9/11. Understandably, most agencies and networks are multifunctional and multidimensional in design and operation, with mandates in relation to several threats, such as drugs plus crime plus terrorism. This is true of entities based partly or fully in the region, such as

CISN and the Caribbean Customs Law Enforcement Council (CCLEC), which are not solely intelligence entities. It also is true of entities that are located within the United States but are critical to the functionality of the networks in the region, such as the Joint Inter-Agency Task Force-South (JIATF-S), which is based in Key West, Florida.[12] As one might appreciate, the HIV/AIDS threat has an 'intelligence' logic different from that for drugs, terrorism, or crime. Thus, information-sharing generally is not a problem. Indeed, the problem for state and NGO officials in some of the smaller nations is one of information overload.

Strategy of Adaptation

In delivering a national media address to the St Lucian nation on March 6, 2003, Prime Minister Kenny Anthony observed:

> The reality is that because of the relaxed manner in which we are accustomed to going about our daily lives, countries like ours are seen as points of weakness, potential launching pads for acts of terror or other mischief, targeted at other countries and their associated interests. We must ensure, through our vigilance and concerted and deliberate action, that our countries serve no such purpose.[13]

Among other things, this plea, which is relevant only in a matter of degree to every jurisdiction in the Caribbean Basin, is a plea for adaptation. It is a plea in the context of the terrorism-related dynamics and United States–Caribbean geopolitical and geoeconomic dealings. Yet it is more than this; it is a plea for adaptation that is salient to the entire security landscape and is pertinent to all the threats and apprehensions.

Curiously enough, some scholars have long made similar entreaties. One example will suffice. Clearly a decade before the message by Prime Minister Anthony, one writer noted:

> Something common to all Caribbean societies is the friendly, trusting, and open nature of their peoples and institutions. This is a characteristic which, when transmitted to the security arena, may make these societies more politically and militarily penetrable, and susceptible to both internal and external threats. Trust and openness are partly due to the relative stability of the region, the absence of authoritarian politics, except once each in Cuba, Grenada, Guyana, and Dominica, and the predominance of liberal democracy where a premium is placed on civil and political rights. It is,

> therefore, relatively easy to gain access to many political leaders and security-sensitive facilities, such as power stations, water supply systems, and communications networks. Greater security consciousness should be exercised to mitigate the circumstances where Caribbean leaders and sensitive installations could become unnecessarily vulnerable.
>
> Expanded security consciousness is especially important in a place like Guyana where the country's size (214,970 km^2) and population distribution – mostly along the coasts – leave vast areas of the country without effective security. It was this circumstance that allowed a group of Americans, Colombians, and Guyanese to build an illegal airstrip at Waranama, four hundred miles from the capital, Georgetown. The Colombians and Americans were able to enter the country illegally and bring a generator, a water pump, two airplane engines, six transmitting sets, tool kits, arms and ammunition, and other supplies over a four-month period. The operations were to be part of an international drug processing and transshipment network involving Trinidad and Tobago, Miami, and Colombia. In January 1989 several of the conspirators were arrested and charged and the equipment was confiscated.[14]

The underlying precept of the Adaptation Strategy is simple: *Caribbean security elites and practitioners should undertake periodic threat assessments of their national and regional security landscapes and make adaptations in modes, methods, policies, and practices commensurate with the changing dynamics and needs.* As the majority of issues facing Caribbean nations are transnational, it is essential that the assessments have both national and international components. It is also critical that Caribbean states play meaningful roles in defining the terms of the assessments, to ensure that the scope and content of the reviews and the resulting agendas for action are consonant with their national and regional interests. As two strategy experts have pointed out, 'Strategy begins with national objectives (sometimes called national interests)'.[15] Too often, Caribbean nations are pliant surrogates for the pursuit of interests of powerful states, IGOs, and INGOs that fund studies and, consequently, influence their findings and the consequent follow-up action, sometimes unduly so.

The security engagement zones discussed earlier provide institutional scope for the pursuit of assessments. They could be undertaken in the context of the agencies and networks shown in Table. 21.1. Hence, the timing of the assessments could be set in the context of the modus operandi of the agencies or networks: annually or biennially at summits, general assemblies, annual conferences and the like, or as determined by the relevant officials within those agencies or networks. Alternatively, those agencies or networks could establish review bodies that would report to the relevant high officials. Of course, such international level assessments do not preclude the creation of national task forces or commissions to deal with particular national anomalies or actual or perceived increases in the scope and intensity of threats.

Importantly, these assessments, whether national or international, should not be held hostage in either design or deliver to the vicissitudes of partisan domestic politics. As several chapters in this volume have shown, some of this periodic assessment and resulting adaptation already occurs in some areas, both nationally and regionally. Nevertheless, assessments tend to be more ad hoc than regularised, institutionalised, or sustained as part of a culture of security management. Moreover, there are several occasions where assessments become ends in themselves, either to placate a domestic constituency or a foreign government or agency, with little attention to implementation of their recommendations. Sometimes this results from poor design of the assessment, where the mandate is too expansive and the process unwieldy. It also is the case that changes among the political and bureaucratic elites sometimes undermine the priority accorded the assessments and their outcomes. At times, resource constraints and administrative lethargy effectively put the death knell on the execution of projects.

Strategy Calculus

It was noted earlier that the Engagement Strategy and the Adaptation Strategy are not incompatible. More than this, though, bilateral and multilateral pursuits should not be viewed in zero-sum terms. Thus, pursuit of the Adaptation Strategy makes it incumbent on security policy makers to keep in mind the following considerations:

- Calculus No.1: prudence suggests that thought be given to the combination of bilateral and multilateral measures that best suit the national (and regional) interests. This Calculus requires policy makers to bear the following in mind:
  - the nature and salience of the threats;
  - their national capabilities;
  - time considerations; and
  - the efficacy of proceeding unilaterally or collectively.
- Calculus No. 2: pursuit of bilateral measures should not contradict or undermine multilateral efforts initiated earlier. It should be added here

that an important tenet of the Adaptation Strategy is the right of security elites and practitioners to review multilateral engagement pursuits in relation to their continuing necessity and utility.

- Calculus No. 3: there exists a correlation between engagement and institutional capacity. Leaders should be mindful of the institutional capacity implications of pursuing numerous bilateral mechanisms or several combinations of bilateral and multilateral ones. This is especially important as they are also pursuing bilateral and multilateral initiatives outside the security area, in relation to trade, investment, intellectual property, telecommunications, and other areas. This Calculus is even more important for leaders in the very small states. In addition, it is crucial in relation to the security practitioners of all nations whose operational lives become extremely stressful and less than efficient as they strive to execute what policy makers sign.[16]
- Calculus No. 4: accept what is true for all states: that even with the necessity for and pursuit of multilateral engagement, states will have national interests they feel obliged to pursue unilaterally or bilaterally and doing this may collide with regional, hemispheric, or international strategy or tactics.
- Calculus No. 5: accept that because of Calculus No. 4, conflicts over sovereignty, strategy, or resources are likely to occur and it would be prudent to establish mechanisms for conflict resolution as multilateral engagements are contemplated. Moreover, the onus lies on both the conflicting parties and the other actors in the zone affected to secure speedy and amicable resolution of conflicts that arise.
- Calculus No. 6: none of the threats and challenges, whether core or peripheral, is amedable to easy defeat or resolution, even if state actors had all the requisite capabilities. Therefore, political elites should avoid platitudes and posturing that raise expectations about quick fixes.

In pursuing the Adaptation Strategy, especially in relation to multilateral engagement, policy makers might find it useful to note the caution issued elsewhere about multilateralism.[17] While multilateralism has several virtues, it also has its limitations. One of them is the propensity for incrementalism, which is driven by several factors. Among them is bureaucratic power politics, both within domestic agencies and international organisations. The reality of power asymmetries and the fact that both state and non-state actors often have to be involved are also important considerations. Plus, there is the need for the larger state and non-state actors in the engagement zones to guard against leadership becoming dictation. All of this means that (a) the process of policy decision making and project design is likely to be time-consuming, and (b) the delivery of the multilateral project(s) might be delayed, to the point often where little appears to be happening, except to the keen observers of the scene.

Overall, the Adaptation Strategy does not preclude the preparation of threat- or issue-specific strategies; indeed, it accommodates them. Broadly speaking, for a region like the Caribbean, there are three strategy levels. The first, which I call Level One Strategies, involves strategies for specific threats or security areas – military defence, narcotics, drugs, HIV/AIDS, terrorism, and the like. Level Two Strategies entail articulation of national security strategies. In the context of multilateralism, there is a third level: Level Three Strategies, which are designed and executed at the regional, hemispheric, or international systemic level. All three levels of strategy are important. However, in circumstances of technical, institutional, and other constraints, which loom large in the Caribbean, one can think of a desire-necessity matrix in which it would be desirable to have all three, but necessary to have at least the first and third level strategies. Note, though, that articulation of a First or Third Level Strategy in the absence of a national security strategy – a Level Two strategy – places the onus on national policy elites to clearly define national interests and provide appropriate parameters to guide the formulation of the strategy.

Trade-Offs

As with any strategy, consideration has to be given to the subject of trade-offs. Making choice therefore becomes a key consideration. This brings into focus the resource allocation challenge to which I alluded earlier and which I examine elsewhere.[18] The security challenges discussed throughout this volume present clear and present dangers to Caribbean nations, although some are less clear and less present than others. Consequently, policy makers are obliged to channel considerable economic and other resources to meeting those threats. Not that the resources allocated to meeting them are adequate; they are not.

However, policy makers have to be mindful that notwithstanding the nature, scope, and gravity of the security challenges, security is not the only item on the national policy agenda. Important too are education, health, housing, roads, and other matters that are critical for economic and political governance and have consequential if not causal connections to the security challenges. Therefore, resources also have to be allocated to these areas. Thus, trade-offs become a critical matter. This could be inordinately difficult. As Barry Buzan noted, and quite correctly:

> The making of national security policy requires choices about both the objectives of policy (ends), and the techniques, resources, instruments, and actions, which will be used to implement it (means). Even if one assumes that neither political nor perceptual problems interfere with the process, these choices are not straightforward.[19]

Yet, it is not merely the specific trade-offs that are important. Crucial, too, is the process of making those decisions, which is hardly ever easy. This is especially so in times of extreme resource scarcity, or when the resources involved for the security engagement are 'significant' or appear to be so. The acceptability of the decision by the sectors of society negatively affected by the trade-offs and the willingness of those sectors to endure the consequential sacrifices that could hinge on the extent to which they were consulted or included in some way in the decision making process. Thus inclusiveness, transparency, and participation become essential features of the decision making process.

The issue of trade-offs is not purely an economic one; it also is a political one, as it involves the essence of politics in Lasswellian terms – who gets what, how, and when. This raises the matter of political power and the exercise of that power, making it necessary for us to remember that the strategies under discussion are being pursued in an overall context of political democracy, central to which is the importance of political restraint by the wielders of political power. In this respect, it is useful to note the prescient observation by James Madison in *The Federalist*, No. 51: 'In framing a government which is to be administered by men over men the great difficulty lies in this: you must first enable the government to control the governed; and in the next place oblige it to control itself'.[20]

The challenge to which James Madison referred becomes accentuated when it comes to national security. This is because security threats tend to result in a shift in the balance of power between people and power elites in the favour of the latter, either through conscious assertion by the elites or with the explicit or default approval of the members of society. This increases the probability that political power could be exercised in ways that result in excessive intrusion of the state into the affairs of citizens. Worse, perhaps, is the exercise of power that restricts or undermines core political values and citizens' rights and freedoms – of speech, press, movement, and privacy, among others.

Moreover, especially when there are disputes over the severity or intensity of threats, in the sense used in Chapter One, the question is raised: Whose security really is threatened – that of the nation or that of the ruling regime? The contemporary history of the Caribbean provides several examples where the ruling elites conflated national security and regime security, and exercised political power in a way that undermined and subverted the rights and freedoms of citizens as they 'protected the national interests of the state'. Haiti, Guyana, Cuba, Suriname, the Dominican Republic, Grenada, and Dominica are among places with clear evidence of this in the past four decades.[21] Thus, it is incumbent on those who control power to ensure that the agents and agencies of security, whether traditional or non-traditional, exercise restraint and temper their exuberance to 'kill the enemy', 'eliminate the threats', and 'protect national security', lest they end up killing the nation while trying to protect the state.

The increased sensitivity to terrorism ever since September 11, 2001, places a new premium on this, especially in parts of the Caribbean with a significant presence of people of Middle Eastern descent or followers of the Islamic religion, such as Trinidad and Tobago, Guyana, and Suriname. In this respect, Prime Minister P.J. Patterson's remarks to the Jamaican Parliament following the September 11 terrorist attack clearly applies to the entire region:

> It is important that we take whatever preventative measures are necessary to protect ourselves even as we join in the international effort. At the same time, it is important that here and elsewhere in the world, reaction to threat of terrorism, does not give rise to religious intolerance and racial prejudice aimed at minority groups, especially those considered to be of the Islamic faith or persons considered to be of suspect loyalties because of their national origin.[22]

Of course, the question about 'security of the regime' or 'security of the nation' often is misplaced, as the threat is manifestly one to both.

Adaptive Engagement

Whether the clear and present dangers are posed to regime, nation, or both, it is reassuring to have the relevant political elites and security practitioners exercise responsiveness and flexibility when the dangers being faced are either aggravated or the circumstances are radically altered. As several of the chapters in this volume have demonstrated, the threats of drugs, crime, and HIV/AIDS have been aggravated in the Caribbean and 9/11 has radically altered the security landscape.

Thus, in the context of engagement and adaptation, it is understandable and noteworthy that the political elites in some places in the region have adopted what might be called *adaptive engagement*, portraits of which are provided in Tables 21.2, 21.3, and 21.4 for Guyana, Jamaica, and St Lucia, respectively. Needless to say, these three nations are not the only ones to pursue adaptive engagement. Note, too, that adaptive engagement has been pursued not only at the national level, but at the regional and hemispheric levels as well. One (CARICOM) regional example is reflected by the decisions issued in the Nassau Declaration on International Terrorism, adopted in October 2001.[23] A few other things are noteworthy. One, the adaptive engagements profiles reflected in Tables 21.2, 21.3, and 21.4 are not necessarily comprehensive portraits of actions taken in those countries. Two, the profiles include immediate actions and proposed actions for new modes and methods. Three, in most cases more than one response instrument is involved. Interesting also is the fact that, while the primary threats prompting the actions are terrorism and crime, in very few cases was the military response instrument considered appropriate.

Table 21.2
Adaptive Engagements in Guyana Pertaining to Crime

Engagement Action	Core Threat Concern	Allied Threats	Primary Engagement Actor	Other Actors (to be) Engaged	Zone(s) of Relevance	Response Instruments
$G100 M to the police force in 2000–01 for weapons, protective gear, transportation, and communications facilities	Crime	Political instability; Drug trafficking	State	Other states; Corporations	National; International	Economic; Political
Commitment to provide $G100 M in 2003–04 to GPF for similar purpose	Crime	Political instability; drug trafficking	State	Other states; Corporations	National; International	Economic; Political
Decision to comprehensively reform intelligence sector	Crime	Drug trafficking; arms trafficking; Terrorism	State	Other states; Corporations	National	Economic; Political; Law Enforcement; Military
Decision to create specialised centre for training on law enforcement, leader-ship, strategy, tactics	Crime	Drug trafficking; Arms trafficking Terrorism	State	Other states; IGOs	National; International	Economic; Political; Law Enforcement
Decision to create SWAT-like 'crime crack force' to complement existing crime-fighting units	Crime	Drug trafficking Arms trafficking Terrorism	State	Other states IGOs	National; International	Economic; Military; Law Enforcement
Review of existing legislation on crime in order to remove loopholes and toughen penalties	Crime	Terrorism; Drug trafficking; Arms trafficking	State	NGOs	National	Political; Economic
Introduction of laws to monitor movement of deportees	Crime	Drug trafficking; Arms trafficking	State	Other states; NGOs	National; International	Political; Economic; Diplomatic
Improve efficiency and processing time of applications for firearms licenses, esp. by business owners	Crime	Political instability; Arms trafficking; Terrorism	State	None	National	Political
Decision to establish a G$20 M Enhanced Welfare Package, with initial fund of $G1 M, for dependents of policemen killed in the line of battle	Crime	Political instability	State	None	National	Economic; Political
Formation of Task Force to oversee the execution of decisions	Crime	All of the above	State	NGOs; Corporations	National	Political; Economic

Notes:

IGO = International Non-governmental Organisation
NGO = Non-governmental Organisation
SWAT = Special Weapons and Tactics

Source: Statement on the Crime Situation and Additional Anti-Crime Initiatives by His Excellency President Bharrat Jagdeo, June 7, 2000, *Office of the President, Georgetown, Guyana.*

Table 21.3
Adaptive Engagements by Jamaica Pertaining to Terrorism

Engagement Action	Core Threat Concern	Allied Threats	Primary Engagement Actor	Other Actors (to be) Engaged	Zone(s) of Relevance	Response Instruments
Increased mobile and foot patrol of airports, especially terminals, airsides, and perimeter fencings	Terrorism	Arms trafficking; Drug trafficking; Crime	State	Other states	National; International	Law Enforcement; Diplomatic; Economic
Drastic reduction in issuance of Air Team and temporary passes to people wanting to enter sterile areas	Terrorism	Arms trafficking; Crime; Drug trafficking	State	Individuals; Corporations	National	Law Enforcement
Increased surveillance at airports	Terrorism	Arms trafficking; Crime; Drug trafficking	State	Individuals; Corporations	National	Law Enforcement
Thorough checks of all vehicles wishing to gain access to restricted areas at airports	Terrorism	Arms trafficking; Crime; Drug trafficking	State	Individuals; Corporations	National	Law Enforcement
More thorough screening of checked and carry-on luggage at airports	Terrorism	Arms trafficking; Crime; Drug trafficking	State	Other states; Individuals; Corporations	National; International	Law Enforcement; Diplomatic
Comprehensive evaluation by Port Authority of port security procedures esp. transshipment terminal and cruise ship ports	Terrorism	Crime; Arms trafficking; Drug trafficking	State	None	National	Law Enforcement
Stringent examination of containers at dock-side and shipside, with appropriate sign-off after each inspection	Terrorism	Arms trafficking; Crime; Drug trafficking	State	Corporations; Multi National Corporations	National	Law Enforcement; Economic
Increased incentives for conventions and groups to come to Jamaica	Terrorism	Political instability	State	Individuals; Corporations; Multi National Corporations	National; International	Economic; Political
Beautification of resort towns	Terrorism	Political instability	State	Individuals; Corporations	National	Economic; Political
Provision of an extra $US 8 M to Operation Grow and creation of a Task Force to approve funds & monitor work	Terrorism	Political instability	State	Corporations; Multi National Corporations	National; International	Economic; Political
Allocation of $US 2.5 M from Operation Grow for TV ads and $US 1 M for print ads between 9-20-01 and 2001 Thanksgiving Day	Terrorism	Political instability	State	Corporations; Multi National Corporations	National; International	Economic; Political
Dispatch to the Middle East in late 2001 of a government-business team to pursue new tourism opportunities	Terrorism	Political instability	State	Corporations; Multi National Corporations	National; International	Economic; Diplomatic; Political

Source: Statement by Prime Minister P.J. Patterson to the Parliament of Jamaica Following the Terrorist Attack on the United States of America, September 25, 2001, *Jamaica Information Service, Kingston, Jamaica.*

Table 21.4
Adaptive Engagements by St Lucia Pertaining to Terrorism

Engagement Action	Core Threat Concern	Allied Threats	Primary Engagement Actor	Other Actors (to be) Engaged	Zone(s) of Relevance	Response Instruments
Purchase and installation of air and sea port metal detectors, X-ray machines, and security patrol vehicles	Terrorism	Drug trafficking; Arms trafficking,	State	Individuals; Other states; Corporations; MNCs	National; International	Economic; Law Enforcement
Passenger tracking and watch list system, and ID badging and tracking systems	Terrorism	Drug trafficking; Arms trafficking	State	Individuals; Other states; Multi National Corporations	National; International	Economic; Law Enforcement
Purchase and installation of communication and video surveillance at sea and air ports	Terrorism	Drug trafficking; Arms trafficking; Crime	State	Individuals; Other states; Corporations	National; international	Economic; Law Enforcement; Diplomatic
Purchase and installation of electronic equipment to detect explosives	Terrorism	Arms trafficking; Crime	State	Individuals; Other states; Corporations	National; International	Economic; Law Enforcement;
Training of air and sea port personnel and review and upgrade of operational systems	Terrorism	Crime; Drug trafficking; Arms trafficking	State	Individuals; Other states	National	Economic; Political
Full passport control	Terrorism	Crime; Drug trafficking;	State	Individuals; Other states	National; International	Law Enforcement; Diplomatic; Political
Tighter control of visas to travel to St Lucia	Terrorism	Arms trafficking; Crime	State	Individuals; Other states	National; International	Diplomatic; Political
Greater restrictions on residents and nationals of some Middle Eastern countries known for terrorism	Terrorism	Crime; Arms trafficking;	State	Individuals; Other states	National; International	Law Enforcement; Diplomatic; Political

Source: Prime Minister's Address on National Security, Castries, St Lucia, March 6, 2003.

Conclusion

It is reasonable to suggest from the foregoing analysis that the challenge and change matrixes of the Caribbean's contemporary security arena are such that the necessity to know 'the enemy' in order to respond and adapt adequately to the shifting dynamics presents a fundamental challenge to security elites and practitioners in the region. It is a fundamental challenge in part because of its powerful inner logic: that the political elites and security practitioners involved also must 'know themselves', so to speak.

Our response to the central question of this chapter – what are some relevant strategies to cope with the challenges confronting states in the region? – suggests that Caribbean security elites and practitioners must not only know; they also must act. And, they must act purposefully in fulfilment of the interests of their nations and citizens, in ways that reflect a willingness and capacity for adaptation. All this gives a powerful timeliness to the words penned in the fourth century by Roman military tactician Vegetius, and confirms the wisdom of remarks by forward-thinking, contemporary statesman, Kenny Anthony.

Closing this chapter also brings us to the final pages of this study. The volume has pursued several aims: to survey the contemporary Caribbean security scene; to assess the actual and potential impact of the September 11, 2001, terrorist attacks on the region; and to examine the terrorism response capacity of Caribbean security agencies and the overall regional security engagement posture.[24] I leave it to your good judgment and that of other readers to evaluate how well these aims have been fulfilled.

Notes

1. Flavius Vegetius Renatus in *On Military Matters*, written in 390 AD. Vegetius was a noted Roman military writer in the fourth century whose writings influenced military strategy and practice from that time up to the nineteenth century. For more about him see *Vegetius: Epitome of Military Science*. Translated with notes and introduction by N.P. Milner (Liverpool, England: Liverpool University Press, 1993).
2. *Prime Minister's Address on National Security*, Castries, St Lucia, March 6, 2003, 1.
3. See Edward N. Luttwak, *Strategy: the Logic of War and Peace* (Cambridge, MA: Harvard University Press, 1987), 239–40.
4. For a useful examination of several corporate approaches to strategy, see Fred Nickols, 'Strategy: Definitions and Meanings,' 2000, available at http://home.att.net/~nickols/strategy_definition.htm.
5. Nickols, Ibid., 7.
6. This term, coined by Charles Lindblom, entered the lexicon of political science and public policy following the publication of his path-breaking article with the same title in the Spring 1959 edition of *Public Administration Review*. The article is reproduced in Jay M. Shafritz and Albert C. Hyde, eds., *Classics of Public Administration* (Chicago: The Dorsey Press, 1987), 273–75.
7. Indeed, the reliance on the United States is such that some engagements would be jeopardised without US funding, if not leadership. Moreover, the 'Caribbean' in some engagements is merely nominal, which raises some troubling questions about whether and to what extent Caribbean interests are served.
8. Some of these challenges were examined in another context elsewhere. See Ivelaw L. Griffith, 'Security Collaboration and Confidence Building in the Americas,' in Jorge I.

Domínguez, ed., *International Security and Democracy: Latin America and the Caribbean in the Post-Cold War World* (Pittsburgh, Pa: Pittsburgh University Press, 1998).

9. James N. Rosenau, *Turbulence in World Politics* (Princeton: Princeton University Press, 1990), 106.
10. For a discussion of some of this, see Everett C. Dolman, 'Military Intelligence and the Problem of Legitimacy: Opening the Model,' in Max G. Manwaring and Anthony James Joes, *Beyond Declaring Victory and Coming Home* (Westport, Conn: Praeger, 2000), 87–105; Lt Col. J. Andrew Lettigrew, III, 'United States Southern Command Information Sharing Projects,' *IA newsletter* (Summer 1999), 3–4, 21; and Robert D. Steele, *The New Craft of Intelligence: Achieving Asymmetric Advantage in the Face of Non-traditional Threats* (Carlisle, PA: Strategic Studies Institute, 2002).
11. This writer was a participant observer at the May 1996 meeting of the CLEIC. I also have had the opportunity to visit several Caribbean JICCs over the years and the JOCC in Trinidad and Tobago in March 2000. The Trinidad and Tobago JOCC is, perhaps, the most sophisticated inter-agency intelligence and operations mechanism in the region except for Cuba.
12. JIATF-S is essentially a United States agency, but it has liaison participation by several Latin American and European nations. This writer had the opportunity to visit JIATF-S in January 2003.
13. *Prime Minister's Address on National Security*, *Ibid*., 1–2.
14. Ivelaw Lloyd Griffith, *The Quest for Security in the Caribbean: Problems and Promises of Subordinate States* (Armonk, NY: M.E. Sharpe, 1993), 277–78.
15. David A. Ochmanek and Steven T. Hosmer, 'The Context for Defense Planning: The Environment, Strategy, and Missions,' in Zalmay M. Khalilzad and David A. Ochmanek, eds., *Strategy and Defense Planning for the 21st Century* (Santa Monica, CA: Rand Corporation, 1997), 39.
16. This point was stressed several times at two different Spring 2003 conferences involving a range of top and middle rank operational officials and policy advisers at which this writer spoke. One was the United States Southern Command Caribbean Maritime Law Conference held in Key West, Florida in January 2003, and the other was the United States-Caribbean Coast Guard Commanders Conference, held in Castries, St Lucia in March 2003. Moreover, it was not the first time this observation was made.
17. See Ivelaw L. Griffith, 'Transnational Crime in the Americas: A Reality Check,' in Jorge I. Domínguez, eds., *The Future of Inter-American Relations* (New York: Routledge, 2000), 78.
18. See my chapter 'Caribbean Security in the Age of Terror: Challenges of Intrusion and Governance,' in Denis Benn and Kenneth O. Hall, eds., *Governance in the Age of Globalization: Caribbean Perspectives* (Kingston, Jamaica: Ian Randle Publishers, 2003), 406–07.
19. Barry Buzan, *People, States, and Fear* (Boulder: Lynne Rienner, 1991), 330.
20. See Samuel Huntington, *Political Order in Changing Societies* (New Haven: Yale University Press, 1968), 7.
21. See, for example, Alma H. Young and Dion E. Phillips, eds., *Militarization in the Non-Hispanic Caribbean* (Boulder, CO: Lynne Rienner, 1986); Griffith, *The Quest for Security in the Caribbean*, Ibid.; and Humberto García Muñiz, *Boots, Boots, Boots: Intervention, Regional Security, and Militarization in the Eastern Caribbean* (Rio Piedras, Puerto Rico: Caribbean Project on Justice and Peace, 1986).
22. See *Statement by Prime Minister P.J Patterson to the Parliament of Jamaica Following the Terrorist Attack on the United States of America, September 25, 2001*, Jamaica Information Service, Kingston, Jamaica, 3.

23. See *Nassau Declaration on International Terrorism: The CARICOM Response Issued at the Conclusion of the Special (Emergency) Meeting of Heads of Government of the Caribbean Community, 11–12 October, 2001*, Nassau, The Bahamas.
24. However, not enough direct attention has been paid to areas such as arms trafficking and intelligence operations, although there is a little discussion on them in this chapter and others. These issues will be examined by this writer elsewhere later.

Contributors

Caroline Allen is a social scientist working on HIV/AIDS in Africa and the Caribbean at the Medical Research Council Social and Public Health Sciences Unit at the University of Glasgow. Her work is part of the UK Department for International Development Knowledge Programme on HIV/AIDS in Developing Countries. She lived in Barbados and Trinidad and Tobago from 1991-2001, working on a variety of sexual and reproductive health research and intervention projects based at the University of the West Indies and the Caribbean Epidemiology Centre (CAREC). Formerly she was behavioural sciences advisor at CAREC's Special Programme on Sexually Transmitted Infections, Port of Spain, Trinidad and Tobago (1999-2001). She has published research on HIV/AIDS, reproductive health, health promotion, gender and the sociology of the body in the Caribbean.

Colvin Bishop is a former officer of the Trinidad and Tobago Defence Force where his last rank was lieutenant colonel. He is a graduate of the Canadian Forces Officer Candidate School, the United States Army Infantry School, the Canadian Forces Staff School, The Canadian Land Forces Command and Staff College, the Pearson Peacekeeping Center in Canada, the National Defence University in Beijing, China, and the United States Army Command and General Staff College. He holds a Bachelor of Science degree in Government from the University of the West Indies, St Augustine, and a Masters in Military Arts and Science from the US Army Command and General Staff College. He is author of 'The Future of Peace Support Operations in the Caribbean', published in *Alert* magazine, an organ of the Jamaica Defence Force.

Peter Clegg is a lecturer in politics and international relations at the University of the West of England, Bristol, in the United Kingdom. His research interests focus on the international political economy of the Commonwealth Caribbean, and the politics of the Eastern Caribbean. He is the author of *The Caribbean Banana Trade: From Colonialism to Globalization* (2002) and has contributed recent articles to *Social and Economic Studies* and the *European Review of Latin American and Caribbean Studies*. Peter teaches courses on Caribbean and Latin American politics, as well as international political economy. Further, he is a member of the Caribbean Board, a group that provides advice on the region to the Foreign and Commonwealth Office.

Jermemy Collymore has been chief administrative officer and coordinator of the Caribbean Disaster Emergency Response Agency (CDERA) since 1991 with overall responsibility for the operational readiness of CDERA, as well as the formulation and coordination of disaster preparedness and response policy for the Caribbean Community region. He holds a BA (Hons) in Geography and an MPhil in Geography, both from the University of West Indies, 1985. He also has done graduate studies in environmental design and planning at Virginia Polytechnic Institute and State University, USA. He has been lecturer in physical planning at the University of the West Indies, Jamaica, program officer, Office of the UN Disaster Relief Coordinator, Pan Caribbean Disaster Preparedness and Prevention Project, and assistant project director, Centre for Resource Management and Environmental Studies, University of the West Indies, Barbados. Jeremy has also been a consultant for UNDRO, the OAS, Canadian International Development Agency, the IDB, and several Caribbean governments.

John Cope is a senior research fellow at the Institute for National Strategic Studies, the research component of the National Defense University (NDU). A retired US Army colonel, he has been military assistant to the Assistant Secretary of State for Inter-American Affairs, and Deputy Chief of Staff, US Southern Command. He has guided the Institute's regional policy research and analysis in support of the Joint Chiefs of Staff and the Office of the Secretary of Defense since 1992. His MA in History is from Duke University, and he is currently in the PhD programme in political science at George Washington University. He has taught at the US Military Academy, the US Army War College, US Marine Corps War College, and the State Department's Foreign Service Institute.

Ramesh Deosaran is professor of criminology and social psychology and director of the Centre for Criminology and Criminal Justice at UWI, Trinidad and Tobago. He is the author/editor of 12 books, the most recent being *The Dynamics of Community Policing: Theory, Practice and Evaluation* (2000) and *Psychonomics and Poverty: Towards Governance and a Civil Society* (2000). Professor Deosaran is editor of the *Caribbean Journal of Criminology and Social Psychology*, editorial consultant to *Police Practice and Research: An International Journal*, and an editorial board member of *Journal of Ethnicity and Criminal Justice* and *A Critical Journal of Crime, Law and Society*. He has published widely in several scholarly journals and research monographs, most recently in *Policing: An International Journal of Police Strategies and Management* (2002) and *Encyclopedia of Crime and Punishment* (2002). Professor Deosaran is consultant to several international organisations, including the IADB, World Bank, ILANUD, UNICRI, and UNDP, and he serves as advisor to several regional governments and international agencies. He also serves as an independent senator in the Parliament of Trinidad and Tobago.

Edmund Dillon is a serving officer of the Trinidad and Tobago Defence Force where he holds the rank of colonel. He is a graduate of the Royal Military Academy, Sandhurst, UK, the Canadian Forces Staff School, the Canadian Land Forces Command and Staff College, the Pearson Peacekeeping Centre in Canada and the United States Command and General Staff College at Fort Leavenworth, Kansas. He has served in several line and staff appointments over the last 28 years in the military. These include the Battalion Second in Command of the First CARICOM Battalion that formed part of the Multinational Force, which participated in OPERATION RESTORE DEMOCRACY in Haiti in 1994. He holds a Bachelor of Science degree in Sociology and Government and a post-graduate Diploma in International Relations from the University of the West Indies, and a Masters in Military Arts and Science from the US Army Command and Staff College. He is currently pursuing a Masters in International Relations at the University of the West Indies, working on the thesis titled 'Rethinking National Security Policy in the Caribbean: The Case of Trinidad and Tobago'.

Norman Girvan, secretary-general of the Association of Caribbean States, is an economist who combines an academic background with experience in government and international organisations. After receiving his PhD in economics from the London School of Economics, he taught at UWI, Jamaica, served in Senegal as senior research fellow at the UN African Institute for Development and Planning in Dakar, was regional coordinator of the Caribbean Technology Policy Studies Project of the University of the West Indies/University of Guyana, and later chief technical director of the National Planning Agency of Jamaica. Dr Girvan also was senior officer and consultant at the UN Center on Transnational Corporations in New York, director of the UWI Consortium Graduate School of Social Sciences, and director of the Sir Arthur Lewis Institute of Social and Economic Studies. He has published 10 books and monographs and over 70 journal articles. Founding president of the Association of Caribbean Economists, he has been adviser and consultant to several governments and international organisations.

Dorith Grant-Wisdom is the director of the College Park Scholars International Studies Program and a member of faculty of the Department of Government and Politics at the University of Maryland. She holds a PhD in Political Science with specialisation in international relations, political economy/international political economy and public policy. Her publications and research interests lie in the areas of globalisation, development, and state-society relations, and focuses on the Caribbean/ Latin American region. She sits on two editorial boards, and is a member of the Democracy, Diversity, and Voice Advisory Board which is a part of the University of Maryland's Democracy Collaborative that brings together an international consortium of over 20 of the world's leading academic centres and citizen engagement organisations.

Clifford E. Griffin is associate professor in the Department of Political Science and Public Administration at North Carolina State University. He specialises in the range of issues that affect development and stability in the wider Caribbean. Along with a number of journal articles and book chapters, he is author of *Democracy and Neoliberalism in the Developing World: Lessons From the Anglophone Caribbean* (Ashgate, 1997). His current major research project is 'The Other Side of US Immigration Reform: The Impact of US Criminal Deportation Policy on Caribbean Democracy'.

Ivelaw L. Griffith, professor of political science and dean of The Honors College at FIU, is a specialist on Caribbean and Inter-American security and narcotics issues who has published several books and numerous scholarly articles. The Royal Military College of Canada, the George Marshall Center for European Security Studies in Germany, and the Center for Hemispheric Defense Studies in Washington, DC, are among places Dr Griffith has been a visiting scholar, and he has been a consultant to Canada's Ministry of Foreign Affairs and International Trade, the OAS, USAID, and other bodies. He has lectured extensively at academic, military, and law enforcement institutions in the Americas and Europe. The MacArthur Foundation, University of Miami's North-South Center, and FIU have funded his research, and he is a recipient of FIU's Award for Excellence in Research. A past president of the Caribbean Studies Association, Professor Griffith serves on the editorial board of *Security and Defense Studies Review* and *The Caribbean Journal of Criminology and Social Psychology.*

Kenneth O. Hall is pro vice chancellor and principal of the Mona Campus, University of the West Indies. He graduated from the UWI, Mona with a Bachelor's degree in History, and subsequently obtained a post-graduate Diploma in International Relations from the Institute of International Relations, in St Augustine. His masters and doctor of philosophy degrees, both in history, are from Queen's University in Canada. He taught history at Mona and at the State University of New York (SUNY) at Oswego, caribbean studies at SUNY, Albany, and american studies at SUNY, Old Westbury. Professor Hall has published widely on caribbean integration. Dr Hall also served as deputy secretary-general of CARICOM from 1994 to 1996. He serves on numerous committees at the university, national, and regional levels, and has participated in policy development relating to a broad range of issues in higher education, such as governance, professional development, enrollment, and program development. He is a member of the University Council of Jamaica and the Board of Directors of the Bank of Jamaica. He is the current chairman of MIND and the National Council on Education, and was appointed chairman of the Caribbean Examinations Council with effect from January 2003.

Janie Hulse is a research assistant for the Western Hemisphere team at the United States Institute for National Strategic Studies. She holds a BSc in Industrial and Labour Relations from Cornell University, and an MSc in Politics of Development in Latin America from the London School of Economics. She has recently been awarded a Rotary World Peace Scholarship to study towards a masters degree in international conflict resolution from Universidad del Salvador in Buenos Aires, Argentina (2004-06).

Isabel Jaramillo Edwards is a research associate in Centro de Estudios Sobre America (CEA) in Havana and associate professor at the Institute of International Relations (ISRI) in Havana and at FLACSO-Cuba at the University of Havana. She has been a visiting scholar at American University, Rutgers University, Florida International University, Georgetown University, Harvard University, University of North Carolina, and at FLACSO-Chile. Some publications by Dr Jaramillo Edwards are: 'The Hemispheric Landscape at the Turn of the Century', in *Army and Politics* (Moscow, 2002); 'Initiatives for Cooperative and Regional Security: Reintegration of Cuba into Regional Projects', in *Security in the Caribbean Basin: The Challenge of Regional Cooperation* (London, 2000); 'Las Migraciones como tema de política exterior de los Estados Unidos' in *Las Corrientes Migratorias y La Actividad Consular de Cara al Siglo XXI* (Havana, 2000); 'Cuba: Política Exterior y Multilateralismo', in *Multilateralismo Latinoamericano, (*Nueva Sociedad-Caracas, 2000); and 'Cuba's Security in the 1990's', in *Security Problems and Political Economy in the Post Cold War* (London and New York, 1996). Her articles have been published in *Fuerzas Armadas y Sociedad, Papeles,* and *Cuadernos de Nuestra America,* among other journals.

Oral Khan, lieutenant colonel in the Jamaica Defence Force, has served in several appointments in the Jamaica Regiment from Platoon Commander to Battalion Second in Command. His other significant appointments include commandant for the Caribbean Junior Command and Staff Course; staff officer for operations and training in the Defence Force Headquarters; and security coordinator in the Ministry of National Security. His military education and training has taken him to courses in Canada, the United Kingdom and the United States of America. A graduate of the University of the West Indies, he holds a Bachelors degree in Management Studies and a Masters in Development Studies. He is also a graduate of the United States Army Command and General Staff College and holds the Masters in Military Arts and Science degree. He is the recipient of the General Service medal (Grenada), and also the Medal of Honour for Meritorious Service to the Jamaica Defence Force.

Thomas Klak is professor of geography at Miami University of Ohio and adjunct professor of geography at Ohio State University. His research analyses the theories, discourses, and practices of economic and social development in global context. He is the editor of *Globalization and Neoliberalism: The Caribbean Context* (1998), and coauthor of *Alternative Capitalisms: Geographies of 'Emerging Regions'* (2003) and *The Contemporary Caribbean* (2004).

W. Andy Knight is professor of international relations at the University of Alberta in Edmonton, Canada. Currently lead editor of *Global Governance Journal: A Review of Multilateralism and International Organizations*, he is a former vice chair of the Academic Council on the UN System. He also served as chair of the International Organization Section of the International Studies Association. Andy has published extensively in the fields of international relations and international organisation. His most recent books include: *Adapting the United Nations to a Post-Modern World: Lessons Learned* (2001), *A Changing United Nations: Multilateral Evolution and the Quest for Global Governance* (2000), and *The United Nations and Arms Embargoes Verification* (1998). Among his recent journal articles is one written with Randolph B. Persaud in Spring 2001 entitled *Latin American Politics and Society*.

Rear Admiral Hardley M. Lewin, who holds an MBA from UWI, Jamaica, is chief of staff of the Jamaica Defence Force (JDF). He enlisted in the JDF in 1971, completed his initial officer training at the Britannia Royal Naval College in 1972, and was granted a commission in the rank of second lieutenant. He was assigned to the JDF Coast Guard and, since 1975, he has commanded every JDF ship. Admiral Lewin has had several overseas appointments including commanding officer of the Caribbean Peacekeeping Forces during Operation Urgent Fury in Grenada (1983–85). His professional education includes the US Coast Guard Search and Rescue School, Royal Naval Long Navigation Course, Canadian Coast Guard Marine Emergencies Management Course, and the Royal Naval Staff Course. He has served as second-in-command of the JDF Support and Services Battalion, as commanding officer of the JDF Coast Guard, and as commandant of the Jamaica Junior Command and Staff Course (now Caribbean Junior Command and Staff Course). He is a recipient of the award of Medal of Honour for Meritorious Service, and the General Service Medal for service in Grenada.

Anthony P. Maingot is professor of sociology at Florida International University in Miami. He received his PhD at the University of Florida, and has taught at Yale University (1966-72), where he was director of the Antilles Research Program, the University of the West Indies, Trinidad (1972-74), and at FIU since 1974. He was a member of the Constitutional Reform Commission of Trinidad, 1971-1974, and has held visiting appointments at the Institute of Developing Economies, Japan, the Institute d'Etudes Politiques, Universite d'aix-en-Provence in France, The Rand Corporation in California, and the North-South Center, University of Miami. A past president of the Caribbean Studies Association, Dr Maingot has received FIU's Distinguished Researcher Award and the Professional Excellence Award from the State University System. He is the author of six monographs and 75 refereed articles and book chapters. Co-author of a *Short History of the West Indies,* now in the 4th edition, his most recent books are *Small Country Development and International Labor Flows* and *The United States and the Caribbean.* He is founding editor of *Hemisphere*, a magazine of Latin American and Caribbean Studies, and serves on the editorial boards of *International Migration* (Geneva) and *Anuario Social y Político de FLACSO* (Costa Rica).

Roger McLean, is a lecturer in the Department of Economics, University of the West Indies, St Augustine, Trinidad. He is also a senior research associate attached to the Health Economics Unit in the Department of Economics. Mr McLean has been conducting research and working in the area of HIV/AIDS for the past six years, focusing on such issues as the macroeconomic impact of HIV/AIDS in Caribbean economies and the cost of the response to the epidemic at both the national and regional levels, and has published on modelling the macroeconomic impact of HIV/AIDS in the Caribbean. Roger has also conducted a number of situational and response analyses on HIV/AIDS for Caribbean territories and has assisted in the formulation of national strategic plans to address the epidemic. He is presently a member of the International AIDS Economics Network (IAEN) and the International Association of Physicians in AIDS Care (IPAC).

Raymond J. Milefsky is the specialist in land and maritime international boundaries and sovereignty issues for the US Department of State, Office of the Geographer and Global Issues, which provides geographic guidance and cartographic and imagery support to policy and legal bureaus in the department in the resolution of boundary, borderland, and territorial disputes. His office ensures that US government cartographic products depict international boundaries in conformity with geographic reality, treaties, and US foreign policy. He worked previously with National Imagery and Mapping Agency as an international boundaries and geographic names specialist. He has an MA from the American University, Washington, DC (Soviet and East European studies), and a BA from Brigham Young University (Russian and Japanese).

Christopher Mitchell is professor of politics at New York University, where he specialises in inter-American relations, migration studies, and Latin American politics. His publications include *New Perspectives in Latin American Studies* (Stanford University Press, 1988), and *Western Hemisphere Immigration and United States Foreign Policy* (Penn State Press, 1992). In the Caribbean, Dr Mitchell has visited Cuba, Jamaica, Barbados, Puerto Rico, and the Dominican Republic, and he has been an official observer of the most recent three Dominican presidential elections. He has held research grants from the Council on Foreign Relations and from the Ford Foundation, and serves on the Editorial Board of the *International Migration Review*.

Trevor Munroe is professor of government and politics at the University of the West Indies, Jamaica. He holds a first class honours degree from the University of the West Indies and a doctorate from Oxford University which he attended as a Jamaican Rhodes Scholar. Professor Munroe has also been the recipient of two Fulbright Fellowships which he took up as a Visiting Scholar at Harvard University. He has authored eight academic books, a number of journal articles, book chapters and working papers, primarily on issues of globalisation and democratic governance in the Caribbean. Professor Munroe received the Vice Chancellor's Award for Teaching in 2000 and is now the recipient of a two-year fellowship from the UWI to conduct research on strengthening democracy in the Caribbean. Dr Munroe has been serving since 1998 as a senator in the Jamaican Parliament where he has been an advocate of tough anti-corruption legislation, and sweeping constitutional reform while serving on Legislative Committees that deal with governance-related issues. He also is the head of one of Jamaica's major trade unions and a director of the Jamaica Confederation of Trade Unions.

Keith Nurse is senior lecturer at the Institute of International Relations, University of the West Indies, Trinidad and Tobago. He is president of the Association of Caribbean Economists and a member of the Caribbean Reference Group on Trade Policy. He is the academic coordinator of the Arts and Cultural Enterprise Management program at the Festival Centre of the Creative Arts, UWI. Dr Nurse has published on the global political economy of the clothing, banana, tourism, copyright and cultural industries. In addition, he has conducted research on development issues including security, gender, and poverty.

Ransford W. Palmer is professor of economics and chair of the Department of Economics at Howard University. He has published widely on development and migration issues of the Caribbean. His recent books include, *Pilgrims from the Sun: West Indian Migration to America* (Twayne Publishers, 1995), *The Repositioning of United States-Caribbean Relations* (Praeger 1997), and *US-Caribbean Relations: Their Impact on Peoples and Culture* (Praeger, 1998). Dr Palmer is a former president of the Caribbean Studies Association.

Emilio Pantojas-García, a political sociologist, is researcher in the Centro de Investigaciones Sociales, University of Puerto Rico, Río Piedras Campus. He is the author of *Development Strategies as Ideology: Puerto Rico's Export-Led Industrialization Experience* (Lynne Rienner/University of Puerto Rico Press, 1990) and co-editor, with Gerardo González Núñez, of *El Caribe en la Era de la Globalización* (Publicaciones Puertorriqueñas/Centro de Investigaciones Sociales, 2002). He has also published extensively in journals in English, Spanish, and French on Caribbean economic development issues. A Fulbright Scholar in 1987, Pantojas-García currently is a member of the Editorial Board of *Latin American Research Review* and vice president of the Caribbean Studies Association.

Elizabeth Riley has a BA (Hons) in Geography from the University of West Indies and MA in Environment and Development from the University of Manchester, United Kingdom. She is programme manager for Mitigation and Research at CDERA with overall responsibility for programmes and the implementation of initiatives under this area. Earlier, she headed the Sustainable Development Unit at the Ministry of Physical Development and Environment (formerly Ministry of Environment, Energy and Natural Resources) in Barbados. She has also worked in the field of renewable energy and was attached to the Center for Resource Management and Environmental Studies (CERMES) at the University of the West Indies. She also has contributed to several environmental studies and policy papers while at the University of the West Indies and the Ministry of Physical Development and Environment, and has written and presented technical papers in disaster management while at CDERA.

Stephen Vasciannie, Bachelor of Science (Econ), UWI, MA (Jurisprudence), DPhil, Oxford, LLM Cantab., is professor of International Law and acting head of the Department of Government at the University of the West Indies, Mona. His main research interests are in the areas of the Law of the Sea, Human Rights and International Investment Law. His books include *Land-Locked and Geographically Disadvantaged States in the Law of the Sea* (Oxford University Press, 1990) and *International Law and Selected Human Rights in Jamaica* (Norman Manley Law School, 2002). Professor Vasciannie was the Smuts Visiting Research Fellow in Commonwealth Studies at Cambridge University for 2001-02, and has been a weekly columnist on local and international affairs for Jamaica's *Gleaner* newspaper since 1995.

Afterword: Rethinking Approaches to Security in the Caribbean*

Rear Admiral Hardley Lewin

Background

The greatest threats to security in the Caribbean are those that are collectively described as transnational. Transnational threats are organised criminal activities that transcend national borders. They include, but are not restricted to: illicit traffic in drugs, arms and ammunition, terrorism, money laundering, and corruption. Cocaine is not produced in the Caribbean, but huge quantities transit the region, given its strategic location between the major suppliers in South America and the major markets of North America and Europe. Significant quantities of marijuana are cultivated in several Caribbean countries. However, the Caribbean is much more than a mere conduit for the movement of illicit drugs, and there are many reasons why countries within the region should be extremely concerned.

Among the reasons to be concerned about the transit of illicit drugs are:

- the link to increased levels of crime and violence;
- the connection to the trade and use of illegal arms and ammunition;
- the potential for the corruption of state officials and institutions;
- the negative effect on legitimate business (money laundering);
- the increase in the level of drug abuse and its attendant social consequences;
- the creation of a negative reputation for states and their citizens; and
- the link to the funding or facilitation of acts of terrorism.

In short, drugs pose a serious threat to Caribbean democracies and the Caribbean way of life. Regional states do not need to experience and re-learn for themselves the bitter lessons of those states that failed to do the right things and take action while there was time. The 1992 West Indian Commission Report to CARICOM summed up the problem as follows:

> Nothing poses greater threats to civil society in Caribbean countries than the drug problem and nothing exemplifies the powerlessness of regional governments more. This is the magnitude of the damage that drug abuse and trafficking hold for our Community. It is a many-layer[ed] danger. At base is the human destruction implicit in drug addiction, but implicit also is the corruption of individuals and systems by the sheer enormity of the inducements of the illegal drug trade in relatively poor societies. On top of all this lie the implications for governance itself at the hands of both external agencies engaged in international interdiction and drug barons themselves the 'Dons' of the Modern Caribbean who threaten governments from within.

The Outlook

It has been more than a decade since that report was issued, and the question arises: Has this ominous observation from the Commission generated the kind of national and or regional response that it deserves? There is little or no evidence to suggest this, but the old threats remain. These old threats have probably taken greater hold of Caribbean societies at a time when our fragile economies have fewer resources to be put at the disposal of the security mechanisms of our states and less ability to make the kinds of social interventions required to maintain hope among our most vulnerable citizens. Poor, fragile economies present tempting opportunities for corruption and the emerging threats of global trade liberalisation and the possible decline in economic development foster the growth of transnational threats.

Terrorism, once thought to be far removed from the Caribbean region, is now a threat of more immediate concern. Caribbean peoples should be reminded that the downing of a Cubana commercial aircraft in 1976 off the coast of Barbados was an act of terrorism. This was long before *terrorism* became a buzzword. In the same way that Cold War politics played itself out in different states within the region, so too will the terrorist strike at his declared enemies whenever and wherever he sees opportunities. Caribbean states are as vulnerable as states in other regions.

The effects of the new global war on terror are two-fold: not only can Caribbean states suffer at the hands of terrorist organisations that threaten to or carry out acts of terrorism, but also at the hands of those states that, in pursuit of terrorist organisations, threaten to or impose sanctions or penalties where they perceive that certain security standards are not being met. Often, these standards require very costly security systems, equipment and a high level of training.

In either case, the implications for tourism, on which so many Caribbean islands depend, are serious. The region can experience serious fallout on tourist arrivals from a single travel advisory issued in North America or Europe. This has been amply demonstrated over and over again. At times the advisory against travel may be general in nature, not targeting the Caribbean as a region. Such advisories are sufficient to have deleterious effects on regional economies.

HIV/AIDS and the effects of natural disasters have been added to the list of issues that have an adverse impact on the region, if only from the point of view that they increase economic vulnerabilities and thereby create increased opportunities for the penetration of transnational problems. The effects of natural disasters, especially those posed by hurricanes, will not go away, and the full effect of the HIV/AIDS epidemic is still to be felt.

In attempting to define the threats to their security, Caribbean states must be fully cognizant of developments within neighbouring states. To ignore or fail to grasp the reality and implications of your neighbour's problems is tantamount to playing Russian roulette with your own security. The nature of transnational activities, including terrorism, is such that the global move towards open borders and free trade can facilitate these very threats.

Thus, the outlook on security in the Caribbean is a very daunting one, which presents severe challenges to regional governments and peoples. As daunting as it seems, however, the sooner Caribbean states step forward to confront and deal with the challenges the better. These challenges are not, and should never be considered to be, insurmountable. However, they require appropriate levels of mental flexibility, clear understanding, strong leadership, and a firm resolve to win.

Proposed Approach

Any approach to the challenges outlined, whether at a national or regional level, has to be viewed against the background of a clear understanding of the problem. In other words, the nature of the problem must be clearly and accurately framed and with an honest appraisal of where the interests of states and the region lie. These assessments must be anticipatory in nature and precautionary in ambit. One would not want to be developing strategies today for yesterday's problems. The true nature, magnitude and implications of the threat have to be widely communicated as the solidarity and cooperation of all citizens must be mobilised. This requires an education programme that is effective and sustainable.

If there is a reasonable 'buy in' to the challenges it is not beyond the capacity of most Caribbean states to develop reasonable strategic plans that are largely home grown. Where capacity gaps exist, there is no shortage of technical assistance from traditional friends and partners. It is important, through, that Caribbean nations recognise that the responsibility for addressing their transnational problems rests within our own borders and with our own nationals. It is no longer good enough to be shielded by a big brother and to respond only to external stimulus, when under duress, whether real or imagined.

A new proactive approach must begin with a return to some basic law enforcement concepts. These are deterrence, detection, apprehension, judicial engagement, and correctional action. Law enforcement requires a presence that is akin to having 'policemen on the beat'. Where a presence is not established in an area, the psychological effect is that the area is abandoned by the states' law enforcement mechanisms. Deterrence is achieved when the potential law breaker feels that there is a strong chance of being detected and desists from his or her unlawful intent. Where deterrence fails, the means must be available to detect this fact followed by the ability to do something about it; that is, to apprehend.

After apprehension, comes the need for quick and efficient judicial disposition. This includes not only court facilities and proper staffing, but a set of robust modern laws that are relevant and that will not easily fall prey to the ingenuity of smart lawyers, who exploit technical deficiencies and the relative inexperience of some prosecutors in several countries. After conviction and sentencing, the correctional component takes over. The requirement is for prison systems geared toward punishment and rehabilitation that reduce recidivism. It is self-defeating if the prison systems are no more than institutions of higher criminal learning.

It is around these five basic components that states must build an appropriate security apparatus, mindful of current and future threats. The consideration of each component in turn would see the emergence of each of the following issues: a) kind of force(s) required (constabulary, military and paramilitary); b) size and shape of force(s); c) kinds of equipment; and d) command, control, communication and intelligence. It would be very easy for any country without any kind of security/defence agency to learn from the lessons of others, follow the approach outlined and implement its plans.

Of course, this is not the case in Caribbean countries. Each state has a constabulary agency, and customs and immigration entities. In addition to the above agencies, several countries have military establishments. In Caribbean countries, changes to the status quo of the state agencies would be fiercely resisted. The tendency is to protect one's own little fiefdom at all costs and without any consideration of the national good. The message here is that implementation of any new security apparatus or structures would face severe challenges including even sabotage. Can government and opposition parties agree on these issues? It would be prudent to involve opposition parties in the process from the very beginning, because the necessary changes may have to be forced over the protestations of those who feel threatened by those changes.

Regardless of the structures that emerge from this framework there has to be a component or unit whose sole purpose is to counter corruption. Well equipped, staffed and trained security forces can be rendered ineffective by corrupt individuals within their ranks. If left unchecked, corruption can grow to such proportions that the entire organisation may have to be disbanded and restarted on an entirely different basis.

In addressing the emergent structures, care must be taken not to fall into the trap of templating. Each state, while considering other models from elsewhere, will understand that it is their home-grown adaptations that will last.

It should also be understood that anything implemented should be constantly reviewed and appropriate adjustments made. Too often plans implemented give the appearance of being cast in stone simply because there is a reluctance to make changes, as this would signal having made an error. This should not be the case. The dynamics of current and future threats require extreme flexibility in structure, strategies and tactics.

If each state were to respond to the needs of its own security responsibilities and put its house in order at the national level, the next logical step would be to deal with the issues of cooperation and coordination across borders. It would seem that a bottom up approach would be most appropriate and achievable. The tendency, thus far, is to seek hemispheric or regional agreements followed by subregional ones. The reverse might have produced more robust and usable agreements with fewer needs for reservations.

It is well accepted that no country can deal with the problems of transnational crime on its own. The United States of America provides leadership in this hemisphere, and close cooperative links are maintained with the United Kingdom and Canada. In relation to our traditional partners, the USA, UK and Canada, much more can be done to increase the levels of cooperation and support received. To do so, every party must be frank with each other in all engagements and display a willingness to transcend traditional suspicions. If this is achieved, then issues of sovereignty can be addressed in a manner that satisfies all parties. Security assistance can be leveraged to extract the maximum 'bang for the buck' and the collective minds can be freed to employ new daring thinking and approaches.

A clear demonstration of will and purpose needs to be found and engaged. Success on the part of Caribbean states can trigger a backlash from drug lords who will not necessarily roll over and die, but seek to break the will of the government and people through violent responses. It is well that all are committed to an even greater level of resolve than that which triggered the backlash in the first instance.

Conclusion

In this Age of Terror, the search for a secure environment within the Caribbean takes on greater proportions. Regional state responses must not only be geared to create an effective security apparatus, but must involve the building of solidarity with the people and the harnessing of their support and cooperation. The task at hand is best summed up by the following statement adapted from a Staff College précis on the subject of the 'Principles of War – Selection and Maintenance of the Aim':

> Security Forces successes alone will not stamp out the threats to security; they may drive it deeper underground or force the criminal elements to allow their activities to lie dormant for a period. The only sure way is to remove the conditions which stimulated criminality in the first place.

There should be a joint politico-security forces aim, namely, to afford protection against criminal elements while at the same time raising the standard of living, improving health and educational facilities, engendering faith in democratically-elected government by demonstrating justice and fairplay, and generally by winning the support of the people. No amount of foreign interference or assistance, short of complete domination, will remedy a deteriorated internal situation unless the people concerned take action for themselves. A well-defined security aim is vital, but success on the security side will be useless unless the complementary political aim is achieved. The cause, not just the effect, of the problem, must be removed.

Note

* Text of the February 1, 2003 luncheon address at the January 31–February 1, 2003 conference of project authors, which was held in Kingston, Jamaica and cosponsored by the Jamaica Defence Force, the University of the West Indies, and The Honors College, Florida International University.

Index